CADCAM

*principles, practice
and manufacturing
management*

CADCAM
• •

principles, practice and manufacturing management

Second Edition

Chris McMahon
Department of Mechanical Engineering,
University of Bristol

Jimmie Browne
Computer Integrated Manufacturing Research Unit,
The National University of Ireland, Galway

ADDISON-WESLEY
Harlow, England • Reading, Massachusetts • Menlo Park, California
New York • Don Mills, Ontario • Amsterdam • Bonn • Sydney • Singapore
Tokyo • Madrid • San Juan • Milan • Mexico City • Seoul • Taipei

© Addison Wesley Longman Limited 1998

Addison Wesley Longman Limited
Edinburgh Gate
Harlow
Essex CM20 2JE
England

and Associated Companies throughout the World.

Cover designed by Designers & Partners, Oxford, UK incorporating figure by the author
Typeset by 35 in 9/12 pt Stone Serif
Printed and bound in the United States of America

First printed 1998. Reprinted 1998

ISBN 0–201–17819–2

British Library Cataloguing-in-Publication Data
McMahon, Chris.
    CADCAM : principles, practice, and manufacturing management /
Chris McMahon, Jimmie Browne. — 2nd ed.
        p. cm.
    Includes bibliographical references and index.
    ISBN 0–201–17819–2 (alk. paper)
    1. CAD/CAM systems. I. Browne, Jimmie. II. Title.
TS155.6.M3953   1998
670'.285––dc21   98–2557
                                                         CIP

To Sue, Rebecca, Douglas and Madeleine
and Maeve, Lorcan, Shane, Ronan and Fergus

Contents

··

Part three **Production planning and control** *411*

Preface

·····················

Introduction

·················

Throughout the life cycle of engineering products, computers have a prominent, often central role. In the process of product design and manufacture, this role is becoming increasingly important as competitive pressures call for improvements in product performance and quality, and for reductions in development time-scales. Computers assist design engineers to improve the productivity with which they carry out their work. Through simulation or analysis they allow the performance of a product to be evaluated before a prototype is made. They aid the organization of complex systems, and the communication of data within the engineering team. These applications may collectively be termed CADCAM: computer-aided design and computer-aided manufacture.

The purpose of this book is to provide a tutorial and a reference source for student and professional engineers who have an interest in the application of computers in product design and manufacture. Through sixteen chapters that provide a comprehensive overview of the application of computers in the product introduction process, the reader is guided through the process of defining a product design with the aid of computers, then developing manufacturing plans and instructions for the product from the design, and finally planning and managing the operation of the manufacturing system itself. Throughout, we seek both to explain underlying principles and to provide insights from applications, and we also seek to provide extensive references to books, research papers and on-line material to assist the reader in finding more information about the topics we present. In some cases we have omitted a detailed discussion of wide-ranging topics such as robotics and techniques for design analysis, because the subjects are in our view properly covered in dedicated textbooks. In these cases we again provide pointers to sources that we have found useful.

The material we present is intended to be suitable for senior or final year undergraduates and graduate students, principally in mechanical engineering (hence a particular emphasis on design), but also in manufacturing systems and industrial engineering. We hope that the material will also be of value to practising engineers in similar disciplines. It has been organized such that the text may be followed without the necessity to pursue theoretical detail, much of which has been placed in boxed sections or appendices. The chapter content has also been organized such that different routes may be taken through the material (identified at the end of this

Preface), depending on whether the reader wishes to have an overview of the topics, to explore the theoretical foundations of the material, or to understand current research issues and developments. Exercises are provided so that the reader may check his or her progress with the material, and projects allow the concepts that have been introduced to be explored through practical applications.

New in this edition

Since the first edition of this book was published, a number of important developments have taken place in CADCAM, in the standards that apply to the topic, and in the engineering environment in which CADCAM is applied. The primary purpose of this second edition is therefore to update the text to describe these developments. At the same time, the opportunity has been taken to make a general revision of the contents of the book, to expand the number of case-study type applications examples and exercises, and to introduce project material.

In the first edition, concurrent engineering was introduced as an important driver for improved product quality and reduced development time-scales. In this edition it receives further emphasis, as does the modelling and management of product data. Opportunity has also been taken to generally update and expand material, especially on geometric modelling, database management systems, communications, graphics and product data exchange standards, parametric and variational approaches to geometric modelling, interfaces between CAD and design analysis, and process planning. In particular, the section on standards emphasizes recent developments in international standards, and extends description of *de facto* standards in CADCAM. New material has been incorporated on mesh generation for finite element analysis, the application of artificial intelligence in design, Taguchi methods for the design of experiments, robotics, the extended enterprise and distribution planning and control. As in the first edition, the material is divided into a number of parts that are each designed to be able to be read as stand-alone sections covering key areas in the subject. A development for this edition is the addition of a new final section to discuss emerging issues in CADCAM, including product data management, assembly and tolerance modelling, the impact of the global networks, and design for the environment.

As noted, this edition has a greatly increased emphasis on practical examples and on projects. A number of applications examples have been drawn from current manufacturing practice, to illustrate how the principles that are presented are being applied in a manufacturing context. The reader will also have the opportunity to explore applications through two projects that are developed through the first two parts of the book. The first project involves the development, from computer-aided design through to analysis and manufacture, of a single part. The second project explores the same process for a small electro-mechanical assembly. The projects are first explained in some detail in Chapter 1, and then at the end of each chapter the next stage in the development of the project is introduced, to allow the reader to explore concepts introduced in that chapter.

This edition also introduces some changes in the presentation and organization of material. In the treatment of geometric transformations the use of column vectors for coordinate data has been adopted in order to bring the book in line with engineering practice. The first edition used row vectors for coordinate data, as is common practice in computer graphics texts. The alternative approaches are described when the topic is first introduced. The main change in organization is the moving of the discussion of parametric and variational modelling from Chapter 6 to Chapter 8, where it has been extended and is now linked to feature-based approaches. Some of the material on engineering data management has also been moved from Chapter 5 to Chapter 16, where it is incorporated into a much wider discussion of product data management. Finally, some material has been removed or reduced, in particular the discussion of vector display devices and some aspects of the GKS graphics standard.

PART CONTENTS

Part One: Computer-aided design

This first part is concerned with the fundamentals of the modelling process by which designs are defined using computers, and with exploration of applications of the CAD model within the design process.

▶ **Chapter 1 The design process and the role of CAD:** This chapter introduces CAD and places it in the context of the design process.

▶ **Chapter 2 Defining the model:** This chapter provides an overview of the techniques for representing the design using drawings, diagrams and three-dimensional computer models, including wire-frame, surface and solid modelling approaches.

▶ **Chapter 3 Techniques for geometric modelling:** This chapter provides details of the fundamentals of the representations used in geometric modelling, including parametric curves and surfaces and techniques for solid modelling.

▶ **Chapter 4 Elements of interactive computer graphics:** This chapter provides an overview of the display and user interaction techniques used in CADCAM, from two-dimensional graphics to techniques for visual realism. The chapter includes an overview of computer graphics hardware.

▶ **Chapter 5 Entity manipulation and data storage:** The manipulation of elements of the CAD model and techniques for its storage are described in this chapter, including an overview of database management systems and details of the relational database approach.

▶ **Chapter 6 Applying the CAD model in design:** This chapter describes applications aspects of CAD, and also presents details of methods for system customization and links to analysis, including geometric analysis and mesh preparation for finite element analysis.

▶ **Chapter 7 Standards for CAD:** This chapter provides an overview of the standards that apply to computer graphics, to networks, and to the exchange of product data.

▶ **Chapter 8 Expanding the capability of CAD:** This reviews developments aimed at improving the utility of CAD through incorporation of techniques from artificial intelligence, and through improved representational techniques such as parametric, variational and feature-based modelling approaches.

Part Two: The design/manufacture interface

This part is concerned with activities at the design/manufacture interface, such as the organization of the product development activity, and preparation of process plans and manufacturing instructions from the design data.

▶ **Chapter 9 The design/manufacture interface:** This chapter introduces the subjects at the interface between design and manufacture, and in particular describes design for manufacture and assembly, and process planning.

▶ **Chapter 10 The total approach to product development:** This chapter reviews techniques and strategies for a systems approach to product development and quality in manufacture at the design/manufacture interface. In particular, organizational approaches to concurrent engineering, and Taguchi methods for off-line quality control, are described.

▶ **Chapter 11 The link to machine control:** The operation and programming of numerical control machine tools and robotic devices, and techniques for rapid prototyping, are reviewed in this chapter.

Part Three: Production planning and control

This part is concerned with the planning and control of the flow of work through a factory floor. It considers production planning and control issues at all levels in the factory and indeed back to suppliers and forward to distributors.

▶ **Chapter 12 Introduction to production planning and control:** This chapter introduces a typology of manufacturing systems and presents an overview of the production management system in terms of a hierarchy of production planning and control systems. It seeks to present planning and control in the context of the extended enterprise model of manufacturing systems.

▶ **Chapter 13 Requirements planning systems:** This chapter presents an overview of business planning and master scheduling systems and a detailed review of the operations of a requirements planning system. Reference is also made to the operation of material requirements planning systems and distribution requirements planning in practice.

▶ **Chapter 14 Shop floor control systems:** This chapter presents the structure of a shop floor control system in terms of a factory coordination system and a production activity control system. The chapter also includes a review of widely used scheduling techniques.

▶ **Chapter 15 Just in time:** This chapter offers an overview of the just in time (JIT) approach to manufacturing systems design and operation which requires a holistic approach to manufacturing with a strong focus on product and process design as well as production planning and control.

Part Four: Future directions for CADCAM

In this part the way in which CADCAM is developing in response to the pressures for global manufacturing and reduced environmental impact are considered.

▶ **Chapter 16 Emerging challenges in CADCAM:** This chapter reviews current developments in CADCAM including new approaches to product modelling, multimedia, the global networks and computer-supported cooperative work, and design for the environment.

Routes through the material

The first three parts of the book are designed to be largely self-contained introductions to computer-aided design, to computer-aided manufacture and to production planning and control respectively. The material may also be subdivided in different ways according to the requirements of the reader, as follows:

A **general introduction** to CADCAM, giving an overview of techniques and applications, but largely omitting detailed theoretical discussions, is given in Chapters 1 (introduction to CAD), 2 (introduction to geometric modelling), part of 6 (CAD applications), 9 (the design/manufacture interface), part of 10 (techniques for a systems approach to product development), 12 (introduction to production planning and control) and 15 (introduction to JIT).

A **detailed treatment** of analytical and computing principles is given in Chapters 3 (geometric modelling), 4 (computer graphics), 5 (model manipulation and data storage), parts of 6 (geometric analysis and FE mesh generation), part of 10 (Taguchi methods), 11 (techniques of computer-aided manufacture), 13 (requirements planning systems) and 14 (shop floor control systems).

Discussions of **current developments** that would be useful to a reader who is generally familiar with CADCAM techniques are given in Chapters 7 (networks and standards), 8 (artificial intelligence in design plus developments in modelling) and 16 (emerging challenges in CADCAM). Parts of chapters 10 (systems approaches) and 15 (JIT) would also be useful in this context.

Acknowledgements

In the first edition of this book we acknowledged the inspiration and support of students and colleagues over many years that had led to the book being written. In this second edition we acknowledge our continued indebtedness in this regard, in particular to our research students and research assistants, the results of whose studies have led to much of the new material incorporated here. We are also for this edition grateful to the users and reviewers of the first edition of the book whose thoughtful comments and feedback were of great assistance in planning and developing the revisions to the text.

Very many people have assisted in the production of the book by allowing their material to be used. We are grateful in particular to Chris Amoah, Bob Barr, Malcolm Blunston, Jack Bones, Richard Bowden, Peter Brett, Geoffrey Brewin, Steve Bruford, Steve Cobert, Peter Coleman, Julian Cooke, Jonathan Corney, Ian Dawkins, Roger Day, Janardan Devlukia, Jeremy Davies, Jim Duggan, Kevin Fitzgerald, Geoff Hall, Jennifer Hand, John Hawley, Paul Higgins, Ken Huff, Sean Jackson, John Kidd, Kevin Kilgannon, David Kite, John Kitchingman, Praba Kugathasan, Gordon Little, Yaowu Liu, David Pitt, Bob Poulter, Marion Ryan, Toufik Sator, Janet Seaton, Ted Talbot, Jim Taylor, David Thomas, Paul Walker, Brian Wall, John Wall, Gordon Webber and Jean Weston for providing figures, examples and other case study material. Kevin Kilgannon kindly prepared the figures and many of the examples in Part Three, and we are grateful also for the contribution of Paddy Jordan and Shane Lillis to the preparation of case studies in this part. Rose Crossland and Michael Mead kindly permitted us to reuse material they had written on object orientation and EXPRESS respectively. We are also especially grateful to Otto Salomons, who commented on the material on assembly and tolerance modelling, and provided valuable information about FROOM, and to Kazem Alemzadeh, Peter Brett, Gordon Clarke, Bob Poulter and Clive Wishart, who provided figures and allowed their material to be used as a basis for the Project exercises in Parts One and Two.

To those who have undertaken the onerous task of reading and checking the manuscript we owe a special debt of thanks, especially to our researchers mentioned above, to Ram Balakrishnan, Irfan Kaymaz, Pat McMahon and Ulrich Riedel, and to the anonymous copy editor and proofreaders whose contribution is most welcome. We remain grateful to Andrew Harrison for his review of the mathematical material in Part One. The errors that remain are our own. Thanks are also due in particular to Gillian Davis, for her secretarial assistance throughout the work, and to Anna Faherty, Alison Martin, Dylan Reisenberger, Michael Strang and colleagues at Addison Wesley Longman, whose enthusiasm and diligence has brought this book to production.

Finally, we must express our continued gratitude to our wives and families, without whose patience and forbearance over many months the work would never have been completed. The book is dedicated to them.

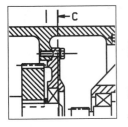

PART ONE

Computer-aided design

The foundation for the application of computers in the product development process is the development of models of products using computer-aided design (CAD). Information from these models then forms the basis for design analysis, for planning and organization of the manufacturing activity, and for the control of machines which manufacture the products.

Many properties of products have to be modelled, including form, dimension, tolerance and structure. In all of these areas, geometry, images and spatial manipulation are very important. For this reason, CAD is founded on computational geometry and computer graphics. In this part of the book we shall begin by exploring these technologies and how they are applied to modelling. We shall then go on to consider applications which use the model, and standards and current trends in the development of design computing.

Chapter 1 introduces CAD and places it in the context of the design process. Chapter 2 is concerned with the techniques for representing the design using drawings, diagrams and three-dimensional computer models, and the fundamentals of these techniques are developed in more depth in Chapter 3. Chapter 4 is concerned with the display of the model using computer graphics, and with the techniques of user interaction. Chapter 5 continues the theme with discussion of the manipulation of elements of the CAD model, and techniques for its storage. The final three chapters are particularly concerned with applications and with future developments. Chapter 6 describes the application of CAD in a number of practical contexts, and also presents details of links to analysis and of methods for system customization. Chapter 7 provides an overview of the standards that apply to computer graphics, to networks and to the exchange of product data, and Chapter 8 reviews developments aimed at improving the utility of CAD through incorporation of techniques from artificial intelligence and multimedia, and through improved representational methods.

1 The design process and the role of CAD

Chapter objectives

When you have completed studying material in this chapter you should be able to:

▶ outline the nature and role of the design process, and understand the application of concurrent engineering in this process;
▶ describe the role of modelling in describing, assessing and communicating designs;
▶ describe the variety of types of model used in design;
▶ describe the role of the computer in design as an agent for creating, manipulating, communicating and applying models of design;
▶ describe the role of the computer either in assisting with or automating existing design methods, or in providing new tools for the designer;
▶ outline a general architecture for CAD systems.

Chapter contents

1.1 The design process

There is practically no aspect of our lives today which is not influenced by the work of engineers. The buildings and equipment we use, the vehicles we travel in and the roads and rails upon which they travel are all direct products of engineering activity. The food we eat is grown and processed with the assistance of engineering products, and engineers design and construct the equipment which prints our books, manufactures our medicines and produces our television images. Engineering and

3

manufacturing together form the largest single economic activity of most western countries, and provide the basis for our prosperity.

If we compare today's engineering products with those of 40 years ago we will find a startling increase in performance, quality and sophistication. Many of the products are of great complexity, and this improvement has been achieved by organizing large teams of people to collaborate in the products' development and manufacture. Today, these teams work under increasing pressure to develop products of high performance and reliability at low cost and in shorter and shorter time-scales.

In view of this pressure, it is not surprising that engineers have turned to machines to assist them in the task of product development and manufacture. The machines involved are computers, and their task is information processing: they are used to assist in the definition and processing of information connected with the design of products, and with the organization and management of the manufacturing systems which make them.

The thrust of this book will be to consider, firstly, how computers are used in the generation and management of the design information that describes products, and secondly, how they are used in the management of information about the manufacturing system which makes the products. Before we set off on this route, let us consider what is typically involved in bringing a product to market, so that we may better understand the place of computers in the process.

In a market economy, product development will be in response to a perceived market need, and this need will usually be identified in the form of a **design brief**, which will be the basis for the subsequent product development. This brief will be taken up by the product **designers**, who will explore ways in which the brief might be met, and will eventually develop the most promising of these into detailed instructions for manufacture. In this, they are assisted by **design analysts**, who use analysis and simulation techniques to test the fitness for purpose of the design proposals, and **development engineers** who carry out experimental work on the test rigs and on prototypes to make detailed refinements of the design. This group may also be supported by **research engineers**, who carry out experimental or theoretical work to fill in gaps in our understanding of materials, processes or techniques.

Once the design has been developed in detail it is taken up by the **process planner**, who will identify the processes and operations required to manufacture and assemble or construct the product. The detail of these processes, and the detail of the parts of the product, is used by the **production planner and controller** to schedule the parts for production, and to manage this production.

This is of course a very broad-brush description of the engineering process, and the detail at every stage will vary considerably according to the numbers of people involved and the nature and complexity of the product. In this chapter we are particularly concerned with the process of design, and in this respect, aircraft engines or computer systems (for example) are highly complex products in which the design involves large teams and is tightly constrained by technical factors. Conversely, in some areas a design may be the product of a single designer or small team, or factors such as fashion may have a more dominant role.

In recent years there have been several attempts to provide a formal description of the stages or elements of the design process. In view of the range of design situations, it is not surprising that there has been some variation in these descriptions, both in

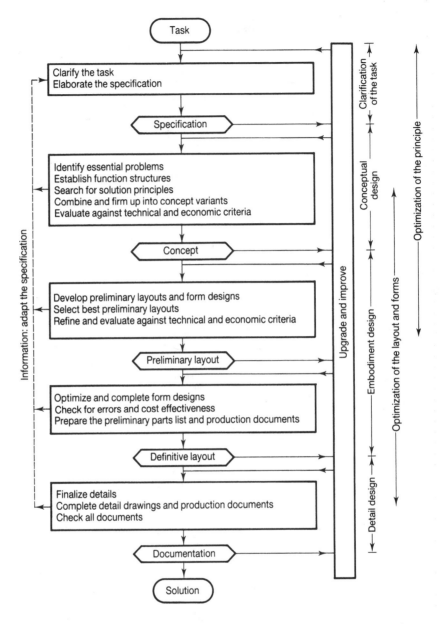

FIGURE 1.1

Steps of the design process according to Pahl and Beitz (1984). (Reproduced by permission of the publishers. © The Design Council.)

terminology and in detail, but in general they agree that design progresses in a step-by-step manner from some statement of need through identification of the problem (the specification of requirements), a search for solutions and development of the chosen solution to manufacture, test and use. These descriptions of design are often called **models of the design process**, and to illustrate these we will consider two models which give different but complementary insights into the process.

The first model is shown in Figure 1.1, and is that proposed by Pahl and Beitz (1984). In this model the design process is described by a flow diagram comprising four main phases which may be summarized as:

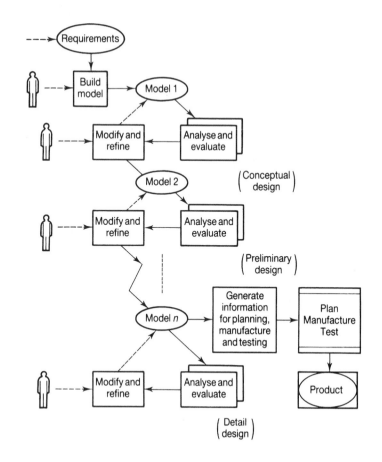

FIGURE 1.2

The design process according to Ohsuga. (Reproduced from Ohsuga (1989) by permission of the publishers. © Elsevier Science Ltd. Kidlington, UK.)

▶ **clarification of the task**, which involves collecting information about the design requirements and the constraints on the design, and describing these in a specification;

▶ **conceptual design**, which involves establishment of the functions to be included in the design, and identification and development of suitable solutions;

▶ **embodiment design**, in which the conceptual solution is developed in more detail, problems are resolved and weak aspects eliminated;

▶ **detail design**, in which the dimensions, tolerances, materials and form of individual components of the design are specified in detail for subsequent manufacture.

Although Figure 1.1 presents a straightforward sequence of stages through the process, in practice the main phases are not always so clearly defined, and there is invariably feedback to previous stages and often iteration between stages.

The second model comes from the work of Ohsuga (1989), and is shown in Figure 1.2. Ohsuga again describes design as a series of stages, in this case progressing from requirements through conceptual design and preliminary design (which is akin to embodiment in the Pahl and Beitz model) to detail design. In this case, however, the various stages of the design process are generalized into a common form in which models of the design are developed through a process of analysis and evaluation leading to modification and refinement of the model. In the early stages of a design, a tentative solution is proposed by the designer. This is evaluated from a number of viewpoints to establish the fitness of the proposed design in relation to the given requirements. If the proposal is unsuitable, then it is modified. The process is repeated until the design is at a point where it can be developed in more depth, and the preliminary design stage will start. In this stage the design is refined, and evaluation and modification repeated at a greater level of detail. Finally, the detail design phase proceeds in a similar fashion to complete the definition of the design for manufacture.

Each of the two models of the design process presented above follows a fairly traditional view in which there is a sequence of design stages, followed by manufacture. Increasingly, however, the pressure to reduce product design and development time-scales is leading companies to conduct design, development, analysis and the preparation of manufacturing information in parallel. This has been variously termed **simultaneous engineering** or **concurrent engineering**, and is pursued in particular by those companies that produce established products, and where new models are required at regular intervals. The topic of concurrent engineering will be addressed again later in this chapter, and in more depth later in the book. For the moment, the sequential models of the design process will be used while the role of modelling and communication in design is considered.

1.2 The role of modelling and communication

The concept of the designer working with **models of designs** is fundamental to the treatment of **computer-aided design** (CAD) in this book. It is important to distinguish here between models of the design process, which essentially attempt to describe the pattern that designers follow in the design of products, and models of the designs themselves. Throughout the design process, design is in the abstract: the physical artefact does not exist, so until it is constructed or manufactured there need to be some models of the design for those involved to evaluate, manipulate and refine. Tomiyama and his co-workers (1989) suggest that such models may exist as different **representations**. The modelled geometry of an engineering component may for example be represented in different ways. If the design is very simple, these may just be ideas in the mind of the designer, but for all except the most elementary designs some more formal representation is needed.

Models of the design are used for a variety of purposes. At the most basic level, they are used by the designer to record and manipulate ideas – as an *aide-mémoire* – and to provide a basis for the evaluation of the design. The design process is rarely undertaken by a single designer, however, and therefore the models have a major role in the **communication** of the design between participants in the process, and to those involved in the manufacture, development and subsequent use of the product.

The description of the design process presented in Figure 1.1 can be used to illustrate the way that representation and communication pervade the process. At the conceptual design stage a representation of the design requirements will be communicated to the designer. Various representations of ideas will be used to evaluate possible solutions, and the chosen solution will be recorded in some way and communicated to the embodiment phase, which may well be undertaken by a different designer. The embodiment phase will generate further models of the design, which will again be communicated to the detail phase, in which the sequence is repeated. A description of the design, with instructions for manufacture, will be communicated to those responsible for manufacture, and it is likely that further representations will be generated for those involved in test, maintenance and use of the design.

As so much design activity is carried out by large teams – the design of automobiles and aircraft, for example, involves thousands of people – the essence of design is the sharing of information between those involved, so communication is of utmost importance.

1.3 Types of design model

The design process model shown in Figure 1.1 gives us a hint of the variety of representations needed in design. There are phrases such as 'develop preliminary layouts' and 'complete detail drawings'. In practice, the designer uses a host of different models depending on what **property** of the design is to be modelled, and who or what is the target, or **receiver**, for any communication (Tjalve *et al.*, 1979). The engineering designer has, at various times, to model the **function** of a design, its **structure** (how the various parts go together), the **form** or shape of the component parts, and the **materials**, **surface condition** and **dimensions** that are required. He or she may also wish to form mathematical models, or computer-based representations, to assist in the evaluation of a design. The potential targets for communication include, among others, fellow designers, manufacturing and workshop staff, and users of the design. For any particular combination of modelled property and receiver there will be a type of model and a technique for its generation that will be most appropriate.

Of all the modelled properties, *form* and *structure* are of particular importance in engineering, and the most appropriate method of representing these has traditionally been graphical. For many engineers – for example, the designers of machines, bridges and vehicles – a major part of their task is to define the shape and arrangement of the component parts of the design. This is conventionally achieved by **drawings** of form. Other engineers are more concerned with the structure of the assembly of standard elements to form a design, with the way these elements are connected together, and with the flows (e.g. of energy or material) between parts (this approach is often called a **systems engineering** approach). Examples in this latter case are electric or hydraulic circuit design, or the design of process plant, and in these domains the representation of designs through **diagrams** showing structure, or system arrangement, is of paramount importance. (This is not to say that the electrical or fluid power systems engineer is not ultimately concerned with the physical layout of components. Rather, a greater part of the design process can be conducted without detailed consideration of form.)

The target receiver for the communication influences in particular the technique that is used for the generation of the model. In the early stages of a design, the designer will often explore ideas by sketching, with little or no detail. When information is being generated for manufacture, however, a more diligent technique is required, and drawings and diagrams will be carefully produced to show all necessary detail.

Finally, in order for any communication to be successful, the 'language' that is employed must be agreed and understood by all those involved. The complexity of design in many domains, and the crucial necessity to avoid misinterpretation and ambiguity in instructing how something must be made, mean that the design models must conform to agreed standards that define the syntax of the languages. This subject will be considered again in the next chapter, which will briefly review the conventional representation of designs using drawings and diagrams.

Example 1.1 *Modelled properties in design*

To illustrate the concepts that have been presented in this section, consider the properties modelled by designers firstly in designing automotive engine components, and secondly in electronic circuit design. Figure 1.3 shows a drawing of an automotive component which is annotated to demonstrate different modelled properties, and Figure 1.4 shows a diagram of a simple electrical circuit to illustrate the different

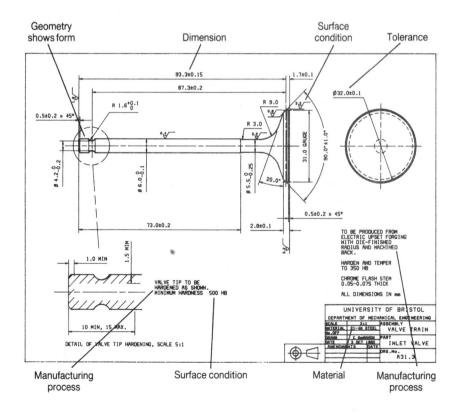

FIGURE 1.3
Modelled properties represented in a drawing.

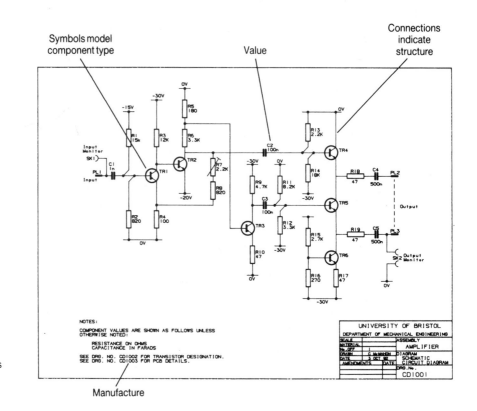

Symbols model component type

Value

Connections indicate structure

Manufacture

FIGURE 1.4

Modelled properties represented in a diagram.

properties represented in such a model. The purpose of drawings and diagrams is to represent those attributes of engineering products that must be defined in order for the products to be made.

1.4 Application of design models

The previous section concentrated on those models of design that are created by the designer, and emphasized that form and structure are the predominant modelled properties in design. Let us turn now to the receiver of the communication, and consider the sort of actions that are taken with the design information that is received. These may be divided into two main classifications: **evaluating** actions, taken to assess the properties or merit of the design, and **generative** actions that generate information from the model for use downstream of the design process, usually in order to progress its manufacture. In each case the actions involve the extraction of information from the design representation, and the combination of this with further information to form a new model. This is shown diagrammatically in Figure 1.5.

Consider now, as an example, the evaluation of the connecting rods which connect the crankshaft of an automotive engine to its pistons. Figure 1.6(a) shows a drawing of these three components produced from a CAD model. A design analyst might use this for the following assessments:

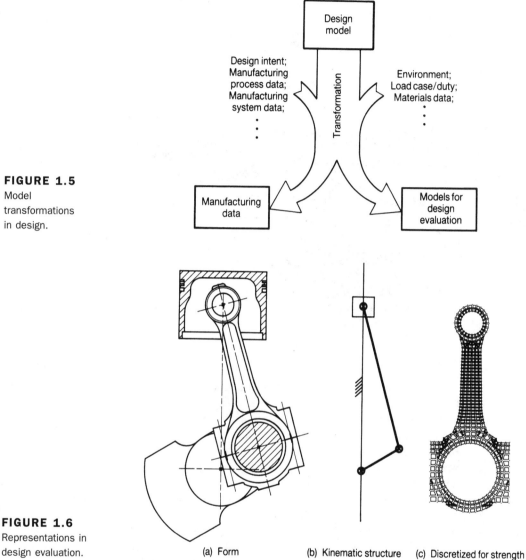

FIGURE 1.5
Model
transformations
in design.

FIGURE 1.6
Representations in
design evaluation.

(a) Form　　　　(b) Kinematic structure　　(c) Discretized for strength

▶ a visual assessment, by inspection of the drawing or CAD model, to ensure that there are no obvious weak areas;

▶ an assessment of the mass of the components, by analysis using the CAD model;

▶ an evaluation of loads in the components, by considering them as parts of a mechanism, as shown in Figure 1.6(b);

▶ an evaluation of stresses, for example using a finite element analysis model as in Figure 1.6(c).

At a later stage, detailed drawings will exist of the components of the design, and from these, manufacturing engineers will extract information for tooling and for the control of production machines.

1.5 Concurrent engineering

In a traditional design process, broadly complete design descriptions are produced in the form of engineering drawings and diagrams, and these are then issued by the design department of a company for analytical evaluation, and for the preparation of plans and instructions for manufacture. Inevitably, the manufacturing specialists and design analysts find aspects of the design that they feel should be improved, and so the design is returned to the design department for modification and reissue of the drawings. In some cases, reissue may occur many times – one large aerospace manufacturer is said to change each drawing an average of 4.5 times before final release – and thus the whole process is both time consuming and costly. Furthermore, because the considerations of manufacturing and other specialists are taken into account after the design drawings have been produced, the design department tends to concentrate on functional aspects of the design at the expense of ease of manufacture, maintainability and so on. Concurrent engineering aims to overcome all of these limitations, by bringing together a design team with the appropriate combination of specialist expertise to consider, early in the design process, all elements of the product life cycle from conception through manufacture and use in service to maintenance and disposal.

The traditional approach to product development is often described as an 'over the wall' approach, because each department involved in the process tends to complete their work and then metaphorically throw it over the wall to the next department. These barriers in communication between phases of product development are broken down in concurrent engineering to enable faster and more responsive product development and a higher product quality. In Figure 1.7 (based on Prasad (1995) and Solhenius (1992)), the sequential and concurrent approaches are compared.

Of course, there are circumstances in which concurrent engineering is not necessarily the best approach, especially where there is very high uncertainty in the product development process, or where a very radical design concept is being developed. In these cases, it might, for example, be more appropriate to develop the functional aspects of a design to a good degree of certainty *before* proceeding to evaluate manufacturing and other life cycle issues (AitSahlia *et al.*, 1995).

1.6 Modelling using CAD

During the design process, the design is progressively refined, in the abstract, until it is completely defined for manufacture or construction. To support the development of the design, designers construct a series of models of various aspects of the design using a number of representation techniques. Sequentially or concurrently, others involved in the evaluation of the design and in the manufacture of the product extract

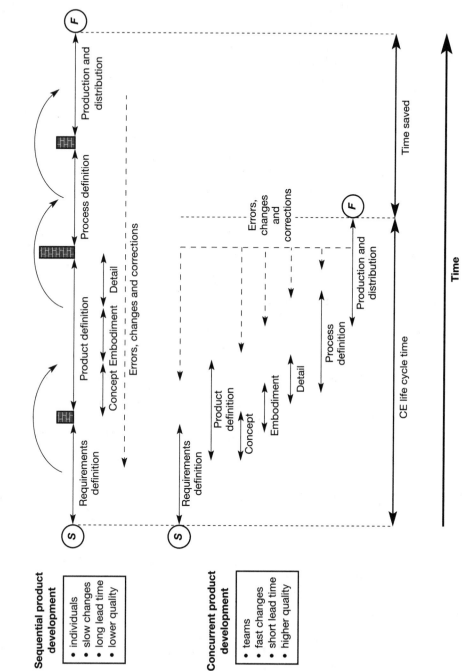

FIGURE 1.7
Sequential versus
concurrent product
development from
start, S to finish, F.

Sequential product development

- individuals
- slow changes
- long lead time
- lower quality

Concurrent product development

- teams
- fast changes
- short lead time
- higher quality

Time

Time saved

CE life cycle time

Sequential product development

Requirements definition
Product definition
Concept Embodiment Detail
Process definition
Production and distribution
Errors, changes and corrections

Concurrent product development

Requirements definition
Product definition
Concept
Embodiment
Detail
Process definition
Production and distribution
Errors, changes and corrections

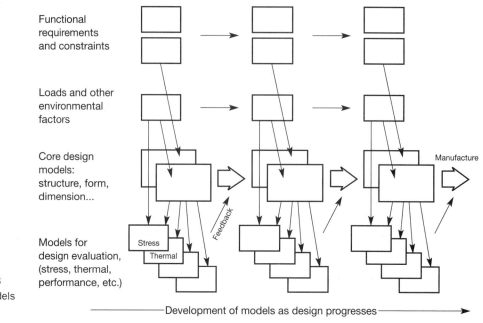

Functional requirements and constraints

Loads and other environmental factors

Core design models: structure, form, dimension...

Manufacture

Models for design evaluation, (stress, thermal, performance, etc.)

Feedback

Development of models as design progresses

FIGURE 1.8

The use of models in design.

information from these models and, in the process, form new models to assist them in their work. Figure 1.8 shows this development in a concurrent engineering process. This figure shows models of the information required for manufacture of the product – the form, dimension, surface condition, structure and so on, being developed as the core of the design process. In parallel, the following are also developed:

▶ models of the functional and other customer requirements for the design, because these may also develop and change as the design progresses;

▶ models of constraints on the design, imposed for example by available materials and manufacturing processes;

▶ models of loads imposed on the design;

▶ models used to evaluate the performance of the design – for example, for stress or thermal analysis, or for aerodynamic assessment.

In this book, the role of CAD in the design process will be presented within the context of this description.

The aim of CAD is to apply computers to both the modelling and communication of designs. There have been two different approaches – which are often used together – namely:

▶ at a basic level, to use computers to automate or assist in such tasks as the production of drawings or diagrams and the generation of lists of parts in a design;

▶ at a more advanced level, to provide new techniques which give the designer enhanced facilities to assist in the design process.

The bulk of the development in commercial CAD systems has been in modelling the form of products (i.e. in providing techniques to assist in the representation of form using conventional drawings or new modelling techniques) or in systems to assist in the production of diagrams and the subsequent evaluation of designs represented by these diagrams.

The driving force behind the provision of computer assistance for conventional modelling techniques has been the desire to improve the productivity of the designer by the automation of the more repetitive and tedious aspects of design, and also to improve the precision of the design models. New techniques have been developed in an attempt to overcome perceived limitations in conventional practice – particularly in dealing with complexity – for example, in the complexity of form of some designs such as automobile bodies, or the intricacy of structure of products such as integrated circuits. CAD should therefore enable the designer to tackle a task more quickly and accurately, or in a way that could not be achieved by other means. Of course, in many cases, both these benefits may be obtained.

In Figure 1.8, models of the design are shown being developed and refined throughout the design process, and being applied at various stages to the evaluation of the design, or to the generation of information for manufacture. This corresponds with the view that CAD should involve the development of a central design description on which all applications in design and manufacture should feed. This implies that computer-based techniques for the analysis and simulation of the design, and for the generation of manufacturing instructions, should be closely integrated with the techniques for modelling the form and structure of the design. In addition, a central design description forms an excellent basis for the simultaneous development of all aspects of a design in concurrent engineering activities.

In principle, CAD could be applied throughout the design process, but in practice its impact on the early stages, where very imprecise representations such as sketches are used extensively, has been limited. It must also be stressed that at present CAD does not help the designer in the more creative parts of design, such as the generation of possible design solutions, or in those aspects that involve complex reasoning about the design – for example, in assessing by visual examination of drawings whether a component may be made, or whether it matches the specification. These aspects are, however, the subject of considerable current research, and possible routes for the future development of CAD systems will be considered in Chapter 8.

1.7 A CAD system architecture

So far, CAD systems have been described in very general terms. More specifically, they can be thought of as comprising:

▶ **hardware**: the computer and associated peripheral equipment;

▶ **software**: the computer program(s) running on the hardware;

▶ data: the data structure created and manipulated by the software;

▶ human knowledge and activities.

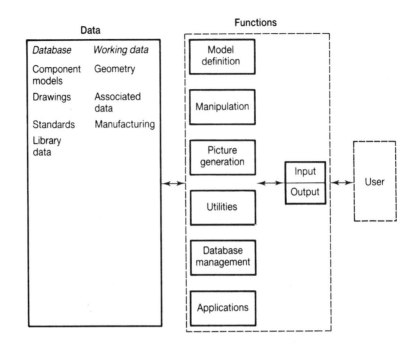

FIGURE 1.9
The architecture of
a computer-aided
design system.

CAD systems are no more than computer programs (although often large and complex), perhaps using specialized computing hardware. The software normally comprises a number of different elements or functions that process the data stored in the database in different ways. These are represented diagrammatically in Figure 1.9, and include elements for:

▶ **model definition**: for example, to add geometric elements to a model of the form of a component;

▶ **model manipulation**: to move, copy, delete, edit or otherwise modify elements in the design model;

▶ **picture generation**: to generate images of the design model on a computer screen or on some hard-copy device;

▶ **user interaction**: to handle commands input by the user and to present output to the user about the operation of the system;

▶ **database management**: for the management of the files that make up the database;

▶ **applications**: these elements of the software do not modify the design model, but use it to generate information for evaluation, analysis or manufacture;

▶ **utilities**: a 'catch-all' term for parts of the software that do not directly affect the design model, but modify the operation of the system in some way (e.g. to select the colour to be used for display, or the units to be used for construction of a part model).

These features may be provided by multiple programs operating on a common database, or by a single program encompassing all of the elements.

This description of the architecture of CAD systems has been used to guide the structure of the first part of this book. The next two chapters will discuss computer techniques for the modelling of designs, while Chapter 4 will outline techniques for the display of these models, and for user interaction with the system (essentially the elements of interactive computer graphics). Chapter 5 will introduce the data structures used to store CAD models, and will then describe some of the approaches used in the manipulation of descriptions of geometry. Applications of the model in design will be covered in Chapter 6, and, in Part Two, applications in manufacture will be addressed. The final chapters of Part One will discuss standards that have been established in CAD data representation, presentation and communication, and the ways in which CAD is currently developing to enhance its usefulness.

1.8 Conclusion

In this chapter the scene has been set for the discussion of computer-aided design. In particular, the various stages in the design process have been examined, as have the ways models of design are devised throughout this process. These models are developed using a variety of representations, and they model a range of properties of the design. Their role involves both describing the design while it is still an abstract concept, and communicating this description throughout the product introduction process. The view has been presented that CAD provides techniques both for automating aspects of this modelling of designs, and for modelling designs in new ways. From this view, a general description of a CAD system in terms of elements for model definition, manipulation and storage was presented, and this description will be used to guide the structure of the first part of this book.

References and further reading

AitSahlia F., Johnson E. and Will P. (1995). Is concurrent engineering always a sensible proposition? *IEEE Transactions on Engineering Management*. **42**(2), 166–70.

Chasen S. H. (1981). Historical highlights of interactive computer graphics. *Mechanical Engineering*. November, 32–41.

Computer-aided Design. **21**(5), June 1989 (special issue commemorating 21 years of the journal, with many interesting review articles).

Cross N. (1994). *Engineering Design Methods: Strategies for Product Design*. 2nd. edn. Chichester: John Wiley.

Finger S. and Dixon J. R. (1989). A review of research in mechanical engineering design, Part I: Descriptive, prescriptive, and computer-based models of design processes. *Research in Engineering Design*. **1**(1), 51–68.

Finger S. and Dixon J. R. (1989). A review of research in mechanical engineering design, Part II: Representations, analysis, and design for the life cycle. *Research in Engineering Design*. **1**(2), 121–38.

French M. J. (1985). *Conceptual Design for Engineers*. London: The Design Council/Springer.

Hubka, V. (1982). *Principles of Engineering Design*. London: Butterworth Scientific.

Kidd P. T. (1994). *Agile Manufacturing: Forging New Frontiers*. Harlow: Addison Wesley Longman.

Nevins J. L. and Whitney D. E. (eds) (1989). *Concurrent Design of Products and Processes: A Strategy for the Next Generation in Manufacturing*. New York: McGraw-Hill.

Ohsuga S. (1989). Towards intelligent CAD systems. *Computer-aided Design*. **21**(5), 315–37.

Pahl G. and Beitz W. (1984). *Engineering Design*. London: The Design Council/Springer.

Prasad B. (1995). Sequential versus concurrent engineering – an analogy. *Concurrent Engineering: Research and Applications*. **3**(4), 250–5.

Prasad B. (1996a). *Concurrent Engineering Fundamentals, Vol. 1: Integrated Product and Process Organisation*. Englewood Cliffs, NJ: PTR Prentice Hall.

Prasad B. (1996b). *Concurrent Engineering Fundamentals, Vol. 2: Integrated Product Development*. Englewood Cliffs, NJ: PTR Prentice Hall.

Pugh S. (1991). *Total Design*. Harlow: Addison Wesley Longman.

Salzberg S. and Watkins M. (1990). Managing information for concurrent engineering: challenges and barriers. *Research in Engineering Design*. **2**(1), 35–52.

Solhenius G. (1992). Concurrent engineering. *Annals of the CIRP*. **41**(2), 645–55.

Suh Nam P. (1990). *The Principles of Design*. New York: Oxford University Press.

Tjalve E., Andreasen M. M. and Frackmann Schmidt F. (1979). *Engineering Graphic Modelling*. London: Newnes-Butterworths.

Tomiyama T., Kiriyama T., Takeda H., Xue D. and Yoshikawa H. (1989). Metamodel: A key to intelligent CAD systems. *Research in Engineering Design*. **1**(1), 19–34.

Exercises

1.1 Select a design project or exercise with which you have been involved, and try to describe the models that you used in its development. What modelled properties were represented in these?

1.2 Research the design textbooks in your library. Are the models of the design process that they present consistent with the models discussed here? In what ways do they differ?

1.3 What are the differences between the sequential approach to the product development process and the concurrent engineering approach? Why should the latter be adopted?

1.4 Under what circumstances might it be appropriate to adopt a sequential engineering or hybrid approach, rather than a fully concurrent engineering approach?

1.5 Select an engineering product with which you are familiar, and then try to identify the range of engineering and other specialists that would have an input into its product development process.

1.6 Using a simplified description of the design process, consider where computational aids might be of assistance to the designer. What features of computers are likely to contribute to their usefulness, and what features may limit their application?

1.7 Distinguish between models of the design process and models of designs.

1.8 Give examples of the use of the different **representations** in modelling a given property of a product.

1.9 Consider a computer program with which you are familiar – for example, a text editor or a spreadsheet. Try to identify the functional elements of this program, and the nature of the data on which these act.

1.10 Explore the command structures of CAD systems to which you have access. Are you able to subdivide the functions into the categories given in Section 1.7? Are all the functions provided by a single program, or by multiple programs?

Projects

In this book, two projects will be developed chapter by chapter in Parts One and Two to allow the reader to explore through simple example applications some of the concepts that are being developed. The projects involve the development of CAD models of a single part, and of a small electro-mechanical assembly, and then the use of those models in analysis and in manufacturing data preparation. At the end of each chapter, the next stage in the development of the project will be introduced, and background study to support the project work will be proposed.

The two projects are:

1. To design, model and then manufacture a single part. The part that is proposed is a chess piece (although other parts would be suitable), and ideally the work would be done in conjunction with others so that a chess set can be designed and made. Figure 1.10 shows a photograph of some typical chess pieces designed using CAD for CNC manufacture. The main objectives of the project are to:

   ▶ produce models of the chess piece using wire-frame, surface and solid modelling;
   ▶ use these models to prepare manufacturing instructions for the chess piece using CNC machining.

FIGURE 1.10
Examples of CNC-machined chess pieces.

The chess piece is a part that may be made just by turning, or may involve turning and milling. It is a suitable subject for a small, flexible manufacturing cell, if available.

2. To model, analyse and manufacture a small electro-mechanical assembly. The artefact that is proposed is a strain gauge load cell, with the signal amplification electronics mounted on a circuit board attached to the load cell, although in principle any simple assembly could be used as the topic for the project. A drawing of the load cell is given in Figure 1.11, and a diagram for the electronics circuit is given in Figure 1.12. The main objectives of the project are to:

▶ produce a full set of two-dimensional engineering drawings and diagrams of the artefact;
▶ produce a solid model of the artefact;
▶ produce a finite element model of the main mechanical member of the load cell, and to use this to examine its stress distribution;
▶ manufacture the mechanical member of the load cell by CNC machining.

Additional, subsidiary objectives for each project will be introduced as the chapters develop.

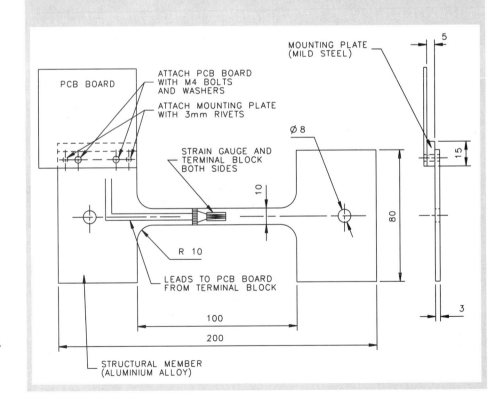

FIGURE 1.11

Drawing of a load cell.

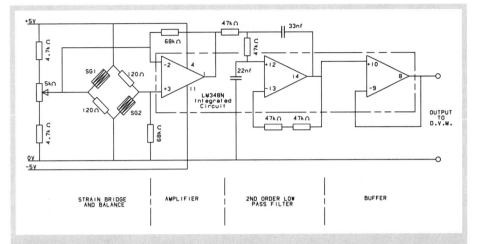

FIGURE 1.12

Circuit diagram for load cell electronics. (Note: SG1, 2 = strain gauges; D.V.M. = digital volt meter.)

Project tasks at this stage are as follows:

Project 1 Chess piece Select a chess piece to design, and then produce sketches of concept designs to develop in subsequent chapters.

Project 2 Load cell Plan the drawings and diagrams that will be needed to represent the artefact. Decide how the parts list is to be made. Research for information about standard parts (e.g. fasteners and electronic parts) to be incorporated in the design.

2 Defining the model

Chapter objectives

When you have completed studying material in this chapter you should be able to:

▶ describe the principal languages for defining engineering designs using drawings and diagrams;

▶ understand the ways in which computers may contribute to modelling of geometry, and of symbols and connections, in drawings and diagrams;

▶ understand the new ways in which computers may be used to generate models of the three-dimensional form of engineering artefacts;

▶ distinguish between the wire-frame, surface and solid modelling schemes for three-dimensional descriptions of geometry;

▶ describe examples of the geometric elements used in the three-dimensional modelling schemes, and outline the method of modelling using these elements.

Chapter contents

2.1 Introduction

In Chapter 1 the range of models that are used to describe engineering designs was introduced, and it was observed that two types of model predominate: firstly, models of **form**, traditionally involving drawings of components and their arrangement in assemblies, and secondly, models of **structure**, traditionally involving diagrams that show the components of a system and how they are connected. It was also seen that successful communication requires the language of communication to be well defined and understood by both the transmitter and the receiver of the message. In the case of engineering drawings and diagrams the rules or **syntax** for their production have been developed over many years, and are now well formalized in standards promoted by the standards organizations of many countries and, in some cases, even companies.

In this chapter the conventional approach to representing models of form and structure by drawings and diagrams will first be broadly reviewed. This will be followed by an exploration of the ways in which computer graphics and computational geometry may assist in modelling using drawings and diagrams, and in alternative representations of form using three-dimensional geometric modelling.

2.2 Established design representations

2.2.1 The representation of form using drawings

The technique of representing three-dimensional forms in two-dimensional space by means of engineering drawings – on paper or on a computer screen – is formally known as **descriptive geometry**. The subject has its origins in antiquity. Parallel projection to create an image of the geometry of a structure was known in Roman times, and projection into multiple picture planes was practised in the Middle Ages, in particular in architectural drawing, but the rationale of the technique as used today has been developed from principles proposed by the French military engineer Gaspard Monge (1746–1818). Monge formalized the method of representing shape by projecting views of an object (in his case military engineering works) into two mutually perpendicular planes: a vertical plane on which elevations were drawn, and a horizontal plane on which plans were drawn (Booker, 1979).

The essence of Mongian projection is still applied today. Three-dimensional forms are represented in two dimensions by mapping points on the object into multiple mutually perpendicular planes of projection using parallel projectors that are normal to the planes of projection. From the projection of *points* may be derived the projection of *edges* of the object, and from the *edges* the *surfaces* that bound the object. Projection into two-dimensional space is obtained by 'unfolding' the multiple perpendicular planes of projection into a single plane, an operation that also relates the projection planes to each other in a formal manner. As an example, let us consider Figure 2.1, which shows a simple object surrounded by a box, the faces of which form the planes of projection.

Figure 2.1 also shows some of the many other conventions used in the production of engineering drawings. These are described in detail in standards such as the American National Standards Institute Y14 series, or British Standard Institution's BS308 (1990), but in summary:

▶ Different line-styles have different meanings on a drawing. For example, edges that are hidden from view are shown as dashed lines, and chain-dashed lines are used to signify axes of symmetry.

▶ The internal form of shapes is described by imagining part of the object removed to show internal detail in a **sectional view**.

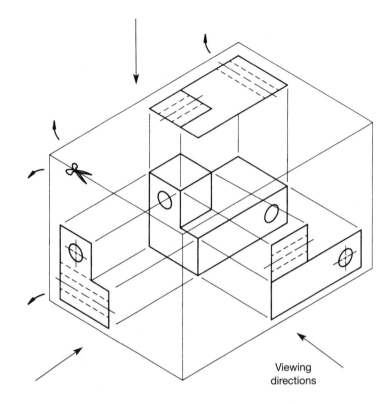

FIGURE 2.1
Orthographic projection of a simple shape.

Viewing directions

▶ Two principal conventions exist to specify how views should be related to each other on a drawing. One, known as **third angle projection**, has been widely adopted in North America and to a certain extent in the United Kingdom and elsewhere. In third angle projection, the projection plane is between the object and the viewer, as shown in Figure 2.1. This is the convention that which will be adopted here. The alternative, **first angle projection**, is more common in continental Europe. In first angle projection, the projection plane is behind the part with respect to the viewer.

▶ Projection into a single plane that is not, in general, aligned with any of the main faces of an object is known as **pictorial projection**. If parallel projectors are used, as for example in Figure 2.2, then scale information is preserved. In some cases, such as the representation of buildings or of large engineering products, visual impression is important, and in such cases **perspective projection** is widely used: Figure 2.3 gives an example for the geometry of Figures 2.1 and 2.2. Perspective projection has the added merit of giving a depth cue to assist in interpreting the drawing.

▶ Dimensions are not measured directly from the drawing geometry, but instead are identified using a symbolic representation that also allows tolerance and surface condition information to be incorporated on the drawing.

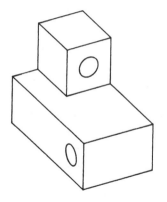

FIGURE 2.2
Parallel pictorial
projection of a
simple shape.

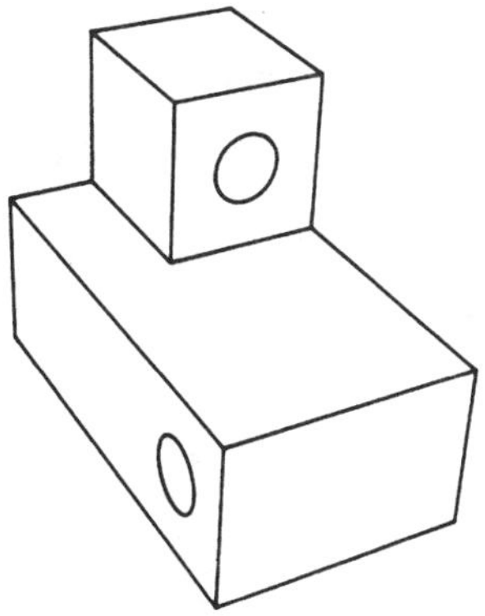

FIGURE 2.3
Perspective
projection of a
simple shape.

▶ Extensive use is also made of symbolic representations as a form of shorthand to allow the repetitive drawing of complex shapes, such as threads and gears, to be avoided.

2.2.2 The representation of structure using diagrams

In engineering diagrams the logical or physical structure of a system, in terms of the assembly of the primitive parts and the relationship between these, is shown by a series of **symbols** joined by **connections**. The rules for the symbols, and for the connections, are again governed by conventions that have been established in standards. The guidelines and conventions for the preparation of diagrams are reasonably common to all disciplines – in the United Kingdom they are described, for example, in British Standard BS5070, and in the United States again in the ANSI Y14 series – but the syntax for symbols varies somewhat between disciplines. Figure 2.4 shows examples of symbols from electrical and fluid power engineering. The interested reader is referred again to the appropriate standards: American standards are contained in the American National Standards Institute Y32 series, and relevant British Standards are BS3939 for electrical symbols, BS2917 for fluid power systems elements and BS1553 for general engineering symbols.

Direction control valve   Make contact   n–p–n transistor

Shuttle valve   Link   p–n diode

FIGURE 2.4

Examples of
electrical and fluid
power symbols.

Differential cylinder   Battery   Variable resistor

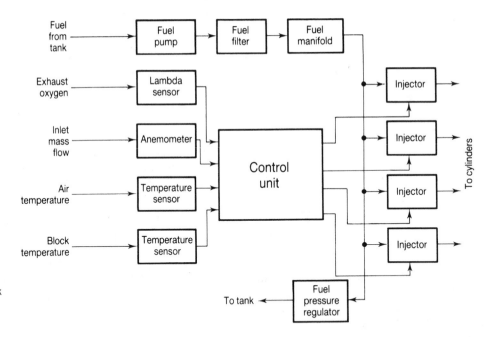

FIGURE 2.5

Example of a block
diagram (for a fuel
injection system).

It has been noted that different drawing types and styles are required at different
stages in the design process. The same is true for diagrams: at an early stage in the
design process it may only be possible to define overall relationships between parts
of a system, and a block diagram may be most appropriate, as shown in Figure 2.5. As
a design is prepared for manufacture, detailed wiring or piping diagrams are required.

By exploiting representations such as block diagrams, the designer is able to subdivide a design problem into smaller, more manageable elements. These in turn may

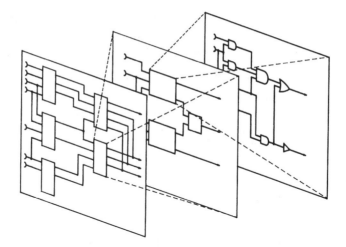

FIGURE 2.6
A hierarchical
arrangement of
diagrams.

be subdivided, such that a hierarchical decomposition of the problem is obtained. One powerful design technique, much used by systems engineers, is to carry out this decomposition at successively lower and more detailed levels of design. This is known as **top-down** design. The practice is encouraged by a feature of diagrammatic representation which allows a symbol at one level to represent a diagram at a more detailed level. An illustration of this is shown in Figure 2.6. It will be seen later that this characteristic of diagrams has been widely exploited in some branches of CAD.

2.2.3 Strengths and weaknesses of conventional representations

Conventional representations of designs have great strengths, and have served the engineer well for many years. Practically any product, from precision machinery to large structures such as bridges, aircraft or buildings, can be represented by Mongian projection (although it may take in the order of 100 000 drawings and other documents to define something as complex as an aircraft). Diagrams may be used to represent virtually any system that may be devised. The existence of established syntaxes also means that all in the engineering business – from technical director to skilled machinist on the shop floor – understand and can interpret the standards.

There are, however, several limitations in the conventional approaches. Firstly, skill is required in the construction and interpretation of drawings. Secondly, it is possible to have conflicting or erroneous models – perhaps views on a drawing that do not correspond, or diagrams with unmatched connections on symbols. Finally, complexity in the product may stretch the techniques to their limits. For example, certain geometries may be very difficult to represent using drawings – particularly where there are complex, doubly curved surfaces such as on automobile or aircraft bodies. In disciplines such as electronic systems design, the sheer number of elements in an integrated circuit or in a computer system may be impossibly laborious to represent using diagrams produced by hand.

Extraction of information from drawings and diagrams

It has been stressed that the main model representation of a design is used to generate further models for assessment and for generation of manufacturing information. It is here that perhaps the greatest weakness of conventional methods lies. The generation of the new models requires the engineer to identify visually the information required from a drawing or diagram. In this lies the shortcoming. Drawings are easily misread – either because of ambiguity or error in the drawing or simply because of human error in the interpretation. In other cases the understanding of a drawing – for example, of a complex shape – may be correct, but different from other interpretations of the same drawing. One automotive company reported a 2–3% variation in performance of engines that were identical except that certain of the more complex castings were produced from patterns made by different pattern-makers – and yet all the patterns were 'correct to drawing'. Whenever there is a transcription from a drawing to extract information there is a risk of error or misinterpretation.

2.3 The computer representation of drawings and diagrams

In Chapter 1 it was noted that CAD may contribute to automating and improving existing techniques, or to providing new methods. The computer generation of drawings and diagrams falls largely into the first category, and seeks to improve the design modelling process by increasing both the speed with which designs may be represented, and the accuracy of representation. It achieves this in part by providing semi-automatic facilities for such tasks as the annotation of drawings with dimensions and labels, or for complex constructions, but especially by facilitating the repetitive use of drawing geometry. In doing so it substantially reduces the risk of transcription errors in the propagation of geometry through the design process, and, as shall be seen later, in the extraction of geometric information for analysis and manufacture.

2.3.1 Computer-aided draughting

At this stage in considering the computer representation of drawings, we are only concerned with the representation of the geometry. The processes of displaying and manipulating the model, and of annotating it to show dimension, material and other data, will be discussed in later chapters. The representation itself is, in general, identical to that used in normal draughting. The same standards will be used wherever possible, and the drawing will be a collection of points, lines, arcs, conic sections and other curves (single geometric elements are often called **entities**) arranged in a two-dimensional plane. Some examples of the geometric entity types available on a popular personal-computer-based CAD system are shown in Figure 2.7. These entities will normally be defined by the system in terms of numeric values for their point coordinate or other data. For example, a line might be defined by the x and y coordinate values of the start and end points, and an arc by the x and y coordinates of the centre point, and the radius and start and end angles.

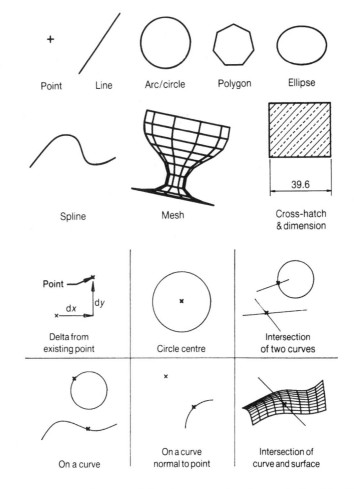

FIGURE 2.7
Geometric entity types available on a PC-based CAD system.

Point   Line   Arc/circle   Polygon   Ellipse

Spline   Mesh   Cross-hatch & dimension

39.6

Point   dx   dy

Delta from existing point   Circle centre   Intersection of two curves

On a curve   On a curve normal to point   Intersection of curve and surface

FIGURE 2.8
Methods for point construction.

In manual drawing, the size of the representation is constrained by the physical size of the drawing sheet, and thus artefacts of different sizes are accommodated by changing the scale of drawing. In CAD such constraints do not exist. The model is constructed by a set of computational procedures which generate curves within a two-dimensional (*x–y*) coordinate system that is limited only by constraints on the size of numbers that may be effectively stored and manipulated by the computer (on one system the coordinate system limits are, for example, 9 999 999 mm or inches in any direction, and this is well below the limits imposed by the computer representation of data). As a consequence, in CAD, drawings should be constructed at *full size* (whether for a bridge or for a precision instrument). It is only when the drawing is reproduced on a computer screen or hard copy such as a plot that the scale of reproduction is important.

CAD also provides the designer with a rich variety of techniques for the definition of geometric entities. These are perhaps best illustrated by examples from a typical commercial system. Figures 2.8–2.10 illustrate a small number of the many methods available in one system for the definition of points, lines and arcs respectively (as an

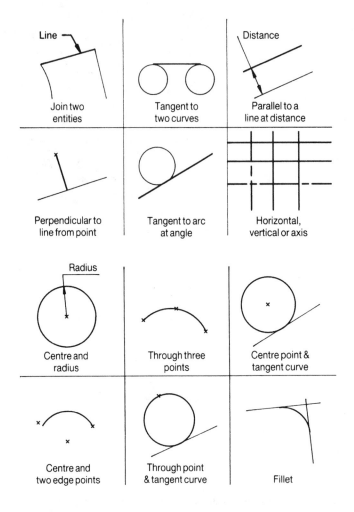

FIGURE 2.9
Methods for line
construction.

FIGURE 2.10
Methods for arc
construction.

exercise, the reader might investigate the methods available on the CAD system to which he or she has access). The facilities for point generation are of particular note: in CAD the model is often developed from a network of points upon which other geometric entities are constructed. These points may be point entities themselves, or implied points related to other entities or intersections. They may also be put in by the designer by entering a coordinate value or by pointing to a position on a computer screen. To assist construction, many systems offer the facility to generate a grid pattern in the construction plane of the system such that user-indicated positions are constrained to lie at grid points. Other facilities are those which allow new geometric entities to be constructed from existing curves, in particular the blending routines for generating fillet arcs, as shown in Figure 2.10.

Because the component geometry may be defined precisely, and may be constructed at full size, the risk of error in the creation and interrogation of a computer-based drawing is lower than for the manual equivalent. In Chapter 6, it will be seen that this benefit is enhanced with functions to create dimensions and other annotation directly from the stored model. This, combined with the facility to reuse stored models, and to manipulate the database, is a powerful aid to the engineer.

2.3.2 Computer-aided schematic drawing

Computer-aided schematic drawing involves using the computer to assist in the production of schematic diagrams. Once again, the appearance of a computer-generated diagram is effectively the same as a manually drawn diagram, and again it is constructed broadly as a collection of lines and arcs. In this case, however, the lines and arcs are aggregated into **symbols** and **connections**, and the user constructs the diagram essentially by placing symbols into position within the two-dimensional construction space, and then connecting the symbols with series of lines that represent the connections.

Many draughting systems have the facility to group together a collection of entities into a superentity that may be known as a **pattern**, a **template** or a **symbol**. They are also able to draw a series of connected lines (perhaps called a **polyline**), possibly constrained to be parallel to the x- and y-axes of the coordinate system. A diagram might, for example, be constructed as a series of patterns connected by polylines. Such systems are useful for the draughting of schematic diagrams, but contain no explicit information within the database concerning the symbols connected by a given polyline, or the 'connections' available on a given symbol. For such facilities we must look to systems that are dedicated to the production of schematic diagrams. Such systems often form a part of computer-aided engineering facilities used for the definition, simulation and manufacture of electronic devices and equipment.

In a dedicated computer-aided schematic system, the basic building blocks of the system will be symbols which are explicitly defined to have connection points, and connectors which are constructed between a connection point on one symbol to one or more other symbols, or to other connectors. It is then possible to extract from a diagram made up of such building blocks a list of the symbols (i.e. the devices they represent) and of the way in which they are connected. This is known as a **netlist**. Such a representation may be used to identify unused connection points on symbols and uncompleted connections. Furthermore, inputs and outputs on a schematic diagram may be modelled, and one schematic may then be used to model the structure of a device represented by a symbol (with connection points as inputs and outputs) on a higher-level schematic. Finally, models of the operation of the devices within a circuit may be combined, using the netlist, to model for simulation the system represented by a schematic.

Figure 2.11 shows a diagram drawn using a computer-aided schematic system, as it would appear on the screen display of the system. In disciplines such as integrated circuit design a whole hierarchy of diagrams may be used, as suggested in Figure 2.6, from a block diagram at the highest level, down to transistor-level representation at the lowest level. The ability to represent designs in such a hierarchical fashion is of great value in top-down design.

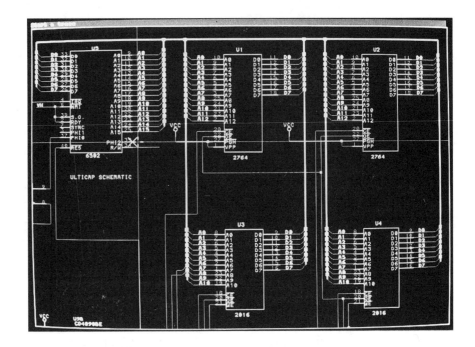

FIGURE 2.11
Diagram drawn with
a computer-aided
schematic system.
(Reproduced by
permission of ULTI-
mate Technology
(UK) Ltd.)

2.4 Three-dimensional modelling schemes

In Section 2.2.3 some of the limitations of orthographic projection as a means of representing engineering geometries were noted. As a consequence of these limitations, various methods have been developed for the representation of geometry using schemes which do not rely on projection into planar space. These schemes involve the construction of a single representation of the component geometry in **three-dimensional** space. By using a single representation, the potential for error inherent in the use of multiple views of a component is avoided. Perhaps more importantly, however, a single representation is potentially far more useful as a basis for applications that involve interrogating the model to extract information for analysis and manufacture.

The methods that have been developed for three-dimensional modelling involve the representation of geometry as a collection of lines and other curves, or of surfaces, or of solids in space. These methods will be considered in turn below, but first it is appropriate to explain some terminologies. It has been seen that drawings are constructed in a two-dimensional coordinate system. Three-dimensional (3D) models are constructed in 3D space – typically in a right-handed **cartesian** coordinate system, as shown in Figure 2.12. There will normally be a fixed coordinate system which is used for the overall definition of the model – we will call this the **global coordinate system** (GCS) – and, in addition, a movable **work coordinate system** (WCS) may be used to assist in the construction of the model. Observe, for example, that the definition of an arc or a conic section curve is aided by using a coordinate system whose x–y plane is parallel to the plane of the curve, as shown in Figure 2.13.

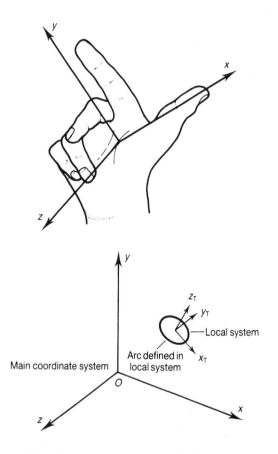

FIGURE 2.12
The right-handed
coordinate system.

FIGURE 2.13
Use of a local
coordinate system.

The geometric entities themselves are normally **instances** of geometric forms known as **primitives**, for which dimensions and orientation are **instantiated** for each entity in the representation. For example, a primitive entity might be an arc of a circle, the dimensions of which would be instantiated to particular values of radius, start and end angle and spatial orientation in a given case.

2.4.1 Wire-frame geometry

The first of the 3D schemes, and computationally the most straightforward, is the wire-frame scheme. In this the geometry is defined as a series of lines and curves representing the edges of, and perhaps sections through, the object. The name of the scheme arises from the wire-like appearance of the models when viewed on a computer screen or hard copy.

Wire-frame representation may be regarded as an extension into a third dimension of the techniques used for draughting. The entities used are generally the same as those used for draughting, although the data stored to define the entities must be extended. For points and lines this simply means adding a z value to the coordinate data, but for arcs and other planar curves the plane in which the curve lies has to be defined. This might involve, for example, referencing the WCS in which an arc is defined.

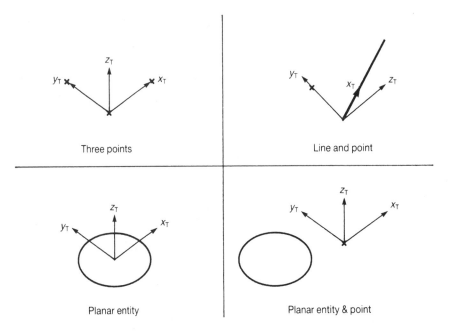

FIGURE 2.14
Methods for defining
local coordinate
systems.

The construction techniques used for the definition of wire-frame geometry are
again broadly similar to those for draughting, but with certain extensions. One that
has already been mentioned is the use of movable WCSs, and in general a number
of ways of defining WCSs from existing points or from existing coordinate systems
are provided. Some examples of methods offered by one CAD system are shown in
Figure 2.14. In the first method, the origin and x-direction of the coordinate system
are defined by two points. The y-direction is defined by the third point. In definition
by a line and point, the end points of the line define the origin and x-direction, and
the y-direction is again defined by a point. In definition by a planar entity, the centre and 0° position on the entity define the origin and x-direction. The y-direction
is at the 90° direction on the entity. The final method is identical, except that the
origin of the coordinate system is offset to a point. Associated with the WCS are
the concepts of the work plane and the working depth. Often, planar entities such
as arcs and conic sections are constructed by default in a plane (the work plane) parallel to the x–y plane of the WCS at a z-axis value equal to the working depth. The
work plane is also used for projected intersections and points: it is often useful to be
able to use apparent intersections of entities when viewed along the z-axis, even
though the entities may not physically intersect in space. In such cases the intersection points are projected into the work plane, as shown in Figure 2.15.

The wire-frame scheme is relatively straightforward to use, and is the most eco-
nomical of the 3D schemes in terms of computer time and memory requirements.
The scheme is particularly useful for preliminary layout work, for solving some geometric problems or for establishing overall spatial relationships for a design. It may
also be useful in some cases where dynamic manipulation of the display or of the
model is required (e.g. in animating the movement of a mechanism), but it exhibits

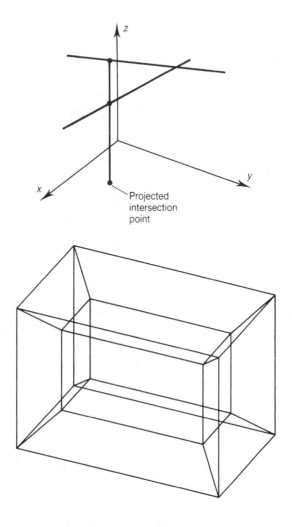

FIGURE 2.15
Projected
intersection of
entities.

FIGURE 2.16
Ambiguity in wire-
frame models.

a number of serious deficiencies when used to model engineering artefacts. These include:

▶ Ambiguity in representation, and possible nonsense objects. The classic example in this respect is the block with bevelled faces and a central hole shown in Figure 2.16. Is the hole from front to back, from top to bottom or from left to right?

▶ Deficiencies in pictorial representation. Parallel projection can make the orientation of models difficult to interpret – for example, it is not possible to say which corner of the block in Figure 2.16 is nearest to the viewer. Complex models are difficult to interpret (consider, for example, the buildings shown in Figure 2.17), and do not allow automatic viewing with hidden lines removed. Silhouette edges (e.g. of cylinders) may not normally be generated. Some improvement may be obtained with **depth cueing**, in which lines further away from the viewer are displayed less intensely to give an impression of depth.

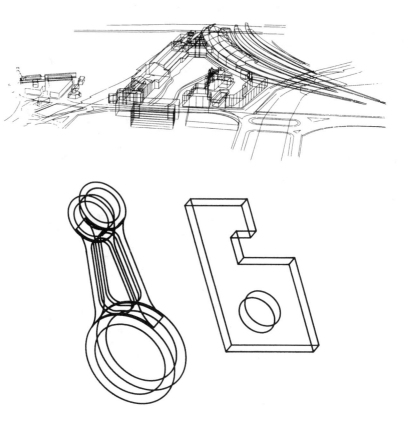

FIGURE 2.17
A wire-frame model of a group of buildings.

FIGURE 2.18
Shapes constructed with 2.5D representation.

▶ The ability to calculate mechanical properties, or geometric intersections, is limited.

▶ Wire-frame geometry is of limited value as a basis for manufacture or analysis.

Two classes of shapes for which a simple, wire-frame representation *is* often adequate are those shapes defined by projecting a planar profile along its normal, or by rotating a planar profile about an axis. Sheet metal components, or those cut from plates, often fall into the first category, and turned or other rotationally symmetric components into the second. Such shapes are not two dimensional, but neither do they require sophisticated 3D schemes for their representation. As a consequence, an intermediate representation, often called 'two-and-a-half-dimensional' or 2.5D, has been developed, and may be considered a subset of the wire-frame scheme. Examples of shapes constructed using 2.5D modelling are shown in Figure 2.18.

2.4.2 The surface representation scheme

Many of the ambiguities of wire-frame models are overcome by using the second of the three main 3D representation schemes – surface modelling. As the name implies, this scheme involves representing the model by specifying some or all of the surfaces on the component. Once again the representation generally involves a series of geometric entities, with each surface forming a single entity. The most elementary

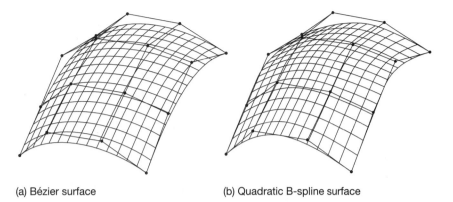

FIGURE 2.19
Examples of surfaces defined from points.

(a) Bézier surface   (b) Quadratic B-spline surface

of surface types is the flat plane, which may be defined in a number of ways including between two parallel lines, through three points or through a line and a point. Other surface definitions generally fall into one of three main categories. In the first category, surfaces are fitted to arrays of data points called **control points**, and the surface is generated either to pass through or to interpolate the points. The second category comprises surfaces which are based on curves: the surfaces may be imagined as forming a skin on top of a wire-frame skeleton. In the third and final category, surfaces are defined to interpolate between other surfaces, for example in the definition of blends.

Figure 2.19 shows examples of surfaces in the first category, which interpolate rectangular arrays of control points. The particular surfaces shown in this diagram are of types known as Bézier and B-spline surfaces, the mathematical basis for which will be introduced in the next chapter.

Figure 2.20 shows examples of a number of surfaces in the second category that are defined from one or more curves, including:

▶ A **tabulated cylinder**, which is defined by projecting a generating curve along a vector.

▶ A **ruled surface**, which is produced by linear interpolation between two different generating or edge curves. The effect is of a surface generated by moving a straight line with its end points resting on the edge curves.

▶ A **surface of revolution**, produced by revolving a generating curve about a centre line or vector. This surface is particularly useful when modelling turned parts, or parts which possess axial symmetry. Commercial CAD systems will often provide the facility to revolve multiple curves in a profile with a single command.

▶ A **swept surface** – in a sense an extension of the surface of revolution – where the defining curve is swept along an arbitrary spine curve instead of a circular arc.

▶ A **sculptured** or **curve-mesh** surface. This is among the most general of the surface types, and is defined by a grid of generating curves which intersect to form a patchwork of surface patches. Examples of this type of surface include the Coons patch, which we will meet again in the next chapter, and the Gordon surface (Mortenson, 1985).

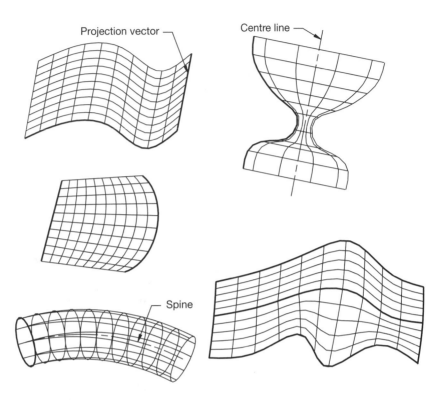

FIGURE 2.20

Examples of surfaces defined from curves.

Bold lines = generating curves

Figure 2.21 shows examples of surfaces in the third category, which interpolate between surfaces. This category may include chamfer surfaces, but largely comprises **fillet surfaces** that are analogous to the fillet arc in curve construction, and that are defined as surfaces connecting two other surfaces in a smooth transition. Fillet surfaces may be considered to be the result of rolling a sphere around the intersection between two surfaces. Fillet surfaces are generally either of a constant or of a smoothly changing radius of curvature. Fillet and chamfer surfaces are shown in Figure 2.21.

Each of the three categories above describe the way in which the surface is **defined**. The underlying mathematical basis of the surface, and the way that it is stored by the system, may in fact be the same for surfaces defined in different ways, and indeed there has been a trend towards more uniform representations in commercial modellers. Thus, in a particular system, a fillet surface, a curve-mesh surface and a surface interpolated through a grid of points might be stored in the same way. Real systems also often allow **composite** surfaces, which comprise a number of elemental surfaces joined together such that they appear to the system user to be a single surface.

In each of Figures 2.19–2.21 it should be noted that the surfaces are shown as meshes of intersecting curves. This is only for display purposes – the surfaces are continuous, with every point on the surface defined by the mathematical relationship used in its definition.

In general, real artefacts are represented using surface geometry by an assembly of surface 'patches'. A complete car body, for example, may require several hundred

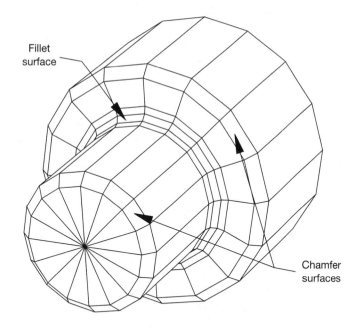

Fillet
surface

Chamfer
surfaces

FIGURE 2.21
Examples of
surfaces defined
from other surfaces.

patches. As noted by Pratt in Rooney and Steadman (1987), there are a number of distinct methods for defining multi-surface objects with 'free-form' surfaces in existing commercial systems. These include:

▶ To work initially in terms of a set of plane cross-sectional curves, not necessarily all in parallel planes. The system **skins** or blends the cross-sections to give a smooth surface, either by using a guiding spine to define swept surfaces, as shown in Figure 2.20, or by **lofting** over sets of curves. Examples of the skinning and lofting facilities offered by a commercial CADCAM system are shown in Figure 2.22. It should be noted that the surfaces shown in these cases often comprise multiple connected surface patches. This approach is most appropriate to shapes such as automotive engine ports and manifolds, pump volutes and so on.

▶ To establish an array of points in space, through which are fitted two sets of intersecting curves, with intersections at a number of the points, to give a curvilinear mesh. Surface patches of the curve-mesh type shown in Figure 2.20 are then fitted to the intersecting curves.

▶ To fit a surface directly to the point set without generating intermediate interpolating curves. The surface types shown in Figure 2.19 are typically used for this purpose.

In real engineering components the surfaces are also often more complex than those shown in the examples above. Even for relatively simple shapes, such as the blended, intersecting cylinders shown in Figure 2.23(a), the surfaces defining the cylinders are not complete surfaces of revolution or ruled surfaces, but parts of these elementary surfaces, bounded by intersections or joins with other surfaces. For many years CAD systems were limited in their ability to model such shapes using bounded

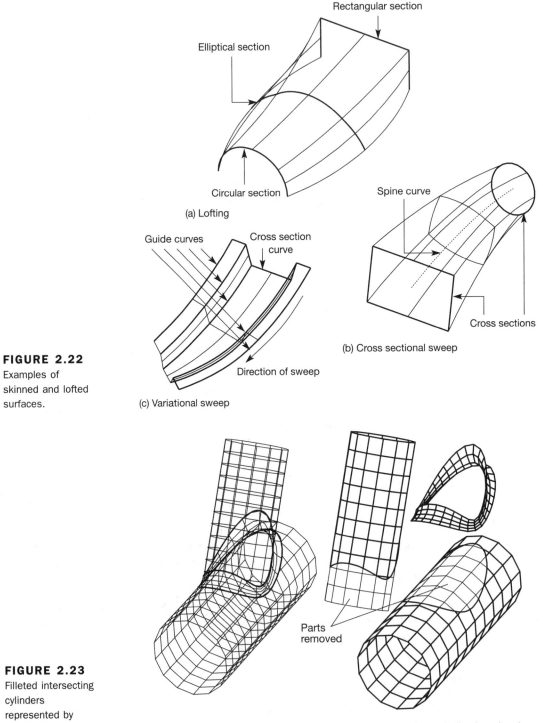

FIGURE 2.22
Examples of skinned and lofted surfaces.

(a) Lofting

(b) Cross sectional sweep

(c) Variational sweep

FIGURE 2.23
Filleted intersecting cylinders represented by trimmed surfaces.

(a) Trimmed surfaces

(b) Individual surfaces, indicating trimming

surfaces, but more recently the facility to trim or extend surfaces to curve or surface bounds, and to remove 'holes' from surfaces, has become the norm. Figure 2.23(b) shows the individual surfaces used in Figure 2.23(a), and how the surfaces representing the cylinders are defined by trimming them to the edges of the fillet surface.

The surface modelling scheme has been particularly widely applied in those areas of engineering where smoothly varying, or **faired**, surfaces are used – for example, in shipbuilding or aircraft manufacture. In these industries, complex shapes were traditionally defined by the process known as **lofting**, in which a series of cross-sections would be blended by smooth curves, often drawn with the aid of a thin, flexible metal or wooden strip known as a **spline**. Weights were often used to fix points through which the spline had to pass, while in other instances the strips would be fixed to wooden templates representing the cross-sections. Curves and sections were usually drawn full size, and the only place with room for this sort of activity was often the loft of the company's engineering offices – hence the name lofting, and the term **lofted surfaces**.

Surface modelling has also made great inroads in those branches of engineering, such as automobile or mould and die manufacture, in which extensive use has traditionally been made of physical models of parts of complex shape. In the automotive industry, for example, full-size clay models of body shapes are used for styling purposes, and subsequently to provide master models to define the vehicle form. Surface modelling has allowed the shape of these models to be captured and used for engineering models and for the preparation of instructions for the manufacture of dies for the sheet metal work. Surface models show very significant advantages over wire-frame models in the links to manufacture and to analysis, as we shall see in later chapters.

Computer-generated surfaces have also been used widely outside of engineering. For example, one of the early applications was in the definition of families of shoe lasts, and in the unfolding or 'development' of shapes for the cutting out of shoe leather. More recently, surface models have been used to manufacture dies for injection-moulded soles of shoes, and they are also applied in other areas of the garment industry, and in such fields as pottery and glass making.

It is in modelling artefacts such as the automobile body that the strengths and weaknesses of the surface method may be seen. Strengths are that ambiguities inherent in wire-frame models are for the most part eliminated, and the surface model provides an excellent basis for the generation of manufacturing information (e.g. for the machining of dies for sheet metal presswork) and of analysis data (e.g. finite element models for body stiffness calculations). In addition, almost arbitrarily complex forms may be precisely modelled, and the models may be distributed to all those in the product development process who require access to them.

Surface representations have several drawbacks, however. In general they are more computationally demanding than wire-frame, and they also require rather more skill in their construction and use (these considerations apply in particular to the more free-form surface types such as sculptured surfaces). Models of any complexity are difficult to interpret unless viewed with hidden surfaces removed.

There is also, as in the case of wire-frame representations, nothing inherent in the surface modelling scheme to prevent ambiguous or erroneous models. Surfaces

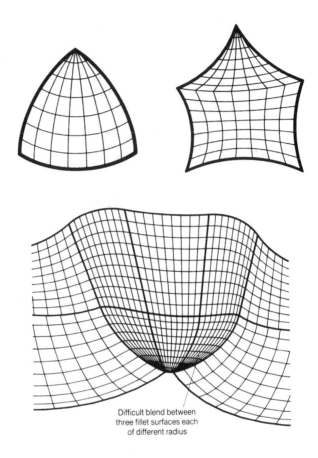

FIGURE 2.24
Three- and five-sided
patches.

FIGURE 2.25
Surface patches on
an automotive
wheel.

Difficult blend between
three fillet surfaces each
of different radius

may be discontinuous, or may intersect with themselves or with each other. Visual inspection of the model is required to identify physically impossible geometries. In general, there is no connectivity between surfaces. If one surface changes then it is the designer's task to resolve any consequences of that change on adjacent surfaces (e.g. if an edge is shared). There is also no indication of the part of the model that is 'solid' – in other words, the representation of an object is simply in terms of a collection of surfaces with no higher-level information about the solid object.

Finally, there are certain surface geometries that are difficult to represent using current surface modelling schemes. As noted, many early systems were not able to represent bounded or trimmed surfaces and some surface forms still present difficulties to current-generation modellers. The surfaces shown in Figures 2.19–2.21 fall into the generic category of four-sided **patches**. Shapes that are not easily described by such forms – for example, three- or five-sided patch shapes (Figure 2.24) – may be difficult to represent, although system capability is improving all the time in this respect. A good example in this respect is the three-sided blend between three fillet surfaces of different fillet radii which occurs at a corner. Figure 2.25 shows a case of this type. In conventional pattern making this form might simply be created by blending modelling clay in the internal corner of a wooden pattern. For many CAD systems this surface would require a laborious construction and it would be difficult to ensure tangency between adjacent surfaces.

2.4.3 Solid modelling

This chapter has so far considered geometric representations of objects that are essentially partial models – the two-dimensional projection of the edges of shapes, or the three-dimensional representation of edges or surfaces. In each case, the solid form of the object has to be inferred from the model. For many engineering purposes these representations are satisfactory, but the increasing application of computers to engineering analysis, or to the generation of manufacturing information, means that an ideal representation should be as complete as possible. An 'informationally complete' representation would, in the words of Requicha and Voelcker (1982), 'permit (at least in principle) *any* well-defined geometric property of any represented solid to be calculated automatically'. Furthermore, the more complete the representation, the smaller the requirement for human transcription between models, and thus the smaller the risk of errors in transcription. The techniques of **solid modelling** have been developed with the aim of providing such a representation, with some success, such that it is now the representation of choice for the most advanced CAD applications.

Solid modelling is a natural extension from the use of essentially 'one-dimensional' entities (curves) or 'two-dimensional' entities (surfaces), to the modelling of shape using three-dimensional solids. Woodwark (1986) proposes that a successful scheme for representing solids should be:

▶ complete and unambiguous;

▶ appropriate for the world of engineering objects;

▶ practical to use with existing computers.

We have seen that the wire-frame and surface schemes fall down on the first of these conditions. Many methods have been proposed for solid modelling, of which none yet is entirely satisfactory, but two have been partially successful, and have come successively to dominate the development of practical systems. These are the constructive approach, of which the most widely applied variant is the **constructive solid geometry** method (termed CSG or C-rep for short, and also known as the set-theoretic or Boolean method) which achieved early prominence in CAD, and the **boundary representation** method (sometimes called B-rep for short, and also termed the graph-based method) which dominates in today's applications. Other techniques will be considered in the next chapter, when some of the theoretical aspects of solid modelling will be discussed in more detail.

Constructive solid geometry

In the constructive solid geometry method, models are constructed using combinations of simple solid **primitives**, such as cuboids, cylinders, spheres, cones and the like. The primitives used by one solid modelling system are shown in Figure 2.26.

The alternative name for the CSG method, set-theoretic modelling, arises from the way in which primitives are combined using the union, intersection and difference

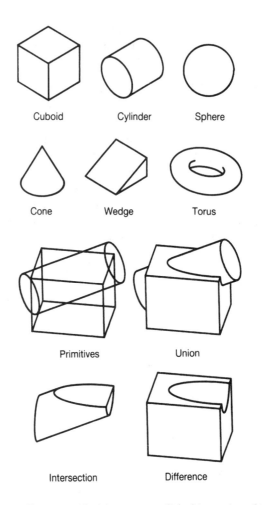

FIGURE 2.26
Primitives offered by
a solid modelling
system.

Cuboid   Cylinder   Sphere

Cone   Wedge   Torus

Primitives   Union

FIGURE 2.27
Boolean operations
on a block and
cylinder.

Intersection   Difference

operators of set theory. For example, given two solid objects A and B, then the **union** operator encompasses all points in space that are contained in ('members of') A OR B (expressed by the Boolean expression A ∪ B). The **intersection** operator similarly encompasses all points that are contained in A AND B, expressed as A ∩ B. There are two results of difference operations between the two objects: those points contained in A AND NOT B (A ∩ B̄ also written A − B) and those contained in B AND NOT A (B ∩ Ā also written B − A). Figure 2.27 shows the effect of these operators on a block and a cylinder. The results of the operations are further, composite solids, which may be combined with other primitive or composite solids to create additional shapes. For example, to create the model shown in Figure 2.28, four primitives – two rect-angular blocks and two cylinders – were required. In more representative engineer-ing components, hundreds of primitives (or, to be more precise, copies or **instances** of primitives at particular locations and orientations in space) may be required, mak-ing the input process potentially protracted.

CSG models have the advantage that they are very compact, and are guaranteed to model valid solids unambiguously. The method of constructing CSG models is

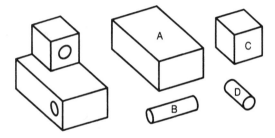

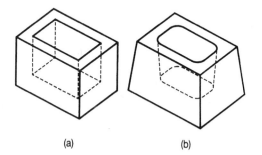

Object = (A − B) ∪ (C − D)

FIGURE 2.28
Constructive solid
model of a simple
block.

FIGURE 2.29
Solid models of a
simple block.

(a)   (b)

such that quite complex shapes may be developed relatively quickly, within the limitations of the set of primitives available within the system. Models are, however, stored in an **unevaluated** form in which the edges and surfaces that result from the combination of the primitives have to be computed when required (e.g. when a display of the model is being generated), with an attendant performance penalty. The calculation of intersections between the surfaces of the primitives, for the purposes of evaluation or other analysis of the model, is one of the key computational issues in CSG. The consequences have been firstly that the range of geometric primitives is often limited to those with planar or quadric surfaces which have reasonably straightforward line/surface or surface/surface intersection algorithms, and secondly that geometric complexity rapidly leads to performance degradation. In modelling terms this means that many features found on engineering components (particularly those produced using such manufacturing processes as forging or casting) such as fillet blends, or draft to allow the component to be withdrawn from the mould or die, may be difficult or time consuming to produce using CSG techniques, although implicit blending facilities are available in research solid modellers using the CSG approach. The simple shape shown in Figure 2.29(a) required just two instances of primitives and one Boolean operation (although in fact there are several ways in which this model could have been defined: a CSG model is not, in general, a unique representation of an object). With taper applied to the walls of the box, and internal fillet radii (as shown in Figure 2.29(b)), 22 instances of primitives and 21 Boolean operations were required. More complex forms, such as those found in automobile body panels, are for practical purposes impossible to model using CSG with the sort of primitive set shown in Figure 2.26, and systems cannot easily incorporate more general surface patches.

Boundary representation

Surface models contain no information about connections between surfaces, nor about which part of an object is solid. If information is added about connectivity between surfaces (which will be called **faces** here), and in addition the solid side of any face is identified, then this forms the elements of the second of the main solid modelling approaches – the boundary representation scheme. Real systems go further than this, and incorporate methods for checking the topological consistency of models (i.e. that there are no extra or missing faces or connections) and also that the models are not geometrically anomalous. Topological consistency is in part achieved by using a data structure in which faces are linked (with the appropriate adjacency relationships) with their bounding edges, which are in turn linked to their bounding vertices (end points) in a uniform structure. Geometric consistency is also achieved by ensuring that the model defines the boundary of a 'reasonable' solid object, as noted by Mäntylä (1988), in which:

▶ faces of the model do not intersect each other except at common vertices or edges;

▶ the boundaries of the faces are simple **loops** of edges that do not intersect themselves;

▶ the set of faces of the model close to form the complete skin of the model with no missing parts.

The third condition disallows 'open' objects. The first two disallow self-intersecting objects, and are enforced by ensuring that the surface of the boundary solid forms what is known mathematically as a '2-manifold', in which every point on the surface has a full two-dimensional neighbourhood of other points on the surface – in other words, every point on the part can be imagined as being surrounded by a disk of surface which could be unfolded flat (Mäntylä, 1988). In Section 3.4 below, methods that are used to ensure the geometrical and topological consistency of boundary models will be discussed in more detail.

The simplest form of boundary model is one that represents all faces as flat planes or **facets**. A curved surface, such as a cylinder, is represented in such a model as a series of facets that approximate the surface, as shown in Figure 2.30. Such a representation, known as a **polyhedral** model, is computationally relatively straightforward, and therefore has performance advantages, which make it widely used in

FIGURE 2.30
Faceted
representation of
a cylinder.

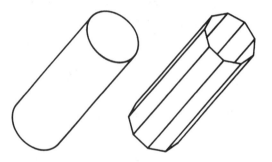

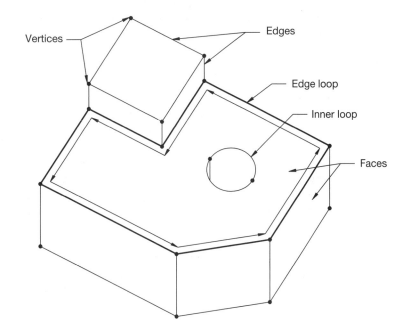

FIGURE 2.31
Elements of a
boundary
representation
model.

visualization packages, games, flight simulators and the like. The approach is, however, clearly limited in the extent to which it can model 'real' shapes such as engineering components. These demand the ability to model general curved surfaces. Early modellers were often limited to quadric surfaces such as cylinders, cones and spheres, partly for the reasons of intersection computation discussed above, although most commercial B-rep modellers now incorporate free-form surface technology, in particular using as a basis for the geometric description of curves and surfaces the **non-uniform rational B-spline** (NURBS), which will be described in more detail in the next chapter. The faces of such boundary representation models are effectively trimmed surfaces, bounded by external and internal loops of edges, as shown in Figure 2.31.

By contrast to CSG modellers, boundary models store information about the faces and edges of a model explicitly in an **evaluated** form. This confers performance advantages on the method, because information for certain applications of the model can be extracted directly from the data structure. Such applications include the generation of images of the model for viewing purposes, and the calculation of the surface area of models – simply the sum of the surface areas of each of the faces. A disadvantage of the representation is, however, that the amount of data stored is relatively large, and therefore boundary representation models tend to require large data files.

Practical systems

As noted, the different techniques used in CSG and B-rep modelling confer different advantages and disadvantages on the respective methods. CSG models tend to be more robust (in other words, less prone to numerical or computational errors or limitations), and have performance advantages where membership test (i.e. identifying whether a point lies in an object) is required. B-rep models tend to offer improved performance in display generation, and more flexibility in the forms that may be modelled. For these reasons many early practical systems were hybrids of the two techniques, and used dual representations. For example, a CSG modeller might use a faceted boundary representation for display purposes and for certain approximate analyses to exploit the advantages of the B-rep technique, but might reserve the precise set-theoretic representation for production of drawing geometry and accurate geometric analysis. Many boundary representation systems also draw on techniques from CSG. In general, the facility for set-theoretic combination of solids, and data input by using predefined primitives such as cylinders, blocks, spheres and wedges, is included in boundary representation systems, and some systems which use boundary representation data storage may also maintain a record of the set-theoretic operations carried out during the course of building a model.

The B-rep scheme has come to be the more widely applied representation in real systems. This is for three main reasons. The first is the geometric limitations of CSG that were noted above. The performance of B-rep systems is very much superior to that of CSG systems for models of any significant engineering complexity. The second reason is that conversion from CSG to B-rep is relatively straightforward through evaluation of the CSG model. The converse is not true. There is no general algorithm for the conversion of B-rep models to CSG, and thus there is no general interchangeability between the two approaches. The third reason is that there is an increasing tendency for commercial modelling systems to combine solid modelling techniques with surface and wire-frame representations in a more or less unified framework, from which the user may choose the most appropriate technique for a given problem. The use of edges (curves) and faces (surfaces) as the basis for solids in a B-rep system facilitates this approach. Such systems generally offer the facility to convert between schemes – for example, to revert from a B-rep solid model to a model consisting of surfaces attached to a wire frame.

Non-manifold models

The non-homogeneous approach to modelling described above relaxes the topological restrictions placed on conventional boundary models, by allowing geometric combinations and constructs beyond that necessary for modelling manifold solids (e.g. many faces meeting at an edge, models in which multiple parts touch one another, or models with faces and edges that are not part of a closed solid). This is known as **non-manifold** modelling, as opposed to conventional boundary modelling, in which space is unambiguously divided into solid and space by the boundaries of manifold solids (Woodwark, 1992). Examples of the two types of model are shown in Figure 2.32. Figure 2.32(a) shows a manifold model, in which each point on the surface of the object is surrounded by a disk of surface. Figure 2.32(b) shows a non-manifold model in which there are a points with one neighbouring face (e.g. on the edge of the separate triangle), with three neighbouring faces (where the L-shaped plate joins the main block) and with no neighbouring faces (on the disconnected line known as a **dangling edge**) (Mäntylä, 1988).

FIGURE 2.32
Manifold and non-manifold models.
(Reprinted from Shah and Mäntylä (1995) © John Wiley and Sons, Inc.)

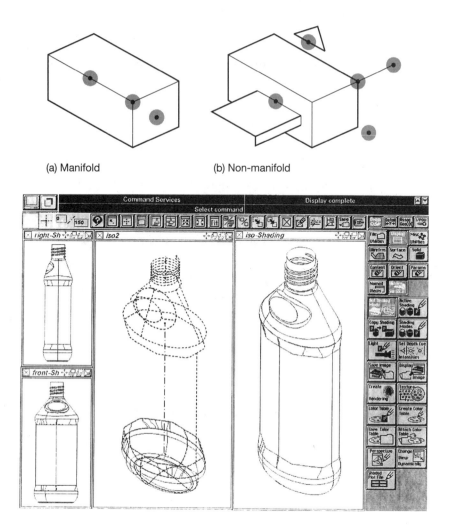

(a) Manifold   (b) Non-manifold

FIGURE 2.33
An example of a hybrid geometric model. (Reproduced by permission of Intergraph (UK) Ltd.)

As an example of the application of a commercial non-manifold modeller, consider the model of a bottle shown in Figure 2.33. The basis for this model is a wire frame constructed using lines and NURBS curves. This is shown in the centre of the figure. Surfaces, again using the NURBS representation, have been added to the wire frame. The thread at the neck has been added as a solid by projecting a cross-section along a spiral curve, whilst maintaining the section normal to the cylinder representing the neck. The oval protrusion on the taper leading to the neck is again solid geometry, obtained by projecting a profile, with draft, onto a surface.

2.5 Conclusion
·····················

In this chapter it has been explained that the conventional representation of engineering products is through the use of drawings and diagrams, which principally model the form and structure of the product respectively. Well-established standards and conventions define the way in which such drawings and diagrams should be constructed, and also define the use of symbolic representations and other shorthand notations for their efficient production.

The first way in which computer-aided design is used in modelling is to allow conventional representations to be used more efficiently: to reduce the risk of error in creating and using drawings and diagrams. The second way is through the use of new techniques for representing the three-dimensional form of components. In this, three techniques predominate:

▶ wire-frame representations, in which the component geometry is represented largely as a collection of curves;

▶ surface representations, in which the component geometry is represented as a collection of surfaces, often attached to a wire frame;

▶ solid modelling, in which the component is represented either as a set-theoretic combination of geometric primitives, or as a collection of faces, edges and vertices defining the boundary of the part.

Increasingly, hybrid systems offering a variety of geometric representations are the norm in CAD. Increasingly also, the three-dimensional model is seen as a central contribution to the integration of design and manufacturing facilities within a company.

References and further reading

American National Standards Institute, Y14 series of standards: e.g. Y14.1 Drawing Sheet Size and Format; Y14.2 Line Converting and Lettering; Y14.3 Multi and Sectional View Drawings; Y14.5 Dimensioning and Tolerancing; Y14.15 Electrical and Electronic Diagrams.

American National Standards Institute, Y32 series of standards: e.g. Y32.4 Graphic Symbols for Heating, Ventilating and Air Conditioning; Y32.10 Graphic Symbols for Fluid Power Diagrams.

Booker P. J. (1979). *A History of Engineering Drawing*. Bury St Edmunds: Northgate.

British Standards Institution (1990). *BS308: Parts 1–3, Engineering Drawing Practice*.

British Standards Institution (1988). *BS5070, Drawing Practice for Engineering Diagrams*.

British Standards Institution (1985). *BS1553, Graphical Symbols for General Engineering*.

British Standards Institution (1985). *BS2917, Graphical Symbols Used on Diagrams for Fluid Power Systems and Components*.

British Standards Institution (1985). *BS3939, Graphical Symbols for Electrical Power, Telecommunication and Electronic Diagrams*.

Davids B. L., Robotham A. J. and Yarwood A. (1991). *Computer-aided Drawing and Design*. London: Chapman & Hall.

Gasson P. C. (1983). *The Geometry of Spatial Forms*. Chichester: Ellis Horwood.

Groover M. P. and Zimmers E. W. (1984). CAD/CAM: *Computer-aided Design and Manufacturing*. Englewood Cliffs NJ: Prentice Hall.

Mäntylä M. (1988). *An Introduction to Solid Modelling*. Rockville, IN: Computer Science Press.

Mortenson M. E. (1985). *Geometric Modelling*. New York: John Wiley.

O'Reilly W. P. (1986). *Computer Aided Electronic Engineering*. Wokingham: Van Nostrand Reinhold.

Requicha A. A. G. and Voelcker H. B. (1982). Solid modelling: a historical summary and contemporary assessment. *IEEE Computer Graphics and Applications*. 2(2), 9–24.

Rooney J. and Steadman P. (eds) (1987). *Principles of Computer-aided Design*. London: Pitman.

Shah J. J. and Mäntylä M. (1995). *Parametric and Feature-based CAD/CAM*. New York: John Wiley.

Taylor D. L. (1992). *Computer-aided Design*. Reading, MA: Addison Wesley Longman.

Voelcker H. B. (1992). New directions in solid modelling? In *Int. Conf. on Manufacturing Automation*, University of Hong Kong, August, pp. 157–68.

Woodwark J. (1986). *Computing Shape*. London: Butterworth.

Woodwark J. (1992). *G-Words. Keywords for Geometric Computing and its Applications*. Winchester: Information Geometers.

Exercises

. . . .

2.1   Discuss the properties of artefacts which may be straightforward to model using a computer, and those which may be difficult (*hint*: consider aesthetics, feel!).

2.2   When would you use a diagram rather than a drawing to model a property of an object?

2.3   A hierarchical sequence of diagrams may be used to decompose a design into different levels of detail. Do you think that a similar decomposition may be applied in drawing, and in three-dimensional modelling?

2.4   List the curve types on a CAD system to which you have access, and sketch the methods offered for the construction of each entity type.

2.5   What are the advantages of using a specialized schematic drawing program rather than a general draughting package for the production of diagrams?

2.6   What methods can you think of for defining new work coordinate system origin and orientation?

2.7   Figure 2.34 shows a drawing of a poppet valve. Sketch how this valve could be represented using a CADCAM system employing (a) wire-frame modelling, (b) surface modelling or (c) solid modelling using the CSG method.

2.8   Suggest how a surface might be fitted to the point set shown in Figure 2.35 by (a) skinning over a set of curves fitted to the points, (b) applying a curve-mesh surface to an intersecting set of curves through the points, and (c) fitting a surface directly to the

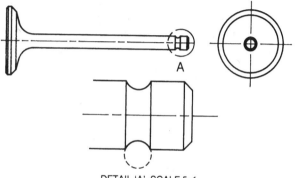

FIGURE 2.34

A poppet valve.

DETAIL 'A', SCALE 5:1

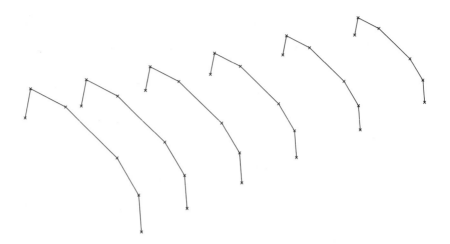

FIGURE 2.35

A point set.

point set. If possible, use a similar point set to explore the surfacing capabilities of a CAD system.

2.9 Describe the geometric modelling facilities available on a CAD system to which you have access. If the system has surface modelling capabilities, sketch the range of surfaces and explain their definition methods. If the system has a solid modelling capability, is it of the CSG or B-rep variety?

2.10 Suggest the most appropriate computer modelling system for:
(a) Producing drawings and manufacturing data for flame-cut and drilled plates for fabricated structures.
(b) Modelling assemblies of fully machined parts, for which mass properties and interference checking are required.
(c) Visualization of the motion of a robot arm.
(d) Modelling automobile body panels.
Give reasons for your choices.

2.11 You have been asked to advise a company on the selection of a CAD system for its design and manufacturing activities. The company manufactures moulds for plastic containers for the packaging industry. What advice would you give the company about the geometric modelling capabilities of the system?

2.12 Suggest alternative ways of modelling the shape shown in Figure 2.28 using constructive solid geometry.

2.13 What faces, edges and vertices would model the object shown in Figure 2.28 as a boundary representation model? How would the object appear if the system was only capable of defining faceted B-rep models?

2.14 Show how the shape shown in Figure 2.28 may be modelled by a surface modeller that does not have a facility to model trimmed surfaces. How would the shape appear as a wire frame?

2.15 What are the results of applying the Boolean intersection, union and difference operations to the two primitives shown in Figure 2.36? Prepare a three-view orthographic projection of the result of a union operation.

2.16 Why do you think that conversion between CSG and B-rep has been relatively straightforward, but that the reverse has proved difficult?

2.17 Outline what is meant by non-manifold modelling, and suggest where this approach may be appropriate.

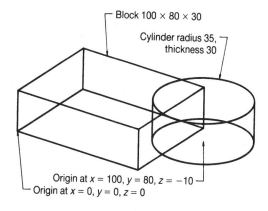

Block 100 × 80 × 30

Cylinder radius 35, thickness 30

Origin at x = 100, y = 80, z = −10
Origin at x = 0, y = 0, z = 0

FIGURE 2.36
Two geometric
primitives.

Projects

For more information about the subjects for project work, please refer to the end of Chapter 1.

The project activity for this chapter is to produce geometry for engineering drawings and three-dimensional models for the artefacts that are the subjects of the projects. Specific project tasks are:

Project 1 Chess piece Produce wire-frame models of the chess piece designs, starting with 2D sections of the rotationally symmetric aspects of the parts. Choose a single design to develop further, and add surfaces to the wire-frame model. Produce also a solid model of the same geometry.

Project 2 Load cell Produce a set of 2D drawings and diagrams of the load cell, showing at least (i) a general arrangement of the whole device together with a parts list, (ii) a detail drawing of the main structural member, and (iii) a diagram of the electronic circuit. Do not add dimensions to the drawings yet.

Techniques for geometric modelling

Chapter objectives

When you have completed studying material in this chapter you should be able to:
- ▶ **describe the reasons for the use of parametric and piecewise representations in computational geometry;**
- ▶ **understand the Hermite and Bézier parametric cubic curve types, and the Bézier–Bernstein polynomial functions;**
- ▶ **understand the continuous second-derivative cubic spline, and the B-spline curves;**
- ▶ **describe the bicubic, Bézier and B-spline surface forms;**
- ▶ **describe the various techniques for the solid modelling of geometry.**

Chapter contents

3.1 Introduction

Computer representations of geometry have so far been considered in a qualitative fashion, in order to establish the broad range and scope of the techniques that are involved. In this chapter, curve, surface and solid modelling will be described in more detail, with the aim of giving the reader an understanding of the nature of the modelling techniques and of their theoretical basis. This has a significant mathematical content, which in general will be separated from the main body of the text so that it may be omitted by the reader interested mainly in an overview of the techniques. Conversely, the reader who wishes to pursue the theoretical aspects in more detail is referred to the texts cited in the references, in particular to the works of Farin (1988),

Faux and Pratt (1979), Mäntylä (1988), Mortenson (1985) and Risler (1992), for a more comprehensive study.

The most mathematically straightforward geometric entities are curves, and therefore the treatment of curve descriptions which follows will be the most complete. Surface geometry is often a more or less straightforward extension of the concepts employed for curves, and will therefore be presented in a rather more cursory fashion in Section 3.3. In Section 3.4, the techniques that may be applied to extend surface descriptions to those of solids will be touched upon, and this section will also consider some of the techniques that are unique to solid modelling, both in terms of geometric representation and to ensure topological and geometric consistency in models.

3.2 Representations of curves

As a prelude to the discussion of representations for curves, let us first examine why there is a requirement for alternative geometric representations to those of classical geometry. Most readers will be familiar with the expressions:

$$y = mx + c \qquad \textbf{(3.1)}$$

$$ax + by + c = 0 \qquad \textbf{(3.2)}$$

and:

$$ax^2 + by^2 + 2kxy + 2fx + 2gy + d = 0 \qquad \textbf{(3.3)}$$

which are the **explicit** equation of a straight line and the **implicit** equations of a straight line and a conic section curve respectively. Why are these not adequate for CAD? There is an evident problem with the explicit expression for a straight line, in that the slope, m, of the line is infinite for a line parallel to the y-axis. Near-vertical lines will have very large slopes, and these may be difficult to define using a computer because very large real numbers may lead to numerical problems. The implicit forms deal with curves of any slope, but have limitations (in common with the explicit forms) in that:

▶ They represent unbounded geometry: Equation (3.2) defines an infinite line, and Equation (3.3) a complete conic section curve. In CAD, however, geometric representation would normally be of a line between two points, and often a part of an ellipse or an arc of a circle.

▶ Curves are often multi-valued. For example, for a given value of x in Equation (3.3) there are two values of y. Ideally, a unique point on the curve would be defined by a single value of a variable defining the curve.

▶ It is often necessary in CAD (e.g. for display purposes, as will be seen later) to evaluate an orderly sequence of points on a geometric entity. Implicit equations do not offer a natural procedure for evaluating points on a curve (consider the conic section curve again: incrementing x by equal intervals gives a very uneven sequence of points on the curve; some values of x may not yield points on the curve).

▶ The equation for the curve will depend upon the coordinate system used.

These difficulties might be overcome by the appropriate programming of the CAD system, but there are further factors which make alternative representations attractive. First of all, it has been noted that faired shapes are commonplace in engineering. Consider, for example, the cross-section of an aerofoil. This is often defined to be a smooth curve passing though a series of points at various distances along the chord of the aerofoil (where the chord runs from the front of the aerofoil section to the back), as shown in Figure 3.1. This shape is simply not amenable to representation by a classical geometric entity such as a conic section curve.

Other curves that may be algebraically or computationally difficult to represent using conventional geometric entities are seen when the intersections between solids or surfaces are examined. Even relatively simple surface forms such as cylinders give rise to complex intersection curves, as shown in Figure 3.2. It may be convenient to approximate such intersection curves by fitting a curve to a series of points computed at the intersection.

The need, therefore, is for a representation of curves that overcomes the limitations of the analytic forms, and also allows the modelling of faired shapes – of shapes which may be said to **interpolate** a series of points. The solution that has been adopted in CAD is to describe geometric entities using a **parametric** form, and to

FIGURE 3.1
An aerofoil section.

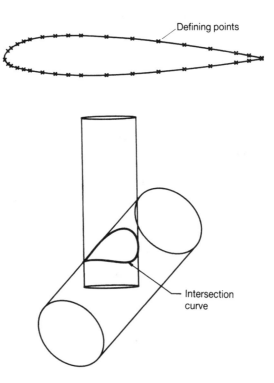

FIGURE 3.2
Intersection of two cylinders.

FIGURE 3.3
Parametric curve,
surface and solid.

Curve   Surface   Solid

interpolate large numbers of linearly independent conditions (such as points) using **composite** entities that are formed piecewise from a number of segments.

3.2.1 The parametric representation of geometry

The parametric representation of geometry essentially involves expressing relationships for the x, y and (if appropriate) z coordinates of points on a curve or surface or in a solid not in terms of each other but of one or more independent variables known as **parameters**. For a curve, a single parameter is used: x, y and z are each expressed in terms of a single variable, typically u. For a surface, two parameters, typically written as u and v, are used, and x, y and z are functions of both of these. For solids, three parameters u, v and w are used. A parametric curve, surface and solid are shown in Figure 3.3, which also shows how such entities are often displayed using CAD systems. For example, the surface is displayed by means of a mesh of curves drawn on the surface at equal increments of the defining parameters u and v (i.e. at constant u and varying v and vice versa). The same form of display may also be seen in the surfaces shown in Figures 2.19 to 2.21.

The form of the relationship between the coordinate positions and the parameters could be quite arbitrary, but in practice only a small number of representations are widely used. The most widespread of these are based on the cubic polynomial, which will be considered next after the bracketed section below introducing the mathematical basis of the parametric method.

The parametric representation of geometric entities

The parametric form of geometric entities involves describing the entity not in terms of expressions such as $y = f(x)$, or $g(x,y) = 0$, which relate the variables describing positions on the entities to each other, but by sets of functions relating positional variables to variation of one or more auxiliary variables or **parameters**. Consider, for example, the general space curve shown in Figure 3.4. There is a parameter, u, associated with the curve, and whose value increases as the curve is traversed from one end to the other. The position of any point on the curve is given by the vector expression:

$$\mathbf{p} = \mathbf{p}(u) \tag{3.4}$$

which is equivalent to:

$$x = x(u) \qquad y = y(u) \qquad z = z(u)$$

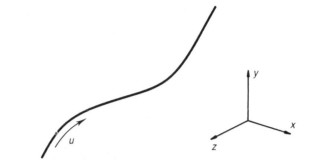

FIGURE 3.4
A general space
curve.

In other words, each of the main space variables x, y and z is a function of the parameter u. More generally, if $\mathbf{p} = (p_1, p_2, \ldots, p_n)$ is a coordinate vector of n-dimensional space, and $\mathbf{u} = (u_1, u_2, \ldots, u_k)$ is an ordered set ($k \leqslant n$) of parameters, then a functional relation of the form:

$$\mathbf{p} = \mathbf{p(u)} \tag{3.5}$$

defines a k-dimensional geometric entity in n-dimensional space. Each of the n component coordinates p_i of $\mathbf{p}$ is a function of all the k parameters u_i of $\mathbf{u}$.

For example, let us consider three-dimensional Euclidean space, for which $n = 3$. For $k = 2$ we have, writing $\mathbf{u} = (u, v)$:

$$x = x(u, v) \qquad y = y(u, v) \qquad z = z(u, v) \tag{3.6}$$

which defines, in general, a curved surface. Similarly, for $k = 3$, we have (with $\mathbf{u} = (u, v, w)$) a solid, and for $k = 1$ (i.e. $\mathbf{u} = (u)$), we obtain Equation (3.4), defining a three-dimensional space curve. In each case, the geometric entity can be evaluated directly for an arbitrary parameter vector $\mathbf{u}$, with none of the difficulties of solving equations presented in implicit form.

As a simple example of a parametric representation, consider a line from a point at x_0, y_0, z_0 to x_1, y_1, z_1. This can be written as:

$$x = x_0 + fu \qquad y = y_0 + gu \qquad z = z_0 + hu \tag{3.7}$$

where x_0, y_0, z_0 is the point corresponding to a zero value of the parameter u. There are two common conventions for the variation of the parameter along the line. The first is that the parameter varies between 0 and 1 along the segment (in which case $f = x_1 - x_0$, $g = y_1 - y_0$ and $h = z_1 - z_0$). The second convention (the **normalized** form) makes u correspond to the real distance along the line, in which case $[f, g, h]$ is a unit vector in the direction of the line.

A further example is the parametric representation of an arc in the $x - y$ plane, that is:

$$x = x_c + r \cos \theta \qquad y = y_c + r \sin \theta \qquad z = 0 \tag{3.8}$$

from which it may be seen that an orderly series of points on the arc may be defined by taking equal increments of the parameter θ, and, furthermore, the arc may be unambiguously bounded by specifying two limiting values of θ.

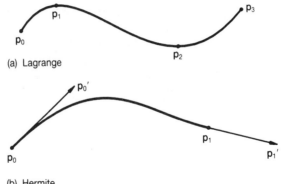

FIGURE 3.5

Lagrange and
Hermite
interpolation.

(a) Lagrange

(b) Hermite

3.2.2 Parametric cubic polynomial curves

In three-dimensional modelling a geometric representation is required that will describe non-planar curves, but which will also avoid computational difficulties and unwanted undulations that might be introduced by high-order polynomial curves. These requirements are satisfied by the cubic polynomial (the lowest-order polynomial that can describe a non-planar curve), which has therefore become very popular as a basis for computational geometry.

Just as two points may be joined by a line, and three points by an arc of a circle, so may four points provide the boundary conditions for a cubic polynomial, as shown in Figure 3.5(a). The fitting of a curve through points is known as Lagrange interpolation, after the famous French mathematician of that name. A cubic curve may equally well be defined to fit two points and two slope conditions at the points, as shown in Figure 3.5(b), which is known as Hermite interpolation after the nineteenth-century mathematician of that name. This latter form has some advantages where close control of the curve slope is desired, and also as a basis of piecewise curves, as will be seen in a later section, and has therefore been widely used. Polynomial geometric forms expressed in the Hermite basis are often known as Ferguson or Coons representations after their pioneering use by these men in the early 1960s. Both Hermite and Lagrange interpolation are described in the bracketed section below which considers cubic polynomials in more depth.

The solution of cubic polynomial curves

Let us consider a cubic polynomial to interpolate points in three-dimensional space. We can write:

$$x = a_1 + b_1u + c_1u^2 + d_1u^3 \qquad\qquad \textbf{(3.9)}$$

$$y = a_2 + b_2u + c_2u^2 + d_2u^3 \qquad\qquad \textbf{(3.10)}$$

$$z = a_3 + b_3u + c_3u^2 + d_3u^3 \qquad\qquad \textbf{(3.11)}$$

We have 12 unknowns and we can therefore, using Lagrange interpolation, solve these equations with four points, each of which provides three boundary conditions. By choosing suitable values for u to correspond to each point and by substituting values of u, x, y and z at each point it is possible to solve for the unknowns. The cubic curve could equally well be defined using Hermite interpolation by specifying two points and two tangent vectors at the points. The cubic is again defined by Equations (3.9)–(3.11), which can be expressed in vector form as:

$$\mathbf{p} = \mathbf{p}(u) = \mathbf{k}_0 + \mathbf{k}_1 u + \mathbf{k}_2 u^2 + \mathbf{k}_3 u^3 \tag{3.12}$$

or:

$$\mathbf{p}(u) = \sum_{u=0}^{3} \mathbf{k}_i u^i$$

where $\mathbf{k}_0 - \mathbf{k}_3$ are unknown vectors, corresponding to a_1 to a_3, b_1 to b_3 and so on in Equations (3.9)–(3.11). The tangent vector (informally the 'slope') of the curve is (denoting $\mathrm{d}\mathbf{p}/\mathrm{d}u$ by $\mathbf{p}'(u)$):

$$\mathbf{p}' = \mathbf{p}'(u) = \mathbf{k}_1 + 2\mathbf{k}_2 u + 3\mathbf{k}_3 u^2 \tag{3.13}$$

Using the end points $\mathbf{p}_0$ and $\mathbf{p}_1$, and the end slopes $\mathbf{p}_0'$ and $\mathbf{p}_1'$, we can substitute in Equations (3.12) and (3.13) to derive the unknowns. It is usual to assign $u = 0$ and $u = 1$ to the two ends of the segment, with $0 < u < 1$ between. Thus:

$$\begin{aligned}
\mathbf{k}_0 &= \mathbf{p}_0 \\
\mathbf{k}_0 + \mathbf{k}_1 + \mathbf{k}_2 + \mathbf{k}_3 &= \mathbf{p}_1 \\
\mathbf{k}_1 &= \mathbf{p}_0' \\
\mathbf{k}_1 + 2\mathbf{k}_2 + 3\mathbf{k}_3 &= \mathbf{p}_1'
\end{aligned} \tag{3.14}$$

Solving for $\mathbf{k}_0$ to $\mathbf{k}_3$ we obtain:

$$\begin{aligned}
\mathbf{k}_0 &= \mathbf{p}_0 \\
\mathbf{k}_1 &= \mathbf{p}_0' \\
\mathbf{k}_2 &= 3(\mathbf{p}_1 - \mathbf{p}_0) - 2\mathbf{p}_0' - \mathbf{p}_1' \\
\mathbf{k}_3 &= 2(\mathbf{p}_0 - \mathbf{p}_1) + \mathbf{p}_0' + \mathbf{p}_1'
\end{aligned} \tag{3.15}$$

Thus, by substitution in Equation (3.12), we obtain:

$$\begin{aligned}
\mathbf{p} = \mathbf{p}(u) = {} & \mathbf{p}_0(1 - 3u^2 + 2u^3) + \mathbf{p}_1(3u^2 - 2u^3) + \\
& \mathbf{p}_0'(u - 2u^2 + u^3) + \mathbf{p}_1'(-u^2 + u^3)
\end{aligned} \tag{3.16}$$

or, in matrix notation, $\mathbf{p} = \mathbf{UCS}$ where:

$$
\begin{array}{ccccc}
\mathbf{p} & = & \mathbf{U} & \mathbf{C} & \mathbf{S}
\end{array}
$$

$$
\mathbf{p} = \mathbf{p}(u) = \begin{bmatrix} 1 & u & u^2 & u^3 \end{bmatrix}
\begin{bmatrix}
1 & 0 & 0 & 0 \\
0 & 0 & 1 & 0 \\
-3 & 3 & -2 & -1 \\
2 & -2 & 1 & 1
\end{bmatrix}
\begin{bmatrix}
\mathbf{p}_0 \\
\mathbf{p}_1 \\
\mathbf{p}_0' \\
\mathbf{p}_1'
\end{bmatrix} \tag{3.17}
$$

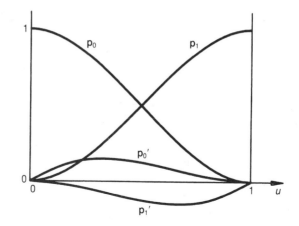

FIGURE 3.6
Blending functions
for a Hermite cubic
curve.

Equation (3.16) from the boxed section above gives the general form of a cubic polynomial in the Hermite basis as:

$$\mathbf{p} = \mathbf{p}(u) = \mathbf{p}_0(1 - 3u^2 + 2u^3) + \mathbf{p}_1(3u^2 - 2u^3) +$$
$$\mathbf{p}_0'(u - 2u^2 + u^3) + \mathbf{p}_1'(-u^2 + u^3) \quad\quad\quad \textbf{(3.16)}$$

which on examination shows that the position of the curve for any value of u is the sum of a number of functions in u multiplied by the boundary conditions $\mathbf{p}_0$, $\mathbf{p}_1$, $\mathbf{p}_0'$, $\mathbf{p}_1'$. We can plot each of these functions as **blending functions** (also known as **basis functions**), as shown in Figure 3.6. The concept of blending functions is an important one, which will be returned to in later sections. Their significance is that the shape of *any* Hermite cubic of the same parametric interval may be expressed as a function simply of the defining points and slopes multiplied by invariant interpolation functions, each representing the 'influence' of the point or slope on the shape of the curve.

Example 3.1 *Calculation of a Hermite curve*

As an example of the use of Hermite interpolation, let us calculate the parametric mid-point of the Hermite cubic curve that fits the points $\mathbf{p}_0 = (1, 1)$, $\mathbf{p}_1 = (6, 5)$ and the tangent vectors $\mathbf{p}_0' = (0, 4)$, $\mathbf{p}_1' = (4, 0)$. At the parametric mid-point, $u = 0.5$ (recall that u varies in the range 0 to 1 along the curve). Substituting this value and the values for $\mathbf{p}_0$, $\mathbf{p}_1$, $\mathbf{p}_0'$, and $\mathbf{p}_1'$ into Equation (3.16), we obtain:

$$x(0.5) = 1[1 - 3(0.5^2) + 2(0.5^3)] + 6[3(0.5^2)] - 2(0.5^3)] +$$
$$0[0.5 - 2(0.5^2) + (0.5^3)] + 4[-(0.5^2) + (0.5^3)]$$
$$= 1 \times 0.5 + 6 \times 0.5 + 0 \times 0.125 - 4 \times 0.125$$

and:

$$y(0.5) = 1[1 - 3(0.5^2) + 2(0.5^3)] + 5[3(0.5^2) - 2(0.5^3)] +$$
$$4[0.5 - 2(0.5^2) + (0.5^3)] + 0[-(0.5^2) + (0.5^3)]$$
$$= 1 \times 0.5 + 5 \times 0.5 + 4 \times 0.125 - 0 \times 0.125$$

which give $\mathbf{p}(0.5) = (3, 3.5)$.

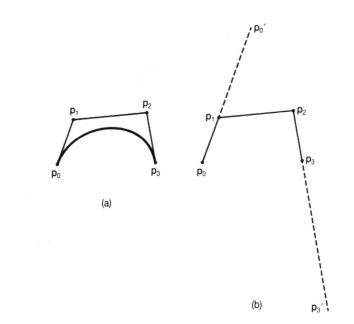

FIGURE 3.7
Cubic Bézier curves.

3.2.3 Bézier curves

The use of points and tangent vectors to provide boundary values for curves is not attractive for interactive design, because the user may not have much feel for slopes entered as numerical values. It is nevertheless useful to be able to control the slope of a curve, as well as the points through which the curve passes. This difficulty was resolved by Pierre Bézier, of the French car company Renault, who pioneered the use of computer modelling of surfaces in design. His UNISURF system, used since 1972 (Bézier, 1986), has been applied to define body panel design for several cars.

Bézier used a **control polygon** for curves, in place of points and tangent vectors (Figure 3.7(a)). This polygon is **approximated** by a polynomial curve whose degree is one less than the number of polygon vertices (which are also known as **control points** or track points). Figure 3.7(a) shows a four-point polygon which is approximated by a cubic curve in which $\mathbf{p}_0$ and $\mathbf{p}_3$ are equivalent to $\mathbf{p}_0$ and $\mathbf{p}_1$ for the Hermite basis cubic polynomial. The mid-vertices $\mathbf{p}_1$ and $\mathbf{p}_2$ are defined to be 1/3 of the way along the tangent vectors at $\mathbf{p}_0$ and $\mathbf{p}_3$ respectively (this is shown in Figure 3.7(b); the value of 1/3 is used because it is the inverse of the degree of the Bézier curve). The mathematics of the resultant cubic curve is outlined in the bracketed section below.

Bézier polynomial curves

For the Bézier cubic polynomial, referring to Figure 3.7(b), we can write:

$$\mathbf{p}_0' = 3(\mathbf{p}_1 - \mathbf{p}_0) \tag{3.18}$$

$$\mathbf{p}_3' = 3(\mathbf{p}_3 - \mathbf{p}_2) \tag{3.19}$$

Substituting these into Equation (3.16) and gathering terms, we obtain:

$$\mathbf{p} = \mathbf{p}(u) = \mathbf{p}_0(1 - 3u + 3u^2 - u^3) + \mathbf{p}_1(3u - 6u^2 + 3u^3) +$$
$$\mathbf{p}_2(3u^2 - 3u^3) + \mathbf{p}_3(u^3) \tag{3.20}$$

which may be expressed in matrix form as:

$$\mathbf{p} = \qquad\qquad \mathbf{U} \qquad\qquad \mathbf{M} \qquad \mathbf{P}$$

$$\mathbf{p} = \mathbf{p}(u) = \begin{bmatrix} 1 & u & u^2 & u^3 \end{bmatrix} \begin{bmatrix} 1 & 0 & 0 & 0 \\ -3 & 3 & 0 & 0 \\ 3 & -6 & 3 & 0 \\ -1 & 3 & -3 & 1 \end{bmatrix} \begin{bmatrix} \mathbf{p}_0 \\ \mathbf{p}_1 \\ \mathbf{p}_2 \\ \mathbf{p}_3 \end{bmatrix} \tag{3.21}$$

The Bézier control points provide an easier way of controlling the shape of the polynomial than the tangent vectors $\mathbf{p}_0'$ and $\mathbf{p}_1'$ of the Hermite formulation. Again, the curve can best be considered to be a combination of blending functions representing the influence that each control point has on the curve, as shown in Figure 3.8.

The cubic polynomial is an example of more general curves that may be fitted to control polygons with arbitrary numbers of track points. The curve passes through the first and last points of the control polygon, and is tangential at these end points to the vectors between the first and last pairs of points respectively. In the intermediate part the curves exhibit the useful **variation diminishing** property where the curve smooths the control points. More formally, the interpolating curve does not have more intersections with any plane than a polygon through the control points, and does not change direction more frequently than the control polygon, and therefore the Bézier curve will not introduce any unexpected behaviour – it will smooth even rapidly varying point sets. Since the blending functions sum to one for any value of u, the curve also lies within the **convex hull** of the defining control points (this is the minimal convex region enclosing the control points). For example, a cubic Bézier curve lies entirely within the tetrahedron formed by the control points. Figure 3.9 shows Bézier curves of various degrees that illustrate these features. The calculation of a four-point Bézier curve is also shown in Example 3.2 below.

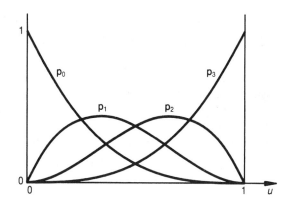

FIGURE 3.8

Blending functions for a cubic Bézier curve.

FIGURE 3.9
Various Bézier curves (showing control polygons).

The general Bézier curve is also known as a Bézier–Bernstein polynomial, because the Bézier technique applies a vector formulation of a method of polynomial approximation developed by Bernstein earlier this century. The algebra of this formulation is outlined in the bracketed section below.

Bézier–Bernstein polynomials

The general expression for a Bézier–Bernstein polynomial is:

$$\mathbf{p}(u) = \sum_{i=0}^{n} \frac{n!}{(n-i)!i!} u^i (1-u)^{n-i} \mathbf{p}_i \qquad 0 \leq u \leq 1 \tag{3.22}$$

(note that $0! = 1$ here, and $u^i = 1$ when u and $i = 0$), which may be written:

$$\mathbf{p}(u) = \sum_{i=0}^{n} B_{i,n}(u)\mathbf{p}_i \qquad 0 \leq u \leq 1 \tag{3.23}$$

where the blending functions $B_{i,n}(u)$ are given by:

$$B_{i,n}(u) = C(n,i)u^i(1-u)^{n-i} \quad \text{and} \quad C(n,i) = n!/[i!(n-i)!]$$

and where $\mathbf{p}_0, \mathbf{p}_1, \ldots, \mathbf{p}_n$ are the position vectors of the $n+1$ vertices of a generalized characteristic polygon.

Example 3.2 *Calculation of a Bézier curve*
....

The values of a Bézier curve fitting a given sequence of points may be calculated by using Equation (3.22), or we may use Equation (3.20) directly if the curve is cubic – fitting four points. For example, let us compute the values of a curve fitting points $\mathbf{p}_0 = (1, 1)$, $\mathbf{p}_1 = (3, 6)$, $\mathbf{p}_2 = (5, 7)$, $\mathbf{p}_3 = (7, 2)$ at $u = 0.4$ and $u = 0.6$. Substituting for the point values in Equation (3.20) we obtain:

$$x(u) = 1(1 - 3u + 3u^2 - u^3) + 3(3u - 6u^2 + 3u^3) + 5(3u^2 - 3u^3) + 7(u^3)$$

and:

$$y(u) = 1(1 - 3u + 3u^2 - u^3) + 6(3u - 6u^2 + 3u^3) + 7(3u^2 - 3u^3) + 2(u^3)$$

which, on evaluating the blending functions for $u = 0.4$ and $u = 0.6$, gives $\mathbf{p}(0.4) =$ (3.4, 4.952) and $\mathbf{p}(0.6) = $ (4.6, 5.248).

3.2.4 General considerations for multi-variable curve fitting

Bézier curves **approximate** points without, in general, passing through them (apart from the first and last in a set, as noted). Bézier curves are also only capable of being **globally modified**: their blending functions are non-zero in the whole range $0 < u < 1$, and therefore moving one of the points in the control polygon affects every position on the curve (apart from the end points), as shown in Figure 3.10(a). Other curve formulations have different characteristics in these respects. In some, the **interpolation** of the point set is achieved, which means that the curve passes through each of the defining points. It has already been noted that this is particularly useful for modelling faired shapes such as are found in aircraft or ships, where the locations of a number of points on curves are precisely known. Other formulations also achieve the desirable objective of **local modification**, in which the movement of one control point only affects the shape of the curve in the vicinity of the point, as shown in Figure 3.10(b).

A further important characteristic of a curve is its degree of continuity. Continuity is characterized as C^0, C^1, . . . , C^n, where the nth derivative of its parametric form is continuous. A polygon, comprising a series of lines, has discontinuities of slope and all higher derivatives at each of the polygon vertices. It is C^0 continuous. Interpolating curves have various degrees of continuity: in C^1 (first-derivative) continuity, the direction and magnitude of the tangent vector (which we will again refer to informally

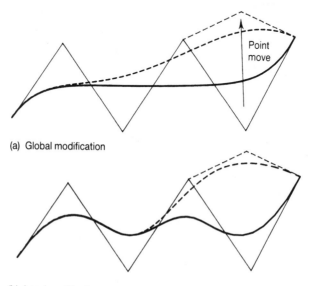

(a) Global modification

FIGURE 3.10

Global and local modification of curves.

(b) Local modification

as slope) of a curve in parametric space is continuous; in C^2 continuity, the first and second ('curvature') derivatives in parametric space are continuous. As an example, let us consider a line that is tangential to an arc. At the join between the line and arc the slopes of the two curves are the same, but their curvatures are different (the line has zero curvature, and the arc has curvature equal to the inverse of its radius). A composite curve formed from the line and the arc is thus first-derivative continuous, but has discontinuities in the second derivative.

Parametric (C) continuity does not necessarily imply geometric (G) continuity. Two curve segments which have tangent vectors with a common direction but not magnitude at their joining point are G^1 but not C^1 continuous. A parametric curve may have continuous derivatives but might or might not have geometrically continuous slope or curvature, which G^1 and G^2 imply.

3.2.5 Cubic spline curves

In the Bézier formulation, the use of continuous blending functions to approximate a set of control points was seen. When interpolating points, however, a different approach is often taken, in which a series of curve segments are joined end to end to form a **composite** curve. Let us consider fitting a curve to a series of points. It has been noted that cubic curves are the lowest-order polynomials capable of defining non-planar curves, and in principle a series of Hermite basis cubics could be joined to form a suitable composite curve, as shown in Figure 3.11(a). It would, however, be inconvenient to ask the user to enter the tangent vector for each point in the point set, and therefore it is more usual in composite cubic curves to use as boundary conditions continuity in first and second derivatives at intermediate points. A curve defined on such a basis is known as a continuous second-derivative **cubic spline** curve. Note here the analogy with the wooden or metal spline used for lofting, as mentioned in Chapter 2 above, although the cubic spline does not assume identical shapes to its physical counterpart.

The bracketed section opposite outlines how a continuous second-derivative cubic spline curve may be defined by considering the way in which the knot points and slope and curvature continuity at these points provide the boundary conditions for each of the curve segments. The advantage of this form is that it is not necessary

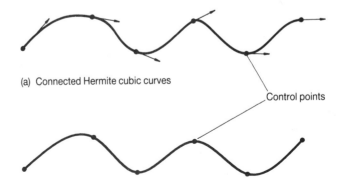

(a) Connected Hermite cubic curves

Control points

FIGURE 3.11

Piecewise continuous curves.

FIGURE 3.12
Global modification
of a cubic spline
curve.

to define slopes at the intermediate knot points. A disadvantage is that only global modification of the resulting curve is possible – as shown in Figure 3.12, where the result of moving one point on a spline curve is shown (it may be noted that the effect of the change in the data point is quite small at remote points on the curve – the curve's behaviour is said to be damped). Some CAD systems offer a modified version of this spline formulation, in which the user may optionally enter slope or tangent vector values at intermediate points, and thus gain control of local curvature, and achieve some degree of local modification, but in such cases second-derivative continuity is lost at these points.

The cubic spline formulation

Consider fitting a spline through a series of n points (Figure 3.11(b)). Each span is a separate cubic segment, with slope and curvature continuity at the points, which may also be known as control points, or in this case **knot points**. For n points, there are $n - 1$ spans, giving $4(n - 1)$ coefficient vectors (four coefficient vectors for each of the segments). The number of point boundary conditions or constraints is $2(n - 1)$, plus $(n - 2)$ 'slope' conditions and $(n - 2)$ 'curvature' conditions. There are thus two remaining conditions to be satisfied, and this is typically achieved by asking the user to enter the slope or tangent vector at the start and end points, or perhaps by specifying zero curvature at each end point. The segment coefficient vectors may then be obtained by solving the resulting simultaneous equations.

To construct a parametric spline with n control or knot points, a sequence of parameter values (called a **knot vector**):

$$(U_0, U_1, \ldots, U_{n-1}) \quad U_{j+1} > U_j$$

must be chosen for the knot points. The simplest choice is a uniform knot vector, in which the parameter value is zero at the first point, and is incremented by one for each subsequent point. Such an approach may, however, lead to pitfalls, for the magnitudes of the derivatives at knot points are a function of the parametrization, and a uniform knot vector for unevenly spaced points may lead to problems, such as unwanted loops in the curve. An ideal parametrization would be to use accumulated curve length, but clearly this cannot be used until the curve is defined, and therefore would require an iterative procedure. A commonly used compromise is to use accumulated chord length, where $U_0 = 0$, and:

$$U_{i+1} = U_i + d_{i+1} \quad i = 0,1,2, \ldots, n - 1$$

where d_i is the distance between $\mathbf{p}_{i-1}$ and $\mathbf{p}_i$.

In some cases, higher-order curves than cubics may be used for splines. In general, a polynomial spline of degree n is constructed piecewise by a sequence of n-degree polynomials defined over consecutive intervals of the independent variable. These polynomials are matched in value and derivative to order $n - 1$ at the knot points. They clearly also exhibit discontinuities in the nth derivative at the knot points, and therefore polynomials of higher order than cubic are often used in representing shapes where high-order continuity is needed, for example for profiles of cams used in mechanisms, or for certain aerodynamic analyses.

3.2.6 B-spline curves

Neither the Bézier nor the cubic spline curve formulations allow local modification of curves, and Bézier polynomials are, in addition, somewhat constrained in the number of points that they may approximate without the degree of the curve becoming inconveniently high. Both of these limitations are overcome by a generalization of the Bézier approach known as the **B-spline** method, which again uses blending functions to combine the influence of a series of control or track points in an approximate curve. For a series of $n + 1$ points $\mathbf{p}_i$, the formulation is:

$$\mathbf{p}(u) = \sum_{i=0}^{n} N_{i,k}(u)\mathbf{p}_i \tag{3.24}$$

where the B-spline blending functions are $N_{i,k}$. This equation may be compared with Equation (3.23) for Bézier curves. The important difference lies in the way in which the blending polynomials are defined. In Bézier curves, the degree of these polynomials is determined by the number of track points, whereas in B-spline curves the degree may be specified independently of the number of track points (within certain limits). Furthermore, the blending functions for Bézier curves are non-zero over the entire interval of the parameter u, but for B-spline curves they may be non-zero for a limited range of the parameter (the bracketed section below gives the mathematical basis for these blending curves, although it should be noted that the recursive form shown is seldom used in practical algorithms, for which the user is referred to specialist texts such as Rockwood and Chambers (1996)). Since each blending curve corresponds to a particular point, moving the point will modify the curve only for that range of the parameter for which the blending function was non-zero.

B-spline polynomials

The blending polynomials for B-spline curves are themselves splines (it is for that reason that they are so named), and they have the useful property in computing terms that they may be defined recursively in terms of B-spline polynomials of lower order. Specifically, a B-spline polynomial of order k (or degree $k - 1$) is defined using:

$$N_{i,k}(u) = \frac{(u - U_{i+1-k})}{(U_i - U_{i+1-k})} N_{i-1,k-1}(u) + \frac{(U_{i+1} - u)}{(U_{i+1} - U_{i+2-k})} N_{i,k-1}(u) \qquad (3.25)$$

where $0/0 = 0$, and with the limiting condition (for $k = 1$) of:

$$N_{i,1}(u) = \begin{cases} 1 & \text{if } U_i \leqslant u \leqslant U_{i+1} \\ 0 & \text{otherwise} \end{cases} \qquad (3.26)$$

The U_i are again the **knot values**, which relate the parametric variable u to the $\mathbf{p}_i$ control points, and may be defined in any ascending numerical order. All of the knot values together form the **knot vector**, and integer knots are commonly used for convenience. Each blending polynomial of order k is non-zero over k intervals of this knot vector, and thus the total number of values in the vector for a given set of points is $n + 1 + k$.

B-spline curves are best illustrated by examples of the blending functions, and of their application to the approximation of a set of points. Figure 3.13 shows blending functions of order 2 (linear), order 3 (quadratic) and order 4 (cubic) on an integer knot vector. Figure 3.14 shows how these functions may be used to define a curve that approximates five points, and it will be observed that, unlike the Bézier curve, the B-spline curves do not pass through the first and last points except when linear blending functions are used. However, behaviour analogous to the Bézier curve at the start and end can also be obtained using B-spline curves, as explained in detail in the bracketed section overleaf.

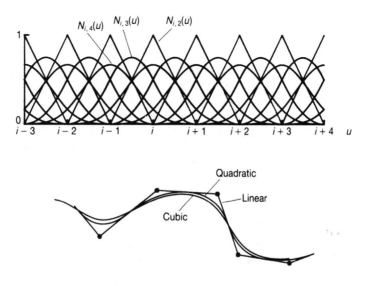

FIGURE 3.13

B-spline blending functions on an integer knot vector.

FIGURE 3.14

Five-point curve approximated using the blending functions in Figure 3.13.

B-spline start and end points

The B-spline curve can be made to pass through start and end points, and to be tangential to the first and last vectors in a control polygon, by adding knots at each end of the knot vector, in which case the range of the parameter u for the curve is given by:

$$0 \leq u \leq n - k + 2 \qquad (3.27)$$

For example, the cubic (order 4) blending functions to approximate eight track points will be defined on the knot vector 000012345555, as shown in Figure 3.15(a). Examples of curves generated using these blending functions are given in Figure 3.15(b), which also shows the localized effect of moving one of the track points, and marks the positions of the parametric knots on the curve.

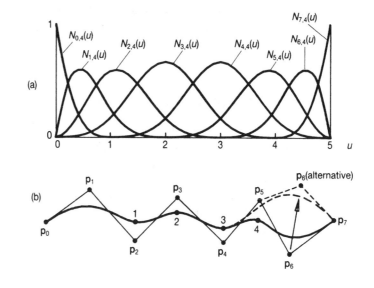

(a)

(b)

FIGURE 3.15
Cubic B-spline
curves.

In the opening remarks of this section it was noted that B-spline curves are a generalization of Bézier curves. In fact, if we define B-spline polynomials of order k for a set of k knot points, the blending functions are identical to those for a Bézier curve. As the polynomial order is reduced, the local influence of each track point becomes more marked. The influence of track points can be further increased by repeating points, which has the effect of first pulling the curve towards the point, and then causing the curve to pass through the point, as shown in Figure 3.16. This figure also shows that the B-spline curves are tangential to the lines between the first and last pairs of points at the ends (a property they share with Bézier curves), and that a series of knot points in a line will lead to a straight section of curve.

Although it was stated in the bracketed section on B-spline polynomials above that integer knots are commonly used for convenience in B-spline formulation, the knot points, U_i, may be at arbitrary ascending numerical values and the methods

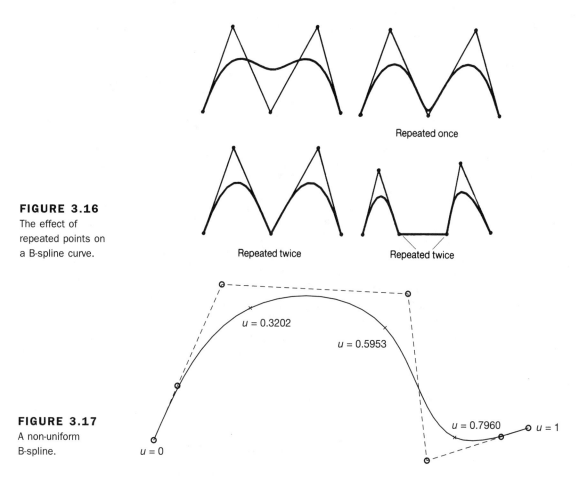

FIGURE 3.16
The effect of
repeated points on
a B-spline curve.

Repeated once

Repeated twice   Repeated twice

FIGURE 3.17
A non-uniform
B-spline.

$u = 0.3202$

$u = 0.5953$

$u = 0.7960$ $u = 1$

$u = 0$

described above will all still work. A B-spline defined on a non-uniform knot vector is called a non-uniform B-spline. Figure 3.17 shows as an example a curve defined in a commercial CAD system which is represented as a non-uniform B-spline on the parameter increment $0 \leqslant u \leqslant 1$, with knots at the u values shown.

3.2.7 Rational curves

The cubic spline, Bézier and B-spline curves form the core of the techniques used in CAD for the representation of free-form curves and data. In engineering design, however, standard analytic shapes such as arcs, cylinders, cones, lines and planes predominate, with the consequence that models of geometry will often involve both free-form and analytic geometry. In addition, there may be a requirement to model analytic geometry using a 'free-form' modelling technique, and this is difficult, particularly for conics and other quadric forms. An ideal modelling method would allow the representation of both analytic and free-form curves in a single unified form. A unified representation would also have the advantage of reducing the database complexity and the number of procedures required in a CAD system for the display and

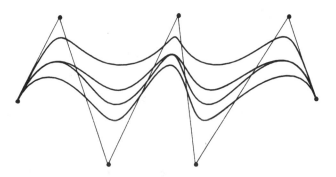

FIGURE 3.18
NURBS curves on
the same point set.

manipulation of geometric entities (e.g. a system may require a separate procedure to display each of the geometric entities, or to calculate the intersection between any pair of entity types).

The class of curves that is known as **rational polynomials** is capable of exactly representing conic and more general quadric functions, and also representing the various polynomial types that we have already met. The mathematical basis of the rational polynomials is briefly described in the bracketed section below, and it is noted that a number of CAD systems today use rational polynomials for the representation of geometry, or for the transformation of geometry between different representations. A very widely used form is the **non-uniform rational B-spline**, or **NURBS**, so called because it is a rational B-spline function allowing a non-uniform knot vector. NURBS is capable of representing in a single form non-rational B-splines and Bézier curves, as well as linear and quadric analytic curves, and may be used in approximating or interpolatory mode. To illustrate the flexibility of the technique, Figure 3.18 shows a number of NURBS curves of order 4 constructed using the same point set, but with different weighting factors in the homogeneous coordinate system.

Rational polynomials

Rational polynomials are functions in which one polynomial curve is divided by another. In particular, they make use of homogeneous coordinates, in which three-dimensional points of the form $[x\ y\ z]^{\mathrm{T}}$ are mapped to four dimensions with an additional coordinate dimension w using the form $[xw\ yw\ zw\ w]^{\mathrm{T}}$, where $w > 0$ (see also Section 4.5.1). The term w is a weighting or scale factor. The rational form of the polynomials that we have used in this chapter is obtained by using homogeneous coordinates in the polynomial expressions, and then dividing the xw, yw and zw coordinates of each point by their homogeneous weighting coordinates. In this way, the rational form of the Bézier curve is:

$$\mathbf{p}(u) = \frac{\displaystyle\sum_{i=0}^{n} w_i B_{i,n}(u)\mathbf{p}_i}{\displaystyle\sum_{i=0}^{n} w_i B_{i,n}(u)} \qquad 0 \leqslant u \leqslant 1 \tag{3.28}$$

and it may be seen that if all $w_i = 1$ then the conventional Bézier expression (3.23) is obtained, since $\sum\limits_{i=0}^{n} B_{i,n}(u) = 1$. Similarly, the rational form of the B-spline curve, or the non-uniform rational B-spline (NURBS), is given by:

$$\mathbf{p}(u) = \frac{\sum\limits_{i=0}^{n} w_i N_{i,k}(u)\mathbf{p}_i}{\sum\limits_{i=0}^{n} w_i N_{i,k}(u)} \tag{3.29}$$

where the $N_{i,k}$ are the B-spline blending functions defined in Equations (3.25) and (3.26).

3.3 Techniques for surface modelling

In the previous section the general form of the parametric representation of a surface was observed to be:

$$x = x(u,v) \qquad y = y(u,v) \qquad z = z(u,v) \tag{3.6}$$

and some of the more important polynomial representations of curves were described. The most widely used techniques for the modelling of free-form surfaces are, not surprisingly, extensions into the second parametric dimension of the polynomial curve techniques, and the resultant surface types share many of the characteristics of the curve forms. The mathematical basis of the techniques is again a more or less simple extension of that of the curve forms, but the detail of the algebra is once more beyond the scope of this book. We will therefore confine ourselves to noting the form of the surface equations, where appropriate, and to describing in qualitative terms the characteristics of the surface forms.

3.3.1 The surface patch

In Chapter 2 the concept of the surface **patch** was introduced. Just as the curve **segment** is the fundamental building block for curve entities (where a curve may be either a single segment, as in a Bézier curve, or a piecewise collection of segments, as in spline curves), so the patch is the fundamental building block for surfaces. Also, just as the parametric variable u varies monotonically along the segment, so the two variables u and v vary across the patch – the patch may be termed **biparametric**. The parametric variables often lie in the range 0 to 1, although other parametric intervals may be used if appropriate. Fixing the value of one of the parametric variables results in a curve on the patch in terms of the other variable (known as an **isoparametric** curve). The result of doing this for a variety of values of u and v is an intersecting mesh of curves on the patch. Figure 3.19, for example, shows a surface with u and v in the range 0 to 1, with curves at intervals of u and v of 0.1.

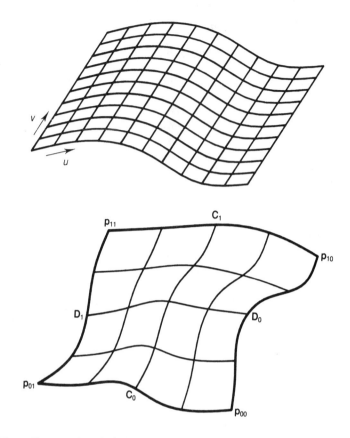

FIGURE 3.19
Surface display with
u and v increments
of 0.1.

FIGURE 3.20
Linearly blended
patch.

3.3.2 The Coons patch

The more general surface forms – the **sculptured surfaces** – often involve interpolation across an intersecting mesh of curves that in effect comprise a rectangular grid of patches, each bounded by four boundary curves. A variety of techniques have been developed for interpolating between such boundary curves, of which perhaps the simplest is the linearly blended Coons patch described in detail in the bracketed section below. Figure 3.20 shows surface paths defined using this formulation. Linear blending has limitations, however, and higher-order blending functions such as cubics are used for formulations that allow tangency continuity between adjacent patches. The term Coons patch is nevertheless used generically to include other patches which are blendings of arbitrary boundaries (Woodwark, 1992).

The linearly blended Coons patch

This patch definition technique blends the four boundary curves of arbitrary parametric form $\mathbf{C}_i(u)$ and $\mathbf{D}_j(v)$ (see Figure 3.20), with the linear blending functions:

$$f(t) = 1 - t \qquad g(t) = t \tag{3.30}$$

Simply applying the blending functions to the curves would give incorrect results, especially at the corners of the patch, and therefore functions of the corner points $\mathbf{p}_{ij}$ must also be introduced into the equation:

$$\mathbf{p}(u,v) = \mathbf{C}_0(u)f(v) + \mathbf{C}_1(u)g(v) + \mathbf{D}_0(v)f(u) + \mathbf{D}_1(v)g(u) -$$
$$\mathbf{p}_{00}f(u)f(v) - \mathbf{p}_{01}f(u)g(v) - \mathbf{p}_{10}g(u)f(v) - \mathbf{p}_{11}g(u)g(v) \qquad \textbf{(3.31)}$$

3.3.3 The bicubic patch

Just as the parametric cubic segment is widely used in the representation of curves, so is the parametric cubic widely used in surface modelling as an edge curve (perhaps as part of a spline), and the equivalent surface form – the bicubic patch – is also an important entity for surface descriptions defined in terms of point and tangent vector information (also known as **tensor** or **cartesian product** surfaces). The algebraic details of the patch are given below.

The bicubic patch

The general form of the expressions for a bicubic patch is given by:

$$\mathbf{p}(u,v) = \sum_{i=0}^{3} \sum_{j=0}^{3} \mathbf{k}_{ij} u^i v^j \qquad \textbf{(3.32)}$$

which may be compared with Equation (3.12) for the parametric cubic curve. Equation (3.32) is a vector equation with 16 unknown parameters $\mathbf{k}_{ij}$. These might be found by Lagrange interpolation through points, in which case 16 points, for example in a 4×4 grid, would be required. Hermite interpolation through points and tangent vectors may also be used, as for curves, but, in this case, simply using the four corner points and the tangent vectors at the corners (two at each point) does not provide sufficient constraints. The remaining four boundary conditions are normally supplied by the **cross-derivative vectors** $\partial^2\mathbf{p}/\partial u\partial v$ at each corner. These partial derivatives are commonly known as the **twist vectors** because they are said to be a measure of 'twist' in the surface. However, although mathematically convenient, they are not a quantity for which the designer will generally have much feel, and therefore implementations of bicubic patches in the Hermite basis generally have to interpolate the twist vectors in some fashion, or to assume that they are zero, and both of these routes may lead to unsatisfactory results.

3.3.4 Bézier surfaces

In the same way that the Bézier curve uses the more tractable control polygon in place of control points and tangent vectors, so too does the Bézier surface formulation use a **characteristic polygon** (also called a **characteristic mesh**) in place

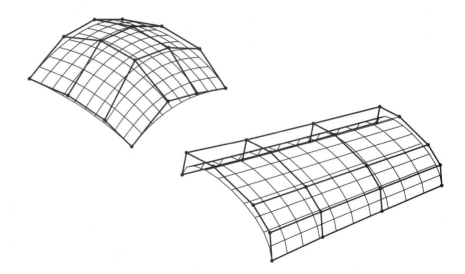

FIGURE 3.21
Examples of Bézier surfaces.

of points and tangent and twist vectors. Points on the Bézier surface are given by a simple extension of the expression for a curve (Equation (3.23)):

$$\mathbf{p}(u,v) = \sum_{i=0}^{m} \sum_{j=0}^{n} B_{i,m}(u)B_{j,n}(v)\mathbf{p}_{ij} \qquad u,v \in [0, 1] \tag{3.33}$$

where $\mathbf{p}_{ij}$ are the vertices of the characteristic polygon and $B_{i,m}$ and $B_{j,n}$ are the blending functions as defined for curves.

Examples of Bézier surfaces and their respective control polygons are shown in Figure 3.21. These show that the surfaces share a number of characteristics with Bézier curves, in particular that the surfaces pass through the corner points of the characteristic polygon only, and have edge curves that are tangential to the edges of the characteristic polygon at the corner points. Furthermore, the surfaces are variation diminishing, and have a convex hull property.

Bézier surfaces share a number of the limitations of the related curves. They only allow global modification, and they are somewhat constraining if smooth transition between adjacent patches is to be achieved – a limitation that is made more acute by the rather intractable nature (both computationally and from the point of view of the user) of characteristic polygons with many points.

3.3.5 B-spline surfaces

The limitations of the Bézier surface are largely overcome by the B-spline surface formulation. This formulation shares certain characteristics with the Bézier scheme, and also with the B-spline curve scheme. The surface again approximates a characteristic polygon (as shown in Figure 3.22) and (generally) passes through the corner points of the polygon, where its edges are tangential to the edges of the polygon (the word 'generally' is used here because B-splines may also be defined using periodic

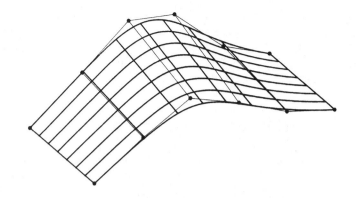

FIGURE 3.22
B-spline surface.

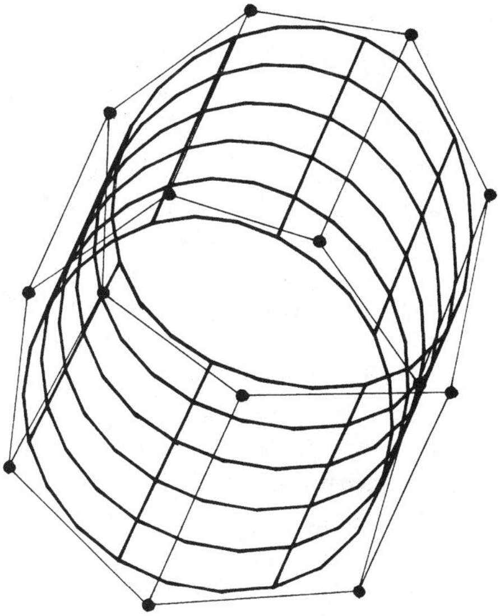

FIGURE 3.23
B-spline surface
with closed
boundary and
periodic blend in
u-direction.

blending functions that are all the same shape; Figure 3.23 shows the effect of using a periodic blending function in combination with a closed control polygon, in which control points on two edges of a mesh are connected). Just as the control point of a curve only influences the shape of the curve over a limited range of the parametric variable, *u*, so a control point of the surface influences the surface only over a limited ('rectangular') portion of the parametric space of variables *u* and *v*. The extent of the influence of a control point, and hence the degree of approximation of the control polygon, may be varied by varying the order of the B-spline blending curves employed.

The expression for the B-spline surfaces is again a straightforward extension of the curve case (given in Equation (3.24)):

$$\mathbf{p}(u,v) = \sum_{i=0}^{m} \sum_{j=0}^{n} N_{i,k}(u) N_{j,l}(v) \mathbf{p}_{ij}$$

(3.34)

where $\mathbf{p}_{ij}$ are the vertices of the defining polygon and $N_{i,k}$ and $N_{j,l}$ are blending functions of the same form as those for B-spline curves, as given in Equations (3.25) and (3.26). From Equation (3.34) it may be seen that blending functions of differing order (k and l) might be used in the two parametric directions, although normally the same order will be used.

3.4 Techniques for volume modelling

In Section 2.4 the constructive solid geometry and boundary representation schemes for volume modelling were introduced, and the overall use of such schemes was discussed in general terms. Again, a detailed treatment of their mathematical and theoretical background is inappropriate to this book. Instead, a taste of some of the problems addressed by the developers of solid modelling systems will be given in this section, by way of illustration. Those readers whose appetites are suitably whetted are encouraged to refer to texts such as those by Mäntylä (1988), Mortenson (1985) and Woodwark (1986) for more extensive treatments. This section will also consider briefly some alternative methods that have been proposed for the representation of solids.

3.4.1 Boundary models

So far this chapter has considered representations of the geometry of shapes, but has given little consideration to their **topology**, which describes the way in which the different elements of a shape are connected together. In the boundary representation scheme for solid models, as was seen in the last chapter, the definition of the solid comes from combining the geometric information about the faces, edges and vertices of an object with the topological data on how these are connected. One of the central problems of boundary modelling, then, is how to ensure that the models defined by the system will always be topologically valid, even during interactive modification. This is done in two ways: firstly by the appropriate choice of data structure, and secondly by ensuring that models conform to a set of mathematical rules that control the topology.

An alternative name for boundary representation models is **graph-based models**, so called because the face, edge and vertex data is stored as **nodes** in a graph, with pointers, or branches, between the nodes to indicate connectivity. The graphs are known as directed graphs, because the direction of the links between nodes is important. Figure 3.24 shows an example of such a graph (represented as a table) for a tetrahedron. It may be seen that there are two unidirectional pointers between each pair of nodes representing adjacent elements. While this means that some data may be redundant, it can speed up the performance of the system.

The topological consistency of the model can be determined by examining the graph for its adherence to certain rules. For example, for a convex body without holes, the rules are that (Mortenson, 1985):

▶ faces should be bounded by a single ring or **loop** of edges;

▶ each edge should adjoin exactly two faces and have a vertex at each end;

▶ at least three edges should meet at each vertex;

▶ Euler's rule should apply. This rule is named after the Swiss mathematician Leonhard Euler (1707–83), and states that:

$$V - E + F = 2 \qquad \qquad (3.35)$$

where V is the number of vertices, E the number of edges, and F the number of faces.

For bodies with holes, protrusions from faces and re-entrant faces, a modified version of Euler's rule known as the Euler-Poincaré formula applies. This states that, if H is the number of interior edge loops or holes in faces, P the number of passages or through holes and B the number of separate bodies then:

$$V - E + F - H + 2P = 2B \qquad \qquad (3.36)$$

Figure 3.25 shows a boundary representation solid with protrusions and depressions on faces, together with a through hole, to which this expression has been applied. The representation of the cylindrical hole in this figure is of particular note. A completely cylindrical face meets itself along one edge, and therefore, to ensure that edges join exactly two faces, cylinders are often represented by **two** semi-cylindrical

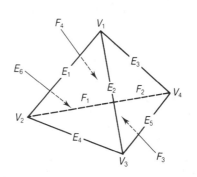

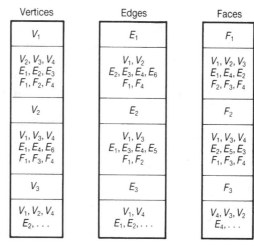

Vertices	Edges	Faces
V_1	E_1	F_1
V_2, V_3, V_4 E_1, E_2, E_3 F_1, F_2, F_4	V_1, V_2 E_2, E_3, E_4, E_6 F_1, F_4	V_1, V_2, V_3 E_1, E_4, E_2 F_2, F_3, F_4
V_2	E_2	F_2
V_1, V_3, V_4 E_1, E_4, E_6 F_1, F_3, F_4	V_1, V_3 E_1, E_3, E_4, E_5 F_1, F_2	V_1, V_3, V_4 E_2, E_5, E_3 F_1, F_3, F_4
V_3	E_3	F_3
V_1, V_2, V_4 $E_2, \dots$	V_1, V_4 $E_1, E_2, \dots$	V_4, V_3, V_2 $E_4, \dots$

FIGURE 3.24
Graph representation for a tetrahedron. (Reproduced from Mortenson (1985) by permission of the publishers. © John Wiley & Sons, Inc.)

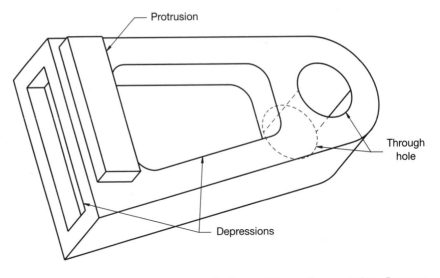

FIGURE 3.25

Protrusions, depressions and holes in a boundary representation solid.

	Vertices	Edges	Faces	Holes	Passages
Basic shape	8	12	6		
Protrusion adds	8	12	5	1	
Depression with sharp corners adds	8	12	5	1	
Depression with filleted corners adds	16	24	9	1	
Through hole adds	4	6	2	2	1

faces. Introducing a cylindrical hole into a body therefore introduces two faces, six edges, four vertices, a through hole and two interior loops in faces, as shown in Figure 3.25.

The way that the Euler–Poincaré formula is used to ensure topological consistency is to restrict the way the model may be manipulated during construction. Legitimate operations on the model are defined using a series of manipulation operators known as **Euler operators**. These specify the combinations of edge, vertex and face that may be added or removed in a single operation to maintain the validity of the formula.

In both research and commercial systems there are a number of variations on the approach both to storing the relationships between model entities and to the maintenance of valid models during construction. In particular, modellers that allow non-manifold models, as introduced in Chapter 2, are not able to enforce strict validity conditions during construction. The approach of one commercial modelling system is to use as its basic representation a topological representation of faces, edge loops, edges and vertices, of which boundary representation solids form a subset when the topological and geometric conditions for validity are met.

3.4.2 Constructive solid geometry

In constructive solid geometry (CSG), which we may remind ourselves involves the construction of a model by the set-theoretic combination of geometric primitives such as cylinders, rectangular blocks and the like, a directed graph is again used for the data structure for the model. In this case, however, the graph is of a particular type

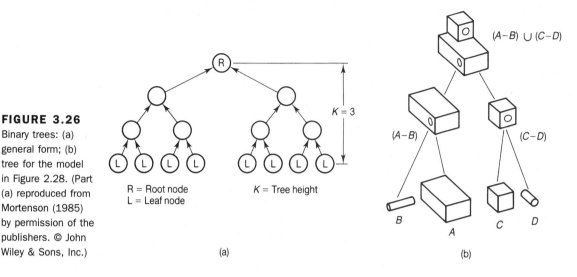

FIGURE 3.26
Binary trees: (a) general form; (b) tree for the model in Figure 2.28. (Part (a) reproduced from Mortenson (1985) by permission of the publishers. © John Wiley & Sons, Inc.)

R = Root node
L = Leaf node

K = Tree height

(a)

(b)

known as a **binary tree**, in which nodes are connected by 'branches' to a root node. Any node may have only one 'parent' node and two 'child' nodes. The root node has no parent, and the nodes with no children are known as leaf nodes. In the CSG model, the leaves are geometric primitives, and the root node and internal nodes comprise the Boolean set operations that construct the model. Figure 3.26 shows the general form of a binary tree, and the specific tree for the model shown in Figure 2.28.

The primitives themselves may be defined in a number of different ways. In some systems they may be bounded solids of the type shown in Figure 2.26, but in other cases they may be derived from intersections of simpler primitives known as **half-spaces**. These are surfaces, such as infinite planes and cylinders, that divide coordinate space into solid and space. A unit cube, for example, may be constructed by the intersection of six planar half-spaces, parallel to the $y - z$, $z - x$ and $x - y$ planes and through $x = 0$, $x = 1$, $y = 0$, $y = 1$, $z = 0$ and $z = 1$ respectively.

One of the main problems of set-theoretic modelling is in achieving the efficient calculation of the intersections between the elements of the model. For complex models with many instances of primitives this can be very computationally intensive. The intensity of this task may be reduced by such means as spatial division of the model such that intersections are only tested for primitives in proximity to each other.

3.4.3 Other modelling techniques

Although the boundary and constructive solid geometry techniques are commercially by far the most widely applied techniques, other methods of modelling have been developed, and three of these – pure primitive instancing, cell decomposition and spatial occupancy enumeration – are mentioned here for completeness.

Pure primitive instancing is the simplest of the techniques, and involves describing models by varying the dimensions of single primitives recalled from a library. The technique may be applied to shapes within families of parts which are

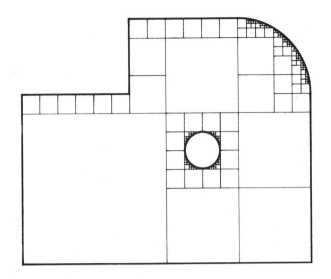

FIGURE 3.27
An example of quadtree subdivision.

geometrically and topologically, but not dimensionally, similar – such as shafts, beams and so on – and is only of very limited value as a design tool.

In **cell decomposition**, the model is described by the assembly of a number of small elemental shapes that are joined together without intersecting – in effect rather like constructive solid geometry but with only a 'joining' operation in place of the set-theoretic operators. Although the technique is not used widely in geometric modelling, it is the basis of finite element analysis (see Chapter 6), in which the analysis of a complex shape is approximated by the analysis of an assembly of simple elements representing the shape.

Spatial occupancy enumeration is similar to cell decomposition, in that the model is divided into a number of small elements, but in this case it involves identifying which of a regular grid of cubic volumes are wholly or partly occupied by the object being modelled. Again, the technique is not used widely in geometric modelling, but associated methods of subdividing two-dimensional and three-dimensional space, known respectively as **quadtree** and **octree** subdivision, are being increasingly applied, for example to the automatic generation of information from solid models. These techniques involve successive or recursive subdivision of a region into square (quadtree) and cubic (octree) shapes. The names come from the reference of each square to four subsidiary squares in quadtree subdivision, and of each cube to eight subsidiary cubes in octree. Representation is based on 4-ary and 8-ary tree structures. When a shape is being approximated the subdivision continues until each square or cube is full of the shape, or empty, or until some predetermined resolution is reached. Figure 3.27 shows an example of a quadtree subdivision for a simple shape.

3.4.4 Construction methods

The construction of solid models by the assembly of instances of primitives or by the identification of faces, edges and vertices is quite a tedious process, and therefore a number of alternative methods of generating the model have been developed. The most important of these are the sweep techniques, which involve taking two-dimensional

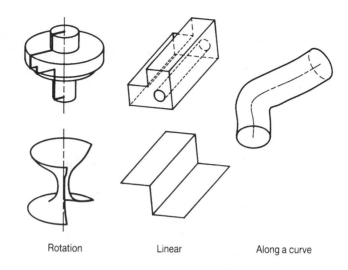

FIGURE 3.28
Examples of sweep
operations.

Rotation   Linear   Along a curve

profiles (generally comprising lines and arcs) and generating solids by projecting them either normal to the plane in which they are constructed, or along a curve (to form a 'pipe-like' shape), or by revolving them around a centre line to form a solid of revolution. Such techniques naturally give rise to edge loops, faces and vertex structures, although linear and rotational sweep algorithms have also been developed for CSG. Examples of these three operations are shown in Figure 3.28.

3.5 Conclusion

There are three main representations used for the three-dimensional modelling of geometry in CAD. These are the wire-frame, surface and solid modelling schemes. This chapter has noted in particular that:

▶ geometric entities are often represented using parametric forms;

▶ of the parametric formulations, the cubic polynomial is particularly widely applied;

▶ the concept of blending the influence of points or curves to determine the shape of a curve or surface is widely applied;

▶ preferred curve and surface representations are often those that smooth data points (they are variation diminishing) and those that allow the form of the entity to be locally modified;

▶ large numbers of independent variables are fitted by the use of piecewise continuous segmented curves known as spline curves;

▶ in volume modelling the approach is to use methods that automatically ensure geometrical and topological validity.

As a result of these considerations a small number of curve and surface types have come to dominate. These include the parametric cubic spline curves and the bicubic patch surface, Bézier curves and surfaces, B-spline curves and surfaces, and the rational curves and surfaces, in particular rational B-splines and non-uniform rational

B-spline curves and surfaces. The last of these formulations, known colloquially as NURBS, has come to have a large influence in geometric modelling because it is capable of exactly representing other spline curves as well as arcs and conic sections. Commercial systems are extensively based on NURBS geometric representations, and also are normally developed as integrated systems in which all geometric entities (curve, surface and solid) are represented in a unified scheme capable of modelling both non-manifold geometry and manifold solids.

References and further reading

Barnhill R. E. (1983). A survey of the representation and design of surfaces. *IEEE Computer-Graphics and Applications*. **3**(7), 9–16.

Bézier P. (1986). *The Mathematical Basis of the UNISURF CAD System*. London: Butterworth.

Bowyer A. and Woodwark J. R. (1983). *A Programmer's Geometry*. London: Butterworth.

Farin G. (1988). *Curves and Surfaces for Computer-aided Geometric Design*. New York: Academic Press.

Faux I. D. and Pratt M. J. (1979). *Computational Geometry for Design and Manufacture*. Chichester: Ellis Horwood.

Mäntylä M. (1988). *An Introduction to Solid Modelling*. Rockville, IN: Computer Science Press.

Mortenson M. E. (1985). *Geometric Modelling*. New York: John Wiley.

Piegl L. (1991). On NURBS: a survey. *IEEE Computer Graphics and Applications*. **11**(1), 55–71.

Preparata F. P. and Shamos M. I. (1985). *Computational Geometry: An Introduction*. New York: Springer.

Risler J.-J. (1992). *Mathematical Methods for CAD*. Cambridge: Cambridge University Press.

Rockwood A. and Chambers P. (1996). *Interactive Curves and Surfaces*. San Francisco: Morgan Kaufman (includes a computer disk with a multimedia tutorial).

Rooney J. and Steadman P. (eds) (1987). *Principles of Computer-aided Design*. London: Pitman.

Shah J. J. and Mäntylä M. (1995). *Parametric and Feature-based CAD/CAM*. New York: John Wiley.

Taylor D. L. (1992). *Computer-aided Design*. Reading, MA: Addison Wesley Longman.

Woodwark J. (1986). *Computing Shape*. London: Butterworth.

Woodwark J. (1992). *G-Words. Keywords for Geometric Computing and its Applications*. Winchester: Information Geometers.

Exercises

3.1 Write down implicit, explicit and parametric expressions for a line and for a circle centred at $x = 0$, $y = 0$.

3.2 Calculate the intersections of a line from (1, 1) to (5, 3) with an ellipse, centred at (4, 2) and with semi-major axis dimension = 3, semi-minor = 2. The semi-major axis is horizontal (*hint*: it may be useful to consider the line in a parametric form, and to move the ellipse centre to the origin).

3.3 Explain the terms convex hull; variation diminishing; second-derivative continuous; control point; and local modification.

3.4 Explain why parametric representations have proved popular in computational geometry.

3.5 Calculate the coefficients for the functions $x = x(u)$, $y = y(u)$ for a Hermite interpolation parametric cubic curve through the points:

$$\mathbf{p}_1 = (1, 2) \qquad \mathbf{p}_2 = (5, 6)$$

with the start and end tangent vectors:

$$\mathbf{p}_1' = (1, 1) \qquad \mathbf{p}_2' = (1, 0)$$

Sketch the curve and the blending functions for the defining points and vectors of a parametric cubic curve.

3.6 Write down the formulae for the Bézier–Bernstein blending functions for a five-point curve.

3.7 A cubic Bézier curve is defined by the points (1, 1), (2, 3) (4, 4) and (6, 1). Calculate the coordinates of the parametric mid-point of this curve, and verify that its gradient (dy/dx) is $\frac{1}{7}$ at this point. Use this information to sketch the curve.

3.8 Solution of the coefficients of a cubic spline curve may be achieved by solving simultaneous equations in the form:

$$\mathbf{Ak} = \mathbf{b}$$

for each variable x, y and z, where $\mathbf{A}$ is a matrix of terms in $(1, u, u^2, u^3)$, $\mathbf{k}$ a column vector of spline segment coefficients, and $\mathbf{b}$ a column vector of constraints (point, slope and curvature). Form $\mathbf{A}$, $\mathbf{k}$ and $\mathbf{b}$ for a three-segment spline, assuming that start and end curvatures are zero.

3.9 Sketch the second-derivative continuous cubic spline curve that fits points $\mathbf{p}_0 = (50, 50)$, $\mathbf{p}_1 = (100, 50)$, $\mathbf{p}_2 = (100, 100)$, $\mathbf{p}_3 = (150, 100)$, $\mathbf{p}_4 = (150, 50)$, $\mathbf{p}_5 = (200, 50)$, $\mathbf{p}_6 = (200, 100)$, $\mathbf{p}_7 = (250, 100)$. What information is required in addition to the point values to enable a second-derivative cubic curve to be defined, and why is this additional information required? Suggest a parameter value for each control point in the curve.

3.10 Develop the general form of a B-spline blending function of degree 3.

3.11 Using the blending curves in Figure 3.15(a) sketch the B-spline curve that interpolates the point set $\mathbf{p}_0 = (1, 1)$, $\mathbf{p}_1 = (4, 1)$, $\mathbf{p}_2 = (5, 4)$, $\mathbf{p}_3 = (7, 2)$, $\mathbf{p}_4 = (7, 2)$, $\mathbf{p}_5 = (7, 2)$, $\mathbf{p}_6 = (9, 4)$, $\mathbf{p}_7 = (12, 4)$. What is the range of the parameter u over which $\mathbf{p}_4$ influences the shape of the curve? Estimate the coordinates of the curve at $u = 2.5$. What would be the shape of the curve if a B-spline of order 2 were fitted to the same point set?

3.12 What is the difference between the linearly blended and the twist vector forms of surface patch? Given points $\mathbf{p}_0 = (100, 100, 0)$, $\mathbf{p}_1 = (100, 200, 0)$, $\mathbf{p}_2 = (200, 100, 0)$, $\mathbf{p}_3 = (200, 200, 0)$, $\mathbf{p}_4 = (200, 150, 25)$, calculate the parametric mid-point of a linearly blended patch bounded by lines joining $\mathbf{p}_0$ with $\mathbf{p}_1$, $\mathbf{p}_1$ with $\mathbf{p}_3$ and $\mathbf{p}_0$ with $\mathbf{p}_2$ and an arc through $\mathbf{p}_2$, $\mathbf{p}_4$ and $\mathbf{p}_3$.

3.13 Use a CAD system to demonstrate the following curve features:

▶ global modification of cubic spline curves and Bézier curves;
▶ local modification of B-spline curves;
▶ the convex hull properties of Bézier curves;
▶ the effect of repeating point selection for each curve type.

3.14 Why is the rational form of polynomial functions used in geometric modelling? Compute the parametric mid-point of a rational Bézier through points $\mathbf{p}_0 = (0, 0)$, $\mathbf{p}_1 = (50, 50)$, $\mathbf{p}_2 = (100, 0)$, if the weight for points $\mathbf{p}_0$ and $\mathbf{p}_2$ is 1, and for $\mathbf{p}_1$ is 2.

3.15 Write down the general expression for a NURBS surface.

3.16 Distinguish between pure primitive instancing, cell decomposition and spatial occupancy enumeration.

3.17 Show how a square with diagonal corners at $x = 0$, $y = 0$, and $x = 8$, $y = 8$, with a square hole removed with diagonal corners at $x = 1$, $y = 5$, and $x = 3$, $y = 7$, may be represented by quadtree subdivision. Draw the 4-ary tree for the subdivision, marking which squares are filled and which are empty.

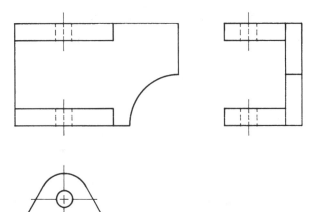

FIGURE 3.29

Three views of a non-functional component.

3.18 Figure 3.29 shows three orthogonal views of a non-functional component. For this shape:

▶ Show that it conforms to the Euler–Poincaré formula (Equation (3.36)).
▶ Show how it may be constructed using a constructive solid geometry solid modelling approach. Draw the binary tree for the model.
▶ Show how sweep operations may be used to define the model.
▶ Suggest how spatial occupancy enumeration might be used to model the shape.

Projects

For more information about the subjects for project work, please refer to the end of Chapter 1.

The project activity for this chapter is largely investigative, to learn how the CAD system can work, what some of the advanced features are, and how it stores its geometry. Specific project tasks are:

Project 1 Chess piece Investigate the use of fillets, blends and chamfering in the solid and surface models of the chess piece. Produce sections through the model at different angles, and then investigate the curve types used to represent the sections. Explore the entity representations used for the model.

Project 2 Load cell Identify the entity types used in the drawings and solid models used for this project. Produce a solid model of the structural member of the load cell. Show how it may be produced using set-theoretic operations on primitives and/or by construction operations such as sweeping a profile. If a boundary representation modeller is used, inspect the faces, edges and vertices of the model, and check that the Euler–Poincaré relationship is followed.

4 Elements of interactive computer graphics

Chapter objectives

When you have completed studying material in this chapter you should be able to:

- ▶ understand the elements of two- and three-dimensional computer graphics and the computer hardware that is used for graphics;
- ▶ explain the clipping, windowing and vector display operations of two-dimensional computer graphics;
- ▶ describe the three-dimensional viewing transformation, and explain the use of homogeneous coordinates;
- ▶ outline the basis of perspective projection;
- ▶ describe the role of hidden-line and hidden-surface removal in generating visually realistic images;
- ▶ describe the principal methods of user interaction, and the specialized hardware that is used for this aspect of system operation;
- ▶ describe the use of windowing systems in user interface design.

Chapter contents

4.1 Introduction

In previous chapters we have seen how the computer may be used to generate models of designs which may be applied at various stages in the design process. The designer and others who use the models need facilities to display them as they are being developed, and to interact with the models and with the CAD system itself.

Design models are primarily geometric or graphical in nature, and therefore the way in which this is achieved is principally through **computer graphics**, with the interaction with the user handled by the system's **user interface**.

This chapter, then, will explore the principles of computer graphics, and of user interface design. It will first consider the nature of computer graphics in general, and will then examine in some detail the specialized hardware used for graphics. Elements of two- and three-dimensional computer graphics will then be introduced, followed by a discussion of techniques that are used to achieve visual realism in the display of geometric models. The chapter will conclude with a presentation of techniques and equipment for user interaction, and with a discussion of the various styles of user interface that may be found in CAD systems.

4.2 Introduction to computer graphics

Computer graphics are a topic of great importance in computing. We have all come across applications of computer graphics in everyday life – for example, in television titles and weather forecast presentations, or in video games. Computer graphics have had a significant impact because they are an extremely effective medium for communication between people and computers – the human eye can absorb the information content of a graph, a pictorial image or a geometric shape much faster than that of a table of numbers or a text file.

There are a number of variations in the characteristics of computer graphics that may be classified into three categories as follows:

▶ The first category defines the control the user has over the image. In **passive** computer graphics the user has no control; in **interactive** graphics the user may interact with the graphics and with the programs generating them.

▶ The second category concerns the way the image is generated. In **vector** graphics the image comprises a number of lines, whereas **raster** graphics involve the manipulation of the colour and/or intensity of points, known as picture elements or **pixels**, in a matrix making up the image.

▶ The third category distinguishes between **image-space** graphics, in which the image itself is directly manipulated to create a picture – as for example in programs such as Microsoft® Paintbrush® (Figure 4.1) – and **object-space** graphics, in which the image is a representation of a separate model. In this latter case, it is the separate model which is manipulated. For example, in a flight simulator, the 'pilot' of the simulator is presented with a continuously changing image of the computer model of the simulator's surroundings.

CAD may be categorized as an application of interactive object-space graphics, in that the objective is to develop interactively a model of a design. It also involves both vector graphics and raster graphics. Line drawings and diagrams make extensive use of vector graphics, and they are also used in the production of 'wire-frame' images for three-dimensional models of all types, although raster hardware is practically universally used for the display of the line images. Raster graphics are used extensively for the display of surface and solid models, and highly realistic displays can be

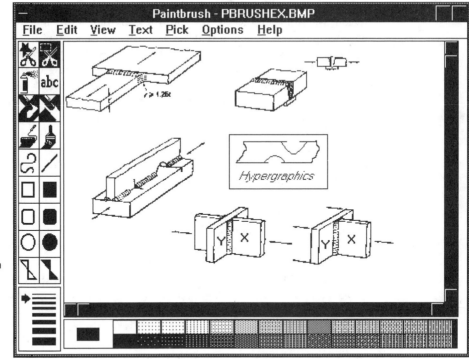

achieved with the use of appropriate **rendering** software to generate the image of
the model.

4.3 Computer graphics hardware

Historically, computers were text- and number-based devices, and required specialized and often very expensive hardware for the display of graphics images, for plotting the image onto hard copy, and for interaction with the user. As graphics have
become a more everyday part of computer applications this hardware has become
part of the standard facilities of computing equipment. Nevertheless, it is still appropriate to review in broad terms the hardware specifically associated with computer
graphics. This section will do so for equipment used in the generation of images. This
will be divided into two categories: **display devices**, for the display of images to
the user, and **plotting devices**, for the generation of hard copy. Later in this chapter we will return to the subject of hardware, when, in Section 4.6, **interface devices**
for interacting with the system and model are considered.

4.3.1 Display devices: the raster-scan CRT

The display device is nowadays almost invariably a visual display unit (**VDU**) of the
raster-scan type, although, historically, calligraphic or **vector** displays, which drew

the picture by constructing an arbitrarily oriented series of lines or vectors on the screen, were important in CAD from the early days until the late 1980s. Raster displays employ the principle that the intensity of each pixel in a rectangular matrix that covers the screen is controlled. The matrix is displayed on the screen surface as a raster, that is as a succession of equidistant linear arrays of pixels known as scan lines, in the manner of a television screen. The most popular display of this kind is the cathode ray tube (CRT), which is a true raster-scan device in that the raster is scanned onto the screen by a deflected electron beam, typically at a **refresh rate** (or rate of repetition of the display of an image) of 50 to 100 Hz.

The display receives its information about the status of pixels from some sort of display memory. A common method is to store a matrix of pixel intensity values in a **digital frame buffer**. In the simplest case, for monochrome images, each pixel can be represented by a single bit in the frame buffer, with 0 representing black, and 1 white (or vice versa). If colour or shades of grey (grey scale) are required, additional bits are allocated to each pixel, so for example 4 bits per pixel would allow $2^4 = 16$, and 8 bits per pixel $2^8 = 256$ colours or shades of grey. Sixteen colours are satisfactory to distinguish between different elements on the screen, but when the production of smoothly shaded images is required, the more extensive range offered by 256 colours is appropriate, and high-performance graphics devices generally assign 24 bits per pixel, or 8 bits to represent the intensity of each of the separate red, green and blue guns of the CRT. An alternative approach is for the 256 colours of an 8-bit display to be selected from a **palette** in which each of the 256 possibilities is cross-referred to a colour in a look-up table, again generally taking one of 256 levels for each of red, green and blue to give over 16 million different colour possibilities.

An alternative method to specifying the level of each of the additive primary colours directly is to employ the three concepts of saturation, hue and lightness (Foley *et al.*, 1996):

▶ **saturation** is used to indicate the proportion of white in the colour, for example to distinguish between shades of blue: royal blue is highly saturated, whereas sky blue is unsaturated, as are pastel shades in general; the primary colours are highly saturated; and white is produced by using equal levels of all three primary colours;

▶ **hue** is used to distinguish between primary and mixed colours, for example to differentiate between blue, yellow and green;

▶ **lightness**, or **intensity**, is used to describe the overall level of brightness of the colour, where zero intensity corresponds to black.

An additional term is **brightness**, used to refer to the intensity of a light-emitting object such as a light bulb.

Modern raster displays have resolutions that vary from the order of 640×480 pixels to 1800×1600 pixels or higher, and are typically either 8-bit/pixel or 24-bit/pixel devices. The latter for a 1280×1024 device implies a frame buffer of nearly 4 megabytes, and thus it is only with the advent of relatively cheap semi-conductor memory that raster devices became very popular for CAD applications.

4.3.2 Display devices: other raster-type displays

Other display technologies also use the raster principle. The most widespread of these are the **liquid crystal displays** (LCDs) which use the technology employed in wrist watches and pocket calculators, and which have become very popular for portable personal computers because they are thin and flat, and because they have a very low power consumption. LCDs use crossed polarizers sandwiching a very thin (0.01 mm) liquid crystal layer, itself between layers onto which are deposited thin grid wires aligned horizontally on one layer, and vertically on the other. The liquid crystal norm-ally rotates polarized light through 90° so that it can pass through the two crossed polarizers. When horizontal and vertical grid wires have an electric potential applied, the resultant field energizes the crystal at the position of the crossed wires, such that it no longer rotates polarized light. Light is thus absorbed, and a dark spot is shown on the display. The complete display is formed by energizing points on the display in a raster-scan fashion, row by row. The effect of energizing the crystal lasts for a few hundred milliseconds, giving the display persistence. A weakness of the LCD is that this persistence is relatively long, making viewing of any dynamic change difficult. Also, the contrast that a standard liquid crystal device can provide, and its ability to display colour, are limited. In all these respects, **active matrix displays** (of which a widely applied type are also known as **thin film transistor** (TFT) displays) offer substantial improvement. These are LCD panels that have a transistor at each grid point on the display, used to allow the crystals to change their state quickly, and to provide a memory of the state of the grid point so that it may be held on continually thus increasing its brightness. The crystals can also be dyed to provide colour (Foley *et al.*, 1996).

There are a number of other display technologies. A further type of raster display that again allows very thin displays is the **plasma panel**, in which each pixel is formed by a neon-tube-type action on an inert gas sandwiched between two glass panels. This type of display does give high contrast, but again colour capability is poor. Some portable computers use **electroluminescent** (EL) displays, in which a matrix grid of wires is used to address a layer of electroluminescent material with a high electric field, as an alternative to LCDs, and **projection CRTs** allow large screen images by projecting the light from three very bright monochrome displays with red, green and blue filters.

Although raster devices have come to dominate computer graphics, they have two significant drawbacks. Their resolution is relatively poor, and the discrete nature of the display means that slanting lines and curves in the image are far from smooth – they display a **staircasing** effect, as shown in Figure 4.2(a). Some very high-resolution dis-plays have been produced, and VDUs with effective resolutions in excess of 3000 × 2000 points have been marketed, but perhaps a more effective remedy for staircas-ing is a technique that smooths sharp edges by modifying the intensity of pixels at steps, known as **antialiasing**. For example, if a line is considered to be 1 pixel wide, then pixel intensity might be set to be proportional to the area of the pixel covered by the line. Figure 4.2(b) shows the effect of applying such an antialiasing approach to the line shown in Figure 4.2(a).

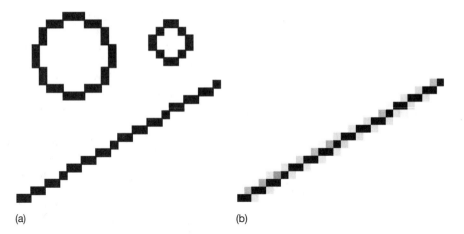

FIGURE 4.2
(a) Imprecision and
(b) antialiasing in
the raster display.

(a)

(b)

4.3.3 The link between computer and display

For many years CAD was carried out using computer terminals connected to central computers, where the central computer resource was often shared between several terminals. In many cases the communications speed between terminal and central computer imposed a limitation on the system performance, which was gradually counteracted by incorporating local computing power into the terminal to handle graphical manipulation and user interaction. This has today developed to the point where computing is for the most part **distributed**, where each user terminal is a computer in its own right. This is the practice adopted in personal computers, and also in the high-performance engineering **workstation**, in which a central processing unit (CPU), semi-conductor memory and backing disk storage are combined with a display in a single unit. Often, a dedicated display processing unit (DPU) may also be included to deal with the very intensive computation required for graphics. The general arrangement of a workstation is shown in Figure 4.3. Workstations and, increasingly, personal computers may be linked together to allow the exchange of data and programs and the sharing of peripherals through **networks**, an example of which is shown diagrammatically in Figure 4.4 (the reader is referred to Chapter 7 for a discussion of this subject in more depth).

A single workstation is not always appropriate for all CAD tasks. A user may wish to use a large computer for some very intensive analytical computation, and then to display the results at a workstation. Alternatively, a network may have more powerful computers that provide computing and storage resources to other workstations. To cater for these circumstances a **client–server** method of operation has been developed, in which a **server process** provides some service to a separate **client process**. For example, in computer graphics a server process may display images and handle user interaction on behalf of the client. The client and server may be two processes operating on the same workstation, or they might be processes operating on different computers, perhaps of differing makes and sizes, on a network. The server process takes messages or **requests**, describing the required action across the network from a client process, and then returns messages describing **events**, for example resulting from user interactions, to the client. Figure 4.5 shows this in diagrammatic

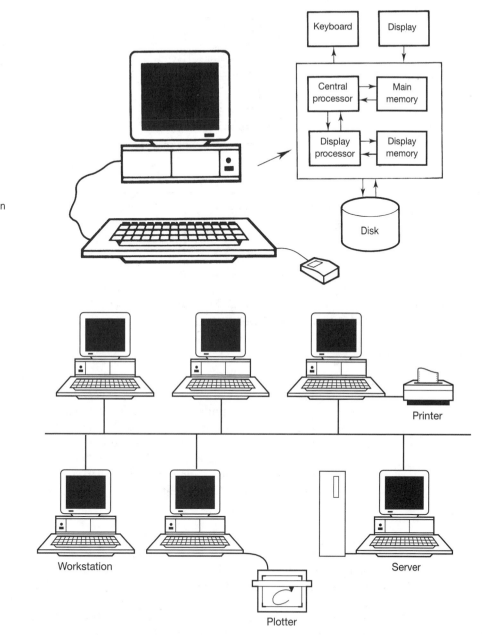

FIGURE 4.3
The general arrangement of an engineering workstation.

FIGURE 4.4
A local area network.

form. Two complaints concerning this method are the high volume of information that must be sent across the network for graphics applications, and the difficulty of synchronizing display and user interaction. Nevertheless, it is a mode of operation that is a standard practice in workstation-based applications.

Also a standard practice is for high-performance workstations to have graphics capabilities that allow most display functions, including viewpoint rotation with

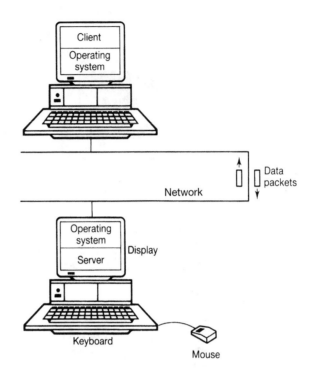

FIGURE 4.5
Client–server
communication
across the network.

hidden-surface removal, to be carried out in real time, even on moderately complex models. Future developments may include large, very high-resolution displays that overcome some of the size limitations of existing devices compared with traditional drawing boards. This may depend on the development of large flat-panel displays for high-resolution television. There may also be a move towards displays that give a virtual three-dimensional image. In recent years such devices have been developed, either using images of different colour or plane polarization viewed through special glasses, or using a vibrating mirror that produces a three-dimensional virtual image by changing its focal point.

4.3.4 Hard-copy devices

The term **hard copy** is used in computer graphics for a copy of an image on some permanent or semi-permanent media such as paper, photographic emulsion or draughting film. There are many ways of obtaining hard copy ranging from laser printers to photographing the screen. The most important methods make use of various plotting devices that may again be divided into vector and raster types.

Vector plotters

Vector plotters are analogous to vector displays in that they produce an image by plotting a sequence of straight lines by moving a pen relative to paper/drawing film or vice versa. Pen plotters may allow for multiple pen types to give different line thicknesses or colours. They generally give high-quality output, and can address as many as 40 points per millimetre, but they are rather slow and do not easily allow for polygonal areas to be filled with solid colour, or a grey scale.

Raster plotters

Several forms of raster-scan plotter have been devised for generating hard-copy images as a matrix of points. The main variation is in the method of 'printing' the points onto the media. This includes dot-matrix devices using the impact of needles on inked ribbons to achieve a resolution of a few hundred points per line (although it can be as high as 10 points per millimetre), and electrostatic and laser-based xerographic devices capable of producing 16 (electrostatic) to 60 (laser) points per millimetre (400–1500 points per inch) and plotting up to A0 size and larger. In the latter case multi-pass electrostatic plotters have been used for full-colour plots up to 1016 mm (40 in) wide, and laser printers of similar widths are produced for the printing of large drawings.

There are other methods for image generation, and the pace of technical development in this field is rapid. **Ink-jet** printers spray ink, often of different colours, from tiny jets in a print head that traverses across the paper. A variety of **thermal** devices transfer wax, ink or dye by the selective heating of fine printing pins. In all of these technologies, resolutions of 75–150 points per millimetre (300–600 points per inch) may be addressed, although the dot size for these devices may be in the order of 0.2–0.5 mm (0.008–0.020 in).

Figure 4.6 shows a portion of an electrostatic plot of a drawing reproduced at full size, as an example of both the raster representation of vector graphics and the

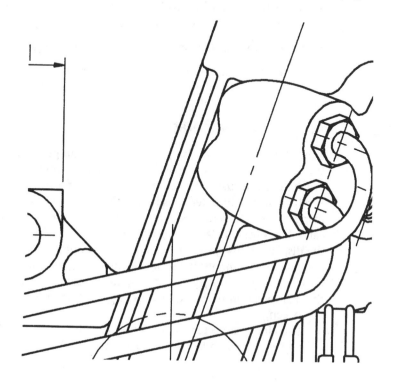

FIGURE 4.6
A portion of an electrostatic plot of a drawing. (Reproduced by permission of TRW Steering Systems Ltd.)

quality that can be achieved by electrostatic plotting technology. Many of the illustrations in this book have, in turn, been produced originally using a pen plotter.

4.4 Two-dimensional computer graphics

We can now explore the principles of computer graphics as applied to the generation of images of designs. The model of a design is actually represented using real-valued numbers in two or three dimensions. A representation is drawn on a VDU screen which is two dimensional (in principle) with the display being defined by integer numerical coordinates. The central aim of computer graphics in CAD is to perform the transformation from design model to display in an efficient manner. A range of geometric representations must be accommodated.

The next section will deal with the general case of image generation for three-dimensional models. For the moment, however, the relatively simple case of two-dimensional graphics will be presented. The essential steps of the process are to:

▶ convert the geometric representation of the model to a form that may be manipulated easily by the graphics routines – for the most part, this means converting curves and text to a series of lines (often termed image **vectors**);

▶ map, or **transform**, the lines from the coordinate system in which they are defined – the model coordinate system – to the coordinate system of the screen;

▶ select those lines that will be visible within the display area on the screen, and discard the remainder – this is known as the **clipping** step;

▶ instruct the display device to draw the visible lines.

The same sequence can be applied to the generation of an image for a plotter. The individual steps in the sequence will now be considered in turn.

4.4.1 Vector generation

Many CAD systems display graphics images simply as a large collection of lines on the screen, whether the image being displayed involves lines, circles, text, surfaces or whatever. At first sight this may seem rather a strange way of going about things. Surely modern computer displays are capable of drawing circles or text? It is true that many are, but nevertheless the use of vectors for display is quite sensible (and the early developers of CAD had no choice!). This is because vector representation allows the display of any geometric entity – including splines and surfaces – as well as text and graphical symbols. It also means that the graphical routines of the program only have to deal with one type of geometric element – the line – and it greatly simplifies the manipulation of images, for example if text or geometry is scaled or rotated on the screen.

The aim of a vector display of a curve is to use sufficient display lines for the curve to appear smooth. The number needed is controlled by the **display tolerance**,

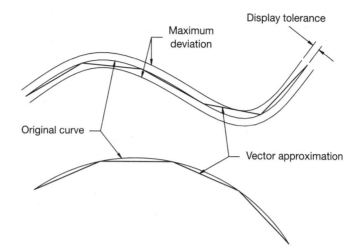

FIGURE 4.7
Display tolerance.

which is the maximum deviation of the vector representation from the true curve shape, as shown in Figure 4.7. In practice, lines are drawn between points on the nominal curve shape, and therefore for arcs, ellipses and so on the permissible deviation is inside the curve. The number of vectors used is a trade-off between appearance of the entities and display performance. A coarse display tolerance implies very polygonal curves. A fine tolerance implies that it is necessary to calculate a large number of curve points, and this can be computationally expensive, although much effort has gone into the development of efficient methods of vectorization, using incremental methods, or taking advantage of symmetry, for example. The calculation of the vector representation of a circle is shown in Example 4.1 below.

The reader may recall at this stage the point made in Chapter 3 concerning the merit of parametric representations of geometry for the generation of sequences of points on curves and surfaces. The generation for display purposes of orderly sequences of points on geometric entities is one of the reasons why parametric techniques are favoured in CAD.

4.4.2 The windowing transformation

The next step is to map or **transform** the vectors from the model coordinate system to the coordinate system of the display screen. The user may wish to display only that part of the model selected using **display control** commands such as **zoom** and **pan**. The image itself may not occupy all of the display screen. Parts of the screen may be allocated to text for user interaction, and the user may wish to show multiple views of the model on the same screen. These requirements are met by using the concepts of **windows** and **viewports**. The window is in effect an imaginary rectangular frame or boundary (of variable size and shape) through which the user looks onto the model. The viewport is the area on the screen in which the contents of the window are to be displayed as an image. This is shown in Figure 4.8 (normally,

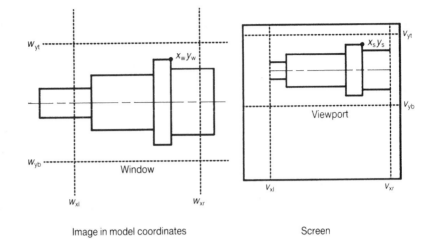

Window

Image in model coordinates

Viewport

Screen

FIGURE 4.8
Window and
viewport.

the aspect ratios of window and viewport are the same, although the figure shows the distortion that can be achieved by making the shapes different). The task in generating the display is one of mapping vectors from the window to the viewport, and the general process of mapping from the model coordinate system to the screen coordinate system is known as a **viewing transformation**.

The general viewing transformation allows any desired scaling, rotation and translation to be applied to the model coordinate definition of the picture. This will be considered in the next section of this chapter. The less general case, in which no rotation is applied, is called the **windowing transformation**.

Using the notation shown in Figure 4.8, we can write expressions for the transformation of a point (x_w, y_w) in model coordinates to x_s, y_s in screen coordinates as follows (Newman and Sproull, 1979):

$$x_s = \frac{(v_{xr} - v_{xl})}{(w_{xr} - w_{xl})}(x_w - w_{xl}) + v_{xl}$$

(4.1)

$$y_s = \frac{(v_{yt} - v_{yb})}{(w_{yt} - w_{yb})}(y_w - w_{yb}) + v_{yb}$$

which can be reduced to the form:

$$x_s = ax_w + b$$

(4.2)

$$y_s = cy_w + d$$

The values of a, b, c and d may be computed when the window and viewport are defined, so each point (generally a line end) may be transformed by a computation involving only two multiplications and two additions. The application of this transformation to a line is shown in Example 4.1 below.

Example 4.1 *Drawing of an arc as a series of vectors*

A circle of radius 25.0 mm, centred at $x = 100.0$, $y = 150.0$, is to be drawn as a series of lines by a two-dimensional draughting system. The maximum display tolerance used is 1.0 mm. Calculate the number of lines required to display the circle within this tolerance, and calculate the screen coordinates of the first of the lines. The window bounds are (40.0, 100.0) and (160.0, 200.0), and the viewport bounds are at pixel locations (0, 50), (480, 450).

The display tolerance is the maximum deviation of the vector representation from the true curve shape. Since this is a circle, this deviation is inside the curve for all vectors. The circle is thus described by a polygon of minimum inscribed radius 24.0 mm and maximum outscribed radius 25.0 mm. Each side of the polygon subtends a maximum angle $A = 2 \cos^{-1}(24/25) = 32.52°$. Thus, the minimum number of lines is 12 (because an integer number is required), and each line subtends 30°, as shown in Figure 4.9. The tolerance in this case is approximately 0.85 mm. This figure also shows that the coordinates of the first line in the display are (125.0, 150.0), (121.651, 162.5).

The expressions for the window transformation in this case are:

$$x_s = \frac{(480 - 0)}{(160.0 - 40.0)}(x_w - 40.0) + 0$$

$$y_s = \frac{(450 - 50)}{(200.0 - 100.0)}(y_w - 100.0) + 50$$

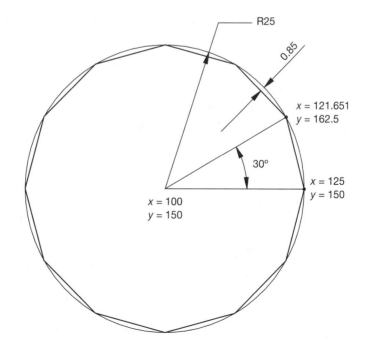

FIGURE 4.9

Vector
representation
of a circle.

rounded to the nearest integer. These may be applied to the line coordinates to give viewport coordinates of (340, 250), (327, 300).

••

4.4.3 Clipping

When the window only shows a part of the model, then those vectors outside the window may lead to undesirable effects if mapped to the screen – they might, for example, write over a text area of the screen, or over another window, or have their coordinates set to the screen boundary values. In any case, it is necessary to identify quickly and efficiently which vectors or parts of vectors are within the window, and to discard the rest. The operation that achieves this is known as **clipping**. Many algorithms have been developed for clipping various graphical elements, using both software and special graphics hardware. A particularly famous algorithm, developed by two of the pioneers of computer graphics, Dan Cohen and Ivan Sutherland, illustrates well the principles involved, and is included as an example in Appendix A.

4.4.4 Line drawing

When this stage is reached, the graphics program has a collection or perhaps a stream of clipped transformed vectors to form the image. All that remains is to draw them on the display, in which respect we will consider as an illustration two aspects of line drawing:

▶ drawing a line on a raster display by setting the appropriate bits in the frame buffer;

▶ instructing a remote process to draw a vector.

The former will apply in cases where the video controller is closely connected to the main CAD processor – for example, when a workstation or personal computer is being used. The discussion of the instruction of a remote process to draw a line is included in part to illustrate the network load imposed by computer graphics.

Drawing lines on raster displays

Line drawing on raster displays is basically a matter of representing a continuous graphical element by a series of discrete points. Examination of Figure 4.10(a) shows that the problem is one of deciding which pixels are near to the line segment, and therefore should be illuminated, and at the same time maintaining an apparently uniform line thickness, all at a rate of perhaps many thousands of vectors per second. Most computer graphics texts contain examples of algorithms for line drawing. For example, Figures 4.10(b), (c) and (d) show how the line drawn in Figure 4.10(a) would be plotted using three different algorithms given in Newman and Sproull (1979). The third algorithm, due to Bresenham, is particularly widely used, because it uses only integer arithmetic, and may be performed incrementally.

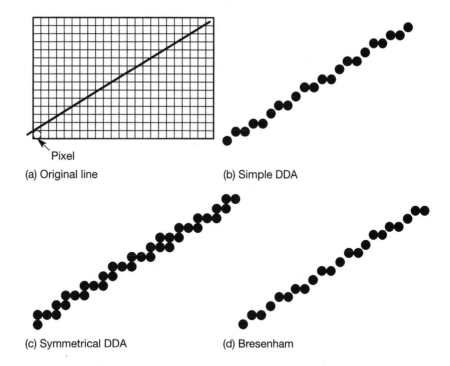

FIGURE 4.10
Line drawing on
raster displays.

(a) Original line

Pixel

(b) Simple DDA

(c) Symmetrical DDA

(d) Bresenham

Transmitting vector information across a network

In order to transmit a graphical instruction of any sort from one device to another, it must be encoded using a **protocol** – a set of rules that control the exchange of data between the communicating devices. A number of protocols exist governing the graphical communication between computers and display terminals, and also between two devices on a network, using the client–server model described earlier in this chapter.

In the client–server approach, the client process will encode the graphics instruction in the appropriate protocol, and then send it across the network to the server process (perhaps after storing a number of messages in a temporary store called a **buffer**). The server process decodes the message and then sets the appropriate bits in display memory, as outlined above.

The instructions to draw lines will normally involve commands to move the attention point to an x, y coordinate position on the screen, and to draw a line from the current attention point to a new x, y point. Positions are generally expressed as integer coordinate pairs. If 2-byte integers are used for each value, then 8 bytes are required for the coordinate data, and in addition information about the required function and drawing style is required. Even if this can be transmitted very compactly (additional data is usually needed for addressing and error checking purposes), at least 10 bytes will normally be required to draw a single line. Display manipulation for a display comprising hundreds or thousands of vectors will thus involve significant network traffic, and the network transmission speed will not normally match the line drawing rate of a modern workstation.

4.4.5 Graphics libraries

It should be noted that libraries of graphics procedures and subroutines exist which make it unnecessary for programmers to program the operations described in this section. Routines for the manipulation of display memory, in particular, will be provided by the equipment manufacturer. The libraries are closely related to the development of standards for computer graphics, and will therefore be discussed further in Chapter 7.

4.4.6 Summary of two-dimensional computer graphics

We have seen that a sequence of operations is required to transform the data from the applications data (in this case the drawing or model) to an image on the screen. This sequence may be thought of as a **pipeline** of operations between the data and the screen. The order in which operations take place depends to some extent on what hardware is available. One possible sequence is shown in Figure 4.11. An alternative sequence, in which clipping takes place after transformation, and therefore in integer screen coordinates, might be more appropriate if hardware is available for these two operations. The notion of a pipeline is even more apposite if the stages of the sequence are allocated to separate hardware units.

FIGURE 4.11
Stages in the graphics pipeline.

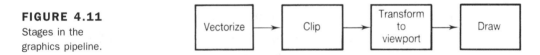

4.5 Three-dimensional computer graphics

The elements of three-dimensional computer graphics are broadly the same as those for two-dimensional graphics: the model is converted to a simple graphical representation such as a collection of vectors; these are then clipped to the window boundary, transformed to screen coordinates and displayed in a viewport on the screen. (There may often be multiple viewports on the screen, each displaying a separate view on the model.) The simplest case of three-dimensional graphics involves parallel projection of vectors: in this case it differs from the two-dimensional sequence only in that the windowing transformation is replaced by the more general **viewing transformation**. The clipping step becomes a little more complex if a pictorial **perspective projection** is applied, and it will be seen in Section 4.6 that extensive computation is required to remove hidden lines and surfaces from the model.

4.5.1 Viewing transformations

In the general viewing transformation the x–y plane of the model coordinate system is not parallel to the x–y plane of the screen coordinate system, and therefore the

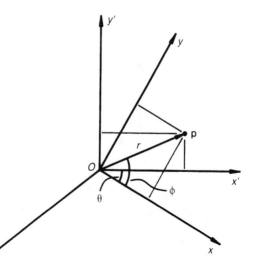

FIGURE 4.12
Rotation about the
z-axis.

transformation has to include a rotation step to align these before the windowing transformation may be applied. The arithmetic of this transformation, and of the associated translation and scaling operations required where the origins and scales of the coordinate systems do not coincide, are given in the remainder of this section. The reader who wishes to omit this detail may proceed directly to Section 4.5.2 below.

As an example of an element of a viewing transformation, consider rotation about the z-axis of the model coordinate system, as shown in Figure 4.12. The model is defined in coordinate system $Oxyz$, and the coordinates of a point, $\mathbf{p}$, are required in system $Ox'y'z'$, aligned with the screen coordinate system. Using polar coordinates in the $Ox'y'$ plane, we can write:

$$x' = r \cos (\phi - \theta)$$

$$y' = r \sin (\phi - \theta) \tag{4.3}$$

$$z' = z$$

Now $x = r \cos \phi$ and $y = r \sin \phi$. Thus:

$$x' = x \cos \theta + y \sin \theta$$

$$y' = -x \sin \theta + y \cos \theta \tag{4.4}$$

$$z' = z$$

which may be expressed in matrix form as:

$$\mathbf{p}' = \begin{bmatrix} x' \\ y' \\ z' \end{bmatrix} = \begin{bmatrix} \cos \theta & \sin \theta & 0 \\ -\sin \theta & \cos \theta & 0 \\ 0 & 0 & 1 \end{bmatrix} \begin{bmatrix} x \\ y \\ z \end{bmatrix} = \mathbf{B}_z \mathbf{p} \tag{4.5}$$

for rotation about Ox and Oy, the equivalent expressions are:

$$\mathbf{p'} = \begin{bmatrix} x' \\ y' \\ z' \end{bmatrix} = \begin{bmatrix} 1 & 0 & 0 \\ 0 & \cos\theta & \sin\theta \\ 0 & -\sin\theta & \cos\theta \end{bmatrix} \begin{bmatrix} x \\ y \\ z \end{bmatrix} = \mathbf{B}_x\mathbf{p} \tag{4.6}$$

and:

$$\mathbf{p'} = \begin{bmatrix} x' \\ y' \\ z' \end{bmatrix} = \begin{bmatrix} \cos\theta & 0 & -\sin\theta \\ 0 & 1 & 0 \\ \sin\theta & 0 & \cos\theta \end{bmatrix} \begin{bmatrix} x \\ y \\ z \end{bmatrix} = \mathbf{B}_y\mathbf{p} \tag{4.7}$$

and **any** rotation between coordinate systems may be expressed as a combination of individual rotations about one, two or three axes. The matrices for these individual rotations may be multiplied together to give a single matrix for any rotation.

Coordinate points are represented in Equations (4.5)–(4.7), and elsewhere in this book, using column vectors, as is the standard practice in engineering mathematics. The reader should note that it is a common practice in computer graphics texts to use row vectors for positional data (the first edition of this book also adopted the convention of using row vectors), in which case Equation (4.5) would be written as:

$$\mathbf{p'} = \begin{bmatrix} x' & y' & z' \end{bmatrix} = \begin{bmatrix} x & y & z \end{bmatrix} \begin{bmatrix} \cos\theta & -\sin\theta & 0 \\ \sin\theta & \cos\theta & 0 \\ 0 & 0 & 1 \end{bmatrix} = \mathbf{p}\mathbf{B}_z \tag{4.5a}$$

Viewing could be achieved by applying a rotation to align the model and viewing coordinate systems as before, then using a windowing transformation to apply scaling and translation, but it would be preferable to combine the two operations into a single transformation. If the windowing transformation is examined again it is seen that it comprises a **scaling** and a **translation**. Scaling with respect to the coordinate system origin and translation between coordinate systems are shown in Figures 4.13 and 4.14 respectively. Using the notation of Figure 4.13 we obtain, for scaling of the coordinate system by a factor of S (the inverse is used here in order to be consistent with the presentation of object transformations in the next chapter):

$$x' = x/S$$

$$y' = y/S \tag{4.8}$$

$$z' = z/S$$

or, in matrix form:

$$\begin{bmatrix} x' \\ y' \\ z' \end{bmatrix} = \begin{bmatrix} 1/S & 0 & 0 \\ 0 & 1/S & 0 \\ 0 & 0 & 1/S \end{bmatrix} \begin{bmatrix} x \\ y \\ z \end{bmatrix} \tag{4.9}$$

and for translation (Figure 4.14):

$$x' = x - dx$$

$$y' = y - dy \tag{4.10}$$

$$z' = z - dz$$

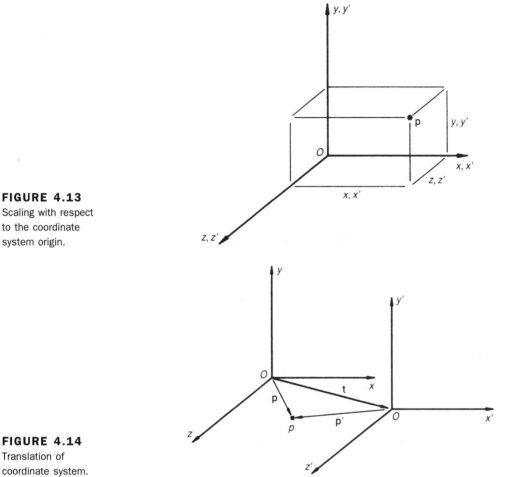

FIGURE 4.13
Scaling with respect
to the coordinate
system origin.

FIGURE 4.14
Translation of
coordinate system.

which is a **vector** operation ($\mathbf{p}' = \mathbf{p} - \mathbf{t}$, where $\mathbf{p} = [x\ y\ z]^T$ and $\mathbf{t} = [dx\ dy\ dz]^T$), and therefore not compatible with the other matrix forms. This limitation may be overcome by the use of a mathematical device known as **homogeneous coordinates**. This involves representing the three-element position vectors by four-element vectors of the form:

$$[wx \quad wy \quad wz \quad w]^T \tag{4.11}$$

where w is the scale factor, which we will normally take to be unity. Using homogeneous coordinates, translation can be expressed in matrix form as:

$$\begin{bmatrix} x' \\ y' \\ z' \\ 1 \end{bmatrix} = \begin{bmatrix} 1 & 0 & 0 & -dx \\ 0 & 1 & 0 & -dy \\ 0 & 0 & 1 & -dz \\ 0 & 0 & 0 & 1 \end{bmatrix} \begin{bmatrix} x \\ y \\ z \\ 1 \end{bmatrix} \tag{4.12}$$

and rotation and scaling in the form:

$$\begin{bmatrix} x' \\ y' \\ z' \\ 1 \end{bmatrix} = \begin{bmatrix} & & & 0 \\ & M & & 0 \\ & & & 0 \\ 0 & 0 & 0 & 1 \end{bmatrix} \begin{bmatrix} x \\ y \\ z \\ 1 \end{bmatrix}$$

(4.13)

where **M** is the appropriate 3×3 rotation or scaling matrix. The transformations are thus consistent – or homogeneous – and we can use:

$$\mathbf{p}'' = \mathbf{A_2}\mathbf{p}' = \mathbf{A_2}\mathbf{A_1}\mathbf{p}$$

$$\mathbf{p}''' = \mathbf{A_3}\mathbf{p}'' = \mathbf{A_3}\mathbf{A_2}\mathbf{A_1}\mathbf{p}$$

Matrices may be **concatenated** (multiplied together in sequence) for any desired transformation.

Example 4.2 *The use of homogeneous coordinates*

An arc is defined in the Oxy plane of a coordinate system $Ox_ay_az_a$ and centred at (100, 100, 0). $Ox_ay_az_a$ is rotated by $45°$ anticlockwise about the Ox_a-axis with respect to system $Ox_wy_wz_w$ (see Figure 4.15). The origin of $Ox_ay_az_a$ is at (50, 0, 0) in $Ox_wy_wz_w$ and the Ox-axes of the two systems are coincident. Evaluate the transformation matrices required in the generation of vectors in $Ox_wy_wz_w$ for display of the arc.

The transformation sequence that is required is:

(a) Align the Oxy planes of $Ox_ay_az_a$ and $Ox_wy_az_w$. This is a clockwise coordinate system **rotation** about Ox_a. Thus:

$$\begin{bmatrix} x' \\ y' \\ z' \\ 1 \end{bmatrix} = \begin{bmatrix} 1 & 0 & 0 & 0 \\ 0 & \cos 45° & \sin 45° & 0 \\ 0 & -\sin 45° & \cos 45° & 0 \\ 0 & 0 & 0 & 1 \end{bmatrix} \begin{bmatrix} x \\ y \\ z \\ 1 \end{bmatrix}$$

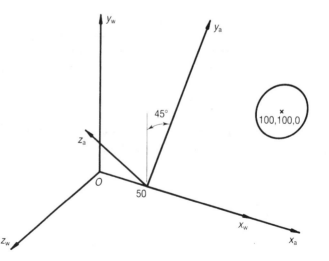

FIGURE 4.15
Coordinate system
transformation.

(b) Align the origins of the two systems. This is a **translation**, that is:

$$
\begin{bmatrix} x' \\ y' \\ z' \\ 1 \end{bmatrix} = \begin{bmatrix} 1 & 0 & 0 & 50 \\ 0 & 1 & 0 & 0 \\ 0 & 0 & 1 & 0 \\ 0 & 0 & 0 & 1 \end{bmatrix} \begin{bmatrix} x \\ y \\ z \\ 1 \end{bmatrix}
$$

(c) Concatenate the matrices of (a) and (b), with the result:

$$
\begin{bmatrix} x' \\ y' \\ z' \\ 1 \end{bmatrix} = \begin{bmatrix} 1 & 0 & 0 & 50 \\ 0 & 0.7071 & 0.7071 & 0 \\ 0 & -0.7071 & 0.7071 & 0 \\ 0 & 0 & 0 & 1 \end{bmatrix} \begin{bmatrix} x \\ y \\ z \\ 1 \end{bmatrix}
$$

So, for example, the centre of the circle is located in $Ox_w y_w z_w$ at $x = 150$, $y = 70.71$, $z = -70.71$.

• •

The use of homogeneous coordinates is an important technique with many applications in addition to the generation of viewing transformations in computer graphics. One of these – the translation, rotation and scaling of objects in CAD – will be described in the next chapter, and the technique is also important in robotics and in mechanisms analysis, where homogeneous coordinates are used to express the relationship between the elements of mechanical linkages.

Let us return briefly to the viewing transformation, and introduce the concept of the **eye coordinate system**. This has its origin at the eye, and the $Ox_e y_e$ plane is parallel to the screen. The viewing transformation thus becomes:

$$
\begin{bmatrix} x_e \\ y_e \\ z_e \\ 1 \end{bmatrix} = \mathbf{V} \begin{bmatrix} x_m \\ y_m \\ z_m \\ 1 \end{bmatrix}
\tag{4.14}
$$

where the subscript m refers to model coordinates, and $\mathbf{V}$ is the viewing transformation. The convention is sometimes adopted that the eye coordinate system is left-handed, so that the z_e-axis points away from the viewer to preserve the intuitive notion of depth. In general, however, model coordinate systems are right-handed systems.

4.5.2 Perspective projection

Perspective projection is often used for pictorial projection of large objects, where parallel projection would give a distorted visual impression. As a general rule it can be said that perspective projection should be used to represent an object that is so large that it would normally be viewed with a significant perspective effect – a vehicle or a building, for example. If the object is small (e.g. if it may be hand-held) then parallel projection is adequate. Perspective projection involves converging projectors and may be generated by first transforming points to the eye coordinate system using

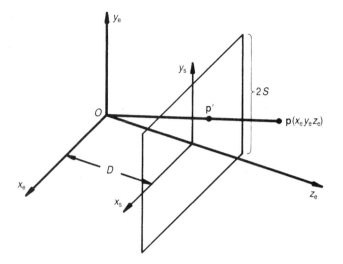

FIGURE 4.16
Perspective projection of a point. (Reproduced from Newman and Sproull (1979) by permission of the publishers. © The McGraw-Hill Companies)

a parallel viewing transformation, and then projecting each point onto the plane of the display screen by a projector passing through the eye coordinate system origin. Projected points may then be connected with lines to generate a vector display. Referring to Figure 4.16, and considering the projected image of the point **p** by similar triangles:

$$\frac{x_s}{D} = \frac{x_e}{z_e} \qquad \frac{y_s}{D} = \frac{y_e}{z_e} \tag{4.15}$$

The numbers x_s and y_s can be normalized (i.e. converted into dimensionless fractions in the range -1 to $+1$) by dividing by the screen size:

$$x_s = \frac{Dx_e}{Sz_e} \qquad y_s = \frac{Dy_e}{Sz_e} \tag{4.16}$$

In this equation the ratio D/S can be thought of as being analogous to the focal length of a lens. If D/S is small the focal length will be short (equivalent to a wide-angle lens). If D/S is large, it will be long (equivalent to a telephoto).

In the perspective projection described above, the z values required to identify the relative depth of objects, for example for hidden-line removal, are not projected. This limitation can be overcome by use of a homogeneous coordinate **perspective transformation**, which is given below without its derivation (Watt, 1993):

$$\begin{bmatrix} X \\ Y \\ Z \\ w \end{bmatrix} = \begin{bmatrix} D/S & 0 & 0 & 0 \\ 0 & D/S & 0 & 0 \\ 0 & 0 & F/(F-D) & -DF/(F-D) \\ 0 & 1 & 1 & 0 \end{bmatrix} \begin{bmatrix} x_e \\ y_e \\ z_e \\ 1 \end{bmatrix} \tag{4.17}$$

where $x_s = X/w$, $y_s = Y/w$, $z_s = Z/w$, $w = z_e$, and F is the z_e value of the furthest point from the origin.

There are several other formulations for perspective projection, as given, for example, in Foley *et al.* (1996).

4.6 Techniques for visual realism
··

The graphical techniques that have been discussed so far will display all parts of the object to the viewer, simply as a collection of lines. Now, if real objects are observed, internal detail and back faces will be obscured from view, shadows will be cast, and surfaces will take on different intensities and hues according to the local lighting conditions. CAD systems have become celebrated in recent years for their ability to simulate such 'realistic' viewing conditions. In this section some of the techniques that promote this will be introduced.

The generation of realistic images involves the application of techniques in two distinct areas: the removal of hidden surfaces from the image, and the shading or colouring of the visible surfaces in a manner appropriate to the modelled lighting conditions. These techniques are founded on the use of colour raster display technologies, because in such displays each individual pixel may be set to a different colour and intensity in order to give the impression of continuous areas of colour and shade. An allied group of procedures for vector displays and plotters that is used to achieve the more limited realism of removing obscured edges and surface curves is called **hidden-line removal**. These procedures predate **hidden-surface removal** because of the early predominance of vector devices, and therefore it is these that we will address first.

4.6.1 Hidden-line removal

In hidden-line (sometimes called hidden-edge) removal, edges or other vectors in the model that are obscured by visible surfaces are omitted from the display of the image, or displayed as dashed rather than full lines. An alternative name for the techniques is visible line identification. The process of generating a hidden-line image is similar to the clipping process, and also involves the segmentation and partial display of partly obscured edges. The essential difference between the two processes is that hidden-line removal involves testing edges in the model against multiple, often irregularly shaped, boundaries. It is therefore a lengthy process: certainly the approach in which each edge is tested against every face in the object is very computationally expensive, although techniques such as the application of boxing tests (generating an imaginary box around parts of the image, and testing for visibility of the box rather than the full model geometry) and spatial subdivision of the model have been applied to improve performance.

Testing edges in the model against general surfaces is difficult. It is much easier to test against flat faces only. Consequently, many CAD systems apply a technique called **tessellation** to subdivide surfaces into planar polygons for hidden-line removal (and, as will be seen, for hidden-surface work also). Figure 4.17 shows a true hidden-line image of an object, and the corresponding image from a tessellated approximation.

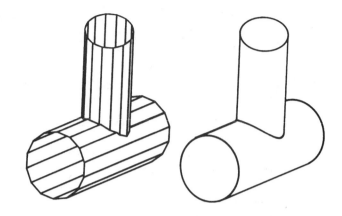

FIGURE 4.17
Comparison of
tessellated and true
hidden-line removal.

Hidden-line removal involves primarily object-space techniques, in that the algorithms generally operate on a model-level representation of the edges and faces. The result of the algorithms is edges that are visible from a particular viewpoint, and which may subsequently be displayed on a graphics screen, or plotted on a pen or other vector plotter.

4.6.2 Hidden-surface removal

Hidden-surface removal (also called **visible surface determination**) is, by contrast, more generally an **image-space** process: an image of an object is generated at a particular resolution by manipulating pixels on a raster display, exploiting the ability of raster devices to display shaded areas. The image-space approach means that performance of hidden-surface techniques is much less sensitive to model complexity than that of hidden-line algorithms. This is because the limited resolution of the raster display means that it is not necessary to devote large computing effort to the generation of fine scene detail for complex models. However, it is necessary to recompute the display for any change in scale.

One of the simplest hidden-surface algorithms is the **depth-buffer** or **z-buffer** algorithm. This algorithm uses the frame buffer for the display to store colour values for the pixels, and an additional buffer, called the z-buffer, to store a current z value for each pixel. This z value represents the depth or distance from the viewing point of the nearest object to the pixel that has been processed by the algorithm. The equivalent pixel in the frame buffer stores the shade of that object. The algorithm works by first setting the depth for each pixel to the furthest possible value, and the colour to a background colour. Each object in the model is then processed, and, for each pixel in the projection of the object, if the depth of the object from the viewpoint is less than the current depth, the depth and colour values for that pixel are replaced by the values for the new object. When all objects in the model are processed, the frame buffer contains the hidden-surface image of the model.

The depth-buffer approach is rather a 'brute-force' approach, and requires a large amount of memory for the buffers, but it is amenable to hardware implementation, and with the declining cost of semi-conductor memory has become a popular technique. There are many other approaches to hidden-surface removal, however, which exploit image or model characteristics in order to improve efficiency, especially when implemented in software.

The image characteristics that are exploited are forms of **coherence**, which is a term that describes the generally slow change in moving images with time, and the often gradual change in colour and shade within an image. A good way of grasping the concept of coherence is to consider the display of a television picture: **temporal** coherence concerns change in time, and means that one frame is often very similar to the next; the similarity between adjacent lines of the image is called **scan-line** coherence, while the similarity in colour between adjacent parts of the picture is an example of **spatial** coherence.

Finally, much hidden-surface removal also relies heavily on polygonal, tessellated representations of surfaces and faces, as shown in Figure 4.17 (the depth-buffer approach can use any model representation for which a depth and shade at an arbitrary point can be computed, although it often also uses a polygonal representation). The basic principle applied is to sort the polygons in some way in order to identify which faces are visible. One sorting technique that is widely applied, known as scan conversion, also determines which pixels lie within the projected image of a given polygon. A well-known hidden-surface algorithm based on a line-by-line scan conversion of the image is included in Section A.2 of Appendix A as an illustration of the approach, although it must be noted that many techniques have been developed, as given in (Griffiths (1978)), and well described in texts such as Newman and Sproull (1979) and Foley *et al.* (1996).

4.6.3 Light and shade

The hidden-surface algorithm will evaluate which face is visible at a particular pixel on the screen, but further information is required to determine the particular colour to display. This comes from a consideration of the colour and orientation of the visible face, and of the illumination simulated in the image, which may generally be of one of two forms:

▶ **Diffuse** illumination, in which light of equal intensity strikes the object from all directions. This is akin to the ambient light reflected from walls and ceilings or transmitted through cloud, and can be represented by an ambient intensity I_a.

▶ **Point-source** illumination, such as that from the sun, or from light bulbs, candles and so on, which has values of intensity, I_p, and location, which will be represented by the vector **p** from the point of interest on the face to the point source.

Sometimes **directed** sources, which have intensity, location and direction, may be modelled.

The simplest type of reflection to model is diffuse reflection, in which the incident light is reflected in all directions. If the proportion of incident light reflected from a given surface is R, then the surface brightness I_s is the sum of the brightness owing to ambient illumination and that owing to point sources, given by:

$$I_s = I_a R + \sum_{i=0}^{m} [I_{pi} R(\mathbf{p}_i \bullet \mathbf{n})] \qquad\qquad (4.18)$$

where $\mathbf{n}$ is the surface normal, and $\bullet$ indicates that the vector dot product is applied. We will ignore distance to the source here.

The realism of the model is substantially improved by the incorporation of **specular reflection** from the surface. This is the reflection of light at or near its angle of incidence which gives a surface a shiny or glossy characteristic. A perfect, mirror-like surface will have exactly equal angles of incidence and reflection. The shine of a painted surface, on the other hand, will arise from some degree of scatter of the reflected light – the greater the scatter, the duller the appearance of the surface. A very simple incorporation of specular reflection into Equation (4.18) involves adding a term as follows:

$$I_s = I_a R + \sum_{i=0}^{m} \{I_{pi} [R_d (\mathbf{p}_i \bullet \mathbf{n}) + R_s \cos^n \phi]\} \qquad\qquad (4.19)$$

where ϕ is the angle between the viewing vector and the reflection vector, and R_d and R_s are the diffuse and specular reflectivity respectively. The term $\cos^n \phi$ is Phong's (1975) empirical reflection model in which, for a perfect reflector, n is infinite, for a very glossy surface n is large, and, for a more matt surface, n is lower. This model is illustrated in Figure 4.18.

The Phong model, developed by Bui-Tuong Phong at the University of Utah (where much work on visual realism was carried out), gives a pleasing result, but is not based in the physics of reflection. A number of other models have been introduced which attempt to model the behaviour or real surfaces, and also include the effects of directionality in the light sources (Foley et al., 1996). The more sophisticated CAD systems also allow features such as transparency and the mapping of textures onto surfaces.

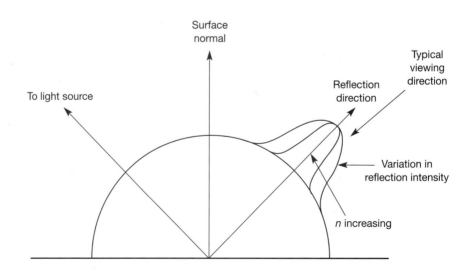

FIGURE 4.18
The Phong illumination rule. (After Watt (1993) by permission of Addison Wesley Longman Limited.)

(a) Flat shading

(b) Gouraud shading

(c) Phong shading

FIGURE 4.19
Comparison of
shading algorithms.

Even the most sophisticated illumination and reflection models will fail to give a realistic picture unless some attempt is made to account for the discrete nature of the faceted model. Figure 4.19(a) clearly shows the sharp changes in shade which occur at edges when constant or **flat** shading of each polygon is used. This can be resolved if the shade is varied across each polygon such that the shade at a polygon's edge matches that of its neighbour. Two techniques are used in particular to achieve this:

▶ **Gouraud** shading, developed by Henri Gouraud (1971), which computes surface normals at polygon vertex points, either from the underlying surface representation, or by averaging the normals of the polygons that meet at the point, and uses these to determine vertex intensities which are then linearly interpolated across the polygon;

▶ **Phong** shading, also developed by Bui-Tuong Phong (1975), which interpolates the surface normal vectors themselves across polygons (based on average vectors at edges), and uses these interpolated vectors in shading models at each pixel in the image.

Because the Phong method interpolates vector rather than scalar values, it is more computationally intensive than the Gouraud technique, but gives a more faithful reproduction of highlights in specular reflection. By computing pixel shade using interpolated surface normals, highlights in the centres of polygons are much more likely to be shown than in the Gouraud case where interpolation uses scalar values at polygon vertices. Phong shading also reduces an undesirable effect known as Mach banding where there are variations in intensity at adjacent facets.

Figures 4.19(a), (b) and (c) show images generated using flat shading and the Gouraud and Phong techniques respectively. Note that in each image the underlying faceted representation may be seen in the silhouette of the image.

4.6.4 Ray tracing and radiosity

Two further techniques which give the highest image quality at the expense of a high computational load remain to be discussed. These are respectively **ray tracing** or **ray casting** and **radiosity**. The first of these techniques comprises a series of algorithms which generate images by considering the path of a ray of light arriving at each pixel on the screen. The path is traced to the points where it meets surfaces in the scene. The ray tracing may be used simply to identify visible surfaces, or it may allow shadows, reflection and refraction to be considered by calculating the surface intensity at the intersection points from three contributions: the local colour due to the illumination of the surface by direct and ambient light, a contribution from the reflection of a ray coming from the reflection direction, and a contribution from a transmitted ray coming from a refraction direction, if the surface is translucent. The path of each refracted and reflected ray is traced to further intersections, and the process is continued for a predetermined number of levels of intersection – for example, in Figure 4.20 three levels are shown.

Ray tracing normally operates on a precise rather than faceted representation, and thus the efficiency of line to surface intersection calculation is key, because of the number of intersections that need to be calculated. In a typical scene many millions of intersections may need to be calculated, and if the surfaces are based on non-uniform rational B-splines then the computational load of the process may be very high (although there are many ways of improving efficiency, such as spatial or hierarchical partitioning of the model, as noted in Watt (1993) and Foley *et al.* (1996)).

In standard ray tracing, rays continue from intersection to intersection as infinitely thin beams, which results in sharp shadows and reflection and refraction. Real

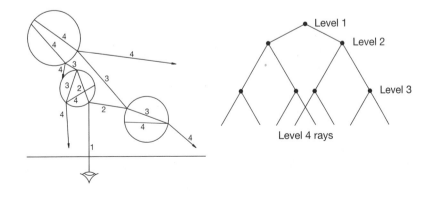

FIGURE 4.20

Intersection levels in ray tracing. (After Watt (1993) by permission of Addison Wesley Longman Ltd.)

scenes tend to be rather more diffuse owing to surface imperfections and scattering in translucent materials. A more realistic effect may be achieved by using 'bundles' of rays per pixel, and allowing some randomness in the paths followed (Cook *et al.*, 1984). By such means ray tracing may be able to go some way towards modelling diffuse illumination, but essentially it is a vehicle for handling specular reflection and refraction.

The radiosity method has exactly opposite characteristics to ray tracing. It was developed to account for the interaction of diffuse light between elements in a scene, but it cannot cope with sharp specular reflection. The method was developed at Cornell University in the early 1980s (Goral *et al.*, 1984), and uses techniques from radiant heat transfer in which the rate of light emission (or radiosity) from each surface in a scene is computed in terms of all of the other surfaces and sources of light. The method is an object-space algorithm, solving for intensity at discrete surface patches within an environment. Once this has been computed, images may be rendered for different viewpoints simply by determining visible surfaces and interpolating surface shades as required.

For each surface patch, *i*, the radiosity, B_i (the energy per unit area leaving the patch per unit time) is the sum of energy emitted from the patch E_i and reflected energy from other patches, given by:

$$B_i = E_i + R_i \sum_{j=1}^{n} B_j F_{ij} \qquad (4.20)$$

where R_i is the proportion of the incident light reflected (and is related to, but not identical to, the diffuse reflection coefficient used above), and F_{ij} is a form factor which determines the fraction of the energy leaving patch *j* which arrives at patch *i*.

The complexity of the radiosity method arises from the requirement to compute form factors for each pair of surface patches in the scene, and also to solve the set of *n* simultaneous equations to find the B_i values. This means that the radiosity method, like ray tracing, is particularly computationally intensive, although both methods benefit from the application of parallel processing techniques.

Radiosity may be used to achieve very high standards of realism for scenes such as room interiors, which makes it potentially very suitable for building design, interior and furnishing design and so on. Ray tracing on the other hand is more appropriate to the modelling of objects such as motor vehicles or consumer durables with glossy surfaces. More routine hidden-surface viewing – for example, to walk through the prototype Boeing 777, or to view an oil rig in position in the North Sea – is still likely to use conventional faceted representation and Gouraud or Phong shading.

4.7 Interacting with the system and the model

So far, this chapter has discussed how images of the computer model may be generated and displayed on the display screen. A major emphasis in CAD is on its *interactive* nature, and thus the techniques that are used to allow the user to interact with the model, and with the CAD system that is generating the model, will now be described. Within this area there are three main facets:

▶ actions by the user to **control** the operation of the system, and the presentation to the user of information and feedback relating to system operation;

▶ **entry of data** by the user for use by the system;

▶ **selection** by the user of parts of the model to be used in construction, or to be manipulated by the system.

Each of these aspects is dealt with by the system's **user interface**. Different styles of user interface offer diverse methods of program control, data entry and selection, which will be discussed later in this section. First, however, it is appropriate to describe briefly the specialist hardware that supplements, in a graphical environment, the traditional keyboard for user interaction.

4.7.1 Hardware for user interaction

In conventional user interaction, the user enters data and selects or enters commands through keystrokes made on a keyboard. In a system in which interactive graphics are used, these actions are generally supplemented by the activities of:

▶ **positioning**, or **location**, generally for data entry within the program;

▶ **pointing** to, or **picking**, graphical or other elements on the display screen, for object or command selection.

A useful concept is to think of the software as being controlled either by continually sampling the state of the input devices that the user may use, or by being interrupted by a series of **events**. A keyboard keystroke is an event, and so is the action of picking or locating, which is usually signalled to the computer by the user pressing a **button** associated with interactive devices used for the action. The devices themselves will be classified here as positioning or pointing devices, corresponding to the division between locating and picking. However, through the appropriate use of software, pointing devices may be used for positioning and vice versa, such that in general it is only necessary for any system to use (at any one time) one device for both locating and picking.

Positioning devices

The CAD user inputs positional information for such tasks as the location of geometry within the model, or for the indication of parts of an image to be magnified in a zoom or other display control operation. In many cases position may be precisely indicated by the entering of coordinate values, or by construction of locating points in the model, but where an approximate location is satisfactory, position may be given by a positioning device.

In most applications in CAD the position will ultimately be required with respect to the model, but nevertheless position will normally be entered with respect to the display screen, or to some other surface, for which purpose a feedback mechanism known as a screen **cursor** is used. The purpose of the cursor is to indicate the current screen position to the user. It normally takes the form of a cross-hair on the

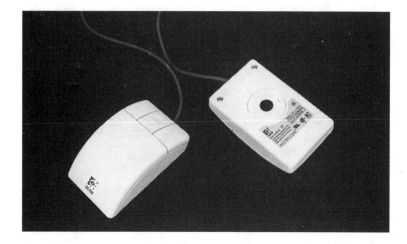

FIGURE 4.21
The mechanical mouse. (Reproduced by permission of Logitech SA.)

screen. The movement of the positioning device by the user is normally reflected in movement of the cursor, and a button on the positioning device or a keyboard keystroke is used to indicate a specific position.

A wide variety of devices may be used for positioning. These include joysticks, similar to those used on arcade and home computer games, thumbwheels, which use a wheel for each direction of cursor movement, roller balls, in which a ball is rolled about a fixed position, and touch-sensitive pads. By far the most widespread device in present use is the mouse (Figure 4.21), which is a mechanical or optical device, developed originally at the Stanford Research Institute, that provides **relative** positional data as it is moved over a flat surface. Mechanical implementations have mechanisms that sense the rotation of a ball in the underside of the mouse as it moves across a surface, and translate this into signals for control of the cursor. Optical designs include devices that sense their motion across a pad printed with a grid pattern. Generally, two or three push-buttons are provided on the top surface of the mouse to allow the user to signal to the program.

The mouse is fitted to most modern workstations and personal computers. Its success comes in part from its being a combination of a positioning device and comfortably located push-buttons, thus allowing many program operations to be carried out without use of the keyboard.

The positioning devices mentioned above are suitable only for screen position input (which may then be translated into a position on a model by the inverse of the windowing and viewing transformations that have been introduced in previous sections in this chapter). The mouse suffers from cumulative errors if lifted from the surface or rotated, and cannot be used for tracing data from paper. For this purpose a digitizer is used (Figure 4.22). Digitizers are available up to larger than D/A0 size and essentially allow positional information with reference to a surface external to the computer display to be recorded to an accuracy of typically 0.25 mm (usually by positioning a cross-hair in a hand-held device called a **puck**, as shown in Figure 4.22, or pointing a pen-like stylus). It is difficult, however, to be consistent and repeatable when using a digitizing puck by hand.

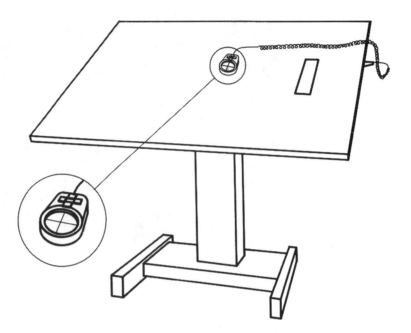

FIGURE 4.22
The digitizer.

Certain digitizers work by means of a grid of wires embedded in the digitizer surface with each carrying a uniquely coded signal. A small coil in the puck or stylus can pick up this signal to indicate position. Other devices use as measuring techniques the resistance of a thin layer of conducting material on the surface of the digitizer, or the time taken for ultrasound to travel from the stylus to microphones. Small digitizers, with a surface area of the order of 275 mm × 275 mm (11 in × 11 in), are known as **graphics tablets**. These may also be used for cursor control (by continuous sampling of the stylus/puck position) and, using their absolute positioning features, for program option selection, as shall be seen later in this section.

Pointing devices

Historically, pointing devices were important in CAD because of the widespread use of the **light-pen**, which could be pointed at illuminated parts of vector displays to select lines in the image. The ubiquitous use of raster displays has meant that the light-pen is rarely used today, and selection of items of interest in an image is instead achieved by the user indicating a position in the image with a positioning device, and then the software computing which relevant element of the display is nearest to the position indicated.

4.7.2 The user interface

CAD systems may be considered as comprising a large number of functions for creating or manipulating the design model. For example a function might create a line in the database parallel to another line at a given distance. To carry out this action, the user would have to:

▶ indicate to the system that this function is required;

▶ select an existing line in the model;

▶ enter the required offset, and indicate the side on which the new line is required.

These actions are examples of the user interface operations of program control, data entry and selection that were introduced at the beginning of this section. Each of these will now be explored in turn.

Program control

The user of a CAD program needs to be able to control, through the program's user interface, the software functions to be applied and the way these functions should operate. Many different styles of user interface have been implemented, but the approaches adopted fall into three broad classes:

▶ **command** entry, in which the user enters a series of characters, essentially as a line of text, which is then interpreted by the system to determine the required action, and very often the data to be used, or the entities to which the action is to be applied;

▶ **menu** entry, in which the user is presented with a list of possible options and invited to select from them: data entry or entity selection is normally prompted by the system once a command has been selected; often, the available options are presented to the user pictorially using **icons**;

▶ **direct manipulation**, in which the function to be carried out is implicit in the way the user manipulates the visual representation of objects on the screen – for example, to use a mouse to drag a pictorial representation of a file to a pictorial representation of a printer in order to print the file.

Very often the user interfaces of real systems will either offer a mixture of styles (in particular menu entry and direct manipulation), or allow the user to choose the way in which the system will be used.

Command-based systems

Command-based systems operate by reading a command and its parameters entered by the user, carrying out the required actions, and then waiting for the next command. The commands themselves may often comprise English-like words. The main commands are indicated by the permitted **major** words, and the options relating to the command by **minor** words. Many systems also allow commands to be abbreviated, either through the use of an alternative form (e.g. 'dimension' might be abbreviated by 'dm'), or by allowing the user to type only those characters of the command required for its unique identification ('dimension' in this case might be entered as 'dim'). The command is itself sometimes followed by the name of an object on which to carry out the command. The general form of command may thus be summarized as:

command {optional parameters} target_object

An imaginary dialogue between a user and a CAD system to draw a line parallel at a distance might be (user entry in **bold**, system response in *italics*, user action between <angle brackets>):

LINE PARALLEL_AT_DISTANCE
Select the base line
<User selects line, by pointing with screen cursor>
Enter the offset distance
100
Indicate side
<User indicates which side of base line using cursor>

The command line is rather verbose, and an abbreviated entry such as **LN PD** is more likely to be used. Some systems may also allow users to name geometric entities, and thus to enter command and data simultaneously. The same example might now be:

LN PD line10 100 XLARGE

which would be interpreted as 'draw a line, parallel at a distance to "line10", offset distance 100, on the side of "line10" that maximizes x'.

Command systems are generally more taxing to the user than menu-driven systems. They are more prone to erroneous entry, and they need comprehensive facilities to guide the user ('help systems') which are, however, difficult to provide effectively. For effective operation, commands should be memorized, and complex systems can therefore require substantial training and experience. On the positive side, however, in trained hands they are fast and extremely flexible, and they are also easy to customize because commands can be collected together into command files, as we shall see in Chapter 6.

Menu-driven systems

The menu-driven approach contrasts markedly with the command approach. The basic principle is that the user is at any time presented with a list or **menu** of the functions or function groupings that are available to be selected. The user selects from the list, and then perhaps from further lists of available suboptions until the function is specified fully, at which point data is entered, or items selected for the operation. In many systems the menus may be regarded as forming an inverted tree, with the main command groupings at the first level (e.g. in a CAD context, construct, modify, delete, move), and more specific functions at lower levels. Figure 4.23 shows a part of a hypothetical menu tree for a CAD system, with the selection route for the example of a line drawn parallel to another line at a distance highlighted.

In many systems there are two groups of menus: a main or primary group for model construction and modification, and a secondary menu giving general functions that may be applied at any time, even in the midst of another operation. Such general functions include display manipulation – zoom and pan – and construction colours and line-styles. Figure 4.24 shows a typical screen layout for a system with

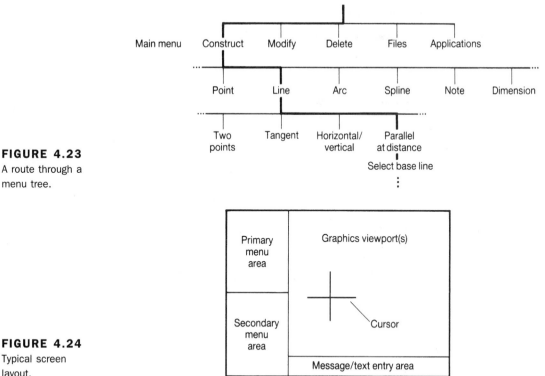

FIGURE 4.23
A route through a menu tree.

FIGURE 4.24
Typical screen layout.

primary and secondary menus adjacent to a graphics construction viewport. Very often, the different parts of the screen are formed by different windows within a windowing user interface (see Section 4.7.3 below).

Traditionally, menus have been displayed as a series of text items on the screen, and the appropriate text item selected in a variety of ways, for example by entering a number or letter on the keyboard (perhaps in combination with another key such as Esc or Alt), by using function keys, or by pointing to the menu item with a graphics or text cursor. Most systems allow both keystroke and cursor entry. Many systems also use graphical symbols, known as **icons**, for menu items, with selection normally by means of a screen cursor controlled by a mouse. A further method, but no longer widely used, is to present the menu as a series of locations or symbols on a printed sheet overlaid on a graphics tablet. The user makes command selections by pointing to the appropriate options with the tablet pen or puck.

Well-designed menu systems are generally easy to learn and require little training, although the very complexity of modern CAD systems often leads to several levels in the 'menu tree', and novices may find it difficult to remember how specific functions may be found. Menu-driven systems also require little typing skill (in particular when graphical menus or cursor selection are used), and pose little problem of erroneous selection. They are, however, rather slow to use (although this may be alleviated by allowing the user to 'type-ahead' menu selections), and are rather less flexible than command systems.

Direct manipulation

The **direct manipulation** style of user interface has been developed in particular from pioneering work at the Xerox Corporation's Palo Alto Research Centre from the mid-1970s, and has been made highly popular by Apple® Macintosh™ computers and the Microsoft® Windows™ systems. In such systems the items that may be manipulated are represented visually on the screen. Text and geometric entities are displayed in the usual way, but files, disks and other objects may be represented by icons. The user carries out actions by selecting items with a cursor, and then indicating the required action by the way the items are manipulated by movement of the mouse. For example, text or geometric entities might be moved by 'dragging and dropping' selected items by holding a mouse button down, moving the items with the mouse and releasing the button when the items are correctly placed. A similar technique might be used to move icons representing files to an icon showing a waste-basket to delete them, or to an icon of a disk drive to copy them to a floppy disk.

Direct manipulation systems are considered very easy to learn and use, but again in comparison with command systems they can be rather slow, especially for a skilled computer user with good typing skills. They are perhaps most valuable when used in conjunction with command or menu-driven interfaces.

Selection of model elements

The selection of geometric entities from the screen has already been mentioned several times in this chapter. Whereas menu selection using a graphics cursor is reasonably easy to implement – it simply involves correlating the cursor position with a limited number of locations or areas on the screen – entity selection is much more difficult. The essential process is that the user points to the entity to be selected, generally with a graphical cursor, and indicates selection with a button press. The software then has to identify which entity is displayed closest to the cursor position – potentially a time-consuming process if the distance from the cursor to the entity has to be calculated for a large number of entities in a complicated model.

Lengthy computation in entity selection is often avoided by use of a modified form of the clipping procedure introduced earlier in this chapter. An imaginary 'window' is drawn around the cursor position, and minimum distance calculations only carried out for the entities that fall within this window. Even this, however, is time consuming if the entity vectors have to be recomputed whenever selection is required, and therefore the display vectors for an image are often stored in a **display file** (which will be described in detail in Chapter 6), and the selection operations act on this file.

In some cases there may be many entities at the same minimum distance from the cursor, or it may be necessary to distinguish between, for example, selection of a vertex, an edge, a face or a body in a boundary representation solid. In such cases the system will usually highlight the candidate entities in turn, and ask the user to indicate which entity is correct, or a 'filter' mechanism may allow the user to restrict the types of entity considered in the selection.

Finally, there are many instances in which the user will wish to select a group of entities simultaneously. Systems will usually provide a number of other techniques for selection (which again may make use of the data stored in a display file, perhaps with a clipping-type algorithm). These include:

▶ selecting all displayed entities;

▶ selecting all entities of a given colour or line-style;

▶ allowing entities to be named or numbered, and selection by name/number;

▶ selecting all entities inside (or outside) a region on the screen. The region is often, but not always, rectangular.

Provision of feedback to the user

A basic principle of user interface design is that the user should always be provided with feedback about what is happening within the system. For example, the command **DELETE line10** might be echoed by the system response *One entity deleted*. Such feedback is particularly important when the user is making a selection from the screen, or when an operation is likely to take more than 1 or 2 seconds. User selection is usually reflected in the selected item – a menu option or a displayed entity perhaps – being highlighted by a change of colour or by some sort of marker. Markers are used in particular to indicate face or body selection in boundary models (e.g. by drawing a box around the selected body) or for monochrome displays where colour change is not an option. Typical marks are small circles or squares placed on the centre of an entity, near the selection point, or in the corners of a box bounding the entity.

To indicate that an operation is likely to take some time, the display of an icon such as an hour glass or watch face, or a message such as 'THINKING . . .' is used. More active indicators such as a dial showing the percentage of the operation completed, or a record of the stage reached in a calculation, are even more helpful. Often, a portion of the user interface will be allocated as a message area, as shown in Figure 4.24.

Several other forms of feedback are used in CAD. For example, when the cursor is used to indicate a bounded area on the screen, the bounding box is often shown dynamically as the cursor is used (a technique, also used in line, curve and surface construction, known as 'rubber-banding'). Two particularly conspicuous ways of attracting the user's attention are to sound a buzzer and to cause part of the display to flash. Overuse of such features is rather annoying to the user, however, and they are thus generally reserved for error conditions.

4.7.3 Windows and user interface management systems

As well as pioneering the development of direct manipulation command entry, the Xerox PARC, and subsequently the Apple Macintosh and workstation manufacturers such as Sun Microsystems, instigated the use of the style of user interface in which the display screen is divided into a number of discrete, resizeable areas, each providing a 'virtual screen' associated with a separate system activity. They are known rather confusingly as **windows** although they are a different concept from the use of windows

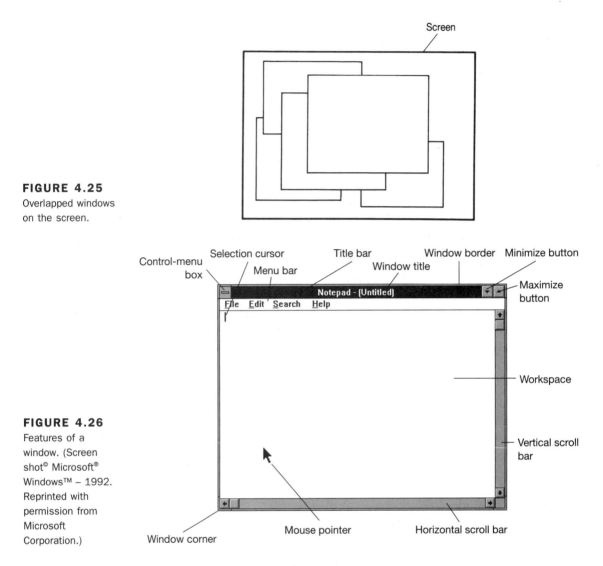

FIGURE 4.25
Overlapped windows
on the screen.

FIGURE 4.26
Features of a
window. (Screen
shot© Microsoft®
Windows™ – 1992.
Reprinted with
permission from
Microsoft
Corporation.)

to define the viewing bounds on a model that we met earlier in this chapter. The windows style is most widely used for operating system environments in which the user may interact with a number of different program applications. For example, a user might perhaps edit a file in one window, by copying text from another edit window, while compiling a program module and monitoring messages in other windows.

Windows may either be arranged side by side and without overlapping on the screen in a manner known as **tiling**, or more usually be overlapped rather like a number of sheets of paper on a desk, as shown in Figure 4.25. An individual window might typically have the features shown in Figure 4.26, and the system itself will usually allow windows to be **popped** into view or hidden from view, and moved or resized by manipulation of keyboard keys or the drag and resize marks on the window boundary (usually with a mouse). The interface style is known as the **WIMP** style, because it is based on the use of windows, icons, mice and pop-up (or pull-down) menus – menus that are temporarily displayed on the screen. Many user interfaces of CAD systems and other engineering software systems are now implemented in the WIMP format, in particular those that may be executed on personal computers. The trend is important because it allows users to work within a uniform interface environment, and also facilitates the moving and copying of data between applications through copying and pasting commands.

The interface environment itself is controlled by a **window manager**, which manages the allocation and use of areas of the screen, and interacts with the **window system** which actually creates and manipulates the windows, and manages the interaction with the user through the keyboard, mouse and other interaction devices. Some window systems are **policy free**, which means that different window managers, each with different styles of window presentation, and perhaps of user interaction, may interact with the same window system (Foley *et al.*, 1996). Other window systems impose a certain style on the window manager, which means that the 'look and feel' of the windows conforms to a set pattern. This is less flexible for the systems programmer, but means that the user will experience a more consistent interface.

In some cases, the facilities discussed in this section are built into systems that may be used by developers of applications programs (such as CAD systems) to provide all of the features of a user interface in a standard form. Such systems are known as user interface management systems, or **UIMSs**, and they typically provide the applications developer with facilities to create and manipulate windows, to display menus and to process user input, all with a uniform style. The UIMS may itself be based on a windowing system, which is used to carry out the display manipulation and to deal with the event management associated with user interaction.

Finally, window systems may be combined with the client–server model introduced in Section 4.2.1 above. In such systems a number of windows on a screen, managed by a server process, may display the output from processes executing on one or more separate computers. Perhaps most importantly, such systems have been designed to allow applications developers to be independent of the physical device used to display the output: an application running on one computer should be able to use a server operating on any other computer in the network, independently of operating system and hardware. We shall deal with this further when standards are discussed in Chapter 7.

4.8 Conclusion

The graphical nature of much communication has made computer graphics a core technology in engineering computing. The widespread use of the technology has been made possible by the development of low-cost hardware for the display of graphics images and for user interaction, and by the development of many techniques for the generation and manipulation of two- and three-dimensional graphics. These techniques are capable of a high degree of visual realism in the display of the engineering model, and dynamic manipulation of shaded images of engineering parts is a commonplace capability in CAD systems.

Also commonplace are windows-based user interfaces that make extensive use of icons, pop-up and pull-down menus and the direct manipulation interface style. Increasingly, these interfaces are adopting a more uniform look and feel that will reduce the effort required in system familiarization, and will facilitate the development of a computing toolkit for engineers.

References and further reading

Brown J. R. and Cunningham S. (1989). *Programming the User Interface, Principles and Examples*. Chichester: John Wiley.

Cook R. L., Porter T. and Carpenter L. (1984). Distributed ray tracing. *Computer Graphics.* **18**(3), 137–45.

Dewey B. R. (1988). *Computer Graphics for Engineers*. New York: Harper & Row.

Foley J. D., Van Dam A., Feiner S. and Hughes J. (1996). *Computer Graphics, Principles and Practice. 2nd Edition in C*. Reading, MA: Addison Wesley Longman.

Glassner A. S. (ed.) (1989). *An Introduction to Ray Tracing*. London: Academic Press.

Goral C., Torrance K. E., Greenberg D. P. and Battaile B. (1984). Modelling the interaction of light between diffuse surfaces. *Computer Graphics.* **18**(3), 212–22.

Gouraud H. (1971). Continuous shading of curved surfaces, *IEEE Transaction on Computers*. June, 623–9.

Griffiths J. G. (1978). A bibliography of hidden-line and hidden-surface algorithms. *Computer-aided Design*. **10**(3), 203–6.

Ingham P. (1989). *CAD Systems in Mechanical and Production Engineering*. London: Heinemann-Newnes.

Jones O. (1989). *An Introduction to the X Window System*. Englewood Cliffs, NJ: Prentice Hall.

Jones P. F. (1992). *CAD/CAM: Features, Applications and Management*. Basingstoke: Macmillan.

Newman W. M. and Sproull R. F. (1979). *Principles of Interactive Computer Graphics*. New York: McGraw-Hill.

Phong, Bui-Tuong (1975). Illumination for computer generated pictures. *Communications of the ACM*, **18**(6), 311–17.

Plastock R. A. and Kalley G. (1986). *Computer Graphics*. New York: Schaum/McGraw-Hill.

Scientific American (1991). Special issue on Computing (September).

Taylor D. L. (1992). *Computer-aided Design*. Reading, MA: Addison Wesley Longman.

Watt A. H. (1993). *3D Computer Graphics*. 2nd edn. Harlow: Addison Wesley Longman.

Whitted T. (1980). An improved illumination model for shaded display. *Communications of the ACM.* **23**(6), 343–9.

Woodwark J. (1986). *Computing Shape*. London: Butterworth.

Exercises

4.1 Distinguish between vector and raster graphics, between object- and image-space graphics, and between passive and interactive graphics.

4.2 What would you understand by the following description of a display device: an 8-bit/pixel, 60 Hz refresh rate colour raster device of 1280 × 1024 resolution?

4.3 The contents of a window bounded by coordinate pairs (52.6, −15.15), (182.6, 86.41) are to be displayed without distortion in a viewport comprising all of a graphics display of 1024 × 800 resolution. Write down the window transformation for lines in the image, and calculate the screen coordinates of a line with window coordinates (124.0, 56.0), (141.0, 56.0).

4.4 How many lines would be required to display a circle of diameter 120 mm within a display tolerance of 0.25 mm? What would the actual display tolerance be for this number of lines? Would it be a sensible tolerance if the expressions for the window transformation are $x_s = 5x_w - 100$, $y_s = 5y_w$, and the viewport occupies all of a screen of resolution 1024 × 1024 pixels?

4.5 Describe the basic types of coordinate transformation in CAD, and then show how these may all be calculated using matrix operations through the use of homogeneous coordinates (in each case give an example of a matrix for the transformation). How may a general rotation transformation be expressed in terms of a combination of other transformations?

4.6 A local coordinate system is defined by three points in the global coordinate system as follows: origin (100, 100, 100), point on x-axis (200, 100, 100), point on y-axis (100, 200, 100). Develop the transformation matrix for transforming points defined in the local system to the global system. Each system is right-handed.

4.7 Compute the screen coordinates of the corners of a 100 mm cube, centred at (0, 0, 1000) in the eye coordinate system, when displayed using perspective projection on a 400 mm square screen of resolution 1024 × 1024. The screen is 300 mm from the eye. What is the appearance on the screen of a wire-frame image of the cube?

4.8 Outline the steps required to generate a hidden-surface image using the depth-buffer approach, and then comment on the relative merits of this approach compared with the scan-line algorithm.

4.9 Outline how scan-line coherence contributes to the efficient computation of hidden-surface images, and then show how a scan-line algorithm may be applied to the geometry shown in Figure 4.17.

4.10 A scene is illuminated by two point light sources at (1000, 1000, 500) and (0, 1000, 1000), and is viewed towards the origin from a point on the z-axis. The relative ambient intensity is 0.2, and that of each point source 0.6. What is the relative intensity of a point at (0, 0, 0) on a surface of reflective index $R = 0.5$, aligned with the Oxy plane?

4.11 Explain the contribution to the calculation of surface intensity of each of the terms in Equation (4.19), and then calculate the Phong surface intensity for the problem given in Exercise 4.10 if the reflection is specular with diffuse reflectivity 0.4, specular reflectivity 0.6, and $n = 2$.

4.12 Explain why Phong shading is more computationally demanding than Gouraud shading, but achieves better results, in particular for specular reflection.

4.13 If you have access to a modelling system, compare the image quality for hidden-surface removal using flat, Gouraud and Phong shading subject to different illumination schemes, and for models with varying degrees of coarseness of faceting.

4.14 Outline the approach of the ray-tracing and radiosity methods for the rendering of scenes in computer graphics, and then explain which technique you would use to display (a) an automobile and (b) the interior of a house, and why.

4.15 To demonstrate the importance of hand–eye coordination in the operation of pointing and positioning devices in CAD, try operating a mouse or graphics tablet turned through 45°.

4.16 Suggest how the command-based approach to the user interface in Section 4.7.2 may be developed for the construction of lines between two points and between entered coordinate values, and for the construction of an arc through a point and tangent to a line. Consider operation with and without named geometric entities.

4.17 If you have access to a CAD system with a menu-based user interface, draw the inverted tree for the geometric construction elements of its menu. What methods of feedback are provided by the system?

4.18 Compare and contrast the command-based, menu-based and direct manipulation styles of user interface. Which do you feel is the most appropriate to the operation of CAD systems in a window-based environment?

4.19 What are the main elements of a WIMP-style user interface?

4.20 Select a computer program which uses graphical icons in its user interface, ideally a CADCAM system. Write down the functions or objects associated with each of the icons. Do the graphical symbols used make intuitive sense? Can you suggest different symbols that would have more meaning to you?

4.21 How does a user interface management system differ from a window management system? What do you understand by the term 'look and feel' applied to a user interface? Select a windowing system that you use, describe its look and feel, and show how different programs that use the system adopt this style.

Projects

For more information about the subjects for project work, please refer to the end of Chapter 1.

The project activity for this chapter is to explore the use of computer graphics in the modelling of the artefacts. Specific project tasks are:

Project 1 Chess piece Produce hidden-line images of the chess piece. Produce shaded images of the chess piece using as many rendering techniques as possible – flat, Gouraud, Phong, ray-traced and radiosity. Explore the effect of varying illumination position and intensity, and surface properties. Use both parallel and perspective projections, viewing from different directions.

Project 2 Load cell Explore the use of two-dimensional computer graphics in the display of the load cell drawings. Explore the effect on the display of variations in display tolerance.

5 Entity manipulation and data storage

Chapter objectives

When you have completed studying material in this chapter you should be able to:

- ▶ outline the main ways in which a CAD model may be manipulated by transformation and by editing;
- ▶ understand the process of object transformation, and the place of homogeneous coordinates in this process;
- ▶ outline the main requirements of a data structure for interactive modelling, and describe a simple data structure for entity storage;
- ▶ outline the concepts of associativity and attributes;
- ▶ describe the role of object-oriented programming techniques in CAD;
- ▶ outline the use of databases in engineering data management.

Chapter contents

5.1 Introduction

A common thread running through the first part of this book is that the user of a CAD system *interactively* creates, manipulates and applies computer-based models while in the process of defining a product. It is in no small part through this interactive process that CAD offers benefits over conventional draughting. Modifying hand-drawn drawings is a slow, tedious process, as is the copying or tracing of detail from one part of a drawing to another, or from one drawing to another. A well-designed CAD system should allow ease of repetition of detail, rapid modification of entities, and modification and reuse of existing models. For this to be achieved effectively, the

CAD user has to be provided with a rich set of facilities for entity manipulation. The system also has to be based on a storage of the model in a computer data structure that facilitates interactive modification. In this chapter both of these aspects of CAD system design will be considered.

The question of how to store the model goes beyond the identification of a suitable data structure for interactive work. In a traditional design office there may have been many designers working on drawings on their drawing boards, but a store would also be maintained of the completed drawings, together with an index or register of these. Project files would also be kept to store calculations, records of meetings, technical data, test reports and so on. An equivalent to such archiving facilities has to be provided in a computerized design office. This chapter will consider how in a computerized system the CAD models may be stored and indexed in a computer database, and will introduce the fundamentals of the relational database technology used for engineering data management.

5.2 Manipulation of the model

The facilities available to the traditional designer for the modification of drawings are very limited. Unwanted parts of the drawing have to be laboriously erased, normally by hand using an eraser and erasing shield. If it is necessary to move some geometry around the drawing, or to copy some repeated detail, this will involve a tedious repetition of the construction, unless it is possible to trace the work – itself a relatively time-consuming task. In CAD the situation is very different: original construction may sometimes take as long as using traditional methods (perhaps longer), but when changes are required the computer system has the advantage (both in time and in terms of accuracy – there will not be transcription errors in copying geometry using CAD). Furthermore, in manual drawing small changes are relatively easy but large changes are difficult. In CAD, the effort required to make a major change will often be only a little more than that required for some minor changes. (A note of caution is required here: if a small change is made to a CAD-produced drawing, it is generally still necessary to replot the drawing after the change has been made, and this can be time consuming.)

What, then, are the facilities that are typically provided for manipulation of the model? In general, they may be divided into four groups of functions:

▶ Those that apply the **transformations** of translation, rotation and scaling to elements of the model. This may involve either **moving** the geometry or **copying** it to create one or more duplicate sets of entities in the data structure.

▶ Those that allow the user to make changes to individual geometric elements to **trim** or **extend** them to their intersections with other elements.

▶ Functions for the temporary or permanent deletion of entities from the model (temporary deletion is usually used to simplify the display, to improve performance, or to make viewing and selection easier).

▶ Miscellaneous functions that, for example, allow entities to be grouped together.

In this section, each of these will be dealt with in turn, first concentrating on the important group of functions that involve transformations of entities.

5.2.1 Object transformations

In Section 4.4.1 it was seen how the position of an object defined in one coordinate system could be expressed in terms of a second system through a **coordinate transformation**. In such a transformation, the object may be considered to be stationary, and the coordinate system to move. When the entities of a CAD model are manipulated by moving them around, or by taking one or more copies at different locations and orientations, a very similar process is undertaken. In this case we imagine the coordinate system to be stationary, and the object to move. Not surprisingly, the mathematical operations of the manipulation, which are called **object transformation**, are very similar to those of the coordinate transformation.

Let us refresh our memories by reviewing the main arguments relating to coordinate transformation. Firstly, recall that there are three main constituent operations: translation (or linear movement), rotation about the origin, and scaling with respect to the origin. These may be described in terms of a vector subtraction ($\mathbf{p}' = \mathbf{p} - \mathbf{t}$) for translation, where $\mathbf{t}$ is the translation vector, and matrix multiplications ($\mathbf{p}' = \mathbf{Bp}$) for the other operations, where $\mathbf{p}$ is an initial x, y, z position vector, $\mathbf{p}'$ a transformed position, and $\mathbf{B}$ a 3×3 matrix to describe rotation or scaling. Secondly, it may be recalled that it is more convenient to express all operations in terms of matrix multiplications, and this may be achieved by using a device known as **homogeneous coordinates**, in which the x, y, z position vector is mapped to a four-element vector $[x \ y \ z \ 1]^T$. Thus, coordinate translation may be expressed in matrix form, and the translation matrix may be combined with the others by concatenation to describe transformations involving arbitrary combinations of translation, rotation and scaling by single transformation matrices.

Now let us examine the object transformation case. Firstly, consider the translation of a point in space from $\mathbf{p}$ to $\mathbf{p}'$, as shown in Figure 5.1. In vector terms this

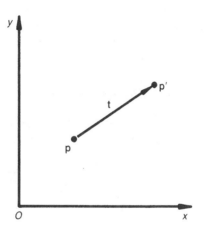

FIGURE 5.1
Translation.

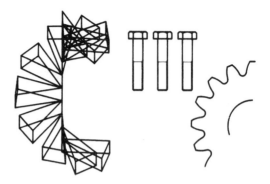

FIGURE 5.2

Examples of copying transformations.

may be expressed as:

$$\mathbf{p}' = \mathbf{p} + \mathbf{t} \tag{5.1}$$

where $\mathbf{t} = [dx\ dy\ dz]^T$, or, in matrix terms using homogeneous coordinates:

$$\mathbf{p}' = \begin{bmatrix} x' \\ y' \\ z' \\ 1 \end{bmatrix} = \begin{bmatrix} 1 & 0 & 0 & dx \\ 0 & 1 & 0 & dy \\ 0 & 0 & 1 & dz \\ 0 & 0 & 0 & 1 \end{bmatrix} \begin{bmatrix} x \\ y \\ z \\ 1 \end{bmatrix} \tag{5.2}$$

and we may see by comparison with Equation (4.10) that object transformation involves an equivalent displacement to the coordinate transformation but in the opposite sense.

We also find that object rotation and scaling operations are similar to coordinate system rotation and scaling. The mathematical bases of these two transformations are described in the bracketed section below. More complex transformations, such as the mirroring of an object through an arbitrary line or plane, are again derived by combining elemental operations. Example 5.1 shows as an illustration the derivation of a transformation matrix for the mirroring of points through a line in the *Oxy* plane. Figure 5.2 in turn shows some examples of geometry copied using the transformation commands of a CAD system. The 'spiral staircase' in particular was constructed by using a transformation involving simultaneous translation and rotation.

Object transformations

Rotation of a point in an anticlockwise direction (which we will take to be positive) about the *z*-axis, as shown in Figure 5.3, is given by the expressions:

$$\begin{aligned} x' &= r \cos (\phi + \theta) \\ y' &= r \sin (\phi + \theta) \\ z' &= z \end{aligned} \tag{5.3}$$

Now $x = r \cos \phi$ and $y = r \sin \phi$. Thus, expanding the elements of Equation (5.3)

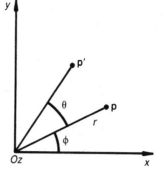

FIGURE 5.3
Rotation of a point about *Oz*.

and substituting:

$$x' = x \cos \theta - y \sin \theta$$
$$y' = x \sin \theta + y \cos \theta \qquad (5.4)$$
$$z' = z$$

which may be expressed in matrix form using homogeneous coordinates as:

$$\mathbf{p}' = \begin{bmatrix} x' \\ y' \\ z' \\ 1 \end{bmatrix} = \begin{bmatrix} \cos \theta & -\sin \theta & 0 & 0 \\ \sin \theta & \cos \theta & 0 & 0 \\ 0 & 0 & 1 & 0 \\ 0 & 0 & 0 & 1 \end{bmatrix} \begin{bmatrix} x \\ y \\ z \\ 1 \end{bmatrix} = \mathbf{B}_z \mathbf{p} \qquad (5.5)$$

and we may see by inspection that this matrix is the transpose of the matrix for coordinate rotation (Equation (4.5)). In other words, rotating the object through $+\theta$ has the same effect as rotating the coordinate axes through $-\theta$. Equivalent expressions for rotations about *Ox* and *Oy* are:

$$\mathbf{p}' = \begin{bmatrix} x' \\ y' \\ z' \\ 1 \end{bmatrix} = \begin{bmatrix} 1 & 0 & 0 & 0 \\ 0 & \cos \theta & -\sin \theta & 0 \\ 0 & \sin \theta & \cos \theta & 0 \\ 0 & 0 & 0 & 1 \end{bmatrix} \begin{bmatrix} x \\ y \\ z \\ 1 \end{bmatrix} = \mathbf{B}_x \mathbf{p} \qquad (5.5a)$$

and:

$$\mathbf{p}' = \begin{bmatrix} x' \\ y' \\ z' \\ 1 \end{bmatrix} = \begin{bmatrix} \cos \theta & 0 & \sin \theta & 0 \\ 0 & 1 & 0 & 0 \\ -\sin \theta & 0 & \cos \theta & 0 \\ 0 & 0 & 0 & 1 \end{bmatrix} \begin{bmatrix} x \\ y \\ z \\ 1 \end{bmatrix} = \mathbf{B}_y \mathbf{p} \qquad (5.5b)$$

Rotations out of the principal planes are again formed by combining rotations about *Ox*, *Oy* and *Oz*, as in the coordinate transformation case.

Finally, if we wish to change the scale of an object in the directions of the individual axes of the coordinate system by scaling factors (S_x S_y S_z) then:

$$\mathbf{p}' = \begin{bmatrix} x' \\ y' \\ z' \\ 1 \end{bmatrix} = \begin{bmatrix} S_x & 0 & 0 & 0 \\ 0 & S_y & 0 & 0 \\ 0 & 0 & S_z & 0 \\ 0 & 0 & 0 & 1 \end{bmatrix} \begin{bmatrix} x \\ y \\ z \\ 1 \end{bmatrix} \qquad (5.6)$$

provides the appropriate transformation using homogeneous coordinates. If a **negative** scaling factor is used, then the object is reflected (or **mirrored**) in the coordinate plane normal to the corresponding axis.

Example 5.1 *The mirror transformation*

As an example of an object transformation, consider the mirroring (or reflection) of three points through a line at an angle of 30° to the Ox axis with its origin at $x = 16$, $y = 24$. The points are located as shown in Figure 5.4.

The steps required in the transformation are as follows:

1. Move to the origin. This is a translation, for which the matrix is (note that a 3×3 matrix is used because the transformation is in the x–y plane only):

$$\mathbf{A} = \begin{bmatrix} 1 & 0 & -16 \\ 0 & 1 & -24 \\ 0 & 0 & 1 \end{bmatrix}$$

2. Rotate through $-30°$. The matrix for this operation is (where $c(x) = \cos x$, $s(x) = \sin x$):

$$\mathbf{B} = \begin{bmatrix} c(-30) & -s(-30) & 0 \\ s(-30) & c(-30) & 0 \\ 0 & 0 & 1 \end{bmatrix}$$

3. Mirror through the Ox axis. The matrix for this operation is:

$$\mathbf{C} = \begin{bmatrix} 1 & 0 & 0 \\ 0 & -1 & 0 \\ 0 & 0 & 1 \end{bmatrix}$$

4. Carry out the inverse actions to **A** and **B**, for which the matrices are:

$$\mathbf{D} = \begin{bmatrix} c(30) & -s(30) & 0 \\ s(30) & c(30) & 0 \\ 0 & 0 & 1 \end{bmatrix} \quad \mathbf{E} = \begin{bmatrix} 1 & 0 & 16 \\ 0 & 1 & 24 \\ 0 & 0 & 1 \end{bmatrix}$$

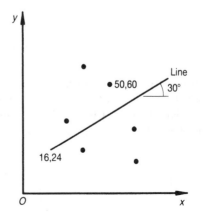

FIGURE 5.4

Reflection of points through a line.

Concatenating these matrices together, we get:

$$\mathbf{EDCBA} = \begin{bmatrix} 0.5 & 0.866 & -12.78 \\ 0.866 & -0.5 & 22.14 \\ 0 & 0 & 1 \end{bmatrix}$$

which may be applied to the points to be transformed. For example, the point at $x = 50$, $y = 60$ transforms to $x = 64.18$, $y = 35.44$.

••

Some CAD systems may offer variations or extensions to the entity transformations described above, such as the following, for example:

▶ Allowing the properties of entities, such as their colour or construction level (this will be discussed later in this chapter), to be varied as they are transformed.

▶ Allowing an image of those entities that are being transformed to replace the cursor (the effect is rather as if the user is dragging the entities around the screen with the cursor); the user may then view the effect of a transformation before placing the entities in position.

▶ Updating connecting entities to reflect the result of a translation. This is sometimes known as **stretching**. In boundary representation manipulation, the moving or **lifting** of faces entails the updating of adjacent loops of edges. Examples of such operations are shown in Figure 5.5.

▶ Incorporating the transformation into a construction scheme for solid geometry, as in the linear and rotational sweep operations described in Section 3.4.4.

5.2.2 Trim and extend operations

The second important group of entity manipulation functions involves the trimming or extending (sometimes called relimiting) of entities to their intersections with other

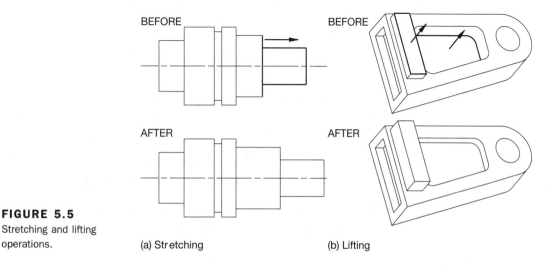

FIGURE 5.5
Stretching and lifting operations.

(a) Stretching   (b) Lifting

BEFORE   BEFORE

AFTER   AFTER

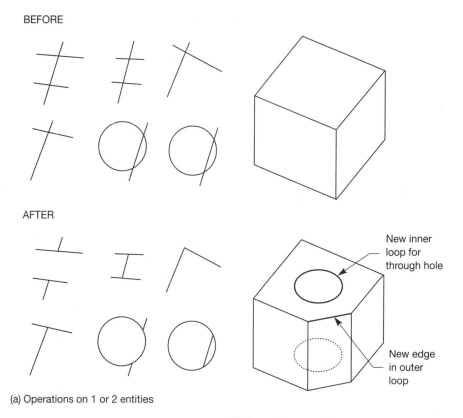

BEFORE

AFTER

New inner
loop for
through hole

New edge
in outer
loop

(a) Operations on 1 or 2 entities

(b) Operations on a B-rep

FIGURE 5.6
Various entity trim
operations.

geometry. Trimming involves removal of a part of the entity bounded by one or more bounding intersections. Extending involves, fairly clearly, the extension of an entity to one or more boundaries. Trim/extend operations may be applied to all sorts of geometry, and are best described by pictures, rather than words. Figure 5.6(a) shows such pictures of a variety of operations involving one or two boundary entities. Other points that should be noted regarding these functions are:

▶ In certain cases a trim operation may change the line-style (or **font**) of part of a curve rather than remove it – for example, to indicate that it is a hidden line. **View-dependent fonts** are used to allow the font of an entity to be modified according to the direction in which it is viewed, and are used mainly to indicate hidden lines in multi-view images of wire-frame drawings.

▶ The screen cursor is normally used to indicate which part of any entity is to be modified. For example, the rule might be that the part nearest the cursor is the part that is left after trimming. The cursor is also used to resolve any ambiguity regarding which intersection to use (e.g. where a line intersects a circle, as shown in Figure 5.6(a)).

▶ The trimming of surfaces in boundary representation systems normally involves modifying the loop of edges that define the boundary of a face, or adding an internal edge loop around a hole in the face. Figure 5.6(b) shows this operation for the trimming of an edge and a hole in a face.

5.2.3 Other functions

There are many other functions that are included in CAD systems to assist the user with the editing of the model, and it would be impossible to list all of them. Nevertheless, some of the more important can be noted. These involve:

▶ The deletion of entities from the model. This may involve, as has been noted, either permanent or temporary deletion, the latter sometimes being called **blanking** or **hiding**. Deletion is, of course, a somewhat drastic operation, but some systems offer the admirable facility to reverse the last operation, even if it has involved deleting everything. Many will no doubt agree that such **undo** operations should be mandatory features of all computer programs!

▶ The collection of a number of entities together, such that they may be manipulated as a single entity, sometimes referred to as a **group** or a **block**.

▶ The modification of entity features such as their colour or line-style.

▶ Facilities for the manipulation of control points for curves such as the Bézier and B-spline types, for the addition of extra control points, and perhaps to convert curves from one basis to another or to modify the order of a curve. For example, a cubic spline curve might be converted to a non-uniform rational B-spline curve, or additional control points might be inserted into a Bézier curve. In some cases, groups of control points on a surface are able to be manipulated together, to allow surface features to be moved and modified.

5.3 Introduction to model storage

Computer programs may be regarded fundamentally as comprising algorithms or functions acting on data structures. This book has so far concentrated on the algorithms – the functionality – of CAD, although the subject of data structures has been touched upon where this is particularly important to the modelling technique, for example in solid modelling. This present section will concentrate on simple data structures that give an example of how CAD systems store the model on which the model creation and manipulation algorithms act. This section does not claim to offer a detailed description of the data structures that might be used by a major CADCAM system, but rather illustrates some of the ideas that underlie CAD data structures, in particular through discussion of:

▶ a data structure for interactive modelling using two- and three-dimensional wireframe and surface geometry, where the relationships *between* geometric entities are less crucial than in solid geometry;

▶ the storage of image vectors in a **display file**;

▶ the association of geometric entities with those used in their construction – **associativity** between entities;

▶ the association of non-geometric data with the geometric model through the use of **attributes**;

▶ the collection of design models into a database, and in particular the use of **engineering data management systems** (EDMSs).

5.4 Data structures for interactive modelling

The specification for a data structure to support interactive modelling is really quite demanding. Consider some of the requirements imposed by a typical system, for which the structure should:

▶ allow **interactive** manipulation – addition, modification and deletion – of data;

▶ support multiple types of data element – geometric, textual, dimensions, labels, tool paths, finite elements and so on;

▶ allow properties such as pen number, line-style, colour and so on to be associated with geometric elements;

▶ allow association between data elements where this is important to the model;

▶ provide facilities for the retrieval of parts of the data structure released by deletions or other modifications (sometimes called **garbage collection**);

▶ perhaps provide a facility to store commonly used geometry once, with repeated references to the geometry stored as **instances**;

▶ be compact – to minimize disk storage and main memory requirements;

▶ allow models of various sizes, and comprising various combinations of entities, to be defined;

▶ provide as efficient an access to the data as possible.

These requirements between them pose significant constraints on the design of the data structure. For example, each entity type will in general require different amounts of data: a point may be defined by three floating-point numbers representing its x, y and z coordinates; a spline, or the other hand, will require many data items: perhaps the coefficients for each segment and the parameter value at each point. Furthermore, for entities such as text notes or spline curves the data will be of variable quantity. In principle, storage could be allocated in a separate array for each entity type (imagine here each array forming a **table** of entities). This would, however, be a poor use of storage space because different models may comprise very different numbers of the various entity types, and therefore the arrays will be inefficiently used, unless dynamic memory allocation, in which memory is allocated to variables as required, is available.

Each entity type will also, in general, require integer as well as floating-point data (and perhaps character data or other data types also), and so our system should be able to cope with this. For example, for a spline, the coordinates of the knot points, or the segment coefficients, are floating-point data items, but the curve colour and style, and the number of knot points, are integer values.

5.4.1 A simple data structure

A simple data structure that does allow arbitrary quantities of data for each entity, and arbitrary combinations of entities, comprises a list or table of entities, with cross-references (or **pointers**) from this list to separate arrays of floating-point, integer and other data specific to the entities. This is shown schematically in Figure 5.7. We will refer to the tables in this structure as an **entity table**, a **real data table** for floating-point data and an **integer data table**. In the entity table, a series of slots, each containing a number of elements of the array used for the table, are assigned one per entity. These contain general data (applicable to **any** entity type) such as the entity type, line-style or colour together with pointers to the more specific entity data in the data tables. For example, a line will have real data for the x, y and z co-ordinates of the start and end points, but no integer data is required. A spline curve might have the number of knot points stored in the integer table, while the curve parameter at each knot point, together with the segment coefficients and/or the knot point coordinates, are stored in the real data table.

The entity table contains additional pointers in each slot. These point from the entity slot to the entities following and perhaps preceding it in the list, so that data may be arbitrarily added, deleted and moved in the list and yet the sequence will

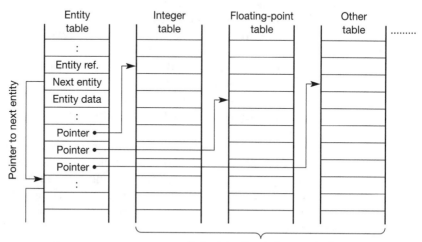

FIGURE 5.7

Entity table and entity data tables.

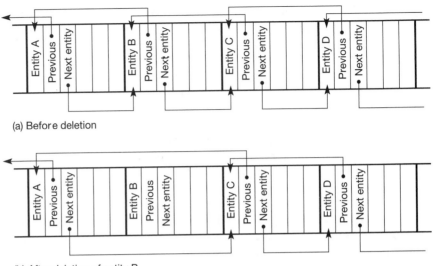

(a) Before deletion

(b) After deletion of entity B

FIGURE 5.8

Entities in a linked list.

remain the same. This type of data structure is known as a **linked list**. If there are pointers in two directions from each entry in the list, then the structure is known as a **doubly linked list**. Deletion of an entity from such a structure is straightforward. Consider, for example, the entities A, B and C in an entity table, as shown in Figure 5.8. Deletion of entity B is achieved by modifying the 'next entity' pointer of entity A to point to entity C, and the 'previous entity' pointer of entity C to point to entity A. The slot that is freed by the deletion of entity B may then be used by a new entity, since the pointers may be to any location in the array storing the entity data. An **undo** operation, to restore erroneously deleted entities, may be implemented by storing the details of the links that have been modified, and recreating these links if required, providing that the slots have not been reused for new entities. It should be noted while the linked list arrangement makes it straightforward to reuse space in the entity table released by deleted entities, reuse of space released in the other tables is more difficult. Some systems have required the user explicitly to request the **compressing** of the data structure to free the model space used by deleted entities.

Certain entities, such as arcs and other conic sections, are planar, and therefore it is necessary to store information about the orientation of their construction planes together with the data defining the size and location of the entity. This might be achieved by storing the matrix describing the transformation between the construction plane and the principal coordinate system, perhaps as a view entity that may be referred to by many geometric entities.

General entity data

As noted, the entity table is a series of slots, one for each entity and containing general data applicable to most entities. Let us now examine in a little more detail what this general data might comprise. The list in Table 5.1 includes some of the items

Table 5.1 General entity data

Data	Notes
Entity type	For example, 1 = point, 2 = line, 3 = arc, etc.
Entity sequence number	Allocated as entities are created
Entity number	Entity position in table
Pointer to integer data Pointer to real data	In a range depending on maximum model size, e.g. 0–524 287
View or coordinate system of definition	Coordinate system for planar entities: for example, in the range 0–1023
Pen number	For example, in the range 0–7
Curve font or style	For example, in the range 0–7, representing such values as full, dashed, chain-dashed and centre line
Entity colour	Range perhaps 0–255
Is entity blanked?	(i.e. temporarily deleted from display) – either yes or no
Is entity grouped?	Either yes or no
Level or layer number	Level numbers may be in the range 0–255 or 0–1023, although in some cases they may be limited only by the storage limits of integer numbers

that should be considered (but note that the pointers used to point to other entities in the linked list are not included here).

A note of further explanation is required regarding some of these items. An **entity sequence number** might be allocated in sequence to each entity as it is defined. This would allow the construction sequence to be stored even if entities were allocated entity table slots out of sequence – for example, if slots released by previously deleted entities were used. An entity number based on an absolute position in the table would allow direct reference from one entity to another. The curve **font** represents the style to be used for the drawing of lines and curves. Some systems also allow the thickness of entities to be varied (typically by drawing multiple vectors). A **group** or **block** is an entity that represents a collection of other entities, grouped together so that they may be treated as one item for selection and manipulation purposes. The **level** or **layer** is a number allocated to entities to assist in partitioning the drawing/model. For example, all entities in a particular element of the model could be given the same level number, or perhaps the drawing border or annotation text might all be placed on the same level. The subject will be addressed again under the topic of draughting in the next chapter.

Twelve items of data are listed in Table 5.1, and more may be required by some systems. What does this imply for the amount of memory that is needed to store the model? If separate variables are allocated to each item of data, then a compact way of storing one entity would use three 1-byte Boolean (or logical) values for the three yes/no items, three 4-byte integers for the entity number and the pointers to real and integer data, and 2-byte integers for the remainder of the values because their range is less than 0–32 767. This means that each entity would still occupy 27 bytes of storage before any of the entity-type specific data is stored. How might this requirement be reduced?

If Table 5.1 is inspected again, it may be seen that many of the data items may only assume a limited range of values. It is not really necessary to allocate pen number, line-style or colour to ranges greater than those suggested in the table. A range of 128 possible entity types would likewise be satisfactory for most systems. Now, such numbers can be represented by a relatively small number of bits: 3 for the range 0–7, 8 for the range 0–255 and so on. Furthermore, the Boolean (yes/no) values can each be represented by a single bit. It is therefore possible to pack the 12 data items shown in Table 5.1 into a small number of bytes of data, perhaps declared as a number of integers. This data representation may be termed **bit-packed**, and allows significant compression of the system storage requirements.

5.4.2 Display files

There are a number of interactive display manipulation operations that are carried out very regularly in CAD. These include:

▶ Redrawing of the display to 'clean up' unwanted clutter on the screen or to restore parts of the image that have been corrupted. For many systems entity deletion or modification involves redrawing entities in the background colour, thus leaving gaps where the remaining geometry is crossed by deleted entities.

▶ Selection of entities from the screen. This was discussed in some depth in the previous chapter.

▶ Rotation of the viewing point for a three-dimensional model.

In each of these cases, and also when an entity is redrawn in background colour during deletion or when it is moved, there is some merit in working not with the base entity data, but with a display file that stores the displayable vectors or polygons for an entity. For example, in the selection of a surface without use of a display file it would be necessary to recompute the surface display in order to identify which path is nearest to the cursor. With a display file it is only necessary to find the nearest displayed vector and to cross-reference back to the entity. Similarly, redisplay of the image and drawing of the entity vectors in the background colour can be very rapid if precalculated vectors or polygons for each entity are used.

Display files also lend themselves to fast image manipulation or **zoom** facilities. Instead of recomputing the entire image for a zoom within the existing window boundary, the display file vectors are used, leading to some loss in display resolution for curves, but generally faster display control. Such operations are sometimes facilitated by storing the display vectors in the display file to a greater precision than that required by the display device, and by 'zooming' by powers of 2 (i.e. 2 ×, 4 ×, 8 ×, 16 × zooms, for example). In three-dimensional manipulation, high-performance display hardware is able to carry out dynamic image rotation and hidden-surface removal and shading for polygonal models stored in display files.

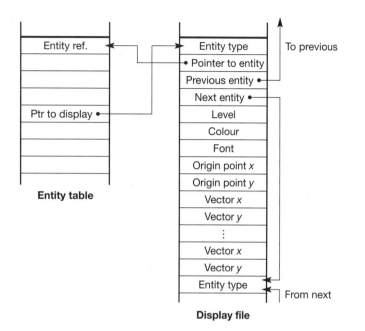

FIGURE 5.9

A display file entry.

The display file is another case where the linked list is a good candidate data structure. Figure 5.9 shows a typical structure for a display file containing image vectors, as might be used in a two-dimensional draughting package, or a three-dimensional system without dynamic image rotation. The file comprises a linked list of entity entries, with each entry containing the sequence of vectors used to draw the entity, together with data on the entity colour, and perhaps also entity type, display font and level information that could be used to support entity selection by these criteria (e.g. select all arcs, or all dashed lines). By using a linked list, entities may be manipulated or deleted without having to rebuild the display file. The display file is also cross-referenced to the main entity data by means of bidirectional pointers, so that the file may be updated as modifications are made to the main model data.

5.4.3 Associative geometry and attributes

The data structure that has been outlined in this section only defines random collections of lines, arcs and other entities, with no data on any relationships between these other than grouping. This simple approach is only used in relatively elementary systems. We have seen already in Chapter 3 that in solid modelling the topological relationships between entities must be stored together with the geometric data. In systems based on all types of geometric representation from wire-frame to solid, it is also common to include in the data storage associations between one part of the model and those other parts used in its definition. At the entity level, for example, this involves including in the entity data reference to those entities used in its construction. One way in which this may be done is to expand the entity type description to include a subtype or form – for example, for lines form 1 might be between

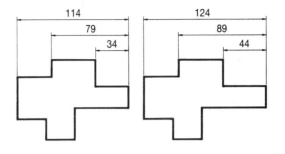

FIGURE 5.10
The updating of associative dimensions.

screen positions, form 2 between entered coordinates, form 3 between two points, form 4 tangent to two curves and so on – and to store in the entity data pointers to the entities used in construction, and the locations of any screen positions used. With such an arrangement it is possible for modification of one entity to be reflected in the dependent entities, either automatically or at the request of the user. This facility, known as **associative** geometry, is particularly useful for updating dimensions to reflect changes in a drawing, as shown in Figure 5.10, although in the writers' experience it is sometimes difficult to construct geometry in such a way as to take advantage of associativity between other geometry.

For the most sophisticated systems, associativity extends far beyond simple entity-to-entity references to include all sorts of data dependencies. For example, a drawing of a part may be constructed by arranging a number of hidden-line views of a solid model on a drawing sheet, and then adding dimensions to those views. In a fully associative system, if the underlying solid model is changed, the geometry shown in the drawing views, and the dimensions attached to this geometry, will change to reflect the underlying model changes, as shown in the example below. Associativity is thus one of the mechanisms by which integration is achieved in CAD-CAM. Association can be extended to all manner of data derived from the CAD model. For example, representations for stress analysis or for control of a machine tool may be derived from the design model. Within limits, associativity allows design changes to be propagated through the processes that depend on the design model for input.

Example 5.2 *The application of associative geometry*

Figure 5.11 shows an example of a drawing that has been produced by taking views on a solid model and arranging them on a drawing sheet. The views are arranged correctly with respect to each other for orthographic projection. If any change is made in the model then this is reflected in the drawing using associativity between the drawing and model. The cross-hatched view is made by automatically sectioning the model and applying hatching to the cut face, and the enlarged view is also made automatically from the underlying geometry. The dimensions themselves are applied to part edges using context-sensitive dimensioning in which the dimension style is inferred from the edges selected. The dimensions on the drawing are also associative with the part edges, so that both geometry and dimensions are updated to reflect changes in the underlying geometry.

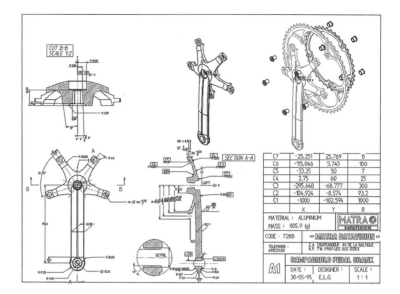

	X	Y	R
C7	-25.251	25.769	8
C6	-115.046	5.745	100
C5	-33.25	50	7
C4	2.75	60	25
C3	-295.648	-68.777	300
C2	-104.924	-8.574	93.2
C1	-1000	-102.594	1000

MATERIAL : ALUMINUM
MASS : 805.9 (g)
CODE : 7288
= MATRA DATAVISION =
TELEPHONE : Z.A. COURTABOEUF AV DE LA BALTIQUE
69822400 B.P. 716 91961 LES ULIS CEDEX
CAMPAGNOLO PEDAL CRANK
A1 DATE : 30/05/95 DESIGNER : E.L.G SCALE : 1 : 1

FIGURE 5.11
Application of
associative
dimensions.
(Courtesy of MATRA
Datavision Ltd.)

Attributes

In addition to associating entities with each other, we can also associate non-geometric data with the geometric model through the use of **attributes**. These are typically name–value pairs, where the name is an alphanumeric character string, and the value may be a string or a number. They are again linked with design model elements through pointers from the elements to the attributes. Each element, which might be an entity in a drawing, or a body in a solid model, may be associated with a number of attributes, and each attribute with a number of model elements, in what is known as a many–many arrangement. The classic use of attributes is for the preparation of parts lists or 'bills of materials' from a computer-based drawing or model. The bill of materials is a structured, hierarchical decomposition of the parts, sub-assemblies and assemblies in an engineering product, together with information about required quantities, part numbers, supplier data and drawing or CAD model references. Example 5.3 shows how a simple single-level bill of materials might be identified from an annotated engineering drawing.

Example 5.3 *Bill of materials from attribute data*

In order to prepare a bill of materials directly from a CAD file the geometry relating to each individual component of the assembly is associated with attributes giving such details as the part name and number, supplier and price. Figure 5.12 shows a very simple assembly, together with the attribute data associated with the parts. Table 5.2 shows a bill of materials derived from the attributes in the figure.

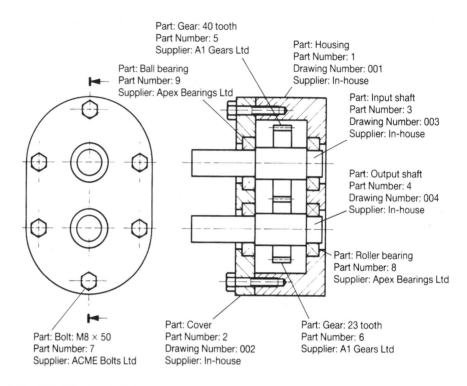

Part: Gear: 40 tooth
Part Number: 5
Supplier: A1 Gears Ltd

Part: Housing
Part Number: 1
Drawing Number: 001
Supplier: In-house

Part: Ball bearing
Part Number: 9
Supplier: Apex Bearings Ltd

Part: Input shaft
Part Number: 3
Drawing Number: 003
Supplier: In-house

Part: Output shaft
Part Number: 4
Drawing Number: 004
Supplier: In-house

Part: Roller bearing
Part Number: 8
Supplier: Apex Bearings Ltd

Part: Bolt: M8 × 50
Part Number: 7
Supplier: ACME Bolts Ltd

Part: Cover
Part Number: 2
Drawing Number: 002
Supplier: In-house

Part: Gear: 23 tooth
Part Number: 6
Supplier: A1 Gears Ltd

FIGURE 5.12
Assembly annotated
with attribute data.

Table 5.2 Bill of materials

Part name	Part number	Drawing number	Number required	Supplier name
Housing	1	001	1	In-house
Cover	2	002	1	In-house
Input shaft	3	003	1	In-house
Output shaft	4	004	1	In-house
Gear: 40 tooth	5		1	A1 Gears Ltd
Gear: 23 tooth	6		1	A1 Gears Ltd
Bolt: M8 × 50	7		6	ACME Bolts Ltd
Roller bearing	8		2	Apex Bearings Ltd
Ball bearing	9		2	Apex Bearings Ltd

5.5 Object-oriented representations

Many commercial CAD systems are very large computer programs indeed: sizes in the order of 100 MB for the program and associated files are commonplace. A problem with large programs is that they tend to be difficult to maintain – in other words, the software organization that develops and supports the system has to spend a large amount of its time correcting faults in the software, and taking into account the existing features of the system when designing additions and modifications. Those readers who have themselves programmed can perhaps appreciate the difficulties in maintaining large programs that may be worked on by hundreds of programmers over many years.

In addition to the problem of maintenance, it is often very difficult to reuse software that has been written for a particular purpose, and therefore a lot of software development effort is spent rewriting elements of programs for functions that have already been coded. One of the reasons for these restrictions is that program procedures tend to be rather dependent on the data structures employed, and vice versa. For example, let us consider a CAD system employing the data structures identified in Section 5.3.1 above. If it is wished to introduce a new geometric entity that does not quite match this data structure, the system developers are faced with recoding their existing program to match the new entity. This difficulty may be overcome by the use of a comparatively new programming paradigm (style) known as **object-oriented programming**.

In traditional procedural computer programs or models, data is moved through a series of procedures which act upon it. An object-oriented model, on the other hand, consists of a set of autonomous **objects**, each containing their own data, which communicate by a tightly defined interface (this communication is sometimes characterized as **message passing**). When an object receives a message, it acts upon its own data using its own procedures (often referred to as **methods**). This **procedural and data abstraction**, where both the data and the methods (or behaviour) which characterize a particular type (or **class**) of object are identified, is one of the four defining concepts of object orientation. The other three are **encapsulation**, **inheritance** and **polymorphism**.

Encapsulation is the hiding of private data and methods within an object, leaving only public properties visible. This makes modifying the data or methods of a class of objects that is already in use in a program or model much safer; the programmer is free to modify private data and methods, for example to fix a problem or improve performance, knowing that the only changes this will cause in the remainder of the program can be checked by examining the effect on the public data and methods of this particular class. Thus the combination of abstraction and encapsulation localizes the effect of changes to data and methods, allowing larger and more complicated models to be built, modified and maintained than with the traditional procedural approach.

Inheritance is used to create **class hierarchies**. A set of objects that differ only in their data values is said to belong to the same class. Classes are arranged in an inheritance hierarchy, where a child class may inherit both data and methods from its parent class or classes (classes above it in the hierarchy) but will also have its own, specialized, data and methods. An inheritance relationship between two classes, (e.g. in a model of a car, the class AlloyWheel is the child of the class Wheel) may be interpreted as an 'is a' relationship in natural language (e.g. 'an alloy wheel is a wheel'). One of the major benefits of inheritance is the opportunities offered for reuse of existing classes in new contexts. If a requirement arises for modelling an aluminium wheel, it can inherit from the existing Wheel class. Or, if a large alloy wheel is required, it could inherit from AlloyWheel. The other important mechanism for reuse is containment (or aggregation) which is represented in natural language as a 'has a' relationship (e.g. 'a car has four wheels'). If a model of a lorry (truck) is required at a later date, the new Lorry class can contain, and hence reuse, the existing Wheel class.

Polymorphism is the property of an object responding appropriately, according to its class, to a standard message (or method invocation). There are many examples of abstract concepts which could usefully be represented as standard messages, aiding clarity and legibility: for example, multiplication. A message sent to an integer telling it to multiply itself by itself should perform an integer multiplication. In a polymorphic implementation, the same message when received by a matrix would perform a matrix multiplication, and so on. Polymorphism becomes particularly useful in objected-oriented (OO) programming when combined with **late-binding**, where the exact class of an object is not known until run-time – the same piece of code can be invoked on different classes of object and each will respond appropriately. For example, consider a program to calculate the total area of a set of different shapes, selected at run-time from a pick-list by the user; the high-level code sends a standard message to each shape instructing it to return its area, and simply adds the results. This usually reduces the total amount of code required and also aids legibility because the high-level code is not cluttered with details concerning how to calculate the area of a square, a triangle and so on. Most importantly, if a new shape class is added, the high-level code requires no alteration.

It could be argued that some of the principles of OO programming (OOP) can be adhered to without using an OO language – C programmers, for example, try to achieve data and method abstraction by collecting related variables and functions in small modular implementation files, to encapsulate private data and functions within the scope of the implementation file and to achieve a limited form of polymorphism simply through consistent function naming. More sophisticated techniques that use features of the operating system to allow the dynamic addition of new program components at run-time are also used. The principles of OOP are an extrapolation of 'good programming practice', not a revolution.

The history of object orientation

Object-oriented programming began its history in the 1960s with the development of Simula67, a discrete event simulation language. Smalltalk, developed at Xerox Palo Alto Research Center (Xerox PARC) in the 1970s, is still considered by many to be the OOP language which is most true to the principles of object orientation; but has never really been widely adopted in the commercial programming community. Xerox was the originator of the graphical user interface (GUI) and Smalltalk was the first language to adopt the now universal paradigm of representing GUI entities such as windows, icons and menus as objects.

Work in the area of knowledge representation and models of human reasoning has been highly influential in the development of OOP. Frames, proposed in 1975 by Marvin Minsky, and their less structured and hierarchical predecessor, semantic nets, are knowledge representation systems based on networks of objects with procedural and data abstraction and inheritance and also with default data values. Knowledge

Representation Language (KRL), developed by Bobrow and Winograd in the late 1970s at Xerox PARC, was an attempt to integrate frames into a practical language.

Over the next 20 years, as GUIs became widespread and software systems became larger and more complex and the principles of object orientation became more necessary to handle this complexity, OOP gradually moved into the mainstream of computing practice; OO extensions to already widely used languages eased the process. Bjarne Stroustrup of AT&T Laboratories designed and implemented a superset of the C language called C++ (Stroustrup, 1997), the first version of which was released in 1983. Although criticized by OOP purists as compromising the principles of object orientation due to its origins in C (e.g. the syntax distinguishes between base-typed variables such as characters, floating-point values, etc., and objects) and also for its provision of 'dangerous' features such as direct access to pointers (object addresses) and explicit casts (where the programmer can freely change the type/class of a variable/object), it is probably the most widely used OO language today. Recently, Java has become very significant in the OOP community. In 1995 the first version of Java was released by Sun Microsystems; Java is, arguably, a pure OO language with a similar but simpler syntax to C++, but with safety features such as no pointers and automatic garbage collection. Java programs are composed of software components which can be distributed anywhere on the World-Wide Web (WWW – see Chapter 16), and can be dynamically extended by the addition of new components. Complete platform independence and the ability to write distributed programs easily, achieved via the WWW, are probably Java's most innovative features.

Object orientation in CAD

Today OOP is the approach of choice in CAD system development. System entities are divided into class hierarchies. Messages instruct objects to draw themselves, or perhaps to move, change colour or change style. New entity types may be added without difficulty, and may inherit some procedures (e.g. change colour or line-style, delete or blank itself) from the class of entities. Furthermore, the message-passing facility between objects affords the possibility of extensive associations between different entities: the example below shows how such associativity has been used in the modelling of a mechanism.

Example 5.4 *The use of object orientation and associativity*

Figure 5.13 shows the solid geometry for a crank-slider mechanism which has been modelled using software with an object-oriented and associative data structure. In this model the centre lines and link positions of the mechanism were constructed using points, lines and arcs, with associativity to reflect the relationships between the mechanism elements, and then the geometry for the crank, connecting rod and piston was itself associated with the point and centre-line geometry as discrete objects. With these relationships, changes in the position of the crank may be automatically reflected in the other elements of the mechanism, as shown in the figure.

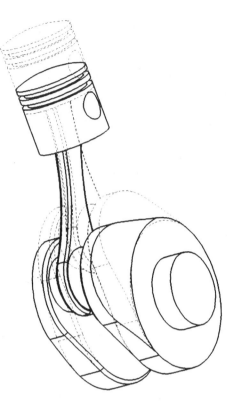

FIGURE 5.13

A mechanism
animated using an
associative data
structure.
(Reproduced by
permission of
Intergraph (UK) Ltd.)

5.6 Database considerations

Our considerations so far have only dealt with the structure of the interactive model file. In CAD systems there is a requirement to store individual models in a sort of automated 'drawing store' from which straightforward retrieval is required. In addition, the store should be able to hold other data such as standard part or symbol data, program files, numerical control and finite element information. Certain systems store models, or **parts**, as files which are really like snapshots of the interactive data structures at a given moment in time. In addition, they typically define a number of other file types which, together with the parts, are stored as standard operating system binary files.

One of the additional classes of file that is very widely found allows collections of entities to be defined by selection from a part file and subsequently to be inserted (typically at any scale, orientation and location) into any part file. Names for files of this type include **patterns**, **templates**, **shapes** and **symbols**. There are variations in the way in which these entity collections are inserted into the part data. In some cases, copies of the entities are added to the part data, and these copies may subsequently be manipulated just as any other entities. Another approach is to insert an **instance** of the entities in the part, at an appropriate scale and orientation, but not to copy the data – simply to cross-reference to the **master** (a copy of which would probably be placed in the part file to allow instances to be taken). The term pattern is more frequently applied to the former approach. In some systems both of these facilities are included.

Disadvantages with the part file style of storage

The part file approach to the system database is very widely applied among systems of all sizes and complexities. However, the main disadvantage with this style is precisely that information is stored in a format analogous to a drawing – as an independent collection of geometric elements. If an assembly model uses data from models of individual components, then if a modification is made to a component model it will not automatically be reflected in the assembly model. Any associativity between geometric elements is within part files only. Similarly, if the geometry of a standard component is stored as a pattern, then, if the component shape is changed, the model files using that pattern would all have to be changed individually.

Finally, there is little information in the filing system – unless embedded in the filename – that allows us to associate other product information – analysis information, process planning data and so on – with the part file in a consistent fashion.

5.6.1 Integrated databases

A good deal of effort has gone into database structure for CAD – with attention given to the possibility of using standard database programs to handle the data. As an illustration, in architectural work some systems are very highly structured on the symbol-instance form (e.g. doors, windows and other standard features are defined only once and any drawing merely cross-references the latest definition of the feature). A similar approach may be taken in general engineering CAD, in order to avoid duplication of data within the database. In this case, an assembly model will be a collection of references to component models elsewhere in the database, together with the appropriate transformations to orient and place the models in the assembly. A drawing might then consist of the requisite views of the model, together with dimensions and other annotation. Parts lists are generated directly by interrogation of the three-dimensional assembly, rather than through attributes attached to individual entities.

Figure 5.14 shows examples of how a commercial system that takes this approach is structured. The system filestore is divided into a number of project areas and a 'standards' area for standard component data. A particular assembly draws on models from within its project area, but also from the archive of another project. In a 'part-file'-based system the data for the components would have been copied into the assembly drawing file, and once done the control over this data would have been lost. In the system represented in Figure 5.14 the data is protected from inadvertent or inappropriate modification. A constraint on such an approach is that careful management of the system is required, in particular in organizing the cross-references required to different parts of the database, although this is a task which may be assisted or automated by software.

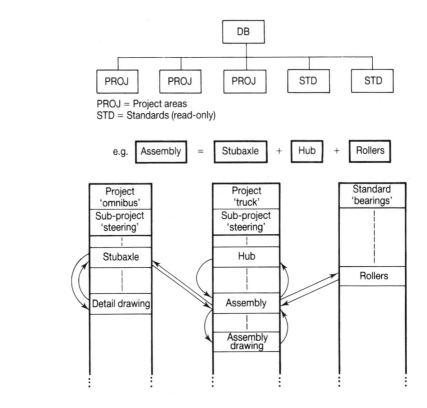

FIGURE 5.14
A project-oriented database organization. (Reproduced by permission of Matra Datavision (UK) Ltd.)

5.6.2 Engineering data management systems

Let us now step even further back from the detail of the part representation and consider the overall management of the database. Some large companies will have hundreds of thousands of model files, drawing files and other CAD data files in store, and in some cases they will be continually reusing these over a period of many years (consider for example the design of a large passenger aircraft or of a generating station). They therefore need systems to index and manage these large quantities of data in a sort of electronic drawing vault. These systems are used by designers to enquire what data is available on a particular project; where it is stored; when models were constructed and by whom; and so on. Designers spend an enormous amount of time searching for data of all sorts: some estimates suggest that they spend as much as 30% of their time actually searching for or through information that is contained in existing drawings and other product data. A system to assist a design team in the indexing, browsing and searching of their design data may be termed an engineering data management system (EDMS). In addition to a data repository, an EDMS also provides:

▶ mechanisms for data security that ensure that data is available and easily accessible to all who need access, but that only those with the appropriate authority can access data;

▶ checks that particular data items are unique – that is, for a given reference, only one data item may exist in the system;

▶ version control mechanisms that log changes and issues of drawings and other files.

The more comprehensive EDMSs are also used to manage data across multiple computing systems – for example, to allow files to be transferred between a CAD system based on a network of workstations and a mainframe computer used for archiving.

5.6.3 Relational databases

The data repository aspects of EDMSs are normally constructed on top of commercial database management systems (DBMSs). These provide the data storage and indexing mechanisms, and handle such aspects as system security and the computing problems associated with shared and simultaneous access to data (the system has to allow simultaneous access by multiple users, both for retrieval and entry/updating of data).

A variety of approaches to database organization have been developed over the years. These share a number of common concepts. These are:

▶ Databases contain **records**, comprising data elements in **fields**.

▶ Elements may be of a variety of data **types** such as numbers, dates and text.

▶ Database contents are catalogued in **data dictionaries**.

▶ Operations on databases – adding, modifying or deleting data – are called **transactions**.

▶ DBMSs provide multi-user access, concurrency control, query capability and security of databases.

The dominant database approach in the 1960s was the so-called **hierarchical** approach, in which data is organized into hierarchical 'tree' structures. This was followed in the 1970s by the more general **network** approach, defined by the 'Conference on Data Systems Languages' (CODASYL), which allowed less restrictive relationships between data elements than the simple hierarchical tree. However, these approaches have today largely been displaced by the **relational** database method, based on a formal methodology and relational algebra developed by Codd at IBM in the 1960s and 1970s (Codd, 1970; Ullman, 1980), in which data is represented in **relations** resembling two-dimensional tables of values. The rows of relations comprise the database records, also known as **tuples**, and the columns are the fields, also called **attributes**. The data types and field descriptions for a particular relation comprise the **schema** for that relation.

The relations which together make up a database are defined by the database schema, which comprises the schemas for the relations in the database, and the integrity constraints that specify legal entries or combinations of entries in the tables. The strength of the relational database approach comes from the ability to manipulate the data tables, and in particular to combine data from two relations to form new, virtual relations. **Join** operations are used to combine tuples from two relations that share a common field. Tuples are joined where the value of a specified tuple in one relation equals the value of a specified tuple in another. By such a means, complex data sets may be generated whilst using straightforward tables.

Relational algebra (adapted from Parsaye et al. (1989) with permission © John Wiley and Sons Inc.)

The operations that manipulate a relational database are based on a formal relational algebra, based on a well-defined logical structure. The five fundamental operations in relational algebra are **selection**, **projection**, **product**, **union** and **set difference**. In addition, **joins** may be defined in terms of product and selection. Selection and projection are **unary** operations that operate on a single relation. The other three operate on pairs of relations and are **binary**.

The selection operation selects rows from a table that satisfy a given predicate. For example, the predicate 'Plant=Bristol' in a machine tool table (Machine-tool) would select those tuples for which the attribute Plant is 'Bristol':

Machine-name	Machine-ID	Plant	Workshop
CNC lathe	1203	Bristol	Turning cell
Machining centre	1309	Galway	Transmissions cell
Five-axis mill	1567	Galway	Die shop
Machining centre	1809	Bristol	Workshop 'A'

The projection operation removes certain columns from a table. For example, to see just the Machine-name, Machine-ID and Plant fields in the Machine-tool table the workshop column would be projected out of the table:

Machine-name	Machine-ID	Plant
CNC lathe	1203	Bristol
Machining centre	1309	Galway
Five-axis mill	1567	Galway
Machining centre	1809	Bristol

The product operator multiplies two tables so that if one table has N rows and I columns, and the other M rows and J columns, the product table has $(N*M)$ rows and $I + J$ columns. For example, the product of:

Machine-name	Machine-ID	Plant
CNC lathe	1203	Bristol
Machining centre	1309	Galway

and a Machine–purchase-date relation:

Machine-ID	Purchase-date
1203	1986
1309	1994

is a table with $2 \times 2 = 4$ rows, with the first three columns from the first table, and the last two from the second:

Machine-name	Machine-ID	Plane	Machine-ID	Purchase-date
CNC lathe	1203	Bristol	1203	1986
CNC lathe	1203	Bristol	1309	1994
Machining centre	1309	Galway	1203	1986
Machining centre	1309	Galway	1203	1994

This does not make much sense, so the table is cleaned up by first selecting those rows where the names in the second and fourth columns match to get:

Machine-name	Machine-ID	Plant	Machine-ID	Purchase-date
CNC lathe	1203	Bristol	1203	1986
Machining centre	1309	Galway	1309	1994

and then projecting out one of the name fields to get the table *Machine-date*:

Machine-name	Machine-ID	Plant	Purchase-date
CNC lathe	1203	Bristol	1986
Machining centre	1309	Galway	1994

A **union** operation between two tables with N and M rows respectively results in a table with $(N + M)$ rows. It will only in general make sense if the schemas of the two tables match.

The **difference** operator (A – B) is used to find records that are in one relation, but not in another. For example, find all Part-name in the Product-composition table below that are parts of a gearbox but not of a pump by specifying:

Project Part-name ((Select Product = gearbox (Product-composition)) –
(Select Product = pump (Product-composition)))

Product-composition

Product	Part-name	Part-no.	Qty
gearbox	pinion	1006	2
gearbox	shaft	1385	2
gearbox	bearing	2876	4
pump	impeller	2346	1
pump	housing	2477	1
pump	bearing	2877	2
motor	rotor	1135	1
motor	shaft	2655	1
motor	bearing	2878	2

the result of this query is then:

Part-name
pinion
shaft

The intersection between two relations (records in A that are also in B) can be defined in terms of differences: $A - (A - B)$.

Joining tables

Although not one of the basic relational operators, **join** can be very useful. It allows a predicate to be applied to all rows formed by concatenating rows from A and rows from B. For example, if we have three rows in A and seven in B we can form 21 possible rows to apply the predicate to, where the predicate would typically be that the value of a field in A and B is the same. As an example, let us consider how we can find products that contain parts manufactured by the Briman Manufacturing Co., given the Product-composition table above, and the Suppliers table:

Suppliers

Supplier-name	Part-no.
Pump Parts Ltd	2376
Bearings-r-us	2876
Bearings-r-us	2877
Bearings-r-us	2878
Gearworks Ltd	1006
Briman Mfg Co.	1385
•	•
•	•

The first step is W = Join (Product-composition, Suppliers, Part-No):

Product	Part-name	Part-No	Qty	Supplier-name
gearbox	pinion	1006	2	Gearworks Ltd
gearbox	shaft	1385	2	Briman Mfg Co.
gearbox	bearing	2876	4	Bearings-r-us
pump	impeller	2346	1	Pump-parts Ltd
pump	housing	2477	1	Bricast Ltd
pump	bearing	2877	2	Bearings-r-us
motor	rotor	1135	1	Briman Mfg Co.
motor	shaft	2655	1	Briman Mfg. Co.
motor	bearing	2878	2	Bearings-r-us

The next step would be to select only those records for which the Supplier-name is Briman Mfg Co. to give:

Product	Part-name	Part-No	Qty	Supplier-name
gearbox	shaft	1385	2	Briman Mfg Co.
motor	rotor	1135	1	Briman Mfg Co.
motor	shaft	2655	1	Briman Mfg Co.

5.6.4 The SQL query language

The relational algebra provides a concise language for representing queries, but is not necessarily easy to use or to interface to programs. This has led to the development of query languages – in effect high-level programming languages specialized for data or information retrieval. The most widely used relational language is SQL (pronounced 'sequel') – the structured query language – developed by IBM in the mid-1970s, and now an ANSI standard.

SQL uses query **expressions** that result in relations. Expressions are of the form:

SELECT Attribute$_1$, Attribute$_2$, . . . , Attribute$_n$
FROM Relation$_1$, Relation$_2$, . . . , Relation$_n$
WHERE Predicate;

to which are added optional clauses for arranging the presentation of results:

ORDER BY
GROUP BY
HAVING

SELECT corresponds, confusingly, to the projection operation in the relational algebra. It is used to list the attributes desired in the table produced by the query, where * means select all attributes from the relation(s). The **FROM** clause is used to specify the list of relations to be used in executing the query, and the **WHERE** clause corresponds to the selection predicate of the relational algebra. Where present it consists of a predicate involving attributes of the relations in the 'where' clause. For example:

> **SELECT** Machine-name
> **FROM** Machine-tool
> **WHERE** Plant = 'Bristol';

yields a list comprising 'CNC lathe' and 'Machining centre', and:

> **SELECT** Product, Part-name, Qty
> **FROM** Product-composition
> **WHERE** Qty > 2;

yields a list of products and their constituent parts and quantities for which the number required of the part is greater than two, that is:

Product	Part-name	Part-No	Qty
gearbox	bearing	2876	4

In addition to the standard relational predicates (<, >, =, etc.) built-in predicates include **BETWEEN** (for ranges), **IN** (for membership) and **LIKE** (for text pattern matching, e.g. **WHERE** Plant **LIKE** 'B%' would match any city name beginning with B ('_' matches a single character)).

ORDER BY allows the order in which the retrieval is controlled to be controlled. For example, **ORDER BY** Qty orders rows according to the value of Qty. If **ORDER BY** is not used, the order of rows may vary from query to query. Ascending or descending order can be specified by **ASC** or **DESC** respectively.

GROUP BY and **HAVING** allow rows to be arranged into groups, and then for operations to be performed on those groups. **GROUP BY** makes **SELECT** display one line for each group of selected rows with the same values of one or more specified columns or expressions. **HAVING** is used to specify which **GROUP BY** elements are to be listed.

For example, to display the earliest purchase date for each machine in a plant from the Machine-date table used in the relational algebra section above (but assuming that it is populated with rather more data), the following command might be used:

> **SELECT** Plant, MIN(Purchase-date)
> **FROM** Machine-date
> **GROUP BY** Plant;

This would give a table with two columns, the first listing plant names, and the second the earliest purchase date for machines in the corresponding plant. The clause MIN() used here, and its counterpart MAX(), are group functions, meaningful only in queries.

To apply only to particular machine types, the **WHERE** clause is used:

SELECT Plant, MIN(Purchase-date)
WHERE Machine-name = 'CNC lathe'
FROM Machine-date
GROUP BY Plant;

In addition to providing a standard mechanism for the querying of relational databases, SQL provides the means of specifying the schema for data tables, and then populating these with data and manipulating the data. The appropriate clauses are readily understood because they use English expressions such as CREATE TABLE for specifying the attributes and data types used in a table, DELETE for deleting records, INSERT INTO *tablename* to add records to a table and so on. Furthermore, SQL may be used from high-level languages in addition to its interactive mode.

5.6.5 Using a relational database for design

So how might a company's design information be stored in a relational DBMS (RDBMS)? Let us consider a very simple example to illustrate the sort of thinking that goes into an EDMS. We can imagine that concerning CAD model records, a company may wish to store information about individual CAD files, and also details about projects and about the design staff involved in the projects. This suggests three relations, perhaps with fields as follows:

CAD-MODEL relation – field descriptions:
Model-number   – integer number
Model-title   – character string
Project-title   – character string
Designer   – character string
Date-of-creation   – date format
Revision-number   – integer number
File-location   – character string

PROJECT relation – field descriptions:
Project-title   – character string
Project-manager   – character string
Start-date   – date format
Client   – character string

EMPLOYEE relation – field descriptions:
Employee-name   – character string
Employee-ID   – integer number
Telephone-number – integer number
Desk-location   – character string

The product relations need to allow a hierarchical breakdown of a product into subassemblies and individual parts. Again, simple relation schemas for this purpose might be:

PART relation – field descriptions:
Part-name   – character string
PartAssembly-ID   – integer number
Part-source   – character string
Part-reference   – character string
CAD-model-number – integer number

where Part-source indicates the supplier, or perhaps the internal source for parts manufactured in-house, and Part-reference gives the internal catalogue number or supplier's number, and:

ASSEMBLY relation – field descriptions:
Assembly-name   – character string
PartAssembly-ID   – integer number
Assembly-source   – character string
Assembly-reference – character string

PART-OF relation – field descriptions:
PartAssembly-ID   – integer number
Has-constituent-part   – integer number
Location-orientation – transformation matrix

In this schema, there will be a record entry in the PART-OF relation for each assembly to subassembly or each assembly to part relationship. The 'Has-constituent-part' field may refer to the ID number either of a subassembly or of a part. Through the PART-OF relation, a hierarchical description of the product can be built up. The 'Location-orientation' field will describe the physical location of the part in the assembly, and its orientation. A convenient way to store this information is as a transformation matrix which allows translations and rotations to be defined together in a convenient manner. A CAD model of an assembly may then be built up by using the PART-OF records, and collecting together the CAD models of the individual parts and locating them using the transformation matrix. The DBMS itself will typically allow rules to be entered to determine what can and cannot be entered into a relation. For example, a rule might be that a CAD model number must be unique. The DBMS will also usually provide facilities to generate interactive menus with which the user can enter and retrieve data from the database and prepare reports of the database contents (which might be used, for example, to investigate project status or to prepare parts lists).

Of course, the relations presented above just give an indication of the sort of techniques used to store product data in a database. Real systems will have very many more relations, and much more complex relation definitions to allow all manner of product data and relationships to be modelled.

5.6.6 Object-oriented databases

Currently, the majority of database applications still use a relational database management system (RDBMS) but, despite still being relatively new technology, object-oriented database management systems (OO DBMSs) are gradually gaining wider usage.

An OO DBMS stores the data for each object in a single place, indexed by a unique object identifier (object ID), rather than scattering the data between different tables as in traditional relational systems. Relationships (links) between objects are usually represented directly using the object ID and thus object links are followed, not by performing joins, but by using the object IDs directly. An OO DBMS will usually provide support for run-time schema querying – where applications can query meta-data about the objects, for example the class name, the names and types of the class attributes and methods, the name of the class, the super- and subclasses, etc.

Hybrid OO–relational products exist which enable object representations to be made in relational databases. Truly OO DBMSs are less widely used, and they usually allow **methods** to be stored in the database schema as well as data structures – those which do not are termed *passive*. Such systems offer considerable advantages of speed over hybrid systems when following object links. Most OO DBMSs also provide some support for object versioning.

5.7 Conclusion

The power of CAD arises in large part from the ability to manipulate the design database, and to make substantial reuse of the data – both in other designs and elsewhere in the design and manufacturing process. Facilities that promote this include extensive editing features and transformation functions to allow data to be moved and copied in a variety of ways. These functions are supported by data structures that allow interactive manipulation of the data to be readily achieved.

The storage and manipulation of CAD data has traditionally often been at a part or 'drawing' level. Increasingly, however, the organization of the overall database is seen as being of particular importance – indeed to be a key to the integration of CAD with parallel and downstream activities. This organization involves on the one hand indexing and storing all of the CAD data held by a company in a form that may be searched and accessed very easily. On the other hand it involves linking of CAD data with all manner of other product data held by the company. For the moment this largely means part, analysis, manufacturing and supplier data that is included together with product configuration information in an engineering data management system (EDMS) database. In Chapter 16 we will return to this topic when we discuss product data management (PDM) and product modelling, which involve the extension of the EDMS approach to include information about workflow within a company, and a wider range of product-related data, including all manner of **unstructured** data such as reports, memoranda, customer and service feedback and so on.

References and further reading

Booch G. (1991). *Object-Oriented Design With Applications*. Menlo Park, CA: Benjamin/ Cummings.

Born C. A., Rasdorf W. J. and Fulton R. E. (eds) (1990). *Engineering Data Management: The Technology for Integration. Proc. 1990 ASME International Computers in Engineering Conference*, Boston, MA.

Coad P. and Yourdon E. (1991). *Object-Oriented Design*. Englewood Cliffs, NJ: Prentice Hall.

Codd E. F. (1970). A relational model for large shared data banks. *Communications of the ACM*. **13**, 377–87.

Date C. J. (1981). *An Introduction to Database Systems*. 3rd edn. Reading, MA: Addison Wesley Longman.

Dittrich K., Dayal U. and Buchmann A. P. (eds) (1991). *Object-Oriented Database Systems*. New York: Springer.

Eastman C. M. and Fereshetian N. (1994). Information models for use in product design: a comparison. *Computer-aided Design*. **26**(7), 551–72.

Foley J. D., Van Dam A., Feiner S. and Hughes J. (1996). *Computer Graphics, Principles and Practice. 2nd edition in C*. Reading, MA: Addison Wesley Longman.

Gorlen K. E., Orlow S. M. and Plexico P. S. (1990). *Data Abstraction and Object-oriented Programming in C++*. Chichester: John Wiley.

Ingham P. (1989). *CAD Systems in Mechanical and Production Engineering*. London: Heinemann-Newnes.

Jackson P. (1990). *Introduction to Expert Systems*. 2nd edn. Reading, MA: Addison Wesley Longman.

Newman W. M. and Sproull R. F. (1979). *Principles of Interactive Computer Graphics*. New York: McGraw-Hill.

Parsaye K., Chignell M., Khoshafian S. and Wong H. (1989). *Intelligent Databases*. New York: Wiley.

Rumbaugh J., Blaha M., Premerlani W., Eddy F. and Lorensen, W. (1991). *Object-Oriented Modeling and Design*. Englewood Cliffs, NJ: Prentice Hall.

Saxena V. (ed.) (1991). *Engineering Databases: An Enterprise Resource. Proc. 1991 ASME International Computers in Engineering Conference*, Santa Clara, CA.

Shaw N. K., Bloor M. Susan and de Pennington A. (1989). Product data models. *Research in Engineering Design*. **1**(1), 43–50.

Stroustrup B. (1997). *The C++ Programming Language*. 3rd. edn. Reading, MA: Addison Wesley Longman.

Ullman J. (1980). *Principles of Relational Database Systems*. New York: Computer Science Press.

Warman E. A. (1990). Object-oriented programming and CAD. *Journal of Engineering Design*. **1**(1), 37–46.

Exercises

5.1 If you have access to a CAD system, list the facilities that it provides for manipulation of the design model. In particular, give details of any transformation functions, and sketch the operation of entity trim functions.

5.2 Write down the principal types of object transformation. Why are homogeneous coordinates often used?

5.3 Calculate the two-dimensional homogeneous transformation matrix to mirror points through the line defined in the *Oxy* plane by the two points (3, 3), (11, 9).

5.4 Calculate the three-dimensional homogeneous transformation matrix to carry out a transformation comprising a translation of 20 mm in the *z*-direction together with a rotation of 20° about a line parallel to the *z*-axis through (20, 20, 0).

5.5 Calculate the three-dimensional homogeneous transformation matrix to carry out a transformation involving rotation of 20° about an axis parallel to the *z*-axis through $x = 50$, $y = 50$, $z = 50$, followed by a rotation of 45° about an axis parallel to the *x*-axis through the same centre point.

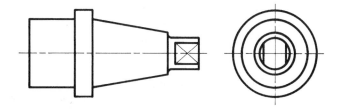

FIGURE 5.15
A machined shaft.

5.6 Trimming and extending commands often involve an interactive sequence such as 'Select entity to be trimmed; select bounding entities'. Suggest how this sequence may be applied to the trimming operations shown in Figure 5.6, and write down the steps required by the CAD system in computing the result.

5.7 Explain how linked lists and data pointers may be used in data structures for CAD systems.

5.8 Consider a two-dimensional draughting system. Geometric entities include points, lines, arcs, ellipses and cubic splines. There are 26 other entity types. Entities are to be drawn in four curve fonts and eight colours, and the system is to allow temporary deletion and grouping of entities, and up to 256 layers. Assuming a maximum of 16 384 entities, and 65 536 real or integer data elements (maximum 256 per entity), each of 4 bytes, specify:
   (a) the general entity data to be stored for each entity, and the number of bits required for each item of data;
   (b) the minimum number of 32-bit words required for the general data for one entity;
   (c) the real and integer data for each entity type;
   (d) the storage in bytes for a drawing comprising 20 points, 250 lines, 105 arcs and 5 ellipses.

5.9 Figure 5.15 shows a drawing of a machined shaft. Sketch how a three-dimensional model of this would be represented using (a) wire-frame geometry and (b) constructive solid geometry, and then compare the likely storage requirements for the entities comprising the two models (you need not consider how the binary tree describing model (b) would be stored).

5.10 Suggest how a display file may be used to:
   (a) identify entities by single selection;
   (b) identify entities inside or outside a region;
   (c) support a fast 'zoom' facility to zoom by a factor of 2, 4, 8 or 16.

5.11 Discuss how the entity storage scheme of Exercise 5.7 might be extended to allow associative dimensions and associative geometry. What would be the effect in an associative system of extending the length of the shaft in Figure 5.15 by 15 mm?

5.12 Suggest how attributes may be used in conjunction with geometric entities to incorporate part number and quantity information into an assembly drawing. Then suggest how this attribute information might be combined with part name, drawing number and supplier data in an engineering drawing database system. How might part information be collected from a *series* of assembly and subassembly drawings?

5.13 Explain why object orientation is preferable to the conventional approach to software engineering, and then briefly outline the four defining concepts of object orientation.

5.14 Where might there be advantages in adopting an object-oriented approach to the data organization and structure for modelling engineering assemblies?

5.15 If you have access to a CAD system, explore the file types which it uses to store data. Do they correspond to the part and pattern files identified in this chapter? Does the database support assembly modelling by reference to the parts which make up the assembly? Is the system linked to an engineering database management system?

5.16 Outline what you think might be the important issues of data management and security for an engineering data management system to manage design information stored on many computers spread over several sites of an engineering company.

5.17 Explain the terms record, field, tuple, transaction and relation in the context of relational databases.

5.18 Identify the binary relational algebra operators, and state briefly what their function is. Then write down the result of the following operation on the Product-composition table given in Section 5.6.3 and reproduced below:

Project Part-name ((Select Product = gearbox (Product-composition)) – (Select Product = motor (Product-composition)))

Product-composition

Product	Part-name	Part-No	Qty
gearbox	pinion	1006	2
gearbox	shaft	1385	2
gearbox	bearing	2876	4
pump	impeller	2346	1
pump	housing	2477	1
pump	bearing	2877	2
motor	rotor	1135	1
motor	shaft	2655	1
motor	bearing	2878	2

5.19 Outline the structure of an SQL query expression, and then indicate which terms in the expression are mandatory. Write a query to obtain a relation comprising the part-names and part-numbers for which quantities of 1 are required from the Product-composition table given in Exercise 5.18. The rows of the table should be ordered in descending part number order.

5.20 Suggest how the database relation schema given in Section 5.6.5 above might be used to represent the assembly-part hierarchy shown in Figure 5.16. Fasteners and minor parts have been omitted from the diagram. Details of the other parts are as follows:

The layshaft, mainshaft, housing and cover are sourced in-house from Main Works, and have part references MW1, MW2, MW3 and MW4 respectively. CAD models of each of these have names CAD_MW1.prt and so on. Bearings are sourced from Bearing Company Ltd, and each have references BCL7308. You may ignore the location and orientation of the parts.

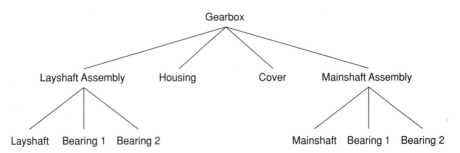

FIGURE 5.16
A simple assembly hierarchy.

Projects

For more information about the subjects for project work, please refer to the end of Chapter 1.

The project activity for this chapter is to explore the use of transformations in the modelling of the artefacts, and to investigate the way in which they are stored by the CAD system. Specific project tasks are concentrated on the load cell, and are:

Project 1 Chess piece Investigate and report how the entities in the chess piece models are stored in the CAD system.

Project 2 Load cell Show how the load cell drawings may be constructed through the use of entity transformations – especially mirroring through axes of symmetry. If associative geometry is available, show how the load cell structural member can be constructed using associative geometry and associative dimensions, and show the effect of varying part of the geometry on the remaining geometry and the dimensions. Suggest how the load cell assembly may be stored in an engineering data management system, and draw its part-assembly hierarchy.

6 Applying the CAD model in design

Chapter objectives

When you have completed studying material in this chapter you should be able to:

▶ make judgements about the most appropriate application of two-dimensional draughting and three-dimensional modelling in CAD;

▶ understand how CAD models may be used for geometric analysis, and for the generation of models for finite element analysis;

▶ understand how CAD systems may be customized by the use of a variety of different approaches;

▶ understand how customization may be applied in particular to part families and parametric geometry.

Chapter contents

6.1 Introduction

The first part of this book has dealt with the more fundamental aspects of CAD, such as the underlying modelling representations and computing techniques. We now begin to build upon these fundamentals by dealing with the application of the technology, in particular within the design process. Wider application within the product manufacturing cycle will be explored further in Part Two of the book. At this stage discussion will be centred on how the designer should best describe designs using the two- and three-dimensional modelling tools available; on how the designer and design analyst can exploit the CAD model in their assessment of the design's fitness for purpose; and on how systems may be customized to automate aspects of design.

6.2 Applications to draughting

Many of the facilities that make the CAD method useful for the production of engineering drawings have already been noted. Sophisticated geometric construction facilities allow the rapid production of views of the part and the precise construction of difficult geometry, and once constructed this geometry may be edited and manipulated by a variety of transformation techniques. But a drawing comprises not just geometry but also a range of annotating entities, such as dimensions and cross-hatching. In this section the facilities typically provided for annotation will be explored, after first reviewing the use of layers in the organization of the drawing.

6.2.1 Drawing organization

The partitioning of a drawing or model may be assisted by the use of **layers** or levels, as introduced in Section 5.4. Essentially a layer is just a number, usually in a limited range, with which entities are associated. By giving the same layer number to entities which are related to each other – for example, to all in a given view – the user may partition a drawing to improve performance and to make viewing and manipulation more straightforward. This is because the system will provide the facility to make entity selection by layer or by layer range. So for example the user might elect to display only the levels of one view (thus making zoom and pan operations much faster), or might move all of the entities in a range of layers in order to reposition a view within a drawing.

In some systems the layer facility is enhanced by allowing layers to have different status, the entities of an **active** layer being displayed and selectable. Those of a **reference** layer will be displayed but not selectable, while an **inactive** layer will not be displayed. New construction will go onto the **current** layer. Layers are rather like a series of transparent overlays which may be viewed at will.

The usefulness of layers depends on the extent to which the user is prepared to use them systematically to organize a model. A model with a poor layer organization may take hours to decipher, and this is why many organizations insist that their design staff work to a well-defined layer allocation strategy, and maintain a record of the layer contents. (In industries where there is regular exchange of engineering data this is so important that standards have emerged for the structuring of CAD data – for example, in the British Standard 1192 (1990) for construction drawing practice.) Table 6.1 shows an example of a layer allocation scheme, and Figure 6.1 shows how a drawing might be subdivided according to such a scheme.

6.2.2 Annotating the drawing

In addition to lines and curves, drawings also contain other elements that give information, such as the dimensions, surface condition, materials and tolerances of the design. CAD systems provide functions to generate this annotation as draughting entities. Furthermore, since the part geometry is stored within the database, generation of a dimension usually just involves pointing to the entities to which it applies: the numeric value is produced by the system without risk of transcription error.

Table 6.1 Layer allocation scheme

Layer numbers	Example contents
0–99	Main geometry, subdivided according to assembly components, or to spatial organization of the drawing (e.g. 0–9 for first view etc.).
100–199	Dimensions and annotation associated with level N-100.
200	Drawing border
201–209	Border annotation and general notes
210–219	Machining information, tool paths, etc.
220–229	Materials data
230–239	Auxiliary models and construction for analysis
240–255	Miscellaneous

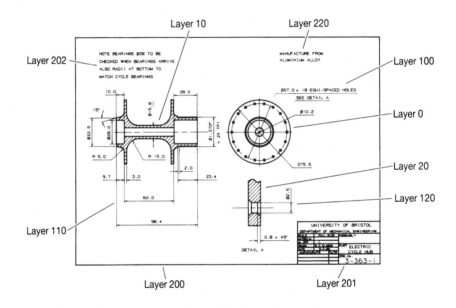

FIGURE 6.1

The use of a layer allocation scheme.

Examples of the draughting entities available within one PC-based CAD system are shown in Figure 6.2.

Another aspect of drawing annotation in which CAD may offer substantial improvement over manual techniques is in the cross-hatching of sectional views. The system software computes the intersections of the hatch lines in a standard pattern with the selected **boundary**, or **profile**, and then trims the line to these. In order to make the computation more straightforward, the boundary is often again represented as a **polygon** which approximates the true profile to within a specified tolerance. In some cases multiple boundaries, and/or one or more islands within the boundary, may be allowed, as shown in Figure 6.3.

A note of caution

Despite the apparent ease with which dimensions and hatching may be constructed using a modern CAD system, the annotation of drawings is regarded as a bottleneck

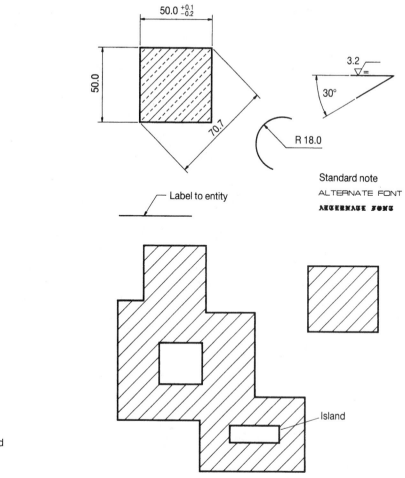

FIGURE 6.2

Draughting entities of an example system.

FIGURE 6.3

Multiple profiles and islands in a cross-hatch boundary.

in the computer-aided draughting process by some users. It is difficult to identify precise reasons for this, but the following factors may contribute, and new users should certainly be alert to these:

▶ Dimensioning systems are designed to be compatible with many different draughting standards, but inevitably systems may deviate slightly from some company practice: some users are very sensitive to this and may spend a long time 'editing' dimensions until they are satisfied with them.

▶ In their effort to make their software as flexible as possible – for example, to address a wide range of drawing standards – system developers may inadvertently make it rather complex. Novice users may therefore find the draughting functions of a system rather daunting.

▶ It may be more difficult to lay out dimensions on a crowded drawing using a CAD system than by hand.

▶ Software may be sensitive to small errors in construction. Some early hatching software was inordinately sensitive, for example, to small breaks in profiles.

6.2.3 Examples of system application

As examples of the application of CAD to two-dimensional draughting, let us examine case study material from three different engineering fields: building services engineering, mechanical handling and printing machinery.

Building services engineering essentially involves the design, installation and maintenance of the heating, ventilating and other services (electricity, water and gas) of a building. The installation has to follow the constraints of the physical structure of the building closely, and in addition the various services should integrate well with each other.

The building services engineer is able to exploit CAD in a variety of ways. Firstly, schematic diagrams representing the pipework, trunking and wiring of the services may be superimposed on drawings of the physical structure of the building, thus obviating the need to redraw these repeatedly. This is often assisted by the layer facility of a system. Water pipes and fittings may be shown on one series of layers, the ventilation ducting on another and so on, as shown in Figures 6.4 and 6.5 (the use of

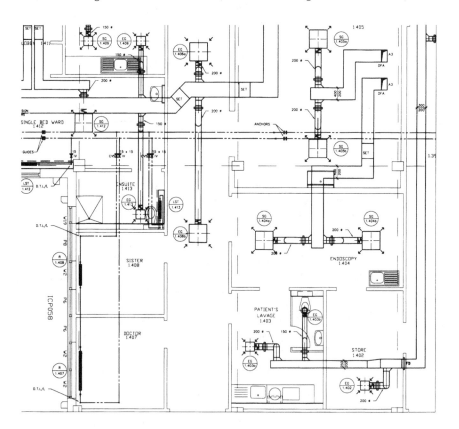

FIGURE 6.4

Heating and ventilating duct work on a building services drawing. (Reproduced by permission of Kennedy & Donkin.)

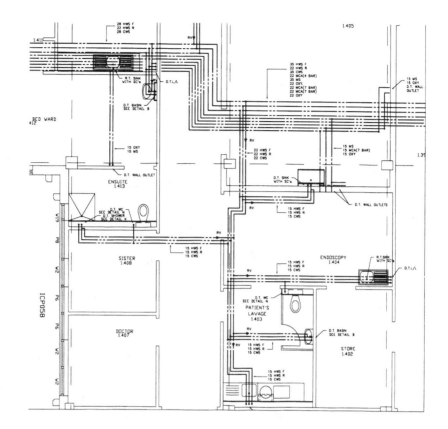

FIGURE 6.5

Water and other pipes and fittings on a building services drawing. (Reproduced by permission of Kennedy & Donkin.)

different colours may also be helpful). By displaying different sets of services simultaneously, the designer may also check that interfaces between services are correct and that there are no conflicts, for example between pipework.

The development of most mechanical assemblies is generally from initial *layout* drawings that are used to explore conceptual arrangements, through *detail* drawings of individual components for manufacture, to *assembly* drawings that show arrangement of components. The repetitive aspect of CAD in this process is generally from the reuse of part geometry. For example, component geometry may be extracted from a layout and used as the basis of the detail drawing. The detail geometry may subsequently be combined with that from other details in the assembly. This sequence, for elements of a mechanical handling machine, is shown in Figures 6.6 to 6.8. Figure 6.6 shows a layout of part of a motor drive, on which the torque arm which constrains the motor is shown in bold. Figure 6.7 shows the detail drawing for this torque arm, and the assembly of the drive is shown in Figure 6.8. It may be seen that the assembly drawing in fact makes extensive use of the geometry from the layout. The repetitive use of geometry may also have advantages in that the risk of error in transcribing geometry between drawings is greatly reduced.

In the third of our examples, concerning the mechanical design of printing press components, geometry reuse is again an important issue. Printing presses make extensive use of parts which are turned (and therefore axisymmetric), or are effectively

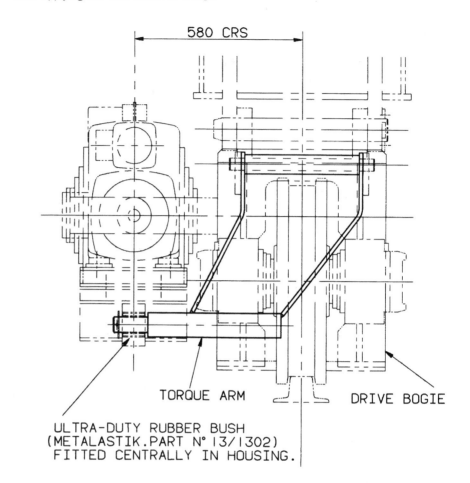

FIGURE 6.6
Layout drawing of a motor drive. (Reproduced by permission of Strachan and Henshaw Ltd.)

580 CRS

TORQUE ARM

DRIVE BOGIE

ULTRA-DUTY RUBBER BUSH (METALASTIK.PART N° 13/1302) FITTED CENTRALLY IN HOUSING.

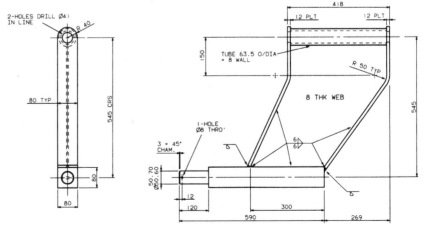

FIGURE 6.7
Detail drawing of a torque arm. (Reproduced by permission of Strachan and Henshaw Ltd.)

2-HOLES DRILL Ø41 IN LINE

R 40

80 TYP

80

80

545 CRS

418

12 PLT

12 PLT

TUBE 63.5 O/DIA × 8 WALL

150

R 50 TYP

8 THK WEB

545

1-HOLE Ø8 THRO'

3 × 45° CHAM.

50.70 Ø50.60

12

120

590

300

269

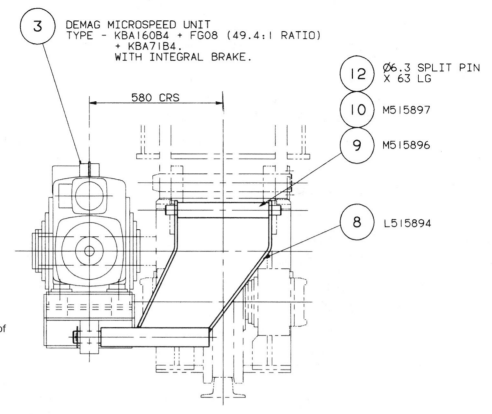

FIGURE 6.8
Assembly drawing of a motor drive. (Reproduced by permission of Strachan and Henshaw Ltd.)

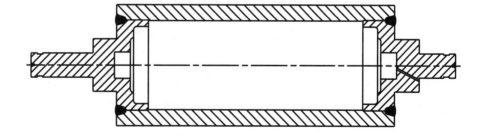

FIGURE 6.9
Drawing of a printing roller. (Reproduced by permission of Strachan Henshaw Machinery Ltd.)

planar, and therefore two-dimensional representations are quite adequate. Examples are:

1. A print roller, shown in Figure 6.9, which is a part for which variants are regularly designed. The ends of the roller remain substantially invariant, while the cylinder diameters and length may vary. Drawing geometry may thus often be produced by scaling and editing an existing drawing.

2. The side frames for the press, which are effectively large plates with a number of precision holes in them. Precision alignment of the parts of the press is crucial to its satisfactory operation. By using computer-based drawings, error-free data transcription to manufacture is ensured, and the dimensions of the repeated holes in the part can be accomplished quickly and accurately.

6.2.4 Guidelines for draughting

Let us complete this section by reviewing guidelines for the production of drawings using computers, and also by noting some limitations. The first guideline is that the greatest productivity advantage is obtained when there is some repetitive element in the drawing task, or the drawing geometry forms a basis for design analysis or the production of manufacturing data. Repetition may arise within a single drawing, for example through component symmetry, through reuse of geometry between drawings in the concept/detail sequence, or through use of library data or existing designs.

The second guideline is that CAD geometry should be drawn accurately, at full size, to exploit automatic dimensioning facilities. The user should also ensure that there is no duplication or superposition of geometry, and that lines are not inadvertently segmented (two or more lines are used when only one is appropriate). Multiple copies of geometry are a common fault among novice users (with raster screens it is sometimes not possible to notice when they occur), and segmented lines often arise from inappropriate use of transformation facilities such as mirroring.

The limitations of dimensioning were noted at the end of Section 6.2.2. The effect of these can be minimized by firstly leaving rather more space for dimensions than necessary for hand-drawn drawings, and secondly by being tolerant of small deviations in the standard of dimensions from company or personal practice. A general guideline is that one should not expect to be able to work in precisely the same way with a CAD system as with pencil and paper. Those who are prepared to adapt are most likely to be successful.

Two final comments are both rather negative. Firstly, many users find the size of VDU screens too small. In particular, constant changes of zoom scale are considered awkward and time consuming. Secondly, small changes to drawings may take a relatively long time using CAD because of the time taken to retrieve the drawing from file, and to produce a new plot. More positively, each of these criticisms is gradually being resolved by improved hardware design and performance.

6.3 Three-dimensional modelling applications

In the 1980s an often quoted aim of computer-integrated manufacture (CIM) was to integrate the design, analysis and manufacturing activities of a company around a central computing database, one of the core elements being three-dimensional geometric models of the product. Significant advances have been made, and for many companies a database of three-dimensional (3D) models forms the basis for product development by the concurrent engineering team, while the number of products that are completely modelled in three dimensions grows each year. Nevertheless, the spread of 3D modelling is perhaps slower than might be expected, and the production of conventional drawings remains a substantial activity in CAD. Let us examine for a moment why this might be so. Firstly, we have seen that certain geometries, such as castings and forgings involving complex blended surfaces, remain relatively difficult to model using the available 3D modelling techniques. For example, substantial skill and computer power is required to model the cast components of an engine with all the relevant details. Secondly, high hardware performance is required to model complex multi-part assemblies. Thirdly, a computer system is required to view a 3D CAD model, whereas a drawing may be copied and easily distributed. Finally, and perhaps most importantly, many properties other than geometry are modelled in an engineering drawing. These include dimension, tolerance, surface condition and treatment, material and manufacturing process and perhaps assembly and operational data. These are described in a drawing in a systematic, formal way that is well understood in engineering. This is not yet true for 3D geometric models. There is as yet no generally agreed way of modelling and communicating the various non-geometric data associated with engineering components (although this is the subject of research and development). This means that, even if a 3D database is used, orthographic projection drawings developed from the 3D models are often used for the formal communication of the design intent to suppliers and to manufacture.

The limitations of 3D modelling are gradually being resolved by research and development, and by the inexorable increase in computer power. Techniques are also being developed for the incorporation of tolerances and surface attributes into modelling schemes. Increasingly, therefore, 3D modelling will become the norm in engineering, incorporated into product modelling approaches comprising multiple, interlinked representations describing different facets of the product, as we have seen in the previous chapter when product modelling was discussed. For the moment, however, a pragmatic approach is advocated in choosing whether to use 3D modelling. In particular, considerable advantage may be obtained by using 3D geometric modelling for those cases where:

▶   geometries are intrinsically difficult to represent using conventional techniques, such as vehicle body panels and moulds for plastic parts;

▶   the use of CAD avoids the need to build physical mock-ups: the Boeing 777, as has been noted, is the first aircraft built by Boeing for which a physical mock-up was not required because a 'digital mock-up' was developed;

▶   the 3D model forms a natural basis for manufacture – for example, for those parts machined by CNC machine tools – or for analysis through the automatic generation of analysis data files;

▶   the 3D model may be used for geometric problem solving – for example, in the design of parts involving non-rectilinear geometries or complex surface intersections, such as sheet metal parts.

6.3.1 The use of 3D modelling for 2D representation

One application of a 3D model is in the generation of an engineering drawing by arranging multiple views of the model on a drawing sheet and then annotating these

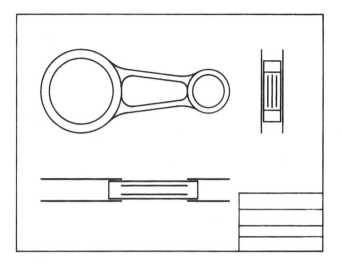

FIGURE 6.10
Arrangement of views of a wire-frame model on a drawing sheet.

views with dimensions, labels and notes. If the underlying 3D model is of the solid or surface type, then automatic hidden-line removal may be used on the drawing views. If the model is of the wire-frame type, then view-dependent editing facilities may be provided to change curve fonts and thicknesses, and to remove hidden geometry. Figure 6.10 shows an example of a wire-frame model and the arrangement of views of this model on a drawing sheet. The approach ensures consistency in the geometry between the views of a drawing, but it may be seen that interpretation is not entirely straightforward.

Of much more value is the automatic dimension updating facility offered by fully associative modelling systems. As noted in the last chapter, in such systems the views on the solid model that are placed on the drawing sheet are associated with the solid-model geometry from which they are derived. As the underlying model changes, the dimensions attached to the drawing view geometry may be updated automatically to reflect the changes.

6.3.2 Three-dimensional modelling for geometric problem solving

Even where drawings are used for data representation, there is merit in using 3D modelling to solve geometric problems, in particular where these involve surface intersections or investigation of clearances. In these respects modelling features which are particularly useful include:

▶ the generation of curves (generally spline curves) that represent the intersection between two surfaces;

▶ the generation of sections through models, for example showing spline curves where surfaces are intersected;

▶ the facility to **develop** (or unroll flat) certain surfaces.

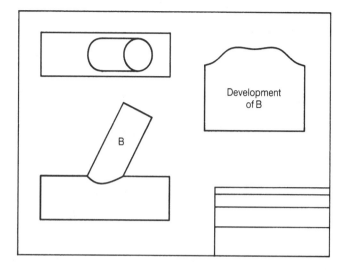

FIGURE 6.11
The use of geometry developed from the three-dimensional model.

Often, a model of all of the part geometry is unnecessary to investigate a particular problem. Instead, a local model of the geometry of interest – perhaps only two or three surfaces – may be sufficient.

As an illustration of the use of surface intersections and surface development let us continue with the example of two intersecting tubes (which may represent fabricated pipework). Figure 6.11 shows a drawing in which the curve of intersection between the two tubes is taken from a 3D model, as is the developed shape of one tube.

6.3.3 Examples of 3D modelling

There may be great advantage in 3D modelling when used to design complex moulded shapes for visualization or manufacture. One company in which these considerations apply is Electrolux, which makes electrical appliances such as washing machines and vacuum cleaners. The latter are made from several large, complex mouldings which mate together to form the body and handle of the cleaner, and whose shape and appearance is very important to the image of the product.

The conventional route from design to manufacture for vacuum cleaner parts is for detail drawings to be produced from layout drawings, and for these to be used for the manufacture of prototype mould tools. Normally, modifications are required to these prototype tools, necessitating a redesign–remanufacture sequence, with consequent delay in the product release. Electrolux achieves a significantly reduced product lead time by bypassing the conventional engineering design drawing stage and producing injection moulding tools for major components directly from full 3D computer models of the parts. It also manufactures prototype parts by using rapid prototyping techniques that allow physical models to be produced automatically from the CAD geometry (as will be discussed in Chapter 11), and by milling parts directly from solid plastic blocks using manufacturing information taken from the CAD model. Figure 6.12, for example, shows a geometric model of a part of a cleaner handle, and

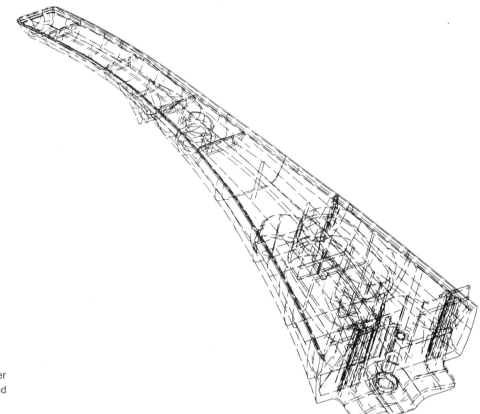

FIGURE 6.12

A geometric model of a vacuum cleaner handle. (Reproduced by permission of Electrolux.)

Figure 6.13 shows the machined-from-solid prototype parts (light) and production mouldings (dark) for the part.

Electrolux reports that the 3D computer-generated models provide a basis for the manufacture of prototype parts that may be considered as equivalent to 'first-off' mouldings from completed moulding tools. This gives confidence in the models, and allows tools to be produced which require very few corrections (thus giving the lead-time saving). The models also form the basis for part visualization and for the preparation of models for analysis – for example, of mould filling and cooling rates.

A second industry in which parts of complex shape are used, and in which expensive tools have to be produced in short lead times, is the automotive industry. The body of an automobile comprises hundreds of sheet metal panels that are joined together by spot-welding and other welding techniques, by bonding or by mechanical joints between panels. The assembled body, before painting, is called the **body-in-white**. All of the panels of a modern vehicle are defined using 3D surface or solid models which are the basis for the manufacture of press tools and for the analysis and subsequent inspection of the body.

In automobile design the external body shape itself is usually first defined using a clay model hand-crafted from concept sketches and drawings. This model is then

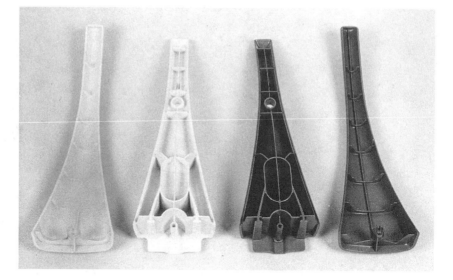

FIGURE 6.13
Prototype and production plastic parts. (Reproduced by permission of Electrolux.)

FIGURE 6.14
A five-axis milling machine for the production of automobile body models. (Reproduced by permission of Rover Group.)

scanned using a large combined milling and coordinate measuring machine (Figure 6.14), and the scanned data is used as the basis for curves to which surfaces are fitted. Figure 6.15 shows the surfaces describing an automobile body which were generated in this fashion. These surfaces define the shape of the **external** body panels of the vehicle, the modelling of which is the start of the generation of a mass of data describing the body-in-white. This includes models of all of the internal panels

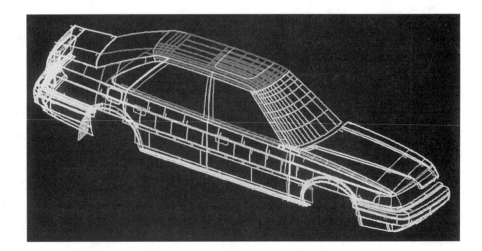

FIGURE 6.15

A surfaced model of a car body. (Reproduced by permission of Rover Group.)

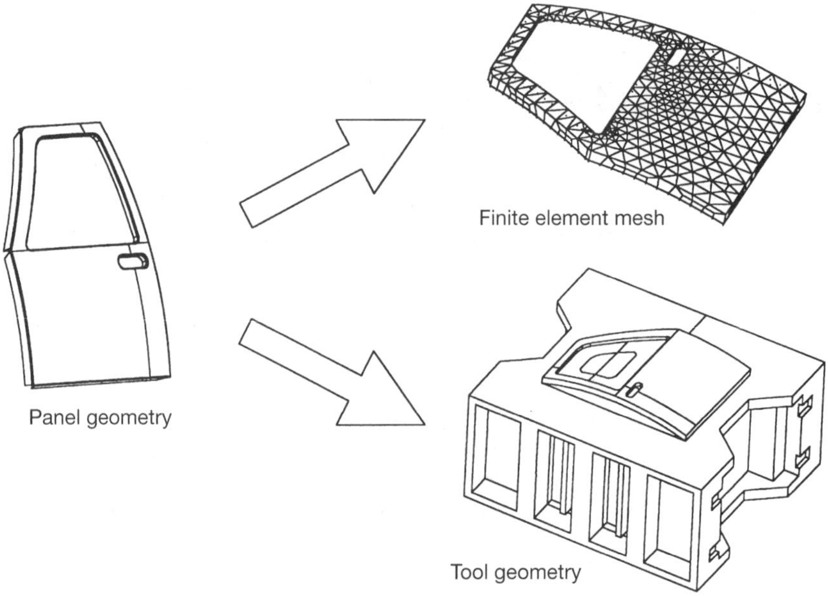

FIGURE 6.16

The models used in automobile body-in-white design. (Reproduced from Kugathasan and McMahon (1997) by kind permission of International Conference on Engineering Design 97.)

Panel geometry

Finite element mesh

Tool geometry

of the body, models to evaluate the structural performance and crashworthiness of the body, models for process planning and for manufacture of the press tools, and models to allow the acoustic performance of the body to be evaluated. Figure 6.16 shows diagrammatically the relationship between some of these models used in body-in-white design.

The internal panels of a vehicle can be among the most complicated surface models that are produced in engineering, owing to the very complex collections of holes, cut-outs, bosses and ribs that may be incorporated on a panel. Models of the largest of these panels, such as the underbody of a vehicle, can comprise very many surface patches.

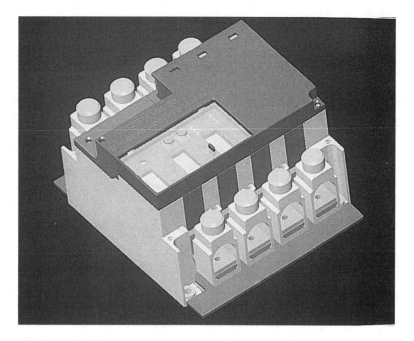

FIGURE 6.17
MEM residual
current device.
(Reproduced by
permission of
MEM500.)

The use of the solid model as a basis for downstream activities was important for the MEM500 Company of Birmingham, UK, a manufacturer of electrical equipment which it supplies worldwide. MEM was able to exploit 3D geometric models of the design of a residual current device shown in Figure 6.17, in three important ways:

▶ To assist their designers and managers in the visualization of the design, so that market viability could be assessed and project funding could be obtained.

▶ To allow engineers to modify the design easily and quickly if it was necessary to do so after design review and testing.

▶ To use the models as a basis for production of physical rapid prototypes directly from the CAD geometry (see also Chapter 11). The first prototype was made in about five days using stereolithography (SLA).

As a result, design time for the new product was cut by more than 50%, from four months to less than eight weeks (SDRC, 1997).

6.3.4 Approaches to 3D modelling

The choice of a modelling scheme should depend on identification of the required properties to be modelled during the design process, together with the type of representation to be used at different stages in the development of the design. The computer aids to be used should be checked to identify whether they are capable of supporting the full range of attributes to be modelled, and that the receiver of any communication is able to receive it in computer-based form (e.g. if the modelling of tolerance is important, will the CAD systems support it; and will the manufacturing organizations be able to receive CAD models in computer-based form, or only as drawings?). Suggested applications for the different 3D modelling techniques are:

Wire-frame models: the generation of view data for 2D draughting; modelling of geometrically simple shapes such as sheet metal components and space frames.

Surface models: used where machining data, volume analysis and picture generation are required, or for the packaging of complex shapes. Used also while a full solid modelling capability is not available, or is inappropriate.

Solid models: are particularly valid for full digital mock-up, assembly evaluation, mass property analysis and interference checking, and for visualization of assemblies.

Once it has been decided that a 3D model is appropriate, the user should answer the questions:

▶ Is it necessary to model all of the component or assembly, or would a limited model, for example of those surfaces to be machined, be adequate?

▶ Are the modelling tools and the system performance adequate for the task? If not, is it possible to simplify the model in order to reduce the complexity of the problem?

6.4 The integration of design analysis and CAD

Many models are used within the design process. As the design is developed the main models represent its structure and form. Gradually, detail of material, dimension and surface condition are added. Successive models form the basis for the **evaluation** of the design, and the **generation** of further information, especially for manufacture. This section will address in particular design evaluation – the generation of information about the design that allows a judgement to be made about its fitness for purpose.

A design has to be judged in many respects. It has for example to have adequate structural, thermal and dynamic performance, satisfactory weight and weight distribution, and resistance to wear and to damage by corrosion and impact. In general, different techniques are required to evaluate the design in each of these respects. In some, data may be extracted directly from the design geometry – either by inspection (e.g. an engineer may be able to identify the susceptibility to corrosion simply from an inspection of design geometry and a knowledge of the materials involved), or by direct manipulation of the model by some algorithm. In most cases, however, it is necessary to use a supplementary model of the design that we will term an auxiliary model (McMahon *et al.*, 1995). Examples of auxiliary models are mathematical models used in automatic control, or finite element models for stress analysis. Auxiliary models may be transient – developed for the purposes of making an assessment, but no longer required except for the purposes of documenting the design process once the assessment is made. They may also be more permanent, and developed and refined as the design progresses. For example, a finite element model may be refined or adapted in the light of changes in the emerging design.

In some cases the properties of a design will be complex functions of its other properties. For example, an evaluation of the durability of an automotive suspension system would be based on an evaluation of stress states in the component parts, in turn based on analysis of the loads arising from dynamic loading of the suspension system through the tyre and from cornering and braking loads. Product performance properties may thus be evaluated from other attributes, through a series of auxiliary models constructed for different purposes. This implies a series of potentially complex interconnections and interactions between the many models used in the design process. To generate the auxiliary models themselves, the designer often has to extract information from the geometric representation, and combine this with information about loads, material properties and so on. It is in this area, and in the direct manipulation of geometric models for analysis, that the CAD system is of most assistance.

6.4.1 Direct assessment from the geometric model

The scope of direct assessment is mainly confined to the extraction of geometric property data from the model. This includes:

▶ the slope and curvature of curves;

▶ normal vectors and curvature of surfaces;

▶ perimeter, area, centre of area and moments of area of closed planar profiles;

▶ volume, surface area, mass and inertial properties of closed volumes and volumes defined by swept profiles.

In this section, discussion will be largely confined to the computation of the geometric properties of profiles, and of volumes derived by sweeping profiles. These and other **geometric analyses** essentially involve subdivision of the region of interest into a number of elemental shapes, and the numerical integration of the properties of those shapes, generally by simple summation. These analyses are based on the standard integral functions that give the properties of closed planar profiles and of closed volumes. For example, for an arbitrary planar profile the key area properties are:

$$\text{Area} = \iint dx \, dy$$

$$\text{First moment about } Ox = \iint x \, dx \, dy$$

$$\text{First moment about } Oy = \iint y \, dx \, dy \qquad \textbf{(6.1)}$$

$$\text{Second moment about } Ox = \iint x^2 \, dx \, dy$$

$$\text{Second moment about } Oy = \iint y^2 \, dx \, dy$$

The actual numerical integration of these integral functions is achieved in CAD by using similar geometric approximations to those used in computer graphics. Curves in profiles are approximated by sequences of lines forming a polygonal boundary, and numerical integration is carried out for the lines in this boundary. By taking this approach, arbitrary profiles may be used as the basis for geometric analysis: the shape may comprise multiple boundaries with internal islands, and these may include various curve types – they are all reduced for the purposes of analysis to a series of lines that approximate the shape to a certain tolerance. The computational problem is therefore reduced to that of determining the properties of an arbitrary polygon. This may be achieved by summing the properties of the trapeziums formed by each line and the coordinate system axes, or the triangles formed by each vector and an arbitrary point. The mathematical basis of the numerical integration, and of one approach using the summation of trapeziums, is outlined in the bracketed section below.

The mathematical basis of 2D section analysis

Wilson and Farrior (1976) show how the 2D integrals for the properties of closed planar profiles above can be transformed for computational purposes using Green's theorem into 1D line integrals, for both simply and multiply connected regions. Green's theorem for a general curve L bounding a region R indicates that:

$$\iint_R \left(\frac{\partial M}{\partial X} + \frac{\partial N}{\partial Y} \right) dx\, dy = \int_L (M\, dy - N\, dx) \qquad (6.2)$$

When this theorem is used with $M = 0$, then:

$$Area = \iint_R dx\, dy = \int_L y\, dx \qquad (6.3)$$

As noted, for analytic boundary curves the integrals may be evaluated approximately by considering a series of lines approximating the curves. Let us consider the analysis of the area, centre of area and second moment of area of a planar shape, as shown in Figure 6.18. It is assumed that the shape lies wholly within the $+x$, $+y$ quadrant of the defining coordinate system, and that it is described as a series of lines. The properties are therefore obtained by considering trapeziums formed by the profile lines and the coordinate system axes.

Consider trapezium $\mathbf{p}_{i-1}$, $\mathbf{p}_i$, B, A in Figure 6.19. We can write (with respect to the x-axis):

$$Area = (x_i - x_{i-1}) \times (y_{i-1} + y_i)/2 \qquad (6.4)$$

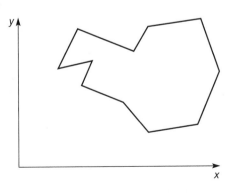

FIGURE 6.18

Planar shape for analysis.

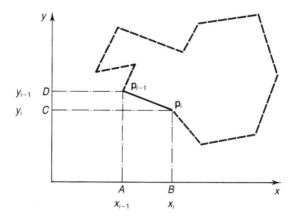

FIGURE 6.19

Analysis of a polygon.

and, for the y value:

$$\text{Centre of area} = (y_i^2 + y_i y_{i-1} + y_{i-1}^2)/3(y_i + y_{i-1}) \qquad \textbf{(6.5)}$$

The second moment of area about Ox, I_{Ox}, is given by:

$$I_{Ox} = (x_i - x_{i-1}) \times (y_{i-1}^3 + y_{i-1}^2 y_i + y_{i-1} y_i^2 + y_i^3)/12 \qquad \textbf{(6.6)}$$

Similar expressions apply for the trapezium $\mathbf{p}_{i-1}$, $\mathbf{p}_i$, C,D, with respect to Oy. The properties for the whole shape are achieved by summing these values for each trapezium, proceeding around the boundary in either direction. For example, for the whole polygon in Figure 6.19, taking $\mathbf{p}_0 = \mathbf{p}_n$:

$$\text{Area} = \sum_{i=1}^{n} (x_i - x_{i-1}) \times (y_{i-1} + y_i)/2 \qquad \textbf{(6.7)}$$

Centre of area x_c, y_c, taking a weighted average:

$$y_c = \left[\sum_{i=1}^{n} (x_i - x_{i-1}) \times (y_i^2 + y_i y_{i-1} + y_{i-1}^2) \right]/6 \times \text{Area} \qquad \textbf{(6.8)}$$

$$x_c = \left[\sum_{i=1}^{n} (y_i - y_{i-1}) \times (x_i^2 + x_i x_{i-1} + x_{i-1}^2) \right]/6 \times \text{Area} \qquad \textbf{(6.9)}$$

Second moment of area about Ox:

$$I_{Ox} = \sum_{i=1}^{n} (x_i - x_{i-1}) \times (y_{i-1}^3 + y_{i-1}^2 y_i + y_{i-1} y_i^2 + y_i^3)/12 \qquad \textbf{(6.10)}$$

and about Oy:

$$I_{Oy} = \sum_{i=1}^{n} (y_i - y_{i-1}) \times (x_{i-1}^3 + x_{i-1}^2 x_i + x_{i-1} x_i^2 + x_i^3)/12 \qquad \textbf{(6.11)}$$

The sign of the results depends on the direction taken, and so absolute values should be used.

Three-dimensional section analysis

Three-dimensional analysis functions commonly provided in CAD systems include those for planar shapes projected in the z-direction (Figure 6.20) and for profiles revolved around one of the principal axes of the coordinate system (Figure 6.21). The techniques used in these cases are relatively simple extensions of those required for the computation of area properties for closed profiles. For example, the volume of a profile projected in the z-direction is simply the projection distance multiplied by the area of the profile. For rotated profiles, the mass properties may be obtained by summing the properties of a series of truncated cones defined by the lines in the profile. When dealing with volumes of revolution, caution should be taken to ensure that the region does not cross the axis of revolution, or an ill-defined problem will result. For further details on the theoretical background to such analyses, the reader is again referred to Wilson and Farrior (1976).

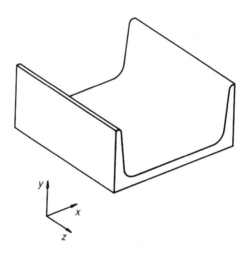

FIGURE 6.20

A shape projected in the z-direction.

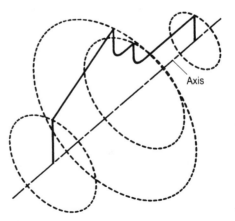

FIGURE 6.21

A shape rotated about axis.

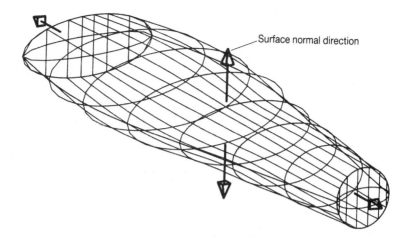

Surface normal direction

FIGURE 6.22
A surface-bounded
shape for volumetric
analysis.

Analysis of 3D surface-bounded shapes or solids

The section analysis techniques above may be extended into three dimensions for analysis of the volumes bounded by surfaces. In this case the summation involves numerical integration over the surfaces themselves, for example by summing the volumes of the prismatic shapes defined by projecting the polygonal faces of the body to the origin. For a convex body, the sign is given by the direction of the normal to the surface. Figure 6.22 shows an example of a surface-bounded body. This figure also shows the surface normals which are used by the system to determine which side of a surface is solid. It may be necessary with surface models for the user to ensure (by inspection) that the boundary is closed and does not include any overlapping surfaces.

Finally, consider the volumetric evaluation of a solid body. An approach may be to use a modification to the ray-tracing approach used for hidden-surface removal in computer graphics, as introduced in Section 4.6.4. In this case a series of 'rays' is projected at a solid model and intersection between these and the faces of the model computed. Approximate mass properties may be obtained by summing the properties of the ray segments within the body, and the precision obtained may be varied by varying the number of rays used for the analysis.

6.4.2 Generation of new models from the geometric model

The example of the use in mechanisms analysis of a model of the design other than the geometric model has already been introduced. The kinematic or dynamic analysis of a mechanism is based on a knowledge of its structure and topology – the constituent links, and how they are joined to other links through joints – together with the loads and the mass properties of the links. In a mechanism, the link dimensions and connections may easily be identified by inspection of the geometric model. The mass properties may also be extracted from the geometry using the techniques given in Section 6.4.1. The CAD model thus provides a good basis for generation of input for such analysis.

6.4.3 Finite element analysis

Of the many analyses that may be applied in engineering design, one family of techniques, known as the finite element method (FEM), has come to dominate. The method is applied to all manner of analytical tasks such as stress, vibration, thermal, electromagnetic and fluid flow analyses (it is in fact applicable to any field problem) and the method is well described in texts such as Zienkiewicz and Taylor (1989, 1991). The FEM solves complex problems, as does geometric analysis, by the numerical solution of a large number of simpler problems that together approximate the true solution. Typically, the problem **domain** – the region that is being modelled (e.g. an engineering component) – is subdivided into a number of simple primitive shapes, known as **finite elements** (where finite implies 'not infinitesimal', rather than 'not infinite'), which are defined and located by the position of points in the domain known as **nodes**. The elements are joined to adjacent elements along common faces and edges, where they may share nodes, in particular at element corners. The collection of nodes and elements describing the whole model is known as a **mesh**. To the mesh are applied boundary conditions, such as specified loads, temperatures and displacements. The distribution of the property of interest within the element is approximated by some shape function (e.g. describing element strain in a stress/displacement analysis), which may be described by a set of equations. The equations for all of the elements in the mesh may be solved simultaneously, by numerical analysis, to obtain an approximate solution to the whole problem.

This section will consider the preparation of data for the FEM, and how this may be helped by the extraction of information from the design model.

Finite element modelling

There are essentially three stages involved in applying the FEM to an engineering problem:

▶ proposing some idealization of the problem – for example, an approximation of the geometry, material properties, constraints and loads – and using this idealization as the basis for the generation of an input into an analysis;

▶ execution, or **processing** of the analysis;

▶ interpretation of the results.

The first part, data preparation, is commonly known as **pre-processing**, while the interpretation is called **post-processing** – they occur respectively before and after the processing of the analysis. The various activities of the pre-processing phase are shown in more detail in Figure 6.23. It can be seen from this figure that a significant part of the pre-processing involves deciding how the geometry may be approximated for the purposes of the analysis, and then how this approximation may be subdivided into the nodes and elements of a mesh.

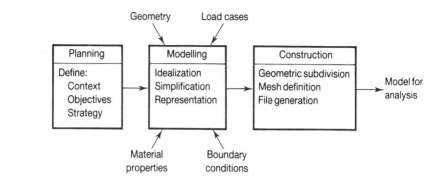

FIGURE 6.23
Stages in finite
element
pre-processing.

Graphical aids for pre-processing

The subdivision of the part geometry into a suitable mesh of nodes and elements for finite element analysis is known as **mesh generation**, and this activity has become a very important part of computer-aided engineering. The quality of the mesh is critical to the overall quality of the analysis, and historically much of the effort of model preparation has been involved in mesh generation. To carry out the geometry subdivision by hand and then to transcribe the node and element information into numerical data for input into the finite element program is very time consuming and error prone, and it is also difficult to identify errors in the mesh – such as unconnected or missing elements – from numerical data. A number of graphical techniques have therefore been developed to assist both in the subdivision of shapes and in examining meshes for geometric and topological correctness.

A large number of approaches to mesh generation have been developed, such that it is now possible to obtain satisfactory meshes for quite complex geometries automatically or semi-automatically. A useful classification of the approaches to mesh generation has been proposed by Ho-Le (1988), and we will use an adaptation of his classification here. For simplicity the examples shown here are for the most part for 2D (planar) meshes only, although the techniques shown are for the most part extendible to three dimensions.

Ho-Le's classification is based on the sequence in which nodes and elements are constructed in the mesh, and on the method for obtaining an initial distribution of nodes or elements. A graphical interpretation of the classification is shown in Figure 6.24, from which it may be seen that three broad classes of approach are further subdivided into six techniques that are more or less widely used.

The most common approach to mesh generation that has been used for many years by most commercial mesh generation systems is the **mapped element** technique. In this approach the geometry is divided into simple regions (e.g. of three or four sides (in two dimensions), or four, five or six faces (in three dimensions)), into the parametric space of which meshes are mapped from unit triangles, squares, wedges or cubes (Figure 6.25(a)). The meshes so produced are sometimes called **structured meshes** because of their regular nature (Mottram and Shaw, 1996). Figure 6.26 shows an example of such a mesh using both triangular and quadrilateral elements. Transition regions are used to join areas of different mesh density (Figure 6.25(e)). The second approach in the classification, **conformal mapping**, is a variant of the mapped

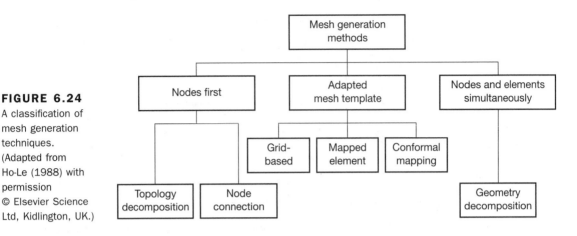

FIGURE 6.24
A classification of
mesh generation
techniques.
(Adapted from
Ho-Le (1988) with
permission
© Elsevier Science
Ltd, Kidlington, UK.)

element approach, in which the mapping is from one polygon space to another. It is more general than the mapped element approach, but is difficult to control.

Structured meshes for complex geometries often require quite considerable skill on the part of the analyst, both in the initial subdivision of the shape and in the determination of the required density of nodes and elements, but a well-constructed structured mesh is likely to give good analysis results. The remainder of the techniques that we will consider produce meshes with more or less irregular forms or topologies, which are therefore often known as **unstructured** or **free** meshes (Mottram and Shaw, 1996). The approaches that produce such meshes form the basis for those techniques for automatic mesh generation with little or no human intervention. The particular techniques are as follows:

▶ The **topology decomposition** method works by recursively removing triangles from a polygonal part boundary, by connecting vertices, until only a triangular region remains (Figure 6.25(b)). Each of the triangular regions so obtained may then be meshed by a straightforward decomposition procedure.

▶ In the **node connection** approach (Figure 6.25(c)), nodes are first added to the polygon boundary at some appropriate distribution, interior nodes are generated – for example, by dividing the area into a number of zones and generating smoothing random nodes in these zones – and then the nodes are connected to form elements. These are usually triangular for 2D meshes, or tetrahedral for 3D meshes. The element formation is typically achieved by Delauney triangulation (Cavendish *et al.*, 1985), the basis of which is described in the bracketed section on page 192.

▶ The **grid-based** approach is based on mapping of a standard grid onto the shape to be meshed, cutting the grid at a boundary, and then moving nodes near the boundary onto the boundary (Figure 6.25(d)). Related techniques are the **quadtree** and **octree** methods for recursive subdivision of shapes into squares or cubes (Yerry and Shephard, 1984), as introduced in Section 3.4.3 in the context of volume modelling.

BEFORE

AFTER

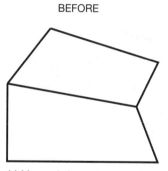 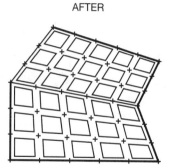

(a) Mapped element approach

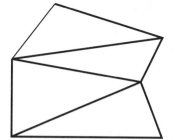 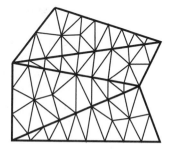

(b) Topology decomposition

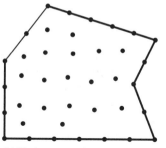 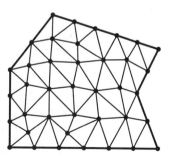

(c) Node connection approach

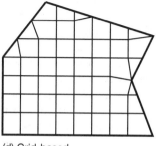 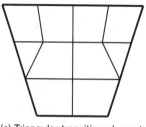

(d) Grid-based

(e) Triangular transition elements

FIGURE 6.25
Approaches to FE
mesh generation.
(Adapted from
Ho-Le (1988) with
permission ©
Elsevier Science Ltd,
Kidlington, UK.)

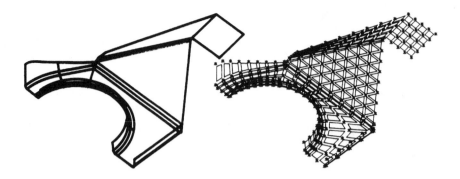

▶ The **geometry decomposition** approaches, which generate nodes and elements simultaneously, involve a number of iterative or recursive methods for geometric subdivision. For example, one approach inserts nodes into the boundary of a convex object, then divides the object roughly in middle of its 'longest axis', inserts nodes into the 'split line' so obtained, and repeats the process recursively for the two halves so formed, until some specified mesh precision is obtained. Another geometry decomposition approach is the **advancing front** method, in which successive layers of elements are defined around the boundary of a body, each layer inside the previous, until the whole body is filled.

Delauney triangulation

Delauney triangulation is a technique for joining the points in a 2D space with triangles, and in a 3D space with tetrahedra. It has the merit that, for the 2D case at least, the shape of the resulting triangles is good for finite element analysis – they have the largest possible internal minimum angles for the point set, and thin, wedge-shaped triangles are avoided. The triangulation is also unique – it is independent of the order of the sample points for all but trivial cases.

The triangulation technique is closely related to the **Direchlet** or **Voronoi tesselation** for the point set. For the 2D case, these tesselations divide the region between the points into a number of polygonal regions called tiles, in which each point is the interior point for a single tile. All other positions within the tile are closer to the interior point than any interior point of another tile. The Direchlet tesselation appears as a set of polygons, the line of which are mid-way between pairs of points in the space. The Delauney triangulation is generated by connecting all points that share a common tile edge (Bourke, 1989). Figure 6.27(a) shows the Direchlet tesselation and Delauney triangles for a small set of points in 2D space.

The triangulation is carried out by repeatedly considering points in a space, and testing them against existing triangles. For each triangle in the mesh, a circumcircle is formed that passes through the points of the triangle. If a point being considered lies within the circumcircle of one or more triangles, then

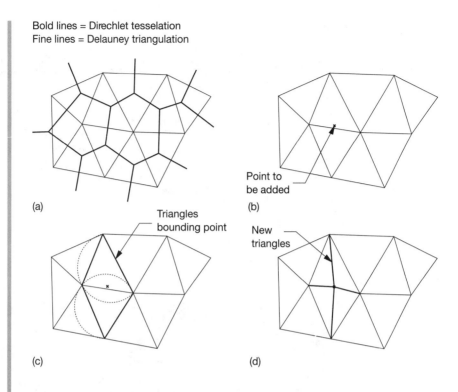

Bold lines = Direchlet tesselation
Fine lines = Delauney triangulation

(a)

(b)

Point to
be added

Triangles
bounding point

New
triangles

(c)

(d)

FIGURE 6.27
Delauney
triangulation and
Direchlet
tessalation.

these triangles are deleted and replaced by new triangles formed between the point being tested and the vertices of the polygon enclosing the deleted triangles. This process is first started by drawing a supertriangle that encloses all of the points being considered, and then each point in the point set is tested. When all points have been considered, triangles connected to the vertices of the supertriangle are deleted (Bourke, 1989). Figures 6.27(b)–(d) show the three stages in the consideration of a point in an existing mesh.

Many modern CADCAM systems include a number of techniques for both mapped element and automatic mesh generation. For example, Figure 6.28 shows a comparison of mapped and free meshes for the same part geometry produced using the same software system. There is still considerable discussion of the merits of the two approaches. Free meshing allows complex geometries to be meshed in very much less time than traditional mapped meshing would have required, but many analysts suggest that caution should be exercised in the use of automatic meshes. In particular, poorly shaped elements may be generated, and the distribution of elements may be inadequate to give a satisfactory modelling of stress distribution, especially where there are large stress gradients. Similar comments could be made about the use of mapped meshing by an inexperienced user, and therefore a general comment is that the satisfactory application of FEM requires an understanding of the theoretical basis of the approach and of the practical limitations of its application.

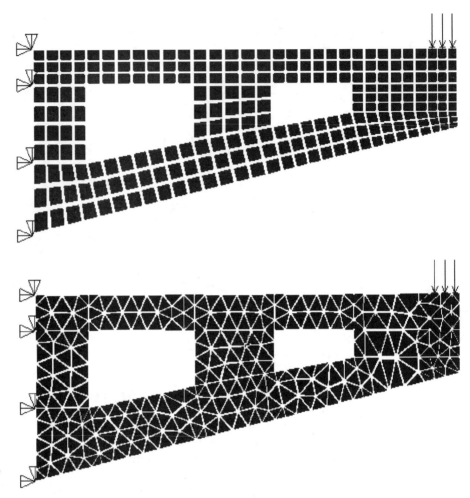

FIGURE 6.28
An example part
with (a) mapped
meshes and (b) free
meshes.

Some of the limitations of automatic meshing may be overcome by the use of **mesh adaptation** techniques which locally modify mesh density – either by moving or adding nodes and elements, or by systematic subdivision of elements – based on an error estimation from an analysis, and on stress gradients within the model (Drake and Manoranjan, 1996). An alternative approach to refinement is to modify the polynomial basis used for the interpolation of displacement within the element.

Graphical aids to pre-processing

Graphical and visual techniques also contribute to data preparation. It is impossible to check the correctness of large data files in any other way. Simply plotting the mesh is useful, although it can be confusing with 3D models unless hidden lines are removed (as shown in Figure 6.29). Plotting will not, however, detect all errors, and therefore special techniques (e.g. element **shrinking**, in which the element is shown

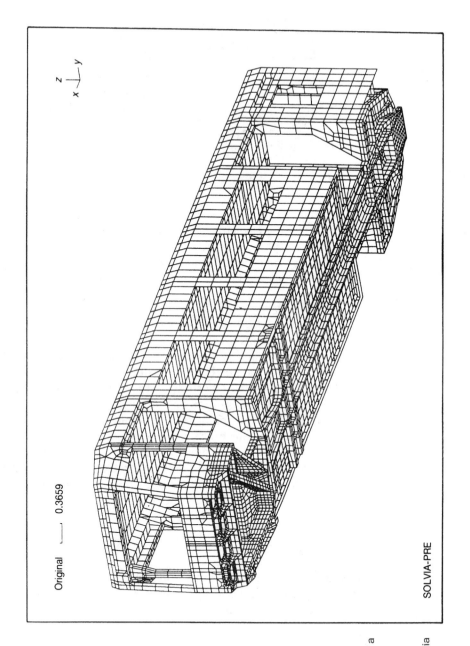

Original ⌐———⌐ 0.3659

SOLVIA-PRE

FIGURE 6.29
Hidden-line plot of a mesh of a railway vehicle body. (Reproduced by permission of Solvia Engineering AB.)

FIGURE 6.30

Principal stresses in the loaded example part – the figure also shows the deformation of the part.

smaller than its true size, as shown in Figure 6.28) have been developed to find such things as missing elements or elements of incorrect thickness.

Finally, graphical aids are also used in pre-processing to allow the user to inspect the boundary conditions. Figure 6.28 shows symbols used by a typical pre-processor to represent loads and displacement constraints in stress analysis.

Graphical aids to post-processing

At the post-processing stage the examination of results is again complicated by the sheer volume of numerical output that often results from the FEM. Aids for interpretation of results are practically essential. The most widespread are techniques for displaying results, especially stresses, strains and temperatures, as plots, such as the contour plot (Figure 6.30 shows a plot of principal stress in the loaded part of Figure 6.28). The introduction of colour graphics has made contour plotting even more effective because colour bands are very easy to interpret. Displacements can also be shown as contours, but the most popular way of exhibiting them is by way of a plot of displaced shape, magnified by some suitable factor as also shown in Figure 6.30. The displaced shape is useful for showing the way in which a structure 'works' under particular loads, although it can be misleading if too large a scaling (displacement amplification) factor is chosen.

Interfaces to CAD

Clearly one of the bases for the FE model is the component geometry. Transcription errors can be minimized if the CAD model can be used directly for the development of the mesh. This is achievable in one of two ways:

▶ The CAD system may interface to a dedicated FE pre-processor, or to the preprocessor in an analysis suite, which must therefore be capable of receiving geometric data from the CAD system. Increasingly, this is facilitated by the development of data exchange standards such as IGES and STEP, as will be discussed in the next chapter.

▶ The CAD system may itself incorporate a mesh generator, such that FE models may be generated directly from the component geometry. (There may be other

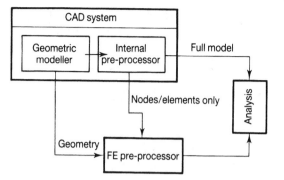

FIGURE 6.31
Alternative routes to
FE model
generation.

variations, in which the CAD system incorporates an FE solver, or the FE system incorporates a geometric modeller.)

These two approaches are summarized diagrammatically in Figure 6.31, together with a third, compromise approach in which the mesh is generated by the CAD system, and the FE modeller adds the boundary condition and material data.

At first sight it would appear eminently sensible to use the second approach in order to take full advantage of the existing geometric descriptions in the CAD system database. In practice, however, there are a number of limitations:

▶ Specialized pre-processor software sometimes has more advanced facilities than those provided by CAD systems (although some CAD vendors specialize in mesh generation, and their systems have very significant FE mesh generation capability). Companies may also wish to use different software for different tasks, to take advantage of their various merits.

▶ The geometry used for FE analysis is generally a simplified or idealized version of the geometrical model in the CAD system. The simplification or removal of detail is by no means an easy task and depends on the analyst's judgement and experience (e.g. Figure 6.29 above shows the simplification in representing a railway coach bodyshell). Furthermore, the definition of the simplified geometry for a mesh generator is only a relatively small part of the total mesh generation task, and therefore efficiency of geometry manipulation is a minor consideration in the task.

The chosen meshing route is to some extent a matter for pragmatism – if the geometry is complex and the meshing approach is straightforward, then the reuse of the CAD model geometry is important. If the geometry is relatively straightforward, but the model is complex (in particular, for example, if customization or complex material characterization aspects of the pre-processor are important), then the approach should be based on the most appropriate pre-processor. What is important is to ensure that, if at all possible, the geometric idealization is based directly on the CAD model geometry to minimize the risk of error. In the longer term, the development of data exchange standards of wide scope, such as the ISO STEP initiative, will allow the increasing interoperability of software, and shared use of databases.

6.5 System customization and design automation

So far we have discussed those aspects of the application of CAD that involve facilities provided either as parts of systems or by third-party software vendors. In many cases, however, a company which uses CAD may wish to develop the system to meet its specific needs – for example, to provide features not included in the base system, to automate routine tasks such as the completion of housekeeping records, or to incorporate in-house analytical methods. Such tasks may be grouped under the general heading of **system customization**. The topic is particularly important, because in many applications it may be the key to the profitable use of CAD.

In many companies, particularly those which regularly produce designs or design elements that are simple variations on a standard theme, the automation of routine tasks may extend to drawing or geometric modelling activities for standard components of variable dimensions, or even to automation of the design to the extent of including design rules, algorithms and calculations in the CAD system. This whole area has seen an explosion of developments in recent years. Systems are in widespread use in which variations in shapes can be generated automatically according to algebraic expressions or relationships between dimensional parameters. Other systems exist in which rules and algorithms can be captured to allow design expertise to be incorporated into knowledge-based engineering systems in order to automate to some extent the production of standard designs or design elements. In more experimental approaches, techniques from artificial intelligence have been applied to CAD problems. We will return to all of these topics in Chapter 8, when we discuss techniques for adding intelligence to CAD. In this present chapter we will consider those techniques that can allow standard CAD systems to be customized by the incorporation of system commands into command files or into high-level languages, or the provision of interfaces to external computer programs. Thus, for example, the steps required to draw or model a component may be programmed and combined with code to compute the dimensions and to process user input.

6.5.1 The scope of customization and design automation

The scope of system customization is extremely broad. At one end of the spectrum it includes such simple facilities as providing the ability to execute a small series of commands in a single step, perhaps by selection of an **icon** on the screen. This might be used, for instance, by a designer to set the colour, line-style and level numbers to be used for a drawing. At the other extreme it may involve the automation of major parts of the design task. Within these two extremes some examples of customization activities include 'housekeeping' tasks such as the completion of drawing title blocks and drawing records, and the incorporation of simple analytical routines for component assessment or other design analysis.

The most important aspects of customization are in the extraction of data from a model for use in some other application, or in the drawing or modelling of parts which are variations on a theme. The data extraction aspects are typically for the application of specialized product-specific design analysis programs, but can also be used to integrate major applications with each other. For example, one of the leading computational fluid dynamics (CFD) programs is incorporated into one of the principal mesh generator/CAD modeller packages through the latter's customization facilities.

The modelling of product families can to a great extent be achieved with parametric or variational modelling (see Chapter 8), but if the construction is based on any significant calculation, or if the arrangement of the parts or features of the artefact varies, then a customized approach is still likely to be required. By product family we mean those parts that conform to a standard pattern, for which the dimensions and other aspects of the designs are based on rules that may be expressed by analysis, relationships or tabulated values. Most are broadly geometrically and topologically invariant, but they vary in dimensions – for example, simple parts such as bearings, fasteners, gears and pulleys fall into this category. For more complex parts such as engine pistons or automotive brake components the detail of the geometry and topological arrangement may vary, as may the dimensions. For small assemblies such as pumps and valves the individual parts and their relation to each other vary. Quite major artefacts such as road bridges, motors and gearboxes may also be regarded as essentially standard products, customized to particular applications. All these examples come under the heading of **parametric designs**, in which the part or product may be described in terms of variable parameters, which are varied to produce variations on the artefact. For example, standard metric bolts may be identified in terms of the dimensions shown in Figure 6.32, all of which are related to the nominal bolt size, but in a particular design may be based on the output from a bolted joint calculation.

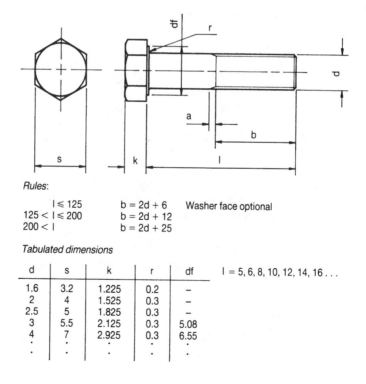

Rules:

$l \leq 125$	$b = 2d + 6$ Washer face optional
$125 < l \leq 200$	$b = 2d + 12$
$200 < l$	$b = 2d + 25$

Tabulated dimensions

d	s	k	r	df	$l = 5, 6, 8, 10, 12, 14, 16 \ldots$
1.6	3.2	1.225	0.2	–	
2	4	1.525	0.3	–	
2.5	5	1.825	0.3	–	
3	5.5	2.125	0.3	5.08	
4	7	2.925	0.3	6.55	
.	.	.	.	.	

FIGURE 6.32
Standard metric bolts: rules and data for a parametric program.

6.5.2 Typical facilities for system customization

As might be expected, those selling CAD systems provide a range of facilities to deal with this variety of tasks. These may be broadly classified into the following categories:

▶ Customizable user interfaces.

▶ **Key-log files**, which allow a series of commands to be recorded, and played back at will.

▶ **Macro languages**, which again allow commands to be recorded in and executed from a file, but with control (such as branching and looping), data entry and user selection commands added.

▶ **Graphics programming languages**, which provide facilities for system commands to be executed as high-level language statements, generally from a hybrid language that is interpreted by the CAD system. The language will normally also offer the data manipulation, program control and data entry facilities that are typical of high-level languages such as Pascal or C.

▶ An application programming interface (API) for the high-level language in which the system was written. Historically, CAD systems were likely to have been written using the FORTRAN language, but C or more probably C++ are today the languages of choice. An API in these languages will normally comprise a library of data structures and procedures for the creation and manipulation of entities in the system database, for extraction of system and entity data, and for user interaction. Procedures will also be defined to bind (also known as link) user-generated code with the system program.

Let us now examine each of these in more depth.

Customizing the user interface

In Chapter 4 the different styles of user interface that are used in CAD were examined. Some types of interface, in particular those that use menus of commands displayed as text or icons on the screen, may be customized in that the user may specify which commands, or sequence of commands, are executed following the selection of a given icon or overlay location. This can be particularly useful in complex systems with lengthy menu selection or command-entry sequences. Operations that are used very regularly may be assigned to icons or to menu options. For example, a user who is predominantly concerned with data preparation for FE analysis, and who uses only a small range of commands, may have the interface customized to allow each of these commands to be selected by a single operation.

Key-log files

Key-log files typically allow all user selections (menu choices, screen position indications, data entry and so on) to be recorded in a file and played back whenever required.

Example applications include operations such as setting up the system to operate in a certain way (e.g. for a particular style of dimensioning), recording start-up sequences (e.g. retrieving a drawing border, scaling the display area and setting levels), recording plot sequences and so on. Some systems allow numeric values to be stored as variables, and by using this facility some limited variation in the construction of geometry may be achieved, but key-logs are normally not sufficiently flexible for parametric parts, because data entry and program control methods are not included.

Macro languages

Where the method of program control is by command entry, then the use of macro languages may allow a customization facility that overcomes many of the limitations of key-logs. Macro languages are methods of allowing sequences of commands to be collected together in a disk file and executed as a single command. They are widely used in operating systems (which are predominantly command-entry systems), the DOS batch file and the Unix command file being two well-known examples. Simply allowing commands to be collected together would, however, just be equivalent to a key-log. Some of the flexibility of a full programming language is introduced by the addition of command constructs specifically for use in a macro file. These include for example:

▶ the facility to ask the user questions, and to store the response, for example as a character variable;

▶ the facility to include parameters, entered by the user on the command line that calls the macro file, in the command sequences;

▶ control constructs, such as branching or looping within the file;

▶ arithmetic operations and named variables.

As an example, let us assume a 2D draughting system with a simple command language as introduced in Section 4.6.2, and that this language has the following command to construct a line between two coordinate pairs:

LN EC x1 y1 x2 y2

meaning 'line, enter coordinates, with coordinate values x1 and y1 for one end and x2 and y2 for the other'. A macro to draw a box between two positions might be:

```
MACRO BOX
LN EC %1 %2 %3 %2
LN EC %3 %2 %3 %4
LN EC %3 %4 %1 %4
LN EC %1 %4 %1 %2
END
```

where %n means 'use parameter n from the command line'. The command to draw a box between positions 0, 0 and 100, 50 would be entered:

BOX 0 0 100 50

Graphics programming languages

The next step on from a macro language is to use a full programming language, with program statements replacing the interactive commands or menu selections that operate the system. Many of the major CAD systems incorporate such languages, usually based on one or more of the established high-level languages. The languages are different, however, in that they only operate as part of the CAD system itself and programs written using the language cannot be executed except as part of the operation of the CAD system. Usually, the system will include an interpreter to execute programs written in the language. This interpreter will normally either read the source code directly (as would a BASIC interpreter on a home computer), or read a file produced by a 'compiler' for the language.

The features of the programming languages include those conventionally found in many high-level languages, such as declarable variables and arrays, control and data manipulation statements, file handling and so on. They also include statements for CAD entity creation and manipulation, and for use of the system's user interface – for example, to display menus to the user, or to ask the user to select entities from the screen or to enter some data. The system entities themselves are often treated as variables. They have to be declared within the program as individual variables or arrays, and geometric or other entities may then be assigned to the variable name, just as numeric values are assigned to numeric variables. Examples of applications of such languages include programs to:

▶ draw standard components, such as bearings or fasteners, in which the component dimensions are stored in arrays within the program;

▶ draw components on the basis of dimensions entered by the user and/or calculated within the programs; examples include test pieces, shafts, gears, valves and even complete assemblies;

▶ customize construction, dimensioning, numerical control or other functions to the requirements of a particular company;

▶ carry out housekeeping duties, such as filling in title block text.

Clearly, the actual form of the program will vary greatly from application to application, but an example of typical program elements, for the construction of parametric part geometry such as that shown in Figure 6.32, is shown in Table 6.2. Appendix B also shows excerpts from a simple program using a Pascal-like language to construct a simple parametric object – a hexagonal nut.

Application programming interfaces (APIs)

Because graphics programming languages are generally interpreted, or compile to a 'pseudo-interpreted' code that comprises calls to the main program procedures, their execution speed is generally fairly slow. Also, because they are not widely used, the implementations of the languages may be less robust than their more celebrated

Table 6.2 Typical elements of a parametric program

1 Initialization	Declare variables and arrays. Assign initial values to variables.
2 Option selection	Allow the user to select options for the program – for example, the type of component or the view required.
3 Data input	Allow the user to input dimensions that specify the component and a reference position for construction.
4 Derived data calculation	Calculate data derived from the input data.
5 Construction	Construct the geometry.
6 Further options	Including deletion of incorrect geometry or return to Stage 2 for further selection.

siblings, such as Pascal, C or C++. Finally, they also have limitations in that they cannot make use of function and procedure libraries for numerical analysis and for graphics, and they often have a relatively limited range of core programming features; for example, the disk file handling facilities may be less extensive than in a mainstream language. Graphics languages are therefore generally limited to low-performance tasks which involve graphics only, or to simple analysis with limited disk file I/O. If it is necessary to use system or library routines or functions then it is preferable to use a compiled language such as C++ for the system customization.

As explained in the introduction to this section, the API normally comprises a library of procedures that may be used for a variety of system functions such as:

Access the data values for model entities

Add, modify and delete geometric entities

Manage part and other files

Access and set system values such as line-style and colour

Create views

Interact with the operator

Output non-graphical data to the graphics screen

Dimension drawings

Add user functions to the applications such as numerical control functions and finite element data preparation

The range of tasks that may be carried out if an API is used is practically unlimited: in principle a completely restyled system is possible. Applications include those listed for graphics programming languages above, and in addition:

▶ implementing system security or accounting;

▶ providing graphical output from analysis programs;

▶ automatically loading parts (e.g. the previous file worked on by the user) when the system is first executed;

▶ incorporating analysis or simulation programs within the CAD system.

Figure 6.33 shows as an example output from a program for the analysis of planar mechanisms. In this program the mechanism configuration is identified interactively from the CAD geometry, and the link motion is drawn by using transformations to move the geometry for the links. The CAD system is also used for the preparation of graphical output from the program.

Our second example of the use of an API concerns the automation of the design of specialized fabricated pipe networks. The networks use a standard design for the pipe junctions and pipe bends, but each bend is custom designed and fabricated according to the bend angle and pipe size. The company designing the pipe networks also wishes to know the lengths of pipe required for each network, the cutting details for each pipe section, and the pipe fittings and flanges required for the networks. The company achieved an automated system by writing an application in which the centre lines of the pipes are modelled as lines, and the junction points and bend locations are modelled as labelled points, with attributes used to record with the network details of pipe and flange sizes. One API application is used to mark up a network model, and once this has been achieved a second application processes this model to obtain, without user intervention, a pipe cutting list for the network and detail drawings of each pipe bend.

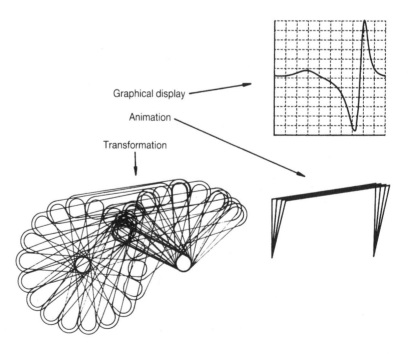

Graphical display

Animation

Transformation

FIGURE 6.33
Example features of a mechanism analysis program developed with an API.

6.5.3 Concluding remarks

The development in modern systems of techniques for automatic parametric modelling, and the growth of knowledge-based systems for design, has perhaps meant that customization facilities are less important for user companies than they used to be. Engineering companies generally wish to concentrate their efforts on their core engineering skills, not on the software engineering effort needed for the development and support of custom facilities. However, the facilities that are provided for system customization not only allow companies to tailor systems to their particular requirements, but also allow third parties to develop add-on facilities for systems. One very well-known PC-based CAD system has achieved a great deal of success in part because it has adopted a very 'open' approach to its system. It has used a straightforward, ASCII part representation that therefore allows third-party developers to access part models, and it has also provided a graphics programming language and software developers' toolkits that have allowed many companies to produce software to work with the system and to enhance its capability. Examples of such enhancements include parametric drawing facilities for standard fasteners, special analysis programs, database conversion software, software for manufacturing applications and so on. Many software vendors are enhancing their systems in this respect by also providing 'toolkits' to allow third parties to develop applications software, and to allow this software to be easily incorporated within the system. The commercial success of future systems may depend on the extent to which they support such development.

6.6 Conclusion

The spectrum of application of CAD is very wide, and industrial practice currently sees activities ranging from computerization of traditional drawing activities through to the complete three-dimensional digital mock-up of aircraft and automobiles. Applications also range from stand-alone systems to extensive integration of CAD with other aspects of product modelling, analysis and simulation. In this chapter the circumstances under which different CAD representation techniques might be applied have been examined, and a pragmatic approach to the choice of technique has been advocated. The full integration of all aspects of design, design analysis and manufacture requires compatible representations of all modelled properties, and the addressing of this issue is a continuing theme.

There have been over the years many claims made about the productivity advantages of CAD. Some of the claims previously made for drawing productivity may have been rather optimistic, but major gains may be made in the customization of a CAD approach to the particular needs of a company. This chapter has outlined the techniques that are used to this end, and has noted the scope of system customization. Increasingly, some of the aspects addressed by customization tools – for example, the programming of families of parts – are being incorporated as standard features of software. Increasingly, also, more sophisticated programming techniques, such as those of artificial intelligence, are being incorporated in the customization tools. This subject will be discussed again in Chapter 8 when the leading-edge developments of CAD are considered.

References and further reading

American Society of Mechanical Engineers. Proceedings of the Computers in Engineering Conferences (a series of conferences containing many interesting papers on computer applications in engineering).

Bourke P. (1989). Triangulate: an algorithm for interpolating irregularly-spaced data with applications in terrain modelling. *Pan-Pacific Computer Conference*, Beijing.

British Standards Institution (1990). *BS1192: Construction Drawing Practice, Part 5: Guide for structuring of computer graphic information*.

Cavendish J. C., Field D. A. and Frey W. H. (1985). An approach to automatic three-dimensional finite element mesh generation. *International Journal of Numerical Methods in Engineering*. **21**, 329–47.

Drake R. and Manoranjan V. S. (1996). Method of dynamic mesh adaptation. *International Journal of Numerical Methods in Engineering*. **39**(6), 939–49.

Ho-Le K. (1988). Finite element mesh generation methods: a review and classification. *Computer-aided Design*. **20**(1), 27–38.

Institution of Mechanical Engineers. Proceedings of the Effective CADCAM Conferences (a series of conferences containing many interesting papers on the practical application of CADCAM).

Kugathasan P. and McMahon C. A. (1997). Generation of viewpoint dependent models for the product introduction process. *Proc. Int. Conf. Engineering Design*, Tampere, **3**, 299–302.

McMahon C. A., Meng X., Brown K. N. and Sims Williams J. H. (1995). A parallel multi-attribute transformation model of design. *Proc. 7th Int. Conf. on Design Theory and Methodology*, 17–21 September 1995, Ward A. C. (ed.), Boston, Ma: ASME, DE-Vol 83, Vol. 2, 341–50.

Mottram J. T. and Shaw C. T. (1996). *Using Finite Elements in Mechanical Design*. London: McGraw-Hill.

NAFEMS (1986). *A Finite Element Primer*. Glasgow: NAFEMS.

Rooney J. and Steadman P. (eds) (1987). *Principles of Computer-aided Design*. London: Pitman.

SDRC (1997). *MEM Electrifies the Market*, SDRC UK Ltd., Hitchin, Herts, UK.

Shephard M. S. (1985). Finite element modelling within an integrated geometric modelling environment: Part 1 – Mesh Generation. *Engineering with Computers*. **1**(1), 61–71.

Shephard M. S. and Finnigan P. M. (1988). Integration of geometric modelling and advanced finite element preprocessing. *Finite Elements in Analysis and Design*, **4**, 147–62.

Wilson H. B. and Farrior D. S. (1976). Computation of geometrical and inertial properties for general areas and volumes of revolution. *Computer-aided Design*. **8**(4), 257–63.

Yerry M. A. and Shephard M. S. (1984). Automatic three-dimensional mesh generation by the modified octree method. *International Journal of Numerical Methods in Engineering*. **20**, 1965–90.

Zienkiewicz O. C. and Taylor R. L. (1989). *The Finite Element Method: Basic Formulation and Linear Problems*. Vol. 1. London: McGraw-Hill.

Zienkiewicz O. C. and Taylor R. L. (1991). *The Finite Element Method: Solid and Fluid Mechanics, Dynamics and Non-Linearity*. Vol. 2. London: McGraw-Hill.

Zienkiewicz O. C. and Zhu J. Z. (1991). Adaptivity and mesh generation. *International Journal of Numerical Methods in Engineering*. **32**, 783–810.

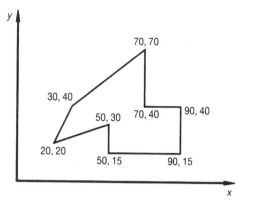

FIGURE 6.34
A profile for
geometric analysis.

Exercises

6.1 Discuss how layers or levels may be used in the organization of an engineering drawing. Can you suggest applications in which there may be particular benefit in using layers? What do you understand by the terms **reference**, **inactive**, **active** and **current** in the context of layers?

6.2 You have been asked to advise a company on the selection of a CAD system for its design and manufacturing activities. The company manufactures moulded parts for consumer durables and the automotive industry. What geometric modelling approach would you advise the company to choose, and what benefits would the CAD system offer the company?

6.3 If you have access to a CAD draughting system, use it to cross-hatch a variety of sectional views of components. Explore the effect of varying the tolerance with which the cross-hatch profiles are represented, if the system allows you to do so. What is the effect of a coarse tolerance?

6.4 Develop an expression for the computation of the volume of a body defined by projecting a polygon normal to its plane of definition, and then use this expression to determine the volume of a 10 mm thick body whose profile is shown in Figure 6.34.

6.5 Using Equations (6.7), (6.10) and (6.11) above, write a program to estimate the area and second moments of area of a circle of radius 50 units, centred at $x = 100$, $y = 100$, assuming that the circle may be approximated by a polygon. What is the error in the estimation of the values if the circle is approximated by (a) an eight-sided polygon and (b) a 24-sided polygon?

6.6 An expression for the volume of a cone is:

$$\text{Volume} = \pi d^2 h/12$$

where d is the major diameter of the cone and h the height. Using this, develop an expression for the volume obtained by revolving a planar profile in the Oxy plane about the Ox axis through 360°. Figure 6.35 shows such a profile. Calculate the volume of revolution for this profile revolved about the Ox axis.

6.7 A two-dimensional ray-tracing approach to the computation of the area properties of closed profiles involves the construction of parallel lines intersecting the profiles, and then the generation of intersection points between the lines and the profile. Area properties are obtained by summing the properties of rectangles whose width equals the separation between the lines, and whose length is the distance between intersection

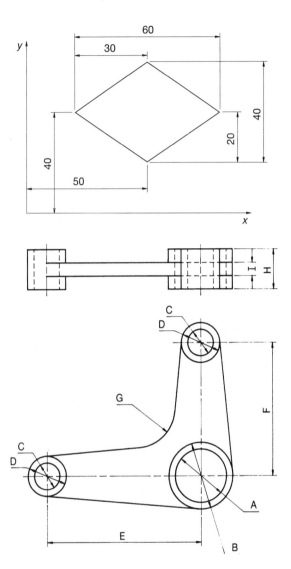

FIGURE 6.35

A profile for a
rotational sweep.

FIGURE 6.36

A bell-crank link.

points for each line. Using this approach find out the accuracy of estimation of the area of a circle 50 units radius if the line separation is (a) 6 and (b) 12 units. You may assume that a line passes through the centre of the circle in each case.

6.8 Discuss how computer graphics may contribute to the generation of models for finite element analysis, and to the subsequent interpretation of results from the analysis.

6.9 Suggest the relative advantages and disadvantages of structured and unstructured meshing for finite element analysis.

6.10 Suggest how the part shown in Figure 6.36 may be subdivided into four-sided regions for meshing for finite element analysis, using a two-dimensional approximation to the three-dimensional shape. Sketch the subdivision of these regions into nodes and elements.

6.11 Figure 6.34 shows an irregular planar polygon in the *Oxy* plane. For this polygon:

(a) Show how it might be divided into quadrilateral finite elements with sides approximately 10 mm long using a mapped element approach.

(b) Show how it might be divided into triangular finite elements with sides about 10 mm long using any two of the node connection, the topology decomposition or the grid-based approaches.

6.12 Exercise 6.10 suggests approximation of the geometry shown in Figure 6.36 by two-dimensional simplification. Suggest how a similar simplification may be used to estimate the mass properties of the shape (and if possible use a CAD system to estimate the mass, centre of mass and other properties of the part). How might more accurate geometric analyses be carried out for the part?

6.13 Outline the steps of a parametric program to draw the two views shown in Figure 6.36 for variable component dimensions. Sketch the entities required in each view, and write down how the program would construct these entities for the input dimensions. If an appropriate CAD system is available write a program to draw these views, given that dimensions A to I are variables.

6.14 Outline the differences between the key-log, macro, graphics programming language and applications programming interface (API) approaches to CADCAM system customization.

6.15 Discuss how you consider the customization capabilities of CADCAM systems should develop in the future.

Projects

$\bullet$

For more information about the subjects for project work, please refer to the end of Chapter 1.

The project activity for this chapter is to explore the facilties in a CAD system for the annotation of the drawings of the project parts, and the application of the CAD models in design analysis. Specific project tasks are:

Project 1 Chess piece Investigate the geometric properties of the chess piece you have defined. Use the geometric analysis functions to calculate volume, mass, centre of mass, surface area and moments of inertia of the part. If possible, carry out the analysis using both surface and solid models of the part, and also compare the analysis results with those for an axisymmetric part, computing the analyses from the two-dimensional profile.

Project 2 Load cell Investigate the geometric properties of the main structural member of the load cell. Use the geometric analysis functions to calculate volume, mass, centre of mass, surface area and moments of inertia of the part. Compare the results of analyses using a two-dimensional profile and a three-dimensional model.

Develop a finite element model for the main structural member of the load cell, loaded as shown in Figure 6.37. If possible, develop both a mapped mesh and a free mesh to model the part, which may be represented by a two-dimensional mesh with thickness. In the case of the mapped mesh, show clearly how the part is subdivided into regions for meshing.

If you have access to a parametric programming language or an API, develop a program to draw a two-dimensional profile of the load cell structural member as a parametric part. Choose a suitable set of defining dimensions for the part.

FIGURE 6.37

Loading of the load cell for finite element analysis.

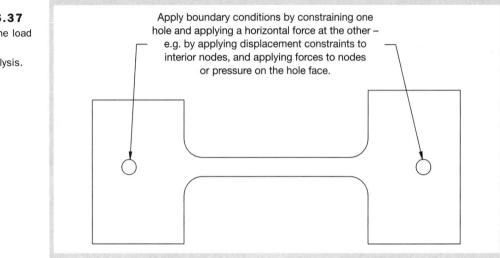

Apply boundary conditions by constraining one hole and applying a horizontal force at the other – e.g. by applying displacement constraints to interior nodes, and applying forces to nodes or pressure on the hole face.

7 Standards for CAD

···

Chapter objectives

When you have completed studying material in this chapter you should be able to:

- ▶ **understand the role of standards in CADCAM;**
- ▶ **understand the way in which standards are applied to graphics, communication and data exchange;**
- ▶ **outline the contribution of graphics standards and packages, and of the X Window System, to computer graphics;**
- ▶ **describe the application of IGES, and of STEP, in CADCAM data exchange;**
- ▶ **outline approaches to computer networking and communications, and the elements of the ISO OSI and TCP/IP approaches to open communications systems.**

Chapter contents

7.1 Introduction

·····················

A critical concern of CAD and of CAM is the communication of design and manufacturing data within an engineering organization and indeed between those organizations involved in the manufacture of a product. The early development of the technology led, however, to a number of software systems and hardware types that were essentially incompatible with each other. Each system vendor used a unique data structure for the storage of the computer models. Each computer manufacturer used a different operating system and, often, there were different rules or protocols for the communication of data between computers (where this was even possible), and from computers to terminals and peripheral devices. While this diversity allowed the very rapid development of the technology, it meant that the computing systems existed in 'islands of automation' that were essentially incapable of communicating with each other, effectively preventing exploitation of one of the potential strengths of the technology.

The divergence in data formats, and in hardware and operating system specifications, also had the effect of tying companies to particular CADCAM systems, while the software vendors found themselves constrained in their choice of hardware by the variety of protocols and operating systems, and by their penchant for modifying hardware in order to improve its performance or usability.

The wish to improve the accessibility of computer languages led early on to the establishment of standards for these. In the same way, the difficulties of incompatibility led to pressure for hardware, software and database standards to isolate programs and programmers from the peculiarities of particular hardware. These allow systems to communicate with each other, and provide some uniformity in the appearance and mode of operation of programs. These standards apply in various situations. Those for computer languages, operating systems and for the presentation of graphics are mainly employed by the software engineers who develop the systems. Communications standards mainly apply at system builder level, while those for the exchange of data influence the activities of the users themselves (although clearly the writing of systems that conform to the standards is a task for the software engineer also). This chapter will concentrate on those standards that apply especially to CADCAM systems and to engineering software – those for computer graphics, for user interface development, and for the exchange of engineering data.

7.2 Graphics and computing standards

Standards in any discipline are not simply imposed by the organizations that are responsible for their development – bodies such as the International Organization for Standardization (ISO), the British Standards Institution (BSI) or the American National Standards Institute (ANSI). Instead, they are developed and approved by committees of experts, usually through a long process of discussion involving drafts, ballots and feedback. They often grow out of standard practice in an industry, although sometimes a new standard may try to influence the direction or pace of development. In the computing industry, established practice is often strongly influenced by a particularly successful approach, company or product that comes to have a strong impact on other products. Sometimes some aspect of a successful product – for example, a language, a file format or a protocol – will form the basis for a standard, but in other cases, even though it may not be officially adopted by a standards body, an approach may be so widely used that it becomes what is known as a *de facto* standard. This is particularly true in the area of peripheral equipment, where for example the protocols used by Tektronix for serial graphics communication for terminals, and the language designed by Hewlett Packard for pen plotters, HPGL, have been very influential. In this chapter we will examine both official and *de facto* standards used in CAD.

Our first concern will be the underlying methods that are used to incorporate graphics into computer programs. In a CAD data structure and indeed in considering data exchange in CAD, a single entity such as a dimension may be quite graphically complex, comprising text and a number of lines. From the computer graphics point of view, the entity will comprise a number of separate graphics primitives. In this section we will deal with the standards that allow such primitives to be drawn on a screen or other graphics device. We will also deal with those graphics standards that allow exchange of images and pictures (rather than CAD models), and govern the interface between the user and the CAD system.

7.2.1 Standards for computer graphics

Standards in computer graphics grew from low-level, device-dependent collections of subroutines supplied by graphics hardware manufacturers into higher-level, device-independent packages designed to introduce a measure of portability to application programs. These packages were first produced by academic or commercial organizations, and typically consisted of a series of subroutines to set up graphics windows and viewports, and to draw simple graphics primitives within them. As well as offering some device independence, they also saved the programmer from developing algorithms for graphics, and allowed new algorithms to be introduced by the package supplier as these became available.

Siggraph CORE

By the late 1970s there were a number of graphics packages in existence, but to achieve portability on a wide scale an industry-wide standard was required. In 1977, the Graphics Standards Planning Committee of the Special Interest Group on Graphics (Siggraph) of the Association for Computing Machinery (ACM) introduced the Core Graphics System (CORE for short), and subsequently refined it in 1979. CORE provided a standardized set of commands to control the construction and display of graphics images, and was independent of hardware or of language. Thus a program written using CORE could be run on any system that had implemented the standard. CORE initially provided for line drawing for both two- and three-dimensional graphics, and in its later versions also included raster operations such as area fill.

Other graphics standards

A little after the CORE system appeared in the United States, work in Europe led to the development of the Graphics Kernel System, or GKS. This standard was initially for two-dimensional graphics, and its development was strongly influenced by the work on CORE (indeed they are practically equivalent for a subset of two-dimensional functions). GKS was adopted as an ISO/ANSI standard, and was extended to cover three-dimensional graphics through the development of GKS-3D. GKS implementations have been made by many hardware manufacturers, for many languages. In Section 7.2.2 below we briefly explore the features of GKS, as an example of a graphics standard.

Although applied in areas as diverse as scientific computing, graphical imaging systems and CAD, GKS is not very satisfactory for dynamic graphics, nor as a tool for programming large graphics applications, for which a variety of alternative approaches have been developed. These include a further standard, the Programmer's Hierarchical Interactive Graphics System (PHIGS), together with a number of proprietary or widely adopted approaches including the X Window System and more recently the OpenGL graphics system, both of which we will explore in more depth later in this section. The PHIGS standard itself has evolved from GKS and CORE, and has features that are derived from each of the earlier standards. For example, input devices and operating modes in PHIGS are the same as those in GKS, while the viewing functions are similar to those in 3D CORE. PHIGS also offers an extended set of primitive graphical elements from which images and models may be constructed, and additional features such as hidden-line and hidden-surface manipulation.

GKS, PHIGS and the other approaches described above are concerned with methods for drawing or plotting graphical entities, and with handling the interaction between the user and the graphics hardware. There is a further set of important graphics standards concerning the storage and exchange of images produced using computer graphics. These standards may be divided into those concerned with images that are a collection of graphics primitives (mainly simple entities, e.g. line, arcs and text), and those concerned with images stored as **bitmaps** (ordered collections of pixels). The former include the Computer Graphics Metafile (CGM), which establishes a format for device-independent definition, capture, storage and transfer of (principally) vector graphics images (in particular those from the GKS, CORE and PHIGS standards), and the companion Computer Graphics Interface (CGI), which provides a procedural interface for the CGM primitives. The latter include a bewilderingly large number of bitmap storage formats including the Graphics Interchange Format (GIF), Tag Image File Format (TIFF or TIF), the Windows™ Bitmap Format (BMP) and many others. We will return to the these in Section 7.2.3 below, after first exploring the basic concepts of the GKS standard.

7.2.2 The Graphics Kernel System (GKS)

As an example of the way in which graphics standards are implemented, and the facilities that they provide, let us look in more detail at the elements of GKS. The standard itself is essentially a form of computer language comprising a series of commands for graphical operations. The graphical parts of a program may be designed as a series of these GKS commands, which are then implemented as procedure, function or subroutine calls within one of the languages to which GKS is bound (such as the C language). Only the GKS names of commands are shown here. For each language to which GKS is bound, these names equate to subroutine or procedure names which are actually used by the programmer in implementing graphics using GKS. This is necessary to accommodate GKS to the specific syntax of each of these languages, and also to allow for symbol naming restrictions: FORTRAN, for example, does not allow names longer than six characters.

GKS is based on a number of elements that may be drawn in an image, known as graphical **primitives**. The basic set of primitives have the reserved word names POLYLINE (to draw a multi-element line), POLYMARKER (to draw points), FILL AREA (for raster fill operations) and TEXT, although some implementations extend this basic set. The syntax of commands for these primitives is:

POLYLINE (n, X, Y)
POLYMARKER (n, X, Y)
FILL AREA (n, X, Y)
TEXT $(x, y, \text{'text string'})$

where n is the number of data points, x is a single and X an array of x coordinates, y is a single and Y an array of y coordinates, and 'text string' is the text to be plotted. For example, if $X = (2.0, 5.0, 3.5, 2.0)$ and $Y = (2.0, 2.0, 5.0, 2.0)$, then POLYLINE $(4, X, Y)$ will draw a triangle with vertices at $x_1 = 2$, $y_1 = 2$, $x_2 = 5$, $y_2 = 2$, $x_3 = 3.5$, $y_3 = 5$.

GKS draws graphical elements into a window defined using a real-valued user coordinate system and transformed into a viewport defined using **normalized device coordinates** (NDCs), in which coordinate values are defined to lie within the range $0 \leqslant x \leqslant 1$ and $0 \leqslant y \leqslant 1$. The viewport is mapped to the device coordinate system of the display hardware by specifying the device characteristics in a **workstation** definition. This allows the programmer using GKS to write for a variety of hardware without making substantial alterations to the program. Multiple windows and viewports may be defined using the commands SET WINDOW (n, x_1, x_2, y_1, y_2) and SET VIEWPORT (n, x_1, x_2, y_1, y_2), where n is the window/viewport number, and $(x_1 y_1)$ and $(x_2 y_2)$ the lower left and upper right corners respectively of the window or viewport. Other commands allow clipping to be switched on and off, and the relative priority of overlapping windows may be assigned with the SET VIEWPORT INPUT PRIORITY command.

Display characteristics for primitives, such as line-style and thickness, colour, text font and text angle, are defined by **attributes**, the values of which are set using the SET command. For example, the SET POLYLINE INDEX (2) specifies that lines should be drawn in a dashed line-style. Each primitive has its own particular meanings for different values of INDEX. GKS also allows attributes to be **bundled**, that is grouped together and modified as a single entity.

The discussions on data structures in Chapter 5 described mechanisms for aggregating entity data into groups which may then be manipulated as a single entity. GKS has a similar facility in the SEGMENT function, which allows commands to be grouped together to describe shapes which may then be manipulated as a single item. Segments are created by delimiting a collection of commands by the statements CREATE SEGMENT (n) – where n is the segment number – and CLOSE SEGMENT. Once defined, the segment may be deleted using the DELETE SEGMENT (n) command, and transformed using the matrix methods that were outlined in Chapter 5. These are applied using the command SET SEGMENT TRANSFORMATION $(n, \mathbf{M})$, where n is again the segment number and $\mathbf{M}$ a transformation matrix in homogeneous form.

Other GKS facilities

It has only been possible within the constraints of this section to provide an overview of some of the features of GKS. Other features of the standard include the handling of user interaction (using a variety of input devices, and comprising facilities for menu selection, element selection from the screen and numerical data entry) and a wide range of levels of operation for input and output (Hopgood *et al.*, 1986).

7.2.3 Standards for exchanging images

The purpose of GKS and other similar standards is to allow graphics to be drawn on a display device by an application program. For example, a CAD system might generate graphics primitives from the CAD model, and display them on the screen using GKS procedure calls. In this process, there are three levels of representation. The CAD model itself comprises geometric, annotation and other entities stored in the CAD system data structure. This model is converted by the CAD system into a series of graphics primitives (e.g. lines of different colour and line-style), and these are then displayed on the screen using the graphics procedures, typically by setting the values of the pixels in a rectangular raster array. The raster array is represented by a region of computer memory known as a bitmap. The three representation levels are therefore CAD entities, graphics primitives and bitmap respectively, as shown in Figure 7.1.

The CAD data structure allows persistent storage of the underlying model, but the process of generating the image from the model is quite time consuming (and requires a software system capable of interpreting the CAD model), and therefore in many cases it may be worthwhile to use and store persistent representations of the images themselves. We may for example wish to use an image in some other application – for example, to incorporate a picture from a CAD system in a technical manual. For these purposes a large number of image storage formats have been developed. These may be divided according to the representation level used for the storage. Images stored at the level of the graphics primitives are stored in **graphics metafiles**, which store graphical data containing device-independent descriptions of pictures. Images stored at the level of the bitmap are stored by making a structured, persistent representation of the bitmap.

A graphics metafile is a formatted computer file containing graphics commands and data. It may be either a trail of the graphics commands used to generate a picture, or a 'snapshot' of the elements that make up the picture. A key feature of a metafile is that it is resolution independent, and can therefore be displayed at different

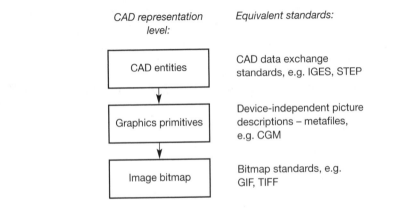

FIGURE 7.1
Representation
levels in computer
graphics.

sizes and scales, and on devices of different resolution. An important metafile standard is the **Computer Graphics Metafile** (CGM – ISO 8632, 1992), which allows pictures to be described as collections of graphics primitives including lines, polylines, arcs, ellipses, filled areas, text and markers such as points or crosses (each of the constructs in GKS has an equivalent in CGM). Attributes allow colours, line widths, text styles and other presentation characteristics to be defined, and additional information in the file allows data precision, font and image types and other details to be specified. The data is stored in one of three encoding formats: Character Encoding, which uses ASCII characters, including control codes; Binary Encoding, which uses binary numbers to represent the data; and Clear Text Encoding, which uses only the printable character set. The last format is verbose, but easy for humans to read, whereas the other two formats are compact but difficult to read (Arnold and Bono, 1988). A brief example of clear-text-encoded CGM, describing two lines of different colours (the numbers in the LINECOLR command are red, green and blue intensity on a scale 0–255; in the LINE command are x, y values), shows the ease with which that format can be read:

```
... BEGPIC;
COLRMODE DIRECT;
BEGPIC BODY;
LINECOLR (0 255 255)
LINE (0,0)(10,10)
LINECOLR(255 255 0)
LINE (0,10)(10,0)
ENDPIC; ...
```

While the CGM provides a means of storing a picture description, a second standard known as the **Computer Graphics Interface** (CGI – ISO 9636) describes an idealized abstract graphics device (known as a virtual device) capable of accepting input and generating, storing and manipulating pictures (Arnold and Bono, 1988). It provides an interface to this idealized device through a **Virtual Device Interface** (VDI). The CGI provides elements for generating and controlling the appearance of graphics primitives (a similar set to that used in CGM), acquiring and setting graphics device characteristics and states, controlling graphics devices, manipulating primitive segments and obtaining graphics input. It also provides functions for creating and manipulating raster bitmaps. The CGI is designed to specify the exchange of information at the level of the VDI, while the CGM captures the descriptions of pictures at the level of the CGI (Arnold and Bono, 1988).

Bitmaps

At the lowest level in the computer graphics hierarchy is the pixel raster displayed on a graphics device. Each pixel in the raster will be assigned a number to allow the value of the pixel colour to be set. One bit per pixel allows only 'black-and-white' images. Colour bitmaps commonly assign 4, 8 or 24 bits/pixel to give 16 or 256 colours, or 256 levels of each of the red, green and blue colour guns respectively

Table 7.1 Common bitmap file storage formats

Format name	File suffix	Compressed	Notes
Windows bitmap format	BMP	No	Proprietary. Came into use with Windows 3.0.
ZSoft file format	PCX	Yes	Proprietary. One of the oldest and most common formats.
Tagged Image File Format	TIFF/TIF	Optional	Widely used, especially for desktop publishing. Several compression schemes.
Graphics Interchange Format	GIF	Yes	Developed and owned by CompuServe. Widely used for the World-Wide Web (WWW).
Joint Photographic Experts Group	JPEG	Yes	ISO/IEC 10918. Uses 'lossy' image compression (removes imperceptible detail) for maximal image compression.
TARGA file format	TGA	No	Proprietary, from Truevision. The first popular format for high-resolution images.

(where multiple bits per pixel are used, the term **pixmap** should strictly be used, but we will retain the term bitmap here (Foley *et al.*, 1996)). The simplest way of storing a bitmap is simply to write the numbers that the pixels represent to the file, together with a header giving information about the file. This is known as uncompressed storage, and is fast but can lead to large files because the size of the file is at least (number of pixels * number of bits/pixel)/8 bytes. The size of the stored file can be reduced by file compression, which takes advantage of coherence in the image (see Chapter 4), for example by recording a series of pixels of the same value as a colour value and a number of occurrences.

A large number of bitmap storage formats have been developed over the years for a variety of purposes. Some of those in common use are shown in Table 7.1.

7.2.4 The X Window System

The pace of change in computer graphics is very rapid, in particular in the area of networked systems, and in the dynamic image manipulation capabilities of graphics hardware. In both respects GKS and PHIGS are limited, and therefore new approaches have been developed to take account of these developments. In this section and the next we will examine two examples of approaches – the X Window System (X) and the Open Graphics Language (OpenGL) – that come into this category and that have widespread application. Both approaches provide not only a standard approach for graphics, but also a means of programming the whole user interface. This is particularly important in modern systems where multiple software packages operate within the same window system. In the early days of CAD, each software system had its own user interface, and there was little compatibility between suppliers. Software suppliers could choose to implement their software without using standards, and indeed many developed specialized hardware to give their systems a performance advantage. Today, the user community wishes its software to operate with a common user interface style, and multi-tasking and multi-processing systems mean that multiple software systems can run simultaneously on the same hardware. Software must therefore be compatible with the window management system and user interface.

No standards exist for window management and the associated user interface that have been approved by the major standards organizations, but a small number of approaches have come to dominate the computer market such that they are in effect *de facto* standards. In particular, the Microsoft® Windows™ products have become ubiquitous for PC hardware, and for workstations the X Window System from the Massachusetts Institute of Technology is an important approach. The former is dedicated to a particular hardware type, but the X Window System allows the development of software systems that may all execute together on a common hardware platform, and that may execute on many different hardware platforms. Furthermore, it enables a user sitting at one computer to execute programs on a remote computer, even of a different type, and still interact with the programs locally. It is the X Window System that we will now discuss.

The X Window System (called X for short) grew out of a project called Athena, initiated in 1984 at the Massachusetts Institute of Technology, which had the aim of allowing computer applications to display output on different hardware from that on which they execute. This work was originally carried out to enable teaching at MIT to use networked graphics workstations from a variety of manufacturers, but the system was made generally available in the late 1980s, and has been widely adopted. In 1988, MIT established a consortium to develop the X Window System and to have it adopted as an ANSI standard. (The X Window System is now managed by the Open Group, formed in 1996 by consolidation of the X/Open Company Ltd and the Open Software Foundation.) Much of the early exploitation of X is based on its revision level 11 (known as X11).

X is an example of a windowing and graphics system that uses the client-server model, as described in Chapter 4. It is capable of simultaneously displaying output from several **client** processes, running on diverse host computers connected via a network to the computer managing the display (the **server** process runs on this computer, and controls not only the screen but also the keyboard and a pointing device such as a mouse with up to five buttons). The output may be displayed in windows using different interface styles, and may incorporate both bitmapped and two-dimensional graphics primitives. (In fact, all screen output in X is ultimately bitmapped. Text is output as bitmapped fonts, and graphics primitive operations are converted into bitmaps.) Furthermore, X allows implementation of programs that are device independent (as do the more traditional graphics standards). If a program uses X it should be unnecessary to change the application code to incorporate a new display device.

Communication between the client and the server is via a graphics description language called the X Protocol. Packets of instructions conforming to this protocol may be sent across a network of any sort (see Section 7.4) between client and server processes. The client process itself manages the interaction through a library of graphics and windowing functions known as Xlib. Many of these functions are similar to those in the GKS standard, described above, and include, for example, the drawing of lines, arcs, rectangles, text and bitmaps with up to 32 bits per pixel (a list of example X functions is given in Table 7.2).

Table 7.2 Example X Window System functions

For manipulating windows

XCreateWindow	creates any kind of window
XDestroyWindow	closes a window and its descendants
XDestroySubwindows	closes the descendants of a window
XMoveWindow	moves a window
XConfigureWindow	changes a window configuration
XQueryTree	returns the window hierarchy
XClearWindow	clears a window to the background colour

Basic graphics commands(* = a multiple element version of this function is also available, e.g. XDrawPoints)

XDrawPoint*	draws a point
XDrawLine*	draws a line
XDrawRectangle*	draws a rectangle
XDrawArc*	draws an arc
XFillRectangle*	sets pixels in rectangle to fill pattern
XFillPolygon	sets pixels in polygon to fill pattern
XSetLineAttributes	sets linestyle and other attributes
XSetFillStyle	sets style for pixel fills
XSetBackground	sets background colour/style

Block operations

XCreatePixmap	create a rectangular array of off-screen pixels in the server; may be drawn in/used like a window
XFreePixmap	free a pixmap
XCreateImage	create a rectangular array of pixels in client memory (can copy to/from server)
XDestroyImage	destroys an image

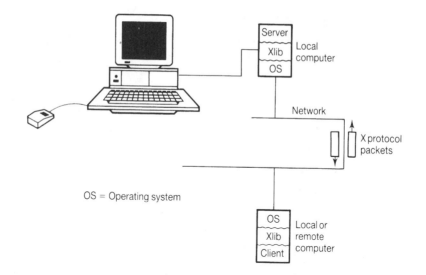

FIGURE 7.2
Client–server
communications
using the X Window
System.

Figure 7.2 shows a schematic arrangement for the client and server communication and the hardware that is controlled by X. Client processes may interact with multiple windows, and in fact multiple clients may interact with a single window. Windows are arranged in a hierarchy: each window may be 'parent' to 'child' windows which are contained entirely within the parent, thus forming a hierarchy of windows on the screen, at the head of which is the 'root' window comprising the whole screen, as shown in Figure 7.3. Otherwise, the way in which the windows are used and arranged on the screen, and the 'look and feel' of the interface, is not dictated by X. Instead, a **window manager**, which is itself a client program, manages the screen and its appearance. The other client programs interact with the window manager in order to obtain screen resources. This, among other things, allows window managers to emulate other windowing systems. Figure 7.4 shows an example of a typical screen appearance generated by a window manager.

Many computer manufacturers and software suppliers have decided to adopt X. All Unix system vendors make it available, and may also incorporate it into their own windowing systems (see discussion of OpenGL in the next section). It has also been implemented for a number of other operating systems and for various hardware. X servers may, for example, be used on personal computers to allow them to be used as X terminals. The look and feel of the X interface may, however, vary from computer to computer depending on the window manager used (although applications using the X protocol will work on all X servers, irrespective of the window manager used). A number of window managers have been developed by the major hardware vendors, although in some cases groups of vendors have joined in consortia to develop a commonly agreed style. More information about X can be found at the Open Software Foundation World-Wide Web site (Opengroup, 1997).

There have also been other developments in the application of X. In its basic form, X, with the Xlib library, allows applications programs to be developed, but it is notoriously difficult to use (windows programming in general is often not straightforward). For this reason a number of toolkits have been developed to assist the programmer

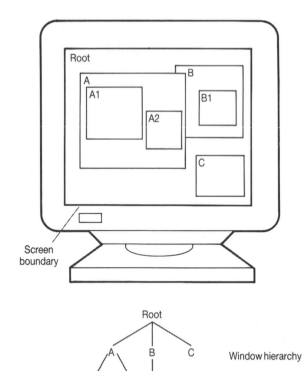

Root

Window hierarchy

FIGURE 7.3
A hierarchy of windows on the screen.

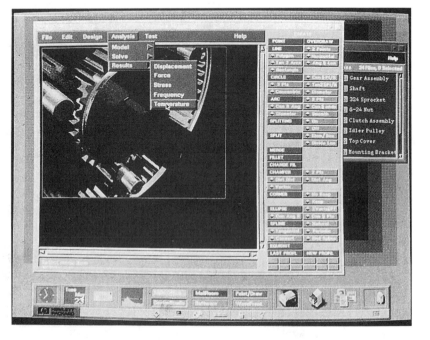

FIGURE 7.4
A typical screen appearance generated by a window manager. (Reproduced by permission of Hewlett-Packard Ltd.)

in building X applications, and it is via these toolkits that the system will for the most part be implemented. A number of utilities have also been written at MIT and elsewhere, and have been included with the system. These include, for example, software for displaying various files, from bitmaps to MPEG 'movie' files (MPEG stands for Motion Picture Expert Group, and is a standard for compressed digital video), and printing and word processing utilities. The continued development of the system is seeing increasing links to existing and developing graphics systems. For example, three-dimensional graphics in the X environment are supported by a combination of PHIGS and X known as PEX (PHIGS Extensions to X), and the OpenGL system that we will now turn to has close links to X.

7.2.5 OpenGL™

X offers a powerful, device-independent means of generating graphical systems and user interfaces, but its device independence and distributed nature means that it can impose a high load on hardware. It also does not exploit to best advantage the graphics accelerator hardware that has been developed to allow dynamic manipulation of three-dimensional models with hidden-surface removal, shading and texturing. For this reason the company Silicon Graphics Inc. (SGI) developed the software interface for graphics hardware known as the Open Graphics Language (OpenGL) that is now controlled by an industry consortium comprising a number of hardware and software vendors that form the OpenGL Architecture Review Board (ARB). OpenGL comprises a set of several hundred procedures and functions that allow a programmer to specify the objects and operations involved in the production of colour graphical images of three-dimensional objects (SGI, 1997). It provides means of drawing and rendering geometric objects (e.g. points, line segments and polygons) and specifying how they should be lit or coloured, and how they should be mapped from the model space to the screen. It is window system independent so that it can be implemented for different window systems – for example, it has been implemented for both X and for Windows NT™.

OpenGL does not require high-performance display hardware to be present, but it does require a frame buffer – memory that stores the raster display bitmap. OpenGL draws directly into the frame buffer, but also allows the use of multiple buffers where, for example, one buffer is displayed while a second is being updated (known as double buffering). OpenGL integrates with X and may use the X server to execute commands, but if the program is running on the same machine as high-performance graphics hardware the X server can be bypassed to obtain the highest performance.

7.3 **Data exchange standards**

In many parts of the engineering industry the increasing application of CAD has been accompanied both by growth in product variety and a broadening of the range of companies involved in the design of a particular product. For example, the traditional approach in the automotive industry was for many component parts to be designed by the car manufacturers themselves, and then manufactured to instructions

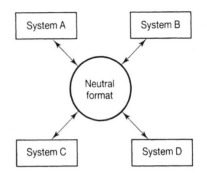

by component suppliers. The trend today is for design authority for an increasing number of components to be delegated to the suppliers, and the extra variety means that these suppliers have to match their designs to a number of variants of particular vehicles. To support this process, a great deal of data concerning vehicle and component designs has to be exchanged between the various companies in the industry. In order for this transfer to be accomplished quickly and accurately, the CAD systems employed by the various manufacturers should be capable of exchanging data with each other.

The easiest way for two companies to exchange data is for them both to use the same CADCAM software, operating at the same revision level. Many of the larger manufacturers have indeed put pressure on their suppliers to adopt the same system as themselves, but a more equitable solution is for the various CADCAM systems in the market to be able to exchange data with each other. In the early days this was achieved by the development of special translator programs to convert data from one particular system into a format acceptable to another. As the number of systems increases, however, this leads to an explosion in the requirements for translator programs – for N systems the number needed is ultimately $N \times (N - 1)$. The solution is to effect the data exchange by first translating into a neutral file format, and then from this neutral format into the target system data structure, as shown in Figure 7.5.

The neutral file solution is easier said than done. Manufacturing today is very much an international business. A given automobile design may be assembled in more than one country, from components manufactured in several countries. Sources of engineering software are less diverse, but nevertheless there is also an international element. The neutral file should therefore be to an internationally agreed standard. The greatest difficulty, however, is the wide variety of representations that are used within the CAD industry. It has already been seen that systems may be for 2D draughting only, or may allow wire-frame, surface or solid models. Even within a given model type there are variations: some systems, for example, limit surface descriptions to a cubic polynomial basis. Others may use polynomials of much higher order, and clearly it will be impossible to translate surfaces from such systems to those that use cubics without at least some loss of precision.

Nevertheless, despite the difficulties, the benefits to be obtained from effective data exchange have led to substantial efforts since the end of the 1970s, prompted in particular by the automotive and aerospace industries (with pressure especially from the military sector). This effort has concentrated especially on the exchange of geometric data which is vital for the description of the *form* of components, and has been partially successful. The development of standards is, however, still very much in progress.

The historical development of CAD data exchange

Perhaps the first significant work in data exchange was the establishment in 1979 of an Initial Graphics Exchange Specification (IGES), supported by the US National Bureau of Standards (and eventually adopted by ANSI in 1981), and now controlled by an organization known as the IGES/PDES Organization (IPO). This standard was developed mainly by major US CAD vendors, and was very much influenced by the CAD and data storage technologies used by a few key players in its development (early versions were based on the Boeing Database Standard Format (DBSF)). The basis for IGES is the storage in a file of details of entities to be transferred between systems. The early IGES dealt with entities used in draughting and simple 3D modelling systems, and incorporated entities that were used by at least three major CAD vendors (version 1.0 (ANS Y14.26M-1981) allowed 34 different entity types). Transfer itself was achieved using a formatted ASCII file capable of being exchanged between any two systems on half-inch magnetic tape (this being the most widely used medium for archival data storage at the time of initial development of the specification). IGES now also allows compressed ASCII format and binary files. Every vendor supporting IGES would write processor software to translate from their proprietary software to the IGES neutral format.

Because of the particular format chosen for IGES files, they are rather long – substantially bigger than the CAD system data files that they represent. The early implementations of IGES translators by the CAD system vendors also tended to be unreliable – in part because of vagueness in the specification, and in part because some vendors only implemented part of the standard. Such difficulties prompted the French company Aerospatiale to develop their own standard, SET (Standard d'Echange et de Transfert), that was eventually adopted by the French national standards body (AFNOR) as a standard in 1985, and has since become widely used in the European aerospace industry. SET uses a similar data model to IGES, but with a very much more compact format.

Limitations of IGES also prompted the German automotive industry to develop a standard of its own, but in this case the objective was to overcome the IGES restriction that only cubic basis surfaces could be represented. The standard VDA/FS was developed particularly to represent higher-order surfaces. A second version has also included topological as well as geometric information.

While these developments were taking place in Europe, work on IGES, and on other experimental standards, continued apace. IGES version 2.0 appeared in 1983, and included entities from finite element and electrical systems applications. Although never an official standard, IGES 2.0 was widely adopted within the CAD industry. At about this time (chronological details are shown in Figure 7.6) work on the development of standards for the exchange of solid modelling data was initiated (IGES at that time allowed wire-frame and limited surface data exchange). One result of this

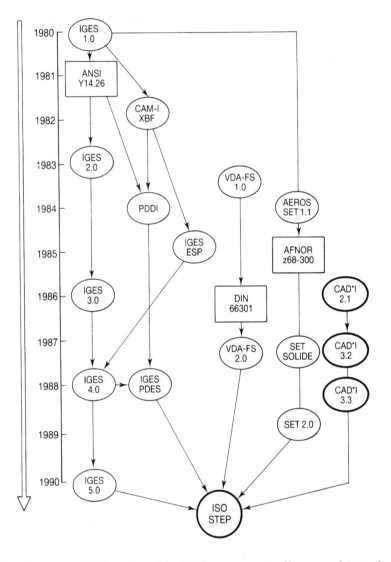

FIGURE 7.6

Chronological highlights of CADCAM data exchange. (Reproduced with permission from Schlechtendahl and Weick (1990). © Harrington Kilbride plc).

work, the Experimental Boundary File (XBF), was eventually merged into the IGES Experimental Solids Proposal (ESP).

In 1986 IGES 1.0 was replaced as an ANSI standard by IGES 3.0, which at the time included over 50 entities in a variety of areas. This version of IGES included some changes in the file format to reduce file sizes and to improve the efficiency with which the files may be processed to and from native CAD system formats. In 1989 version 4.0 was introduced, and incorporated some facilities for the exchange of data describing constructive solid geometry models, originating from the IGES ESP. The transfer of solid models using the alternative boundary representation was incorporated in IGES 5.0 at the beginning of the 1990s.

At the time of writing, the latest version of IGES adopted by ANSI is IGES 5.3, although not all vendors will support this revision of the standard. Perhaps the most widely implemented revision is version 3. IGES is now generally stable and reliable for exchange of simple geometric entities (points, lines, arcs and conics), a little less so for more complex entities such as splines, sometimes poor for annotation and dimensions, and reportedly often poor for 'Group' entities and some other entity constructs (Tailor Made Software, 1997).

7.3.1 An outline of the IGES standard

The IGES standard is essentially a specification for the structure and syntax of a neutral file in ASCII, compressed ASCII or binary format. We will discuss here the ASCII file, which is divided into 80 character records (lines) – the format for punched card data widely used for data processing in the 1960s and 1970s – terminated by semicolons and subdivided into fields by commas. The five sections are:

▶ The **Start Section**, which is set up manually by the person initiating the IGES file, and which contains information that may assist the user at the destination, such as the features of the originating system.

▶ The **Global Section**, which provides in 24 fields the parameters necessary to translate the file, including (field number in brackets) the delimiter characters (1 and 2), sender's identifier (3), filename (4), ID of the software producing the file (5) and version of the IGES processor (6), precision of integer, floating-point and double precision numbers (7 to 11), receiver's identifier (12), model space scale (13), units (14), name of the units (15), maximum number of line thicknesses (16) and maximum line thickness (17), time file generated (18), smallest distance (19) and largest coordinate value (20), person and organization creating the file (21 and 22), IGES version (23) and drafting standard (24).

▶ The **Directory Section**, which is generated by the IGES pre-processor, and which contains an entry for each entity in the file comprising a code representing the entity type and subtype and pointers to the entity data in the next section; two lines comprising 18 fields of eight characters are used for each entry.

▶ The **Parameter Data Section**, which contains the entity-specific data such as coordinate values, annotation text, number of spline data points and so on. The first parameter in each entry identifies the entity type from which the meanings of the remaining parameters may be derived. Each entry has a pointer in columns 66–72 to the directory entry for the entity.

▶ The **Termination Section**, which marks the end of the data file, and contains subtotals of records for data transmission check purposes.

Each record line has an identifier in columns 73–80. The first character of the identifier indicates the file section (start = S, global = G and so on), and the remainder is an integer number starting with one at the beginning of each section. This number is used by IGES for the pointers for the cross-referencing between sections. (The reader may note, in the use of separate directory and parameter sections, and in the cross-referencing between entity entries, a similarity with the data structure presented in Section 5.3.)

Some of the entities that are supported by IGES are shown in Table 7.3 below. Entities such as 142 – curve on a parametric surface – and 144 – trimmed parametric surface – allow edge loops and faces of B-rep geometry to be exchanged. Example 7.1 shows how IGES information is presented for a very simple collection of geometry.

Table 7.3 IGES data types

Geometric entities

100	Circular arc	124	Transformation matrix
102	Composite curve	125	Flash
104	Conic arc	126	Rational B-spline curve
106	Copious data	128	Rational B-spline surface
108	Plane	130	Offset curve
110	Line	132	Connect point
112	Parametric spline curve	134	Node
114	Parametric spline surface	136	Finite element
116	Point	138	Nodal displacement and rotation
118	Ruled surface	140	Offset surface
120	Surface of revolution	142	Curve on a parametric surface
122	Tabulated cylinder	144	Trimmed parametric surface

Annotation entities

202	Angular dimension	216	Linear dimension
206	Diameter dimension	218	Ordinate dimension
208	Flag note	220	Point dimension
210	General label	222	Radius dimension
212	General note	228	General symbol
214	Leader (arrow)	230	Sectioned area

Structure entities

302	Associativity definition		
304	Line font definition	406	Property
306	Macro definition	408	Singular subfigure instance
308	Subfigure definition	410	View
310	Text font definition	412	Rectangular array subfigure
312	Text display template		instance
314	Color definition	414	Circular array subfigure instance
320	Network subfigure definition	416	External reference
402	Associativity instance	418	Node load/constraint
404	Drawing	420	Network subfigure instance
		600–699	Macro instance

Example 7.1 *An example IGES file*

Figure 7.7 shows a line, a point and an arc, the IGES representation for which is shown below.

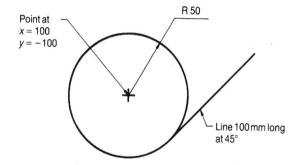

FIGURE 7.7
Geometry for IGES
example.

EXAMPLE IGES FILE   S0000001
1H,,1H;,,,9HMASTERCAM, 1H1,16,8,24,8,56,,1.,1,4HINCH,1,0.01, G0000001
13H850101.010000,0.,100.,,,;   G0000002
    116   1   1   1   1   0 00000000D0000001
    116   0   3   1   D0000002
    124   2   1   1   1   0 00000000D0000003
    124   0   3   1   D0000004
    100   3   1   1   1   3 00000000D0000005
    100   0   3   1   D0000006
    110   4   1   1   1   0 00000000D0000007
    110   0   3   1   D0000008
116,100., −100.,0.;   1P0000001
124,1.,0.,0.,0.,0.,1.,0.,0.,0.,0.,1.,0.;   3P0000002
100,0.,100., −100.,150., −100.,150., −99.99999;   5P0000003
110,135.3553, −135.3553,0.,206.066, −64.64465,0.;   7P0000004
S0000001G0000002D0000008P0000004   T0000001

Note: The parameter entry for the line (110) is $x_1, y_1, z_1, x_2, y_2, z_2$; for the arc (100) is z, x, y of centre, x, y of start point, x, y of end point; and for the point (116) is x, y and z.

7.3.2 The future: STEP

Although IGES has been a dominant standard for CAD data exchange, a number of alternative or variant approaches have been developed over the years, and, furthermore, there has always been some dissatisfaction in the underlying basis for IGES. These factors have led in recent years to an effort to develop an agreed international standard to integrate the previous work, and to provide an improved fundamental basis for standards activities in this area. This effort grew out of the initiation in 1984, by the IGES organization, of the Product Definition Data Interface (PDDI) with the aim of developing a successor to IGES known as the Product Data Exchange Specification (PDES), and the inauguration by the ISO in the same year of Technical Committee 184, Sub-Committee 4 (TC184/SC4), with the aim of coordinating efforts aimed at developing a new standard for the representation of product model data. (The standards activities of the ISO are undertaken by about 200 technical committees, each of which has a number of subcommittees. Technical Committee 184 is responsible for Industrial Automation Systems and Integration, and Sub-Committee 4 with Industrial Data and Global Manufacturing Programming Languages. It is responsible for the development of ISO 10303.) The PDES activity and other world-wide developments such as the large European Community research project 'Computer-Aided Design Interfaces' (ESPRIT Project 322 – CAD*I (Schlechtendahl (1989); ESPRIT is the European Strategic Programme for Research into Information Technology) have been drawn together by the ISO into a single unified standard, ISO 10303. This standard is formally named 'Industrial automation systems and integration – product data representation and exchange', although it is more widely known by the informal acronym STEP (Standard for the Exchange of Product Model data). In the United States by the PDES acronym which has been retained in the term 'Product Data Exchange using STEP' (STEP activity in the United States is the responsibility of the IGES/PDES Organization (IPO), the management functions for which are provided by the US Product Data Association (US PRO)(US PRO, 1997)).

STEP seeks to address a number of limitations of IGES. In particular, IGES was not developed using a formal specification language, nor was it based on information modelling methodologies, and therefore there is vagueness in the specification. It does not clearly distinguish between the logical specification of the standard (the meaning of the data from a CAD system point of view), the applications requirements (how the data will be used in particular applications), and the physical specification for the storage of data in exchange files. IGES does not provide sufficient conformance clauses or test sets for testing how the implementations from different CAD vendors conform to the standard. Furthermore, vendors may choose which aspects of the standard they implement, and therefore there is almost invariably a mismatch between the coverage of processors from different vendors. STEP improves on this in a number of respects (Owen, 1993):

▶ STEP uses a formal model for the data exchange, which is described using an information modelling language called EXPRESS that was developed specifically for STEP. EXPRESS is both human readable and computer processable, and is used to specify the information models in STEP. In IGES the specification describes the format of a physical file which stores all of the geometric and other data. In STEP this data is described in the EXPRESS language, which then maps to the physical file. The physical file does not then need to have a definition of how, for example, a particular entity such as a spline should be represented, but rather how EXPRESS models are represented in the file.

▶ STEP has a three-layer architecture that enables multiple application views and implementations to be defined. The first layer comprises techniques for the implementation of STEP, such as the way in which models are related to the EXPRESS language, and through this to the physical file. The second layer comprises **resource information models** which provide context-independent information such as, for example, the description of the geometry, topology or product structure. Resource models are so called because they provide a resource to the third layer, known as **application protocols**, which contain information related to a particular application domain such as draughting or electrical product modelling. The relationship between these three layers is shown in Figure 7.8.

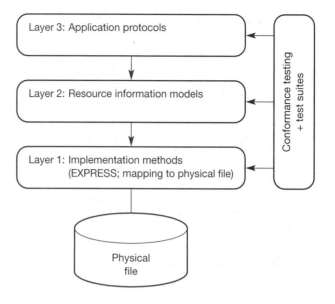

FIGURE 7.8
Relationship
between layers of
the STEP standard.

▶ The application protocols describe constrained subsets of the STEP standard which should ensure that the implementations by different vendors are very much more compatible than IGES implementations. To ensure further conformance, STEP includes a conformance testing methodology and a series of test suites.

ISO TC184/SC4 is subdivided for the purposes of developing STEP into a number of working groups (WGs) covering different aspects of the standard such as STEP development methods, conformance testing procedures and implementation specifications. The standard itself is so large that it is being developed incrementally as a series of separate standards called parts. The intention is that the most important parts will be developed and released first to form a core on which further development of the standard can take place. The parts themselves are divided into seven classes, as follows:

▶ **Introductory (Parts 1–9)**, currently comprising Part 1, Overview and General Principles.

▶ **Description Methods (Parts 11–19)**, comprising Parts 11 and 12 relating to the Express language.

▶ **Implementation Methods (Parts 21–9)**, describing how EXPRESS is mapped to physical files and other storage mechanisms.

▶ **Conformance Testing Methodology and Framework (Parts 31–9)**, which provide methods for testing implementations, and test suites to be used during conformance testing.

▶ **Integrated Resources (Parts 41–99, 101–99)**, which include generic resources such as geometry and structure representation (41–99), and widely used applications such as draughting and finite element analysis (101–99).

▶ **Application Protocols (Parts 201–99)**, which describe implementations of STEP specific to particular industrial applications, and are associated with implementation methods to form the basis of a STEP implementation.

▶ **Abstract test suites (Parts 301–99)**, which provide test suites for each of the Application Protocols.

▶ **Application interpreted constructs (Parts 501–)**, which describe various model entity constructs, and specific modelling approaches.

The current assignment of parts to each class, and their release status, is shown in Table 7.4. Twelve STEP parts were approved as international standards in 1994, with two more in late 1996. These include particularly important parts such as Part 1, which gives an overview of the standard, Part 11, which describes the EXPRESS language, and Part 21, which gives details of the physical file. Of the Integrated Resources, two particularly important parts are Parts 41 and 42. Part 41 is concerned with 'Fundamentals of Product Description and Support', and deals with the product categories (electrical, mechanical, etc.), data types (drawings, diagrams and so on), data usage (engineering, testing, etc.), versioning and assembly relationships. Part 42 is the part which covers 'Geometrical and Topological Representation', essentially modelling as covered in Chapters 1 and 2 of this book.

At the time of writing, work is very much still continuing on the development of STEP, and the development activity is stimulating a great deal of work by system vendors and by researchers throughout the world. When TC184/SC4 was initiated, it was hoped that the initial release of the standard would be achieved in five years, but the process has taken rather longer than planned. The magnitude of the task is very large, however. With all its parts, the standard is very large, and it has to be developed through a Committee Draft (CD) stage, then a Draft International Standard (DIS) stage and final draft stage before being adopted as an international standard. At the CD stage, 16 countries are involved. At the DIS stage, the standards bodies of 90-odd countries have a say in the ballot. The structure of STEP and the development and balloting procedures are well documented in Owen (1993), and the interested reader is also referred to the standard itself, and to the publications and WWW sites of the various standards bodies involved for further information on the development of STEP. (For example, the US National Institute of Standards and Technology (NIST) maintains a web site on TC184/SC4 activities at *http://www.nist.gov/sc4*, and PDES Inc. has a home page at *http://www.scra.org/pdesinc.html*.)

The EXPRESS language

The basic element of the EXPRESS language is the **entity**, which is a named collection of data and constraints and/or operations on that data. The entity data is expressed as a collection of attributes, which may be of a variety of types including strings, real and integer numbers and logical or Boolean values, and ordered or unordered collections of these termed arrays, lists, sets and bags. Arrays and lists are ordered, sets and bags are unordered; sets, lists and bags may have an indeterminate upper bound; each member of a set is unique. The attributes may also be references to other entities, or

Table 7.4 Parts of the STEP standard (note that (I) indicates parts that have been released as an International Standard at the time of writing, (F) parts that are at Final Draft International Standard stage, (D) parts that are at Draft International Standard stage, (C) parts that are at Committee Draft stage and (W) parts that are at Working Draft stage. Abstract test suites for APs have numbers 100 higher than the AP number)

Part	Name	Part	Name
1(I)	Overview and fundamental principles	43(I)	Representation structures
Description Methods		44(I)	Product structure configuration
11(I)	EXPRESS language reference manual	45(F)	Materials
12(I)	EXPRESS-I language reference manual	46(I)	Visual presentation
		47(D)	Shape variation tolerances
Implementation Methods		49(D)	Process structure, property and representation
21(I)	Clear text encoding of the exchange structure	*Integrated Application Resource*	
22(I)	Standard data access interface (SDAI) specification	101(I)	Draughting
		104(C)	Finite element analysis
23(C)	C++ language binding to the SDAI	105(I)	Kinematics
24(C)	C language binding to the SDAI	106(W)	Building construction core model
26(W)	Interface definition language binding to the SDAI	*Application Protocol*	
		201(I)	Explicit draughting
Conformance Testing Methodology and Framework		202(I)	Associative draughting
31(I)	General concepts	203(I)	Configuration controlled design
32(F)	Requirements on testing laboratories and clients	204(C)	Mechanical design using boundary representation
33(C)	Abstract test suites	205(C)	Mechanical design using surface representation
34(C)	Abstract test method	207(D)	Sheet metal die planning and design
35	Abstract test methods for SDAI implementations	208(C)	Life cycle management – change process
Integrated Generic Resources		209(C)	Composite and metallic structural analysis and related design
41(I)	Fundamentals of product description and support	210(C)	Electronic assembly, interconnect and packaging design
42(I)	Geometric and topological representation		

Table 7.4 cont'd

Part	Name	Part	Name
212(C)	Electrotechnical design and installation	231(C)	Process engineering data: process design and process specification of major equipment
213(D)	NC process plans for machined parts		
214(C)	Core data for automotive mechanical design process	232	Technical data packaging core information and exchange
215(W)	Ship arrangement		
216(W)	Ship moulded forms	*Application Interpreted Construct*	
217(C)	Ship piping	501(C)	Edge-based wireframe
218(C)	Ship structures	502(C)	Shell-based wireframe
220	Process planning, manufacture and assembly of layered electronic products	503(C)	Geometrically bounded 2D wireframe
		504(C)	Draughting annotation
		505(C)	Draughting structure and administration
221	Functional data and their schematic representation for process plant	506(C)	Draughting elements
		507(C)	Geometrically bounded surface
222	Exchange of product data for composite structures	508(C)	Non-manifold surface
		509(C)	Manifold surface
223(C)	Exchange of design and manufacturing product information for casting parts	510(C)	Geometrically bounded wireframe
		511(C)	Topologically bounded surface
224(D)	Mechanical product definition for process plans using machining features	512(C)	Faceted boundary representation
		513(C)	Elementary boundary representation
225(D)	Building elements using explicit shape representation	514(C)	Advanced boundary representation
226(W)	Ship mechanical systems		
227(D)	Plant spatial configuration	515(C)	Constructive solid geometry
228	Building services: heating ventilation and air conditioning	516(C)	Mechanical design context
		517(C)	Mechanical design geometric presentation
229	Exchange of design and manufacturing product information for forged parts	518(C)	Mechanical design shaded representation
230(W)	Building structural frame: steelwork		

again to arrays, lists or sets of these. A collection of definitions of entities, and of the data types and constraints associated with these, is known as a **schema**.

An example entity definition is:

```
ENTITY automobile;
            make              :STRING;
            serial_number     :INTEGER;
            engine_size       :REAL;
            colour            :colourtype;
            owner             :person;
            previous_owners :LIST[0:?] OF person;
UNIQUE
        serial_number;
WHERE
        engine_size>0.0;
END_ENTITY;
```

The first three attributes of the entity **automobile** are of the simple base types. The next two are types which will have been defined elsewhere in the schema. The current owner is a **person**, which will be another entity type, and the previous owners are referenced by a (possible empty) LIST of **person**. The **colour** attribute is of type **colourtype**, which could be defined by the statement:

```
TYPE colourtype = ENUMERATION OF
                    (red,
                    black,
                    blue,
                    white);
END_TYPE;
```

which specifies that **colour** must be one of a restricted set of values.

Constraints have been placed on the values of two of the attributes. The **serial_number** must be different from every other in the file, and the **engine_size** must have a value greater than zero. Constraints may be applied in a variety of ways, much as they would be in programming languages.

EXPRESS also has mechanisms for capturing the hierarchical nature of some data types, via the use of SUPERTYPEs and SUBTYPEs, where a subtype is a kind or variety of entity that is its supertype. For example, we might say that **automobile** is a subtype of **road_vehicle** for which the definition might be:

```
ENTITY road_vehicle SUPERTYPE OF ONEOF
                (truck, automobile, bicycle);
END_ENTITY;
```

The definition of **automobile** would have to be modified to reflect the existence of the supertype:

ENTITY automobile SUBTYPE OF
　　　　　　(road__vehicle);

We could also say that **automobile** is a supertype of **saloon__cars** (or **sedans**), **hatchbacks** and **estates** (or **station__wagons**), so building a conceptual tree of information.

The EXPRESS language provides a powerful facility for modelling information in terms of entities and their relationship to each other. Example 7.2 below shows how geometric entities might be defined in EXPRESS, and how instances might be included in the physical file.

Example 7.2 *Using EXPRESS to model geometric entities*

The EXPRESS definition for a point might be:

```
ENTITY point ;
    x-coordinate : REAL ;
    y-coordinate : REAL ;
    z-coordinate : REAL ;
END_ENTITY ;
```

and for a circle:

```
ENTITY circle ;
    centre : point ;
    radius : REAL ;
END_ENTITY ;
```

Actual instances of these on the physical file could be as follows:

```
#15 = POINT (3.3,4.4,5.5) ;
#16 = POINT (6.6,7.7,8.8) ;
#17 = CIRCLE (#15, 5.0) ;
```

There are four additional aspects to EXPRESS that are used in STEP. Firstly, a graphical notation is provided for a subset of EXPRESS, known as EXPRESS-G. Entities and attributes are shown by boxes, and relationships between entities and attributes, or between entities in a class hierarchy, are shown by relationship lines. EXPRESS-G does not allow constraints to be specified. Figure 7.9 shows an example of the use of EXPRESS-G to represent the 'automobile' entity example given in this section.

The second additional aspect of EXPRESS is EXPRESS-I, which is an instantiation language that enables instances of schema or entities or collections of schema instances (models) to be displayed. EXPRESS-I is also used in the specification of abstract test cases used in conformance testing (Owen, 1993). Finally, EXPRESS-M

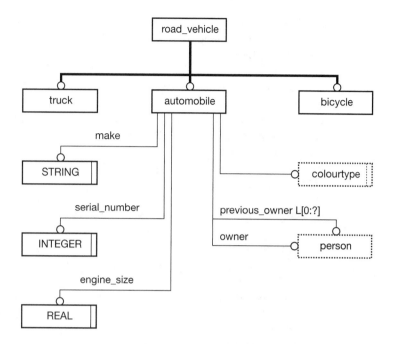

FIGURE 7.9

Example of the use
of EXPRESS-G.

deals with mapping between schemas, and EXPRESS-C extends the capability of
EXPRESS by modelling static and dynamic behavioural properties.

7.3.3 CALS

Continuous Acquisition and Life-cycle Support (CALS) is a US Department of Defense
initiative with the aim of applying computer technology to the process of specifying, ordering, operating, supporting and maintaining the weapons systems used by
the US armed forces, although it can be adopted by any industry, not just the defence
industry. The main thrust of the initiative is a prescription of the formats to be used
for the storage and exchange of computer-based data and information. CALS was
originally called Computer-aided Acquisition and Logistics Support, and was instigated by the US Deputy Secretary of Defense, William Taft, in 1985 with the objectives of accelerating the integration of reliability and maintainability design tools into
contractor CAD/CAE processes, accelerating the automation of contractor processes
for generating logistics technical information (manuals, training materials, etc.) and
increasing the ability of the military to receive, distribute and use logistic technical
information. The initiative led to the publication of the military standard MIL-STD-
1840a, 'Automated Interchange of Technical Information' in 1986, and in revised
form in 1987.

The first stage of CALS prescribes standards for the exchange of product data, and
in particular of technical publications. The text of the publications uses the standard
generalized markup language (**SGML**), which is a language for the marking up or tag-
ging of ASCII text to separate the logical elements of a document (such as chapters,

headings, paragraphs and pictures), and to specify the processing functions to be performed on those elements. The tags that SGML uses to identify document elements are ASCII strings embedded in angled parentheses <> to distinguish them from the rest of the document. We will come across the same approach in Chapter 16 when we discuss the hypertext language HTML that is based on SGML and used for the World-Wide Web. MIL-M-28001 specifies the markup of text using a subset of SGML, and SGML-compatible codes to describe the layout of technical publications to specific requirements. The rules that define possible document structures are contained in document type definitions (DTDs – again in MIL standards), and the procedures that process the elements of the text are contained in programs that use the SGML syntax. In this respect a variation in approach is used for application of CALS outside of the US defence environment. The standards to be used for illustrations and drawings include IGES, the Computer Graphics Metafile (CGM), and the CCITT group 4 facsimile standard for raster formats.

In view of concern over the imprecision in IGES, CALS has developed a further standard (MIL-D-28000, 1987) which defines subsets of IGES to be used for specific applications including technical illustrations, engineering drawings, electronic engineering data, and geometry for manufacture by numerical control machines. Further classes are being developed for 3D piping and tubing, process plant flowsheets, finite element analysis, 3D modelling and other applications. By using subsets of IGES it is hoped to overcome some of the limitations of that standard. Eventually, it is expected that CALS will use the STEP standards for product data, and will also extend into such areas as electronic hardware description and office document exchange. For up-to-date information on CALS, the reader is referred to the US Department of Defense web site on the subject (DoD, 1997).

7.3.4 Another *de facto* standard: DXF

In recent years CAD systems based on personal computers (PCs) have come to dominate the CAD market in terms of the number of copies of software sold. Of the software written for PCs, one program, AutoCAD by AutoDesk Inc., has had a large market share and has been very influential. In part this has been because the company has adopted the approach of making it relatively straightforward for third-party software vendors to develop software to work with AutoCAD or with AutoCAD files. One way in which this was done was to have two formats for the storage of files: a compact binary form (the .DWG format), and a readable form using ASCII, the file structure and format of which AutoDesk publishes and supports. The ASCII representation is known as DXF (short for Data eXchange Format), and is now widely used by many PC-based (and other) CAD systems as a means of storing data in a portable form.

There are four parts to a DXF file, as shown in Table 7.5. It is possible to produce a valid DXF file including just the ENTITIES section.

DXF files can be very long, because they assign two lines in the file to each data item: the first line says what the data item is, and the second gives the value for the item. So, for example, an ENTITIES section containing a single line might be (explanations given in brackets):

SECTION	(beginning of section)
2	
ENTITIES	(entity section label)
0	
LINE	(entity type)
8	
0	(layer number)
10	
–2.154000	(first x coordinate)
20	
1.315000	(first y coordinate)
30	
0.000000	(first z coordinate)
11	
8.341000	(second x coordinate)
21	
10.500000	(second y coordinate)
31	
0.000000	(second z coordinate)
0	
ENDSEC	(end of section)
0	
EOF	(end of file)

AutoDesk has in recent releases of AutoCAD allowed users to define their own DXF entities, but for the most part DXF clearly works best with those entity types that are used in AutoCAD. Two-dimensional draughting geometry is most likely to translate correctly, and high-order geometric entities such as splines and complex surfaces are, along with annotation entities such as dimensions and fill patterns, more likely to cause problems.

Table 7.5 Sections in a DXF file

Section title	Content
HEADER	Values for AutoCAD system variables, such as user interface style and parameters, default layer, dimensioning style, etc.
TABLES	Line-styles, user-defined coordinate systems.
BLOCKS	Definitions of blocks instanced in the model.
ENTITIES	Entity definitions and data.

7.4 Communications standards

Data exchange depends not only on the compatibility of the applications data formats between the communicating systems, but also on compatibility of the physical means of communication. For example, two sites might choose to exchange CAD files using magnetic tapes, but tape sizes and types vary, and even if the same physical tapes are used, different manufacturers may store data on the tapes in dissimilar ways.

Increasingly, computers are arranged to communicate with each other. For example, an engineering workstation might be connected to a supercomputer for the analysis of large finite element models, and to computers in an engineering workshop for the transmission of manufacturing data to machine tools. Such local connections form what is known as **local area networks** (LANs), and involve the connection of digital devices over distances from a few metres up to a few kilometres. Computers that are widely spread geographically – for example, a company's computers on different sites, or machines on a number of university campuses – may also be connected, even if these sites are in different countries or continents! These connections are known as **wide area networks** (WANs). In LANs and WANs, there are again wide variations in the physical means available (twisted pair or coaxial cables, optical fibre links, microwave links and so on), and in the formats or protocols used to encode the data. In order for communication to be successful, closely defined standards for all aspects of the communication are required.

Wide area networks

Communication between digital devices in both LANs and WANs is normally achieved in serial mode (i.e. 1 bit at a time) along a single path (e.g. a pair of wires). WANs usually use telephone-type communications lines, operated either privately or by the public telecommunications companies (and, as a consequence of using such technology, the data transmission rates are generally low: in the order of tens of thousands of bits per second). The data-carrying networks operated by the public utilities are known as **public switched data networks**, or PSDNs. Data is transmitted across such networks either by **circuit switching** or by **packet switching**. In a **circuit-switched public data network** (CSPDN) a physical communication channel is set up between the sending and receiving points of the network, and this channel is then used exclusively for the communication (in the same way that telephone conversations are made). In a **packet-switched public data network** (PSPDN), the information to be transmitted is divided into a number of self-contained message units, each with information about the destination address, and these units or **packets** are sent separately through the network and then reassembled at their destination. The packets are guided through the network by **packet-switching exchanges** (PSEs), which have the equivalent function to telephone exchanges for voice communications. These store packets and then use their destination addresses, together with a **routing directory** which specifies the transmission paths for each address, to identify the outgoing network links along which the packets should be forwarded. Such exchanges are sometimes referred to as **nodes** within the network (indeed, this term is used as a general term for termination points, junction points and devices within a network). Figure 7.10 shows a WAN in diagrammatic form.

Increasingly, the public communications networks use digital transmission and computer-controlled switching. When digital transmission is extended to subscriber equipment then a high-bit-rate switched transmission path will be available at each subscriber outlet, and the network will be capable of supporting both digitized voice

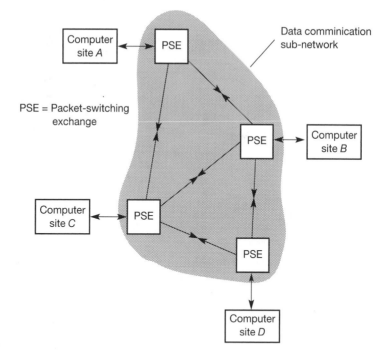

FIGURE 7.10
The topology of a wide area network. (Reproduced with permission from Halsall (1988). © Addison Wesley Longman Ltd.)

and data transmission, without the use of modems, as an **integrated services digital network** (ISDN). The mode of operation in which all information – voice, image, video or other data – is transmitted over broadband versions of such networks by first dividing it into small, fixed size frames and then transmitting it using packet-switching techniques is known as **asynchronous transfer mode** (ATM). ATM uses channel demand to determine how data packets are allocated, and allows better use of available bandwidth (Halsall, 1992).

Local area networks

The techniques used for communication within LANs, and also the physical means of connection between equipment, are quite diverse, and rather different from those employed in WANs. The diversity has arisen in part because of the preferences of the organizations that originally developed the techniques, and in part to accommodate the various applications of LANs.

The most obvious area of difference between a WAN and a LAN is in the topology of the network itself. LAN topology is generally rather simpler than the mesh arrangement shown in Figure 7.10, and will fall into one of four categories: the star, the ring or the bus/tree shown in Figure 7.11, or a variation of the bus or ring known as the hub (Halsall, 1992). We shall concentrate on the last two of these.

The method of controlling access to the network is also achieved in a number of different ways, of which perhaps the most important are the use of a **control token**, and **carrier sense multiple access with collision detection** (CSMA/CD). The former is used with either bus or ring topologies, and essentially controls access to the

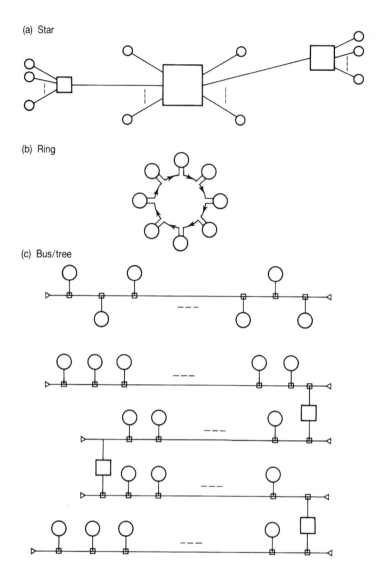

(a) Star

(b) Ring

(c) Bus/tree

FIGURE 7.11
Local area network topologies. (Reproduced with permission from Halsall (1988). © Addison Wesley Longman Ltd.)

network by requiring a transmitting device to have possession of a single control token which is passed from device to device around the network. CSMA/CD, on the other hand, is only used with bus networks. In this method, the various devices in the network are connected to the same cable, and a node may transmit (or **broadcast**) data (in the form of a frame of information with a source and destination address and various other protocol data) when it senses that the cable is inactive. Other nodes on the network 'listen' to the transmissions and receive correctly addressed data. However, it is possible for two nodes to try to broadcast data simultaneously, with consequent corruption of the information. In an attempt to prevent this, the transmitting nodes first sense whether a carrier signal (for another node's data) is present on the cable, and if so delay transmission. If a collision still occurs, then the node that detects this jams the network for a short while (to alert all other nodes) and the transmitting nodes then wait a short random period of time before attempting to retransmit.

The transmission itself is achieved in one of two modes: in **baseband** mode, in which all the available bandwidth of the cable is used for a single high-bit-rate data channel (for example at 10 megabits per second (Mbps) or higher), or in **broadband** mode, in which the available bandwidth is divided to allow a number of (lower-band-width) channels to be transmitted along the same cable. Office systems (of the sort connecting CAD equipment) would probably use baseband transmission on either a token ring or a bus/tree topology network, whereas transmission in a factory environment might well use broadband transmission. The CSMA/CD bus network, generally known as an **Ethernet**, is particularly popular for connecting engineering workstations.

Increasingly, networks themselves are being connected to each other, normally through devices known as **bridges**, which link homogeneous networks, and **routers**, which link dissimilar networks but where all the devices implement compatible protocols (according to the OSI model – see below). Bridges allow traffic intended for a local part of a network to be constrained within that segment, so limiting the total load on the network. Routers usually have software intelligence that allows them to segregate traffic in a complex interconnected network. Where the connection is to a proprietary network architecture, then **gateways**, which perform the necessary protocol conversion between heterogeneous networks, are used to route packets between networks. Figure 7.12 shows a possible configuration in which networks of different topologies might be connected.

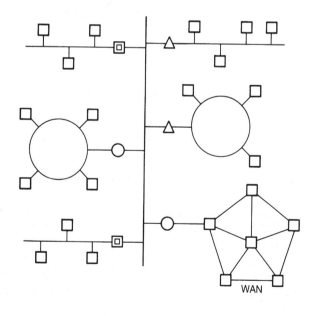

FIGURE 7.12

Configuration of networks of different topology and compatibility.

▣ = Bridge: homogeneous networks

△ = Router: dissimilar but compatible networks (to OSI level 3)

◯ = Gateway: heterogeneous networks

Standards in data exchange

Because WANs necessarily involve connection of equipment to public hardware, internationally agreed standards for the physical connections and for data transmission protocols have been established for many years. These are set in particular by the International Telegraph and Telephone Consultative Committee (CCITT), and include standards identified by letter series. Perhaps the best known are the X-series standards for connection of data terminal equipment (DTEs) to public data networks – X25, for example, concerns the connection of computers to packet-switched networks.

The nature of LANs is such that they may often be restricted to equipment from a single manufacturer, and therefore a number of proprietary networking techniques have been developed; several of these are still in use. They are sometimes known as closed systems, because of the restrictions in the equipment they can connect. Nevertheless, there have also been considerable efforts to establish international standards in the area, and in particular the ISO has adopted the 802 series of standards developed by the American Institute of Electrical and Electronic Engineers. For example, a standard for baseband mode operation under CSMA/CD is ISO 8802.3. This standard is based on the Ethernet method, developed by a group of computing companies at the beginning of the 1980s from research work at the Xerox Palo Alto Research Center. In fact, it differs slightly (e.g. in frame protocol) from the *de facto* Ethernet standard, which is still implemented by most manufacturers.

The ISO has also been very active in promoting open computing systems, to which equipment from diverse manufacturers may be connected. In particular, an ISO reference model for Open Systems Interconnection (OSI) has been developed, which defines a multi-layered approach to communication in both LANs and WANs. These layers cover the spectrum of communications elements from the physical connections between equipment, dealt with by layers 1 and 2, to the interface with the application, covered by layer 7. The intermediate layers deal with data routing, reliability and security, and standard coding. Figure 7.13 shows the various layers and their broad division.

TCP/IP

Concurrently with the ISO development of the OSI standards, the US Department of Defense have for many years funded work on computer communications that led to the development of a collection of interconnected networks, or internet, known as **ARPANET** (after the **Defense Advanced Projects Research Agency** (DARPA)). The ARPANET has gradually been extended over some 20 years to incorporate academic and then other networks to form a global network now known simply as **the Internet**, the development of which has led to the specification of a set of network and application-oriented protocols known as **Transmission Control Protocol/ Internet Protocol** (TCP/IP). These protocols are in the public domain and thus they have been very widely adopted, such that they are the most widely used open system standard. They have influenced the development of the ISO standards, and have been the basis for some, but they are not the same. The Internet has recently experienced explosive growth, as attested to by almost daily media attention.

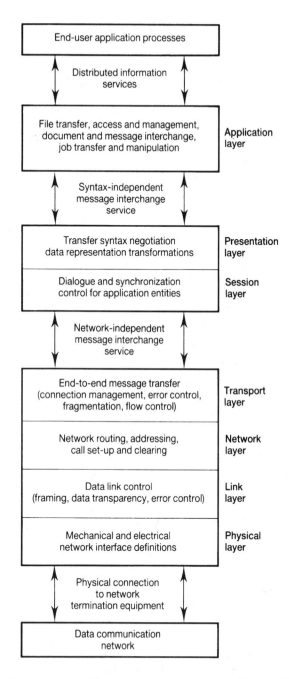

FIGURE 7.13
OSI protocol layer summary. (Reproduced with permission from Halsall (1988). © Addison Wesley Longman Ltd.)

Figure 7.14 shows some of the standards associated with the TCP/IP suite, and their relationship to the ISO reference model. The TCP is the equivalent to the transport layer (level 4) and provides a message transfer service that allows messages to be exchanged simultaneously in two directions. The IP provides a network service between packet-switched networks interconnected by gateways, and is the equivalent

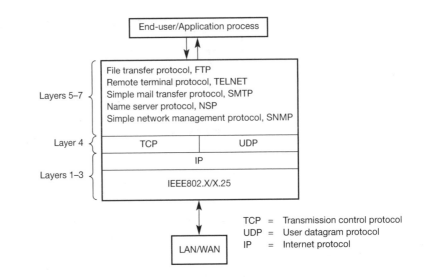

FIGURE 7.14
The TCP/IP Protocol
Suite. (Reproduced
with permission
from Halsall (1992)
© Addison Wesley
Longman.)

to the ISO network layer (level 3). At a higher level are facilities used by application processes (such as the WWW) or the end user which include:

► TELNET, which enables a user or application process on one machine to communicate with an application process on a remote machine. This allows, for example, a user to 'log on' to a remote machine and to use application programs as if his or her terminal were connected directly to the remote machine.

► FTP (File Transfer Protocol), which enables a user of an application program to access and interact with a remote file system, for example to transfer files between one file system and another.

► SMTP (Simple Mail Transfer Protocol), which is used to transfer mail between different mail systems.

► SNMP (Simple Network Management Protocol), which is used for the sending and retrieving of network management information across the network.

Of these, TELNET and FTP will be the most familiar to the reader.

Manufacturing network applications

The computer communications field is developing very rapidly, and therefore it is difficult to be very specific about the way that developments will be made in manufacturing. We can nevertheless learn something about the thinking that goes into communications systems design from existing developments. In this respect the design of two **open systems interconnection environments** (OSIEs), based on the OSI model, are of particular interest in engineering manufacture. These are the **Manufacturing Automation Protocols** (MAPs), proposed by General Motors for factory communications systems, and the **Technical and Office Protocols** (TOPs) proposed by Boeing Computer Services specifically for office equipment. Neither of these proposals appear to have had the impact that might have been expected, but nevertheless the way in which different network features have been selected to match the networks' duties can be seen from a comparison of these.

In a manufacturing environment, the control of machines may mean that it is necessary to be able to guarantee the correct timing of data transmission, and thus MAP uses a token bus mode of operation. Because a very high rate of data transmission may not be required, and because of the diverse range of communications requirements met with factory equipment, the broadband transmission method is used (although only two channels are used). Also, among the ISO facilities provided is the manufacturing message service (MMS), designed specifically for manufacturing environments to enable a computer to control a number of distributed devices. Finally, a reduced set of protocols, operating on a simple, lower-bandwidth cable, is provided for local operation within a manufacturing cell, controlled using the MMS by a cell controller (CC). This **enhanced performance architecture** (EPA) reduces the overhead of the full OSI model.

In an office environment, the actual timing of the data transmission is less important, but absolute speed of transmission is more critical (in view of the size, e.g. of CAD and finite element files). TOP therefore employs CSMA/CD in baseband mode, typically at 10 Mbps. TOP also, by comparison with MAP, omits MMS, but has facilities to assist in the transfer of jobs between computing devices, and the operation of computers as terminals in a device-independent fashion.

Fibre optic links

An alternative to copper connecting wires in LANs is the use of optical fibre connectors. Optical communications offer the advantages of large transmission bandwidth and relative immunity from electromagnetic interference or corrosion problems which make them ideal for industrial environments. Each of the main network architectures and protocols (token ring, CSMA/CD and token bus) has been adapted to the use of fibre optics, but for networks based specifically on fibre optics a new standard, the fibre distributed data interface (FDDI), has been developed by ANSI. The FDDI specifies a network comprising a pair of rings with counter-rotating network traffic, called the primary and secondary ring, that may be used in parallel, or may allow network operation in the event of ring failure. The standard also specifies protocols for data transfer on this network.

The FDDI may be used where very high data transfer rates are required, for example between computers and a file server. The data rate is equivalent to 100 Mbps over each ring. It also offers the prospect of large networks, for example with perhaps 500 stations connected by over 100 km of optical cable, again operating at very high bandwidths. The increasing integration of CADCAM activities, and the very large quantities of network data transfer associated with windows-based user interfaces and large CADCAM models, will make such data transfer capabilities increasingly necessary in the future.

In addition to the FDDI, ANSI has also been instrumental in the development of the Fibre Channel standard for very high-speed fibre optic data communications – in the order of 1 gigabit per second between very large numbers of nodes. As the bandwidth capabilities of fibre optics are further developed there are clear possibilities for significantly higher rates.

7.5 Conclusion

The development of effective and reliable standards is essential if CADCAM is to fulfil its promise as an integrating factor in engineering. These standards have to be in place not just in the area of CADCAM data, but in all aspects of computing relevant to the technology. We have seen in this chapter that extensive standards and industry-wide approaches already exist in computer graphics, in the GKS and PHIGS standards, and the OpenGL graphics system, and in communications, in the form of the TCP/IP and ISO Open Systems Interconnection protocols. In the important area of user interfaces the X Window System and Microsoft's Windows products are very influential, and in CADCAM data exchange itself, the Initial Graphics Exchange Specification (IGES) and the AutoDesk DXF format have been in existence for some years. Although imperfect they have seen widespread use.

The pace of development in computing is such that standards development is sometimes overtaken by events. Often a particular approach will become a *de facto* standard simply through the extent to which it is used, sometimes displacing official standards in the process. We can see this to a certain extent in communications and in graphics and interface standards with the dominance of TCP/IP, and the products of a small number of vendors. In other cases new standards have to be developed almost before the ink is dry on the pages of the existing ones. For example, in CAD-CAM data exchange the ISO is working on new standards for representation and exchange of parts library data (ISO 13584), and in 1996 a Parametrics Group was set up to incorporate into STEP the means for capturing and exchanging the parametric, constraint-based product models that we will meet in the next chapter. Nevertheless, work in CADCAM data exchange over the next few years will concentrate on the development of the STEP standard that has already begun, and on widening the scope of the product data that may be exchanged using the standard. Some people hope that STEP will allow such complete product data description that informal aspects of the design such as design intent and function may also be exchanged. The extent to which these hopes will be realized remains to be seen.

References and further reading

AFNOR (1985). Automatisation industrielle: Representation externes des données de définition de produits. *Specification du standard d'échange et de transfert (SET)*. Version 85.08. Z68300.

ANSI/IEEE Standard 802.3 (1985). *Carrier Sense Multiple Access with Collision Detection*.

ANSI/IEEE Standard 802.4 (1985). *Token-passing Bus Access Method*.

ANSI/IEEE Standard 802.5 (1985). *Token Ring Access Method*.

Arnold D. B. and Bono P. R. (1988). *CGM and CGI. Metafile and Interface Standards for Computer Graphics*. Berlin: Springer.

Chenes R. A. (1989). *Computer-aided Acquisition and Logistic Support, A Revolutionary Evolution*. North Hampton, MA: EMCA.

DoD (1997). CALS Web site. *http://www.acq.osd.mil/cals/calsinfo.html*. Washington, DC: US Department of Defense.

Finkelstein W. and Guertin J. A. R. (1988). *Integrated Logistics Support: The Design Engineering Link*. Bedford: IFS/Springer.

Foley J. D., van Dam A., Feiner, F. K. and Hughes J. F. (1996). *Computer Graphics Principles and Practice. 2nd Edition in C*. Reading, MA: Addison Wesley Longman.

General Motors (1988). *Manufacturing Automation Protocol Specification*. Version 3.0.

Gennusa P. L. (1987). Computer-aided Acquisition and Logistics Support (CALS): recent developments and industry perspective. *SGML Users' Group Bulletin*. **2**(2). 97–8.

Goldfarb C. (1990). *The SGML Handbook*. Oxford: Clarendon Press.

Halsall F. (1988). *Data Communications, Computer Networks and OSI*. 2nd edn. Harlow: Addison Wesley Longman.

Halsall F. (1992). *Data Communications, Computer Networks and Open Systems*. 3rd edn. Harlow: Addison Wesley Longman.

Hopgood F. R. A., Duce D. A., Gallop J. R. and Sutcliffe D. C. (1986). *Introduction to the Graphical Kernel System (GKS)*. 2nd edn. London: Academic Press.

IGES, version x.y. Springfield, VA: National Technical Information Service.

Information Technology Requirements Council (1984). *Technical and Office Protocol*. Version 3.

International Organization for Standardization – ISO – World-Wide Web site. *http://www.iso.ch/*. The source of information about ISO standards.

ISO 7498 (1984). *Information Processing Systems – Open Systems Interconnection – Basic Reference Model*.

ISO 7942 (1985). *Graphical Kernel System (GKS)*.

ISO 8632 (1992). *Computer Graphics – Metafile for the Storage and Transfer of Picture Description Information, Parts 1–4*.

ISO 9592 (1989–92). *Computer Graphics – Programmer's Hierarchical Interactive Graphics System (PHIGS), Parts 1–3 (1989) and Part 4 (1992)*.

ISO 9636 (1991). *Computer Graphics – Interfacing Techniques for Dialogues with Graphical Devices (CGI), Parts 1–6. Note*: ISO 9636 is the Functional Specification, ISO 9637 (1992) covers the data stream binding, and ISO 9638 (1994) the language bindings.

ISO 10303 (1994). *Industrial Automation Systems and Integration – Product Data Representation and Exchange (STEP)*. Parts of this standard are shown by a suffix number. For example, ISO 10303–41 is Part 41: Integrated Generic Resources: Fundamentals of Product Description and Support. ISO TC184/SC4/WG5. Geneva: International Organization for Standardization.

Jones O. (1989). *An Introduction to the X Window System*. Englewood Cliffs. NJ: Prentice Hall.

MIL-D-28000 (1987). *Military specification, Digital Representation for Communication of Product Data: IGES Application Subsets*. Washington, DC: US Department of Defense.

Opengroup (1997). X Window System web site. *http://www.opengroup.org/tech/desktop/x/*. Open Software Foundation.

Owen J. (1993). *STEP An Introduction*. Winchester: Information Geometers.

Plastock R. A. and Kalley G. (1986). *Computer Graphics*. New York: Schaum/McGraw-Hill.

Pountain D. (1989). The X Window System. *Byte*. **14**(1), 353–60.

Schlechtendahl E. G. (ed.) (1989). *ESPRIT Project 322: CAD Data Transfer for Solid Models*. Heidelberg: Springer.

Schlechtendahl E. G. and Weick W. (1990). ESPRIT contributions to the exchange of CAD models. *European CADCAM 1990/91*. London: The CADCAM Association.

Seifert R. (1991). Ethernet: ten years after. *Byte*. **16**(1), 315–22.

SGI (1997). OpenGL Web site. *http://www.sgi.com/Technology/OpenGL/*. Silicon Graphics Inc.

Smith J. M. (1990). *An Introduction to CALS: The Strategy and the Standards*. Twickenham, England: Technology Appraisals.

Stallings W. (1989). When one LAN is not enough. *Byte*. **14**(1), 293–8.

Tailor Made Software (1997). CAD data transfer web site. *http://www.tailormade.com/*.

US Pro (1997). US Pro Web site. *http://www.scra.org/uspro/orgs/uspro.html*. US Product Data Association.

Valenzano A., Demartini C. and Ciminera L. (1992). *MAP and TOP Communications. Standards and Applications*. Harlow: Addison Wesley Longman.

Wilson P. R. (1987). A short history of CAD data transfer. *IEEE Computer Graphics and Applications*. June, 64–7.

Exercises

7.1 Discuss the areas in which standards impinge upon the design and operation of CADCAM systems. Which of these areas is most important from a user's point of view?

7.2 Write out the general form of the GKS commands to draw a rectangle from $x = 0$, $y = 0$ to $x = 150$, $y = 100$, together with the text string 'TEXT NOTE' located at $x = 25$, $y = 50$.

7.3 How should the commands in Exercise 7.2 be modified if (a) a filled rectangle is required and (b) the rectangle and text are to be constructed as a single segment?

7.4 Distinguish between a metafile and a bitmap for the representation of picture information. Give examples of standard formats for each.

7.5 Outline how a CAD drawing file would be stored at different representation levels from a collection of entities in a part file to a collection of pixels in a bitmap. Indicate the relationship between these representations.

7.6 Outline the elements of the client–server model for network computing, and describe how the X Window System fits into this model.

7.7 Which X Window System commands might be used to draw filled rectangles in three different styles in (a) an array of off-screen pixels in the server and (b) a window on the server's screen?

7.8 Outline the five sections of an IGES file for CAD data transfer, and show as an example the representation of an arc within such a file.

7.9 Use a CAD system to generate an IGES file and/or a DXF file for a simple collection of geometry. Examine the file(s) and match the entity entries in the file(s) to the entities in the CAD part.

7.10 Explain why the STEP standard has been developed to replace the IGES standard, and then outline the approach and structure of STEP.

7.11 Suggest how the following arc geometric entities might be modelled in EXPRESS, and how instances of the entities might be stored on the physical file: (a) an arc defined by the x, y and z coordinates of the centre, together with radius and start and end angles; (b) an arc through three predefined points; (c) an arc through a predefined point and tangent to a predefined line.

7.12 Suggest an EXPRESS entity definition for a commercial aircraft, using the following attributes: make, model number, number of engines, maximum speed, number of seats, airline and routes. The attribute routes should allow an arbitrary list of routes on which the aircraft is used to be specified, and the attribute airline should be one of a list of four airlines.

7.13 Outline the standards used in the Continuous Acquisition and Logistics Support approach, and then suggest which of these standards would be used to produce a computer representation of a technical manual for an engineering product. What do you think are the advantages of using the CALS approach for technical documentation?

7.14 Distinguish between a wide area network and a local area network.

7.15 Distinguish between the star, the ring and the bus/tree topologies for local area networks. What do the terms token passing and CSMA/CD signify in the context of the latter two network types?

7.16 Outline the seven levels of the ISI OSI model, and then indicate the parts of the TCP/IP set which correspond to the top five levels.

7.17 Outline the differences between the Manufacturing Automation Protocol (MAP) and the Technical and Office Protocols (TOPs) for networks, and suggest how the features of each protocol match the needs of the working environment.

Projects

For more information about the subjects for project work, please refer to the end of Chapter 1.

The project activity for this chapter is to explore the use of standards for the representation and exchange of the CAD files that have been developed for the chess piece and load cell projects. Specific project tasks are:

Projects 1 and 2 Chess piece and load cell Produce IGES, DXF and STEP representations of the part files used to represent the chess piece and load cell, and then:

▶ explore how well these files can be read by another CAD system;

▶ examine the content of the files for one of the parts (e.g. the detail drawing of the load cell structural member), and relate this content to the description of the file representation for the standard used.

8 Expanding the capability of CAD

Chapter objectives

When you have completed the material in this chapter you should be able to:
- describe the limitations of conventional CAD approaches in providing design information and advice;
- outline the scope for application of artificial intelligence techniques in design;
- outline the main knowledge representation and inference techniques in knowledge-based systems;
- describe the integration of knowledge-based systems and CAD in knowledge-based engineering;
- outline the main approaches to parametric and variational modelling in CAD;
- understand the motivation behind the use of feature-based approaches in CAD, and distinguish between design by features and feature recognition;
- outline the principal techniques of design information systems, and in particular explain the basis of text-oriented databases and hypertext.

Chapter contents

8.1 Introduction

CAD is now so extensively applied that in some companies all design work is done using CAD systems. Despite this considerable success, there is a widespread view that CAD is not yet adequate as an *aid* to the designer in generating a design. CAD is considered to concentrate rather too much on providing means of representing the final form of the design, whereas designers also need a continual stream of advice and information to assist in decision making. For example, a CAD system might allow a finite element model to be developed for analysis of a design, but it would give no advice on what element type to use in the particular circumstances, or on how to model a certain loading condition; it might allow manufacturing instructions to be derived from the design geometry, but it is unlikely to be able to advise the designer whether a certain shape is capable of being economically cast or forged.

Even though CAD systems concentrate on the modelling of designs, the extent to which they are able to model different attributes varies considerably. Shape and dimension are well covered by geometric modelling capabilities, and structure by the hierarchical bills of materials in product data management systems. Other properties, such as tolerance, material, surface condition and function, are, however, much less satisfactorily dealt with – often only by annotation of a conventional drawing or by attaching attributes to a three-dimensional model. A system that captures a complete model of a product will require formal notations for all of the properties of the design.

Furthermore, there is a widespread view that even the geometric aspects of a design are not modelled by traditional CAD systems in the way that is most useful to a designer, or in the way that designers think of them. In the early stages of the design process, the designer may wish simply to sketch ideas, and may be reluctant to specify actual dimensions for a part. As the design progresses, the designer may wish to explore a variety of different dimensions, in order to answer 'what-if' types of questions about the design. And all through the product introduction process, all those who work with the CAD model may wish to use model concepts that have more engineering meaning. We have seen, for example, how a component such as a connecting rod might be represented by a collection of lines and arcs on a draw-ing, or by surfaces on the part, or by instances of solid primitives. A designer, on the other hand, may envisage the part as two 'eyes' joined by a 'shank', or a manufac-turing engineer might think in terms of manufacturing features such as a reamed hole, a blend or a flash-line.

The tasks of the new generation of CAD systems are therefore to represent a wider variety of a design's properties, in terms that are familiar to engineers, and to handle those aspects of engineering practice, and of a company's organization and equipment, that influence design. The way in which it is hoped to achieve this is to bring ideas and techniques from research into artificial intelligence (AI) and informa-tion systems, and also to search for higher-level methods for modelling of the design representations.

In addition to the substantial research work involved in the detailed development of CAD techniques, there has been much recent work on the system architectures that may be appropriate in the future. A recurring theme in this field is the concept of integrated systems, which provide many different computational approaches to assist the designer, and allow the product itself and the production plant, design process and applications to be modelled. The integrating technologies in such sys-tems will be CAD modelling, AI, information systems and databases, and the prod-uct models will be underpinned by new ways of describing products. Figure 8.1 shows one possible arrangement for such a system.

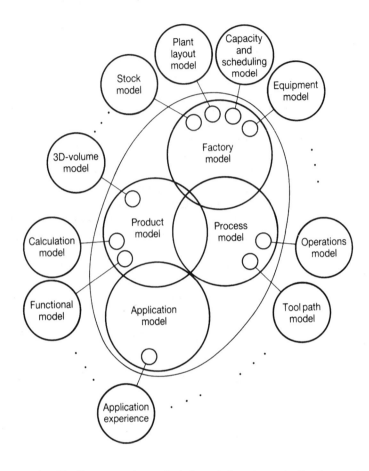

FIGURE 8.1

The connection of product-related models.
(Reproduced from Spur *et al.*, 1989 with permission from Mechanical Engineering Publications Ltd.)

Concurrent with the move towards integrated systems is the increasing globalization of industry. Increasingly, a product may be engineered in one country and assembled in another, perhaps using parts procured from several others. Product development teams need to operate in an integrated manner, but are geographically separated. In order to achieve this, a variety of techniques are developing to support cooperative working, in particular those that exploit the Internet and high-speed communications as will be seen in Chapter 16. The product-related models shown in Figure 8.1 will eventually be distributed and globally accessible.

8.2 Artificial intelligence in design

There are a number of strands of research into artificial intelligence (AI). Only one part of the activity involves trying to produce machines (computers) which simulate intelligent behaviour, and this work is surrounded by much controversy: there are those who dispute that it is feasible or that the tenets of the AI research community are valid. Other less controversial work involves investigating the nature of intelligence, and trying to make machines smarter by learning how to enable them to represent and manipulate real-world knowledge. The application of AI to design is generally concerned with these latter activities: with studying how designers apply human intelligence to design, and with trying to make computer aids to design more knowledgeable.

The main themes in the application of AI are currently to explore the formal representation of design knowledge, and also to develop techniques for reasoning with or applying this knowledge. Computers have traditionally been able to deal with the application of the laws of applied science, expressed for example in mathematical techniques such as finite element analysis. What AI may allow in particular is the representation of heuristic (or 'rule-or-thumb') knowledge that is less easy to express using traditional mathematical approaches. The part of AI that is particularly concerned with the development of such representations is known as **expert systems**, or more generally, **knowledge-based systems**.

Basic concepts

Brachman and Levesque (1985) suggest that a primary concern of AI is 'writing down descriptions of the world in such a way that an intelligent machine can come to new conclusions about its environment by formally manipulating these descriptions'. One can take a less strong view about the role of 'intelligent machines', but nevertheless a characteristic of knowledge-based systems is a formal and explicit representation, stored in a **knowledge base**, of the knowledge pertaining to a given area (or **domain**) of activity. The representation typically uses symbolic (as opposed to numeric) terms defined in a notation or language with semantics which are used to define their meaning and a well-defined syntax governing the form of statements. The symbols define both concepts within the domain and the relationships between them.

The extraction of information from the knowledge base is carried out by a part of the system known as an **inference engine**, which is generally separate from the knowledge base itself. Inference normally involves search and matching in the knowledge base in order to try to meet a goal (e.g. to optimize the parameters of a design, or to diagnose a fault in a machine).

The knowledge base is developed by a process of **knowledge acquisition** – described by Buchanan and Shortliffe (1984) as 'the transfer and transformation of potential problem-solving expertise from some knowledge-source to a program'. This may be achieved in a variety of ways, including **knowledge elicitation** by systematic study of expert behaviour, for example by study of an expert's approach to sample problems, or by a number of interview techniques. The relationships between the elements of a knowledge-based system are shown in Figure 8.2.

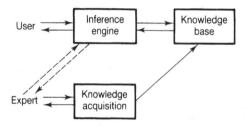

FIGURE 8.2
The elements of a knowledge-based system.

8.2.1 Representing knowledge

Many different knowledge representation techniques have been proposed. In this section we will consider a number that broadly reflect the range of approaches available to the system developer. These are, firstly, a group of knowledge representation techniques that might be used by a knowledge engineer to describe a problem in a conventional knowledge-based system. These are **production systems**, **frames**, and **graphs** and **networks**. Secondly, we will examine an 'automatic' technique for knowledge capture that does not involve the development of a knowledge base, but rather uses the approach of teachable computing networks knows as **neural networks**. Finally, we will explore briefly how uncertainty may be incorporated into knowledge representation through the use of **fuzzy sets and systems**.

Production systems

In production systems, knowledge is represented as a collection of premise–action pairs, called **production rules**, whose general form is:

IF {some combination of conditions is true}
THEN {draw some conclusion or take some action}

For example, a rule that might be applied in the case of bearing selection for the connecting rod example might be:

IF the motion is oscillating AND the load is high AND
the load is fluctuating AND the lubrication is oil spray
THEN bearing type is plain bearing

This rule would be implemented (generally more tersely, but often in an English-like language) in the knowledge base. This rule would be applied together with other rules, such as:

IF application is engine THEN lubrication is oil spray OR pumped oil

and facts such as:

application is engine

in order to complete the knowledge base.

Frame systems

Whereas production systems are used to store heuristic rules and facts, frame systems (or more usually just **frames**) represent knowledge by use of prototypical objects. Frames represent **classes** of such objects as collections of data in slots within the frame, in some ways analogous to the storage of data in C or Pascal structures. An example frame, describing the plain bearing chosen for our connecting rod, is shown in Figure 8.3. This frame belongs to the class of objects known as plain bearings. The particular bearing is described by an instance of the frame, in which slot values are **instantiated** to those appropriate to the bearing. Although the values shown in

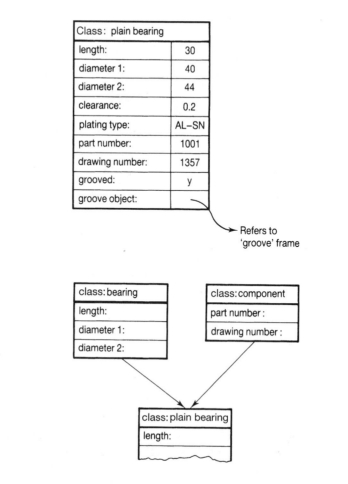

FIGURE 8.3
A frame representation for bearing data.

FIGURE 8.4
Data inheritance.

Figure 8.3 are just numbers or strings, frames generally allow the freedom to use different data types, such as lists or references to procedures. Furthermore, the values of slots may be obtained from other frames by inheritance: a particular class of frames may itself be a subtype of a higher-level class. So, for example, the class 'plain bearing' may be a member of the higher-level class of 'bearing'. Furthermore, a given class may inherit attributes from multiple frame classes – for example, the class of plain bearings may inherit dimensional details from the higher-level class 'bearing', and may inherit part and drawing number slots from the class called 'component', as shown in Figure 8.4. Further properties of frames are that slots may be given default values built into the frame system or inherited from superclasses, and the slots may also refer to procedural attachments – executable code that may manipulate the contents of slots in frames.

Graphs and networks

The hierarchical arrangement of frames may be regarded as a number of entities in a network linked together by inheritances. This concept of primitive entities called

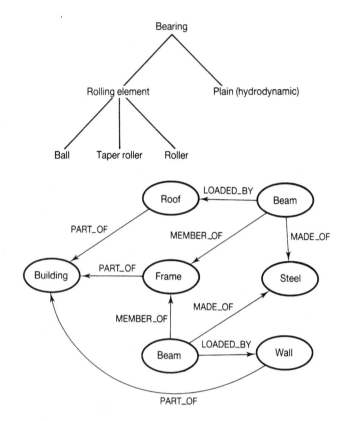

FIGURE 8.5
A simplified hierarchy of bearing types.

FIGURE 8.6
A network of relationships.

nodes being connected together by other primitive entities called **arcs** or **links** is known as a **graph** (of which a network is a particular type). As we have seen, graphs may be used to represent relationships between entities: for example the graph shown in Figure 8.5 (in fact in this case a **tree**) represents classes of bearing. A second example, in this case a more general **associative net**, representing associations between entities in a building structure, is shown in Figure 8.6. It may be seen from this figure that a variety of different association types may be represented by the links.

The reader will note the similarity between the frame representation and the object-oriented approach described in Chapter 5. Increasingly, the representation schemes available in knowledge-based system toolkits are embedded in object-oriented technology.

Hybrid representations

In general, a single representation is not adequate to represent all of the knowledge of a particular domain. The most flexible systems will offer a variety of representation schemes: for instance, an associative net may use frames, stored in some hierarchy, as a means of representing the nodes in the network. The reasoning with the knowledge in such a network might be achieved by rules stored in a production system. For example, let us consider a system to advise on whether a component might be manufactured by casting. A suitable knowledge representation might comprise production rules to describe the **domain knowledge** about casting design, and frames to describe the component being assessed. The domain knowledge will remain more or less static, while the component data will be different for every assessment.

Neural networks

The knowledge representation schemes outlined above are used **explicitly** to represent domain knowledge. An alternative is to use a computing approach in which a general-purpose program or computing device is capable of adapting itself to a particular set of circumstances. This might be appropriate, for example, where knowledge acquisition is too difficult or too expensive. An instance of such an approach is the use of **artificial neural networks**, also known as connectionist models, parallel distributed models or simply neural nets.

Neural networks comprise many simple computational elements called **nodes** or **neurons**, each of which collects by weighted addition the signals from various other nodes to which it is connected in a network (Beale and Jackson, 1990). The arrangement is intended to be somewhat analogous to the arrangement of neurons connected by synapses in the brain. The weighted sum, called the **net input** to the node, is processed by an internal function to give the output of the node. This output may be part of the output from the network, or may provide an input signal to further nodes in the network. The nodes of a network are arranged in layers, with an input layer receiving inputs and an output layer presenting output signals, and with one or more internal or **hidden layer** between these, as shown in Figure 8.7. This diagram shows the weight associated with each path joining one node in the network to another. It is also possible to bypass internal layers, for example to connect input neurons directly to the output. The principle of operation of a neural network is as follows. Firstly, the network is trained by presenting to it a large number of example tables of input signals and their corresponding outputs, known as training instances. The weights of the paths joining the nodes of the network are then

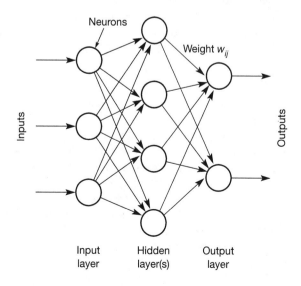

FIGURE 8.7
The structure of an artificial neural network.

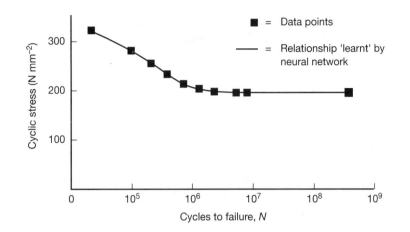

FIGURE 8.8

The learning of a relationship by a neural network.

adjusted by an algorithmic scheme to minimize the difference between the training outputs and the outputs generated by the network for the same set of input values. There are a number of schemes available, of which perhaps the best known is the back propagation approach developed by Rumelhart and his co-workers (1986) and so called because errors are propagated through the layers. Once trained, the network will provide an apparent relationship function between inputs and outputs, and will generate an output for any arbitrary combination of input values.

Neural networks can be trained to learn relationships from the simple – such as that between stress level and number of cycles to failure used in fatigue analysis, as shown in Figure 8.8 – to the more complex, such as, for example, being trained to discriminate between different numbers of passengers on underground railway station platforms, using video camera images as input. They may also be used in such areas as fault diagnosis, image processing or process control. Their use is, however, not simply a matter of presenting a set of training data to a network. The number and arrangement of internal layers is important, and there is a variety of learning techniques and internal functions used in nodes, so that experimentation is needed to identify the arrangement that gives the best result, although increasingly the experimentation is built into the learning arrangement automatically.

Fuzzy sets and systems

In the example rule from a production system given earlier in this section, one of the clauses of the rule states 'IF . . . the load is high . . .'. One of the problems with this sort of rule is that of defining what we mean by a high load. We could identify some value below which the load is not high, and above which it is, but a sudden change in strategy at some arbitrary value might not be sensible. To deal with this sort of linguistic uncertainty, Zadeh introduced the concept of a **fuzzy set** (1965). Conventional sets are said to be **crisp** in that items either belong to a set or they do not. By contrast, a fuzzy set is a collection of objects without clear boundaries. It is defined to be a set of entities in which each entity is not limited by exclusively being a member or not a member of that set. Instead, each entity is allowed to have a partial membership of the set. For a fuzzy set, the function $\mu_B(x)$ represents the

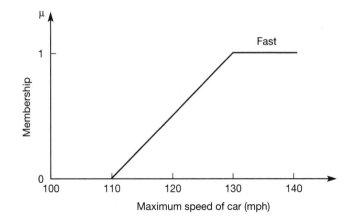

FIGURE 8.9
The fuzzy set for
'fast cars'.

membership function for the set, in which the degree that an element, x, of the universal set X belongs to set B is expressed by a number in the range 0 and 1. So, for example, the membership function for the set of fast cars, based on maximum speed in miles per hour might be as shown in Figure 8.9. From this graph, the membership value for a car with a maximum speed of 120 mph is 0.5, and for 130 mph or above is 1 (i.e. above 130 mph there is no uncertainty that the car is fast). **Fuzzy numbers** may also be used to express numerical vagueness, in that a range of values with different memberships may be assigned to a number. By expressing the terms used in a problem as fuzzy variables, vagueness in the problem can be taken into account, provided that some suitable way can be found of combining multiple fuzzy concepts in a reasoning scheme – and this has been a central issue in research in fuzzy systems.

Fuzzy theory has been developed extensively since its introduction in the 1960s, with applications in many domains (Dubois and Prade, 1980). It has been applied in control, in logic programming (by making the support for the truth of a proposition a **fuzzy** variable), in database retrieval and in a number of engineering applications (Ross, 1995). An algebra has been developed for manipulating fuzzy sets and numbers, and by use of the **extension principle** fuzzy variables can be propagated through functions. Because design is a topic in which there is considerable vagueness and imprecision, especially in its early stages, fuzzy theory has also seen a widespread but currently mainly experimental application in engineering design. In particular, applications to preliminary design have been noted by Wood and Antonsson (1989), who also provide an interesting comparison of fuzzy and probabilistic approaches in Wood *et al.* (1990).

8.2.2 Inference schemes

In order to identify whether the premise of a rule is true, it may be necessary to evaluate whether other rules are true, and these other rules may in turn require the evaluation of further rules. This procedure is known as **inference** from the knowledge base, and the inference mechanism of a system is used for manipulation of the knowledge in order to solve problems. The knowledge may be represented in many ways, although discussion here will be confined to production systems.

Chaining mechanisms

The order in which the elements of the knowledge base are accessed is important to the characteristics of the inference process. Two mechanisms that are widely used are **backward chaining** and **forward chaining**. The purpose of the inference will typically be to achieve some goal – such as to identify the most appropriate bearing for a particular application. Backward chaining involves working backwards from a rule that gives a trial conclusion – for example, from a rule that concludes that a plain bearing is appropriate. The premise of the rule is tested by checking the facts in the knowledge base or by asking the user, and/or by evaluating the rules necessary to determine whether the premise is true. The antecedents of these rules are in turn evaluated, and so on until the only information that is used is facts. This will either prove the rule true – in which case the goal is achieved, or false, in which case alternative conclusions (e.g. that ball bearing is appropriate) are evaluated. Figure 8.10 shows how a simple network of rules may be used for selection of a bearing type, and how backward chaining is used for such selection.

In Figure 8.10 the user of the knowledge-based system would be asked to provide the information about the type of bearing load and speed regime when it is needed by the inference. If, on the other hand, the system starts by collecting this information from the user, then it could work forward, or forward chain, through the rules to the appropriate conclusion, as shown in Figure 8.11.

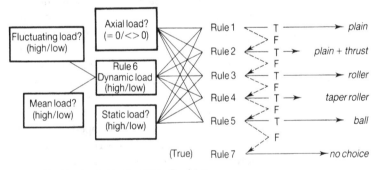

– – – – – – Backtrack moves   T = true;   F = false

Rule 1
IF axial load = 0 **AND** dynamic load = high **AND** static load = low **THEN** choose *plain* bearing

Rule 2
IF axial load <>0 **AND** dynamic load = high **AND** static load = low **THEN** choose *plain + thrust*

Rule 3
IF axial load = 0 **AND** dynamic load = high **AND** static load = high **THEN** choose *roller*

Rule 4
IF axial load <> 0 **AND** dynamic load = high **AND** static load = high **THEN** choose *taper roller*

Rule 5
IF axial load <> 0 **AND** dynamic load = low **AND** static load = low **THEN** choose *ball* bearing

Rule 6
IF fluctuating load = high **AND** mean load = high **THEN** dynamic load = high
                                                    ELSE dynamic load = low

Rule 7
IF (true) **THEN** *no choice*

FIGURE 8.10

Rules for bearing selection.

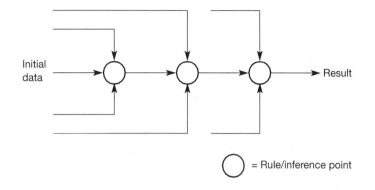

FIGURE 8.11
Forward chaining.

◯ = Rule/inference point

Forward chaining is more appropriate when the number of facts pertaining to a particular problem is fairly limited, but where there are many possible conclusions. Backward chaining is more appropriate if the reverse is true. The reader should also note that a characteristic of the inference that has been described is **search** of a solution space, and the matching of solution patterns to patterns in the knowledge base.

8.2.3 Approaches to the application of AI in design

The examples above show that knowledge-based techniques may be applied to the problems of selection in design. Areas where a similar approach may be taken include the selection of materials, manufacturing processes and analytical techniques. Rule-based approaches may also be applied to problems which involve diagnosis and assessment. There are, in addition, several other classes of design problem for which AI techniques may be particularly relevant, and these will be discussed below.

Decomposition

Engineering products are often highly complex, involving hundreds or thousands of parts, and in the design of such products the interactions between the design activity and other activities – such as manufacture and purchasing – are also very complex. A way of managing complexity that is adopted in many design approaches is to apply a 'divide and conquer' method in which a problem is divided into smaller, more soluble, sub-problems. Much research into the application of AI in design has also followed this approach by studying how designs, and design knowledge and the design process, may be subdivided, or **decomposed**, into smaller elements. Once these smaller problems have been solved, it is then necessary to assemble the results into an overall solution, resolving in the process any conflicts arising from the subdivision.

Decomposition may be achieved in a variety of ways, for example by dividing the problem according to the nature of the solution technique adopted, or by dividing the design itself into a series of elements. An assembly might be divided into subassemblies, and these in turn into individual components. The latter approach suggests a hierarchy of design detail: at the upper levels the overall parameters of the design are established, together with the interfaces between major design elements. The details of these elements are established at lower levels, which may in turn consider the design as a series of separate elements. If the design process progresses from the upper levels to the lower ones this is known as a **top-down** approach to design. Conversely, if the detailed component parameters are established first, and then the results assembled at a higher level, then this is known as **bottom-up** design. In practice, top-down design is widely applied in aerospace, electronics and software design, but in mechanical design a hybrid, part top-down, part bottom-up, approach is often adopted because of the influence of detail design consideration on the overall design approach.

Plan selection and refinement

In many design problems the design approach can, at least in part, be reduced to that of identifying a generic design type and then filling in details of dimensions, materials and component arrangement. In AI this approach is called **plan refinement**, and is a technique that originates from research into medical expert systems. There it is used to select a general treatment approach, and then to refine this to identify drug combinations and amounts appropriate to a particular patient. In terms of our example, the process of selecting a type of bearing to use, and then instantiating the values of the attributes in a frame describing that bearing, can be regarded as a simple example of plan refinement.

Constraint-based reasoning

The particular materials, dimensions and surface treatment and condition selected for a given design will be chosen to ensure that the design is fit for purpose, and that it can be made. If a dimension is such that the design breaks under load, or cannot be made, then the design conflicts with **constraints** imposed by the strength of its materials or the manufacturing process respectively. The more general concept is that a particular design is at a point in a multi-dimensional design space, and that bounds on that space that define feasible (but not necessarily optimal) designs are imposed by constraints, as shown in Figure 8.12. The idea of constraint-based reasoning is that designs can be modelled in a network of design attributes and their associated constraints. A feasible design within the constraint space (if one exists) may be identified by chaining through the network. Figure 8.13 shows part of a simple constraint network for the design of pistons.

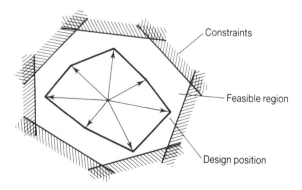

Constraints

Feasible region

Design position

FIGURE 8.12

The design problem as a multi-dimensional constraint space.

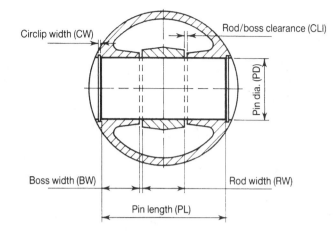

Relationships:
1. Bearing area = Bearing diameter × Length
2. Bearing pressure = Bearing load/Area

Constraints:
3. Pin length ≤ Rod width + (2 × Boss width) + (2 × Clearance)
4. Minimum metal thickness obtained graphically from pin diameter and length, piston diameter and circlip dimensions

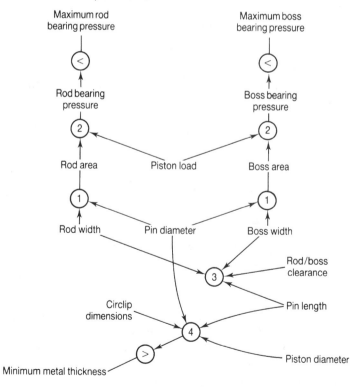

FIGURE 8.13
A constraint network for a piston.

Values in circles refer to inequalities, or to relationships or constraints

Case-based reasoning

Human beings usually make judgements on the basis of past experience, often by drawing connections between the problem to be solved and previous similar problems. When approaching a design problem the designer might ask 'have we ever done anything like this before, or do I know anybody that has?', and would seek to learn from and exploit the previous examples. The technique known as **case-based reasoning** seeks to provide computer-based design tools that emulate this behaviour of searching for analogy. Typically, the system would include a number of examples of design situations, represented in symbolic form and indexed to aid retrieval, together with generalized knowledge about how to transform one or more of these previous situations to work in a new context. An example application would be in **configuration design** – the selection of the arrangement of elements in a design, the relationship between them, and their attributes. In a simple form, known as **select and verify**, a case-based reasoning approach would involve selection of a potential solution from a given set of arrangements, and then verification of the suitability of the approach by testing it against the requirements and constraints of the problem. A more general approach, known as **match, modify and test**, allows the solution to be found by modifying a candidate configuration (Wielinga and Schreiber, 1997; Maher and de Silva Garza, 1997). The reader will notice the similarity of this latter approach to plan selection and refinement.

Grammatical design

The design task can be viewed as involving repeated cycles of considering a partial design, comparing it with the design goal, deciding on a transformation to get closer to the goal and then applying that transformation to the partial design. A transformation may take various forms, including adding detail to a design, modifying an existing structure, or adding new components. Brown (1997) contends that **grammatical design** is a paradigm based directly on this view, and is concerned with identifying a computational basis for representational structures and transformation mechanisms. It does this by providing a mechanism for the generation of design structures by a formal generative system which has three parts:

▶ a 'vocabulary' of design elements that may be incorporated into candidate structures;

▶ a set of transformation rules that transform structural arrangements of the elements into new structures; and

▶ an initial structure.

In just the same way that a grammar of a language describes and provides a framework for the ways that the elements of the language can be legitimately combined, so a design grammar provides a framework – and a formal computable mechanism – for doing design. The framework can be regarded as a mechanism for representing accumulated experience and standard practice, for exploring standard arrangements, or for ensuring that only structures with specific properties are generated. Much research in grammatical design to date has applied to **shape grammars** which consider formalisms for legitimate combinations of geometric elements (Stiny, 1991), although grammars have been applied to architectural planning and building layout, engineering assessment, process planning and structural design amongst other applications.

Truth maintenance

A product design is normally developed over a period of time, as the designer collects information and experiments with different design arrangements. As the design process progresses, assumptions will be made and values assigned to design attributes. These attributes are dependent on values determined by earlier decisions, and, furthermore, different values may be assigned as alternative design strategies are explored in different contexts. The problem of maintaining these different contexts, and the data dependencies that exist in such complex situations, is known as **truth maintenance**.

8.2.4 Knowledge-based engineering

Knowledge-based systems are a general technology, applied in domains as diverse as medicine, banking, engineering and commerce. Most of the techniques we have discussed so far in this chapter could be applied in almost any application domain, but some very specifically engineering-oriented applications of knowledge-based systems do exist. Well known amongst these is the approach known as **knowledge-based engineering** (KBE). KBE is a combination of object-oriented programming, knowledge representation, rule-based systems and CAD, and it tries to exploit the strengths of each of these.

The foundation of KBE is the development, using object-oriented techniques, of a product model. In this model, object class definitions are defined which represent classes of design parts, and product-structure trees are used to identify the hierarchical breakdown of assemblies into subassemblies. The models draw on the general ideas of product structure and product configuration which suggest that we can classify engineering products into a number of hierarchical decompositions – based for example on function, part family, manufacturing process and so on. Information about the design parts is attached to the model using attributes. These can represent any sort of information – dimensions, tolerances, materials, and also relationships between parts and derived values such as weight, cost, manufacturing process data and so on. By using procedural attachments, attributes can also be written as expressions, rules, relationships to other attributes or inputs from other programs or databases. They can also be arranged to prompt for user input if required.

The structured object approach to model representation is **declarative** – the attributes and relationships of the model are declared, but order of computation is not prescribed, and therefore the models are very flexible. Engineers can record knowledge about a product without concern for the order of execution of the program.

The product model, together with rules about the product, allows the production of arbitrary design variants that are instances of the object-oriented model that conform to the rules. Where KBE differs from other knowledge-based systems is that geometric modelling capabilities are incorporated to allow the model to be represented by standard geometric techniques such as surface or boundary representation parts. This allows the parts defined by the model and rule aspects of the system to be represented, and also allows geometric reasoning where it is appropriate, but unlike a conventional CAD system it does not force a very geometry-centred approach to design automation.

KBE has been applied in a large number of design contexts, but in particular in those design domains where products are variations on an established design pattern. Examples of applications have included heat exchanger design, engine part design, even the design of complete wing mechanical structures for aircraft. Example 8.1 gives an example of the application of KBE using a system from one of the major software vendors in the area.

Example 8.1 ***The application of knowledge-based engineering***

Knowledge-based engineering (KBE) offers the possibility of automating repetitive, rule-driven design tasks, and thus to achieve significant reductions in concept design time-scale while at the same time increasing the number of design solutions that are explored. The approach can offer benefits in a wide range of applications, ranging from those where the product is designed to order, to mass production automotive and consumer durable industries. One company that has devoted considerable effort to developing a portfolio of KBE applications is Jaguar Cars, where KBE has been applied to assist in meeting increasing time, cost and customer and legislative demand pressures in design.

Jaguar has developed a wide range of KBE applications that include wheel envelope and ground clearance calculation, internal ergonomics, vehicle side glazing design, windscreen wiped-area evaluation, headlamp feasibility study and body panel reinforcement design. The last two applications are particularly good examples of the use of KBE. In conventional headlamp feasibility, Jaguar would expect a 4–6 week response from its suppliers in evaluating headlamp design proposals. In the Jaguar KBE applications, supplier design rules are incorporated, thus allowing different design proposals to be evaluated very rapidly against the supplier rule base.

A rule base is also used in the application of panel reinforcement design. We have seen in Chapter 6 that an automobile body comprises a large number of sheet metal panels that are welded together to form the body. In many cases an external panel is combined with an internal reinforcement panel to form a sort of sandwich construction, for example in the bonnet (hood) or boot (trunk) lid of the vehicle. Jaguar has incorporated its design rules for panels into a KBE application such that a reinforcing panel can be designed automatically given an external panel surface and a reinforcement pattern. The rules govern pressing direction, draft angles, section dimensions and bend radii, all of which are automatically calculated based on section depth, material thickness and material type. The output from the KBE program is a fully surfaced model of the reinforcing panel, and may typically be achieved in a few minutes rather than hours or days. This allows the company's engineers to explore many different reinforcing patterns. Where at one time only one or two patterns

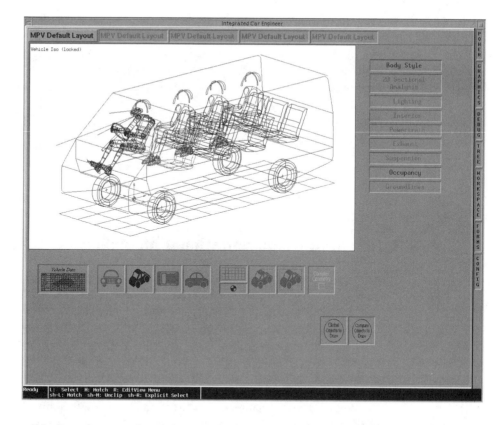

FIGURE 8.14

An example of knowledge-based engineering. (Reproduced by permission of Concentra Ltd.)

might have been explored, in a recent project 11 different bonnet (hood) reinforcement patterns were tried, with the result that the panel was much closer to optimum.

KBE has also been applied to whole-vehicle concept design studies, in order to explore different vehicle configurations. KBE allows rules to be built into the system for configuration of engines, transmissions and suspension systems, and for links to be built into mechanisms analysis, dynamics analysis and the like. Figure 8.14 shows a screen shot from the Vehicle Layout System of the Integrated Car Engineer™ (I.C.E.) suite developed by Concentra, in partnership with Lotus and Tata Technologies, that allows 'top-level' checks on a vehicle design to be rapidly carried out.

8.2.5 Concluding remarks

We have seen that there are very many approaches to the application of knowledge-based and artificially intelligent systems in engineering design, and the applications to engineering in general are even more varied. Broadly, the applications may be classified into those that attempt to automate routine design, in which the heuristics and algorithms for the design of a particular type of product are captured, and those which seek to provide some sort of specialist input, for example in design for manufacture or assembly. An example of the former might be seen where a company that produces automotive parts to an essentially standard design, but with dimensions modified to suit individual manufacturers' vehicles, automates its design activity using a KBE or a plan selection and refinement approach. An example of the latter is a system to rate a product on its ease of assembly, and then to suggest design changes that would improve its assemblability (Swift, 1987). The topic of the application of AI in engineering in general and in engineering design, analysis and manufacture in particular has been the subject of considerable research in recent years, and there are conferences and scientific journals that specialize in publishing research into the field – for example, the journals *AI in Engineering Design, Analysis and Manufacture (AI-EDAM)* and *AI in Engineering,* and the *AI in Design* conference series. The interested reader is referred to these publications, to the special issues on AI in design of the *IEEE Expert* journal (*IEEE Expert*, 1997) and to an AI in design index for the World-Wide Web maintained at Worcester Polytechnic Institute in Massachusetts (Brown D. C., 1997).

8.3 Parametric and variational modelling

In Chapter 6 we saw that in many cases a designer may wish to produce geometry for a product design that is a variation on some previous design. Many companies have products in which parts are variations of standard families, or which use geometry from the design of previous products, but with changes in dimensions. Often, early in design of a new product, the designer knows broadly what is required, but cannot specify exact dimensions, or may want to explore variations in dimensions as the design progresses. In each case facilities are required to allow variations of shapes to be produced in what is known as parametric design.

We saw also in Chapter 6 that the production of a repetitive family of parts type of design can be achieved by programming the commands required to model the part in a computer program or macro, but that this is not a very flexible approach. It is satisfactory for well-defined families of parts for which multiple variants are required, and for which the programming effort is justified. Where skilled programming staff are available, this approach can be very successful. However, for each change in part geometry, the program or macro has to be re-executed to construct the geometry from scratch, and 'what-if' types of investigation of the effect of changes in dimensions have to be carried out by repeatedly executing the program. For these reasons, new approaches to parametric design have been developed that allow modification and reuse of the model as constructed – that is, a parametric design approach that is integrated into the modelling approach of the system, rather than requiring special programs to be written.

The new approaches to parametric design include a number of different techniques that often appear broadly similar to the user; indeed, it may be difficult to distinguish which approach is being used. The techniques allow the user to describe the dimensional attributes of the modelled geometry not only by numbers, but also by expressions that relate the dimensions to the values of variables and/or to other parametric dimensions. The values of variables may be entered by the user, or may be tabulated. This allows a geometric model to be defined first in terms of a general shape and topology, and then for an instance of the shape to be instantiated by entering the appropriate variable values that allow the dimensions to be computed.

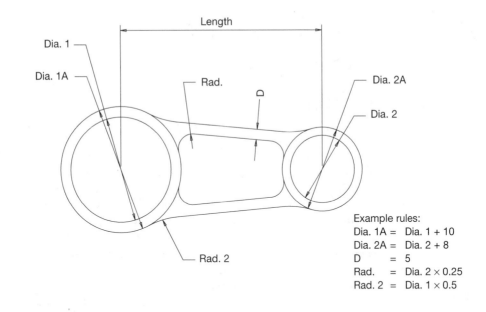

Length

Dia. 1

Dia. 1A

Rad.

D

Dia. 2A

Dia. 2

Example rules:
Dia. 1A = Dia. 1 + 10
Dia. 2A = Dia. 2 + 8
D   = 5
Rad.   = Dia. 2 × 0.25
Rad. 2 = Dia. 1 × 0.5

Rad. 2

FIGURE 8.15
A link as a
parametric object.

Changes to the geometry may be explored very quickly simply by changing the values of key variables. To illustrate, let us consider a simplified version of a connecting link as a parametric design. Figure 8.15 shows the dimensions of the link, and a series of simple expressions that relate the values of these to key dimensions – in this case the bore of the holes in each end of the link. Once this part has been defined as a parametric design, then changing the values of variables Dia.1 or Dia.2 would cause the geometry to be reconstructed to reflect the change in dimensions, again as shown in Figure 8.15.

8.3.1 A classification of parametric design approaches

Roller (1991) proposes that parametric design approaches may be classified into variant programming, expert systems, constructive schemes and numerical constraint solvers. Variant programming is the generation of programs for parts, using macro languages, graphics programming languages or APIs, as described in Chapter 6. Expert systems approaches to parametric design are the KBE approaches described in Section 8.2.4. The commercial approaches to parametric modelling fall mainly under the final two headings. Constructive schemes use the sequence or history of operations by the user to build a part to record the object definition in some way. Numerical constraint solvers allow the dimensions of a part to be defined in terms of relationships and constraints, and generate part variants by applying some sort of constraint satisfaction algorithm. The difference between **parametric** and **variational** approaches is in the type of constraint satisfaction algorithm employed. Parametric systems solve constraints by applying assignments to model variables sequentially, where each assigned value is computed as a function of previously assigned values. Variational systems construct a system of equations representing the constraints, and then solve all the equations simultaneously using a numerical solving procedure or some equivalent method (Shah and Mäntylä, 1995). Both constructive and constraint solving approaches are called parametric modelling in commercial systems.

Constructive schemes

Constructive schemes generate a procedural description of the sequence of modelling operations to build an object, often through storage by the system of a 'journal' or history of command and data entries, and explicit identification in this journal of the input parameter entries, and the use of relationships between model variables. The history file might, for example, record in the form of a tree structure the elements or features of the model, and the Boolean operations used to incorporate them into the part. Changes to the parametric geometry are achieved by modifying input parameters, which results in a recomputation of any derived values, and a repetition of the construction sequence defined in the journal using the revised variables. Shah and Mäntylä (1995) call these models **unidirectionally parametric** or **procedural**, because the sequence of computation is fixed by the procedural representation of the constraints. Such an approach can often be built on top of an existing modeller, and has been employed as a means of adding parametric capabilities to established CADCAM systems. The disadvantage of the procedural approach is the computational effort required to replay the procedure in the event of changes, and the relative lack of flexibility in the parametric relationships and variations that can be explored.

Numerical constraint solvers

Numerical constraint solvers avoid some of the problems of the procedural constructive scheme by replacing the fixed solution sequence of the history journal with more general mechanisms for solving the constraints applied to the part parameters and the relationships between them. Parametric constraint solvers, as noted, solve constraints by computing values as functions of previously assigned values. In variational geometry, by contrast, a complete system of constraint equations is developed and solved simultaneously (and therefore the order of constraint creation is not important).

In a simple form, variational geometry systems involve the identification of a number of characteristic points on a shape, and a number of dimensions which impose constraints on the permissible location of the characteristic points. Consider, for example, the shape shown in Figure 8.16. The characteristic points identified are described by a geometry vector, $\mathbf{x}$, containing their cartesian coordinates:

$$\mathbf{x} = \{X_1, Y_1, Z_1, \ldots, X_N, Y_N, Z_N\}^{\mathrm{T}} \tag{8.1}$$

or:

$$\mathbf{x} = \{x_1, x_2, x_3, \ldots, x_{n-2}, x_{n-1}, x_n\}^{\mathrm{T}}$$

where $n = 3N$ (Light and Gossard, 1982). Dimensions impose constraints on the permissible locations of the characteristic points, and may be expressed analytically by equations of the form:

$$F_i(\mathbf{x}, \mathbf{d}) = 0 \quad i = 1, 2, \ldots, m \tag{8.2}$$

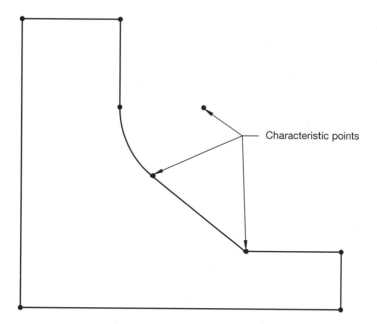

Characteristic points

FIGURE 8.16
Characteristic
points on a two-
dimensional profile.

where **d** is the vector of dimensional values, **x** is the geometry vector and m is the number of constraints.

Constraint equations include those to prevent free-body movement (one point may be 'grounded'), and dimensional constraints such as:

horizontal distance: $X_1 - X_2 - D = 0$

vertical distance: $Y_1 - Y_2 - D = 0$ $\qquad$ **(8.3)**

linear distance: $(X_1 - X_2)^2 + (Y_1 - Y_2)^2 - D^2 = 0$

although geometric constraints (area, for example) may also be applied.

Simultaneous solution of the set of constraining equations, for example by a recursive Newton–Raphson method, yields the geometry vector corresponding to the set of dimensions. A valid dimensioning scheme is therefore one in which the locations of all characteristic points are constrained by the set of equations. The number of constraint equations, m, should equal the number of degrees of coordinate freedom, n. Even if $m = n$ the problem can still, however, be numerically singular if part of the shape is overdimensioned and part is underdimensioned.

In commercial applications, variational systems generally apply to two-dimensional geometric profiles, although they are beginning to be applied to three-dimensional geometry. The 2D profiles are also used in 3D geometry as the basis for extrusion, sweeping and skinning operations, and for feature-based geometry, which we will come across later in this chapter. In many commercial applications, constraining dimensions and other conditions may be automatically identified during construction (using **sketch-based input**, or added interactively by the user). Figure 8.17 shows examples of the constraints that may be applied in a commercial variational

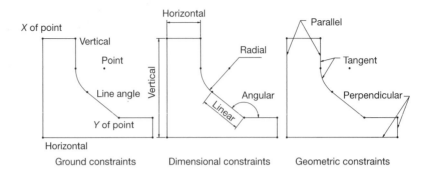

FIGURE 8.17
Constraints applied
to a 2D profile.

geometry system. Variants may be produced by entering values for key dimensions. Other dimensions are then derived or solved.

Of course, commercial variational geometry systems are very much more sophisticated than the simple approach outlined here, and the capabilities are quite considerable, as shown in Example 8.2. The constraint management approach of a commercial system will identify free degrees of freedom, will detect redundant constraints, and may allow incomplete sets of constraints to be entered. It may also (internally) represent sets of constraints in a network graph to identify coupling between constraints to allow large sets of constraints to be decomposed into smaller sets of coupled constraints to improve solution efficiency. Each set of coupled constraints is then solved in sequence to propagate changes through the constraint network. Proponents claim that variational geometry approaches can be faster and more flexible than parametric modelling approaches, because it is not necessary to resolve the entire model completely for all small changes, and because there is much more flexibility in applying and managing constraints.

In CAD system applications the term variational geometry is often used to embrace any technique for applying dimensional constraints to 'free-hand' geometry in order to solve geometric problems, to generate families of shapes, or to allow easy modification of dimensions. The term parametric modelling is also often used to describe any 'dimension-driven' approach to modelling. The success of either approach depends on the sophistication that may be built into relationships between dimensions, and the extent to which other facilities may be linked in with the system. For example, where dimensions have to be chosen to accommodate standard parts (such as fasteners) then they usually have to be constrained to be one of a limited range of preferred values (e.g. the sequence for metric thread sizes is . . . 4, 5, 6, 8, 10, 12, 16, 18, 20 . . . mm). Also, if the part is a member of a family, then a company may wish to be able to deal with the analysis of the part as a family – in which case it might be appropriate to associate a parametric finite element mesh with the parametric part. Finally, and perhaps the most challenging aspect, is that parts often change in configuration as they are scaled – for example, in a bolted flange the number of bolts might be a function of the flange diameter. Some parametric approaches only allow **geometric** parametrization in which the dimensions of a shape may change but not its structure. Parametric systems should include the facility to change the geometric *and* topological arrangement of the model also as dimensions change. This

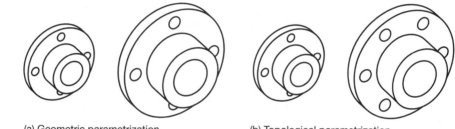

FIGURE 8.18
Geometric and
topological
parametrization.

(a) Geometric parametrization   (b) Topological parametrization

is known as **topological** or **structural** parametrization, in which for example the
number of holes in a flange could change as the flange diameter varies, as shown in
Figure 8.18.

Example 8.2 *Example of the application of a variational modelling system*

Honeywell Air Transport Systems of Phoenix, Arizona, produces on-board flight system computers, display systems and other instrumentation for the cockpits of large
commercial aircraft such as the Boeing 777 and McDonnell Douglas MD-11. The company uses a solid modelling system with a variational capability to support its concurrent engineering strategy by allowing manufacturing engineers, analysts, engineering
and design staff to share models of products, such as that shown in Figure 8.19, before
they are built. It is also able to send IGES files to the technical writers producing
maintenance documentation, and has been able to use stereolithography (SLA) for
the manufacture of rapid prototype parts.

Honeywell's designers use the variational modelling features of the CAD system
to develop features for use in design, and to assist in the development of design

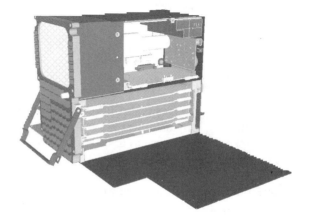

FIGURE 8.19
Honeywell flight
system product.
(Reproduced by
permission of SDRC
and Honeywell Air
Transport Systems.)

concepts. Features are developed by sketching profiles on the faces of objects, and then extruding or protruding what is sketched. Figure 8.19 shows that the geometry of the company's parts is ideally suited to the use of feature geometry of this type. Variational geometry allows parts to be constructed quickly and constraints to be added once the parts have been built. The parts can then be changed very easily by modifying dimensions. The users report that the advantage of the variational approach is that they do not have to know exactly what they want at the initial design stages. They can produce a model of a general idea, bring it up on the screen, and then subsequently constrain and change it very easily. The use of constraints in the variational modelling approach also allows design intent to be built into the model, and the general application of variational 3D modelling has greatly reduced design cycle time.

8.4 Feature-based modelling

Implicit in many of the skills of an expert designer is an ability to manipulate geometric concepts. The packaging of an aircraft's undercarriage mechanism into a compartment in the wing, the recognition of a stress-raising feature likely to lead to component failure, and the development of a plan of the machining operations to manufacture a product all require a very sophisticated geometric reasoning ability. Any truly expert computer program will have to emulate such ability. So far, many of the programs that attempt to apply concepts of AI to design have either skirted around the issue of geometric reasoning, or arranged for the user of the program to make the appropriate interpretations. At best, geometrically limited examples have been attempted.

Part of the difficulty in geometric interpretation is that the methods traditionally used for modelling of geometry in CAD are not semantically very rich. There is no information, for example, to say that a collection of lines and arcs, or of cylinders and cones, represents a drilled and tapped hole. A trained human observer can, nevertheless, interpret such features on a drawing or in a 3D model without difficulty. A rapidly developing technique in CAD is therefore to represent components in terms of higher-level entities that do have some engineering meaning. Such entities are called **features**.

8.4.1 What is a feature?

There are almost as many definitions of features as there are workers in the features research field! Originally features were thought of almost exclusively in their geometric sense. Shapes such as drilled holes, ribs or bosses in castings, grooves in shafts and so on were regarded as typical features. In addition to a geometric meaning, they also had some engineering meaning – features were often related to machining operations, although in some work almost any attribute of a component or part of a component (such as material properties, tolerances and so on) came to be regarded as a feature. In this work we will use Brown's definition (1992):

> A feature is any perceived geometric or functional element or property of an object useful in understanding the function, behaviour or performance of that object.

A more restricted definition that a feature is a prototypical shape with some engineering significance or meaning is, however, widely used. Much of the early work on features came from manufacturing process planning, which is the procedure whereby a plan is determined for the sequence of operations required to manufacture a component. In order to automate this task, it is necessary for computers to be able to recognize on a CAD model of a component those features that may be produced by given machining operations. The process of identifying these features in a CAD model is called **feature recognition**. An alternative to feature recognition is **design by features**, in which the model is constructed from a library of features, rather than geometric primitives. In this way, features have been used as a basis for a number of design activities, including the rapid design of components using standard shape features, and assistance with the interface between CAD and analysis and manufacture. Many major CAD systems now allow modelling with features, as well as employing parametric or variational modelling (which features exploit), but the topic in general is still the subject of extensive research.

8.4.2 Feature recognition

The task in feature recognition is to take an existing solid model and to search its data structure for combinations of geometric elements that correspond to prototypical features. Feature recognition has been based most often on boundary representation (B-rep) modellers because the adjacency relationships between geometric entities are explicitly modelled in such systems. Bronsvoort and Jansen (1993) indicate that recognition methods using boundary representations are all based on matching patterns of faces, edges and vertices, and identify three broad classes of approach:

▶ **Syntactic pattern methods** represent sequences of geometric elements such as line and arc segments to describe 2D geometric patterns as strings of codes. These strings are searched for substrings representing particular geometric elements, or a parser checks whether substrings of the string can be generated by a grammar describing the features. Syntactic pattern methods cannot be applied in three dimensions.

▶ **Rule-based methods** use production rules to describe features, and then search for patterns of entities in the model which match the rules using pattern matching mechanisms, for example in Prolog. The rules are of the form:

> IF (topological conditions AND material conditions AND geometric conditions)

> THEN (shape IS feature_X)

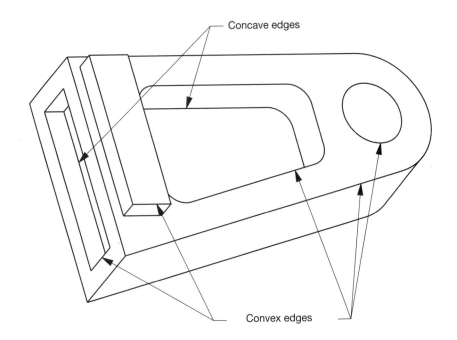

Concave edges

Convex edges

FIGURE 8.20
Concave and convex edges in feature recognition.

Topology alone is not sufficient to recognize features, and other information such as whether an edge is convex or concave, or whether faces are parallel or perpendicular, has to be included in the reasoning (as the **material conditions**) in order for recognition to succeed. For example, a protrusion and depression might have the same face and edge geometry and topology. Discrimination between them may be achieved by considering whether the edges are at concave or convex points on the geometry, as shown in Figure 8.20 (Shah and Mäntylä, 1995).

▶   **Graph-based methods** use either the boundary representation graph or other graphs such as a **face–edge graph** (FEG) to represent the model. The graph is then searched for matches to subgraphs which correspond to feature graphs. In an FEG the faces of the shape are shown as nodes, and shared edges as links. Attributes attached to the links identify whether the edge is concave or convex. An example of a related feature recognition approach is shown in Example 8.3.

In some cases, a combination of approaches may be the best way to identify features.

Example 8.3 *Feature recognition*

As an example of feature recognition consider the identification of machined depressions (pockets) or protrusions on a part as shown in Figure 8.21(a). The aim of the recognition process is to identify pockets or protrusions that may be machined by milling with the tool approach direction as shown in the figure. The recognition process first identifies all faces whose surface normals are perpendicular to the tool approach direction (Figure 8.21(b)). It then uses face–edge graphs for the part to

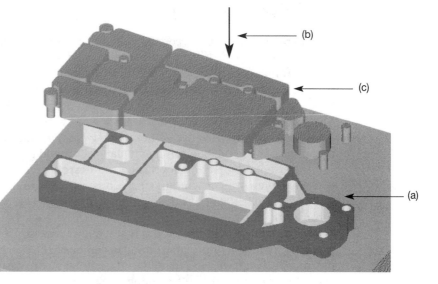

FIGURE 8.21
Recognition of pocket features. (Reproduced by permission of Dr J. Corney the Heriot-Watt Feature Finder reseach group.)

search for loops of connected faces that form complete pockets, or the external profiles of protrusions – including the external profile of the whole part. Figure 8.21(c) shows an example of a set of features identified on a part, using the algorithms that are described more fully in Little *et al.* (1997) and Corney and Clark (1991). Little *et al.* also report the results of applying the Heriot-Watt FeatureFinder algorithm to a series of test pieces that are used to compare the performance of different feature recognition algorithms.

A completely separate approach to feature recognition is the **volume decomposition** approach, which aims to determine the material that has to be removed from a base part to get the required object, and to decompose this material into features generally corresponding to machining operations.

The recognition of features in constructive solid geometry models is potentially more difficult than in B-rep models, because a CSG model is non-unique, and because primitives in proximity to each other can be widely distributed within the model tree. There have been limited experiments in feature recognition based on spatial relationships between the principal axes of primitives. Proposals have also been made that involve attempting to match patterns of primitives (representing features) with the primitives in the model tree. Nevertheless, B-rep remains the main representation on which feature recognition is based (Woodwark, 1988). Even the B-rep-based feature identification schemes have been developed mainly for research programs. Often only simple examples have been used, and in some cases there are significant limitations in the sorts of geometry that may be examined (e.g. models with planar faces only). The recognition rules or algorithms may also be confused by such things as intersecting features (e.g. intersecting holes) and by the other intersections between features that occur in practical engineering geometry.

8.4.3 Design by features

The alternative to feature recognition that is potentially attractive is to develop the design model *ab initio* in terms of features. The designer could carry out a modelling operation that explicitly creates a feature on a part and obviates the need for a program to recognize it. This **design by features** is again the subject of research, and, although some commercial modellers are beginning to adopt feature-based approaches, the associated problems are by no means solved. Once again, a number of techniques have been explored. Here we will examine two representative methods that involve operations akin to the Boolean manipulations of solid primitives in solid modelling.

The first of these techniques is known as **destructive solid geometry**. Features, typically representing machining operations (e.g. drill, mill), are **subtracted** from a workpiece or billet which is the starting point. Figure 8.22 shows a few steps in the construction of such a model. It is as if the user were machining with the computer, and the advantage of the method is that it allows process plans to be generated automatically, and the results of machining operations to be checked as if they were being performed. The drawback is that it is not a natural way to design shapes. The designer needs to have the end result in mind before proceeding, and also needs to be able to think in terms of machining operations when the natural features for the product may be functional, and the designer's skills may not be in this area.

In the second approach to design by features no billet is required. Instead, the user may assemble a representation of an object as a collection of features, by either adding or subtracting features from the model. The method is therefore sometimes called **constructional design by features**. A number of programs have been developed along these lines. Some are very closely integrated with solid modellers and some less so, but are nevertheless able to translate the feature representation into solids. A variety of underlying representations are used, encompassing all of the major solid modelling approaches – B-rep, CSG, and dual representation. An illustration of the construction of a component using features is shown in Figure 8.23.

Features have often been used in the definition of parts made using a single manufacturing technique such as casting, moulding or machining. Figure 8.23 shows an

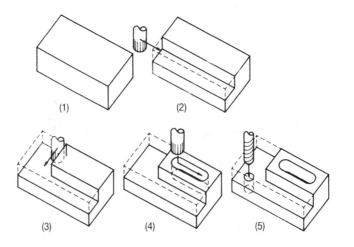

FIGURE 8.22

Steps in an example of 'destructive solid modelling'.

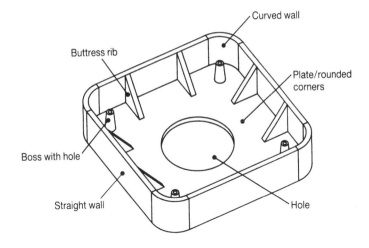

Curved wall

Buttress rib

Plate/rounded corners

Boss with hole

FIGURE 8.23
Design of a plastic moulding by features.

Straight wall

Hole

example of such a part – a plastic injection moulding – that has been defined using instances of features of the six basic types: straight wall, boss, curved wall, hole, plate with rounded corners and rib.

Some design by features systems offer the user a fixed set of features to choose from. In others, the user is allowed to define features for inclusion in a library. Library or user-defined features may be classified as **elementary** – simple features that cannot be decomposed into simpler features – and **composite** features, which are constructed from two or more elementary features. Composite features can be further subdivided into **pattern** features, which have repeated instances of simpler features such as a pattern of bolt holes or a set of gear teeth, and **compound** features, such as counter-bored holes, that are built up from simpler ones (Shah and Mäntylä, 1995). A distinction may also be drawn between **explicit** or **evaluated** or **enumerated** features, in which all the geometric details of the feature are explicitly defined, and **implicit** or **unevaluated** features, which contain information (such as defining parameters) which may be used to define part geometry, the full details of which need to be calculated when required. Examples include threads, knurls, gear teeth and so on, and also operations which define features on other geometry, such as an edge preparation or a lip on a sheet metal part.

A start has also been made on the inclusion of features in the emerging international standard for product data, the so-called STEP standard (ISO 10303, which is discussed in Section 7.3.2). A draft of Part 48, covering form features, was produced, but at the time of writing the future direction of this part of the standard is rather unclear. It is worth noting, however, that the draft standard uses the implicit/enumerated feature classification noted above, and also makes a distinction between different geometric forms including depressions, deformations (bends, embossings, twists, partial cut-outs and tube deformations), protrusions, area features (knurls, threads, markings, couplings) and passages and transitions (edge and corner blends). Classifications of features for process planning and other applications have been proposed (e.g. CAM-I, 1986), although it is very difficult to make an application-independent classification of features (Bronsvoort and Jansen, 1993).

8.4.4 The application of feature-based models

In addition to the applications that have been noted, feature-based approaches have been applied on a research basis to a variety of other engineering tasks, including:

▶ the generation of part programs for numerically controlled machine tools;

▶ the modelling of components to be manufactured using casting and forming processes;

▶ assembly modelling;

▶ the generation of finite element models.

It is likely that this list will grow rapidly in the next few years. A problem that exists with features to date, however, is that different applications tend to require different features (or at least have been modelled by different features in the prototype systems). For example, a manufacturing engineer may view an aircraft part that is to be machined from a forging in terms of the machining operations that are to be carried out, for which the most appropriate features might be pockets. The stress analyst may instead be interested in the ribs between the pockets, and the appropriate features in that case would be ribs. The original designer may have viewed the part primarily in terms of its intended function, and might use a different representation again. One can envisage an explosion of feature types, complicated also by the sheer number of geometric features that are possible. It is not clear how this question will be resolved. It will at least be necessary to associate different meanings with features according to their application. Perhaps we will in future have a central model from which others are derived, or perhaps we will maintain multiple models in different 'feature spaces' and map between these, as suggested by Shah (1988), and described in more detail by Bronsvoort and Jansen (1993). Alternatively, CAD may not develop along the design by features route at all (some argue that it is not a comfortable way for designers to work anyway), and instead a range of feature recognition techniques – one for each application – will be used in conjunction with some more or less conventional modelling technique. In the authors' view a hybrid approach, with the designer constructing a model using one set of features, and mapping and feature recognition algorithms identifying other domain-specific features, is perhaps the most likely scenario.

8.5 Design information systems

A good deal of the application of AI to design, and of the use of feature-based models, is aimed at trying to *automate* aspects of the design process. One sees, for instance, a feature recognition program for use in automatic process planning or an expert system aimed at automatically checking whether a design may be made by casting. While, clearly, enormous benefit could be obtained from computer programs that are able to carry out such tasks, there are some very significant hurdles to be overcome, and there is therefore merit in examining alternative routes to assist the designer.

A number of factors constrain the application of fully automatic systems in design. These include:

▶ An enormous variety of information contributes to a modern design of any complexity, and the task of knowledge elicitation and organization is therefore daunting.

▶ Design data is not always well formulated, and not always complete. Human beings can deal with such data reasonably easily. Even the most 'intelligent' of programs have great difficulty.

▶ Designers (and indeed medical practitioners and other users of expert systems) are sometimes reluctant to assign responsibility for decisions to computer programs, no matter how competent they may appear.

The alternative approach is to provide the designer with the information to make decisions or judgements. The problem is then reduced to the (still not inconsiderable) task of organizing design information such that a match to the designer's requirements can quickly be made.

The information that a designer seeks includes answers to questions concerning the established design practices and procedures in the company, the relevant company, national and international standards, the manufacturing processes for the product, existing similar designs that might be adapted, and the service experience from previous designs. These questions may generally be answered by data from reports, from design guides, from textbooks, from drawing registers and so on. The information is primarily a mixture of text and pictures, interspersed with some numerical data for items such as drawing numbers. By and large, the data is also not highly structured – as would be, for example, a company's stock control or stores accounting records. A term for this sort of information is **informal information**. We will now examine some of the ways it may be organized and managed.

8.5.1 Text databases

Formal, highly structured data is traditionally stored in databases such as the relational type that was introduced in Chapter 5. Textual data – for instance, for the details of books in a library or abstracts of papers in journals – is by contrast often stored as a series of records (one per book or abstract) in **text-oriented databases** that have special facilities for word search. Where the full text of documents is stored, then the databases are called **full-text** databases.

In conventional databases of all sorts, including relational and text-oriented, the search is by set-theoretic combinations of attributes or words. For instance, a relational database for stock control might be searched for all records for which the attribute 'part number' is a certain value AND the attribute 'order status' is 'open' in order to identify outstanding orders for a part. Each criterion will give a set of records for which the attribute match is true. The database enquiry (or **query**) will be satisfied by the Boolean intersection of these two sets. Text-based databases concentrate on **indexing** the occurrence of words in records so that such searches can be carried

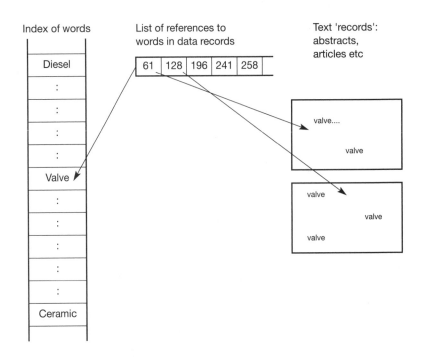

FIGURE 8.24
The structure of a text-oriented database.

out very quickly. Building an index of a database is time consuming, but it is worthwhile to do for infrequently changed items such as records in text databases. A common indexing method is to use an **inverted file** in which, in addition to the text records themselves, the database stores for each word a list of the records in which it appears, as shown in Figure 8.24. It is then very straightforward to find the list of records containing a particular word – because it is contained in the index list. It is also straightforward to find the records that contain particular combinations of words simply by carrying out Boolean operations on the index lists. For example, to find the records containing the words 'information' and 'retrieval' and 'database', the system would compute the Boolean intersection between the index lists for these three words.

More sophisticated searches are possible if the index list stores the position of words in a record in addition to their occurrence. For example, the index might show that the word 'information' occurred in record 3485 at word positions 5, 127, 348, 357 and 543. By recording this additional information, the search can include adjacent words (usually indicated by placing them in inverted commas, e.g. 'information retrieval') or can look for the occurrence of words near each other in a document. Search is also facilitated by the use of **wildcards**, which allow one or more arbitrary characters to be represented by a single character – for example, data* would match onto database, datastore, dataset and so on if * is a wildcard for one or more characters. The system would in this case do the set-theoretic union of all of the index lists for the matched words. Example 8.4 gives an example of search in a text-oriented database.

Example 8.4 *Search in a text-oriented database*

The terms database, datastore, information, retrieval and search have index lists as follows:

database	2, 4, 6, 7, 12, 14, 19, 23, 24, 30, 33, 40
datastore	1, 5, 8, 11, 15, 18, 21, 25, 30, 34, 35, 41
information	1, 2, 6, 7, 10, 11, 15, 17, 19, 24, 25, 30, 33, 34, 40
retrieval	1, 2, 5, 6, 10, 11, 17, 19, 24, 25, 34, 40, 41
search	4, 5, 7, 12, 18, 19, 23, 25, 30, 33, 34

The result of the query:

information AND data* AND (retrieval OR search)

would be carried out as follows. Firstly, the parts in brackets are evaluated, and the wildcards are expanded and treated as union operations in brackets. Thus, the union of the retrieval and search index lists, and of the database and datastore index lists, would be carried out to give the following:

(search OR retrieval)	1, 2, 4, 5, 6, 7, 10, 11, 12, 17, 18, 19, 23, 24, 25, 30, 33, 34, 40, 41
data*	1, 2, 4, 5, 6, 7, 8, 11, 12, 14, 15, 18, 19, 21, 23, 24, 30, 33, 34, 35, 40, 41

The intersection of these with the information index list is then carried out to give the following result:

Result   1, 2, 6, 7, 11, 24, 30, 33, 34, 40

There are limitations of conventional set-theoretic search. In a large database a query might return a very large set of records which satisfy the search criteria, and the user would then have to think of a more restrictive set of words and try again (or laboriously scan through all the identified entries). Conversely, there may be some important reference that has been indexed under the term that the person making the query has not thought of, or perhaps a word may be misspelled, and in these cases the queries would fail to identify useful records. In general, too open a search specification can lead to too many database matches; too restrictive a specification may lead to data being missed. These limitations have led to much research on alternative search and retrieval strategies – for example, to ask the user to identify documents from a search that are useful, and then to use the words in those documents to provide index terms for further searches, or to use thesauri to generate equivalent or alternative words to those that have been used. These techniques come under the title **intelligent information retrieval** (Croft, 1993).

The techniques of text databases are gradually spreading to the indexing and search of more general documents. For example, document management systems deal with documents that are stored as a combination of text and pictures, and pages on the World-Wide Web are also indexed using the same underlying technology.

8.5.2 Hypertext and hypermedia

Another technique that has been developed for loosely structured information is the **hypertext** method (Conklin, 1987), which offers an attractive means of information presentation through a collection of discrete pieces of text and graphics in which individual components (which we term here **nodes**) are connected through a network of links. The hypertext system provides tools for creating and browsing this combination of text, graphics and network. The term hypertext originally applied to linked collections of text. As the information types were expanded to include graphics, sound or other media, the term **hypermedia** was introduced (the term **multimedia** is also used for mixed media which can include images, text, video, sound, etc., but these are not necessarily linked together into an interconnected network), although hypertext is still often used for mixed media systems, and we will use it as a generic term here.

The concept of hypertext was proposed in the 1940s by Vannevar Bush in a far-sighted article in the *Atlantic Monthly* (Bush, 1945). Bush proposed the establishment of a microfilm-based system, called the Memex, in which an enormous library of documents, notes, photographs and sketches would be developed, with a method for establishing a link between any two points (nodes) in the library. The links between related data Bush termed trails, and he suggested that these would be developed by experts who would act as trailblazers! It was not until the 1960s that computers allowed some of these ideas to be put into practice, with early hypertext systems running on the large mainframe systems of the time. Early pioneers included Douglas Engelbart, who also developed the mouse, and Ted Nelson, who coined the term hypertext in 1968 and who developed a system called Xanadu which introduced ideas of a networked, world-wide system for publication (Parsaye *et al.*, 1990). By the 1980s many systems were being introduced, running on workstations and PCs, and the concept of hypertext was popularized by such programs as the Apple Computer HyperCard system, and later help systems for Microsoft Windows and other windowing systems.

Nodes and links

In a hypertext system, nodes are viewed as a series of **pages**, sometimes called **cards**, with **links** to further pages highlighted as an active region of the computer screen associated with a segment of text (a word or a phrase) or an image, known as a **hot-spot** or a **hyperlink**. Active regions are shown by a change in colour, by underlining, by coloured borders for images, and perhaps by changing the appearance of the screen cursor as it passes over the region. The user navigates through the network of pages by selecting the active regions, usually with a mouse button press, in order to follow links between pages. The links may be embedded in the nodes themselves, or may be maintained separately, with cross-reference from the node to the text or graphics content, as shown in Figure 8.25. In one hypertext system, developed to allow existing engineering drawings, pictures and text to be indexed, the links are embedded in a transparent overlay (called a **foreground**) through which the drawing, picture or other data is viewed, as shown in Figure 8.26 (McMahon *et al.*, 1995).

In addition to direct links between pages of information, links in some hypertext systems can be arranged to carry out other actions – for example, to display an expansion of the current hyperlink while a mouse button remains depressed, or perhaps to expand or collapse the display of the current node. Procedures may also be executed from hyperlinks – to carry out searches, to execute programs and so on. The system described in McMahon *et al.* (1995) is capable of carrying out a search of pages indexed in a page database, or execution of external programs, from a hyperlink.

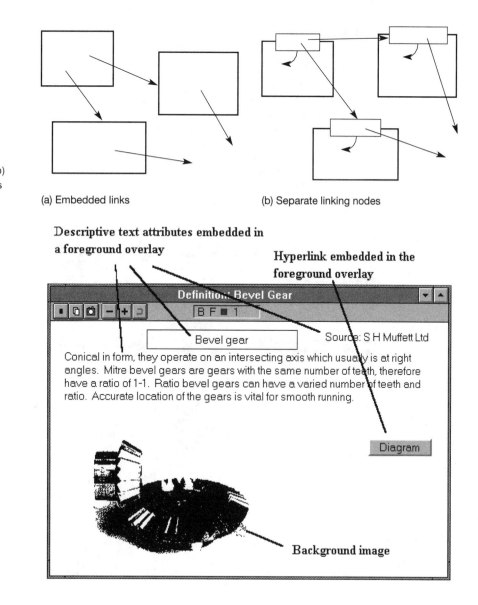

FIGURE 8.25
(a) Embedded or (b) separate hyperlinks in hypertext.

(a) Embedded links   (b) Separate linking nodes

FIGURE 8.26
Hyperlinks embedded in a foreground overlay.

There has been an explosion in hypertext applications in recent years, driven in particular by the phenomenal growth in the World-Wide Web, which we will discuss in Chapter 16 when we consider current developments in CADCAM. In engineering, hypertext has been used for help systems, computer-based technical documentation (e.g. if the text says 'To access knurled sprocket first remove auxiliary widget-drive cover (see <u>Section 4.2</u>)', then '<u>Section 4.2</u>' may be actively linked to the appropriate piece of text), in computer-based handbooks and advice systems, and in computer-aided learning (CAL) systems, among other applications. Example 8.5 shows example pages from a hypertext design handbook for bearing design.

Example 8.5 ## *An example of the application of hypertext*

Hypertext offers the opportunity to develop on-line documents for all sorts of applications, and although the conventional chapter–section hierarchy of conventional documents can be employed, hypertext encourages a division of material into screen-sized portions, and also encourages links between branches of a hierarchy. Figure 8.27 shows example pages from a hypertext handbook for rolling elements bearing design. This application has the following features:

▶ Advice on (i) which bearing type to use in different situations; (ii) bearing designations and codes; (iii) bearing selection and load calculations; (iv) bearing installation and lubrication; (v) example applications.

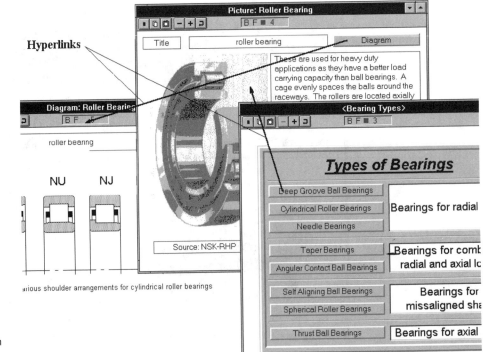

FIGURE 8.27
A hypertext design handbook.

▶ Embedded pictures and drawings.

▶ A database of illustrated examples.

▶ Hyperlinks between pages, as shown in Figure 8.27.

8.6 Conclusion

This chapter has reviewed some of the technologies that may be important in computer aids to design over the next few years. They are still the subject of extensive research, and thus it is likely that some will change considerably before finding widespread commercial implementation. What is also likely is that no single technology will be adequate by itself. Instead, the designer will have at his or her disposal a toolkit of techniques. A multi-windowing engineering workstation will give access to parametric or variational modellers with feature-based design capability and a range of analysis and planning tools, and to these will be added expert systems for heuristic advice, hypertext for browsing though brochures, standards, papers and company information from CD-ROMs or via the Internet and company intranets (an intranet is a network that offers the information-sharing capabilities of the Internet, but within the sites of a single company or corporation), and databases for component and materials information. We will return to these topics in Chapter 16, when we discuss current developments in the World-Wide Web (WWW) and computer-supported cooperative work (CSCW). For the moment let us note that the development of standards will mean that increasingly the designer will be able to switch and move data between the various programs more or less at will, and high-speed networks will allow data to be moved around the world equally at will.

References and further reading

Beale R. and Jackson T. (1990). *Neural Computing: An Introduction.* Bristol: Institute of Physics.

Brachman R. J. and Levesque H. J. (1985). *Readings in Knowledge Representation.* Los Altos, CA: Morgan Kaufmann.

Bronsvoort W. F. and Jansen F. W. (1993). Feature modelling and conversion – key concepts to concurrent engineering. *Computers in Industry.* **21**, 61–86.

Brown D. C. (1997). AI in design webliography. *http//cs.wpi.edu/Research/aidg/AIinD-hotlist.html,* Computer Science Department, Worcester Polytechnic Institute, MA.

Brown D. C. and Chandrasekaran B. (1989). *Design Problem Solving: Knowledge Structures and Control Strategies* (Research Notes in Artificial Intelligence). London: Pitman.

Brown K. N., Sims Williams J. H. and McMahon C. A. (1992). Grammars of features in design. In *Artificial Intelligence in Design, Proc. Conf. on AI in Design,* Pittsburgh (ed. J. Gero). New York: Kluwer Academic.

Brown K. N. (1997). Grammatical design. *IEEE Expert.* **12**(2), 27–33.

Buchanan B. G. and Shortliffe E. H. (1984). *Rule-based Expert Systems: The MYCIN Experiments of the Stanford Heuristic Programming Project.* Harlow: Addison Wesley Longman.

Bush V. (1945). As we may think. *Atlantic Monthly.* **176**, 101–8.

CAM-I (1986). *Part Features for Process Planning.* Report No. R-86-PPP-01, CAM-I Inc., Arlington, TX.

Conklin J. (1987). Hypertext: an introduction and survey. *IEEE Computer*. **20**(9), 17–41.

Corney J. and Clark D. E. R. (1991). Method for finding holes and pockets that connect multiple faces in $2^1/2$D objects. *Computer-aided Design*. **23**(10), 658–68.

Coyne R. D., Rosenman M. A., Radford A. D., Balachandran M. and Gero J. S. (1990). *Knowledge-based Design Systems*. Reading, MA: Addison Wesley Longman.

Croft W. B. (1993). Knowledge-based and statistical approaches to text retrieval. *IEEE Expert*. **8**, 8–12.

Dubois D. and Prade H. (1980). *Fuzzy Sets and Systems: Theory and Applications*. New York: Academic Press.

Gero J. S. (ed.) (1991). *Artificial Intelligence in Design, Proc. Conf. on AI in Design*, Edinburgh, June 1991. Oxford: Butterworth-Heinemann.

IEEE Expert: Intelligent Systems and their Applications (1997). Special issues on AI in design (ed. D. C. Brown and W. P. Birmingham). **12**(2 and 3), March–April, May–June.

ISO 10303 (1994). *Industrial Automation Systems and Integration – Product Data Representation and Exchange* (STEP). Geneva: International Organization for Standardization.

Jackson P. (1990). *Introduction to Expert Systems*. 2nd edn. Harlow: Addison Wesley Longman.

Jared G. E. (1989). Reasoning and using geometric features. In *Geometric Reasoning* (ed. J. Woodwark). Oxford: Oxford University Press.

Jovanovic A. and Bogaerts W. F. L. (1991). Hybrid knowledge-based and hypermedia systems for engineering applications, Tutorial 13. *Avignon '91 Expert Systems and their Applications*, Avignon.

Light R. A. and Gossard D. C. (1982). Modification of geometric models through variational geometry. *Computer-aided Design*. **14**(4), 209–15.

Little G., Tuttle R., Clark D. E. R. and Corney J. (1997). The Heriot-Watt FeatureFinder: a graph-based approach to recognition. *Proc. Computers in Engineering Conference, DETC97/CIE-4276*. Sacramento, CA: ASME Design Engineering Technical Conference.

Maher M. L. and Pu P. (eds) (1997). *Issues and applications of case-based reasoning in design*. Mahwah, NJ: Lawrence Erlbaum.

Maher M. L. and de Silva Garza A. G. (1997). Case-based reasoning in design, *IEEE Expert*. **12**(2), 34–41.

McMahon C. A., Pitt D. J., Yang Y. and Sims Williams J. H. (1995). *Review*: an information management system for informal design data. *Journal of Engineering with Computers*. **11**, 123–35.

Parsaye K., Chignell M., Khoshafian S. and Wong H. (1990). *Intelligent Databases*. New York: John Wiley.

Rada R. (1991). *Hypertext: from Text to Expertext*. London: McGraw-Hill.

Ringland G. A. and Duce D. A. (eds) (1987). *Approaches to Knowledge Representation: an Introduction*. Letchworth: Research Studies Press.

Roller D. (1991). An approach to computer-aided parametric design. *Computer-aided Design*. **23**(5), 385–91.

Ross T. J. (1995). *Fuzzy Logic with Engineering Applications*. New York: McGraw-Hill.

Rumelhart D. E., Hinton G. E. and Williams R. J. (1986). Learning internal representations by back-propagating errors. *Nature*. **323**, 533–6.

Salomons O. W., Houten F. J. A. M. van and Kals H. J. J. (1993). Review of research in feature-based design. *Journal of Manufacturing Systems*. **12**(2), 113–32.

Salzberg S. and Watkins M. (1990). Managing information for concurrent engineering: challenges and barriers. *Research In Engineering Design*. **2**(1), 35–52.

Shah J. J. (1988). Feature transformations between application-specific feature spaces. *Computer-aided Engineering Journal*. December, 247–55.

Shah J. J. (1990). Assessment of features technology. *Computer-aided Design*. **23**(5), 58–66.

Shah J. J. and Mäntylä M. (1995). *Parametric and Feature-based CAD/CAM*. New York: John Wiley.

Shah J. J. and Rogers M. T. (1990). Feature-based reasoning shell: design and implementation. *Computers in Engineering Journal*. January.

Shah J. J., Sreevalsan P., Rogers M., Billo R. and Mathew A. (1988). Current status of features technology. *Report R-88-GM-04.1*. Arlington, TX: Computer Aided Manufacturing – International, Inc.

Shneiderman B. and Kearsley G. (1989). *Hypertext Hands-on!*. Reading, MA: Addison-Wesley.

Spur G., Krause F.-L. and Lehmann C. M. (1989). Integration of methods for knowledge processing and geometric modelling. *Proc. IMechE Effective CADCAM 1989*. C395/055, pp. 57–68.

Stiny G. (1991). The algebras of design. *Research in Engineering Design*. **2**(3), 171–81.

Swift K. G. (1987). *Knowledge-based Design for Manufacture*. London: Kogan Page.

Wielinga R. and Schreiber G. (1997). Configuration-design problem solving. *IEEE Expert*. **12**(2), 49–57.

Wood K. L. and Antonsson E. K. (1989). Computations with imprecise parameters in engineering design: background and theory. *ASME Journal of Mechanisms, Transmission and Automation in Design*. **111**(4), 616–25.

Wood K. L., Antonsson E. K. and Beck J. L. (1990). Representing imprecision in engineering design: comparing fuzzy and probability calculus. *Research in Engineering Design*. **1**, 187–203.

Woodwark J. R. (1988). Some speculations on feature recognition. *Computer-aided Design*. May, 189–96.

Zadeh L. (1965). Fuzzy sets. *Information and Control*. **8**, 338–53.

Exercises

· · · · · · · · · · · · · ·

8.1 What are the functions of the knowledge base and the inference mechanism in knowledge-based systems?

8.2 Outline the principles of forward- and backward-chaining inference in a knowledge base comprising production rules.

8.3 Suggest a set of production rules for fault diagnosis for an automobile that fails to start. Consider, for example, the following cases: flat battery, no fuel, faulty fuel pump, faulty ignition.

8.4 Extend the frame representations shown in Figures 8.3 and 8.4 to include ball bearings and roller bearings as separate classes.

8.5 What do you understand by the terms decomposition, plan selection and refinement, constraint-based reasoning and case-based reasoning in the context of AI in design?

8.6 Outline how the part shown in Figure 6.35 may be represented in a system that uses parametric geometry.

8.7 Figure 8.28 shows a poppet valve, such as might be used in an automotive diesel engine. Show how such a part may be considered as parametric geometry, and suggest dimensions to be used in defining instances of the geometry; then suggest how a cross-sectional profile of the part may be constrained for solving by variational geometry.

8.8 Figure 8.29 shows a profile drawing of a side-frame that is manufactured by cutting from steel plate, together with the key dimensions used in its definition. Outline the principles of variational geometry, and then show how they might be applied to the side-frame profile.

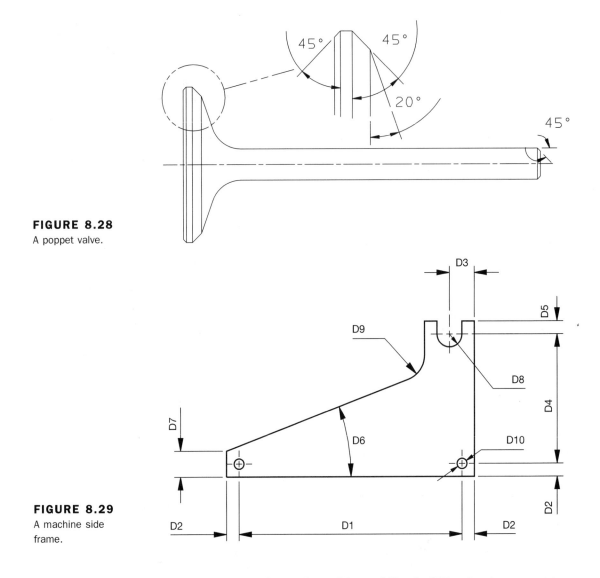

FIGURE 8.28
A poppet valve.

FIGURE 8.29
A machine side frame.

8.9   Why should design features be used for modelling in CAD rather than geometric primitives? Under what circumstances do you think that feature-based design may be particularly appropriate? What are the limitations in the features approach?

8.10 Distinguish between feature recognition and design by features. Then suggest a set of features for the modelling of axisymmetric turned shafts incorporating parallel and tapered portions, chamfers, fillet blends and external threads. What parameters would you use in their definition?

8.11 Why do you think that feature recognition is more straightforward with the boundary representation scheme than with constructive solid geometry?

8.12 What is a text-oriented database system? Outline the basis of a set-theoretic search of such a database using Boolean combinations of keywords.

      In a particular system, words in the index have references to records as follows:

Word	Records
knowledge	3 8 15 24 31 32 40 56 57 58 70 72 74 81
acquisition	3 8 24 40 45 51 57 58 63 66 70 71 75 80 81
technique	1 3 7 15 24 30 32 40 45 56 63 70 77 80 81
techniques	2 8 15 20 25 32 40 45 46 51 57 59 60 64 72
design	3 5 8 12 15 21 24 32 40 42 45 48 56 57 58 63 66 70 72 82

What is the result of the following query?

> design AND knowledge AND acquisition AND technique*

where 'technique*' means any word beginning with 'technique'.

8.13 Define the terms nodes and links in the context of networks, and then show how frame and feature hierarchies and hypertext systems may each be represented by graph models.

8.14 Information search may be classified into query (e.g. of a database) or browse (e.g. of a hypertext system). For what sort of engineering information do you think query would be most appropriate, and for what sort is browse preferable?

8.15 Outline the method of information representation in a hypertext system, a relational database system and a text-oriented database system.

Projects

For more information about the subjects for project work, please refer to the end of Chapter 1.

The project activity for this chapter is to explore how the new technologies for CAD representation that have been introduced in this chapter might be applied in the chess piece and load cell projects, in particular to explore how parametric, variational and feature-based geometry may be used in the modelling of the chess piece and the load cell.

PART TWO

The design/manufacture interface

···

Part Two of this book is concerned with activities at the interface of design and manufacture, in particular with applications of the design model to the generation of manufacturing information, and with actions which may be taken at the design stage to ensure that a product is designed for high quality and for ease of manufacture.

Chapter 9 introduces the subjects at the design/manufacture interface, and in particular describes design for manufacture and assembly, and process planning.

Chapter 10 is concerned with techniques and strategies for a systems approach to product development and quality in manufacture at the design/manufacture interface.

Chapter 11 covers the operation and programming of numerical control machine tools, and introduces the elements of robotics and techniques for rapid prototyping.

9 The design/ manufacture interface

Chapter objectives

When you have completed studying material in this chapter you should be able to:

▶ describe the constraints on product and manufacturing performance of a traditional sequential approach to engineering organization;
▶ understand the role of concurrent engineering and computer-integrated manufacture in engineering;
▶ understand the place of group technology in piece part classification, and in the organizing and planning of manufacture;
▶ describe the main elements of design for manufacture and assembly and outline the steps that may be taken in designing a product for assembly;
▶ outline the elements of process planning and in particular outline the issues in generative process planning.

Chapter contents

9.1 Introduction: the limitations of traditional engineering approaches

The actual processes of using computers to aid design are so fascinating that there is a risk that the designer may forget *why* the work is being undertaken. All design must keep the end product in mind. The aim is to produce an artefact which

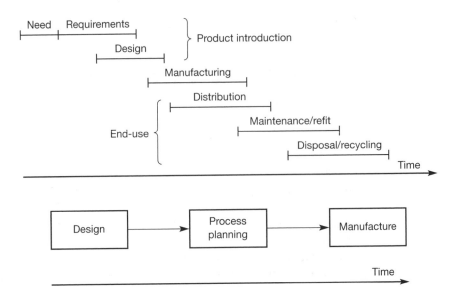

FIGURE 9.1
Product life cycle phases.

FIGURE 9.2
Sequential engineering.

approaches the best means of meeting a need at an appropriate manufacturing cost. The end must be hardware, and in order to achieve this the interface between design and manufacture must be crossed. This interface is the subject of this chapter.

The term product life cycle embraces all of the principal phases in the development and use of a product, including the identification of need; requirements specification; product design; manufacturing; distribution; maintenance and refurbishment; and subsequent disposal or recycling. These phases may be further grouped into product introduction and end-use stages in the life of a product, as shown in Figure 9.1. Traditionally, the design and manufacturing phases were separated and occurred sequentially, with process planning as the activity which bridged the gap between the two phases (Figure 9.2). Thus, the design phase was used to prove a product design and to establish production methods before the product went into production. For many products, the manufacturing phase which followed was characterized by years of steady output, during which it was hoped to recover the costs incurred at the design phase of the product and process introduction. Process planning was a relatively simple step, involving the translation of product and process design requirements into a set of manufacturing instructions which could be interpreted and carried out in the manufacturing facility.

In today's manufacturing environment, however, the expectation of high stable demand is not always realistic. Products are being continually redesigned and a product's useful life in the marketplace is constantly under threat from others with new and improved design features. In addition, firms continually strive to reduce the time taken to put a product on the market. This compression in product life cycle means that manufacturing firms can no longer afford to invest resources in dedicated production facilities, since the product design may change before the production facility has been paid for! Rather, flexible production systems are needed in order to cope not only with existing product designs but also with future redesigns of these products. Above all, techniques are required which allow new products to be designed and manufactured in ever shorter time-scales and at reduced cost.

The segregation of design and manufacturing functions is itself a constraint, irrespective of changes in product life cycle and demand. Communication and collaboration between separate design and manufacturing functions is often poor. As a senior engineer in an automotive component supply company remarked 'we would be given component drawings and be told "make these" – and just have a few weeks to do so: there was no opportunity for any feedback to improve the design or to optimize the manufacturing process'. The problem is also one of inadequacy of communication throughout the product cycle. In Chapter 1 it was observed that, during the design process, representations of designs are developed for communication to the manufacturer. These representations often lack information about function or the reasons why designs have certain features – therefore manufacturing specialists cannot make due allowance for the designer's intent. Conversely, information about design features which lead to failings such as poor reliability and high costs may not get back to the designer.

Subdivision of manufacturing activities into specialist functions also has an adverse effect on quality management, in that quality tends to be seen as the responsibility of the quality control department or inspector, and not of the organization as a whole.

The design–make–test–redesign loop

In many large-volume industries the traditional product development route has been to design and make prototype components, then test them and redesign as necessary (and then retest) to iron out any faults. This process leads to satisfactory (but not optimal) designs at reasonably low cost, but it contributes to long design and development times. The knowledge that components are to be tested and redesigned as necessary also leads to excessive design experimentation without good cause, with the consequence that many products are unreliable when first released onto the market unless an expensive test programme is undertaken.

Summary

All this shows the limitations of traditional approaches. Information on how to achieve product quality, cost and variety is not fed back to the designer at a sufficiently early stage to be effective, so the whole process takes too long. Successful modern companies have devised new approaches, some of which will now be discussed.

9.2 Current themes in manufacturing engineering

Quality

A modern approach to quality replaces the notion of acceptable levels of defects with a *zero-defect* philosophy. The word quality is not used here in the sense of 'luxury', but in the sense of meeting or exceeding the customers' expectations and of not giving cause for disappointment. (It can be argued that exceeding the customers' requirements – for example, in accuracy or surface finish – is also a poor approach to quality because excessive costs are incurred.) Within a company, the term **total quality** implies that the achievement of high quality is the responsibility of everyone in an organization, not just of a single department or group.

Two approaches in particular are characteristic of a 'total quality' approach to engineering. The first is to see things in *systems* terms: products are systems from which a certain performance is required; the manufacturing processes and their disposition for a product constitute a **manufacturing system**; the manufacturing organization itself is a system with certain goals and characteristics. The overall aim is to see that each system fulfils its function. The second approach is to adopt a philosophy of **continuous improvement**. Rather than seeking highly innovative product or manufacturing system designs on a narrow front, all aspects of the product or manufacturing system should be the subject of continuous refinement.

Organizational changes

The demarcation between design and manufacture may mean that quality is lost and that design changes to meet manufacturing requirements are needed at a late stage. These problems may be rectified by increased cooperative working between designers and manufacturing and other specialists throughout the product development phase. In particular, the design of the product and of the manufacturing system which is to make it should be developed hand in hand. This is known as **concurrent engineering**, or **simultaneous engineering** or even **life cycle engineering**, where the whole life cycle of a product is considered concurrently. The first of these terms will be used here.

The practice of concurrent engineering involves developing the design using multi-disciplinary teams, combining expertise from such areas as materials, manufacturing processes, assembly, inspection, maintenance, marketing, performance and end use, and calling on specialist expertise, for example in fatigue and fracture, or in noise and vibration. A process that is typically adopted is for the designers' proposals to be evaluated repeatedly by the team members from early in the conceptual phase of the design.

In conventional engineering organizations the responsibility for a product moves between departments as design gives way to manufacture and so on. Such companies may be organized into 'product engineering' and 'manufacturing engineering' functions, with further subdivision by function. Conversely, in companies organized for concurrent engineering, a product is often the responsibility of a product team that follows the product from its inception to the completion of its production life and beyond. The balance of individual effort within this team, and indeed its leadership, will vary according to the stage in the product life cycle, but the essential composition remains the same. The organization of the company itself will often be according to product group, rather than function.

Techniques

To support the philosophical and organizational changes outlined above, a number of techniques have been devised to assist in product and manufacturing system development. Included amongst these are what shall be termed here 'techniques for quality engineering', which include methods for all stages from the initial identification of the customer requirements to the design of reliable manufacturing operations. The techniques include systematic methods for the allocation of engineering effort to meet product requirements, and methods for the identification of possible failures and of the effects of such failures.

A second group of techniques are those of computer-aided manufacture (**CAM**). Cooperative working between different engineering functions lends itself naturally to the sharing of data and of computational aids. In particular, the component geometry developed through the use of CAD may be reused in the generation of manufacturing instructions for numerically controlled production processes, and in the planning of manufacturing operations through computer-aided process planning (**CAPP**). These activities in turn feed information, together with **bill of materials** data from CAD, into the computer-aided production management (**CAPM**) activity. This integration of all manufacturing activities through the use of linked computer aids and a shared database is sometimes called computer-integrated manufacturing (**CIM**). The data exchange between activities in a CIM environment is shown in Figure 9.3. Although elements of CIM are in place, their comprehensive integration is still a matter of research.

The major research efforts at the interface between CAD and CAM have been in the development of computer-aided process planning systems which attempt to automate the communication process between product designers and manufacturing engineers. However, these systems have tended to concentrate on automating the traditional process planning function, that is the generation of process plans for

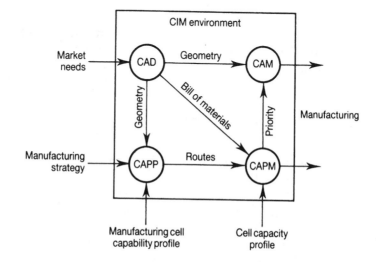

FIGURE 9.3

Data exchange in a CIM environment. (Reproduced from Lucas Engineering and Systems (1988) by permission of Lucas Engineering and Systems.)

FIGURE 9.4

Structure of a CAPP
system.

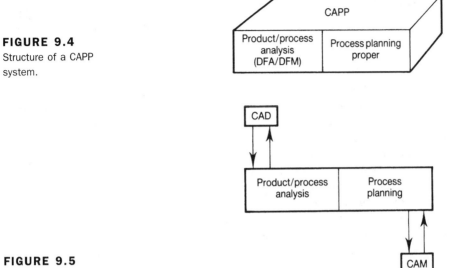

FIGURE 9.5

Data flow to CAPP.

manufacturing. This, in our view, is too narrow a path to enable CADCAM integration. There is a growing awareness of the need to incorporate design for manufacturing and assembly techniques in the domain of computer-aided process planning systems. These are techniques which are used in product/process analysis, an activity which allows the manufacturing function to influence the design process and to ensure that designers are aware of the effects of various design features on the ease of manufacture of a part. Thus, a computer-aided process planning tool can be considered as having two separate functions, product/process analysis and process planning proper, as shown in Figure 9.4. A two-stage process results, in which CAD data is first examined for product/process analysis of the parts, and design for manufacturing assembly guidelines are applied to this design data and the results fed back to the designer, after which redesign may occur. Process planning thereupon receives parts which have been 'passed' by product/process analysis and generates manufacturing instructions for their manufacture. The flow of data is represented in Figure 9.5.

9.3 The organization of this part of the book

This chapter and the next two form Part Two of this book, which will explore aspects of product development and CIM – organizational, philosophical and technical – concerned with the design/manufacture interface. These aspects are equally important at the factory organization and control level, which will be the subject of the third part of this book.

The chapter organization here will broadly follow the technical organization identified in Section 9.2 above. The remainder of this chapter will first outline the part classification approach known as group technology, and will then explore techniques for improving the manufacturability of designs that come under the term design for manufacture and assembly (DFM/A), before outlining the elements of process planning and assembly planning. Chapter 10 will deal with contemporary approaches to product development, and will deal in more depth with the systems engineering and concurrent engineering approaches identified above, as well as outlining the scope and nature of techniques for quality engineering. Chapter 11 will complete this part of the book with a description of manufacturing machines that exploit computers for their control – numerically controlled machine tools and robots – and with an exploration of the application of computing techniques to the preparation of data for machining processes. Later in the book, in Chapter 16, we will return to the topic of assembly, when we consider assembly and tolerance modelling.

The reader should also note that we will return briefly to the subject of design for manufacture in Section 15.4 of Chapter 15, when we discuss the **just in time** approach to manufacturing organization and philosophy.

9.4 **Group technology**

In **group technology** (GT), components are grouped into families on the basis of similarity of such features as part shapes, part finishes, materials, tolerances and required manufacturing processes. Gallagher and Knight (1973) define GT as 'a technique for identifying and bringing together related or similar components in a production process in order to take advantage of their similarities by making use of, for example, the inherent economies of flow-production methods'. GT has been widely used to help to simplify the flow of work through a manufacturing system. In particular, by identifying components which have similar processing characteristics, GT can support the development of product or cell-based plant layouts. The effect of this is to generate simplified material flow patterns in a plant and to allow responsibility and *ownership* for a component or group of components to rest with one group of operators and their supervisor. In addition, simplified material flow patterns frequently result in reduced material transfer times between machines, reduced material handling, reduced component manufacturing lead times, and reduced work in progress. Furthermore, the fact that similar parts are being made on the same machines means that machine set-up times are also frequently reduced, and better use may be made of special tooling. Later, we will see that GT has an important contribution to make to the development of just in time systems (see Chapter 15, Section 15.3).

An important aspect of GT is that it often helps to minimize unnecessary variety of components in a manufacturing plant by making designers aware of existing similar components. Often design engineers are unaware of the existence of similar designs in current production, perhaps because the part numbering system does not carry sufficient information to allow them to retrieve designs from the CAD system. In these circumstances parts effectively tend to be duplicated, perhaps with minor differences which are unnecessary to the parts' role in the end product. Among other problems, unnecessary part numbers lead to a proliferation of paperwork and increased stock.

The use of GT codes to retrieve data is also useful when it comes to process planning. Process planners, rather than starting from zero with each new part to be planned, can review the process plan for a similar part (i.e. a part with a similar GT code) and modify it to develop the process plan for the new part. In fact, this approach is the basis of the variant approach to automated process planning, as we shall see in Section 9.6.

GT forms component families on the basis of the design or manufacturing attributes – sometimes both – of the components in question. A large number of classification systems have been developed, including the Brisch system in the United Kingdom and the Opitz system in Germany. These systems allow the manufacturing systems analyst to code the components manufactured in a plant and to identify families of components which have similar processing requirements and consequently can be manufactured in a GT cell. We will now briefly review coding and classification systems, with particular reference to the Opitz system.

GT-based classification and coding systems are based on the design attributes of parts, the manufacturing attributes of parts or frequently a combination of design and manufacturing attributes. Normally the systems are formed around 10- to 20-digit codes, using simple codes, hierarchical codes or indeed hybrid simple and hierarchical codes. In a simple coding system (sometimes referred to as chain-type systems) each digit in a code always has the same meaning; that is, it always represents the same underlying feature. In a hierarchical system, the meaning attached to an individual digit is dependent on the interpretation of the previous digit. The hierarchical coding system results in a more compact code for each individual component, but of course the decoding for each part number is more complex, which implies that in general more complex algorithms are required to sort parts into particular categories or families.

Classification systems have been developed for a wide range of applications, including forged parts, sheet metal parts, cast parts and indeed machined parts. Machined parts have received by far the most attention, reflecting their relative importance in manufacturing industry. We will review the Opitz system, which although quite old now, is useful from the point of view of understanding the overall approach of such systems.

The Opitz system (see Opitz, 1970), which was designed to incorporate the encoding of design and manufacturing features, has three elements: the first element consists of five digits which describe the geometric form of the component; the second element, consisting of four digits and known as a supplementary code, classifies the size, material, original raw material form and the required accuracy of the component; the third element of the code is considered discretionary and may be used to encode information of a process planning nature, for example operation sequences, required machine tools, required fixtures, etc. The structure of the Opitz system can be understood from Figure 9.6 which is reproduced from Opitz (1970).

A large number of commercially available computer-based systems have been developed to support the creation of GT codes, and indeed the retrieval of part information, part drawings, design information and even process planning information. More recently, the techniques of artificial intelligence have been applied to this area. See, for example, the EXGT system described in Kerr (1991).

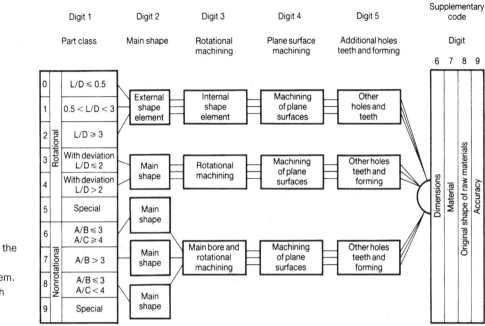

FIGURE 9.6
The structure of the Opitz Group Technology system. (Reproduced with permission from Opitz, 1970.)

9.5 Design for manufacture and assembly

Increasing specialization in industry means that today's designer is often less proficient in manufacturing terms than in the past, when design staff were generally recruited from the machinists and technicians of a company. This situation is exacerbated by the rapid change in manufacturing practice in many industries, and by the global competitive pressures that we have noted. These circumstances have led to significant interest in techniques that assist in **design for manufacture** (DFM). The importance of these techniques can be further underlined by the fact that about 70% of the manufacturing costs of a product (cost of materials, processing and assembly) are determined by design decisions, with production decisions (such as process planning or machine tool selection) responsible for only 20% (Andreasen, 1983).

Traditionally, good manufacturing practice has been recorded in textbooks and in training programmes, and much DFM still takes this form – although generally more systematically organized into design guidelines and tables of 'dos and don'ts'. A recent trend has been to incorporate these guidelines into 'expert systems' for advice on DFM. Another recent development, again amenable to computer implementation, has involved methods for systematically rating a product in terms of its manufacturability, and then suggesting procedures for improving this rating. This has been applied in particular to **design for assembly** (DFA), which has assumed increasing importance because assembly is so labour intensive: as process costs have reduced, owing to improved machines and processes, so assembly costs as a proportion of the total have increased.

Design for manufacture guidelines have been developed for practically every aspect of manufacture, but they may be broadly divided into four groups relating to the **general approach** to DFM, to **selection of manufacturing processes**, to **design for particular processes**, and to **assembly**. A word of warning, however, before we look at these in more detail: the designer should be aware of *all* the requirements and constraints on a design, as discussed earlier in this chapter. For example, many DFM guidelines are contradicted by design for recycling guidelines (e.g. some techniques for rapid assembly make it difficult to disassemble the product), and therefore DFM should be used with care.

Guidelines for the general approach to DFM

General guidelines for DFM may be summarized as follows:

▶ Take advantage of economies of scale:

- design parts to be capable of being used in multiple products;
- minimize the number of separate part types in a product (this also helps to reduce the number of inventory items, and assists assembly and maintenance by, for example, lowering the number of tools required).

▶ Aim to standardize as much as possible:

- use parts of known capability and from known suppliers;
- use parts that are a variation on a standard: try to develop part families.

▶ Use simple, low-cost operations:

- use established technologies as far as possible;
- avoid high-cost technologies unless technically essential;
- choose simple, regular shapes and part assemblies.

Choice of production process

So many factors come into the choice of how to make something that only the most general of overall guidelines may be specified. What shape and size is a component, how strong, how accurate in dimension and what surface finish is required are just a few of the considerations. In some cases the techniques are so well established that the choice is clear (for instance, automotive bodies are almost invariably made by pressing and spot welding sheet steel). Nevertheless, some general guidelines that *do* apply are:

▶ select a process commensurate with the required accuracy and surface finish;

▶ select component dimension and surface finish parameters that allow the widest possible tolerance range and surface finish variation;

▶ make full use of prototypes, but note the variations in strength and other performance measures that can arise between one-off and mass production methods;

▶ make a detailed comparative assessment of available manufacturing systems at the design stage; in particular, carry out an analysis of the sensitivity of part and assembly costs to production volume for different processes.

Guidelines for particular processes

Each process will have its own associated guidelines, and often these will be expressed in the literature by illustrations of good and bad product features. Guidelines, according to the general classes of process, are as follows (Pahl and Beitz, 1984; Matousek, 1963):

▶ **Forming** processes force a material to deform plastically to conform to a die – for example, in forging or extrusion. Design guidelines aim to ensure that:

– the part may be removed from the die – by avoiding undercuts, and by providing tapers;
– the part fills the die – by avoiding very narrow or deep ribs, sharp changes in cross-section and sharp corners, and by designing shapes that occur in unrestrained pressing;
– tooling costs are minimized, for example by using simple shapes and flat die-split planes.

Some examples are shown in Figure 9.7 (Dieter, 1986; Bralla, 1986).

▶ **Moulding** processes involve the filling of a mould with a liquid material – for example, casting or injection moulding. Design guidelines again aim to ensure that parts can be readily removed from moulds, and that tooling costs are minimized by the use of simple shapes with the minimum number of pattern pieces and cores. In addition, the guidelines aim to:

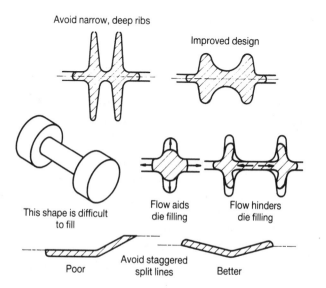

FIGURE 9.7

Examples of design guidelines for forming.

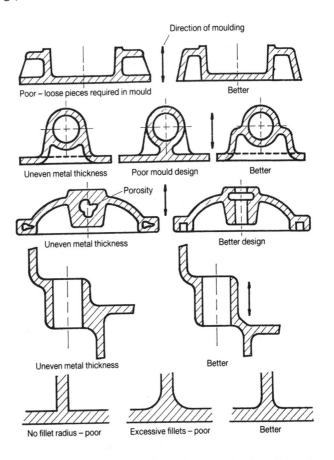

FIGURE 9.8

Examples of design guidelines for moulding. (Council of Ironfoundry Associations, 1956.)

– avoid defects in the moulding by using constant wall sections or gradual changes in section;
– assist any subsequent machining by avoiding sloping surfaces, and by breaking up large surfaces;
– provide accurate location of cores and easy removal of flash.

Examples are shown in Figure 9.8 (Council of Ironfoundry Associations, 1956).

▶ Operations such as machining are **material removal** processes. The many guidelines here are to ensure that material can be easily and cheaply removed with acceptable surface condition, for example by:

– using simple tool shapes;
– aiming for simple, continuous machined surfaces; where there are multiple surfaces to be machined, try to ensure that they are parallel or at right angles to each other;
– providing for adequate clamping;
– providing adequate run-out.

Some examples are shown in Figure 9.9.

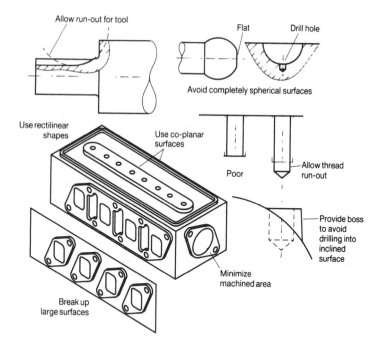

FIGURE 9.9

Examples of design guidelines for machining.

The figures for this section show only a small fraction of the total guidelines appropriate to the particular processes, and of course there are many more operations, such as surface treatment and finishing, that are not described here.

9.5.1 Design for assembly

We now present a summary of the current general rules and guidelines available to assist product designers in improving the ease of assembly of their designs. These guidelines are based on the authors' experiences, and on a study of a wide range of books, articles and papers on this topic, as listed in the references section for this chapter. We look at a detailed application of these guidelines in Section 11.6.5. The guidelines can be categorized into design rules relating to:

1. Consideration of the organizational and environmental conditions which affect assembly.

2. Simplification and standardization of product design.

3. Consideration of the assembly processes and how product design affects their execution.

We shall now discuss each of these issues in turn.

Organizational and environmental conditions

These conditions refer to the organizational context within which product design takes place, and the conditions which affect the planning and performance of manufacture. Of particular importance are:

▶ *The provision of information.* Designers should be supplied with information which will allow them to quantify the consequences of their designs from an assembly as well as a technical perspective.

▶ *Integrated product design and development.* In line with the concept of concurrent engineering discussed above, firms should strive for simultaneous product, production technology, and production system design and development, or at least adopt an interdisciplinary approach to the design of each. Product design should also be integrated with other manufacturing functions which affect it or which it affects, for example marketing and sales (Andreasen, 1983).

▶ *Pre-assembly work.* Product designs, especially for automated assembly or complex products, should be examined for their potential for pre-assembly work, that is work which precedes the main assembly task.

▶ *Flexible sequencing of assembly operations.* Constraint-free sequencing can be approached through (1) allowing arbitrary decomposition of the product into subassemblies, (2) using standard parts and subassemblies, (3) avoiding compulsory assembly sequences (Gairola, 1987).

Simplification and standardization of product design

Designing for simplicity and standardization is as much a question of adopting the correct attitude as it is of obeying specific rules, but some general guidelines are useful.

1. *Minimize the number of parts in a product.* There are two fundamental approaches to minimizing the number of parts in a product. The first is to determine the theoretical minimum number of parts required to guarantee the product's functionality. The second approach is to integrate parts wherever possible, with any potential combination of parts being balanced against the possibility of increased complexity and expenditure in the resulting manufacturing assembly operations.

2. *Minimize product variation and part variety.* Most marketable products sell in a number of styles, with various additional/optional features. Variations of this nature are desirable from a sales point of view, but create numerous problems for assembling the products and should be avoided as far as possible.

3. *Use assembly-orientated construction principles.* These refer to the design principles that determine how the product is to be put together. To achieve simplicity and clarity, and so ease of assembly, product designers should aim for:

   (a) modular construction – that is, construct products from standard building blocks or subassemblies;
   (b) sandwich construction – all components are assembled successively from one direction (usually vertically), with each part added being centred by the preceding part in the assembly sequence; having a product constructed in such a manner reduces robotic assembly to a series of pick and place operations (Laszcs, 1985);
   (c) avoiding close tolerance or high surface quality demands on components.

4. *Use subassemblies*. Dividing a product up into subassemblies and standardizing these subassemblies leads to less variety, increased production runs, and generally a simpler assembly process.

5. *Use a base component*. Each product should, where possible, be designed to have a solid base to which parts can be inserted directly, and which should give coherence to the whole assembly.

Facilitating assembly processes

Although all elements of design for assembly affect the execution of assembly processes, certain considerations in designing products relate directly to assembly processes/operations. These considerations can be classified as follows.

1. *Design for ease of insertion*. In order to facilitate the easy and quick insertion and mating of parts, designers need to consider their designs from the perspective of:

   ▶ favourable insertion directions and movements: 'investigations of 355 insertion processes have shown that forcing a machine to insert from the side would be twice, and from the bottom three times, as expensive as from top downwards' (Gairola, 1987);
   ▶ choosing appropriate materials;
   ▶ enabling fast and efficient insertion procedures.

2. *Design for ease of fastening and joining*. The design rules for joining and fastening can be classified under those relating to the choice of joining/fastening technology (screwing, bonding by adhesive, etc.) and those relating to the use of this technology, that is the allocation and location of fasteners. When a designer is choosing a joining method, systematic listing, classification and assessment of the available joining methods are useful tools for choosing assembly orientated joining techniques (Schraft and Bassler, 1985). Once a particular joining method has been selected, it should be used for as many joints in the assembly as possible.

3. *Design for ease of handling*. Parts handling may consume almost 80% of assembly time (Gairola, 1987). To facilitate handling procedures in general, materials and surfaces should be chosen which are adequate for handling, and all parts should be dimensionally stable.

4. *Design for ease of labelling*. Installing a label on an assembly can be more difficult and labour intensive than installing a part, and there are frequently many unnecessary labels on assemblies. Consequently, significant labour and cost reduction can be achieved by examining the application of labels for redundancy and repetition.

5. *Design for ease of testing*. In general, designers should attempt to move testing of products back as close to their assembly as possible, and reduce the number of tests needed. The overall guidelines of simplification and standardization again apply here.

The question remains as to how the guidelines outlined above can be realized in practice. Browne and O'Gorman (1985) recommend that in the short term designers

```
PART : KEYBOARD                OPERATION TIME        42.5 secs

SERIES OF INDIVIDUAL QUESTIONS.

PART(P) / TASK(T) ...................................... /  PART          2.0 s
MANIPULATE / ORIENT FIRST ................. /  YES           9.0 s
PART FASTENED ...................................... /  YES           0.0 s
FASTENED BY .......................................... /  PRESS FIT     1.5 s
SEPARATE OPERATION ........................... /  YES           2.0 s
EASILY VIEWED ....................................... /  NO            2.0 s
EASILY ACCESSED ................................. /  NO            2.0 s
EASILY ALIGNED ..................................... /  NO            1.5 s
EASILY INSERTED ................................... /  NO            1.0 s
STICKY / SHARP / FRAG / SLIPPERY ....... /  YES           0.5 s
NEST / TANGLE ........................................ /  YES           0.5 s
HEAVY (>10 LB) ....................................... /  NO            0.0 s
REQUIRE TOOLS ..................................... /  YES           0.0 s
TOOLS REQUIRED: .................................. /  SPECIAL       7.5 s
REQUIRE TWO PEOPLE / MECH ASST ..... /  NO            0.0 s
180 DEG SYMMETRY ABOUT X ............... /  YES           0.0 s
180 DEG SYMMETRY ABOUT Y ............... /  NO            0.0 s
180 DEG SYMMETRY ABOUT Z ............... /  YES           0.0 s

MEASUREMENTS OF SAMPLE PART A = 20 : B = 10.: C = 5        (A > B > C)
```

FIGURE 9.10

Individual assembly time for the assembly of a sample part.

should be 'educated' in these rules, which individual companies will refine in the context of their own experience and products. Over a period of time it is likely that the refined guidelines will be incorporated in an expert system. Such a system would be based on a set of characteristics which are desirable in a product/process, and a set of characteristics which should be avoided. Each product/part/process design would be assessed with respect to these characteristics, and the designer advised accordingly. Many such expert systems exist as commercial software packages. A system developed by Graves and Poli (1985) asks the user a series of simple questions about the proposed design and assembly of a product, and assigns approximate times to each assembly operation based on the answers given. The questions, answers and associated times for an example operation from the assembly of a telephone (the fastening of a keyboard to a subassembly) are displayed in Figure 9.10. The first question determines whether the user is referring to an operation which primarily involves a part (e.g. attaching two parts together) or to a task. If the user is referring to a part, then a value of 2 seconds is added to the operation time, and a series of further questions asked about the part characteristics. When a user is specifying a task, he or she is asked to enter an estimate of the time for the task, and the rest of the questions are irrelevant. The questions concerning part characteristics include:

1. Does the part need to be manipulated or orientated first?

2. Does the part need to be fastened, and what fastening operation is used (the user can choose a press/snap, bend or screw operation)?

3. Is a separate operation required to position the part, or is it self-locating?

4. Can the part be easily viewed, accessed, aligned and inserted?

5. Is the part sticky, sharp, fragile or slippery, and can it easily become tangled or nested?

6. Is the part heavy, and does it require tools and/or more than one person or mechanical assistance to move it?

7. Is the part symmetrical about any axis?

Depending on the answers received, the system assigns times and calculates an operation time for each individual operation. In this way a designer can see the implications of his or her design in terms of its total assembly time, and so can assess its ease of assembly.

9.6 An overview of process planning techniques

We have already seen that the procedure whereby the design description of engineering parts and assemblies is converted into instructions for the manufacturing plant is known as **process planning**. The instructions describe in detail the manufacturing process operations which convert parts from rough billets to the finished state, and the assembly operations which subsequently assemble parts into products. The procedure is therefore one of matching component requirements to the capabilities of the available manufacturing plant, and process planning can thus be regarded as the link between engineering design and shop floor manufacturing/assembly.

The chosen process plan for any part or assembly will depend on many factors – in general there is no unique plan which is appropriate for a given circumstance. The factors which will affect the planning decisions include the part geometry, the required accuracy and surface finish, the number to be produced, the material which has been specified by the designer and so on. For example, a very smooth surface finish may call for a grinding operation, and a less fine finish a turning operation, for the same part geometry. Similarly, if small numbers of a turned part are to be produced, it may be appropriate to program a numerically controlled machine tool to carry out a machining operation. For larger numbers an automatic lathe may be more appropriate, while for a one-off a manual lathe might be chosen. In addition to the component-specific factors, the choice of the process plan is also greatly influenced by the available manufacturing plant. In this respect the choice is also whether the part or assembly should be made in-house at all, or bought from another company. This is termed the make-or-buy decision, and is inextricably linked with the early stages of process planning.

A process planning example

As an example of the effect of changes in part attributes on the elements of the process plan, let us consider process planning for an 'impression stop' from a printing machine, a simplified drawing of which is shown in Figure 9.11. This part is produced by a combination of turning and milling of a billet sawn to length from bar stock. The sequence of manufacturing operations using a CNC mill/turn centre (a lathe with a milling head which is capable of carrying out both turning and milling

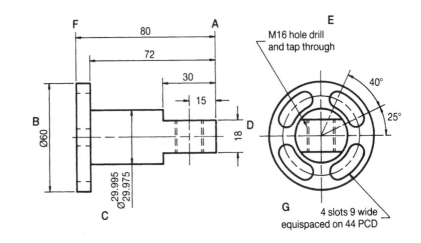

FIGURE 9.11

An example part for process planning. (Reproduced by permission of Strachan Henshaw Machinery Ltd.)

operations) is shown below. The letters in brackets refer to the label of the machined feature on the drawing:

> Face the part (A); turn the 60 mm outside diameter (B); turn the 30 mm nominal diameter with two finish cuts to achieve the correct tolerance (C); mill the two flats (D); drill and tap the M16 hole (E); part off (F); reverse part in chuck; mill the radial slots (G).

All of these operations may be done with a single machine. However, if the tolerance required on the 30 mm nominal diameter was smaller, for example 0.01 mm, then it might be necessary to finish-grind that diameter between centres. This would involve two additional operations on the mill/turn centre to centre-drill the two ends of the part, and a grinding operation on a separate machine. Conversely, if the tolerance was relaxed to 0.1 mm, a single finish cut would be acceptable.

The same example may be used to illustrate the effect of manufacturing plant availability on the process plan. If the mill/turn centre is not available, and manually operated tools must be used, then the plan might become (omitting detail):

> Face; turn outside diameter; turn 30 mm diameter; part off; transport to milling machines; mill flats; transfer to drilling machines; mark up; drill and tap; transfer to milling machines; mill slots.

This is a very much longer sequence, because transport operations are often time consuming and part-finished items may be held up waiting for machines.

A framework for process planning

A useful framework into which process planning may be placed is provided by Gindy (1992) in describing a planning system 'GENPLAN'. This framework shows the procedure working with **component** information – the parts, part features and connectivity – and with **processing systems** information – the available machines, tools and processes. This information is further subdivided into **absolute knowledge** – the geometry and topology of the parts, and the form-generating capabilities of the processes – and the **constrained knowledge** – the part sizes, finishes and accuracy, and the process size envelopes and capabilities. Using this information the process planning procedure is divided chronologically into three stages: the first involves identifying whether the features on a part are capable of being made with the available manufacturing resources; the second stage is to identify the particular operations or processes which may produce the part forms, or the assembly operations, to within the required technical constraints such as surface finish; and the third and final stage involves attempting some form of optimization of the sequence and the detail of the operations to form the process plan.

Computer-aided process planning

In traditional process planning systems the plan is prepared manually. The task involves reasoning about and interpreting engineering drawings, making decisions on how cuts should be made or how parts should be assembled, determining in which order operations should be executed, specifying what tools, machines and fixtures are necessary, and so on. The resulting process plan is therefore very much dependent on the skill and judgement of the planner. The type of plans which a planner produces depends on the individual's technical ability, the nature of his or her experience and even on the person's mood at the time of planning. The use of computer-based decision support systems (**computer-aided process planning**, CAPP) offers potential benefit in terms of reducing the routine clerical work of manufacturing engineers and also providing the opportunity to generate rational, consistent and perhaps optimal plans. Additionally, an integrated CADCAM system can only be developed if there exists a system that can utilize design data from a CAD system and information from manufacturing databases to manufacture the part. CAPP seeks to provide this interface between CAD and CAM.

Two approaches have been used to automate process planning: **variant** and **generative**. The elements of these are outlined below.

Variant process planning

This approach is sometimes referred to as the retrieval method, and has been widely used in machining applications. The basic idea underlying variant process planning is that similar parts will have similar process plans. Computer software is used to identify similar parts, through the use of GT-based coding and classification system (see Section 9.4). Part families are defined and a composite part, which includes all of the features of that family, is developed. A complete process plan for the composite part is then developed and stored in memory. When required, a process plan for an individual part is 'developed' by defining that part in terms of its overlap with the composite part and then retrieving the appropriate segments of the process plan for the composite part. The identification of the appropriate part family and indeed the identification of the overlap between the individual part and the composite part for the family is realized through the use of the GT-based coding system.

Variant process planning systems have been developed for many applications in machining. For example, systems have been developed to support the generation of process plans for rotational or cylindrical machined parts. Rotational parts are parts whose main geometry is based on a cylinder or a variant of a cylinder and which are normally machined on lathes or cylindrical grinders. Also, systems have been developed to support the development of process plans for prismatic parts. These are parts whose main geometry is based around a cube or prism. Typically, such parts are machined on milling machines, boring machines, surface grinders, etc. For a review of such systems see Davies and Darbyshire (1984). Clearly, the variant approach has one great weakness, namely that the system is only capable of planning for parts which fall within the defined part families. Further, the process plan developed by a variant system is rarely complete, except for the simplest of parts, and normally requires the time and effort of an experienced planner to complete it.

The generative approach

In the generative approach a new process plan is generated or synthesized for each individual component. In theory a human planner is not required as the computer system develops a process plan using decision logic and pre-coded algorithms. A number of approaches to generative process planning have been developed, which cover a range of manufacturing domains – Chang (1990) provides an excellent review. Although process planning systems exist in areas such as sheet metal fabrication (De Vin *et al.*, 1994; Shipitalni and Saddan, 1994) and assembly (Yung and Wang, 1988), the greater body of work concerns process plan generation for machined parts including: GENPLAN (Gindy *et al.*, 1993), QTC (Kanumury and Chang, 1991) and PART (Van Houten and Van't Erve, 1992). The components of a generative system, as described by Wang and Li (1991), are as follows.

▶ A part description, which should identify a series of component characteristics, including geometric features, dimensions, tolerances and surface condition.

▶ A subsystem to define the machining parameters, for example using look-up tables and analytical results for cutting parameters.

▶ A subsystem to select and sequence individual operations. Decision logic is used to associate appropriate operations with features of a component, and heuristics and algorithms are used to calculate operation steps, times and sequences.

▶ A database of available machines and tooling.

▶ A report generator which prepares the process plan report.

The key problems in generative systems development are in the first three components. Existing drawing and CAD model representations are not adequate for automatic process planning, and have to be enhanced through the addition of information about component features and other characteristics, either automatically through feature recognition, or through 'design by features', as discussed in Chapter 8. Process capability and parameter representation is made complicated by the sheer number of machines and process/material combinations that must be represented. The identification and sequencing of machining operations is a very complex task, both owing to the number of machining operations and part geometries that have to be catered for, and because of the very large number of operation sequences that become possible for complex parts involving many machining operations. In the remainder of this section we will therefore review these main considerations in generative process planning, concentrating on the main themes of part representation, process capability representation and reasoning about plan generation.

Part representation

Part representation is one of the key foundations of process planning. In order for planning to proceed, a representation of the desired part attributes in terms of shape, dimension, tolerance, materials and surface condition is required. Traditionally, this information has been contained in engineering drawings that have been used by skilled process planners. As three-dimensional geometric modelling was developed, it was thought that it would provide a good basis for process planning, but purely geometric representations were found to be limited in their ability to support process planning (for example, there is little information in a collection of part faces to say that it has a particular engineering significance). For this reason, higher-level part representations have emerged based on **features**, which as we have seen in Chapter 8 are modelling entities which combine geometric and other attributes with information about engineering intent. In that chapter we noted that features may be used through **feature recognition**, in which features are automatically identified from conventional geometric models, or through **design by features**, in which the designer designs directly in terms of features.

Feature recognition or **feature extraction** attempts to recognize collections of geometry of manufacturing significance from the solid model. A typical approach requires features to be recognized from the description of the faces, edges and vertices of a B-rep model. Some systems, such as the PART or QTC II systems, are now able to extract features in a limited way (Chamberlain *et al.*, 1993; Van Houten and Van't Erve, 1992), but feature recognition is as yet restricted in its range of application. The design by features approach, in which the design is defined *ab initio* in terms of features, has emerged as an alternative approach for all but the simplest of part geometries (refer to Chapter 8 for further discussion on this topic).

One approach to design by features is the **destructive solid geometry** (DSG) representation in which features or primitives are all subtracted from a model of the billet for a part. As a DSG model uses only the Boolean difference operator there is a simple association with machining operations since subtracting volumes sequentially is akin to material removal operations in machining. The complexity of parts which can be represented by a finite set of primitives is, however, limited, and the representation of protruding features is awkward and not explicit. Even so, this relative simplicity has led researchers also to investigate the automated conversion of constructive solid geometry (CSG) to DSG by such methods as the convex hull algorithm (Kim, 1992), since process planning would be relatively simple from DSG.

Design by features involves the designer constructing the part geometry using features of known geometry. This results in an explicit representation which allows local geometry to be considered during process planning (although it should be noted that for many commercial CADCAM systems, features are used predominantly for rapid construction of part geometry, and a persistent feature representation is sometimes not maintained). As a high-level description of part geometry, the notion of features has gained acceptance as a representation supporting the generation of process plans

(Salomons *et al.*, 1993). Unfortunately, the desire to capture more than purely geometrical and/or topological information concerning a part has led to a number of application-specific definitions of features. For example, a given component geometry may be required to be described differently by a designer who requires form and function to be expressed, an assembly planner in describing an assembly operation or relationship, or a machinist who requires volumetric material removal operations to be carried out whilst achieving appropriate tolerance levels. An additional difficulty, known as non-uniqueness, is that even within a particular feature schema, dedicated to a specific application, there may still be multiple ways of representing a single geometric form.

Two types of feature description are commonly used in the context of machining process planning: form features, which are recognizable shapes such as cylinders or blocks, which cannot be further decomposed without reducing them to meaningless geometric entities (El Maraghy, 1993); and functional features, describing such geometries as slots, keyways, chamfers, threads, etc. There is a relatively simple correspondence between such features, at least in their volumetric form, and the swept volume of cutting tools or the geometry of stock material since these features are defined specifically for process planning. These types of description are also reasonably natural for designers to use to express form but may not be so good at expressing function.

A further distinction that is used in feature modelling for CAPP is the differentiation, noted in Chapter 8, between positive or **protrusion** features, and negative or **depression** features. Protrusion features are used broadly to define the overall dimensions of a component. Examples of protrusion features are bosses, ribs, blocks or cylinders. Depression features may be holes, slots, chamfers, or any other geometry which describes a volume of material removed from a protrusion feature, as shown in Figure 9.12, which also shows examples of form and functional features.

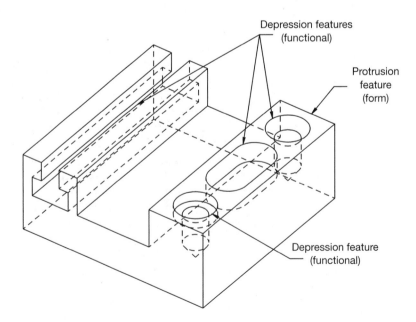

FIGURE 9.12
Features used in CAPP.

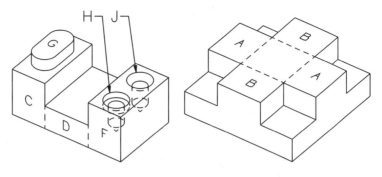

FIGURE 9.13
Topological relationships between features.

(a) Features G and C, C and D and D and F are *adjacent*
Features H and J are *owned* by feature F

(b) Features A-A and B-B *intersect*

Features alone are not sufficient to describe a part geometry. Additionally, some indication of the relationship or connectivity between features is required. These are termed topological relations and further aid the process plan reasoning. Topological relationships are necessary, since the relationship between features can influence such factors as tool access during machining, fixture design, etc., as well as influencing the order in which features are machined. For example, if two rotational features are axially connected and the same turning operation is required to machine both features, it would make sense to machine these features one after the other. If, however, a rotational feature requiring turning is connected to a prismatic feature requiring milling, then a tool change will be necessary. Under these circumstances, it may be sensible to machine other rotational features requiring turning before changing to a milling tool for the prismatic feature. The topological relationship of adjacency, especially in edge–face relationships in B-rep models, is used widely in feature recognition. In addition, Lee *et al.* (1996) suggest that the relationships used in planning should be extended to include intersection between protrusions – **interpenetration** – and intersection between protrusions and depressions, which they term **ownership**. These relationships are shown in Figure 9.13. Interpenetration is important because, when two protrusions interpenetrate, it is necessary to manufacture them simultaneously, as shown in the example in Figure 9.13(b). Ownership is important because often it is necessary to manufacture a protrusion before any depression that it contains is manufactured.

Topological relations between features are also necessary to represent dimensional and geometrical tolerances which are expressed between features. Although tolerances associated with an individual feature may be expressed as attributes of that feature, it is often required to give interfeature dimensions. It is therefore necessary to consider the way in which features are connected, in order to assess overall dimensions and tolerances. In addition, the tolerance data should be available for all intermediate geometries that are reached as the part progresses through its manufacturing route, as decisions on when to carry out inspection operations, and the choice of manufacturing process, depend on tolerance information.

A number of part representations for process planning using features technology have been developed. The GENPLAN system (Gindy *et al.*, 1993) first divides the volumetric features into protrusions, depressions and surfaces. Each of these features is defined using envelope boundaries giving entry/exit and depth boundaries. For example, a blind hole will have an open face, a closed face and a depth, whilst a through hole is expressed by two open faces and a depth. Other approaches have defined different topological relationships, such as precedence, thin section and feature overlaps (Young and Bell, 1993). These relationships not only define the relationship between feature geometries, but also aid the sequencing of material removal operations. For example, a precedence relationship may state that a hole has to be drilled before it is tapped. These issues are discussed further in McMahon *et al.* (1997) which reports a recursive plan generation system that uses Lee *et al.*'s topological relationships between features in a hierarchical part representation to restrict the search space of operation sequences.

Process capability representation

In addition to a part representation, a notation is also required to represent process capability. This should be capable of representing the tolerance and surface condition that can be achieved by the process, the access directions for tools, the machining rates that are achievable, the tool shapes and motions that are used, and the overall size and shape capabilities of the process. The level of detail depends on the final application of the process plan. If detailed process plans (sometimes called **operation plans**) are required, containing information about tool paths, feedrate and so on, then a large amount of data is required concerning not only machine tool specifications but also details of the available tools and set-up limitations.

Detailed manufacturing information is, however, not necessary in **outline process planning**, which involves the identification of candidate sequences of operations that may be used to manufacture a part. Detailed process planning takes these candidate sequences and expands them by adding manufacturing detail regarding machines to be employed, tooling data, material removal rates and so on. During the outline planning stage the application of detailed information is time consuming, and to perform this operation on every possible sequence in a problem domain is not viable. Detailed manufacturing information must, however, be used in operation planning, applied to a small number of plans identified at the outline process planning stage.

A number of approaches have been devised for the representation of manufacturing capabilities in planning systems. The GENPLAN system (Gindy *et al.*, 1993) represents machine tool capabilities as elementary motions and includes some rules for grouping these motions into a particular machined form generating capability. The TIPPS system (Wang and Wysk, 1988) represents capability knowledge in the form of IF . . . THEN **production rules** (see Chapter 8), and facts (or declarative knowledge) are represented by **frames**, for example workpiece geometry, machine tool geometry, etc. The QTC system (Chang, 1990) also uses production rules, in which each feature has attributes which specify its dimensional, tolerance and other parameters, which are retrieved and associated with a particular manufacturing capability.

Plan generation

The task of plan generation is to reason with the part and process capability representations, in order to identify and sequence a series of material removal operations which transform a part from an initial starting billet to a final design geometry. One of the major problems with generating a process plan is the combinatorial explosion of possible sequences. For example, for a component which requires N operations during manufacture, these operations can be sequenced in $N!$ possible ways. Further, if there are, on average, T manufacturing processes capable of undertaking a particular operation, then there are $T.N!$ possible operation sequences. Of course, only a limited number of these sequences will be feasible, but, nevertheless, the generation of a process plan requires searching the problem space to find possible sequences of operations which form a solution. By searching for all possible sequences and selecting the optimum, based on some criterion such as minimum production cost or operational 'best practice', a globally optimum solution to process plan generation is made. Unfortunately, the computing resource associated with full problem space searching is extensive for all but the simplest of part geometries.

In order to overcome the problems associated with full problem space searching, process planning systems seek to eliminate unfeasible sequences at the earliest possible stage, and to identify feasible sequences for eventual sorting into rank order. Sequence elimination is most efficient if substantial parts of the search space may be eliminated in a single step, and therefore techniques for such 'pruning' of the search space are sought. The criteria upon which unfeasible sequences are eliminated can be broadly divided into geometric or manufacturing considerations.

Geometric considerations essentially serve to ensure that the shapes produced are geometrically and topologically feasible throughout the manufacturing sequence, and to eliminate plan sequences which violate this principle. For example, any material removal sequence which results in a void at some intermediate stage is not feasible. Conversely, it is feasible, but usually not sensible, to work in alternate stages on each end of a bar, or to switch between physically separated parts of the workpiece between operations.

Manufacturing considerations describe factors which determine the feasibility of manufacture of a part via a particular processing sequence, and include:

▶ mandatory operation relationships: for example, that a hole must be drilled before it is tapped;

▶ tool approach, fixturing and holding rules: the tool must be able to access the part of the component to be machined, and the component must be capable of being located and supported;

▶ tolerance and surface condition capabilities: the process must be capable of producing the required surface finish and tolerance;

▶ size constraints: the part size must not exceed the capacity of the production machines.

Other manufacturing considerations might be to group all the material removal operations which require a single machining operation (e.g. turning) together, to reduce the set-up and downtime costs associated with part manufacture. Alternatively, on a multi-function machine tool, it may be appropriate to group together as many operations as possible which can be carried out whilst the part is held in a particular fixturing device. These sorts of considerations can often be relaxed or even changed, depending on the demands of the manufacturing environment. For example, optimum plans may differ if parts must be produced in minimum time or if minimum tooling costs are specified. Alternatively, if a particular machine tool requires refurbishment, it may be temporarily eliminated as a manufacturing capability. Optimum plans will therefore be produced which do not rely on the particular machine tool in question.

The act of eliminating unfeasible or non-preferred sequences through geometrical and manufacturing considerations is known as constraining. Methods of imposing constraints on possible operation sequences have generally centred on applying heuristic rules or algorithms. The difficulty with using rules is that, as the complexity of a part and the manufacturing processes capable of producing a part increase, so the number of rules required increases. This leads to a large number of rules which are often stored in a separate database. Factors such as changing the application domain of a process planning system to new parts, or the purchase of a new machine tool with greater manufacturing capability, require that new rules be added to the database, or existing rules modified. Maintenance of such a rule database is often time consuming. Further, as the number of rules increases, they may become contradictory, different rules stating a different course of action for the solution of an identical problem, depending on the operation's location within the sequence.

Algorithms have been used to overcome the need for an extensive database of rules, although they are generally applied to less complicated planning domains, such as sheet metal bend sequencing (Shipitalni and Saddan, 1994). By applying the part description in a rigid format, algorithms may be used to constrain unfeasible sequences by continually applying constraining criteria. Some algorithmic systems act to eliminate unfeasible sequences as soon as some point in a sequence fails to conform to the constraining criteria. More recent applications, using genetic algorithms or simulated annealing, consider a full operation sequence and iteratively develop an optimum solution by promoting the development of favourable sequence segments that fulfil a given criterion, such as minimum manufacturing cost.

The difficulty with algorithms is that they fail to constrain sequences with regard to detailed criteria. Specific problem states which can be accommodated by a particular rule are not easily dealt with by general application algorithms. A solution is to combine algorithms, which initially reduce the number of feasible sequences with regard to general constraints, with rules. The reduced number of sequences allowed by the algorithms means that a smaller number of more specific rules is required for more detailed constraining criteria.

The status of generative process planning

Although a large number of prototype generative process planning systems for machining applications have been reported in the research literature, relatively few truly generative systems are in use in industry. The present research into developing planning systems that combine feature-based representations with artificial intelligence techniques for plan sequencing and application of process capability constraints may provide a framework to incorporate the decision-making process of the planner and make it suitable for automation. Most of the current uses of expert systems in the area of process planning can be regarded as either automated systems or decision support systems. When process planning is concerned with manufacturing operations like machining, which involve generally simple machine movements which may easily be categorized, and which are well understood and supported by mathematical and heuristic models of cutting performance, an expert system approach may prove suitable for the *automatic* generation of process plans. However, for assembly operations, which we will deal with next, no such well-founded evidence or generally accepted categorization of operations exists. Assembly process planning relies heavily on the experience of the process planner and the industry in which he or she is working. Thus expert systems intended for assembly process planning applications are likely to be designed as intelligent decision support systems with the process/manufacturing engineer having the final decision. For assembly planning to develop, it is necessary that the actual assembly operations are clearly understood and defined.

On a more general note, the move away from the traditional sequential approach to the organization of design and manufacture is likely to have a large impact on process planning systems. Traditionally, process planning has formed the link between discrete design and manufacturing activities, but as planning for manufacture is moved earlier in the product introduction process, the role of CAPP will expand. In particular outline process planning systems will be used to give rapid feedback about the manufacturing feasibility of the product early in the design process.

The application of CAPP will also expand beyond the present concentration on machining systems to other manufacturing processes such as presswork and other forming processes, composites manufacture, and of course assembly, which is the topic to which we will now turn.

Assembly process planning

In general terms, assembly is performed by people when volumes are low, by computer-controlled machines and robots when volumes are moderate, and by special-purpose machines when volumes are very high. The assembly process is more complex than might appear at first sight for two reasons: firstly, assembly operations were traditionally performed by manual operators who were considered unskilled, but who in fact were very skilled in terms of manual dexterity, hand–eye coordination, and ability to detect and exert forces, apply pressures and so on; secondly, assembly operations tended to be specific in terms of particular industrial sectors. Thus, for example, a set of assembly skills was built up in the electronics sector, involving initially the insertion of electronic components in printed circuit boards (PCBs) using manual means, semi-automated placement machines and ultimately computer-controlled component insertion machines, so-called DIP (Dual-in-line Package) insertion, component sequencing and VCD (Variable Centre Distance) insertion machines. In more recent times, with the development of SMT (Surface Mount Technology) electronic components, much of this insertion assembly technology has been replaced by SMT lines which include placement machines, solder reflow systems, curing ovens, etc. The assembly skills which are prevalent in the electro-mechanical sector are quite different from those in the electronics sector. A further set of tasks and skills is required in mechanical assembly.

In fact, some work was done in the Charles Stark Draper Laboratory in the United States in the early 1980s on the issue of defining standard assembly operations. Typical assembly tasks were identified by taking apart and reassembling a variety of products (largely electro-mechanical items and their components). All of the items studied could be assembled with various combinations of 12 operations. The operations in question were: simple peg in hole insertion; push and twist insertion; multiple peg in hole insertion; insert peg (vertically) and retainer (horizontal); screw insertion; force fit insertion; remove locating pin; flip part over; provide temporary support; crimp sheet metal; remove temporary support; and join by welding or soldering (Nevins and Whitney, 1978). Based on this set of assembly operations, Bowden and Browne (1987) developed a simple assembly process planning system, using a decision support approach.

Recent research on assembly process planning has concentrated on the assembly of mechanical parts and also on the integration of assembly process planning with the CAD system. This integration is important because the CAD model is the source of much of the data necessary to support the development of the process plan: in particular data on the interrelationship between parts, the surface characteristics of individual parts, etc. However, part of the problem is the lack of a sufficiently complete model to support assembly process planning. This problem in turn stems at least partially from the lack of a complete understanding of the assembly process and indeed the thought process of the assembly process planner as he or she creates a particular process plan. For a detailed review of assembly process planning the interested reader is referred to Chapter 10 of Wang and Li (1991).

9.7 Conclusion

Pressure to achieve improved product quality while at the same time reducing costs and lead times is forcing companies to pay close attention to product design, in particular design for manufacture. This has made the interface between design and manufacture a target for the extensive development of new engineering techniques and organizational approaches. This development continues, with the key word being **integration** – of specialist approaches, of computer applications and of technologies. Although much has been achieved, there are many problems to be solved, and this is therefore likely to be a major area for CADCAM development in the near future.

References and further reading

Alting L. and Zhang H. C. (1989). Computer-aided process planning: the state-of-the-art survey. *International Journal of Production Research*. **27**(4), 553–85.

Andreasen M. (1983). *Design for Assembly*. A collaboration by The Institute for Product Development (IPD), the Technical University of Denmark and Danish Technology Ltd. Kempston: IFS Publications.

Andreasen M., Myrup M. M., Kähler S., Lund T. and Swift K. (1988). *Design for Assembly*. Bedford: IFS Publications/Springer.

Boothroyd G. and Dewhurst P. (1987). *Product Design for Assembly*. Wakefield, RI: Boothroyd and Dewhurst Inc.

Bowden R. and Browne J. (1987). ROBEX – an artificial intelligence based process planning system for robotic assembly. In *Proceedings of the IXth ICPR Conference*, pp. 868–74.

Bralla J. G. (ed.) (1986). *Handbook of Product Design for Manufacturing*. New York: McGraw-Hill.

Browne J. and O'Gorman P. (1985). Product design for small parts assembly. In *Robotic Assembly: International Trends in Manufacturing Technology* (ed. K. Rathmill), pp. 139–55. Kempston: IFS Publications.

Burbidge J. L. (1979). *Group Technology in the Engineering Industry*. London: Mechanical Engineering Publications.

Chamberlain M. A., Joneja A. and Chang T. C. (1993). Protrusion-features handling in design and manufacturing planning. *Computer-aided Design*. **25**(1), 19–28.

Chang T. (1990). *Expert Process Planning for Manufacturing*. Reading, MA: Addison Wesley Longman.

Council of Ironfoundry Associations (1956). *A Practical Guide to the Design of Grey Iron Castings for Engineering Purposes*. London: Council of Ironfoundry Associations.

Davies B. J. and Darbyshire I. L. (1984). The use of expert systems in process planning. *Annals of the CIRP*. **33**(1), 303–6.

De Vin L. J., Streppel A. H. and Kals H. J. J. (1994). Tolerancing and sheet metal bending in small batch part manufacture. *Annals of the CIRP*. **43**(1), 421–4.

Dieter G. E. (1986). *Engineering Design. A Materials and Processing Approach*. New York: McGraw-Hill.

El Maraghy H. A. (1993). Evolutions and future perspectives of CAPP. *Annals of the CIRP*. **42**(2), 739–51.

Gairola A. (1987). Design for assembly: a challenge for expert systems. In *Artificial Intelligence in Manufacturing* (ed. T. Bernold). Amsterdam: Elsevier.

Gallagher C. and Knight W. (1973). *Group Technology*. London: Butterworth.

Gindy N. N. Z. (1992). A product data model for computer-aided process planning systems. In *International Conference on Manufacturing Automation*, University of Hong Kong, pp. 428–33.

Gindy N. N. Z., Huang X. and Ratchev T. M. (1993). Feature-based component model for computer-aided process planning systems. *International Journal of Computer Integrated Manufacturing*. **6**, 20–6.

Graves R. and Poli C. (1985). *Integrated Product Design and Assembly Process Design*. Amherst: Department of Mechanical Engineering, University of Massachusetts.

Kanumury M. and Chang T. C. (1991). Process planning in an automated manufacturing environment. *Journal of Manufacturing Systems*. **10**(1), 67–78.

Kerr R. (1991). *Knowledge-based Manufacturing Management*. Harlow: Addison Wesley Longman.

Kim Y. S. (1992). Recognition of form features using convex decomposition. *Computer-aided Design*. **24**(9), 461–76.

Laszcs J. F. (1985). Product design for robotic and automatic assembly. In *Robotic Assembly: International Trends in Manufacturing Technology* (ed. K. Rathmill), pp. 157–72. Kempston: IFS Publications.

Lee H., Scott J. A., Sims Williams J. H. and Cox D. R. (1996). A symbolic calculus for volumetric reasoning about process plans. *AI EDAM*. **10**, 183–98.

Lucas Engineering and Systems (1988). *The Lucas Manufacturing Systems Handbook: Mini Guides*. Solihull: Lucas Engineering and Systems.

Lyman J. (1984). Surface mounting alters the PC-board scene. *Electronics*. February, 21–2.

Matousek R. (1963). *Engineering Design: a Systematic Approach*. London: Blackie.

McMahon C. A., Cox D. R., Sims Williams J. H. and Scott J. A. (1997). Representation and reasoning in computer-aided process planning. *Proc. Institution of Mechanical Engineers, Journal of Engineering Manufacture*, **211**(B), 473–85.

Nevins J. L. and Whitney D. E. (1978). Computer controlled assembly. *Scientific American*. February, 101–20.

Noble P. (1988). Component choice and PCB design for automation. *New Electronics*. February, 24–6.

Opitz H. (1970). *A Classification System to Describe Workpieces*. Oxford: Pergamon Press.

Pahl G. and Beitz W. (1984). *Engineering Design*. London: The Design Council/Springer.

Salomons O. W., Van Houten F. J. and Kals H. J. (1993). Review of research in feature-based design. *Journal of Manufacturing Systems*. **12**(2), 113–32.

Schraft R. D. and Bassler R. (1985). Considerations for automatic orientated product design, product design for robotic and automatic assembly. In *Robotic Assembly: International Trends in Manufacturing Technology* (ed. K. Rathmill), pp. 173–84. Kempston: IFS Publications.

Shipitalni M. and Saddan D. (1994). Automatic determination of bend sequences in sheet metal products. *Annals of the CIRP*. **43**(1), 23–26.

Steudel H. J. (1984). Computer-aided process planning: past, present and future. *International Journal of Production Research*. **22**(2), 253–66.

Swift K. G. (1987). *Knowledge-Based Design for Manufacture*. London: Kogan Page.

Swift K. and Redford A. H. (1977). Assembly classification as an aid to design and planning for mechanised assembly of small products. *Engineering*. December, 33, 35.

Treer K. (1980). Designing parts for automatic assembly. *Engineering*. July, 16–19.

Van Houten F. M. and Van't Erve A. H. (1992). A feature-based computer-aided process planning system. *International Journal of CADCAM and Computer Graphics*. **7**(3), 335–68.

Wang H. and Li J. (1991). *Computer-aided Process Planning*. Amsterdam: Elsevier.

Wang H. and Ozsoy T. (1991). A scheme to represent features, dimensions, and tolerances in geometric modelling. *Journal of Manufacturing Systems*. **10**(3), 233–40.

Wang H. and Wysk R. A. (1988). A knowledge-based approach for automated process planning. *International Journal of Production Research*. **26**, 999–1014.

Webb R. (1975). Part design can make or break automatic assembly. *Engineering*. February, 64–7.

Young R. I. M. and Bell R. (1993). Design by features: advantages and limitations in machine planning integration. *International Journal of Computer Integrated Manufacturing*. **6**, 105–12.

Yung J. and Wang H. (1988). Automated process planning for mechanical assembly operations. *Proc. 3rd Int. Conf. CADCAM, Robotics and Factories of the Future (CARS and FOF '88)*, Vol. **2**, 131–5.

Exercises

9.1 Select examples of formed, moulded and machined components. Do they conform to the rules outlined in Figures 9.7–9.9? Can you suggest improvements to the designs?

9.2 What is meant by the term 'concurrent engineering'?

9.3 What is group technology? How does group technology form 'component families'?

9.4 Distinguish clearly between 'simple' and 'hierarchical' group technology coding systems. Use an example from the Opitz system to illustrate your answer.

9.5 In terms of design for assembly, outline some appropriate guidelines for:
   (a) The simplification and standardization of product design.
   (b) Facilitation of the assembly process.

9.6 Distinguish clearly between 'variant' and 'generative' process planning.

9.7 Distinguish between protrusion and depression features, and between form and functional features, in the context of computer-aided process planning.

9.8 What is a topological relationship between features? Give examples of relationships, and suggest how they may be used to assist in computer-aided process planning.

9.9 What techniques may be used to reduce the search space in plan generation for computer-aided process planning?

9.10 Outline the issues and problems in assembly planning.

Projects

For more information about the subjects for project work, please refer to the end of Chapter 1.

The project activity for this chapter is to explore issues in the manufacture of the chess piece and load cell that are the project subjects. Specific tasks are:

Project 1 Chess piece, and Project 2 Load cell Produce a process plan for the sequence of operations required to manufacture each part. Classify the chess piece and the load cell structural member using the Opitz group technology classification, or a similar classification.

10 The total approach to product development

Chapter objectives

When you have completed studying the material in this chapter you should be able to:

- ▶ **outline the systems approach to engineering;**
- ▶ **explain the purpose and place of concurrent engineering, and understand the use of team-based and matrix organizational structures;**
- ▶ **understand the total quality approach to engineering, and describe techniques that may contribute to that approach within the design and manufacturing process;**
- ▶ **understand the elements of quality function deployment and of failure mode and effect analysis;**
- ▶ **outline Taguchi's approach to off-line quality control, and in particular to parameter design and design of experiments.**

Chapter contents

10.1 Introduction: the systems approach

In recent years there has been criticism of the preponderance in science of a 'reductionist' philosophy that seeks to understand the natural world by studying its component parts (Checkland, 1981); similarly, engineers have been criticized for paying too much attention to optimizing parts of products or manufacturing processes rather than the whole. These criticisms have been voiced by those who advocate a holistic approach – a concern with the whole rather than with the parts – which may be called the **systems** approach.

The systems approach grew in particular from electronic engineering and computing, where the notion of meeting some overall requirements by assembling elements into a system is particularly apposite. Such engineering applications have been termed **hard systems** because the interfaces between the various elements are well defined. Systems thinking has also been applied to the more fuzzy areas of management and human interactions, which have been termed **soft systems** (Checkland, 1981).

Part of the power of the systems approach is that systems can be subdivided recursively into a hierarchy of subsystems, which can themselves be examined in a holistic fashion. The reader will recall the hierarchical decomposition of an electrical system described by a series of diagrams in Figure 2.6, and the hierarchical decomposition that was applied in adopting an object-oriented approach to programming, or in the network models of hypertext and frame-based systems.

Systems may also be regarded as interacting with other systems. For example, we can regard a particular product design as a system. The characteristics of the product will be influenced by a variety of other systems, such as the manufacturing system that makes it, the service system that maintains it, the environment in which it operates and so on. It may be helpful to consider a simple model that regards designs as:

▶ being driven by **requirements** placed on them (typically by the customer);

▶ being limited by **constraints** imposed by the systems with which the design interacts.

The designer will try to maximize the **utility** of the design (or the value of the design to the customer) in response to the requirements. For instance, the requirements that drive an aircraft design are for long range, low seat-mile costs, low noise, high reliability and durability and so on. The utility of an aircraft will be a very complex function of its performance in these terms, and will involve many trade-offs. The design will be constrained by such factors as:

▶ the characteristics of the environment in which the aircraft will operate: airfield runway and taxiway sizes and weight limits; noise regulations; international safety regulations and so on;

▶ the characteristics of the manufacturing system that will make the aircraft: available manufacturing processes, plant size and location and so on.

The important point is that it is the performance of a design as an entire system that is crucial. For instance, the characteristics of the component parts of the aircraft are not important to the airline or its passengers except in so far as they contribute to the characteristics of the aircraft as a whole.

In Chapter 8 the concept of a multi-dimensional constraint space was introduced in the context of constraint-based reasoning. Using this as a model the requirements may be visualized as forcing a design against constraint boundaries, as shown in Figure 10.1. For early versions of a design these boundaries may be very poorly understood – with the consequence that the design will be simultaneously overdesigned in some respects and unreliable in others (where it inadvertently crosses a constraint bound – consider, for example, the performance of early cars or aircraft). For well-established products, however, much of the design task involves trying to obtain as good an understanding as possible of the design requirements, and of the constraints. For complex products this understanding comes from the work of specialists – in

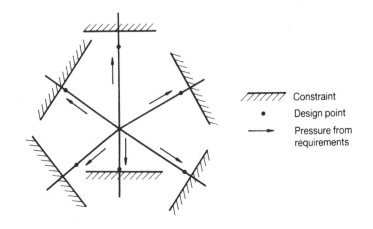

FIGURE 10.1
Design as a
multi-dimensional
state-space.

manufacturing, in reliability, in design analysis and so on. The collaborative working of such specialists in concurrent engineering will be the subject of the next section, and in the remainder of the chapter the philosophy behind current approaches to quality engineering, and a number of the techniques developed to provide a qualitative judgement of product quality, will be outlined.

10.2 Concurrent engineering

The successful design of most established products requires the input of specialists. The design lead time may be short if this specialist input occurs throughout the design phase, thus avoiding costly design–redesign loops. The product lead time can be further reduced by actually designing the manufacturing system at the same time as designing the product. This also allows the designer and manufacturing engineer to trade off parameters interactively to give an optimum design of product and process. This is the process of **concurrent engineering**.

The concurrent engineering process should address the complete life cycle of a product, from prototype and test through manufacture, use, maintenance and repair and (of increasing importance today) to eventual disposal and recycling.

Company organization

To support a concurrent engineering approach, many companies are moving away from a traditional **functional organization**, in which product engineering and manufacturing engineering are separate, and particular specializations are discrete departments. These group individuals according to their knowledge and work specialisms, with each group represented by a separate manager. The move is towards more flexible **project-** or **team-based** organizations, in which the central focus of a group is not a functional discipline, but a project or a class of product.

There are a number of different approaches to team-based design. In some companies the principal grouping is first according to the main class of product. Companies who have grouped this way include an automobile manufacturer that groups

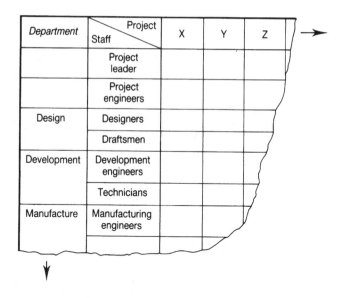

Department	Project / Staff	X	Y	Z	
	Project leader				
	Project engineers				
Design	Designers				
	Draftsmen				
Development	Development engineers				
	Technicians				
Manufacture	Manufacturing engineers				

FIGURE 10.2

Matrix organization of projects and departments.

its main product development teams into small, medium and large cars and off-road, and an aircraft manufacturer that divides broadly into short-, medium- and long-range aircraft classes. From within these main groupings, individual teams are formed for the development of specific products. Ideally, in a team-based organization each project is allocated the appropriate mix of staff at any stage in the project life cycle. In the early stages marketing and concept design specialists would predominate; at the later stages, specialists in maintenance and reliability would be prevalent.

A purely project-based organization may be difficult to manage because it is in a permanent state of flux as people are moved between projects, and therefore in practice the intermediate **matrix organizations** are sometimes used. In such organizations, staff are allocated to departments according to speciality or function, and project teams are then drawn from these departments as required. The term 'matrix' is used because the staff allocation to projects can be shown on a matrix, as in Figure 10.2. Typically, full project teams under a separate project team leader would be used for major new products requiring input from a number of functions. Derivative designs, or work involving minor product changes, might be dealt with purely by the functional organization.

A matrix form of organization can also be used to share expertise between technical specialists, and to ensure that common practices are adopted throughout a company. For example, let us assume that a company makes hydraulic system products that include valves, pumps, actuators and accumulators, manufactured by different manufacturing groups. A matrix organization such as that shown in Figure 10.3 would establish working teams that integrate 'horizontally' to ensure consistent company practice in such areas as design analysis, geometric modelling and manufacturing data generation. Product group practice would be vertically integrated to ensure that the output from one model may be fed into the next.

No single organizational structure is suitable for managing all levels of product complexity and innovation. Each has its strong and weak points, and the balance

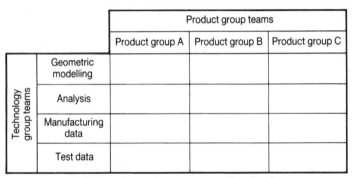

		Product group teams		
		Product group A	Product group B	Product group C
Technology group teams	Geometric modelling			
	Analysis			
	Manufacturing data			
	Test data			

FIGURE 10.3
Matrix organization for technical support teams.

Product groups could be based on product types, e.g. small, medium, large airliners, or on major sub-assemblies, e.g. gearbox, engine, chassis etc.

between these for a particular organization may change with time. The team-based organization is good at concentrating effort on the project and the product, but less satisfactory at developing and sharing specialist skills. The functional organization has the opposite characteristics. The matrix organization seeks to combine the strengths of the two approaches, but at the expense of a lack of clear lines of responsibility and conflicting loyalties. A currently prevailing view is that, whatever organization a company has, it should perhaps be moving towards, or taking on the characteristics of, the opposite organization type. If team based, it should be moving towards a functional alignment in order to facilitate skill development and the sharing of experience. If a functional organization, it should be moving towards project-based organization in order to concentrate team effort on product issues and understanding.

10.3 The total quality approach

We can all identify instances when the failure of some product or service has led to inconvenience, unnecessary expenditure and frustration or annoyance. Perhaps a car part has failed prematurely, with significant repair cost. Perhaps a train has failed to run on time, with the result that we are late for an important meeting. In a restaurant, our meal is cold and has to be returned to the kitchen. All of these instances, and many more, are examples of poor quality products or services. Furthermore, these examples are not rectified simply by 'inspecting' more thoroughly – the poor quality arises from a failure to achieve excellence in some part of an organization.

Within an engineering environment we can recognize more examples of the effects of poor quality. A defective machine setting may lead to components being scrapped, with the attendant rework costs and time delays. Incorrectly packaged components may be damaged in transit. A design that is not adequately protected against corrosion may rust and be unsaleable.

All of these instances of poor quality may also be defined as a failure of the product or service to perform as expected: a failure to satisfy the customer. In each case there is a cost associated with the defective performance. It may be a clear monetary cost, for example in the replacement of the car part, or it may be the 'cost' of high blood pressure when the train is late! This cost has been termed 'quality loss' by the

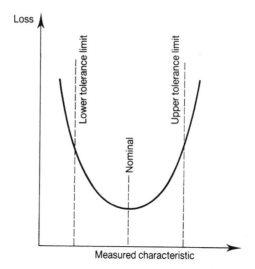

FIGURE 10.4
The quality loss function.

Japanese engineer Genichi Taguchi, and he suggests that deviation of a product from an optimum performance may be described by a **quality loss function**, as shown in Figure 10.4. (More specifically, Taguchi relates the quality of a product to the loss falling on society from the time the product is shipped. The loss function is used as a means of equating variation in the quality of a product or service with a monetary value.) The objective of an organization should be to minimize the quality loss function for its product or service.

Poor quality may arise from the inadequate performance of any part of an organization (even if the result is just that the product is more expensive than it needs to be: there is still a quality loss in the additional cost). The contribution of all parts of an organization to quality has led to the concept of **total quality**, sometimes called **total quality management (TQM)**, because it may be regarded as a management philosophy. The notion is that **everybody** in an organization should be concerned with assuring the quality of their work, and with taking continual steps to try to improve this quality. The policy is one of **continuous improvement**.

Brown *et al.* (1989) identify a total quality organization as one in which success comes from the right balance between the company **culture, structure** and **organization**. They see the culture as implying the combination of company values and management style, and the employees' attitudes and reaction to these values. The structure describes the formal reporting relationships within the organization, and involves here a trade-off between specializations and natural group integration of people, jobs and departments. The systems are the formal and informal procedures employed within the organization to measure the achievement of the company and of its suppliers and competitors.

Key principles of total quality

The company Lucas Engineering and Systems (Lucas, 1988) has identified a number of key principles of total quality from the work of such authors as Deming, Juran and Ishikawa. These may be summarized as:

▶ Adopt a policy of continuous improvement and innovation in all areas, especially training.

▶ Reduce the number of suppliers, and involve them in a policy of continuous improvement also.

▶ Provide on-line techniques for problem identification and solution; in particular, make extensive use of statistical methods.

▶ Make use of multi-disciplinary teams in an open, innovative environment; avoid overbureaucratic imposition of work standards.

Within this context, the term **on-line** is used to describe quality control measures taken at the point of manufacture of the product: an example is a continuous monitoring of the critical product dimensions to ensure that they remain within acceptable limits. The converse of on-line quality control is **off-line** control, and this term is used to describe those activities that take place away from the manufacturing process. These include measures taken at the design stage, in testing and in marketing to ensure high quality. Increasingly, these measures are becoming more important in the overall task of achieving quality.

Techniques for quality engineering

A very wide range of techniques is available for both on-line and off-line quality control in product design and manufacture. Figure 10.5 shows examples of these techniques with indications of the stages in the product introduction process at which they may be applied. The key points of the techniques are summarized opposite:

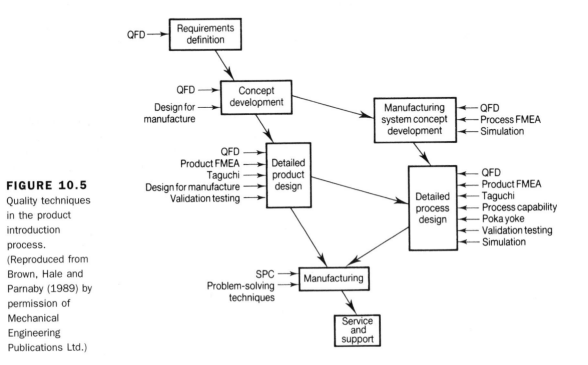

FIGURE 10.5
Quality techniques in the product introduction process. (Reproduced from Brown, Hale and Parnaby (1989) by permission of Mechanical Engineering Publications Ltd.)

▶ **Quality function deployment** (QFD) is a matrix technique for the identification firstly of product or process design requirements (in particular to identify the requirements of the customer), and secondly of where it is most appropriate to expend engineering effort in meeting these requirements.

▶ The term **design for manufacture and assembly** (DFM/DFA) embraces a range of methods that assist in designing a product for ease of manufacture and assembly, and in so doing improving the quality of the product. We have met these in the previous chapter.

▶ **Failure mode and effect analysis** (FMEA) is a systematic technique for the identification of the possible modes of failure of a product or process, and of the likely consequences of such failure.

▶ **Taguchi methods** apply statistical techniques to evaluate the combined effect of various design parameters in order to minimize variation in design performance.

▶ No two manufactured items are ever exactly alike, owing to variations in the processes that make them. **Statistical process control** (SPC) involves the monitoring of process variations in order to distinguish between normal and abnormal causes of these.

▶ **Poka yoke** is the term used to describe the use of foolproof devices within a process to prevent defective products being produced. For example, a part may be shaped in such a way that it is impossible for it to be incorrectly assembled to another part.

▶ **Process capability studies** involve the study of a process in order to identify whether it is capable of manufacturing parts to within the required tolerances.

▶ **Simulation** encompasses a number of techniques for modelling and simulating the operation and performance of a manufacturing process.

▶ **Validation testing** involves a number of test methods for verifying that a product design performs as expected. For example, an automotive suspension component will be subjected to a fatigue test in order to ensure that it has an adequate life.

▶ The term **problem-solving techniques** includes a variety of systematic, graphical and analytical techniques for problem identification and resolution.

Certain of these procedures will be explored in more depth in Section 10.4. In this discussion, the reader will note that computer aids are not in general essential to the application of the philosophies and techniques described. The material is included here because it forms part of the environment in which CADCAM is often applied, and because the techniques will increasingly be assisted by computer.

10.4 Techniques of quality engineering

We have already seen that a wide range of techniques may be applied to assist in achieving high quality products. This section presents details of some of the better known methods.

10.4.1 Quality function deployment

The technique known as quality function deployment (QFD) was developed in Japan in the 1970s as a systematic technique for identifying what features of a product contributed most strongly to high product quality, and therefore where engineering effort should be expended. 'Quality function deployment' is a rather obscure term that comes from the literal translation of the original Japanese name, but it may be helpful to think of the deployment of the functions important to quality through a series of charts or matrices that cover aspects of the product development process from design to the generation of manufacturing instructions. It has been claimed that QFD has been a significant factor in improving product quality and lead time and in reducing design changes – an example result being the virtual elimination of corrosion warranty claims in the Japanese automotive industry.

The basis for the method is the notion that a customer requirement may be related to the approaches that might be taken to fulfil it (these are generally expressed as WHAT is required, and HOW it might be achieved). For example, if the WHAT for a washing machine is high durability, the HOWs might include a stainless steel drum and a high-quality paint finish. The WHATs and the HOWs could simply be listed with relationships shown, but this is not entirely satisfactory because any HOW might contribute to multiple WHATs (e.g. high-quality paint contributes to durability and 'good appearance'), and a given WHAT may be satisfied by multiple HOWs. The solution is to use a matrix method in which the WHATs are listed on the left-hand side (as inputs to the matrix), and the HOWs along the top (as outputs from the matrix). A link between an input and an output may then be made by entering a mark in the appropriate matrix cell.

The essence of QFD is in the identification of links between WHATs and HOWs using the matrix grid. Generally, the degree of the relationship is also shown by the use of different symbols in the cells. Figure 10.6 shows examples of the symbols commonly used – for weak, strong and very strong relationships – together with the overall matrix layout. Usually, numerical values are also used for different degrees of relationship to assist in assessing the value of product features. Typical values are

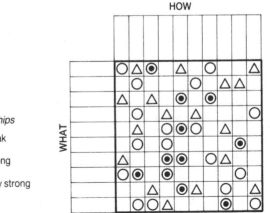

FIGURE 10.6

Elements of QFD charts.

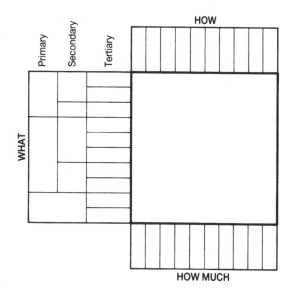

FIGURE 10.7
Basic QFD chart
plus target values
and breakdown of
requirements.

1, 3 and 9 respectively, although others are used by some companies – including negative numbers in some cases. In general, consistency is more important than the specific values chosen.

A bald statement of user requirement is often not very helpful, and therefore in practice this is refined on the left-hand side of the matrix into more detailed statements termed **secondary** and **tertiary** requirements. For example, our washing machine may have 'safe operation' as a primary requirement. One of the secondary requirements might be 'foolproof operation', which might be expressed by the tertiary requirements 'child-proof' and 'simple controls' among others. The 'requirements' are all nevertheless expressed as desirable features. The HOWs, on the other hand, must all be implementable – they must be capable of being translated into engineering action (and these include service or other organizational actions such as 'inspect annually' as well as product features such as 'stainless steel drum'). The HOWs are often qualified according to their area of application, and are normally further qualified by statements signifying HOW MUCH (e.g. what thickness of paint, what depth of case hardening – known as **objective target values**) in a row across the bottom of the chart. The expansion of the basic matrix with this further detail is shown in Figure 10.7.

Figure 10.7 is the basic form of a single chart. Using this, a series of customer requirements may be matched to product features, and specifications may be obtained for the value of the features. Child-proof operation, for instance, might be obtained by the features 'stiff door catch' and 'heavy-to-operate switch', and values may be quoted for the operating loads in each case. The product features do not indicate, however, how they are to be obtained in terms of component characteristics. The real value in QFD is to be able to take the 'output' from this first chart and use it as 'input' to further charts in order to identify these required component characteristics. The output from this second level of charts may then be used as input to a third

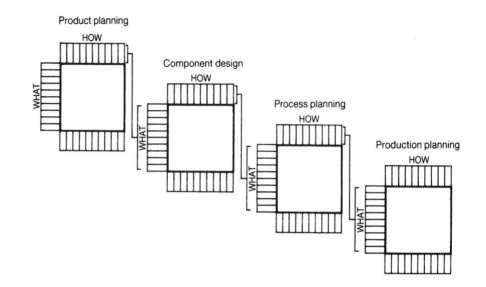

FIGURE 10.8
A cascade of QFD
charts.

level to identify the characteristics required of the processes that make the components, and so on. Conventionally, there are four levels:

1. **product features and functions**, which are identified at the product design stage;

2. **component characteristics**, which correspond to the detail design activity;

3. **process characteristics**, identified at the process planning stage;

4. **production operations** – the generation of operator instructions and on-line quality control documentation at the production planning stage.

These may be imagined as occurring in a sort of cascade, as shown in Figure 10.8, although in practice the various charts may be developed concurrently, particularly if a concurrent engineering approach (for which QFD is ideal) is being pursued. In practice also some organizations use more or fewer levels than those shown.

The reader will appreciate that as QFD charts are being developed they accumulate a great deal of information about a product. They thus have a value as a repository of knowledge and as a training aid. Experience suggests that QFD charts are most valuable when developed over many months or years. They are certainly not a 'quick fix'!

QFD charts may be enhanced in a variety of ways by the addition of further detail around the chart. Figure 10.9 shows a chart with such enhancements, which include:

▶ **A correlation matrix** – the triangular region above the main grid – which shows supporting or conflicting relationships between the HOW items. For example, the attributes 'high latch force' and 'high opening effort' for a washing machine door would support each other, but would conflict with 'low closing effort'. The correlation matrix is thus very good in showing where trade-offs must be made.

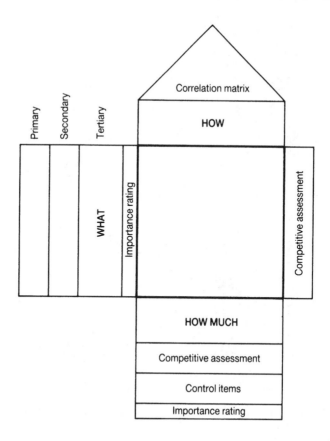

FIGURE 10.9
Full QFD chart
details.

▶ **Weighted requirements:** some requirements are obviously more important
than others. An estimation of relative weightings will normally be made, and
applied to the relationship values.

▶ **Competitive assessments** of rival products both in terms of subjective evaluations of the WHAT factors and more quantitative evaluations of the HOW factors.
The WHAT evaluations are usually plotted for each of a number of competitor
products by recording the subjective assessments – for example, as a rating 1–5
– for each criterion on the right-hand side of the chart. The HOW factors may
also be recorded as rating values on a scale 1–5, or as absolute values in the same
units as the target values. These are plotted across the foot of the chart. In each
case different symbols are used for each competitor. By comparing good performance in terms of customer requirements with the product characteristics, it may
be seen whether the engineering judgement of which factors contribute to good
product performance is correct.

Manufacturers may add further detail to the charts, such that they take on a
rather daunting appearance! Figure 10.10 shows, for example, a QFD chart from a
major automotive manufacturer which includes such aspects as the relevant standards and the degree of technical difficulty of product features, in addition to those

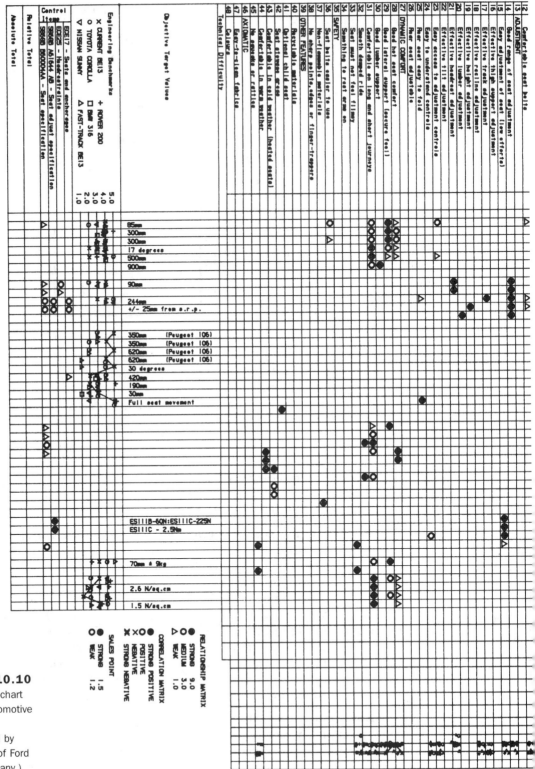

FIGURE 10.10

An example chart from an automotive application. (Reproduced by permission of Ford Motor Company.)

Orientation

Design Requirements

Customer Requirements | Rate of Importance

Left (Customer Requirements):

1 APPEARANCE
2 Concealed hardware
3 Good rear seat appearance
4 Good front seat appearance
5 STATIC COMFORT
6 Easy to get into/out of front seat
7 Good access to rear seats (3 door cars)
8 Comfortable seat (cushion & back)
9 Good rear seat foot-room
10 Good rear seat knee-room
11 Good fabric feel

Right (Design Requirements):

#	Requirement
1	SEAT DIMENSIONS
2	Max.height of back wedges
3	Width between cushion wedges
4	Width between back wedges
5	Cushion top surface angle
6	Cushion length
7	Pad lumber radius
8	ADJUSTMENT DIMENSIONS
9	Range of headrest vertical adjust
10	Range of headrest tilt adjust
11	Range of track adjust
12	Range of height adjust
13	Range of lumbar adjust
14	PACKAGE DIMENSIONS
15	Footroom for ingress/egress (seat fully forward) - 3 door
16	Footroom for ingress/egress (seat fully rearward) - 3 door
17	Knee-room for ingress/egress (seat fully forward)
18	Knee-room for ingress/egress (seat fully rearward)
19	Seat back angle when tipped forward
20	Width between tracks
21	Height under rear of front seat (seat fully rearward)
22	Depth of recess in front seat back panel
23	Seat movement without interfering with rear seat tip
24	Volume of stowage on seat
25	COMPONENT PROPERTIES
26	Hardness of wedges
27	Surface softness
28	Pad hardness
29	Laminate thickness
30	Fabric water vapour permeability
31	Thermal conductivity
32	Cushion vibration transmissibility
33	Heater pad-time to max. temperature
34	Heater pad - maximum temperature
35	Foam flammability
36	OPERATION
37	Max. force/torque to operate seat tracks
38	Max. force/torque to operate seat height adjust
39	Ratio of seat movement to control movement
40	Free-play in mechanisms
41	TESTING
42	Manikin deflection - Lateral Support test
43	Noise from Hydropulse test evaluation
44	Seat cushion pressure distribution - max.pressure gradient
45	Seat cushion pressure distribution - max.pressure
46	Seat back pressure distribution - max.pressure gradient
47	Seat back pressure distribution - max.pressure

Our Company

Quality Plan

Rate of Level Up

Sales Point

Absolute Weight

Demanded Weight

Absolute Total

Relative Total

1.0
2.0
3.0   Customer Benchmarks
4.0
5.0

x CURRENT BE13   + ROVER 200   △ FAST-TRACK

o TOYOTA COROLLA   □ BMW 316

▽ NISSAN SUNNY   ✳ RENAULT CLIO

that we have discussed. Although complex in appearance, the basic principles behind a chart as detailed as this are those that have been outlined in this section.

10.4.2 Failure mode and effect analysis

We have already met in QFD a method for systematically identifying customer requirements, and for indicating where engineering effort should be directed to meet those requirements. **Failure mode and effect analysis (FMEA)** is a complementary technique that aims to identify potential ways in which a product or process might not meet expectations and any possible causes of a failure to do so. The technique also ranks failures and causes to indicate where engineering effort should be expended to reduce failure likelihood and severity.

FMEA is similar to QFD in many ways. It is a technique based on the completion of charts or matrices by a team, and again it may be applied in a hierarchical fashion from product assessment through to the assessment of components and processes.

The basis of FMEA is to try to identify and list all possible ways in which an assembly, a part or a process could fail to conform to its specified requirements. Typical failures in casting, for example, might include component porosity, sand inclusions, poor surface finish, incorrectly filled moulds and so on. The FMEA team should always work by assuming that failures are going to happen, and should seek to answer the question 'what might the customer find objectionable?'.

The first stage of the ranking procedure is then carried out by rating the **severity** of each of the possible failures on a scale of 1 to 10, where 1 implies that the customer would hardly notice the failure, for example a minor blemish in a paint finish, 5 that the customer would be made uncomfortable or be annoyed by the failure, and 9 or 10 would signify a major failure such as a significant safety hazard or a non-compliance with a government regulation.

The next step is to identify for each failure every possible cause, and to rank each of these causes according to the likelihood of its **occurrence**, again on a scale of 1 to 10. In this case 1 indicates that the cause will almost never arise (e.g. less than 1 in 10^6 during the design life), 5 an occasional failure (perhaps 1 in 400 during the design life), and 10 that it will be a regular occurrence.

The final stage of the ranking is to consider what techniques are currently used to try to **detect** a failure cause or **mode**, for example, what quality control mechanisms, such as inspection, are in place, or, if not a subject of inspection, what other means are there for identifying that the failure mode has occurred. These current controls are listed, and the likelihood of detection for each failure cause listed, again using a scale of 1 to 10, where 1 is almost certain detection and 10 a practically undetectable mode.

The three assessments – severity, occurrence and detection – are now multiplied together for each failure mode to give a **risk priority number (RPN)** in the range 1 to 1000, as shown in Figure 10.11, which shows how an FMEA chart is laid out. This number is then used as an aid to indicate the priority of action for each mode – engineering effort should first be concentrated on those modes with a high RPN, to try to reduce the risk of occurrence, or to minimize the severity, or to increase the likelihood of detection, for example by instituting a more stringent quality control regime. For instance, in a safety-critical application of welding, 100% inspection using

Potential failure mode	Potential effect of failure	Potential cause of failure	Current controls	Occurrence	Severity	Detection	Risk priority number
				A 1–10	B 1–10	C 1–10	A×B×C 1–1000

FIGURE 10.11
Failure mode and effects analysis chart.

X-ray techniques might be used in order to reduce the detection rating for a failure mode. It is important to note that RPNs are not absolute indicators that might be used for product comparisons – different teams are likely to come up with different ratings for the same potential failure mode. Instead, FMEA ratings can highlight the necessity for improved design or for changes in production processes or quality control procedures.

The action part of FMEA involves the development of a plan, sometimes called a control plan, to detail the recommended action from the FMEA chart, and to record the new rating for this action. This plan identifies what design change is to be made or how checks are to be implemented and with what frequency, and who is responsible.

FMEA techniques share another characteristic with QFD in that the charts may be regarded as live documents that are developed, amended and updated with time. A constraint in their application, in particular if they are regularly updated, is the amount of clerical work involved in maintaining them. For this reason a number of computer programs have been developed for the production and presentation of FMEA documents. These programs also have features such as:

- the facility to reuse portions of existing FMEA charts as a basis for new reports;
- sort routines to rank entries by RPN;
- facilities to allow data to be moved and copied around a chart;
- word-processor-type commands for text entry and editing, and spreadsheet-style entry for severity, occurrence and detection numbers.

Example FMEA chart

Figure 10.12 shows an example FMEA chart, again from a major automotive manufacturer. This shows, on the left-hand side, a series of columns comprising the part name and number, the potential failure mode, the effects of failure and severity rating, a number of potential causes of failure and occurrence ratings, and methods of detection – known as design verification – and their ratings. These combine to give RPNs for each potential cause.

On the right-hand side of the chart the recommended actions to alleviate each failure cause are listed, together with an indication of responsibility. Also shown are numerical indications of the updated occurrence and detection indices based on action and tests and leading to a 'resulting RPN'.

POTENTIAL FAILURE MODE AND EFFECTS ANALYSIS (DESIGN FMEA)

Ford

Subsystem/Name	Body Closures	Suppliers and Plants Affected	Dalton, Fraser, Henley Assembly Plants
Design Responsibility	Body Engineering	Model Year/Vehicle(s)	199X/Lion 4dr/Wagon
Other Areas Involved	Car Product Dev., Manufacturing, B&A.	Engineering Release Date	9X 03 01
Prepared By	A Tate – X6412 – Ford Body Eng.	FMEA Date (Orig.)	8X 03 22 (Rev.) 8X 08 14

Part Name & Number / Part Function	Potential Failure Mode	Potential Effect(s) of Failure	Severity	Potential Cause(s) of Failure	Occurrence	Design Verification	Detection	RPN	Recommended Action(s)	Area/Individual Responsible & Completion Date	Action Results: Actions Taken	Severity	Occurence	Detection	RPN
Front door L.H. — o Ingress to and egress from vehicle; o Occupant protection from weather, noise and side impact; o Support/anchorage for door hardware including mirror, hinges, latch and window regulator; o Provide proper surface for appearance items – paint and soft trim.	Corroded interior lower door panels	o Deteriorated life of door leading to: o Unsatisfactory appearance due to rust through o Impaired function of interior door hardware	7	o Upper edge of protective wax application specified for interior panels is too low.	6	Vehicle general durability tests, veh T-118 T-109, T-301	7	294	Add laboratory accelerated corrosion testing	A Tate – B&CE 8X 09 30	Based on test results (Test No. 1481) upper edge spec. raised to 125mm.	7	2	2	28
				o Insufficient wax thickness specified	4	Vehicle general durability testing – as above	7	112	Lab. test as above. Conduct Design of Experiments on wax thickness.	Combine w/test for wax upper edge verification	Test results (Test No. 1481) show specified thickness is adequate	7	2	2	28
				o Inappropriate wax formulation specified	2	Physical and Chem. Lab. test – Report no. 1265	2	28	None	A Tate – B&CE 9X 01 15					
				o Entrapped air prevents wax from entering corner/edge areas	5	Design and investigation with non-functioning spray head	8	280	Team evaluation using production spray equipment and specified wax	B&CE & B&A 8X 11 15	Based on test additional holes will be provided in affected area.	7	1	3	21
				o Wax application plugs door drain holes	3	Laboratory test with 'worst-case' wax application and hole size	1	21	None						
				o Insufficient room between panels for spray head egress.	4	Drawing evaluation of spray head access.	4	112	Team evaluation using design aid buck and spray head.	B&CE & B&A 8X 09 15	Evaluation showed adequate access.	7	1	1	7

FIGURE 10.12

An example design FMEA chart. (Reproduced by permission of the Ford Motor Company.)

10.4.3 Taguchi methods

One of the most influential engineers in the field of quality attainment has been Dr Genichi Taguchi. His work has stressed that it is more valuable to introduce quality concepts at the design stage rather than through inspection after manufacture. He has in particular developed a number of statistical techniques for analysing the effects of manufacturing tolerances and of environmental variations on the performance of a product. Although statisticians have not always been in full agreement with the detail of the techniques, the procedures have been reported to be very effective when applied.

We have already come across some of Taguchi's ideas concerning quality loss and the stages of product design. The central idea of quality loss is that any product deviation from specification, **even within allowable limits**, incurs a loss, which is the sum of losses internal and external to the producer, and which may be expressed as a monetary value. A typical **loss function** is shown in Figure 10.13. Now, if this figure is combined with probability distribution functions for component characteristics, shown in Figure 10.14, it will be seen that the higher-quality component has a much lower expected loss than the low-quality component, even though both are nominally entirely within specified limits, because most of the high-quality components lie in the range of values for which quality loss is low.

One of the aims of Taguchi methods is therefore to optimize processes in order to minimize quality loss. This optimization is either around a central target value (e.g. of a component dimension) known as 'Nominal the Best', or aims for a maximum value (e.g. tensile strength) known as 'Larger the Better', or a minimum value (e.g. product shrinkage) known as 'Smaller the Better'.

According to Taguchi *et al.* (1989) the stages in the design process are **system design**, at which the overall form of the system is identified, **parameter design**, when attribute values are specified, and **tolerance design**, when allowable ranges of deviations in the parameter values are defined. The major engineering effort should

FIGURE 10.13
Relationship between quality loss and deviation from target value. (Reproduced from Taguchi, Elsayed and Hsiang (1989) by permission of the publishers. The McGraw-Hill Companies. © Bell Communications Research.)

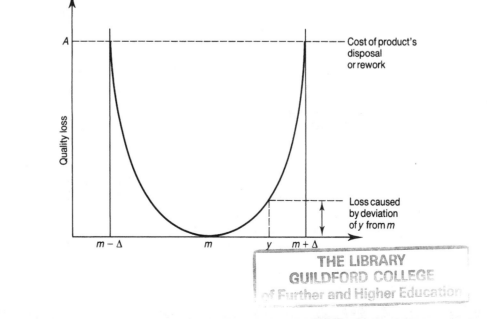

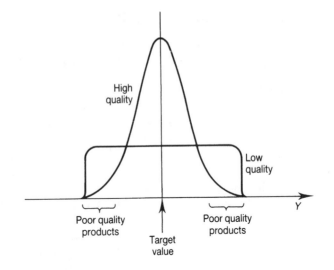

FIGURE 10.14
Probability distribution functions for component characteristics for high- and low-quality products. (Reproduced from Lewis *et al.* (1989) by permission of Mechanical Engineering Publications Ltd.)

be directed towards parameter design in order to ensure a **robust** design, that is one that is as insensitive as possible to normal variations in the product's environment. The environmental factors can include all sorts of items. For example, the factors for a photocopier might be the quality of the paper to be fed – for instance, the coefficient of friction of the surface, or the thickness and stiffness of the paper – as well as such items as temperature, humidity and power source line voltage. A robust design would therefore be one that operates satisfactorily with a wide range of paper grades under widely varying operating conditions. The techniques that are used to identify critical design parameters, to select optimum settings and to guide compromise in the event of conflicting requirements are based on statistical examination of the results of multiple experiments, as described in Taguchi *et al.* (1989).

The variation in design parameters and in the external environment is described by Taguchi as **noise**. Starkey (1992) classifies noise factors into three groups:

▶ **Outer noise**, which comprises variations in operating environment such as variations in temperature and humidity, materials being processed, fuel qualities, human factors among operators and so on.

▶ **Inner noise**, which comprises deterioration in parts and materials owing to wear, corrosion, damage and so on.

▶ **Between-product noise**, which comprises material and manufacturing process variations.

Starkey notes that outer noise is not, in general, under the designer's control, and therefore the design should be robust enough to cope with variations in these factors. Inner and between product noise are more under the designer's control, but often at the cost of more expensive materials or manufacturing processes. There is also the temptation simply to overdesign parts to ensure that they give an adequate performance over their life. The philosophy of robust design suggests that there is an alternative, and that is to mitigate the noise factors so far as possible by selecting design parameters that minimize the sensitivity of the design to noise. This may seem a straightforward notion, but it is complicated by the sheer number of variable parameters in any design – each of the dimensions is a variable, as are material attributes and manufacturing factors such as surface condition or adhesive bond strength. The number of parameter combinations is such that it is impossible to explore in full all of the feasible combinations. To help us here Taguchi provides two techniques:

1. Effort should be concentrated on the maximization of the **signal to noise ratio** (S/N) for parameters of the design.

2. **Experiments** should be used to explore a range of parameter combinations to inform design decisions.

Signal to noise ratio

In communications, acoustics or electrical engineering the signal to noise ratio is defined as the ratio of the wanted signal (e.g. a radio transmission) to unwanted random noise, for example from atmospheric effects. In design use the same broad meaning can be used – for example, the ratio of the variation in material strength to the average value – but the term can also be used to describe the sensitivity of some design performance parameter to variations in an attribute of a part. As an example, let us consider the installation of a disk spring in a machine to achieve a certain spring force. The installed length of the spring is subject to variation owing to manufacturing tolerances, but it is important to minimize the variation in the spring force that results from variation in installed length. The designer has three springs that could be used to achieve the required spring force at the installed length, as shown in Figure 10.15 which shows the characteristics of each of the springs, together with the target spring force (line F–F).

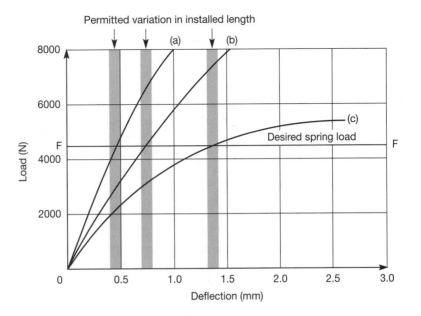

FIGURE 10.15
Load deflection curves for three disk springs.

Also shown on Figure 10.15 is the variation in installed length that is permitted for the design, and the effect that this has on the spring force for each of the springs. It may be seen that, owing to the varying characteristics of disk springs, spring (a) has a ratio of force to force variation of 5.52, and for springs (b) and (c) the values are 8.49 and 26.8 respectively. These values are regarded here as the signal (output) to noise (in this case between-product noise) ratio for the three design cases (note that signal to noise ratio is more conventionally measured using $S/N = 20 \log_{10}(\sigma/\mu)$, where σ is the standard deviation and μ the mean for a set of readings). Robust design thinking in this case points the designer towards spring (c) since for this spring the variability in performance as a proportion of the nominal values is minimized.

The ideas of design signal to noise can be extended to many other applications. The values of resistors in an electric circuit should be selected to make the performance of the circuit as insensitive as possible to the variation in resistor value, to allow low-cost resistors with a wide tolerance band to be selected, and to reduce the sensitivity of the circuit to variations in temperature. Engine combustion chambers should be designed to be as insensitive as possible to variations in fuel quality, and ignition timing should be selected to minimize the effect of variations in timing on the engine performance, even at the expense of achieving less than optimum performance at nominal values. In each design field there will be many cases where the ideas of S/N ratio can be applied.

The ideas of sensitivity to variation can also be applied to the planning of the overall configuration of a design. Gardiner (1984) considers robust designs to be those that are capable of being extended beyond their original capabilities by incremental change, and describes for example the different configurations for the installation of engines on passenger aircraft. By suspending the engines below the wings, it is possible to install different engines without fundamentally compromising the design, whereas if engines are buried in the roots of wings or in the rear of the aircraft fuselage then there will be significant limitations on the freedom to modify the engine installation or to install new engine types. This approach can also be considered in terms of the sensitivity of the design to variation in parameters.

Design of experiments

Signal to noise ratio is a concept that can be explored for a few key parameters of a design, or to make detailed and local design decisions. However, in design there will often be many interacting design parameters, and it may be difficult to isolate a particular parameter for study. In these cases it is necessary to carry out experiments (either physically or analytically) to explore the effect of combinations of parameters. While this may be feasible for small numbers of parameters, it soon becomes unrealistic if many are to be explored because the total number of experiments required is n^p, where p is the number of parameters to be tested and n is the number of values to be used for each parameter. So if there are six variable parameters, each to be tested at three levels, the total number of tests is $3^6 = 729$, and with more realistic cases with many more parameters the number of tests required is very much higher.

The carrying out of a full set of experiments for a given set of variables is called the **full factorial** approach. By building on techniques used by a British agricultural

Table 10.1 Example orthogonal arrays

Array	Number of factors	Number of levels
L_4	3	2
L_8 (see Figure 10.16(a))	7	2
L_9 (see Figure 10.16(b))	4	3
L_{12}	11	2
	1+	2
L_{18}	7	3

FIGURE 10.16
Typical orthogonal
arrays. (After
Starkey (1992) by
permission of
Arnold.)

Trial	Variables						
no.	1	2	3	4	5	6	7
1	1	1	1	1	1	1	1
2	1	1	1	2	2	2	2
3	1	2	2	1	1	2	2
4	1	2	2	2	2	1	1
5	2	1	2	1	2	1	2
6	2	1	2	2	1	2	1
7	2	2	1	1	2	2	1
8	2	2	1	2	1	1	2

(a) L_8 array

Trial	Variables			
no.	A	B	C	D
1	1	1	1	1
2	1	2	2	2
3	1	3	3	3
4	2	1	2	3
5	2	2	3	1
6	2	3	1	2
7	3	1	3	2
8	3	2	1	3
9	3	3	2	1

(b) L_9 array

research station to study variables affecting plant growth, Taguchi developed a technique whereby useful information for design purposes could be obtained from a more limited number of tests. His technique is based on the use of tables known as **orthogonal arrays**, combined, where there are interactions between variables, with charts known as **linear graphs**.

Orthogonal arrays are tables for which the columns show parameters to be tested, and the rows show combinations of parameter values to be used in experimental trials. The parameters are often refered to as **factors**, and the values that the parameters can take are known as **levels**. The tables are called orthogonal because the levels of each factor are equally represented in the trials. In many cases, standard arrays can be used for experimental work. Table 10.1 gives a number of examples, and Phadke (1989) gives 18 standard orthogonal arrays.

If the design factors are independent of each other, then a **lumped parameter model** is used, which simplifies the problem by neglecting intersections between factors. If they are not independent, then **linear graphs** are used to indicate which factors relate to each other to form new factors. They are drawn by plotting the factors that are to be explored as nodes on a graph, and then by showing possible interactions between factors as arcs on the graph. Interactions between factors are themselves assigned as factors. For example, a three-factors problem would have three interactions between factors (X_1X_2, X_1X_2, X_1X_2) and an error factor, to give a total of seven factors which, for two levels, would require an L_8 array, whereas the full factorial tests for this situation would require 128 trials. (For non-independent factors, the number of trials used for two levels per factors is 2^p, where p is the number of factors. In this case $p = 3$, so the number of trials is 2^3.)

Once the trials identified in the orthogonal arrays have been carried out, the observations Y_i are investigated by recording them in a response table and then investigating the variation of dependent variables against the trial parameters using **analysis of means** (ANOM) and **analysis of variance** (ANOVA). In ANOM the overall mean is calculated, and the **main factor effects** (MFE) for each factor are computed for two-level factors by calculating MFE = (ΣY_i at high level – ΣY_i at low level)/0.5N. These may then be plotted to indicate the factor-level combinations that give the best overall performance (and these are not necessarily the combinations that are tested in the experiments). The same approach can be taken to identify the overall and factor means for the S/N ratio.

ANOVA is used to determine the relative importance of factors in the experiment, and to estimate the error variance, by calculating various statistical values for the experiments, including (for a two-level experiment (Ertas and Jones, 1993)):

▶ The **total sum of the squares** of the observations, given by $S_t = S_y - T^2/N$, where S_y is the sum of the squares of each observation, T the sum of all observations and N the total number of observations.

▶ The **sums of squares** for each two-level factor, $S_i = 2(\text{MFE})^2$, and for the error $S_E = S_t - \Sigma S_i$ for all factors and interactions.

▶ The **mean square** for each factor, M_i, and for the error, M_E, given by $M_i = S_i/v_i$ and $M_E = S_E/v_E$ where v_i = number of levels – 1 and $v_E = (N - 1) - \Sigma v_i$.

▶ The **F test**, which is the ratio of sample variances used to identify whether there are significant differences in estimates at known confidence levels. They are calculated using $F_i = M_i/M_E$.

▶ The **per cent of variance**, which is the per cent contribution of factor i to the total variance, given by $P_i = 100(M_i - M_E)/S_t$.

Once calculated, the derived values can be compared with each other from their tabulation or by plotting them.

The approach to MFE calculation can be simplified, with either the mean values for each level plotted, or the difference between level mean and overall mean. An example, for four controllable factors with three levels for each factor, is shown in Figure 10.17, which shows plots of the effects of controllable factors on an independent variable extracted by Starkey from a lumped parameter case study reported in Bendell (1989).

The mean response results give one set of information from the experiments. Further information is obtained by plotting the signal to noise ratio for each of the parameters in the same way, and is shown in Figure 10.18 for the example of Figure 10.17. Where there is a statistical basis for the S/N value, Starkey suggests that the ratio of the mean to the standard deviation should be plotted, expressed in decibels (dB).

From the plots of mean response and S/N ratio for each of the parameters, the values to be used in the design can be selected. In the particular cases shown in the figures, values A_2, C_3 and D_3 were chosen because they were best according to both

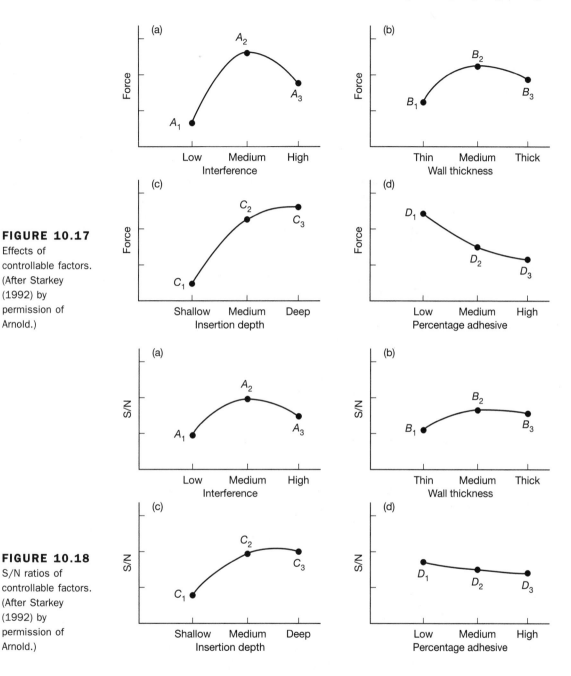

FIGURE 10.17
Effects of controllable factors. (After Starkey (1992) by permission of Arnold.)

FIGURE 10.18
S/N ratios of controllable factors. (After Starkey (1992) by permission of Arnold.)

criteria, while value B_1 was chosen by the engineers on the project, because there was a cost advantage (Starkey, 1992).

The whole domain of robust design using Taguchi methods is receiving significant research and development attention as a result of the quality gains that are claimed to arise from its implementation. Design of experiments is used both for optimization of objective functions and for reducing the sensitivity of engineering designs to uncontrollable noise factors.

10.5 Conclusion

Highly competitive world markets make attention to quality, price and delivery of engineering products of paramount importance. This chapter has presented the view that addressing these issues is partly one of philosophy and organization, and partly of the application of the battery of techniques that are available to the engineer.

In terms of philosophy and organization there are three key issues: firstly, the engineer should be concerned with the performance of the whole product, or of the whole manufacturing organization, which implies that a systems view should be taken; secondly, the product development lead time and product cost and quality may all be improved by the simultaneous application of specialist expertise to the design of the product and of its manufacturing process in concurrent engineering; and finally, quality is the responsibility of the whole organization, and a total quality approach should be adopted.

In the development of the design the designer has traditionally had a number of quantitative, analytical techniques at his or her disposal. To these techniques are added a number of qualitative methods, such as quality function deployment, failure mode and effect analysis, and design for manufacture and assembly, which assist in particular in matching the design to the needs of the customer.

References and further reading

Bedworth D. D., Henderson M. R. and Wolfe P. M. (1991). *Computer-Integrated Design and Manufacturing*. New York: McGraw-Hill.

Bendell A. (ed.) (1989). *Taguchi Methods – Applications in World Industry*. London: IFS Publications and New York: Springer.

Brown A. D., Hale P. R. and Parnaby J. (1989). An integrated approach to quality engineering in support of design for manufacture. *Proc. Institution of Mechanical Engineers*. **203**, 29–38.

Checkland P. (1981). *Systems Thinking, Systems Practice*. Chichester: John Wiley.

Ertas A. and Jones J. C. (1993). *The Engineering Design Process*. New York: John Wiley.

Fowlkes W. Y. and Creveling C. M. (1995). *Engineering Methods for Robust Product Design*. Reading, MA: Addison Wesley Longman.

Ford Motor Company (1988). *Potential Failure Mode and Effects Analysis (FMEA), Instruction Manual*. Dearborn MI: Ford Motor Company.

Gardiner J. P. (1984). Robust and lean designs with state of the art automotive and aircraft examples. In *Design, Innovation and Long Cycles in Economic Development* (ed. C. Freeman). London: Francis Pinter, 143–68.

Lewis S. M., Sexton C. J., New R. E. and Hodgson B. A. (1989). The application of Taguchi methods at the design analysis stage. *IMechE C377/216, Proceedings of the International Conference on Engineering Design, ICED '89*, Harrogate.

Liley J. E. N. (1989). The management of design. *Proc. Institution of Mechanical Engineers, ICED '89*, C377/103, 245–62.

Lucas Engineering and Systems (1988). *The Lucas Manufacturing Systems Handbook: Mini Guides*. Solihull: Lucas Engineering and Systems.

Mallick D. N. and Kouvelis P. (1992). Management of product design: a strategic approach. In *Intelligent Design and Manufacturing* (ed. A. Kusiak). New York: John Wiley.

Phadke M. S. (1989). *Quality Engineering Using Robust Design*. Englewood Cliffs, NJ: Prentice Hall.

Pugh S. (1990). *Total Design*. Harlow: Addison Wesley Longman.

Roy R. and Wield D. (1986). *Product Design and Technological Innovation*. Milton Keynes: Open University Press.

Starkey C. V. (1992). *Engineering Design Decisions*. London: Edward Arnold.

Sullivan L. P. (1986). Quality function deployment. *Quality Progress*. June, 39–50.

Taguchi G., Elsayed E. and Hsiang T. (1989). *Quality Engineering in Production Systems*. New York: McGraw-Hill.

Taguchi G. and Konishi S. (1987). *Orthogonal Arrays and Linear Graphs*. Dearborn, MI: American Supplier Institute.

Exercises

10.1 Select some household artefact – an electrical appliance, for example. Try to write down the requirements placed on the design by the customer, and the constraints imposed upon the design (e.g. by legal requirements, material considerations, etc.). Which constraints do you think are most significant? Also, can you write down a relationship which expresses the utility of the design – for example, to encapsulate the cost/performance trade-off?

10.2 Outline the elements of a matrix approach to the organization of engineering activities. What might be the appropriate elements of a matrix for a company manufacturing a variety of domestic electrical equipment? Or for the technical support functions of a company manufacturing power generation equipment?

10.3 Are there any design circumstances in which concurrent engineering would not be appropriate? Why is it particularly appropriate for the development of designs for products that are mass produced?

10.4 Why do you think many small improvements (in a policy of continuous improvement) are a better way to quality than large leaps?

10.5 Outline the techniques which are available to the engineer for on-line and off-line quality control in product design and manufacture. Which of these do you think are more important at the design stage, and which in manufacturing?

10.6 What do you understand by the terms 'on-line' and 'off-line' in the context of quality management? Give examples of each type of quality control.

10.7 Try to form a product planning quality function deployment chart for a bicycle. What do you learn about the process of building a QFD chart from this exercise?

10.8 After completing Exercise 10.7, form a component planning QFD chart for the saddle of the bicycle. Are you able to go any further and consider process planning?

10.9 Develop a failure mode and effect analysis chart for a bicycle, or for some other simple product with which you are familiar. What do you rate as the most serious potential failure mode? If possible, compare your answers with those of your colleagues.

10.10 How do you feel computers may assist the engineer in the development of QFD and FMEA charts?

10.11 What do you understand by the term 'robust design'? Why should engineering effort be directed in particular towards **parameter design** in order to ensure robust designs?

10.12 Using the spring performance curves given in Figure 10.15, compute the signal to noise ratio for the spring force for each spring given that the installed length is 1.3 ± 0.1 mm, and therefore identify which would be the most robust design selection for this installed length.

10.13 Write down the orthogonal arrays for the cases of four factors each with two levels, and for three factors with three levels for each.

Projects

For more information about the subjects for project work, please refer to the end of Chapter 1.

The project activity for this chapter is to explore how techniques for quality engineering may be applied to the two project artefacts. Specific tasks are:

Project 1 Chess piece Produce a QFD chart for the chess piece.

Project 2 Load cell Produce an FMEA chart for the load cell.

11 The link to machine control

Chapter objectives

When you have completed the material in this chapter you should be able to:
- ► **understand the principles of numerical control (NC) technology and describe the range of machine tools to which it is applied;**
- ► **outline the various routes for part programming in NC;**
- ► **understand the various elements of machine control data programs and be able to interpret a simple program;**
- ► **describe the nature and structure of the APT programming language and understand the role of CLDATA and post-processing in the part programming task;**
- ► **understand the application of CADCAM systems in generating part programs, in particular for complex surface models;**
- ► **outline the nature and scope of rapid prototyping techniques;**
- ► **understand the elements of robotics, and outline their application in assembly and in manufacturing cells.**

Chapter contents

11.1 Introduction

The subject of this chapter is the interface between CAD and the manufacturing processes actually used to make the parts. Process planning – the selection of the manufacturing processes and the planning of individual operations – has been described in Chapter 9. This chapter is now concerned with the computer-controlled machines used in manufacture, and with the extraction of data from the CAD model for the purpose of controlling these machines.

Getting geometric information from the CAD model is of particular relevance to the manufacture of parts directly by machining (i.e. by material removal), and to the manufacture of tooling for forming and moulding processes, again by machining. The use of numerical information for the control of such machining processes is predominantly through the numerical control (NC) of machines, and this topic will form the content of Sections 11.2–11.4 of this chapter. The discussion will concentrate first on the NC of machine tools, and will then describe various approaches to the provision of computer assistance in the programming of NC machines. Sections 11.5–11.7 of the chapter will first describe the techniques for the direct production of arbitrary three-dimensional shapes from CAD models in **rapid prototyping**, and will then go on to give an overview of robot technology, and of the application of robots in assembly and cellular manufacturing.

11.2 Fundamentals of numerical control

In the late 1940s an American named John Parsons devised a method for the manufacture of smooth shapes (such as templates for aircraft wing sections) by recording on punched cards the location of the centres of a large number of holes approximating the shape, and feeding these cards into a machine tool to drive a cutter. The shape resulting from the many holes could be smoothed to give the desired profile. The US Air Force was sufficiently impressed by Parsons' ideas that they contracted the Servomechanisms Laboratory of the Massachusetts Institute of Technology (MIT) to develop the concept into a workable system. At about this time work began on similar concepts in the United Kingdom, and progress was rapid on both sides of the Atlantic, such that numerically controlled tools were being used in production fairly routinely by the mid to late 1950s.

In the intervening years there has been very extensive development, and today numerically controlled devices are used in all manner of industries. Milling machines manufacture the moulds and dies for polymer products ranging from packaging to automobile headlamps, and machine large aircraft components such as bulkheads and wing skins from single billets. Flame-cutting and plasma arc machines cut shapes for railway locomotives and ships from large steel plates. Lasers are manipulated to cut tiny cooling holes in gas turbine parts. Electronic components are inserted into printed circuit boards by NC insertion machines. There is hardly an aspect of discrete-part manufacture that has not been strongly influenced, even revolutionized, by NC. It can also be argued that many industrial robots are essentially numerically controlled devices, in that they are production machines whose motion is determined by a stored program.

The essential features of numerically controlled machines have been established for many years. They comprise a **controller**, known as the **machine control unit**, or **MCU**, capable of reading and interpreting a **stored program** and using the instructions in this to control a machine via **actuation devices**. This arrangement is shown in Figure 11.1. The stored program was originally (usually) recorded on paper tape from which it was read by the MCU, but today the program is normally

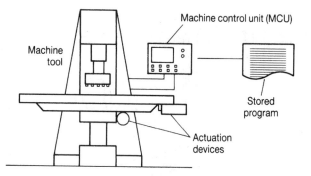

FIGURE 11.1
Arrangement of
a numerically
controlled machine
tool.

stored within the controller, and often communicated to the controller from a remote computer by communications lines. The actuation devices are generally a servo system of some sort. The MCU gives instructions to this system, and monitors both position and velocity output of the system, using this **feedback** data to compensate for errors between the program command and the system response. The feedback is normally provided through sensors such as shaft or position **encoders**.

The arrangement in which the instructions given to servo motors are modified according to the measured response of the system is called **closed-loop control**, and is by far the most prevalent type of NC. Some low-cost and early systems also use the conceptually simpler **open-loop** arrangement in which the controller passes instructions to the actuation system but does not monitor the response.

In machine tools the cutter may typically move in multiple directions with respect to the workpiece, or vice versa, and therefore the controller normally drives more than one machine axis. Examples of machine applications and numbers of axes are as follows:

▶ **two-axis** motion, generally in two orthogonal directions in a plane, which applies to most lathes (Figure 11.2) as well as punch-presses, flame- and plasma arc and cloth-cutting machines, electronic component insertion and some drilling machines;

▶ **three-axis** motion, which is generally along the three principal directions (x, y and z) of the cartesian coordinate system, and applies to milling (Figure 11.3), boring, drilling and coordinate measuring machines, among others;

▶ **four-axis** motion, which typically involves three linear and one rotary axis, or perhaps two x–y motions, as for example for some lathes fitted with supplementary milling heads;

▶ **five-axis** machines, which normally involve three linear (x, y and z) axes, with rotation about two of these – normally x and y – and are generally milling machines (Figure 11.4).

In general, the right-handed coordinate system convention is applied, and positive rotation obeys a right-hand screw rule.

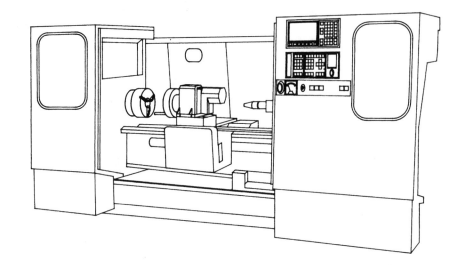

FIGURE 11.2
A CNC lathe.

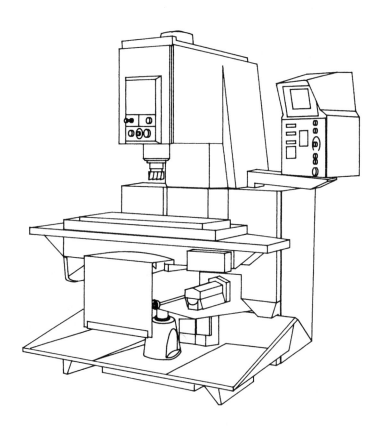

FIGURE 11.3
A CNC milling
machine.

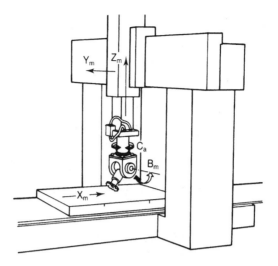

FIGURE 11.4

A five-axis skin mill machine. (Reproduced with permission from Dooner (1987). © The Open University.)

Types of machine motion

The simplest type of machine motion is known as **point-to-point**, and involves moving a tool between specified positions at which some operation is carried out. The actual path taken between these positions is not important. A drilling machine is an example of a machine where only point-to-point control may be required.

A second type of motion is known as **straight-cut**, and in this the machine is capable of moving the cutting tool parallel to only a single machine axis at a controlled rate. This motion type is very restrictive, and is much less widely applied than **contouring** NC. This allows point-to-point and straight-cut motion, and also motions which involve simultaneous precise control of more than one machine axis. Typical contouring motions are straight-line moves between arbitrary positions (known as **linear interpolation**), and arcuate motion, generally in a plane defined by any two machine axes (known as **circular interpolation**). Of course, by employing a large number of short linear moves, any path can be approximated. This method is used for more complex curves (e.g. to machine conic sections or shapes defined by spline curves).

The motion of the tool along a path is controlled to a programmed **feedrate**, generally expressed in terms either of feed per revolution of the spindle (for instance, in mm per revolution (MMPR) or inches per revolution (IPR)) or feed per unit time (e.g. mm per minute (MMPM)). The former is usually used for lathes, and the latter typically for milling machines.

In addition to the motion of the cutter with respect to the workpiece, the controller will also command the operation of the spindle drive, and of features such as the coolant supply, tool (cutter) changes, workpiece clamps and chucks and so on. The more sophisticated of modern controllers will also interface to other production equipment, such as conveyors, automatically guided vehicles or part-changing robots.

11.2.1 Computer numerical control

Early controllers were constructed using thermionic valves and electro-mechanical relays. These were eventually replaced by discrete semiconductors, but until the 1970s controllers had very limited capabilities. There was no facility to store a program within the MCU. The controller could only process one command at a time, and the number and scope of the available commands were very limited. The development of the modern controller was enabled by the incorporation after about 1970 of a computer within the control itself, in so-called **computer numerical control** (CNC), and controllers are invariably now of this type. They allow local program storage and editing and the inclusion of much more sophisticated operation – in terms of the control functions, of the command language used by the controller, and of the input and output facilities, they now almost match those of conventional computers. A block diagram for a CNC system is shown in Figure 11.5. CNC machines have at least a keyboard and alphanumeric screen, and the more sophisticated of recent machines have displays for graphical verification of the tool path, as shown in Figure 11.6.

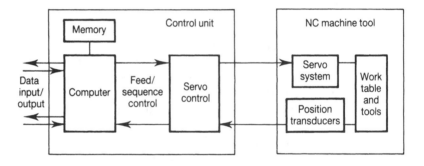

FIGURE 11.5
A block diagram for a CNC system.

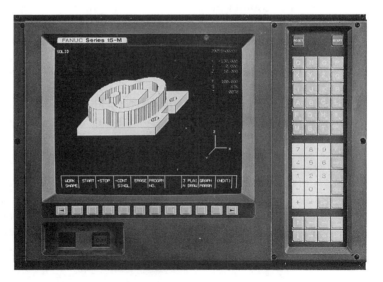

FIGURE 11.6
Graphical display and editing features of a modern CNC controller.
(Reproduced by permission of Fanuc Robotics Ltd.)

Direct and distributed numerical control

As mentioned above, the traditional method for storing a program and transmitting it to a machine tool was punched paper tape. This was a reliable method in the presence of swarf, lubricants and electrical noise in a machine shop, but the paper tapes were very bulky and relatively easily damaged (although metallized tapes overcome this to a certain extent). In some cases magnetic media – in particular enclosed cartridge tapes and the more modern hard-package floppy disks – have been used as storage media, but the preferred way is now to communicate the program to the machine tool directly from another computer.

There are two main ways in which part programs may be communicated to a machine from a remote computer. In **direct numerical control**, part program **instruction blocks** are communicated to machine tools as required from the remote computer. This technique relies on the computer always being available to service the machine tools, and with modern CNC machines has been superseded by **distributed numerical control**, in which the central computer downloads complete programs to CNC machines as required. These machines may store one or more programs in their local storage, and they are thus independent of the central computer, but the distributed arrangement allows flexibility in determining the machine to carry out a particular job. In both distributed and direct numerical control the acronym DNC is used, although the term DNC/CNC may be used for distributed NC because of its dependence on CNC controllers. In addition to the facility for the storage and distribution of part programs, DNC systems of all types often provide facilities for the reporting of machine operation data to central computers for the provision of workshop management information, and for the incorporation of the machine tool and other manufacturing equipment into a larger integrated system – for example, for the coordination in a manufacturing cell of the operation of the CNC machine and of robots used for machine loading and unloading, part conveyors and so on. This wider integration has also been termed **integrated numerical control** (INC) (Hannam, 1996).

For programs within the memory capacity of the controller the DNC approach is fine, but for very large programs (e.g. milling of complex surfaces, which we will come to later) it may be necessary to pass the program to the machine in 'blocks', and to ensure that the machine does not pause in mid-cut as these are being transmitted. Transmission of such programs is known as **trickle feeding**. The DNC/CNC mode of operation has advantages in that the CNC can, if necessary, work independently of the DNC system, and the more lightly loaded host computer can be available for shop floor management tasks such as control of part and cutter movements, and manufacturing cell supervision.

11.2.2 Machining centres

In addition to the developments in machine tool controllers through the expansion of their computing power and the provision of external interfaces, machine tools themselves have continued to develop. This has been in particular in order to extend the capability of single machines to undertake a wide range of machining operations with minimum set-up time and set-up changes, or to allow as many machining operations as possible to be carried out on the same machine. The facilities that are provided in modern machine tools for these purposes are:

▶ Tool magazines and tool handling systems that allow a large number of tools – perhaps a dozen on a lathe or more than 50 on a milling machine – to be stored and loaded on demand.

▶ Pallet loading systems in which the workpiece and its fixtures are loaded onto a pallet and the complete pallet/workpiece assembly is loaded into the machine tool for machining. While one workpiece is being machined, a second can be prepared on its pallet, and workpeice changeover therefore only requires a pallet change. With two pallets this is known as **pendulum loading**. The larger integrated systems will have pallet stands in which multiple workpieces may be stored on pallets, and the pallets may be used to transport workpieces around the manufacturing system.

▶ Multiple machining spindles. For example, a lathe may be provided with a milling spindle so that both turning and milling operations may be carried out on the same machine. This avoids a machine change for the many parts that are essentially turned parts with simple milling or drilling operations, as shown in the process planning example in Section 9.6. Other machines combine milling and grinding spindles to allow these two operations to be incorporated into machining sequences without machine changes.

11.3 Data preparation for numerical control

Another name for the stored program in NC is the **part program**, and the process of writing such programs is known as **part programming**. The task of part programming is that of translating a representation of the geometry of a component – perhaps a drawing – first into a specification for the operations to be carried out by the machine tool, and then into a program of instructions for the controller. Traditionally, this would be done by the part programmer poring over an engineering drawing of the component, sketching the tool paths and carrying out arithmetic and trigonometric calculations for the program. This would then be coded on a coding form before being punched onto paper tape. The whole process was time consuming, error prone and rather tedious.

Many NC machines are still manually programmed, in particular where parts are relatively simple. Today this is helped by the data entry and editing features of the controller, and by programming aids such as canned cycles, which will be discussed later. The programming of complex shapes has always been difficult, however, and from the early days of NC alternative approaches to part programming using computer assistance have been used. These approaches in particular assist with the mathematical calculations for determining cutter path offsets for multiple cuts on a part, and have the additional merit of reducing programming errors. The first of these

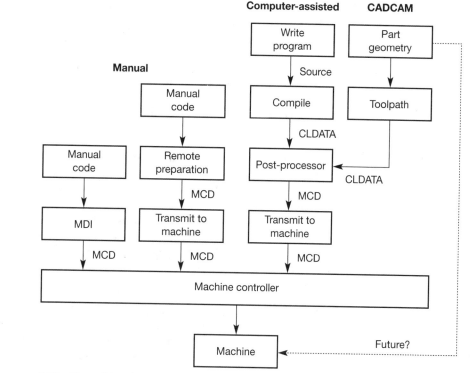

FIGURE 11.7
Alternative routes for part programming.

MDI = Manual Data Input

methods involves computer languages for defining part geometry and cutter motion that compile to give the cutter paths with respect to the workpiece. The second approach involves directly extracting machining data (again in the form of cutter paths) from the CAD model. These alternative routes are shown, together with the manual part programming route, in Figure 11.7. In each of the computer-assisted routes, it will be seen that cutter paths are first produced in a generic (machine-independent) format, and then converted by a program called a **post-processor** into the form suitable for the machine tool (known as **machine control data**, or **MCD**).

The part program itself generally follows a fairly well-defined syntax (although with some variation because of differences between machines and controllers). Unfortunately, this syntax is rather old. Because NC, and indeed computer-aided part programming languages also, were established so early, they have been rather left behind in computing terms. Essentially, the machine receives instructions as a sequence of blocks containing commands to set machine operations and parameters and dimensional and speed data. Each command has an associated identifying letter, and is generally identified by number. They are classified as follows:

▶ The **sequence number** (identifier N) is simply the identifying number for the block, in ascending numerical order (but not necessarily in a continuous sequence).

▶ **Preparatory functions** (identifier G) prepare the MCU for a given operation, typically involving a cutter motion. The importance of these functions is such that MCD is often called colloquially the 'G-code program'.

▶ **Dimensional data** items (identifiers X, Y, Z, A or B) contain the locational and axis orientation data for a cutter move.

▶ **Feed functions** (identifier F) are used to specify the cutter feedrates to be applied.

▶ **Speed functions** (identifier S) are used to specify the spindle speed, or to set up parameters for constant surface speed operation.

▶ **Tool functions** (identifier T) are used to specify the cutter to be used, where there are multiple choices, and also to specify the particular cutter offsets.

▶ **Miscellaneous functions** (identifier M) are used to designate a particular mode of operation, typically to switch a machine function (such as coolant supply or spindle) on or off.

The end of a block is signified by an **end of block** character. These functions may be further classified into **modal** commands, which set a parameter (e.g. the spindle speed) until it is changed by another command of the same type, and **one-shot** commands, which only operate at the time they are issued (such as unclamp chuck).

There are a number of ways of presenting the command data. By convention, data within the block is in the sequence:

N G XYZAB F S T M *eob*

and this sequence has been used in formats known as **fixed sequential** and **tab sequential** which use the order to identify the particular item of data. By far the most common data format, however, is the **word address** form, which uses the identifier letter for each command item to indicate the type of data that follows. There is no need to enter data unless it is required, and thus the format is compact.

There are further variations in the format of data items within the block, in particular for numerical data. This is because different-sized machines typically have different numbers of characters before the decimal place in dimensional data (and inch data will generally have four characters after the decimal place, while metric data will have three). Some machines also allow leading and trailing zeros or decimal points to be omitted. So, for example, the same command might be represented in quite different ways for different machines. The following sequences give identical instructions:

N001 G01 X45. Y75.125 Z150. F.75 S3000 *eob*

or:

N001 G01 X045000 Y075125 Z150000 F075 S3000 *eob*

Of the particular operation types that may be programmed, the preparatory and miscellaneous functions are the most diverse. A list of typical operations in each category and their associated code numbers are given in Tables 11.1 and 11.2 respectively, although the reader should note that the lists are not complete, and that many controllers do not conform to these values. We will come across explanations for many of the terms used in the tables in due course, but note that in particular:

▶ **Absolute** programming implies that coordinate locations are given as absolute values in the machine's coordinate space, whereas **incremental** programming implies that each move is specified as an incremental move from the previous position. Originally, machines would work in either absolute or incremental mode, according to the type of feedback transducers with which they were fitted. Now most machines will allow either mode, although those with incremental encoders have to be moved to a known position on first start-up to initialize the system. It should be noted also that in absolute mode a variable origin can usually be used. For example, in turning, the origin could be at the centre of the end of the workpiece.

Table 11.1 Preparatory commands (G-code)

G00	Point-to-point positioning
G01	Linear interpolation
G02	Clockwise circular interpolation
G03	Counter-clockwise circular interpolation
G04	Dwell
G05	Hold
G33	Thread cutting, constant lead
G40	Cancel tool nose radius compensation
G41	Tool nose radius compensation – left
G42	Tool nose radius compensation – right
G43	Cutter length compensation
G44	Cancel cutter length compensation
G70	Dimensions in inches
G71	Metric dimensions
G90	Absolute dimensions
G91	Incremental dimensions
G92	Datum offset

Table 11.2 Miscellaneous commands (M-code)

M00	Program stop
M01	Optional stop
M02	End of program
M03	Spindle start clockwise
M04	Spindle start counter-clockwise
M05	Spindle stop
M06	Tool change
M07	Mist coolant on
M08	Flood coolant on
M09	Coolant off
M10	Clamp
M11	Unclamp
M13	Spindle clockwise, coolant on
M14	Spindle counter-clockwise, coolant on
M30	End of tape, rewind

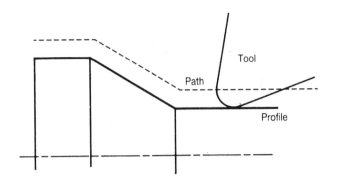

FIGURE 11.8

Profile turning and tool nose radius compensation.

▶ **Cutter compensation**, also known as cutter or tool nose radius compensation (TNRC), is used because most tools – even for turning – do not cut at a single point, but rather on a curved cutting edge. Without TNRC it is necessary for the programmer to program the movement of the centre of the cutter to take account of its orientation with respect to the workpiece. For example, in turning the profile shown in Figure 11.8, the path of the centre of the cutter should be as shown by the chain-dashed line – the cutter path is defined by offsetting the desired profile by the radius of the cutter, and the cutter direction changes at the intersections of the offset curves. Although the computation of these offsets is straightforward, it is tedious and a source of error. TNRC allows the programmer simply to program in terms of the desired profile, and to tell the control to which side of the profile the cutter is. The control then makes the appropriate calculations to define the cutter path. It has the added advantage that cutter nose radius may be varied without changing the program.

▶ **Constant surface speed (CSS)** machining involves the adjustment of spindle speed in order to maintain the speed of the cutter with respect to the workpiece at a constant value. There is generally an optimum cutting speed for metal removal in any machining operation (depending on the cutter type and material to be cut). The variation in cutting radius in turning makes the optimum speed difficult to achieve. A facing cut traverses across the workpiece, and so to achieve optimum cutter speed the spindle speed should be changed continually as the cut progresses. CSS operation is usually included on lathes to allow this. In CSS operation the programmer will specify either a given surface speed or a certain spindle speed when the cutter is at a given radius, and the control will adjust to suit, up to a specified maximum.

Example 11.1 *An example program*

Let us complete this section by considering an example in the form of the simple program below to drill two holes in a plate, as shown in Figure 11.9.

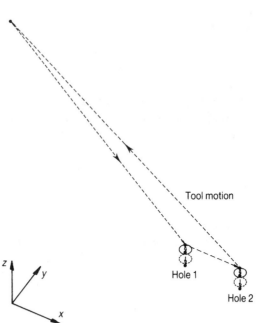

Tool motion

Hole 1

Hole 2

FIGURE 11.9
Toolpath for the
drilling of two holes
in a plate. See
Example 11.1.

Program statement							Explanation
N010	G90						Select absolute
N020	G71						Select metric
N030	G00	X0	Y0	Z300	T01	M06	Load centre drill
N040	G00	X100	Y100	Z25			Above 1st hole
N050	G01	Z17	F400	S3000	M03		Centre drill
N060	G00	Z25	M05				Retract
N070	G00	X150					2nd hole
N080	G01	Z17	F400	S3000	M03		Centre drill
N090	G00	Z25	M05				Retract
N100	G00	X0	Y0	Z300	T02	M06	Load 10 mm diameter drill
N110	G00	X100	Y100	Z25	M08		Above 1st hole
N120	G01	Z3	F350	S2000	M03		Drill
N130	G00	Z25	M05				Retract
N140	G00	X150					2nd hole
N150	G01	Z3	F350	S2000	M03		Drill
N160	G00	Z25	M05	M09			Retract
N170	M00						Program stop
N180	M30						Return to start

11.3.1 Manual programming

Manual part programming implies simply that the person doing the programming – the part programmer – works without computer aids, and determines the MCD program directly. This was originally often a tiresome process, particularly for those parts where a large number of **roughing** cuts were required for bulk material removal, because much detailed trigonometric calculation may be required to establish the cutter path. It is also potentially error prone, because of the risk of making mistakes in entering data.

Some of the tedium of manual part programming is relieved by what one manufacturer calls 'programming productivity aids'. These are features taken from high-level languages, and include:

▶ Special preparatory commands, known as **canned cycles**, for common machining operations that involve repeated moves. These are in a sense equivalent to libraries of standard subroutines/procedures in conventional programming languages, and are applied to operations such as rough cutting of typical volumes, drilling, tapping and threading cycles and so on.

▶ A facility for user-defined sequences of commands, known as **subroutines** or **macros**, that may be called repeatedly in a part program, possibly with variable parameters to provide variable numerical data to the program.

This second facility is sometimes sufficiently powerful that variable parameters can be used to define the dimensions for machining of complete families of simple parts. The use of both canned cycles and a simple subroutine are included in the example below showing the turning of a simple shaft.

Example 11.2 ***The use of canned cycles and subroutines***

The use of canned cycles and subroutines in NC programming is illustrated by the programming of the turning operations on a simple shaft. Figure 11.10 shows a drawing of the component and an annotated program for its manufacture. Figure 11.11 shows the roughing and finishing moves for the program. Note that in this case the syntax of the program is that of the General Electric 1050 series of controllers.

11.3.2 Computer-assisted part programming

The first alternative route to manual part programming is to use a computer language in which to define the part geometry and tool motion, and to let the computer system carry out the offset calculations. Although the computer relieves the part programmer of many of the onerous tasks of programming, it is still necessary to define the sequence of operations, the feeds and speeds, the tools to use and the general cutting movements. The stages of computer-assisted part programming may therefore be summarized as follows:

1. Identify the part geometry, general cutter motions, feeds, speeds and cutter parameters.

2. Code the geometry, cutter motions and general machine instructions into the part programming language. This code is known as the **source**. Widely used languages for this task are Automatically Programmed Tools (APT) and its derivatives, and COMPACT II.

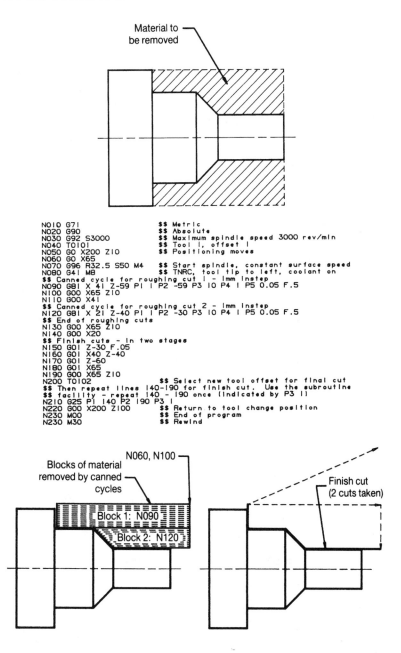

FIGURE 11.10

Example of the use of canned cycles.

FIGURE 11.11

Roughing and finishing operations for the program of Figure 11.10.

3. Compile or **process** the source to produce the machine-independent list of cutter movements and ancillary machine control information, known as the **cutter location data file** (or **CLDATA** for short).

4. **Post-process** (so called because it takes place after processing stage 3) the CLDATA to produce machine control data (MCD) for the particular target machine. The file format of the CLDATA file for the APT programming language is defined in ISO standards.

5. Transmit the MCD to the machine, and test.

The encoding of part geometry and tool motion into a language has now been largely superseded by the direct generation of cutter location data from the CAD model using a CADCAM system (i.e. replacing steps 2 and 3 above), as described in Section 11.3.3. The languages are still in use, however, and furthermore they have formed the basis for the development of the direct generation of tool path data from part geometry in CADCAM. In particular, many CADCAM systems produce output in APT CLDATA format and use the APT language for system customization. For these reasons the APT language will be briefly reviewed in the next section. More complete details of the language are contained in Appendix C.

Automatically Programmed Tools

The **Automatically Programmed Tools** (APT) language was initially developed at MIT and the Illinois Institute of Technology in the late 1950s and early 1960s. The language is a three-dimensional system that can control machines with up to five motion axes. It has also spawned many derivatives and, although some 30 years old, is still in use today.

An APT program comprises language statements that fall into the following four classes:

▶ **geometry statements**, which comprise definitions of those aspects of the part geometry relevant to the machining operations;

▶ **motion statements**, which define the motion of the cutting tool with respect to the part geometry;

▶ **post-processor statements**, which contain machine instructions that are passed unchanged into the CLDATA file to be dealt with by the post-processor;

▶ **auxiliary statements**, which provide additional information to the APT processor giving part name, tolerances to be applied and so on.

The order in which these statements appear is important. The normal program sequence is:

auxiliary statements: to specify part name and post-processor;

geometry statements;

auxiliary and post-processor statements: to define cutter and tolerances, and machining conditions;

motion statements;

auxiliary and post-processor statements: to switch off spindle and coolant, and to stop the program.

The general form of a geometry statement is:

symbol = geometry__word/descriptive data

where symbol is a name for the geometric element (using up to six characters commencing with a letter), and has the same role as a variable name in other high-level languages, and geometry__word is the **major word** name of a geometry type. These include, among others, points, lines, planes, circles, cones, spheres, ruled surfaces and tabulated cylinders. The descriptive data comprises the numeric data required to define the entity, reference to the names of the other entities used in its definition, or qualifying **minor words** to indicate the type of geometry definition to use (for instance; INTOF indicates that the intersection of entities should be used). An example is:

CIR = CIRCLE/CENTER, PT, TANTO, LN

which defines a circle, CIR, tangent to line LN and with its centre at point PT. Appendix C contains a fuller list of geometric definitions.

Once the part geometry has been defined the APT programmer may specify how the cutter is to move, either in absolute or incremental terms, using the commands GOTO/(absolute position) or GODLTA/(incremental move) respectively, or with respect to the part. The latter is achieved by defining cutter moves with respect to geometric entities along paths bound by other entities, using motion words GOFWD (go forward), GOBACK, GORGT (go right) and so on.

Post-processor statements control the operation of the spindle, the feed and other features of the machine tool. Some common post-processor statements are (where the '/' indicates that some descriptive data is needed):

COOLNT/ for coolant control – for example, ON or OFF;
RAPID to select rapid cutter motion;
SPINDL/ to select spindle on/off, speed and direction of rotation;
FEDRAT/ to select feedrate;
TURRET/ to select cutter number;

Auxiliary statements are used to provide information required by the APT processor in processing the source. This includes for example the name of the part being processed and the details necessary for offset calculation, including the cutter size and the accuracy to which approximations should be made when representing curved paths by straight lines.

APT also includes facilities for arithmetic manipulation (using the same notation as FORTRAN) and for looping, and also a subprogram feature known as the **macro** facility. This allows a programmer to program repetitive operations as a single group of statements and to call this group repeatedly within a program. It also allows symbolic parameters (variables) to be used instead of actual values. At the time the macro is called these symbols are instantiated with the actual values to be used. For example, assume that it is necessary to drill a series of holes. Assume also that drill depth (DPTH), spindle speed (SPED), drilling feedrate (DRFR) and clearance of the drill above the part (CLRNC) are variables. We define the macro DRILL as follows:

```
DRILL = MACRO/DPTH, SPED, DRFR, CLRNC
        DX1 = CLRNC*0.9
        DX2 = DPTH + CLRNC – DX1
        RAPID
        GODLTA/0, 0, –DX1
        SPINDL/SPED, CLW
        FEDRAT/DRFR, MMPM
        GODLTA/0, 0, –DX2
        GODLTA/0, 0, DX2
        RAPID
        GODLTA/0, 0, DX1
        SPINDL/OFF
        TERMAC
```

Each time that a drill operation is required, the programmer inserts in the program:

```
CALL/DRILL, DPTH = depth, SPED = spindle speed, DRFR = feedrate,
            CLRNC = clearance
```

thus replacing the several statements that would be required otherwise. An example with typical values might be:

```
CALL/DRILL, DPTH = 100, SPED = 2000, DRFR = 150, CLRNC = 20
```

Although we have used drilling as an example macro here, in many APT systems it is likely that this facility would normally be provided using the **cycle** capability. This feature is used for standard operations. Cycle commands are a form of post-processor statement, in that they are passed straight to the post-processor for conversion into the appropriate machine commands – often themselves canned cycles. For example, a drilling cycle might be:

```
CYCLE/DRILL, R, point, F, depth, IPM, feedrate
```

where the minor word DRILL specifies the cycle type, and the other minor words R, F and IPM indicate the point of termination for the rapid approach, feed into the workpiece and feedrate respectively.

Post-processing

The result of the processing of the APT source is the CLDATA file, as we have seen. This is a binary file, although it is generally possible to obtain a readable version known as a CLPRINT file. The CLDATA file contains details of cutter moves either as a series of absolute linear and/or circular GOTO moves (e.g. GOTO/100,50,0 means move to $x = 100$, $y = 50$, $z = 0$) or relative GODLTA moves, interspersed with post-processor statements for spindle, coolant and feedrate control and so on. This file is converted to a machine-specific MCD file by the post-processor program. Because of the variations not only in the format of MCD files, but also even in the meaning of particular G- and M-codes, these have traditionally been customized programs that are dedicated to particular machine tool/controller combinations (in fact, not only are there differences in the tools and controllers, there are also differences in CLDATA formats, owing to variations in approach by different suppliers of APT, computer and CADCAM systems and other part programming languages).

Generalized post-processors

As the number of NC machine tools employed by a company increases it becomes inconvenient (and expensive) to have to purchase a post-processor for each machine/controller combination. There have therefore been developed in recent years generalized post-processors (sometimes called colloquially 'G-posts') that are able to post-process for almost any machine. To achieve this they may be customized individually by reading at run-time a configuration file that lists the machine tool and controller syntax and characteristics. Typically, the generalized post-processor has a companion program that serves to generate the configuration file, as shown in Figure 11.12, through an interactive question and answer session.

Much of the work in customizing a post-processor simply involves assigning preparatory codes to certain operations and dealing with the particular format of the MCD file. Some machine operations and some APT statements (in particular the CYCLE statement) are, however, very difficult to accommodate in a standard format, and therefore generalized post-processors may incorporate the equivalent of a programming language so that detailed, specialized customization may be done by the user.

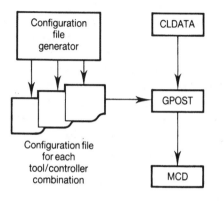

FIGURE 11.12

The generalized post-processor and configuration file generator.

```
              GENERALIZED POSTPROCESSOR                      )  HEADER
                                                             )  DETAILS
              MACHINE NUMBER  8001.0   DATE  20790  PAGE   1  )

   MOOGTURN/ GE 1050 HLX BRISTOL UNIVERSITY

                                          ABX       ABZ     FEED  SPD  ISN   TIME
   $NOZZLE  TURNING
     N0010 G53                                                         0003  .000
     N0020 G54                                                         0003  .000
     N0030 G95                                                         0003  .000
     N0040 G71                                                         0004  .000
     N0050 G90                                                         0005  .000
        FROM    125.00000    25.00000   0.00000
     N0060 T0202 M08                    25.000   125.000               0006  .000
     N0070 G97 S1500 M04                25.000   125.000         1500  0008  .000
     N0080 G00 X50.239 Z99.746          50.239    99.746 999.00 1500  0010  .003
     N0090 G01 X58.724 Z95.503 F.3      58.724    95.503 450.00 1500  0012  .016
     N0100 Z.401 F.1                    58.724      .401 150.00 1500  0014  .650
     N0110 G00 X50.239 Z4.643           50.239     4.643 999.00 1500  0016  .650




      LISTING OF TOOL MOTION AND OTHER COMMANDS CONTINUES


       V
     N1340 X95.276 Z80.86               95.276    80.860 150.00 1500  0214  5.948
     N1350 G00 X86.791 Z85.103          86.791    85.103 999.00 1500  0216  5.949
     N1360 X50. Z125.                   50.000   125.000 999.00 1500  0218  5.953

       ACCUM. CUT TIME =      5.95 MINUTES              )
       ACCUM. DWELL TIME =    0.00 MINUTES              )  SUMMARY OF PROGRAM DURATION
             TAPE LENGTH =   19.48 FEET  (   593.60 CM) )  AND POST-PROCESSOR RESULTS
       NUMBER OF ERRORS =        0                      )
```

FIGURE 11.13

An example post-processor output file.

Post-processor output

A post-processor will produce as output more than simply the MCD file. It will also produce diagnostic and process planning information. Included in the first of these will be indications of violations of machine limits or feedrate errors. Process planning information will often include the length of the tape required to hold the program, and the machining time at programmed feeds and speeds. Examples of such data in a post-processor output file are shown in Figure 11.13.

11.3.3 The CADCAM approach to part programming

The prevalent approach to computer-assisted part programming today is to prepare the part program directly from the CAD part geometry, either by using NC programming commands included in the CADCAM system or by passing the CAD geometry into a dedicated CAM program. (Some systems also have a facility to produce APT source geometry directly from a CAD data file. To this are added auxiliary and post-processor information and cutter motion statements in the conventional way.) The CADCAM approach has a number of advantages over the use of a part programming language, of which the most important is the removal of the need to encode the part geometry and the tool motion. This eliminates the risk of error in interpreting or transcribing the geometry, and greatly reduces the time taken in tool path data preparation.

CADCAM brings additional benefits to part programming through the use of interactive graphics for program editing and verification. CADCAM systems generally provide facilities to:

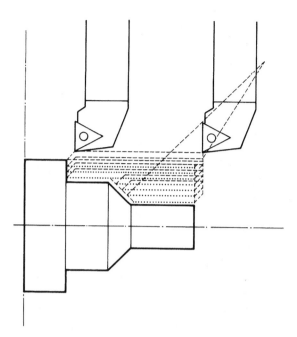

FIGURE 11.14
Example tool
display.

▶ display the programmed motion of the cutter with respect to the workpiece (usually by means of a graphical representation of the cutter), which allows visual verification of the program; an example tool display is shown in Figure 11.14;

▶ edit interactively a tool path with the addition of tool moves, standard cycles and perhaps APT macros (or the equivalent from other languages).

The latter facility is normally greatly aided by access to the system facilities for geometric construction and interaction and for coordinate system manipulation. CADCAM systems also incorporate the most sophisticated algorithms for part program generation – in particular for bulk material removal and for the machining of complex surfaces.

The approach to part programming using CADCAM is thus broadly as follows:

1. The aspects of the part geometry that are important for machining purposes are identified (and perhaps isolated on a separate level or layer); geometry may be edited, or additional geometry added to define boundaries for the tool motion.

2. Tool geometry is defined, perhaps by selecting tools from a library.

3. The desired sequence of machining operations is identified and tool paths are defined interactively for the main machining operations.

4. The tool motion is displayed and may be edited to refine the tool motion, and macro commands or other details may be added for particular machining cycles or operations.

5. A cutter location data (CLDATA) file is produced from the edited tool paths.

6. The CLDATA file is post-processed to MCD, which is then transmitted to the machine tool.

Each of steps 1, 3 and 4 will now be discussed in more depth.

Bounding the tool path

Tool motion is normally defined such that the edge of the tool remains in contact with the part geometry throughout the cut. Tool shape is generally arcuate (lathe tools), or with a square or radiused corner (milling tools). For surface milling, tools are often assumed to have a hemispherical tip (known as a ball-ended cutter). In all cases the CADCAM system will generate a tool path with automatic tool nose radius compensation, and with cutter paths offset for the multiple passes required for roughing.

When it is necessary to bound the motion of the cutter along a particular geometric entity, CADCAM systems often use the concept, taken from APT, that the cutter moves are limited by three surfaces: the **part surface**, the **drive surface** and the **check surface**. The cutter always remains in contact with the part surface. It moves along the drive surface until it reaches the check surface which halts the motion (and which may in turn form a new drive surface along which the cutter will move). The check surface may limit the tool motion in one of three ways, as shown in Figure 11.15, which also shows an example of a hemispherical cutter moving with respect to the three surface types.

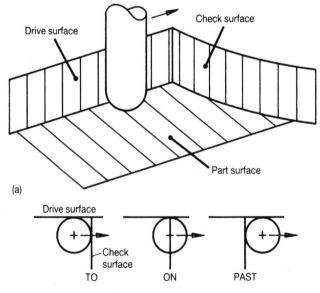

FIGURE 11.15
Part, drive and check surfaces, and constraints on tool motion.

(a)

(b) Constraint of tool motion by check surface

Specifying the cutter path

The more sophisticated CADCAM systems support a wide range of machining operations, broadly divided as follows:

▶ **Lathe** operations include turning, facing, grooving and thread-cutting. Example cutter paths are shown in Figure 11.16.

▶ Two-axis or two and one-half axis ($2\frac{1}{2}$ axis) **milling** and **drilling** operations include point-to-point motion for drilling and **profiling** and **pocketing** operations, as shown in Figure 11.17. Pocketing will typically include facilities for milling around one or more profile(s) within a pocket, and for alternative strategies for material removal, as shown in the figure; $2\frac{1}{2}$ axis machining implies that machine movements are in planes parallel to the *x–y* plane. Moves in the *z*-direction are for drilling or for in-feed or cutter retraction only.

▶ **Surface milling** functions allow surfaces to be machined using **three-axis** or **five-axis** contouring motion by a milling machine. In each case the cutter is traversed along a series of paths at constant surface parameter, or along contour lines. In three-axis motion the cutter axis is maintained vertical, while in five-axis machining the cutter is maintained normal to the surface, or at a fixed angle to the surface normal. Figure 11.18 shows three- and five-axis moves for the milling of a convex surface. Section 11.4 describes the application of surface milling in more detail.

▶ **Cutting** operations include flame- and plasma-cutting devices, and usually involve moving the flame/arc along a profile defined by a series of curves.

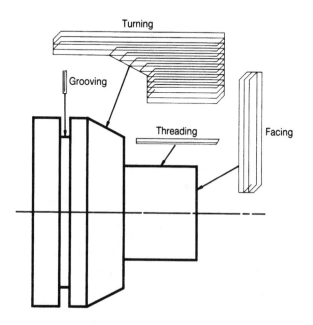

FIGURE 11.16
Example lathe cutter paths.

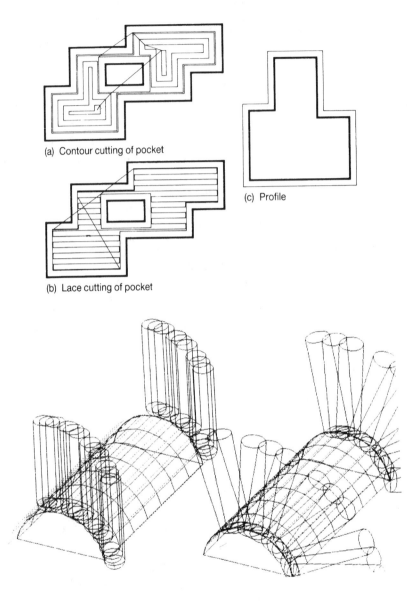

(a) Contour cutting of pocket

(c) Profile

(b) Lace cutting of pocket

FIGURE 11.17
Milling by profiling
and pocketing.

FIGURE 11.18
Three- and five-axis
moves for convex
surface machining.

► **Brake-press** operations are for NC turret presses that process sheet metal, and generally involve producing profiles and cut-outs by repeated use of tools of standard profile (e.g. round, rectangular or D-shaped).

Where significant material removal is required, the software normally allows bulk material removal roughing cuts as well as finishing cuts to define the final form. Sometimes an intermediate semi-finishing cut is allowed. These often use a different strategy. For example, roughing of a die cavity that will be finished by surface milling might be carried out by clearing a series of levels of the cavity each at a constant depth. The finishing will often involve approximating a curve or a surface by a series of straight-line moves, and in this case the accuracy to which the approximation is made is defined by a tolerance specifying the maximum deviation of the approximation from the true geometry. Where the geometry of the part is defined using a parametric entity, the straight-line moves may be defined by equal increments of the entity parameters.

Editing the cutter path

Once the cutter path has been defined, the part programmer will wish to display the cutter motion to verify that it is correct, and may also wish to carry out various **editing** operations. Possible actions include combining cutter paths, adding additional moves for cutter change or perhaps to clear obstacles, or deleting redundant moves. They may also include the addition to the cutter path of commands that will be included in the CLDATA file – for example, for spindle, coolant or feedrate control, or to carry out groups of operations. In some systems these may be defined using the APT MACRO or CYCLE commands, as outlined in Section 11.3.2 above. In the context of part programming using CADCAM, the macro might be used for:

▶ initializing the machining process at the beginning of the program – for example, setting up the post-processor and machine tool;

▶ avoiding clamps or other obstacles within the tool path;

▶ implementing a user-written procedure for hole drilling, boring, tapping and similar operations;

▶ machining a fixed pattern, such as a bolt circle.

The CADCAM system will also normally be able to enter standard operations into the cutter path as CYCLE commands.

Examples of CADCAM application

In the past, NC machines have shown great promise, but the difficulty in programming complex shapes has rather limited their application. The improvement that CADCAM brings in this respect has had a significant influence on component design. In particular, profiling and pocketing are very widely applied in aircraft manufacture to mill from solid components that would previously have been fabricated, and designers of moulded and formed components now have greater freedom to design components with complex doubly curved shapes. Examples 11.3 to 11.5 below illustrate these cases.

Example 11.3 *A turning example*

Figure 11.19 shows an example of a turned shape (an acoustic horn) in which the profile to be turned is defined by a spline curve. The figure shows the part geometry, the roughing cuts and the finishing cut for the shape. Without the use of CADCAM, this part could not have been turned without the manufacture by hand of a template for a copy-lathe. Using CADCAM reduced the manufacturing time from days to hours.

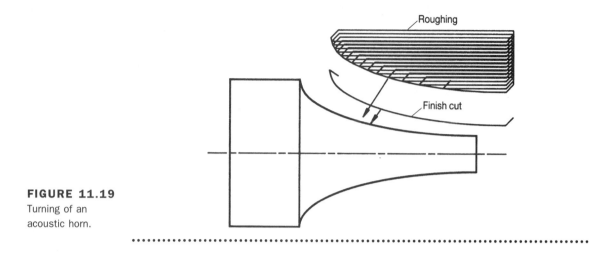

FIGURE 11.19
Turning of an
acoustic horn.

Example 11.4 *Pocket machining*

Figure 11.20 shows an aircraft component which has been machined by a series of profiling and pocketing operations using CADCAM. Component shapes which once would have been fabricated by riveting separate pieces together are often now machined from solid, giving improved structural integrity.

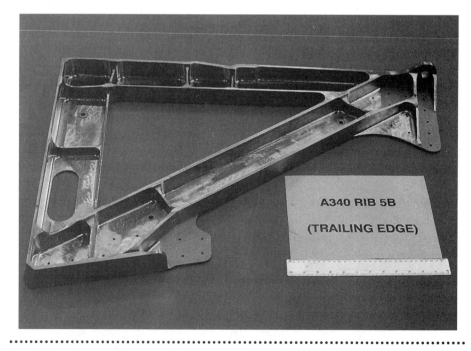

FIGURE 11.20
An aircraft
component
machined by milling
operations.
(Reproduced by
permission of British
Aerospace Airbus
Ltd.)

Example 11.5 *Surface milling*

Figure 11.21 shows a mould that has been machined from a solid block by surface milling. Moulds for complex shapes, in this example for blow-moulded components, may be machined directly from the CAD geometry that defines the shape.

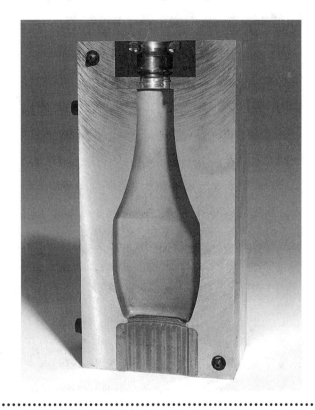

FIGURE 11.21
A mould machined from solid by surface milling. See Example 11.5. (Reproduced by permission of Crown Cork and Seal Group Inc.)

Part programming method selection

Of course, the CADCAM approach to NC data preparation is not without its limitations. In particular, the programs that are produced are often very long – especially those for machining of surfaces, which can have sizes in megabytes. For modern CNC, very much more compact code can be produced for some components through the use of canned cycles, and for many components these may make manual programming quite straightforward. Increasingly, also, CADCAM-like graphical facilities for program editing and verification are being incorporated into controls themselves. We can therefore propose the following broad guidelines for the choice of programming technique:

▶ for point-to-point and straight-line drilling and milling, and for straightforward turning, *manual* programming may often be appropriate;

► for pocket and profile operations, *computer-assisted* or CADCAM approaches are most appropriate;

► for surface milling, and the turning or milling of profiles defined by spline curves, CADCAM is practically essential.

11.4 Machining from 3D models

Let us now consider in more detail the generation of machining information from surface and solid models. At the end of this section we will consider how, by exploiting geometric modelling and 3D visualization techniques, a realistic display of the effect of movement of the machining cutter may be produced, but first we will explore how finishing machining cuts are made that seek to reproduce as accurately as possible the modelled form of complex surfaces. The essential problem is that of machining a surface that may be doubly curved, with wide variations in curvature. The software has to include different strategies appropriate to different types of surface, and also ensure that in the process of machining the cutter does not interfere with parts of the workpiece other than those it is intended to cut.

There are a number of ways in which the cutter can move across the surface, depending on the nature of the cut. We have seen that roughing may use the strategy of clearing the workpiece to a series of different depths. For finish cuts the cutter may follow:

► curves along a surface at constant values of one of the surface parameters – either in a forward and backward motion known as lace cutting, or with all cuts in the same overall direction, called non-lace cutting;

► contours on the surface;

► paths projected on the surface, for example in a series of parallel planes.

These options are illustrated in Figure 11.22.

In surface milling there are two principal categories: three-axis and five-axis machining. In the former the cutter is always at a fixed angle with respect to the work piece – normally aligned with the z-axis – and ball-ended cutters are generally used for the concave surfaces for which the method is most appropriate. This allows the use of relatively low-cost machines, software and controls, but has the disadvantage

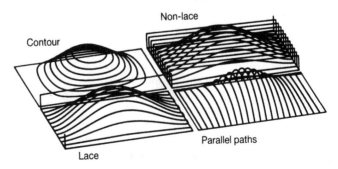

FIGURE 11.22
Cutter paths for surface machining.

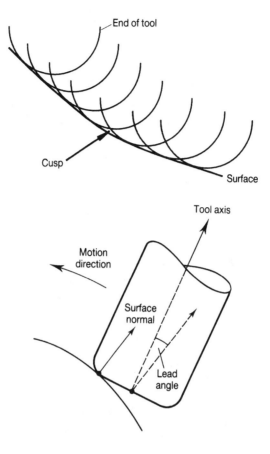

FIGURE 11.23
Cusps between tool passes.

FIGURE 11.24
Inclination of the cutter in five-axis machining. (Reproduced with permission from Dooner (1987). © The Open University.)

that raised cusps are left between cuts, as shown in Figure 11.23. There is clearly a trade-off between cusp size and the number of machining paths used (and the programming software will often compute the number of paths for a given cusp height or vice versa). The current practice of large memory capacity and trickle feed allows very small step-over between adjacent paths, and hence small cusps, but some hand-finishing is still required.

In five-axis work the cutter axis is varied to suit the orientation of the surface. In principle the cutter could be aligned with the surface normal, but in practice it is often inclined so that cutting is not on the bottom but on the side of the cutter, as shown in Figure 11.24 (this is so that the cutter may be more effective by cutting at the largest possible radius). It is also normal in five-axis machining to use square-ended cutters, which practically eliminate the production of cusps, but these cutters are really only appropriate to convex surfaces.

Computing the cutter location

In either three- or five-axis milling the cutter location problem is essentially one of offsetting the cutter contact locus on the surface such that the cutter centre follows the desired path. This is easiest for ball-nosed cutters, for which the centre of the

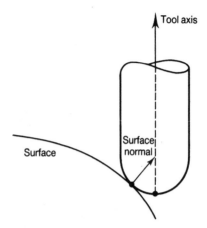

FIGURE 11.25
Location of
spherical-ended
cutter. (Reproduced
with permission
from Dooner (1987).
© The Open
University.)

spherical end is offset by the radius of the end in a direction equal to the surface normal at the contact point (as shown in Figure 11.25). This surface normal may be calculated from the vector product of the partial differentials in the two parametric directions:

$$\mathbf{n} = \partial\mathbf{p}/\partial u \times \partial\mathbf{p}/\partial v \tag{11.1}$$

The sequence of steps to generate a three-axis lace path with a ball-ended cutter would therefore be:

For each value of the parameter v (incremented by equal steps chosen to give the required cusp height), increment u in equal steps (chosen to give the required tolerance), and for each increment:

– calculate the position, $\mathbf{p}$, on the surface at the given value of u and v;
– calculate the surface normal, $\mathbf{n}$, at $\mathbf{p}$;
– calculate the cutter nose centre offset by the radius, r, along $\mathbf{n}$ from $\mathbf{p}$.

The same basic principles, although with rather more algebraic and computational complexity, may be applied to five-axis machining, although here the cutter axis is also arranged to be aligned with the surface normal, or to be tilted slightly, as shown in Figure 11.24.

Gouge detection

When machining concave surfaces, the cutter end radius will ideally be smaller than or equal to the smallest radius on the part, and therefore all of the part surface will be capable of being machined by the cutter. However, this is not always possible and in such cases there is a risk of the cutter interfering with or gouging the surface. It can also occur in five-axis work that the cutter can interfere with the part owing to its orientation. In five-axis work, gouge detection is also more complicated because the whole cutter geometry has to be considered, especially if a concave surface is being machined. Examples of gouge conditions are illustrated in Figure 11.26.

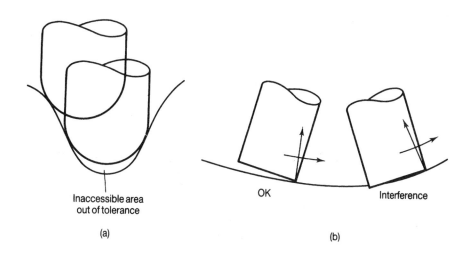

FIGURE 11.26
Examples of potential gouge conditions. (Reproduced with permission from Dooner (1987). © The Open University.)

Inaccessible area out of tolerance

(a)

OK

Interference

(b)

Using the cutter to produce blends

In the chapter on surface modelling it was noted that some surface types, especially blends between other surfaces, may be difficult to model correctly. One straightforward pragmatic approach is to use a cutter nose radius to produce the blend surface by using the APT concepts of part, drive and check surfaces. Some systems allow check surfaces to be defined even if area milling of a surface is being carried out, and a ball-ended cutter will naturally produce a blend of the radius of the ball at the junction between the part and check surfaces.

11.4.1 Tool path generation from solid models

For many years, the main activity in CAM was the machining of surfaces and of profiles bounded by curves. CAM software systems also required considerable expertise in machining on the part of the user – the system would generate the tool motions required to machine a part, but the overall sequence of operations and the cutting conditions, speeds and feeds would be the responsibility of the user of the software. The evolution of the capabilities of CAM has seen significant changes in both of these respects, in particular through the following developments:

▶ Automatic **waterline** or **z-level** machining of solid models, in which a tool path for the machining of a solid model is generated by taking slices through the model at successive depths, and then using area-clear algorithms to program the clearance of material at each depth.

▶ Generation of tool paths in the context of models of the **whole machining environment**. The generation of the tool path considers not just collisions between tool and workpiece, and gouging of the workpiece by the tool, but also interactions between the tool and the part, the billet, clamps, fixtures and the machine tool itself.

▶ **Shaded display** of machine environment and of machining operations. The checking of the tool path is very much facilitated by the generation of full shaded surface models of the machine, clamps, fixtures and parts, and of dynamic display of the state of the part at each stage of the machining process, in order to show the effect of material removal.

▶ **Feature-based machining**, in which the description of a part as a collection of features may be used to call up prototypical machining sequences for particular features, with selection of machining parameters directly from the feature data.

▶ The incorporation of **machining rules** to allow the software to make intelligent decisions about cutting depths, feeds and speeds according to the geometry, tooling and workpiece material.

▶ **Fixture** and **tool libraries**, which may be combined with the tool and part display facilities, and with the rule-based machining.

▶ **Associative machining**, in which the machining operations may be associated with the workpiece geometry and other parameters such that a change in part attributes may be used automatically to recalculate the tool paths. For example, a change in workpiece material could be used to cause the cutting depth and feeds and speeds of a tool path to be recalculated, or a change in geometry could prompt revision of the tool path pattern.

11.5 Rapid prototyping

Earlier, in Chapter 1 of this book, we made reference to a model of the design process developed by Pahl and Beitz (see Figure 1.1). The third phase of this model was referred to as **embodiment design**, in which the conceptual solution is developed in some detail, problems are resolved and weak aspects of the design are eliminated. Frequently during this phase of the design it is necessary to ensure that the embodiment is in fact fit for the intended purpose. This is achieved through **prototyping**. The creation of prototypes is useful from a number of points of view. Firstly, the availability of a prototype facilitates discussion with other colleagues including, for example, marketing and sales personnel and manufacturing engineers, and also with clients and customers. Secondly, prototypes are useful to help the designer to visualize complex structures and surfaces and indeed may be used to check various engineering characteristics, for example the use of models of possible car body design in wind tunnels to check aerodynamic performance.

Up to now we have used the term model to refer to abstract or mathematical representations. Clearly here we are talking about physical models, frequently made of clay and wax. The creation of a physical model is, however, a **time-consuming** task which requires the services of skilled machinists.

For many manufacturing companies, however, time has become a competitive weapon – time as measured in time to market for new products and time to fulfil customer orders. In Chapter 12 we will look in more detail at the nature of 'time-based competition' and offer a more complete discussion on time to market and time to fulfil customer orders. For the moment, it is sufficient to offer the following working definition of time to market.

Time to market refers to the time that elapses from the development of the initial product concept until the product is available to the customer. Companies seek to reduce time to market by implementing concurrent (or simultaneous) engineering (see Chapter 9) and by using rapid prototyping technology.

Technically speaking, rapid prototyping is a term used to describe a number of techniques which rapidly produce solid physical models of components and products using 3D computer data by a group of relatively new manufacturing technologies. The terms **solid-object modelling**, **tool-less manufacturing** and **desktop manufacturing** have also been applied. In general these technologies manufacture products by adding layers of material (or laying down material) rather than by a metal removal process (e.g. machining). In essence rapid prototyping converts 3D CAD data into physical models without the need for special-purpose tooling. Among the better known rapid prototyping processes are stereolithography, selective laser sintering and layered (or laminated) object modelling.

Stereolithography is essentially a type of 3D printing process based on the use of a light-sensitive polymer fluid and a computer-driven laser scanning system. The process starts with a 3D CAD model, which is processed to create a series of very thin horizontal cross-sections or slices. These thin slices are then used to trace the path of the cross-section of the product by controlling a laser which generates an ultraviolet light beam and travels across a vat of photocurable polymer liquid. The laser beam traces the path of the cross-section, changing the liquid into a solid until the appropriate layer or slice is formed or laid down. The CAD model used for stereolithography is in the form of a tesselated set of triangular facets representing the part geometry. Most CAD systems will now produce these .STL format models as a standard file type.

As Figure 11.27 suggests the platen moves until the emerging solid physical model of the component is just below the surface of the light-sensitive polymer, leaving a

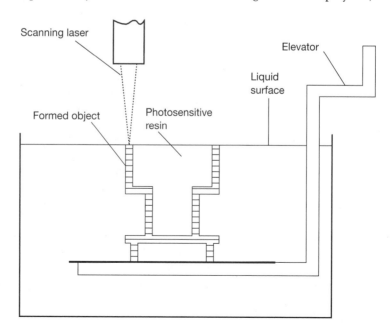

FIGURE 11.27
Stereolithography.

thin layer of polymer fluid between the top of the component and the polymer surface. The scanning laser beam now traces out the shape of the next slice on the thin exposed film of fluid. The laser sets and solidifies the fluid exposed to it. In this way a series of layers are built up eventually to replicate (in solid form) the 3D model from the CAD system.

The value of stereolithography lies in its ability to allow designers to produce prototypes of emerging designs quickly and thus to go through several design iterations quickly. The process is particularly useful for components with complex geometry.

Selective laser sintering (SLS) and **layered object modelling** (LOM) are similar processes to stereolithography in that they take the CAD model and converts it into 'slices' that are used to build the model. However, SLS and LOM use different materials technologies in place of the polymer fluid. SLS works by laying down thin layers of solid polymer powder that the laser sinters as it traces out the 'slice'. As each slice is completed, a further layer of powder is added and sintered to the layer below. LOM works by using a laser to cut profiles from a strip of adhesively backed paper. Layers of paper are bonded to each other to make a part with an appearance rather akin to wood, and with similar density and properites.

There are a number of other rapid prototyping technologies available, and the approach has also been used to make patterns for the rapid production of prototype castings and tools for other processes such as electric discharge machining.

11.6 Robotics technology

The numerically controlled machine tool is an example of a manufacturing device that may be programmed to carry out a particular task. A robot is a further example of such a device, but is more general purpose. Whereas an NC machine tool is designed to move a tool with respect to a workpiece, or vice versa, a robot is a programmable device that is designed to move and manipulate all manner of objects through various programmable motions. Robots have been applied in many different situations, but mainly in the automation of repetitive, unpleasant or hazardous tasks.

Robots have evolved over a period of years from simple mechanical handling devices into machines capable of sensing and reacting to their environment. The early spur for their development was the need for manipulators to work in hazardous environments in atomic energy. In the late 1940s, the Argonne National Laboratory in the United States developed coupled 'master–slave' mechanical manipulators for use in radioactive environments in which a master multiple degree-of-freedom device was guided by an operator, and the slave unit duplicated the master unit's motions. In the 1950s these ideas were extended by various organizations to include electric or hydraulic servo assistance and eventually control by switches or joysticks.

The devices of the 1940s and 1950s required a human operator, and were not able to work unattended. The first industrial robot, capable of autonomous manipulation, was developed in 1959 by Unimation Inc., and through the 1960s there was widespread work in universities and research organizations to develop various manipulator devices, and to link them to sensors, TV cameras and other feedback devices. These efforts continued into the 1970s, with the use of visual and force feedback (Lee *et al.*, 1984).

The 1980s saw an explosion in the industrial application of robotics, with numbers doubling in the period 1985 to 1987. In 1985, for instance, the numbers of robots in Japanese industry was 64 000, and in the United States 13 000, although the definitions of robot on which these numbers are based may not have been completely comparable. By 1987 the numbers were 118 000 and 25 000 respectively (*Industrial Robot* **12**(1), 1985; Bedworth *et al.*, 1991). Robots were applied mainly to repetitive activities such as spot and arc welding, spray painting and coating, machine tool loading and general mechanical handling, and with a particular concentration in automobile body manufacture, for spot welding and painting. Growth continued into the 1990s, but less strongly, and with an increased emphasis on assembly and inspection. More recent development has seen a renewed emphasis on incorporating sensory intelligence into robotic devices, and on widespread applications including processing of meat and other flexible materials, and even applications in surgery.

11.6.1 Robot types and motions

As noted, a robot is a programmable multi-function manipulation device. In other words, it carries out a sequence of motions defined by a stored program, and it can be programmed to carry out different functions or tasks. The basic elements of a robot are shown in Figure 11.28, which shows a machine that comprises:

▶ an **end effector**, which is a device that may be used to grip objects, or to attach various tools or other devices that are to be manipulated;

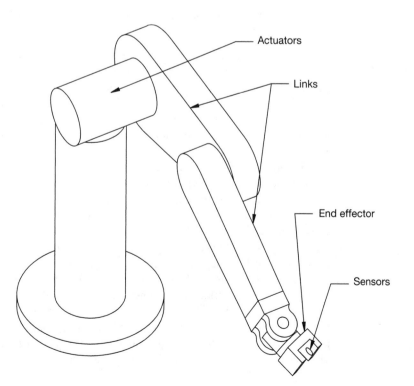

Actuators

Links

End effector

Sensors

FIGURE 11.28
The elements of a robot.

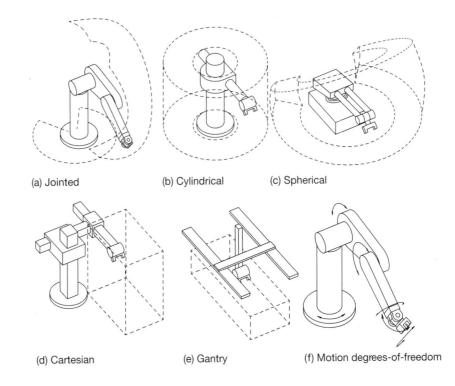

(a) Jointed　　　　　(b) Cylindrical　　　　(c) Spherical

(d) Cartesian　　　　(e) Gantry　　　　(f) Motion degrees-of-freedom

FIGURE 11.29
Robot configurations
and work volumes.

▶ a **linkage** or **mechanism** that manipulates the spatial position and orientation
of the end effector;

▶ **actuators**, including electric motors or hydraulic or (rarely) pneumatic cylinders, that effect the motion of the linkage;

▶ **Sensors** of various descriptions for feedback in the control of the devices.

These elements can be arranged in a number of configurations, which have different characteristics, including load-carrying capability, dexterity and effective **work
volume**, or volume within which the end effector can be manipulated. Figures
11.29(a)–(e) show the arrangement and sketches of the work volumes of five common configurations. The jointed type is very widely used, and is probably the most
dextrous, although at the expense of accuracy. Because of its similarity to the human
shoulder and arm, it is also known as the **anthropomorphic** type, or sometimes
the articulated robot.

The end effector can usually be positioned within the work volume with five or
six degrees of freedom: three linear (x, y and z) and three rotational (α, β and γ).
Generally, three degrees of freedom are provided by the main manipulator, and two
or three by the end effector, as shown in Figure 11.29(f). The type of movement that
may be achieved within the work volume may be broadly divided, as for NC machine
tools, into **point-to-point** motion, in which the path between the start and end
point of a move is unspecified, and **contouring** or **continuous path** motion.
The paths for the latter normally comprise sequences of linear or arcuate motions.

However, whereas for an NC machine tool a linear motion is straightforward, since it involves incrementing the position of each motion axis at a constant rate, for robots of other than the cartesian type linear motion control is complex. For anthropomorphic arms, linear motion may require continuous non-linear adjustment of the position of each joint, and the calculation of these positions can be quite difficult, as the brief introduction to robot kinematics in the bracketed section below shows.

Kinematics of robotic manipulators

The task of a robot manipulator is to move the end effector through a desired set of positions and orientations known as the **trajectory** or path. In order to achieve this, it has to make the appropriate joint movements for each part of the path. The task of motion control is to identify for each element of the path what the required motion is for each joint (the joint trajectory), and then to control the joints using an appropriate control algorithm together with feedback from sensors. The task is summarized in Figure 11.30.

The task of determining the position of the end effector given a set of joint positions is called the **forward kinematics** problem and is relatively straightforward providing that we can use the coordinate system transformation method introduced in Chapter 4. Figure 11.31 shows an anthropomorphic robot with a cartesian coordinate system aligned with each of the joints. Coordinates in the coordinate space of the end effector may be computed in world coordinates simply by performing a series of coordinate system transformations along the chain of links in the robot arm – and the transformation matrices can be multiplied together to give a single matrix if homogeneous coordinates are used.

The task of identifying the required joint positions for a given end-effector position and orientations is called the **inverse kinematics** problem, and is a much more difficult task. Computation of joint positions q_i for each end-effector

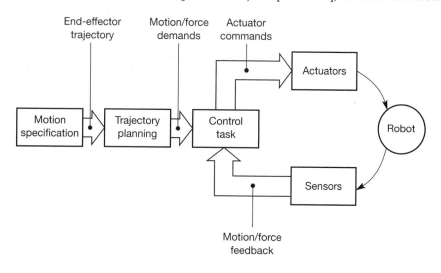

FIGURE 11.30
The robot motion control task.

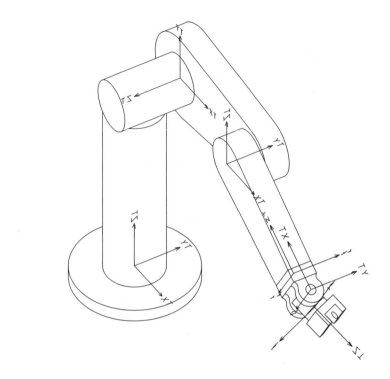

FIGURE 11.31
Robot joint
coordinate systems.

position $\mathbf{p}(t)$ and orientation $\theta(t)$ requires the solution of a set of equations relating these:

$$[\mathbf{p}(t), \theta(t)]^{\mathrm{T}} = \mathbf{f}[q_1, q_2, q_3, q_4, q_5, \ldots, q_n] \qquad \textbf{(11.2)}$$

Some manipulator configurations may have closed solutions, but for the most part the equations are non-linear. They may be solved numerically, or in other ways, but solutions can be computationally intensive.

If only positional control of the manipulator is required, calculation of the trajectory requires that the inverse of $\mathbf{f}$ be solved for each corner point, or **position point**, in the path to give the joint positions for these points. Simple servo schemes can be used to drive each joint to the required position, but because the joints are controlled independently, the path of the end effector between position points is not in general in straight lines. Where joint motions are completely independent of each other, then this is known as **point-to-point** motion. Where each joint is moved during the same time period, and is interpolated during the move according to a consistent scheme, then this is known as **joint interpolation**, and again the motion between position points will not, in general, be in straight lines.

The task of controlling motion along a prescribed path (usually in straight lines) between position points is more difficult still. One approach is to divide each path into a number of smaller segments, and to construct a corresponding series of joint trajectories. If the segments are sufficiently small, the joint increments become small, and the transformation $\mathbf{f}$ in Equation (11.2) becomes a differential transformation, known as the **Jacobian matrix** of the displacement, which is usually linear. The Jacobian contains trigonometric functions of the joint displacement with respect to the joint coordinates before the motion increment, and can be inverted to give joint increments in terms of the change in $\mathbf{p}(t)$ and $\theta(t)$, or $\mathbf{f}$ can be differentiated directly (Luh, 1983).

The above paragraphs only begin to describe the problems of robot control. The controller needs to incorporate velocity as well as positional information along the trajectory to ensure that motion is acceptably smooth, and the control also needs to take account of the dynamic behaviour of the manipulator, which again is highly non-linear. Important dynamic effects include a change in the moments of inertia of the arm with respect to joints during motion, interaction between joints owing to centrifugal and Coriolis accelerations, variations in gravitational forces, and the effect of variations in payload. Because of the complexity of the kinematics and dynamics of robots, they have been the subject of a great deal of study over recent years. The interested reader is referred to the various specialized journals and conferences on the topic. A useful introduction to the topic is the IEEE Computer Society tutorial (Lee *et al.*, 1984).

11.6.2 Accuracy and repeatability

The robot also differs from the machine tool in the accuracy and repeatability that may be achieved for its positioning movements. Machine tools are designed for high stiffness and very accurate movements – accuracies in the order of 0.01 mm can be achieved. Robot performance is much worse than this. They are more usually designed for agility, and the number of degrees of freedom, and thus the required number and nature of their joints, mitigates against high accuracy. In describing their performance, the following terms are used:

▶ **Spatial resolution** is the smallest controllable increment of motion that can be programmed, and is a function of the resolution of the controller and the encoders on the motion axes, and of the size of the robot amongst other factors.

▶ **Accuracy** describes the maximum difference between the actual position reached in a movement and the target or programmed position. If the accuracy is considered during a move then it is termed the **dynamic accuracy**.

▶ **Repeatability** describes the ability of the robot to return to a programmed point, or more specifically the maximum difference between positions for multiple returns to a point. Repeatability is usually much better than accuracy, and this can be important for some applications. For example, for repetitive tasks, poor accuracy can be compensated in programming, provided that repeatability is good, so that the operations can be performed consistently.

▶ **Drift** is the time-dependent tendency of the robot to move from its desired position. This can be in the short term – for example, if a position is held for a long period of time – but more importantly it can be a loss of accuracy and repeatability over a long period of time owing to wear, backlash, drift in electronic equipment and so on. Drift can partly be overcome by regular recalibration of the machine.

For robots the accuracy can sometimes be measured in millimetres (although it is usually much better than this), and the repeatability in the order of tenths of milli-metres, so these are not high-precision devices. The factors that affect accuracy and repeatability include ambient temperature, link and joint stiffness, joint backlash, hysteresis and clearance, computational errors, drive motor resolution and so on. Also very significant is the payload carried by the device. The largest robots are capable of carrying in the order of a tonne, but the smaller robots have payloads in the order of kilograms only, and large payloads can cause significant link deflection. If only joint position and not absolute position is measured, this can have a significant effect on accuracy, although increasingly devices are being developed for in-cycle position measurement and feedback.

11.6.3 Robot programming

A straightforward way of identifying the required manipulator positions for a trajec-tory is to move the robot through the sequence of position points under manual con-trol. This is known as the **teach** or **teach-through** mode of programming, and is usually done in slow motion under the control of a joystick, push-buttons for joint controls, a master–slave arrangement or some similar approach. Once programmed, the motions can be edited and played back repetitively.

An alternative to teaching motion is to program using a programming language or simulation system, and over the years many computer languages have been devel-oped for this purpose. For example, Lee *et al.* (1984) describe nine languages, and present detailed descriptions of a number of these. Some robots use adapted versions of the G-code languages used by NC machine tools. One robot language, known as VAL, was the earliest to be developed for commercial applications, has been widely used and is a good example of how a language may be used for robot control. VAL was developed by the Unimation company in the 1970s, and allows motion control under point-to-point, joint interpolated and cartesian motions (see the box on kine-matics above for an explanation of these terms) in discrete steps or as a continuous path (Shimano, 1979; Unimation, 1980). The language is interpreted, with some arith-metic, branching, looping and subroutine capabilities, as one might expect in a high-level language, and matrix manipulation capabilities for transformation calculation. It also has features to aid in the interactive development of programs, for event trig-gering for robot attachments, and in the interfacing of the robot to sensors for the adjustment of programs to sensor input.

VAL language statements comprise commands that are followed by arguments that may include references to positions or transformations to positions, or by numeric data entry. An example command is:

MOVES POINT1

which instructs the robot to move in a straight line from the current position to the position point labelled POINT1. Further commands are divided into a number of groups for program, trajectory and configuration control, to manipulate positions and variables, and other miscellaneous functions. The classification of these commands, with examples and explanations of their meaning, is given in Table 11.3 An example

Table 11.3 Example instructions in the VAL language

Command group	Description	Example commands ([] = optional argument, <> = variables/symbols)	Meaning
Robot configuration control	To set the robot configuration.	RIGHTY or LEFTY	Change robot configuration to resemble human's right or left arm respectively.
Motion	Command robot movements.	MOVE <location>	Move to predefined location using joint-interpolated motion.
		DRAW [<x>][<y>][<z>]	Move robot along straight line by distance x, y and z in these coordinate directions.
		DEPART <distance>	Move tool the specified distance along current z-axis.
Hand control	Control grasping device at end effector.	OPEN [<h_o>] CLOSE [<h_o>] GRASP <h_o>,[<label>]	Open hand to separation h_o. Close hand to separation h_o. Grasp and check if final opening is less than h_o, if so, go to 'label'.
Integer variable	Set or display integer variable values.	SETI <i.var>=<i.var.2>	Set value of i.var to expression given in i.var.2.
		TYPEI <i.var>	Display value of i.var.
Location assignment and modification	Define and modify the destinations of robot motion.	HERE <location>	Set precision point or transformation to current position.
		SET <pt_or_trans> = <pt_or_trans_2>	Set point or transformation on LHS to equal value or expression on RHS.
Program control	Alter the sequence in which program steps are executed.	GOTO <label>	Unconditional branch to program step identified by label.
		WAIT <channel>	Enter a wait loop until the desired state of an external channel is reached.
Trajectory control	Enable/disable features of the servo/trajectory.	SPEED <value> [ALWAYS] COARSE [ALWAYS]	Set robot speed. ALWAYS = for all subsequent motions. Allow larger errors in position (and therefore faster motion execution).
Miscellaneous	Miscellaneous commands	DELAY <time>	Puts program into idle loop for specified period of time.
		TYPE [<string>]	Display <string> on the system monitor.

of the way some of these might be used in a short program is as follows, with comments and explanations in italics.

1.	SETI PART.NO = 0	*Initialize integer variable for part number.*
2.	SET START = 50.0, 50.0, 50.0	*Initialize location for start of operations.*
3.	SET COLLECT = 200.0, 100.0, 0.0	*Initialize position of workpiece.*
4.	SET UNLOAD = 100.0, 200.0, 0.0	*Initialize unload position.*
5.	MOVE START	*Move to start position.*
6. 100	MOVES COLLECT, 50	*Move to 50 mm above COLLECT position.*
7.	MOVES COLLECT	*Move to COLLECT position.*
8.	GRASP 20	*Close gripper to 20 mm.*
9.	DEPART 50	*Move away from COLLECT position by 50 mm.*
10.	MOVE UNLOAD, 50	*Move to 50 mm above UNLOAD position.*
11.	MOVES UNLOAD	*Move to UNLOAD position.*
12.	OPEN 50	*Open hand to 50 mm to release part.*
13.	SHIFT COLLECT BY 0, 0, 20.0	*Increase COLLECT by 20.0 mm in z-direction.*
14.	SETI PART.NO = PART.NO + 1	*Update part number.*
15.	IF PART.NO NE 4 THEN 100	*Repeat if parts not all processed.*
16.	STOP	

11.6.4 Robot applications

We have already noted that robots have principally been applied to those tasks that are repetitive or hazardous, or both. Two very well-known examples of such applications are in spot welding and in spray painting for automobile body manufacture. An automobile body is manufactured from a large number (it can be hundreds) of pressed steel panels that are joined together largely by making resistance welds known as spot welds on flanges between panels. There are thousands of welds in a body, and the task of making them with manually operated equipment is dirty, noisy and arduous – and one for which it is difficult to ensure consistent quality. Today, the task of welding body panels together to form the unpainted steel body – called the 'body-in-white' – is almost entirely carried out by robots that manipulate spot-welding guns held by their end effectors.

The body-in-white is painted before the interior trim and hardware and the mechanical parts of the vehicle are fitted. Again, this is a repetitive task that requires great consistency to achieve high-quality results. It is also hazardous because of the air-borne droplets that result from the paint spray. Robots can be taught to carry out repeatedly the required movements for a consistent paint finish, and also can be programmed if necessary to deal with different vehicles in a paint line (e.g. to paint a sedan, then a station wagon, then a coupe), with no change in consistency.

Other activities for which consistent, repeated motions make robots valuable include arc welding – for example, the complex manipulation required to weld the joints on a bicycle frame – and machine loading and unloading. We will return to the latter shortly when we discuss cellular manufacturing. Areas of growth in robot application since the mid-1980s have in particular been in assembly of mechanical devices (ranging from small electro-mechanical assemblies to internal combustion engines) and in application outside traditional engineering industry – for example, in aspects of medicine and surgery that require very careful control of cutting implements (Drake *et al.*, 1991), in meat cutting (Wadie and Khodabandehloo, 1995), and of course in the handling of hazardous materials such as explosives or radioactive materials.

11.6.5 Robot application to assembly

Application of robots to automate assembly tasks has proved difficult. Engineers have adopted two main approaches: the development of sophisticated assembly robots incorporating external sensors to allow the robot to adapt to its work surroundings, and the redesign of products to facilitate robot assembly. The first approach involved the development of 'intelligent' sensor-based robots with sufficient accuracy, speed and repeatability, 'universal' grippers and capable of being programmed in task-oriented robot languages. In the authors' experience the second approach of 'design for robot-based assembly' has frequently proved fruitful.

SCARA robots

The SCARA (Selective Compliance Assembly Robot Arm) is an assembly robot developed in the late 1970s and early 1980s by Professor Makino of Yamanashi University, Japan. Results from experiments in assembly research indicated that for some directions stiffness was required while for other directions compliance was required. The SCARA robot was designed to meet these requirements.

Owen (1985) suggests that the majority of assembly tasks consist of single linear motions which move components vertically downwards from a rest position above an item, so that the two objects are in physical contact. Other assembly motions include 'pick and place' actions that transport individual components from feeder devices to pre-assemble positions. Therefore the ideal robot for an assembly task is one which can service a given horizontal surface and has a vertical motion.

Figure 11.32 shows the structure of a SCARA robot. Features of the SCARA structure which facilitate assembly include:

1. Selective compliance, which means that the robot can adapt to slight variations in position.

2. The capability of the robot to cover a large working area.

Design for robot assembly

An outline of a systematic procedure for robot-oriented assembly is presented in Figure 11.33. This procedure applies the guidelines set out in Section 9.5.1.

Review of product range

A large product range and a large variety of product styles require a high degree of flexibility in the assembly system. Generally it is true that the greater the flexibility desired the more expensive the assembly system becomes. This could result in a system that is outside the bounds of economic and technological feasibility.

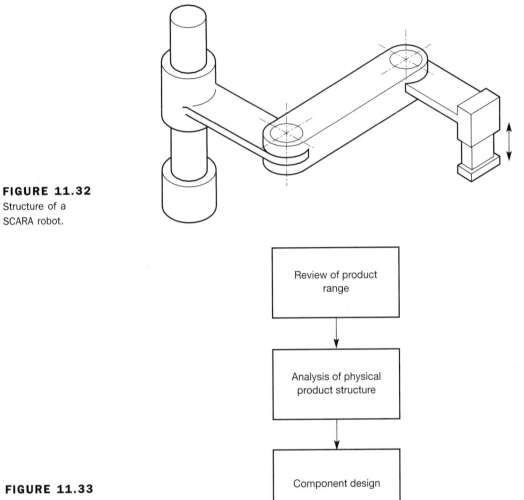

FIGURE 11.32
Structure of a
SCARA robot.

FIGURE 11.33
Robot-oriented
assembly.

Utilization is influenced by the size of the production run assembled on the same equipment. Hence, the designer should avoid variations or ensure that variants can be assembled in the same way. The productivity of the system is a function of the number and length of stoppages. Again there is trade-off between an extremely flexible plant that can accept many variations in components and a range of components with few variations.

Possible ways of satisfying these objectives are to reduce/rationalize the product range or to examine the commonality of parts and subassemblies over the product range, as shown in Figure 11.34, and try to increase the degree of commonality. It is not only production cost savings that accrue from a rationalization of product range, but also organization savings resulting from a possibly smaller product range and/or fewer parts in inventory, fewer parts drawings, etc. Further savings will result from

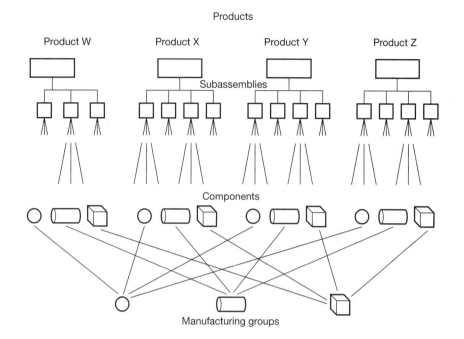

FIGURE 11.34

Parts commonality.

reduced programming, reduction in the number of robot stations, and reduction in the range of robot grippers.

Analysis of physical product structures

The product structure is the outcome of the quantitative structure-level design. This stage of the functional procedure is therefore concerned with the design of product so that robot assembly is facilitated. The product designer works on two levels: a fundamental structure level where techniques and solutions are logically connected, and the quantitative structure level where decisions on distances, tolerances, positioning in space and division into parts are made.

To achieve a product design that is suited to robot-oriented assembly, various product structures should be systematically examined as an aide to alternative design. The alternative product structures are:

▶ The frame – one basic component carrying all other components.

▶ Stacked assembly – the components are assembled by stacking them on top of each other and secured by (usually two) surrounding components.

▶ Composite product – different materials are combined to meet different demands.

▶ Base component product – the base is used for assembly and transport.

▶ Product created from modules – a product composed of larger self-contained parts or functional units with simple relations with the rest of the product.

▶ Building-block system – a system of products which are structured in such a way that all products can be constructed from a number of building blocks.

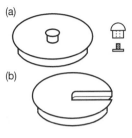

(a)

(b)

The lid (a) consists of three parts which have to be assembled. However these have been integrated into a single plastic moulded part (b) which does not require any assembly.

FIGURE 11.35
Design integration and differentiation.

There are two general but useful design principles at this stage: design for simplicity and design for clarity. Two techniques that have proved valuable and that should be adopted are:

▶ Separate function and form.

▶ Integrate and differentiate.

The first technique, separation of form from function, has been very successfully applied in the electronics industry where the function, as exemplified by a circuit diagram, has been developed separately from the form, that is the PCB layout and physical component selection. At the form stage of the design there are specific rules regarding product design. For example, the axes of the components must be oriented in a north–south or east–west direction. This design is facilitated by the large degree of standardization in electronic components.

An example of the application of the integration and differentiation principle is given in Figure 11.35. Integration results in fewer parts than differentiation.

One method of reducing the difficulty of the assembly task is to reduce the contents of the task by using fewer parts. However, fewer parts may result in more complex moulded or machined parts with a consequent increase in their cost of manufacture. Useful rules include:

▶ Avoid separate connecting elements.

▶ Standardize joining points. If different product styles are needed then all the differently shaped components should have the same connecting points and assembly method. This reduces the need for tooling and set-up.

▶ Replace screwed connections by locking connections. Screwing involves numerous individual steps: ordering of screw, setting up, singling out, feeding, locating, etc.

▶ Reduce the number of assembly parts – individual parts should be combined.

▶ Reduce the extent of the final assembly operation by defining new subassemblies.

▶ Standardize assembly direction and joining by motion along a single axis.

▶ Avoid tight tolerances where possible.

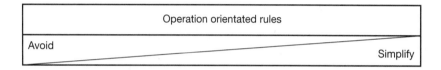

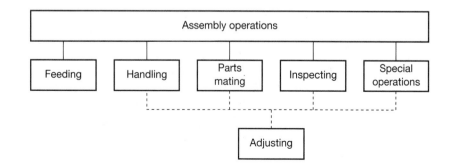

FIGURE 11.36
Direction of
assembly-oriented
design.

Design of components

At this stage of the design procedure the central theme is the avoidance and simplification of assembly operations, as shown in Figure 11.36. There are rules which should be applied to each of the assembly operations outlined in Figure 11.36 in order to achieve design for robot-oriented manufacture:

▶ Feeding
Avoid orientation operations:

- use magazines;
- use bandoliered components;
- integrate the production of components into the assembly, for example springs;
- avoid tangling/nestling.

Facilitate orientation operations:

- avoid clamping or hooking;
- put special faces in the component for orientation;
- avoid components of low quality;
- make the component symmetric;
- or make it clearly asymmetric.

▶ Handling

We can subdivide the handling operation into three stages: picking up, moving and laying down. Thus we simplify the handling operation by: (1) the passive reduction of demands that are made on the handling device, by removing difficulty in the execution of handling functions; and (2) the improvement of the possibilities of handling a part by adding special form elements to the part that support the execution of the handling operation actively. The requirement for handling is further decreased by the integration of components.

▶ Parts mating

– put special faces on the component for guiding purposes, for example lead-in chamfers;
– make all joins simple;
– reduce the number of stop faces;
– insertion should be along a single axis;
– reduce the number of parts and connecting elements by integrating production methods.

For example, in automatic PCB assembly, the probability of successful insertion of IC leads is greater if the leads are pointed than if the leads are straight ended. PCBs are a good example of products where insertions are along a single axis (vertically).

▶ Inspection

– facilitate ease of access to test points.

▶ Adjusting

– design products to facilitate adjust operations.

The design of the individual components may force the designer to return to the second stage of the functional procedure to reconsider the product structure.

Summary of design rules

A summary of the design rules previously discussed is now presented. Essentially there are two design rules: avoid and simplify. This design methodology is shown in Figure 11.37. The rules presented below result from an application of these two basic principles to the area of light engineering assembly. The design rules fall into four categories or levels:

▶ Level 0 – Overall strategy

▶ Level 1 – Product range

▶ Level 2 – Product structure

▶ Level 3 – Component design

Level 0 – Overall strategy

1. Products must be designed for robot-oriented production as well as for performance, reliability, maintainability, safety, aesthetics, etc. This requires the involvement of the production department at an early stage of the design process.

2. Formulate a manufacturing/product strategy. Strategic decisions must be made about the manufacturing system and the product range.

Level 1 – Product range

1. Minimize and, where possible, avoid product variations, or ensure that variations can be assembled in the same way.

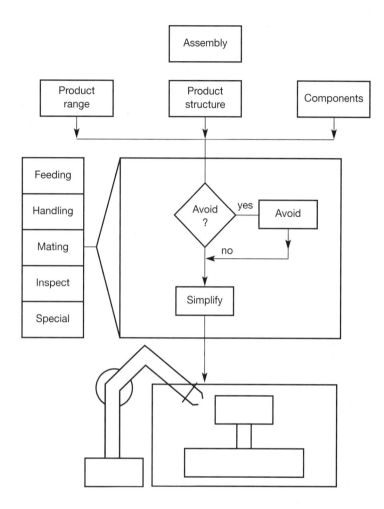

FIGURE 11.37
Design methodology.

2. Rationalize the parts range within the products. This involves parts families, not individual parts.

Level 2 – Product structure

1. Use standard assembly modules where possible.

2. Design the product for simplicity and clarity.

3. Try to reduce the number of parts in the product. This reduces assembly costs but may increase parts costs. Use the integration/differentiation principle.

4. Examine alternative produce structures and use a single one through the product range if possible. Basic product structures include the frame, stacked assembly, composite product, base component product, modular product building block.

5. Avoid joins where possible. Reduce the number of joining operations in the assembly of a product.

6. Standardize joining points.

7. Avoid using separate connecting elements where possible. This also reduces the number of parts to be assembled. It means designing parts so that they can be joined together without the need for a separate part to hold them together.

8. Replace screwed connections by locking connections, where possible. This eliminates parts (screws) and simplifies assembly.

9. Standardize the direction of assembly.

10. Avoid tight tolerances where possible.

11. Ensure that test, inspection and adjust points are freely accessible.

Level 3 – Component design

1. Design components for simplicity and clarity.

2. Use standard components where possible.

3. Avoid, if possible, or simplify parts feeding. This reduces the requirement for an expensive and complex array of parts feeding equipment.

4. Avoid orientation operations where possible.

5. Use magazine parts where possible.

6. Use bandoliered components where possible

7. Integrate the production of components into assembly.

8. Avoid tangling, nesting of components.

9. Facilitate orientation operations.

10. Avoid clamping or hooking if possible.

11. Put easily identifiable orienting faces on components.

12. Avoid using low-quality components.

13. Make the components either symmetric or else totally asymmetric.

14. Avoid, if possible, or simplify the handling operation. (Handling is a non-productive operation and should therefore be avoided.)

15. Simplify and reduce the handling required by the part. Special problems are presented by delicate parts or parts with a precision-ground finish. Reduced handling requirements may mean fewer and/or less versatile grippers are required.

16. Design the part so that handling is facilitated. This may mean the addition of special surfaces that can be grasped by the robot gripper.

17. Simplify the parts mating process. Simplification of this operation can result in shorter assembly time and in a greater probability of successful assembly.

18. Put special guiding faces on the component.

19. Reduce the number of stop faces where possible.

20. Design components to facilitate inspection and permit free access to test and adjust points.

11.7 Cellular manufacturing

Many of the technologies that we have discussed in the first two sections of this book are brought together in the use of cellular manufacturing. Factories were traditionally organized on functional lines, in which all machines of a particular type would be located together, and parts requiring operations from more than one machine type would be transported between areas of the workshop or factory, a process that is time consuming and difficult to control. In cellular manufacturing, the machines required to carry out the operations on particular families of parts are grouped together into a **manufacturing** or **machining cell**, such that parts can be transported easily between machines, and the manufacturing process can be controlled more closely. For example, a company manufacturing a range of fuel pumps might group its machines into cells responsible for machining the cast casings, the pump rotors and the valves respectively, whereas a gas turbine manufacturer might group its machines into cells responsible for blades, disks, rotors, casings, combustion chambers and so on.

Very often there will be a variety of different parts manufactured within a part family, and in order to accommodate the cell to the characteristics of these different parts, it has to be arranged such that it is adaptable in the way it carries out its operations. To achieve this, the following technologies are drawn together in **flexible manufacturing cells**:

► **group technology** to identify and characterize the part families to be manufactured;

► **CNC machine tools** to allow automatic control of machine tools, and to allow programs for each part to be stored and executed on demand;

► **tool handling systems** to allow automated tool changing;

► adaptable and automated **mechanical handling** and **robots** to transport parts between machines, to load machines, and to interface to external material handling;

► **sensor technologies** to read barcodes attached to parts, to sense part orientation and position and so on;

► **digital communications** using networking technologies and communications standards to link together the elements of the cell, and to connect them to the cell controller and through that to the factory production management system.

Figure 11.38 shows how these elements might be employed in a simple system designed to make small parts requiring turning and milling.

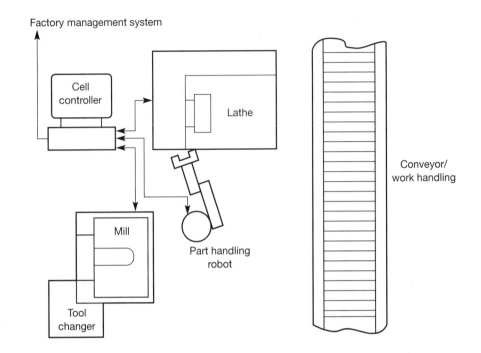

Factory management system

Cell controller

Lathe

Conveyor/ work handling

Mill

Part handling robot

Tool changer

FIGURE 11.38
A simple machining cell configuration.

11.8 Conclusion

The key to the application of CADCAM is the extraction of data from the design model for use in analysis and in manufacture. The main method to date of translating CAD data into manufacturing instructions is in the generation of data for use in computer-controlled production machines. In this chapter the elements of numerical control and robotics technology have been reviewed, and the various methods of generating part programs for NC applications have been outlined. Recent developments in tool-less manufacture have also been noted, and it is likely that the future will see continued development of techniques for manufacture with the minimum of human intervention.

References and further reading

Bedworth D. D., Henderson M. R. and Wolfe P. M. (1991). *Computer-Integrated Design and Manufacturing*. New York: McGraw-Hill.

Browne J. *et al.* (1985). *Product design for small parts assembly in robot assembly* (ed. K. Rathmill). UK: IFSA (Publications) Ltd.

Deitz D. (1990). Stereolithography automates prototyping. *Mechanical Engineering* **112**(2), 35–9.

Dooner M. (1987). *Computer-aided Engineering, PT616: Numerically-Controlled Machine Tools*. Milton Keynes: The Open University.

Drake J. M., Joy M., Goldenberg A. and Kreindler D. (1991). Computer and robotic assisted resection of brain tumours. *Proc 5th Int. Conf. on Advanced Robotics (ICAR)*, Pisa, 888–92.

Faux I. D. and Pratt M. J. (1979). *Computational Geometry for Design and Manufacture*. Chichester: Ellis Horwood.

Groover M. P. (1980). *Automation, Production Systems, and Computer-Aided Manufacturing*. Englewood Cliffs, NJ: Prentice Hall.

Groover M. P. and Zimmers E. W. (1984). *CAD/CAM: Computer-Aided Design and Manufacturing*. Englewood Cliffs, NJ: Prentice Hall.

Hannam R. (1996). *Computer Integrated Manufacturing from Concepts to Realisation*. Harlow: Addison-Wesley.

Jacobs P. F. (1996). *Stereolithography and Other RP&M Technologies from Rapid Prototyping to Rapid Tooling*. Dearborn, MI: Society of Manufacturing Engineers.

Kral I. H. (1987). *Numerical Control Programming in APT*. Englewood Cliff, NJ: Prentice Hall.

Leatham-Jones B. (1987). *Elements of Industrial Robots*. London: Pitman.

Lee C. S. G., Gonzalez R. C. and Fu K. S. (1984). *Tutorial on Robotics*. Silver Spring, MD: IEEE Computer Society Press.

Luh J. Y. S. (1983). An anatomy of industrial robots and their controls. *IEEE Transactions on Automatic Control*. **AC-28**(2), 133–53, and in Lee *et al.* (1984), 5–25.

Malcolm D. R. (1988). *Robotics: An Introduction*. Boston: PWS-Kent.

McKernon P. J. (1991). *Introduction to Robotics*. Reading, MA: Addison Wesley Longman.

Muraski S. J. (1990). Make it in a minute (3D plastic mould making). *Machine Design*. **62**(3), 127–32.

O'Gorman P. D. and Browne J. (1988). *Kitting an international encyclopedia of robotics* (ed. New York: R. C. Dorf). Wiley-Interscience, Vol. **2**, 753–61

Owen T. (1985). *Assembly with Robots*. London: Kogan Page.

Pressman R. S. and Williams J. E. (1977). *Numerical Control and Computer-aided Manufacturing*. New York: John Wiley.

Sharon D., Harstein J. and Yantian G. (1987). *Robotics and Automated Manufacturing*. London: Pitman.

Shimano B. (1979). VAL: a versatile robot programming and control system. *Proc. COMPSAC 79*, 878–83, and in Lee *et al.* (1984), 366–71.

Unimation (1980). *Users Guide to VAL™: a Robot Programming and Control System*. Danbury, CT: Unimation Inc.

Wadie I. H. C. and Khodabandehloo K. (1995). Path generation for robotic cutting of carcasses. *Computers and Electronics in Agriculture*. **12**, 65–80.

Weiss L. E., Gursoz E. L., Prinz F. B., Fussell P. S., Mahalingham S. and Patrick E. P. (1990). A rapid tool manufacturing system based on stereolithography and thermal spraying. *Manufacturing Review*. **3**(1), 40–8.

Woodwark J. (1986). *Computing Shape*. London: Butterworth.

Exercises

11.1 Distinguish between three-axis and five-axis machine tool motion. What are the advantages associated with using a five-axis machine for milling, and when is it appropriate to use this technique?

11.2 What are the units in which feedrate is normally expressed for machine tools? Which of these units are normally used for turning, and why should constant surface speed machining be widely used for turning?

11.3 Explain the following terms in the context of computer-aided manufacture: CLDATA; APT; post-processor; circular interpolation; G- and M-codes.

11.4 Write an MCD program to mill around the four sides of a square block of sides 50 mm, thickness 20 mm, using a 25 mm diameter cutter. Assume that only a finishing cut is required.

11.5 Explain the meaning of the term 'canned cycle', and list some applications for this part programming feature.

11.6 What is the significance of the identifiers N, G, M, S, F and T in a program statement for an NC machine?

11.7 Distinguish between the terms 'major word' and 'minor word' in the context of APT. What are the four types of statement in the APT language? Illustrate how these fit into the structure of an APT program.

11.8 Sketch the geometry that is defined by the following APT statements:

```
P1 = POINT/0,0,0
P2 = POINT/100,0,0
C1 = CIRCLE/CENTER,P1,RADIUS,50
C2 = CIRCLE/CENTER,P2,RADIUS,30
L1 = LINE/LEFT,TANTO,C1,LEFT,TANTO,C2
L2 = LINE/RIGHT,TANTO,C1,RIGHT,TANTO,C2
```

11.9 The APT source for the machining of a milled component is given below. From this source, sketch the geometry and the tool path, and indicate the purpose of each of the post-processor statements.

```
PARTNO      EXAMPLE PART
            MACHIN/MILL,1
            INTOL/.001
            OUTTOL/.001
            CUTTER/.5
SETPT =     POINT/-5,-5,4
P1    =     POINT/0,0,0
P2    =     POINT/0,1.75,0
P3    =     POINT/5,3,0
P4    =     POINT/4,0,0
L1    =     LINE/P1,P2
L2    =     LINE/P1,P4
L3    =     LINE/P2,RIGHT,ATANGL,20,L1
L4    =     LINE/P3,PARLEL,L2
L5    =     LINE/P3,PARLEL,L1
L6    =     LINE/P4,LEFT,ATANGL,70,L2
PL1   =     PLANE/P1,P2,P3
            SPINDL/1000
            FEDRAT/5
            COOLNT/ON
            FROM/SETPT
            GO/TO,L1,TO,PL1,TO,L2
            GOLFT/L1,PAST,L3
            GORGT/L3,PAST,L4
            GORGT/L4,PAST,L5
            GORGT/L5,PAST,L6
```

GORGT/L6,PAST,L2
GORGT/L2,PAST,L1
GOTO/SETPT
COOLNT/OFF
FINI

11.10 Prepare a program in the APT language for the finish milling of the profile shown in Figure 11.39.

11.11 Modify the APT MACRO shown in Section 11.3.2 to drill the hole in two cuts, withdrawing the drill from the workpiece after each.

11.12 Explain the function of the post-processor in computer-assisted part programming.

11.13 What step-over would be required between cutter paths to give a maximum cusp height of 1 mm using a 15 mm diameter ball-ended cutter on a plane horizontal surface?

11.14 Outline the machining operations covered by CADCAM approaches to tool path generation. Can you identify classifications for the approaches to tool path definition for different machine types?

11.15 What are the benefits in using interactive graphics in the generation and checking of tool paths?

11.16 Distinguish between lace, non-lace and contour machining of surfaces.

11.17 Explain the principles of the stereolithography (SLA) and laminated object modelling (LOM) approaches to rapid prototyping, and then explain the steps taken in the preparation of an SLA or LOM part from a CAD model.

11.18 Describe the main robot configurations, and then suggest which configurations would be most suited to (a) paint spraying, (b) loading and unloading of heavy parts onto a machine tool, and (c) simple assembly operations involving vertical placement of parts onto a horizontal surface.

11.19 Indicate the difference between resolution, accuracy and repeatability for a robot. What factors do you think affect each of these three characteristics?

11.20 Outline the steps of a VAL program to take a set of five cubic blocks of sides 50 mm, stacked on top of each other, and place them side by side with 50 mm spacing and aligned with the x-axis.

11.21 Explain how the design rules for part feeding and part mating given in Section 11.6.5 facilitate automated assembly.

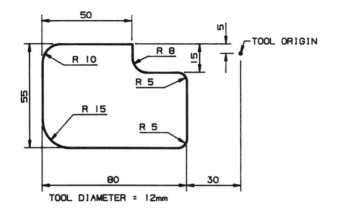

FIGURE 11.39

An example part for APT programming.

Projects

....

For more information about the subjects for project work, please refer to the end of Chapter 1.

The project activity for this chapter is to prepare information for the manufacture of the two project artefacts. Specific tasks are:

Project 1. Chess piece. Produce tool paths for the CNC manufacture of the chess piece as CL DATA, then post-process these, and use the resulting programs to manufacture an example of the part. If a flexible manufacturing cell is available, program the robots to load and unload the machine tool(s), and also program the cell controller to process parts through the cell. As a supplementary or alternative exercise, produce an STL file of the part and then use this for rapid prototyping of the part.

Project 2. Load cell. Produce tool paths for the profile milling of the load cell structural member, post-process these and manufacture an example of the part. Explore the suitability of the artefact for robotic assembly, and then design an assembly cell for the artefact.

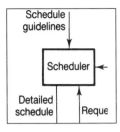

PART THREE

Production planning and control

....

We now go on to consider the issues involved in managing the flow of products through a manufacturing plant in order to produce high-quality products at minimum cost and on time for the customer. The issues involved are more complex than one might imagine at first sight. Typically, a modern manufacturing facility produces a range of reasonably complex products. Frequently these products are manufactured and assembled from a large number of components and subassemblies, some of which are purchased externally. The difficulties arise partially from the fact of having to predict or forecast customer orders in a situation where the time it takes to complete an order is greater than the acceptable lead time to fill an order for a customer. This is compounded by the situation where customers expect the manufacturer to supply particular individual product features at short notice. Further, today's competitive business environment means that the manufacturer who can respond to an order and deliver quickly will gain the business.

A number of approaches and techniques have been developed to respond to these challenges. These systems are normally considered under the headings of production planning and control (PP and C) systems, production management systems (PMS) or indeed computer-aided production management (CAPM) systems. They form the basis of this part of the book. The discussion on these techniques is supported by short presentations of a number of industrial case studies.

12 Introduction to production planning and control

Chapter objectives

When you have completed studying the material in this chapter you should be able to:

▶ differentiate between the major categories of a discrete parts manufacturing system;
▶ articulate a simple typology of manufacturing systems;
▶ outline the overall structure of a production management system;
▶ differentiate clearly between the various levels in a production management system;
▶ understand the role that EDI (electronic data interchange) plays in supporting the linkages between the manufacturing plant, its suppliers and customers;
▶ articulate the thinking behind lean production, in particular in so far as it relates to supply chains;
▶ differentiate between time to market and customer order fulfilment time;
▶ understand the nature of business process reengineering and its relevance to production planning and control systems.

Chapter contents

12.1 Introduction

The planning and control of the flow of work through a manufacturing system is a complex task. Customer orders must be translated into orders for the many components, subassemblies and assemblies which are required to complete that order. Some components are manufactured in-house while others have to be purchased from external suppliers. The availability of all of the necessary components of the end product must be managed so that the customer order is fulfilled in terms of the order specification, cost, quality and delivery date. Clearly the difficulty of the task depends on the complexity of the products in question, the degree of customization of the individual customer orders and the requirements of the customer in terms of the delivery date.

In this chapter we set the scene for the discussion on production planning and control systems by looking at the various types of manufacturing plant and offering a simple typology of manufacturing systems. Also we introduce the structure or architecture of a modern production management system and lay the basis for the detailed discussion which follows in Chapters 13, 14 and 15.

12.2 Discrete parts manufacturing

There are two basic categories of industrial plant: continuous process industries and discrete parts manufacturing. Continuous process industries involve the continuous production of a product, often using chemical as well as physical or mechanical means (e.g. the production of fertilizers or sugar). Discrete parts production involves the production of individual items and is further subdivided into mass, batch and jobbing shop production, as illustrated in Figure 12.1. In this part of the book, the focus is on discrete parts manufacturing.

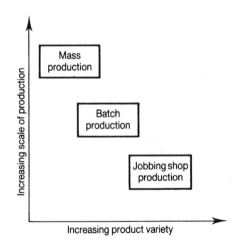

FIGURE 12.1

Classification of discrete production.

Jobbing shop production

The main characteristic of jobbing shop production is very low volume production runs of many different products. These products have a very low level of standardization in that there are few, if any, common components. To produce the different products, the manufacturing firm requires a highly flexible production capability. This implies flexible equipment capable of performing many different tasks, as well as a highly skilled work force. Jobbing shops normally operate a **make to order** or **engineer to order** policy (see Section 12.3). A typical example of the jobbing shop is a subcontract machine shop.

Batch production

Batch production's main characteristic is medium volume production runs of a range of products. Batch production is defined as the production of a product in small batches or lots by a series of operations, each operation typically being carried out on the whole batch before any subsequent operation is started on that batch.

The production system must be reasonably flexible and uses general purpose equipment in order to accommodate varying customer requirements and fluctuations in demand. Batch production can be seen as a situation which lies between the extremes of the pure jobbing shop and pure mass production, and where the quantities required are insufficient to justify mass production. Because of the large variety of jobs involved, batch production has much of the complexity of the jobbing shop. A typical example of batch production is the manufacture and assembly of machine tools.

Mass production

The major characteristic of mass production is large volume production runs of relatively few products. All products are highly standardized. Typically, demand is stable for the products and the product design changes very little over the short to medium term.

The production facilities consist of highly specialized, dedicated machines, and associated tooling. Although these machines are extremely expensive, the cost is allocated over very long production runs. The term *hard automation* or *Detroit style automation* was coined to describe the type of automation associated with mass production. It is hard in the sense that the automation is dedicated and very inflexible. Mass production fits the category of a **make to stock** manufacturing environment (see Section 12.3).

12.3 A typology of manufacturing systems

Today market pressures are forcing companies previously involved in mass production to develop more flexible batch production-oriented systems. This is particularly true of the automotive industry and of manufacturers of consumer goods. Increasingly it seems customers demand a greater variety of products and are unwilling to

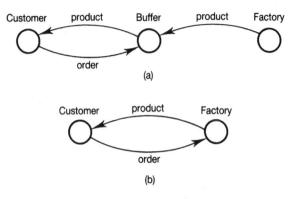

FIGURE 12.2
Evolution of
manufacturing.

accept mass produced products. Customization to consumer needs is the emerging trend. Some go so far as to argue that we are moving towards one of a kind production (OKP) (Higgins, 1991; Wortmann, 1992).

The marketplace has changed dramatically in the last twenty or so years. Customers are no longer satisfied with standard products and are moving in the direction of each consumer demanding a customized product. In the past, products were highly standardized and every customer purchased basically the same product. The manufacturer in this type of system produced the standard products and stored them in a warehouse which acted as a buffer for finished goods inventory. The customer then withdrew the products from the buffer and therefore had minimal interface with the manufacturer. The factory continued to schedule the manufacture of products in order to keep the finished goods inventory at a specific level. Figure 12.2(a) depicts this approach.

Recently, a new approach has evolved whereby the customer interface with the factory is on a different basis. There tends not to be a finished goods inventory buffer from which the customer orders the products. The customer's requirements are now passed to the manufacturer. In some cases the customer orders a partially customized product, and this concept is suggested by Figure 12.2(b).

A typology of manufacturing environments

Four classic types of manufacturing environment have been identified:

▶ Make to stock.

▶ Assemble to order.

▶ Make to order.

▶ Engineer to order.

Make to stock (MTS) implies the manufacture of products based on a well-known and predictable demand pattern. In this environment the interface with the customer is rather distant, the production volume of each sales unit tends to be high and customer delivery time, normally short, is determined by the availability of finished goods inventory. The finished goods inventory acts as a buffer against uncertain demand and stock outs. Figure 12.2(a) portrays a typical MTS system. The MTS system has the advantage of having short delivery time, but inventory costs in the factory are large and customers are unable to express preferences as to the design of the product. The MTS environment also assumes reasonably long and predictable product life cycles.

Assemble to order (ATO) is a system which uses the same core assemblies for products and has the capability to vary other components of the final assembly. A manufacturing environment working on this strategy primarily has contact with the customer only at a sales level. The delivery time is medium to low and customer delivery time is based on the availability of major subassemblies. Demand uncertainty is handled by overplanning components and subassemblies. Assembly only takes place on receipt of a customer order and buffers of modules or options may exist. The product routing in the factory is typically fixed. No final product inventory buffer exists and the customer has limited input into the design of the product.

Make to order (MTO) describes a manufacturing facility which has many of the base components available along with the engineering designs, but the product is not actually completely specified. Manufacturing of the product begins upon receipt of a customer order and the configuration of the product is likely to change from the initial specification during the course of processing. Interaction with the client is extensive, normally involving sales and engineering, while the delivery time ranges from medium to large. Promise for completion of orders is based on the available capacities in manufacturing and engineering.

Finally, **Engineer to order (ETO)** is an extension of the MTO system with the engineering design of the product based on customer requirements and specifications. The same characteristics apply as in the case of MTO, but clearly customer interaction with the product supplier is even greater. True one of a kind products are engineered to order.

Table 12.1 compares and contrasts the various categories of manufacturing system. In reality, very few firms belong specifically to a particular category. Many firms would be classified as **hybrids** of the above. A firm might be a hybrid of MTS and ATO. This implies that it holds assembled products, for which there is a steady demand, in stock, but also has a facility whereby products can be configured according to customer needs. Many observers would argue that over the past twenty years or so manufacturing has moved along the continuum (see Figure 12.3) in a left-to-right direction from 'make to stock' to 'engineer to order' as customers increasingly demand customized products. The availability of computer-based information systems (e.g. materials requirements planning systems of the type described in Chapter 14), modelling and design support tools (e.g. CAD and process planning systems) and computer controlled manufacturing technology (e.g. computer numerically controlled machines and robots) has certainly facilitated this drift away from MTS systems and towards customer-driven manufacturing systems (Stendel and Desruelle, 1992).

FIGURE 12.3
Manufacturing continuum.

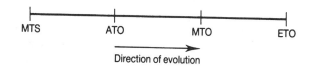

Table 12.1 Contrasts between MTS, ATO and MTO (adapted from Wemmerlov, 1984)

Aspect	MTS	ATO	MTO
Interface between manufacturing and customer	Low/distant	Primarily at sales level	Engineering and sales level
Delivery time	Short	Medium	Long
Production volume of each sales unit	High	Medium	Low
Product range	Low	Medium/high	High
Basis of production planning and control	Forecast	Forecast and backlog	Backlog
Order promising (based on . . .)	Available finished goods inventory	Availability of components and major subassemblies	Capacity for manufacturing or engineering
Handling of demand uncertainty	Safety stocks of sales units	Overplanning of components and subassemblies	Little uncertainty exists
Master scheduling* unit	Sales unit	Major components and subassemblies	End products, subassemblies, stocked fabricated parts
Final assembly schedule	Close correspondence to the master schedule	Determined by customer orders received by order entry	Covers most of the assembly operations
Bill of material† structuring	Standard BOMs (one BOM for each sales item)	Planning BOMs are used	BOMs are unique and created for each customer order

* The master schedule is the planned production schedule, defined by quantity and date, for top level items (normally either finished products or high level (in a bill of material sense) configurations of material); see Chapter 13.
† The engineering document that defines the product is the bill of material, which lists components of each assembly and subassembly (Orlicky, 1975).

12.4 Classification of PMS decisions

The success of a manufacturing business is heavily dependent on the translation of the future vision of the business through all layers in the organization. Unfortunately, in many manufacturing businesses, there is a lack of information flowing between the lower or operational levels and the top management level. To help overcome this it is essential that the manufacturing planning and control activities are described in

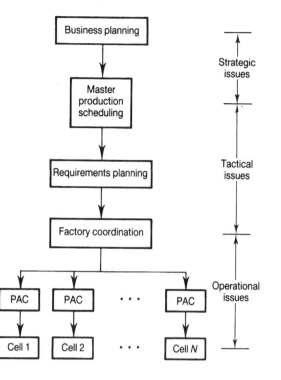

FIGURE 12.4
A simplified
architecture for
production planning
and control.

a logical, consistent and enduring systems framework. Here we define an architecture for production management systems (PMS) which seeks to achieve this goal (for a further treatment see Doumeingts (1990) and Bertrand *et al.* (1991)). We now present an overview of this production management systems architecture and outline it in terms of three main approaches, namely strategic, tactical and operational. The main elements in the architecture, as illustrated in Figure 12.4, are business planning, master production scheduling, requirements planning, factory coordination and production activity control.

The three levels represent different planning horizons. The length of these planning horizons may vary depending on which production environment one is operating in (i.e. job shop, batch, or mass production). The strategic planning horizon may cover one to five years; tactical planning one month to three years; and operational planning real-time to one week.

This PMS architecture reflects a situation where a factory has been subdivided (in so far as possible) into a series of group technology-based cells (see Chapter 9), where each cell is responsible for a family of products, assemblies or components and is managed by a production activity control system. The factory coordination module ensures that the individual cells interact to meet an overall production plan.

Each of the building blocks within the architecture will now be introduced in very general terms. Later, in Chapters 13 and 14, we will treat specific building blocks in greater detail.

Business planning

Business planning provides the plans that are necessary to drive the sales, manufacturing and financial activities of an organization. These plans define the markets to be addressed, the products to be manufactured, the required volumes and resources, and the financial impact of meeting the overall objectives set by the strategic planning systems within the organization. From a manufacturing standpoint, business planning addresses manufacturing strategic planning and long-range production planning. It will be discussed in more detail in Chapter 13.

Master production scheduling

The master production schedule (MPS) is a statement of the anticipated manufacturing schedule for selected items by quantity per planning period. It is a listing of the end items that are to be produced, the quantity of each item to be produced, and when they are to be ready for shipment. End items may be products (in an MTS environment), major assemblies or groups of components (in an ATO environment), or even individual parts used at the highest level in the product structure. The MPS provides the basis for making customer delivery promises, utilizing the capacity of the plant effectively, attaining the strategic objectives of the business as reflected in the long-range production plan, and resolving trade-offs between marketing and manufacturing. Unlike a forecast of demand, the MPS represents a *management commitment* authorizing the procurement of raw material and the production of component items. The MPS is a disaggregation of the long-range production plan developed at the higher level, and directly drives the requirements planning function at the lower level.

Requirements planning

Requirements planning resides in the tactical level of the PMS architecture. The main function of requirements planning is to take the build plan from the master schedule and explode the items in the MPS into its constituent components. This can be achieved using the bill of materials (BOM). (A BOM describes the structure of a product in terms of the assemblies, subassemblies and parts which go to make up the product and the relationship between them.) The requirements planning process results in a series of scheduled planned orders for each assembly, subassembly and component in the BOM. However, to produce a series of planned orders requires much more than the 'explosion' of that product using a BOM. Other facilities, such as lot sizing and pegging, are also required. These will be described further, with examples, in Chapter 13.

Factory coordination

The function of the factory coordination system is to manage the implementation of the MPS throughout the factory. The transition from requirements planning to factory coordination and production activity control marks the transition from tactical planning to short-term or operational planning and control. The problem is to ensure that the MPS which was exploded at the requirements planning stage is realized across the various work cells at the operational level of the factory. Factory coordination is therefore a set of procedures concerned with the planning and controlling of the flow of products at a plant level. These procedures should have close links with the manufacturing systems design task. This design task is concerned with the design of the production environment in terms of the identification and maintenance of product families and an associated product-based layout. The complexity of the factory coordination task is greatly reduced if the production environment is designed efficiently. The requirements planning system develops a set of *planned* orders, which are converted into *actual* orders by the factory coordination system. Factory coordination will be discussed in more detail in Chapter 14.

Production activity control (PAC)

PAC exists at the lowest level of the PMS architecture. PAC describes the principles and techniques used by management to plan in the short term, to control and to evaluate the production activities of the manufacturing organization. As it exists at the operational level of the PMS hierarchy, PAC operates in a very short time horizon, typically between one week and quasi real-time. It is desirable, for greater control, that PAC activities be as close to real-time as possible, and consistent with actual industry requirements. In Chapter 14 we discuss PAC in more detail.

Frequently the term shop floor control (SFC) is used to describe the operational control of the work flow through the factory floor. In our terminology SFC incorporates the combination of the factory coordination system and the production activity control systems.

We have discussed the building blocks that together constitute the production management system. Within our PMS architecture we distinguished the strategic, tactical and operational levels. Essentially we are following the approach of Anthony (1965) who identified three basic levels at which decisions are made. These are described below.

Strategic planning: facilities design

The major decisions at this level of the hierarchy reflect policy formulation, capital investment, physical facilities design and long-term growth and diversification strategies. These decisions are extremely important because, to a great extent, they are responsible for maintaining the competitive capabilities of the firm, determining its rate of growth, and eventually defining its success or failure. An essential characteristic of these strategic decisions is that they have long-lasting effects, thus requiring long planning horizons in their analysis. This, in turn, requires the consideration of uncertainties and risk attitudes in the decision-making process. Specifically, the decisions at this level relate to:

▶ determining the products to be designed, developed and manufactured;

▶ matching products to specific market sectors and hence meeting customer expectations;

▶ the overall design and development of the physical manufacturing system itself.

Management control (tactical planning): aggregate capacity planning

Anthony (1965) defines *management control* as 'the process by which managers assure resources are obtained and used effectively and efficiently in the accomplishment of the organisation's objectives'. The decisions made at this level are re-planned on a relatively frequent basis, perhaps every month or three months. They may deal with several plants, many distribution centres and many regional and local warehouses, with products requiring multi-stage fabrication and assembly processes, that serve broad market areas affected by strong randomness and seasonalities in their demand patterns. They usually involve the consideration of a medium-range time horizon, divided into several periods, and require significant aggregation of relevant managerial information. Typical issues decided on at this stage are:

▶ effective resource utilization and allocation in product design, development and manufacture;

▶ effective budgeting processes, frequently covering a one to three year time horizon;

▶ demand management, master production scheduling, and aggregate production planning.

Operational control: detailed production scheduling

After making an aggregate allocation of the resources of the firm, it is necessary to deal with the day-to-day operational and scheduling decisions. This stage of the decision-making process is termed **operational control**. The operational control decisions require the complete disaggregation of the information generated at higher levels into the details consistent with the managerial procedures followed in daily activities. Some typical decisions made at this level are:

▶ the assignment of customer orders to individual machines;

▶ the sequencing of these orders in the workshop;

▶ inventory accounting and inventory control activities;

▶ despatching, expediting and processing of orders;

▶ vehicular scheduling.

Integration between the PMS levels

In a production planning and control system, entities communicate in different ways. Strategic decisions are translated into tactical statements, which finally are expressed in production activities at the operational level. Although this information flow is complex, two generic classes can be distinguished. The first class concerns *qualitative* (or symbolic) information. This class supports highly abstract statements and therefore is predominant in strategic decision making. The second class consists of *numeric* information. Although its use is not limited to operational layers, this class represents

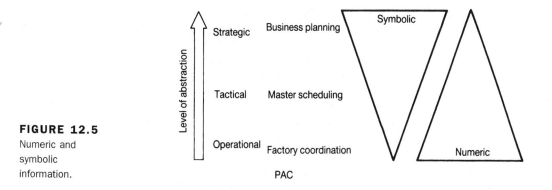

FIGURE 12.5
Numeric and
symbolic
information.

more or less a *quantitative translation* of goals and strategies, which are elaborated in symbolic terms. Figure 12.5 shows an overall representation of the amount of each information type at the different levels.

The importance of symbolic information decreases as we move from the strategic management level down to the operational level. Alternatively, the importance of numeric information grows as we proceed from the higher to the lower level. In the model for PMS presented here, each layer of the hierarchy translates 'some' symbolic information into 'some' numerical information. The translated 'chunk' of information corresponds to the result of a decision-making activity.

One of the main objectives of any production planning and control system must be 'integration' between the different layers in the hierarchy. Some of the main information flows between the different levels in the PMS architecture are now briefly described.

Business planning to MPS: qualitative data passed from business planning to MPS involves guidelines within which the lower level decision categories must operate. This information can include order agreements with suppliers and customers, inventory policies, overtime policies, guidelines on subcontracting and resource utilization levels. The long range production plan (LRPP) is the main quantitative input to MPS. See Chapter 13 for details of the LRPP.

MPS to business planning: the MPS feeds back information to business planning, giving aggregated reports on performance metrics, inventory, capacity and utilization levels.

MPS/requirements planning to factory coordination/PAC: the main inputs from the higher levels to the requirements planning system are the inventory, bill of materials and master production schedule data. The requirements planning module creates a series of 'planned orders' for factory coordination. Some qualitative information is also passed to the operational control layers. This is often in the form of guidelines or goals for the production department. Many of these goals may be conflicting in nature and often rules or heuristics are used to solve these conflicts. Examples of the type of goals are 'achieve lowest production cost', 'meet due dates', 'use overtime if necessary', 'keep work in progress as low as possible', etc.

Factory coordination/PAC to MPS/requirements planning: this information mainly takes the form of reports on achievements against the plan. These reports are aggregated across components, assemblies and products and may include information on meeting due dates, actual manufacturing lead times, number of orders shipped late, inventory levels, bottleneck information, etc.

The competitive success of a manufacturing company depends to a great extent on the complete integration of the various blocks within the production planning and control system. This means that decisions made at the strategic level, however qualitative they may be, must be translated completely down through the system to influence the master schedule. This will, in turn, affect requirements planning and will consequently reach into the operational level or day-to-day activities of the business. Similarly, the constraints at operational level, such as available capacity, must be analysed and fed back up the system into the tactical level. This, in effect, closes a very sensitive control loop which, if carefully monitored, leads to the maximum degree of control. If a company with a well-defined set of strategic goals can achieve maximum control over its manufacturing planning system then it will come one step further to attaining a definite competitive advantage over its rivals.

12.5 Cooperation with suppliers and customers

Earlier, in Section 12.3, we discussed the differences between order-driven manufacturing systems (assemble to order, make to order and engineer to order) and production-driven systems (make to stock). We indicated the drift towards customer-driven and hence order-driven systems. Customer-driven manufacturing requires that manufacturers develop close relationships with their customers in order to understand their precise product needs and be in a position to respond to them rapidly. Manufacturers also realize that their ability to satisfy customer needs is dependent in turn on the ability of the manufacturers' suppliers to deliver raw materials, components, subassemblies, services, etc., of the appropriate quality at the right price and on time.

This recognition of the key role of suppliers and the importance of being 'close to the customer', together with the emergence of modern telecomputing facilities, gave rise to the emergence of the extended enterprise. The extended enterprise arises partly from the attempts of manufacturers to gain competitive advantage from the linkages within their supplier chain and their distribution chain. Furthermore the availability of sophisticated computer- and telecommunications-based networks, and the emergence of data exchange standards, including STEP, PDES, etc., facilitate the creation of competitive advantage by creating enduring and mutually beneficial linkages with suppliers, distributors, etc.

The extended enterprise concept is also in tune with the concept of **core competence** and the **focused factory**. The focused factory is based on the idea that a plant which concentrates on a narrow range of products for a particular market segment is likely to outperform a more traditional plant with a wider range of activities, products and markets. By focusing on particular products, markets, skills, activities and technologies, the firm's objectives are more likely to be achieved without the compromises which are often required to be made in less focused environments. Core

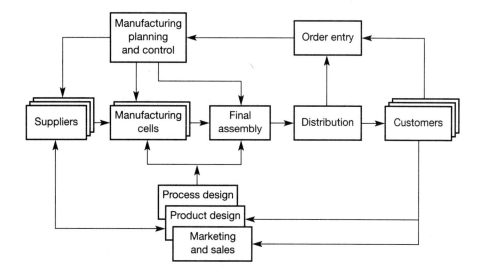

FIGURE 12.6
Integration in manufacturing.

competencies are those competencies which are central to the achievement of the firm's business objectives and which deliver low cost and/or product differentiation.

In a world of increasing specialization, the development of focus and core competence is necessary to achieve world-class performance. But world-class product delivery and service frequently require an amalgam of multiple world-class capabilities. The extended enterprise allows a firm to take advantage of external competencies and resources without owning them. The extended enterprise thus marks a shift in the traditional thinking about the structure and ownership of value-adding activities in the **value stream**. We are accustomed to thinking about a single enterprise with many functional departments, performing functions such as sales, marketing, design, engineering, manufacturing, assembly, distribution, etc. However, within today's global marketplace, entities from different enterprises, or indeed entities which are in themselves nominally independent enterprises, may come together to produce a particular product or service. This 'networking' of enterprises we term the extended enterprise and it is facilitated by today's information and telecommunications technologies. Figure 12.6 presents a simple model of the manufacturing business within the 'value chain' of supplier–manufacturer/assembler–distributor–customer. Up to now the emphasis has been on production planning and control within the 'four walls of the manufacturing plant'. However, as we will see later, the availability of electronic data interchange and sophisticated computer networks means that we now seek plan and control using electronic means across the whole value chain.

JIT (Just in Time), which will be considered in detail in Chapter 15, was probably the first approach to advocate strongly close customer involvement and indeed supplier involvement with the manufacturing company. Among other things, JIT emphasized customer involvement in the final scheduling of production systems and close cooperation with suppliers to ensure high-quality components and timely delivery. Thus already in the early 1980s JIT began to focus the view of manufacturing systems specialists on issues outside the four walls of the manufacturing plant, namely customer and supplier involvement.

12.5.1 EDI (Electronic Data Interchange)

Electronic data interchange (EDI) emerged as a reasonably mature technology in the mid to late 1980s. EDI (also known as paperless trading) may be defined as the electronic transfer from computer to computer (or from application to application) of commercial or administrative transactions using an agreed standard to structure the transaction or message data. Properly installed EDI offers benefits in terms of reduced data errors through the avoidance of double entry of data; reduced costs through improved business processes; reduced lead time, better service and customer support through faster and better business processes. EDI can be used across the value chain to improve the administrative systems and linkages between suppliers and the manufacturing plant and those between the manufacturing plant and its distributors and customers. Initially EDI was used to support business transactions (invoicing, purchase orders, purchase order acknowledgements, dispatch notifications, stock reports, etc.) between suppliers and their customers. However, as Figure 12.7 suggests, EDI and sophisticated computer networks can also facilitate the implementation of JIT ordering and Kanban supply techniques (see Chapter 15) within the value chain using electronic means.

EDI is now beginning to be used to exchange technological product data (Figure 12.7). In fact some analysts use the global term EDE (Electronic Data Exchange) to incorporate EDI and CDI (CADCAM Data Interchange). CDI is extremely important in an era of joint product and component development between suppliers and final assemblers and clearly promotes the realization of concurrent engineering. CDI is facilitated by the development of product data exchange and product modelling systems and standards such as PDES/STEP (see Chapter 7).

Clearly EDI is more than the automation of the transfer of data between business partners. EDI affects the way companies and enterprises interact with each other and the way they do business. For example, in many applications it fundamentally

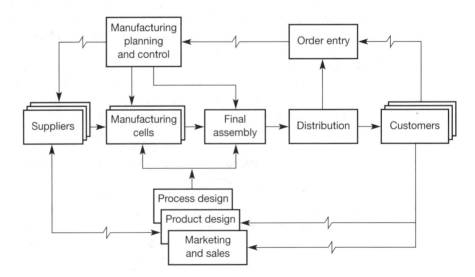

FIGURE 12.7
EDI within the
extended enterprise.

redefines the role of the purchasing organization; radically impacts the business processes used therein by, for example, automating simple but time-consuming activities and freeing up resources for other, more value-adding activities. In other words, EDI is not simply the automation of current methods; it makes newer and better methods possible. Over time EDI brings trading partners closer together, and supports the creation of the extended enterprise. In fact many of today's most advanced manufacturing companies use EDI to exchange production and purchasing information and to support joint (with suppliers and/or customers) engineering development teams. EDI can be said to be a technology which seeks to gain competitive advantage for its users by creating effective and cost-efficient linkages (in the language of Porter (1985) and his value chain model).

12.5.2 Value chain analysis

Manufacturing companies cannot address today's competitive challenges without enlisting the active support of their suppliers and working very closely with their customers. Porter (1985) introduced the concept of the value chain as a device to diagnose and ultimately enhance competitive advantage. Porter suggested that value chain analysis helps a manager to separate the underlying activities a firm performs in designing, producing, marketing and distributing its product. In Porter's own words 'the value chain is not a collection of independent activities but a set of interdependent activities', which are the building blocks of competitive advantage.

The critical points in Porter's work, from our point of view, are that value-adding activities are related by 'linkages in the overall value chain and that linkages can lead to competitive advantage'. In Porter's model, linkages define the relationships between the way one value-adding activity is performed and the cost and performance of another. Linkages can lead to competitive advantage in two ways: optimization and coordination. Linkages also facilitate trade-offs between particular value-adding activities; for example, a superior and therefore more costly product design using high-specification materials may well reduce inspection costs in manufacturing and after-sales service costs. To achieve optimization of linkages or even effective coordination across linkages requires effective information flow. In fact information systems are frequently the basis on which competitive advantage is achieved from linkage. For example, within a particular firm's value chain, competitive advantage can be gained by effectively integrating the design and manufacturing systems through the development and installation of a CADCAM system. In fact the effort to achieve an integrated CADCAM system is a recognition of the value of exploiting the linkage between design and manufacturing to reduce time to market, and to facilitate better product design and manufacturing. This is the realm of concurrent or simultaneous engineering which was discussed in Chapter 10.

Of course linkages also exist between a manufacturing firm's value chain and those of its suppliers, distributors and customers. Suppliers produce components or subassemblies which the manufacturing firm uses to build its own products and whose quality and price impact the quality and price of the firm's products. This fact is implicitly recognized in lean production thinking as we will suggest later when we come to discuss lean supply chains (see Section 12.6.1).

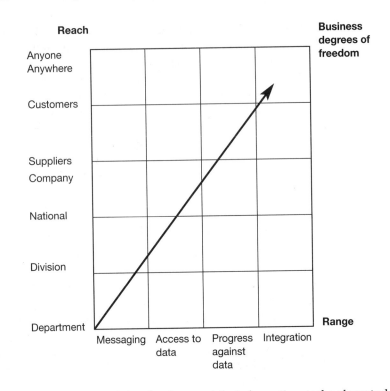

FIGURE 12.8
IT – reach and range.

Much of the thrust of the development in information technology today seeks to realize competitive advantage by exploiting linkages within the value chain, and indeed minimizing the transaction costs that arise from these linkages. We are thinking here particularly of the emergence of global computer networks (the Internet and intranets, for example) and the gradual integration of telecommunications and information technology. Referring to this topic, Keen (1991) uses the terms 'reach' and 'range'. 'Reach' is the extent to which a user can interact with other users across communications networks. 'Range', on the other hand, defines the type of interaction which is possible. At the lowest level the range may be limited to simple messaging using text data. At a higher level it may facilitate the exchange of complex CAD data between machines using different operating systems in different parts of the world.

The ultimate expansion of technology along the 'reach' and 'range' axes will eventually facilitate the integration of business processes and associated data across the globe (see Figure 12.8).

Electronic mail available to all members of a single firm represents a low level of reach and range. Electronic mail available to users on an Internet-style network offers tremendous reach but very little range. The use of EDI technology by manufacturing businesses reflects their attempts to expand their reach back into the supply chain and forward to the customer chain. The development of systems which expand the 'reach' and 'range' of a manufacturer's activities backwards and forwards in the supply chain has tremendous consequences for individual business processes and the way individual tasks are carried out. In many ways this forms the basis for a new area of endeavour, namely **business process re-engineering** (BPR) which we will look at in Section 12.8.

12.6 Lean production

The term 'lean production' was coined by the research team engaged in the IMVP (International Motor Vehicle Programme) research programme (see Womack *et al.*, 1990). Lean production was defined by contrasting it with two existing production systems approaches, namely **craft** production and **mass** production. In craft production skilled workers use relatively simple but very flexible tools to produce one-of-a-kind products to meet precise customer requirements. Consequently craft products are relatively expensive. In mass production highly skilled specialists design products to be made in high volumes by relatively unskilled operators using expensive special-purpose and inflexible machines. Standardized products are turned out in high volumes to be sold at reasonably low prices to customers. The mass producer has typically made very large investments, which it seeks to recover by keeping standard designs in production for as long as possible. The customer compromises variety to acquire low-cost products.

Lean production seeks to combine the advantages of the two methods of production, and seeks to avoid the high cost of craft products and the rigidity and standardization of mass production. Womack *et al.* claim that the origins of lean production go back to the early 1950s, when Toyota concluded that mass production was inappropriate to Japan and set about developing an alternative approach. This alternative approach sought to make a greater variety of vehicles as demanded by the Japanese market, focused on reducing set-up and changeover times at individual processes, developed new human resources ideas and quality ideas, and developed sophisticated supply chains to supply components and subassemblies to the plants. Further, these sophisticated supply chains were duplicated at the distribution and customer end, where a network of distributors and dealers was established. The dealer became part of the production system as Toyota gradually stopped building cars in advance for unknown buyers and slowly converted to a build to order, in reality an assemble to order, system in which the dealer was the first step in the Kanban system, actually sending orders for pre-sold cars to the factory for delivery to specific customers in 2 to 3 weeks. Thus **customer-driven manufacturing**, as distinct from stock-driven production, became a reality.

Since the early 1990s, the International Aerospace Programme (IARP) has been examining business efficiency in leading UK aerospace companies. This research programme, funded by industry and the Department of Trade and Industry (DTI), places particular emphasis on the potential benefits of adopting the lean production techniques developed in the automobile industry. According to Professor Andrew Graves, director of IARP (IMI, 1995), 'lean production can dramatically reduce product development and manufacturing lead times, as well as improve assembly productivity and product quality'. The concepts of lean production are not necessarily restricted to materials supply and inventory alone. Indeed, they can, and should, penetrate all value-adding activities of an enterprise. Professor Graves goes on to say that having learnt certain aspects of lean production – just in time, inventory control and concurrent engineering – 'we must now build and explore more radical changes, in particular to the organisation of R&D, engineering and production'.

12.6.1 Lean supply chains

An interesting aspect of the lean production approach is the role of suppliers in developing and sustaining competitive advantage. We will emphasize this supply chain issue because we see it as an important aspect of production planning and control.

The Japanese supply chain is based on a small number of key suppliers, sometimes called first-tier suppliers, who in turn engage subcontractors in what becomes a **supply pyramid**. There are very close relationships between each link in the chain and its lower-level suppliers – design engineers are engaged early in the design process of the customer company. In the auto industry for example, the first-tier suppliers have full responsibility for component systems and subassemblies that perform to an agreed performance specification in the finished car. The supplier's development team, with support from resident design engineers from the auto manufacturer and the second-tier suppliers, conduct detailed development and engineering (see Womack *et al.*, 1990).

Clearly the supply chains and 'supplier pyramids' require substantial sharing of proprietary information on costing, volumes and production techniques. The relationships between the auto producer and the various tiers of suppliers are managed through regional supplier associations. Through these associations new techniques including SPC (Statistical Process Control), CAD, etc., are disseminated.

The extent of these supply chains can be gauged from the following figures. According to Womack *et al.* Toyota Motor Company accounts for 27% of the total cost of the materials, tools and finished parts required to make a car. The equivalent figure for General Motors in the United States was at that time 70%.

Lean supply chains completely redefine the role of the purchasing organization in the manufacturing firm. Whereas the traditional role of purchasing was to define alternative suppliers, negotiate lower prices and expedite delivery to meet demand, lean manufacturing refocuses and greatly extends the role of the purchasing function. The 'Lean Production' purchasing function must work to develop an extended organization or enterprise based on close collaboration within the supply chain. Essentially the purchasing function must seek to develop partnership relationships with a smaller number of suppliers who themselves form the first tier in a supply pyramid. In the context of the extended enterprise the purchasing department must move towards a role which is essentially that of **external resources** (i.e. supply chain) **management**. This external resource management role supports the early involvement of suppliers in new product development and design, very close customer–supplier relationships in terms of the sharing of cost and technical information previously considered proprietary, and the sharing of specialists, etc.

A recent article in the Business Section of the UK newspaper *Independent on Sunday* (19 March 1995, page 3) indicated the impact of lean supply chains in the UK. A number of Japanese car manufacturers have established final assembly plants in the UK and therefore have economic and business interests in developing UK-based automotive parts suppliers. According to this article the UK is developing a 'two tier manufacturing sector, divided into those companies that supply the Japanese and those that don't'. It seems that the UK-based large Japanese auto manufacturers are putting 'dramatically higher effort into supplier development'. It seems that Toyota, in particular, works with the manufacturing functions in their suppliers, 'other customers tend to work with commercial and purchasing departments but (Toyota) look at the manufacturing systems' and seek to improve them. The methods are passed back down the supply chain, 'at the end of the day, if our own suppliers are not supplying us products of the right quality, that affects us. They are the weakest link in the chain.'

12.7 Time-based competition

Time-based competition refers to gaining advantage by delivering products and services faster than one's competitors. As long ago as 1989 Peters suggested that 'Time is becoming the main battlefield – and weapon – of competition'. It is clear, from many sources, that time has emerged as a dominant factor in determining and sustaining manufacturing and indeed competitive advantage. Suri (1994), while extolling the virtues of QRM (Quick Response Manufacturing), a euphemism for time-based competition within the manufacturing – as opposed to banking, insurance, hospitals, etc. – sector, supports this view. Many other authors, such as Blackburn *et al.* (1992), Charney (1991), Merrills (1989), Peters (1989), Syan and Menon (1994), Muntslag (1993), Parsaei and Sullivan (1993), Pfeifer *et al.* (1994), Stalk (1988) Stalk and Hout (1992), Suri (1988, 1989, 1994) and Warnecke (1993), echo similar sentiments.

Response time is significant from two perspectives:

1. **Time to market** is the time it takes to develop a new product, that is from firm product concept to initial market availability. This is an important competitive issue in markets where technology is changing rapidly and where product life cycles are short and getting shorter.

2. **Customer order fulfilment** time is the time it takes to process an individual customer order. It represents the time a customer must wait from placement of order to delivery of product. We will look at each of these issues separately.

12.7.1 Time to market

As discussed in Chapter 10, concurrent engineering (CE) or simultaneous engineering seeks to reduce time to market for new products while simultaneously increasing product quality and reliability and reducing the manufacturing and maintenance costs, etc. It works right from the initial product ideas through the manufacturing and assembly to the final service and support activities.

Womack *et al.* (1990) have highlighted the success of the Japanese automobile industry in reducing time to market for new products. According to Womack *et al.*, the Japanese auto makers had a 42 month new product introduction cycle in the mid-1980s. Currently they plan for a 24 month cycle. Clark and Fujimoto (1989) studied the strategic and economic impact of reduced time to market. They estimated that each 1 day delay in introducing a new mid-size car to the international market represents 1 million ECUs in lost profits. Jones (1992) agrees that product development time is a critical competitive factor in the automotive sector and quotes statistics which illustrate the superiority of Japanese auto makers: in the mid-1980s, for a comparable project the European and the American auto makers took about 60 months from product concept to market launch, compared with 46 months for the Japanese. Pfeifer *et al.* (1994) make the position very clear when they state 'It is not the best and cheapest which will survive, but the fastest'.

12.7.2 Customer order fulfilment time

We must also look at time in the context of delivery time to individual customers. In the past, manufacturers ensured rapid response to customers by carrying stocks of finished goods. However, this option is no longer available for many manufacturers, because of the increasing tendency of customers to acquire customized products. As indicated earlier, there is an increasing tendency for manufacturers to move away from MTS (Make to Stock) manufacturing systems and move towards ATO (Assemble to Order) and indeed MTO (Make to Order) approaches. The market demand for fast turnaround on increasingly complex and customized products is leading to tremendous development in manufacturing planning and control systems and indeed distribution planning and control systems.

Quick response in retailing

Hammond (1993) provides an excellent overview of the background to and the nature of 'quick response' in the retailing sector. She argues that the growing ability of retailers and manufacturers to collect, transmit and interpret data is enabling far-reaching changes in the buying and selling practices of retailers. These changes are in turn impacting strongly on the manufacturers who supply products to these large retailers. Large retailers enjoy the economies of scale benefits which result from massive product volumes and at the same time exploit their in-depth market knowledge (gained through information technology and telecommunications) to provide products and services carefully tuned to the precise needs of local markets. To exploit their knowledge of aggregate and local market trends, retailers seek to develop a quick response capability in order to respond quickly to customer demand. To achieve 'quick response' these retailers must choose manufacturers (as suppliers) who have the necessary capabilities and then establish coordinating mechanisms to ensure fast and accurate flow of data and product through the supply chain.

According to Hammond (1993) a quick response strategy involves the following necessary elements:

▶ An effective integrated information pipeline (including product identification and tracking systems), EDI facilities, video conference systems to support on-line buyers meetings and the fast flow of information from the retailer to the supplier.

▶ A short product development cycle, that is very short time to market.

▶ Consumer testing to narrow product selections for specified market segments (Benetton has POS (Point of Sale) terminals in key retail outlets, which are electronically connected to the central system in Italy rapidly to capture demand and order information. Benetton uses these sites to collect customer reactions and get early demand information, in order to support better preliminary production plans, and commitments to suppliers). Today large retailers (J. C. Penney in the United States, for example) try to make short-term and frequent commitments based on end-consumer feedback rather than on marketing forecasts.

▶ Effective forecasting and replenishment systems.

▶ Rapid order fulfilment.

▶ Short-cycle manufacturing.

In state-of-the-art continuous product replenishment (CPR) systems, EPOS (Electronic Point of Sale) terminals record when a product is sold and therefore no longer in stock. The information can immediately be transmitted to the manufacturer's computer system which can then automatically organize replenishment of this stock at the appropriate location, whether this is the retailer's own warehouse or direct to the store itself. In a variation on this model, not involving EPOS, 'merchandizers' visit key customers – typically the stores of multiples on a regular (often daily) basis, review their sales and stock positions, agree order levels with retail management, store those orders in hand-held terminals and transmit orders back to the supplier for delivery (normally overnight delivery).

The large US-based multiples are moving towards line site stocking (LSS), where the supplier effectively retains ownership of the product, until the customer orders or buys. The US retailer Wal-Mart has this arrangement with virtually all of its suppliers. Effectively Wal-Mart offers a retailing service to manufacturers, who are paid when the product is sold and taken off the shelves.

Clearly large retailers (the multiples) place tremendous demands on their suppliers. Individual retailers have developed sophisticated codes of practice which place rigorous demands on suppliers in terms of the transport, packaging, labelling and even the precise arrival times of deliveries at the retail stores and/or their regional depots. Increasingly they are requiring the use of EDI technology to support the order placement, delivery and invoicing activity. One case in point is J. Sainsbury plc in the UK which has a 'Primary Distribution Manual' which defines precise standards and requirements for food safety, supplier service standards, packaging and labelling, receipts procedures, invoice processing and finally environmental requirements (e.g. reduction of packaging volume). CPR and LSS are practised today in the United States, are under review by the large multiples in Europe, and are likely to be common practice in Europe in a very short time.

Figure 12.9 indicates the type of environment which manufacturers who supply large retailers are facing. It is essentially an extended enterprise environment.

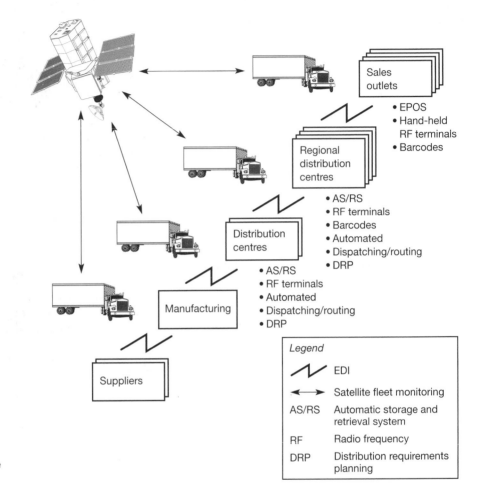

FIGURE 12.9
One scenario of the future supply chain.

12.8 Business process re-engineering

The availability of technologies such as CADCAM, CAPM (Computer-Aided Production Management) and the new opportunities available to work closely with suppliers (supply chain management) and distributors using EDI and telecomputing have not always delivered the level of increases in productivity and timeliness for which management had hoped. Many analysts believe that the heavy investments in technology, particularly information technology, have not delivered their potential, because manufacturing enterprises often use the new technology to automate existing and frequently antiquated ways of doing business (see Lyons, 1995). In many cases the existing business processes remain intact and the new computer systems simply speed them up. Hammer (1990) coined the phrase business process re-engineering (BPR) in an article in the *Harvard Business Review* appropriately subtitled 'Don't automate, obliterate'.

Whereas other approaches, for example total quality management, JIT (Just In Time) and WCM (World-Class Manufacturing) (see Chapter 15), seek to inculcate a culture of 'continuous improvement' into the manufacturing enterprise, BPR offers itself as an approach which promises dramatic, even revolutionary, change in key performance measurements (see McSwiney, 1995). Also, whereas JIT and WCM tend to focus on shop floor operations, for example lot size reduction programmes, set-up reduction programmes, establishment of product-flow-style layouts, BPR tends to focus on 'white-collar' and organizational process styles of activities. In particular BPR tends to be used to analyse the data, work and process flows within and between organizations. According to Davonport (1993) a business process is a set of logically related tasks which are executed to achieve a particular business outcome. Furthermore business processes in general cross organizational boundaries. Hence the redesign or the re-engineering of a business process involves tasks which cut across individual organizations.

The very activity of establishing an integrated supply chain involves creating active linkages between organizations which up to then were mutually exclusive, and developing new ways of working to realize the potential benefit of the new links. Consider the following example. A small manufacturing enterprise (SME), which manufactures sheet metal parts to order, has a major customer who is a major supplier of telecommunications equipment (PABXs – Private Automatic Branch Exchanges). Over the years the companies have developed strong relationships of mutual trust. The SME has developed its internal manufacturing and quality processes to the stage that its customer (the large supplier of telecommunications equipment) now has such confidence in its quality and reliability that the customer has dispensed with the 'incoming inspection' activity and the SME supplier now ships to stock. The customer now wishes to develop an even closer relationship with the supplier and to use EDI technology to automate the linkages between the two companies. The availability of the EDI link allows a complete review of the process by which the two companies interacted.

Let us consider the situation prior to EDI. We will refer to the large telecommunications systems supplier as Company A and the SME supplier of sheet metal components as Company B. Prior to EDI the situation was as follows.

Every 6 months Company A would provide Company B with a statement of its likely requirements for the three components Company B manufactured and supplied to it. It would also indicate its likely 'draw-down' pattern for the components, that is quantities to be supplied every week, every day, etc. Company B was now in a position to plan its own capacity and raw materials orders for the period. Once this 'blanket pseudo-order' had been agreed, Company A would issue actual orders for batches of parts, following as closely as possible the order pattern indicated in the original statement of requirements. Company B would then manufacture and dispatch, with the associated delivery notes, the required volumes of components. On receipt at Company A's premises, the delivery note would be signed and returned to Company B. The returned and signed delivery note to Company B would trigger its accounts person to create an invoice to be posted to Company A. The receipt of the invoice at Company A would trigger its accounts payable to initiate an accounts payment process, which involved an internal check (in Company A) that the parts were indeed received, the raising/signing of a cheque and its dispatch to Company B. This reasonably complex and indeed error-prone process was repeated frequently.

The decision to use EDI technology offered an opportunity to re-engineer the whole process. The outcome can be described as follows: Company A still presents Company B with a blanket 'pseudo-order' for the following 6 months. Company B now has electronic access to the work in progress levels of the components it supplies to Company A. It has agreed a minimum stock level to be located at Company A's premises. It supplies components on a 'two-bin' system to Company A. No orders, dispatch notes or invoices are issued. As the final assembly line in Company A's premises releases finished product to the finished goods warehouse, it calculates the volume of used components supplied by Company B and credits Company B with this. As a result monthly payments are made directly via bank transfer to Company B.

Clearly this is a simple example, but it indicates the possibilities for process redesign inherent in using EDI technology to create extended-enterprise-style relationships and integrated supply chains. Other shared business processes are clearly more complex, and require much deeper analysis to understand them in detail and to develop new improved processes. BPR software tools are available to help in this task of analysis and redesign (see Bradley *et al.*, 1995).

12.9 Conclusion
•••••••••••••••••

In this chapter we have provided a brief introduction to production planning and control systems in the context of the evolving manufacturing system. Further, we have outlined a simplified architecture for a production planning and control system. We have also looked beyond production planning and control, in order to understand the interaction of the production planning systems with customers and suppliers. In the next two chapters we will consider elements of that architecture in more detail.

References and further reading
•••••••••••••••••••••••••••••••••••

Anthony R. N. (1965). *Planning and Control Systems: A Framework for Analysis*. Cambridge, MA: Harvard University Press.

Bertrand J. W. M., Wortmann J. C. and Wijngaard J. (1991). *Production Control: A Structural and Design Oriented Approach*. Amsterdam: Elsevier.

Blackburn J. D., Elrod T. Lindsley W. B. and Zahorik A. J. (1992). The strategic value of response time and product variety. In *Manufacturing Strategy – Process and Content* (ed. C. A. Voss). London: Chapman & Hall, 261–81.

Bradley P., Browne J., Jackson S. and Jagdov H. (1995). BPR – A study of the software tools currently available. *Computer in Industry*.

Browne J. (1995). The extended enterprise – manufacturing and the value chain. In *Balanced Automation Systems – Architecture and design methods* (ed. Luis M. Camarina-Matos and Hamideh Afsarmanesh). London: Chapman & Hall, 5–17.

Browne J., Sackett P. J. and Wortmann J. C. (1994). Industry requirements and associated research issues in the extended enterprise. *Proc. IMSE'94 Workshop on Integrated Manufacturing Systems Engineering*, Grenoble, France, December 12–14 (ed. F. Vernadat).

Browne J., Sackett P. J. and Wortmann J. C. (1995). Future manufacturing systems – towards the extended enterprise. *Computers in Industry*. **25**, 235–54.

Charney C. (1991). *Time to Market: Reducing Product Lead Time*. Dearborn: Society of Manufacturing Engineers.

Chryssolouris G. and Lee M. (1992). An assessment of flexibility in manufacturing systems. *Manufacturing Review*. **5**(2), 105–16.

Clark T. and Fujimoto T. (1989). Product development in the world auto industry. *Brooklyn Papers on Economic Activity*. **3**.

Davenport T. H. (1993). *Process innovation, reengineering work through Information Technology*. Boston, MA: Harvard Business School Press.

Doumeingts G. (1990). Computer aided process planning and computer aided production management. In *Product Development and Production Engineering in Manufacturing Industries* (ed. C. Foulard). New York: Hemisphere.

Foulard C. (Editor) (1990). *Product Development and Production Engineering in Manufacturing Industries*. New York: Taylor & Francis.

Hammer M. (1990). Re-engineering work: Don't automate, obliterate, *Harvard Business Review*. July–August, 104–12.

Hammer M. and Champy J. (1993). *Reenginering the Enterprise*. New York: Harper Collins.

Hammond J. H. (1993). Quick response in retail/manufacturing channels. In *Globalisaton, Technology and Competition* (ed. S. P. Bradley, J. A. Hansman and R. C. Nolan). Boston, MA: Harvard Business School Press.

Hars A., Heib R. Kruse, Chr. Michely J. and Scheer A. W. (1992). Reference models for data engineering. *CIM. Proc. 8th CIM Europe Conference*, Birmingham.

Hauser J. R. and Clausing D. (1988). The house of quality. *Harvard Business Review*. May–June, 63–73.

Hayes R. H., Wheelwright S. C. and Clark K. B. (1988). *Dynamic Manufacturing – Creating the Learning Organisation*. New York: The Free Press.

Higgins P. (1991). Master production scheduling: a key node in an integrated approach to production management systems. PhD Thesis, University College, Galway.

Hirsch B. E. and Thoben K. D. (Editors) (1992). *'One-Of-A-Kind' Production: New Approaches*. Amsterdam: Elsevier.

IMI (1995). Innovative Manufacturing Initiative Newsletter, DTI, UK, Issue 9, Oct. 1995.

Jones D. T. (1992). Beyond the Toyota production system – the era of lean production. In *Manufacturing Strategy – Process and Content* (ed. C. A. Voss). London: Chapman & Hall, 189–210.

Keen P. G. W. (1991). *Shaping the future: business design through information technology*. Boston, MA: Harvard Business School Press.

Kusiak A. (Editor) (1987). *Modern Production Management Systems*. Amsterdam: Elsevier.

Lev B. (Editor) (1986). *Production Management Methods and Studies*. Amsterdam: Elsevier.

Manufacturing engineer in the 21st century. Profile 21, Executive Summary.

Lyons G. (1995). Application of information technology in the redesign and implementation of business processes. In *Re-engineering the Enterprise* (ed. J. Browne and D. O'Sullivan). London: Chapman & Hall.

McSwiney J. (1995). BPR for SMEs. In *Re-engineering the Enterprise* (ed. J. Browne and D. O'Sullivan). London: Chapman & Hall.

Merrills R. (1989). How Northern Telecom competes in time. *Harvard Business Review*. July–August.

Muntslag D. R. (1993). *Managing Customer Order Driven Engineering*. Hilversum: Moret Ernst and Young.

Orlicky J. (1975). *Material Requirements Planning: The New Way of Life in Production and Inventory Management*. New York: McGraw-Hill.

Parsaei H. R. and Sullivan W. G. (1993). *Concurrent Engineering – Contemporary Issues and Modern Design Tools*. London: Chapman & Hall.

Peters T. (1989). Tomorrow's companies. *The Economist*. 4 March.

Pfeifer T., Eversheim W. Konig W. and Weck M. (1994). *Manufacturing Excellence – The Competitive Edge*. London: Chapman & Hall.

Porter M. E. (1985). *Competitive Advantage*. New York: The Free Press.

Porter M. (1988). *Competitive Advantage: Creating and Sustaining Superior Performance*. New York: Free Press.

Pine B. J. (1993). *Mass Customisation, The New Frontier in Business Competition*. Boston, MA: Harvard Business School Press.

Plossol G. W. and Wight O. W. (1967). *Principles and Techniques*. Englewood Cliffs, NJ: Prentice Hall.

Rolstadas A. (1988). *Computer Aided Production Management*. New York: Springer.

Rolstadas A. (1991). CIM and one of a kind production. In *Computer Applications in Production and Engineering* (ed. G. Doumeingts, J. Browne and M. Tomljanovich). Amsterdam: Elsevier Science.

Schonberger R. J. (1987). *World Class Manufacturing Casebook – Implementing JIT and TQC*. New York: The Free Press.

Schonberger R. J. (1990). *Building a Chain of Customers*. London: Hutchinson Business Books.

Stalk G. Jr (1988). Time – the next source of competitive advantage. *Harvard Business Review*. July–August.

Stalk G. Jr and Hout T. M. (1992). *Competing Against Time*. New York: The Free Press.

Stendel H. J. and Desruelle P. (1992). *Manufacturing in the Nineties*. New York: Van Nostrand Reinhold.

Suri R. (1988). RMT puts manufacturing at the helm. *Manufacturing Engineering*. (2).

Suri R. (1989). Lead time reduction through rapid modelling. *Manufacturing Systems*. July.

Suri R. (1994). Common misconceptions and blunders in implementing quick response manufacturing. *Proc. SME AUTOFACT '94 Conference*, Detroit.

Syan C. S. and Menon U. (1994). *Concurrent Engineering – Concepts, Implementation and Practice*. London: Chapman & Hall.

Warnecke H. J. (1993). *The Fractal Company – A Revolution in Corporate Culture*. Berlin: Springer.

Wemmerlov U. (1984). Assemble to order manufacturing: implications for materials management. *Journal of Operations Management*. **4**(4), 347–368.

Womack J. P., Jones D. T. and Roos D. (1990). *The Machine that Changed the World*. New York: Rawson Macmillan.

Wortmann J. C. (1992). Factory of the future: towards an integrated theory for one of a kind production. In *One of a Kind Production* (ed. B. E. Hirsch and K. D. Thoben). Amsterdam: North-Holland.

Exercises
··············

12.1 Distinguish clearly between mass, batch and jobbing shop production.

12.2 Define the terms 'make to stock', 'assemble to order', 'make to order'.

12.3 What is a bill of materials?

12.4 What do you understand by the term 'extended enterprise'?

12.5 Distinguish clearly between 'time to market' and 'customer order fufilment time'.

13 Requirements planning systems

Chapter objectives

When you have completed studying the material in this chapter you should be able to:

- ▶ understand clearly the different roles of the business planning, master production scheduling and requirements planning functions within a production management system;
- ▶ identify the main decision categories in business planning;
- ▶ understand the role of long-range production planning;
- ▶ understand the structure of the master production schedule (MPS) record, and be able to calculate the projected available balance (PAB), the available to promise (ATP) line and the cumulative ATP line in this record;
- ▶ apply relatively simple forecasting techniques to generate forecast demand for the MPS record;
- ▶ understand the structure of a bill of materials (BOM), and understand the logic associated with the processing of bills of materials and the generation of planned orders for assemblies, components etc;
- ▶ understand the concept of pegging in requirements planning systems;
- ▶ apply reasonably simple lot-sizing techniques to convert planned orders into actual orders;
- ▶ understand clearly the net change and regenerative approaches to requirements planning;
- ▶ understand the difficulty of installing requirements planning systems in practice;
- ▶ understand the nature and operation of DRP (Distribution Requirements Planning) systems.

Chapter contents

13.1 Introduction

In this chapter we look at three elements of the PMS architecture described previously. In particular, we focus on the requirements planning element of this architecture, but we will also look briefly at the higher level subsystems, namely business planning and master scheduling. We will also include a short discussion on the implementation of these systems in industry. A large part of the discussion in this chapter is taken up with the actual requirements planning system. Materials requirements planning explodes the requirements of top-level products, defined in the master schedule, through the bill of materials (BOM). A BOM describes the parent–child relationship between an assembly and its component parts. Projected gross demand is then compared to available inventory and open orders over the planning horizon at each level in the BOM. A set of time-phased planned manufacturing and purchase orders is generated on the basis of this comparison. We will introduce this discussion of requirements planning through a simple example.

Firstly, however, before we discuss requirements planning, we will quickly review the techniques used at the master scheduling level, and also provide a brief overview of business planning in so far as it affects production planning and control.

13.2 Business planning

Business planning is a very complex topic with far-reaching implications. Here we will take a brief overview of business planning and focus exclusively on the production planning and control aspects of this important topic. Clearly companies that focus exclusively on the short-term issues to the detriment of longer term planning run the risk of not being in business when the long term comes to pass! Success is built on a vision of what the future will look like and the role that the company perceives itself playing in that vision. The various elements, such as products, technologies, marketing image, customers, suppliers and competitors are important in describing a company's business strategy. Manufacturing must also be included in this vision, as it is an important part of a firm's business planning process.

A manufacturing strategy is formed by the decisions taken in, and in connection with, manufacturing, which have a strategic influence on the company's competitive approach. The purpose of a manufacturing strategy is to direct a company's manufacturing resources in a manner that supports the competitive ability of that company. Manufacturing strategy is devised to support certain order winning criteria (OWC) which have traditionally revolved around the areas of price and quality. In today's business environment, competition is frequently based on delivery performance, and price and quality are considered to be necessary prerequisites for continued existence in the market place.

The following are some different definitions of manufacturing strategy:

A Manufacturing Strategy describes the competitive leverage required of – and made possible by – the production function. It analyses the entire manufacturing function relative to its ability to provide such leverage, on which task it then focuses each element of the manufacturing structure. It also allows the structure to be managed, not just the short-term, operational details of cost, quality and delivery. And it spells out an internally consistent set of structural decisions to forge manufacturing into a strategic weapon. (Skinner, 1974)

. . . a Manufacturing Strategy consists of a sequence of decisions that, over time, enables a business unit to achieve a desired manufacturing structure, infrastructure, and set of specific capabilities. (Hayes and Wheelwright, 1984)

There are six decision categories involved in the development of a manufacturing strategy (see Figure 13.1). These are:

1. Capacity decisions.

2. Facilities decisions.

3. Vertical integration decisions (make or buy).

4. Process decisions.

5. Infrastructure decisions.

6. Human resources decisions.

Each of these decision categories is now briefly discussed. A full discussion on the details of each decision process is beyond the scope of this textbook. The interested reader is referred to Hayes and Wheelwright (1984).

Capacity decisions

Capacity decisions can take many different shapes and forms. They can be expressed for example in terms of production equipment, factory floor space and human

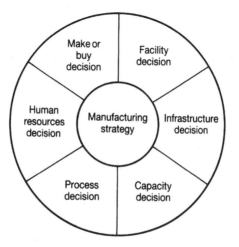

FIGURE 13.1
Composition of manufacturing strategy.

resources. Clearly, decisions regarding equipment or space have different risk levels attached to them. These risks levels are dependent on the amount of investment a firm has to commit. Hence, it is essential when making a capacity decision that all of these factors (i.e. space and equipment) are taken into consideration. The ability to strike a balance between these capacity decisions is critical to the success of the business planning function. The main factors influencing the capacity decisions are as follows:

1. Anticipated future customer demands.

2. The cost of expanding capacity (e.g. the cost of buying new equipment).

3. The technology currently available and the rate of technological change.

4. The manner in which competitors are likely to react (e.g. other competitors may jump on the bandwagon of a capacity increment, which may well result in the creation of excess production in the industry).

   When dealing with capacity decisions, three basic questions need to be answered:

▶ *When* should capacity be added?

▶ *How much* capacity should be added?

▶ *Where should* capacity be added?

Facilities decisions

The capacity and facilities decision categories are closely related. Any decision by a corporation to expand or to shrink its capacity has implications for its facilities decisions and vice versa. This does not imply that other decision categories are not affected. Factors influencing the facilities decision include:

▶ forecast increase or decrease in demand;

▶ technology change;

▶ change in the external environment, including for example, changes in government policies, on shifts in public opinion;

▶ opportunities to make significant impact on the company's competitive position.

Facilities decisions are concerned with the assignment of specific products, customers and markets to individual facilities. One of the first problems that arises, when dealing with the facilities decision, concerns the availability of the shop floor space in a plant in anticipation of a future increase in demand. Examples of other aspects of the facilities decision concern the layout of the plant and the problem of *where* to locate additional plants.

Make or buy decisions

Make or buy decisions are concerned with the choice of which product or process technologies are to be kept in-house and which are to be subcontracted to external suppliers. It is a very important decision within a manufacturing strategy, since it dictates such choices as capacity, facilities, process and, to some extent, infrastructure. The decision is particularly relevant today, given the perception that factories and businesses focused on core competences are likely to be more successful than those which form highly vertically integrated enterprises (see Womack *et al.*, 1991). The aim of the decision is to allow the manufacturing firm to concentrate on that which adds most value and those technologies which enhance its competitive position and strengthen it in terms of its order-winning criteria (OWC) while removing unnecessary management complexity.

Process decisions

Choosing a particular process for a manufacturing plant is becoming a highly important decision in today's manufacturing environment. This is so because the tasks performed in a manufacturing plant are no longer merely a simple case of either jobbing, batch, assembly or continuous processing. In fact, many manufacturing plants involve a combination of these manufacturing processes. When determining a process choice, the issues that need to be addressed include:

▶ *The level of customization:* if a firm's marketing strategy is to provide quality and a high degree of customized products, then the highly flexible nature of job shop processing is more attractive than the alternatives. Thus, the order-winning criteria of a firm can provide guidelines regarding the type of process to select. The relationships between a product and its process are shown in Figure 13.2. As shown in the figure, the level of standardized product increases as we move towards a continuous process.

▶ *The expected volume of product:* the volume of the market demand also influences a process decision. Figure 13.3 shows the relationship between the volume of products produced and the processes employed.

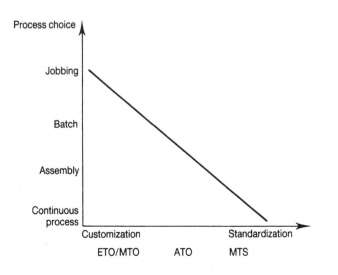

FIGURE 13.2
The relationship between process choice and degree of customization.

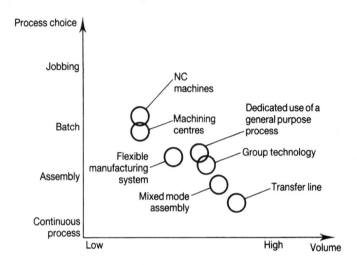

▶ *The requirements of the process:* these refer largely to the level of skill and experience that the personnel of a firm are required to possess.

Other factors that need to be considered include the ability of the firm to integrate the process with existing processes and equipment, the investment required, the firm's competitive ability and the technical and commercial risks involved in employing a particular process. Questions might arise, for example, regarding the maturity of a proposed process, whether or not it uses a proven technology etc.

Infrastructure decisions

Manufacturing infrastructure can be described as the policies and organization by which manufacturing accomplishes its work, specifically production and inventory control systems, cost and quality control systems, workforce management policies and organizational structure (Skinner, 1974).

Human resources decisions

Decisions made in the other categories have a bearing on the human resources decision and conversely successful implementation of the other categories is dependent on the correct human resource structures being in place. This decision category involves two main decisions:

▶ *The design of the organization:* this involves the identification of the individual functions within the organization, the overall organizational structure and the design of the decision-making system.

▶ *The design of the reward system:* these include rewards for compliance with rules, excellent performance, group rewards etc.

13.2.1 The long-range production plan

The long-range production plan is the main quantitative output from the business planning function. This plan is typically stated in terms of units of production, monetary units, groups of products, volumes etc. The long-range production planning process involves many trade-offs in the strategy of a firm and should at least address the following factors:

▶ the total factory (or multi-plant) load;

▶ the make or buy decision on the degree of factory vertical integration;

▶ the degree of capacity flexibility;

▶ investment levels;

▶ product life cycles;

▶ personnel policies and organizational structure.

These issues are all considered over a time-scale of less than or equal to the horizon of the manufacturing strategy and greater than that of the master production schedule (MPS). The plan includes a statement on the volumes of particular product families required to be manufactured, within large time buckets (the units of time into which the planning horizon is divided). The most obvious difference between the strategy and the plan is the change from an emphasis on numbers. The long-range production plan bridges the gap between the language of production (production volumes, time-scales, staff numbers, capacity hours) and that of senior management (revenue, profits, return on investment). The plan provides the interface between the strategy and the MPS. In some companies the plan may be called a 'factory budget', but budgets are usually expressed in financial terms, whereas a production plan should include product numbers as well as financial targets.

13.3 Master production scheduling

A master production schedule (MPS) is generally defined as an anticipated build schedule for manufacturing end items or product options. As such, it is a statement of production, not a statement of market demand. The MPS takes into account capacity limitations and forms the basic communication link with manufacturing.

The availability of a flexible MPS framework is a fundamental requirement in a state of the art manufacturing planning and control system. MPS resides at the interface between the strategic and tactical planning levels in the PMS architecture. As such, it is a key decision-making activity. The demands coming from business planning are translated at the MPS level into demands on the manufacturing system. The MPS becomes *an anticipated statement of production* from which all other schedules at the lower levels are derived.

A detailed review of the functionality of an MPS system is beyond the scope of this book. What we can say is that the MPS is driven by a combination of actual customer orders and forecasts of likely orders. In general we might expect that customer orders would predominate in the early part of the MPS planning horizon and the later part would be made up primarily of forecasts. The *planning horizon* refers to the span of time which the MPS covers. Clearly the planning horizon should extend beyond the longest cumulative lead time* for any MPS item. In general, we can say that MPS items are finished products in the case of make to stock plants and high level (in the BOM) assemblies and items in the case of assemble to order or make to order plants.

Before we look at MPS procedure we will briefly review some of the more widely used forecasting techniques. Such forecasting techniques are frequently used to develop product demand forecasts in an MPS system.

13.3.1 Forecasting

It is worthwhile to offer some definitions of forecasting initially (see Makridakis and Wheelwright (1985) for a comprehensive review of forecasting techniques and methods for industrial and management use):

> To calculate or predict some future event or condition, usually as a result of rational study and analysis of available pertinent data. (Webster's dictionary)

> A forecast is the extrapolation of the past into the future. It is an objective computation involving data as opposed to a prediction which is a subjective estimate incorporating management's anticipation of changes. (APICS dictionary)

> A procedure which enables a company to predict future events upon which decisions controlling the allocation and use of resources can be based. (Friessnig, 1979)

Webster's definition suggests an explanatory or extrinsic approach where outside factors are used to make a forecast. The APICS definition reflects the time-series approach, where statistical analysis of prior experience is used in order to help to predict the future. We will now look at some of the more common time-series and explanatory forecasting techniques that are currently in use.

There are three basic types of forecasting technique: **qualitative**, **quantitative** and **casual**. The first uses qualitative data (expert opinion, for example) and information about special events. It may or may not take the past into consideration. The second, on the other hand, focuses entirely on pattern changes, and thus relies entirely on historical data. The third uses highly refined and specific information about relationships between system elements, and is sufficiently powerful to take special events into account (Chambers *et al.*, 1971).

Here we will concentrate on the quantitative forecasting techniques frequently used by personnel in master scheduling analysis and decisions. The two most import-

* The notion of lead time is fundamental to all discussions on production planning and control systems. Therefore we will offer a formal definition. The APICS dictionary defines lead times as follows: 'A span of time required to perform an activity. In a production and inventory context, the activity in question is normally the procurement of materials or products from an outside supplier or from one's own manufacturing facility. The individual components of any given lead time can include some or all of the following: order preparation time, queue time, move or transportation time, receiving and inspection time.'

Table 13.1 Quantitative forecasting techniques (Adapted from Makridakis and Wheelwright, 1985)

Important groups of forecasting methods	Major forecasting methods	Description
Time-series (history repeats itself; thus the future will be some kind of continuation of the past)	Naive	Simple rules, such as: forecast equals most recent actual value or equals last year's same month + 5%
	Decomposition	A data time is 'broken' down into trend, seasonal, cyclical and random parts
	Simple time-series	Forecasts are obtained by averaging (smoothing) past actual values
	Advanced time-series	Forecasts are obtained as combinations of past actual values and/or past errors
Explanatory (future can be predicted by understanding the factors that explain why some variable of interest varies)	Simple regression	Variations in the variable to be forecast are explained by variations in another variable
	Multiple regression	Variations in the variable to be forecast are explained by variations among more than one other variable
	Econometric models	Systems of simultaneous equations where the interdependence among variables is taken into account
	Multivariate methods	Statistical approaches allowing predictions through analysis of multivariate time-series data
	Monitoring	Non-random fluctuations are identified so that a warning signal can be given

ant groups of forecasting methods in this context are those defined in the **time-series** and **explanatory** categories of Table 13.1, which has been adopted from Makridakis and Wheelwright (1985). We will now review some of the more widely used methods from these two categories.

Simple regression

Simple regression enables the forecaster to predict the value of a particular variable (the dependent variable) based on its relationship to another variable (the independent variable). This relationship is assumed to be linear, that is,

$$\hat{Y} = \alpha + \beta X \tag{13.1}$$

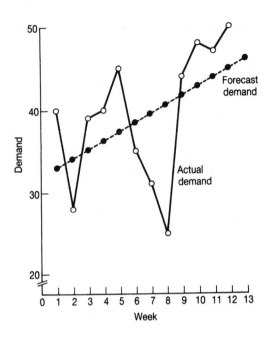

FIGURE 13.4
Actual values with
least squares
regression line.

where X is the independent variable, α and β are constants and $\hat{Y}$ represents the fore-cast value for Y, which is the actual or observed value.

For example a manufacturer may use the simple regression technique to predict the future demand for his products based on historical demand data. In this case the independent variable is time and the dependent variable is the demand for the products. The objective of least squares regression is to draw a line though a set of points that minimizes the distance between the actual observations and the corresponding points on the line. A graphical representation of the regression forecasts in comparison with the observed demand values is shown in Figure 13.4, which illustrates forecast and actual demand for the manufacturer's product for each of 13 weeks.

The values of the regression forecasts are tabulated in Table 13.2. In this, each of the deviations (errors) can be computed as $e_i = Y_i - \hat{Y}_i$, and each of the values on the regression line can be computed as $\hat{Y}_i = \alpha + \beta X_i$. The method of least squares determines the values of α and β in such a way that the sum of the squared deviations $\Sigma e_i^2 = \Sigma(Y_i - \hat{Y}_i)^2$ is minimized. The forecast equation is calculated as follows:

$$\beta = \frac{\Sigma XY - n(\overline{X}\,\overline{Y})}{\Sigma X^2 - n(\overline{X}^2)}$$
$$= \frac{3216 - 12(6.5)\,(39.25)}{650 - 12(6.5)^2} = 1.08 \tag{13.2}$$

$$\alpha = \overline{Y} - (\beta \times \overline{X})$$
$$= 39.25 - (1.08 \times 6.5) = 32.23 \tag{13.3}$$

Substituting these values into Equation (13.1), we obtain:

Table 13.2 Regression

X	Observed demand Y	XY	Forecast $\hat{Y} = \alpha + \beta X$	Absolute error e_i	Squared error e_i^2
1	40	40	33	7	49
2	27	54	34	7	49
3	39	117	35	4	16
4	40	160	36	4	16
5	45	225	38	7	49
6	35	210	39	4	16
7	31	217	40	9	81
8	25	200	41	16	256
9	44	396	42	2	4
10	48	480	43	5	25
11	47	517	44	3	9
12	50	600	45	5	25
$\Sigma X = 78$	$\Sigma Y = 471$	$\Sigma XY = 3216$		$\Sigma e_i = 73$	$\Sigma e_i^2 = 595$
$\Sigma X^2 = 650$	$\Sigma Y^2 = 19\ 235$			MAD = 6.08	MSE = 49.58
$\overline{X} = 6.5$	$\overline{Y} = 39.25$				

$$\hat{Y} = 32.23 + 1.08(X) \tag{13.4}$$

In this calculation, $\overline{Y} = \Sigma Y/n$, $\overline{X} = \Sigma X/n$ and n is the number of observations upon which the regression analysis is based. A continuation of the line $\hat{Y} = \alpha + \beta X$ will give forecast values which are dependent on the X variable. The manufacturer can predict the demand for week 13 using the forecast equation:

$$F_{13} = 32.23 + 1.08(13) = 46 \tag{13.5}$$

The mean of the absolute errors, known as the mean absolute deviation (MAD), and the mean squared error (MSE) are calculated for all forecasts. The relatively low values of the MAD and the MSE indicate that the simple regression technique provides a reasonably accurate forecast in this case.

Simple moving average

Simple moving average provides a means whereby randomness is eliminated from a forecast by taking the average of a number of observed values and using this as the forecast for the following period. The term 'moving average' is used because as each new observation becomes available, a new average can be computed and used as a forecast. It can be mathematically represented by the following equation:

$$F_{t+1} = S_t = \frac{X_t + X_{t-1} + \ldots + X_{t-N+1}}{N} \tag{13.6}$$

Table 13.3 Simple moving average

| Week | Observed demand | Three-week moving average | | | Five-week moving average | | |
		Forecast demand	Absolute error (e_i)	Squared error (e_i^2)	Forecast demand	Absolute error (e_i)	Squared error (e_i^2)
1	40	–	–	–	–	–	–
2	27	–	–	–	–	–	–
3	39	–	–	–	–	–	–
4	40	35	5	25	–	–	–
5	45	35	10	100	–	–	–
6	35	41	6	36	38	3	9
7	31	40	9	81	37	6	36
8	25	37	12	144	38	13	169
9	44	30	14	196	35	9	81
10	48	33	15	225	36	12	144
11	47	39	8	64	37	10	100
12	50	46	4	16	39	11	121
13	–	48	–	–	43	–	–
			$\Sigma(e_i) = 83$	$\Sigma(e_i^2) = 887$		$\Sigma(e_i) = 64$	$\Sigma(e_i^2) = 660$
			MAD = 9.2	MSE = 98.5		MAD = 9.14	MSE = 94.28

where: F_{t+1} = forecast for time $t + 1$, S_t = smoothed value at time t, X_t = actual value at time t, i = time period, N = number of values included in average.

For the manufacturer, Table 13.3 compares the moving average forecast with the actual demand. The three week moving average forecast is equivalent to the average demand for the three previous weeks. Thus for example the forecast of 48 for week 13 is the average demand for weeks 10, 11 and 12. The five week moving average forecast is calculated similarly.

Clearly the observed demand values for at least n periods must be available before an n-period moving average forecast can be made. From Table 13.3 it is clear that the observed demand values for the first three weeks are required before the first three-week moving average forecast can be made. Similarly, the five-week moving average forecast is first available for week 6.

For the three-week moving average forecasts, the smallest value is 30 and the largest value is 48, representing a range of 18. For the five-week moving average forecasts the range is 8 (43–35). Clearly, the greater the number of observations used in the moving average calculation, the greater the smoothing effect on the resulting forecasts.

The mean absolute deviation (MAD) and the mean squared error (MSE) are calculated for both forecasts. In this instance, the five-week moving average forecast is slightly more accurate. In general a larger number of periods should be used to compute the forecast if the historical observations contain a large degree of randomness, or if little change is expected in the underlying pattern. However, if the underlying pattern is changing, or if there is little randomness in the observed values, a small number of periods should be used to calculate the forecast value.

Single exponential smoothing

Single exponential smoothing uses three pieces of data to calculate a one-period-ahead forecast. The data in question is the most recent observation, the most recent forecast and a value for α, where α is the parameter that gives weight to the more recent values. The equation is as follows

$$F_{t+1} = F_t + \alpha(X_t - F_t) \quad \text{or} \quad F_{t+1} = F_t + \alpha e_t \qquad \textbf{(13.7)}$$

where: F_{t+1} = forecast for time $t + 1$, F_t = forecast for time t, X_t = actual value at time t, e_t = error in the forecast at time $t = X_t - F_t$, α = smoothing constant ($0 \leqslant \alpha \leqslant 1$).

Therefore, in fact, the new forecast is the old forecast plus α times the error in the old forecast. For values of α that are close to 1, the new forecast will contain a large adjustment for any error in the previous forecast. For values close to 0, the new forecast will show little adjustment for the error in the previous forecast.

Table 13.4 demonstrates the single exponential forecast with values for α of 0.2 and 0.8. The demand for week 1 is used as the initial forecast for week 2. The remainder of the forecasts are then calculated using the above equation. The smoothing effect on the forecast is more apparent with small values of α.

Table 13.4 Single exponential smoothing

Week	Observed demand	Forecast with $\alpha = 0.2$			Forecast with $\alpha = 0.8$		
		Forecast demand	Absolute error (e_i)	Squared error (e_i^2)	Forecast demand	Absolute error (e_i)	Squared error (e_i^2)
1	40	–	–	–	–	–	–
2	27	40	13	169	40	13	169
3	39	37	2	4	30	9	81
4	40	38	2	4	37	3	9
5	45	38	7	49	39	6	36
6	35	40	5	25	44	9	81
7	31	39	8	64	37	6	36
8	25	37	12	144	32	7	49
9	44	35	9	81	26	18	324
10	48	37	11	121	40	8	64
11	47	39	8	64	46	1	1
12	50	41	9	81	47	3	9
13	–	44	–	–	48	–	–
		$\Sigma(e_i) = 86$	$\Sigma(e_i^2) = 806$		$\Sigma(e_i) = 83$	$\Sigma(e_i^2) = 859$	
		MAD = 7.8	MSE = 73.27		MAD = 7.5	MSE = 78.1	

Seasonal exponential smoothing

Seasonal exponential smoothing was developed by Winter in the 1960s and can handle seasonal data (i.e. a situation where the size of data value depends on the period or season of the year), as well as the existence of an underlying trend in the data values. There are four equations involved in Winter's method, three of which smooth a factor associated with one of the three components of the pattern – randomness, trend and seasonality:

$$S_t = \alpha \frac{X_t}{I_{t-L}} + (1 - \alpha)(S_{t-1} + T_{t-1}) \tag{13.8}$$

$$T_t = \beta(S_t - S_{t-1}) + (1 - \beta)T_{t-1} \tag{13.9}$$

$$I_t = \gamma \frac{X_t}{S_t} + (1 - \gamma) I_{t-L} \tag{13.10}$$

$$F_{t+m} = (S_t + T_t m)I_{t-L+m} \tag{13.11}$$

where: S = smoothed value of the deseasonalized series, T = smoothed value of the trend, I = smoothed value of the seasonal factor, X = actual value, L = length of seasonality (e.g. number of quarters in a year), F_{t+m} = forecast m periods (quarters) after time t, and α, β and γ are constants used to smooth *seasonal data*.

X_t is the actual data value which contains seasonality, while S_t is smoothed and does not. However, seasonality at each period is not perfect, as it contains randomness. Thus it must be smoothed or averaged to remove such randomness. To smooth this seasonality, the equation for I weights the newly computed seasonal factor (X_t) with γ and the most recent seasonal number corresponding to the same season I_{t-L} with $(1 - \gamma)$.

The equation for T_t smooths the *trend* since it weights the incremental trend $(S_t - S_{t-1})$ with β and the previous trend value T_{t-1} with $(1 - \beta)$. In the equation for S_t, the first term is divided by the seasonal factor I_{t-L}. This is done to deseasonalize (eliminate seasonal fluctuations) from X_t.

Table 13.5 demonstrates Winter's method using values of $\alpha = 0.2$, $\beta = 0.1$ and $\gamma = 0.05$. In this example the given data extends over twelve quarters. Over the three years, demand tended to increase from one quarter to the next. However, there is a large reduction in demand for the final quarter of each year (seasonality factor); see Figure 13.5.

Initial values must be determined before any forecast can be made. Thus:

$$S_{L+1} = X_{L+1} \tag{13.12}$$

gives $S_{4+1} = X_{4+1} = 409.00$,

$$I_{1 \le i \le L} = \frac{X_i}{\overline{X}} \tag{13.13}$$

where:

$$\overline{X} = \sum_{i=1}^{L+1} X_i/(L + 1) \tag{13.14}$$

Table 13.5 Seasonal exponential smoothing

Period (quarter)	Actual value X_t	Smoothed deseasonalized value S_t	Smoothed seasonal factor I_t	Smoothed trend value T_t	Forecast when $m = 1$
1	338	–	0.89	–	–
2	378	–	0.99	–	–
3	447	–	1.17	–	–
4	339	–	0.89	–	–
5	409	409.00	0.90	19.92	–
6	447	433.44	0.99	20.37	425
7	546	456.38	1.17	20.63	531
8	422	476.44	0.89	20.57	425
9	493	507.16	0.90	21.59	447
10	572	538.55	0.99	22.57	523
11	638	557.96	1.17	22.25	656
12	457	566.86	0.89	20.92	516
13	–	–	–	–	529

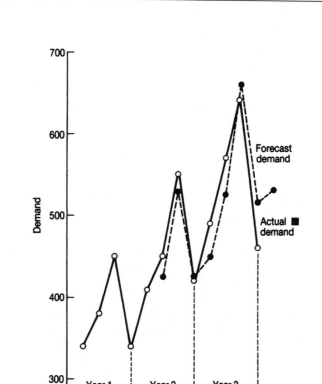

FIGURE 13.5
Graph of actual and forecast figures.

gives

$$I_1 = \frac{338}{(338 + 378 + 447 + 339 + 409)/5} = 0.89$$

and

$$T_{L+1} = [(X_{L+1} - X_1) + (X_{L+2} - X_2) + (X_{L+3} - X_3)]/3L \qquad \textbf{(13.15)}$$

gives

$$T_{4+1} = [(409 - 338) + (447 - 378) + (546 - 447)]/12 = 19.92$$

The other values of S_t, T_t, I_t and F_t are calculated using the formulae given above. For example, the calculations for period 12 are as follows:

$$\begin{aligned} F_{12} &= [S_{11} + T_{11}(1)]I_8 \\ &= (557.96 + 22.25)0.89 = 516.39 \end{aligned} \qquad \textbf{(13.16)}$$

$$\begin{aligned} S_{12} &= (0.2)(X_{12}/I_8) + 0.8(S_{11} + T_{11}) \\ &= 0.2(457/0.89) + 0.8(557.96 + 22.25) = 566.86 \end{aligned} \qquad \textbf{(13.17)}$$

$$\begin{aligned} T_{12} &= 0.1(S_{12} - S_{11}) + 0.9(T_{11}) \\ &= 0.1(566.86 - 557.96) + 0.9(22.25) = 20.91 \end{aligned} \qquad \textbf{(13.18)}$$

$$\begin{aligned} I_{12} &= 0.05(X_{12}/S_{12}) + 0.95(I_8) \\ &= 0.05(457/566.86) + 0.95(0.89) = 0.89 \end{aligned} \qquad \textbf{(13.19)}$$

Forecasts for periods 13, 14, 15 and 16 (year 4) can be obtained by varying the value of m and the seasonal factor I_t:

$$F_{12+m} = [566.86 + 20.92(m)]I_{12-4+m} \qquad \textbf{(13.20)}$$

$$F_{13} = [566.86 + 20.92(1)](0.90) = 529.00 \qquad \textbf{(13.21)}$$

$$F_{14} = [566.86 + 20.92(2)](0.99) = 602.13 \qquad \textbf{(13.22)}$$

$$F_{15} = [566.86 + 20.92(3)](1.17) = 736.65 \qquad \textbf{(13.23)}$$

$$F_{16} = [566.86 + 20.92(4)](0.89) = 578.98 \qquad \textbf{(13.24)}$$

The major difficulty associated with Winter's method lies in the determination of the values for α, β and γ that will minimize MSE or MAD. However, computer-based systems have dramatically reduced the burden of this task.

Forecasts provide an important input to the production planning and control system. In this section we have looked at some of the techniques in use in recent years. Many people argue that we need to apply properly the existing techniques rather than seeking out new forecasting techniques. In the next section we will look at the information contained in a typical master production scheduling record where forecasts are combined with other information, typically actual customer orders and inventory data, to develop the complete MPS record (Higgins and Browne, 1992).

13.3.2 The MPS record

Table 13.6 is an example of the contents of a typical simplified MPS record. It contains for a particular item, in this case Product A, the information which the master

Table 13.6 MPS record

Item Product A						Part number: FP-100							
Week number	1	2	3	4	5	6	7	8	9	10	11	12	13
Manual forecast	50	60	40	60	60								
System forecast	60	60	60	60	60	60	60	60	70	70	70	70	70
Customer order	55	60	20	17	30	5							
Total demand	55	60	40	60	60	60	60	60	70	70	70	70	70
MPS	0	55	40	60	60	60	60	60	70	70	70	70	70
PAB	5	0	0	0	0	0	0	0	0	0	0	0	0
Available to promise	5	−5	20	43	30	55	60	60	70	70	70	70	70
Cumulative ATP	5	0	20	63	93	148	208	268	338	408	478	548	618
PAB(0) = 60													

scheduler needs to carry out his or her function. As can be seen, it consists of a series of forecasts, summaries of the levels of customer orders where appropriate, calculations of projected available balances (PABs), and available to promise (ATP) figures over the planning horizon, in this case thirteen weeks. Later we will review each of the individual lines in this MPS record in some detail.

The master scheduler is able to calculate a figure for total demand, and using the MPS line in Table 13.6 is able to come up with a figure for available inventory. The cumulative (procurement and manufacturing) lead time which is the minimum MPS planning horizon is sometimes referred to as being 'frozen', which indicates that no changes inside this lead time are allowed. Many firms do not like to use the term 'frozen', saying that anything is negotiable – but the negotiations get tougher as the present time approaches. A better term to use might be 'firm', indicating that this lead time represents quantities of end items committed to, and started, in manufacture. **Time fencing** is an extension of the freeze concept. Many firm set time fences which specify periods in which various types of change can be handled, with various levels of required approval. The location of time fences and the nature of the approval required is dependent on the situation. Varying lead times, market conditions and processing flexibility make for different time fences, sometimes at different plants within the same firm. Time fences should be tailored to specific product groups, as lead times may vary widely between product groups.

The eight rows of data outlined in Table 13.6 will now be discussed individually in more detail.

The forecast lines

The manual forecast typically comes from the sales or marketing department and is input directly to the MPS record. Although forecasting is assumed to be the responsibility of sales/marketing, rather than the master scheduling group, the master schedule function may generate a system forecast (using the techniques presented earlier) for the following reasons:

▶ to cross check the sales or manual forecast;

▶ to be used when there is no sales forecast (i.e. further out on the planning horizon);

▶ to be used as an accuracy measurement mechanism.

Table 13.6 shows some sample data for both manual and system forecasts.

Customer orders

The customer demand is input directly by sales or marketing personnel. It is usually assumed that the customer demand is the actual demand and the delivery lead time is fixed. In this example we will assume a two week delivery lead time. Sample data is shown in Table 13.6.

Total demand

The total demand is the demand quantity used with the MPS quantity to calculate a figure for available to promise. It can be the actual customer orders or sales forecast. Figure 13.6 illustrates the various inputs. For example, in order to calculate the total demand, the following rules might be used:

1. If the customer demand is within the demand time fence then the customer demand becomes the total demand.

2. If the customer demand is outside the demand time fence, and a manual forecast exists, then the manual forecast becomes the total demand.

3. If the customer demand is outside the demand time fence and no manual forecast exists, then the system forecast becomes the total demand.

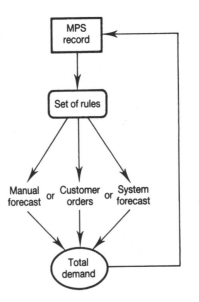

FIGURE 13.6

Generating a figure for total demand.

We can illustrate the method of calculating total demand as follows. Again assuming a lead time of two weeks, the total demand for week 1 is obtained from the customer orders row (rule 1). In week 3, total demand is taken from the manual forecast row (rule 2). Further out, say in week 10, the total demand is assumed equal to the system forecast, i.e. 70. See Table 13.6 for sample data.

Master production schedule (MPS)

This is the line which states the anticipated build schedule for the product. The MPS item is a manufacturing order, which has been automatically calculated or manually manipulated during the development of an MPS. The value for time bucket i is calculated as follows:

$$MPS[i] = MAX(SS + Total\_Demand[i] - PAB[i - 1], 0) \qquad \textbf{(13.25)}$$

e.g.

$$MPS[1] = MAX(0 + 55 - 60, 0) = MAX(-5, 0) = 0 \qquad \textbf{(13.26)}$$

where SS is the safety stock and $PAB[i - 1]$ is the projected available balance for the previous time bucket. In this case the safety stock is assumed equal to zero; i.e. no safety stock. Safety stocks are a quantity of stock maintained in inventory to protect the manufacturing plant against unexpected fluctuations in demand or supply. Thus safety stocks may be considered to be an insurance against unexpected events. Given the high cost of committing capital to support inventory, safety stocks are often considered an expensive option.

Projected available balance (PAB)

The *projected available balance* is the expected number of completed items on hand at the end of each period. The logic associated with the PAB calculation is as follows:

1. For the first period where the actual demand is within delivery lead time:

$$PAB[1] = PAB[0] + MPS[1] - Total\_Demand[1] \qquad \textbf{(13.27)}$$

   For the example listed in Table 13.6:

$$PAB[1] = 60 + 0 - 55 = 5 \qquad \textbf{(13.28)}$$

2. For subsequent periods within the delivery lead time:

$$PAB[i] = PAB[i - 1] + MPS[i] - Total\_Demand[i] \qquad \textbf{(13.29)}$$

   For example, for period 2:

$$PAB[2] = 5 + 55 - 60 = 0 \qquad \textbf{(13.30)}$$

Available to promise (ATP)

The **available to promise** line represents the uncommitted portion of an organization's planned production based on the supply from the master schedule. It is used for two purposes, namely:

▶ to make the maximum use of inventory;

▶ to protect all customer commitments.

The ATP line is subject to constant change and it is important to keep it up to date with new orders, as it is the mechanism by which orders are promised to customers. The ATP is calculated using the following two equations:

$$ATP[1] = PAB[0] + MPS[1] - MIN(Customer\_Orders[1],$$
$$Total\_Demand[1]) \tag{13.31}$$

$$ATP[i] = MPS[i] - MIN(Customer\_Orders[i], Total\_Demand[i]) \tag{13.32}$$

For the example illustrated in Table 13.6, example ATP calculations are as follows:

$$ATP[1] = 60 + 0 - MIN(55, 55) = 5 \tag{13.33}$$

$$ATP[8] = 60 - MIN(0, 60) = 60 \tag{13.34}$$

Cumulative ATP

The cumulative ATP, as the name suggests, is calculated by cumulating the ATP values over time. See Table 13.6.

From MPS to requirements planning

At this stage we have considered the fundamentals of the master production scheduling (MPS) system. As indicated earlier the MPS is a critical input to the requirements planning system. It defines the demand for products or end level items. We are now in a position to consider in detail the role of the requirements planning system, which calculates the demand for lower level (in the BOM) items.

Before doing so it is important to draw attention to one important insight which the originator of the requirements planning approach brought to our attention. Orlicky (1975) differentiated between what he termed *independent* and *dependent* demand items. When we say that the demand for a particular item is independent, we imply that it is not related to the demand for other items. When we say that the demand for an item is dependent we imply that it can be calculated directly by reference to some other item or product. Thus the demand level for independent items can be forecast. MPS items are independent demand items, whose demand is forecast when firm customer orders are not to hand. Items below the MPS level in the bill of materials are considered to exhibit dependent demand. The calculation of the level and timing of the demand for dependent demand items is the main function of the requirements planning system, which we will now go on to discuss.

13.4 Requirements planning
••••••••••••••••••••••••••••••••

As we indicated earlier, requirements planning translates the requirements for end-level items defined in the MPS into time-scheduled requirements for individual assemblies, sub-assemblies and components by exploding the MPS requirements right down

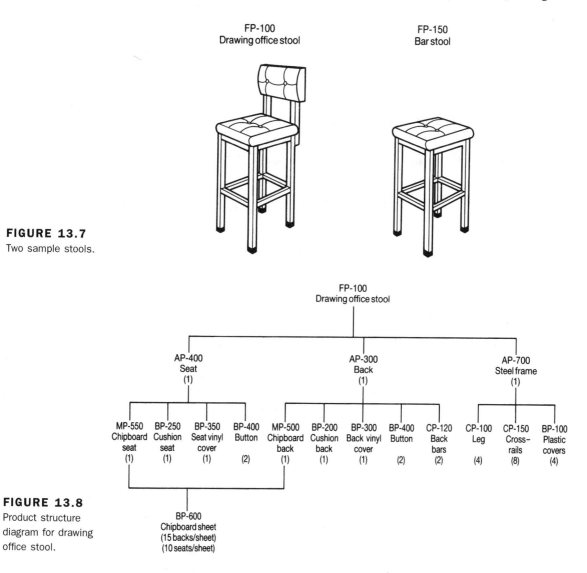

FIGURE 13.7
Two sample stools.

FIGURE 13.8
Product structure
diagram for drawing
office stool.

through the bill of materials (BOM) and offsetting the demand for individual items by the appropriate lead times. We shall present requirements planning through a simple example of the use of the technique. The example has been developed to illustrate the main points of the requirements planning process.

Consider the following situation. Skehana Stools Inc. manufactures two types of stool, namely a drawing office stool and a bar stool (see Figure 13.7). The bill of materials for the drawing office stool, represented by a product structure diagram, is shown in Figure 13.8. Thinking back to our earlier discussion on independent and dependent demand, it is clear that item FP-100 exhibits independent demand, whereas all of the assemblies and components below it in the bill of materials of Figure 13.8 exhibit dependent demand.

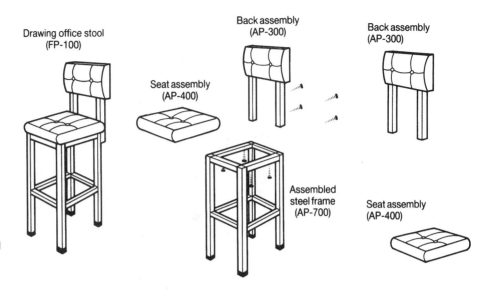

FIGURE 13.9
Drawing office stool
broken into three
subassemblies.

Within the diagram we have indicated the quantity of each item per parent part. Thus, for example, there are four legs per stool assembly. Further, a single chipboard sheet can be cut into ten chipboard seats, or alternatively fifteen chipboard backs. We also indicate the part number. Furthermore, we note that the two products share some common components. The bill of materials (BOM) for the bar stool is similar to that of the office stool, except of course that the back assembly is excluded.

This is typical of the type of situation that requirements planning handles well, i.e. where production covers a range of products with common components and sub-assemblies. In Figure 13.9 we show how the drawing office stool is broken down into three separate subassemblies; namely the back assembly, the seat assembly and the steel frame. The back and seat assemblies are further broken down into their component parts in Figure 13.10. Finally, in Figure 13.11 we show how the steel frame is disassembled.

In Table 13.7, the *master parts* information needed for the example is presented. The information is presented in part number order. The level code refers to the lowest level of the bill of materials at which the component is to be found. In all cases the lead times are given in weeks. The make/buy code indicates whether a part is manufactured in-house or purchased from an external supplier. The lot-sizing policy (see Section 13.4.2) is largely **lot for lot** (L), by which we mean that the net requirement quantity is scheduled as the batch size for the replenishment order. The lot-sizing policy for the buttons and plastic covers is **fixed order quantity**. For these items, 500 units are scheduled as the batch size for the replenishment order.

The first two letters of the part number code indicate the extent to which that part has been processed, namely:

▶ **FP:** finished part. These pieces have been fully processed.

▶ **AP:** assembled part. These pieces have been assembled from the basic component pieces.

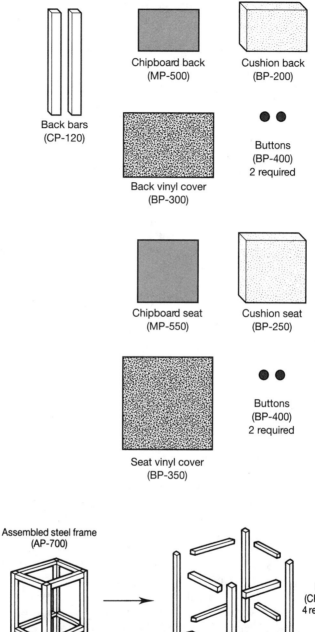

FIGURE 13.10
Seat and back with a breakdown of components.

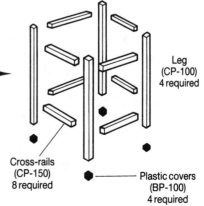

FIGURE 13.11
Frame being broken into its component parts.

Table 13.7 Master parts data

Level	Part number	Lot size	Lead time	Description	Make/buy
0	FP-100	L	1	Drawing office stool	M
0	FP-150	L	1	Bar stool	M
1	AP-300	L	2	Back	M
1	AP-400	L	2	Seat	M
1	AP-700	L	2	Steel frame	M
2	CP-100	L	2	Leg	B
2	CP-120	L	2	Back bars	B
2	CP-150	L	2	Cross-rails	B
2	MP-500	L	1	Chipboard back	M
2	MP-550	L	1	Chipboard seat	M
2	BP-100	500	3	Plastic covers	B
2	BP-200	L	2	Cushion back	B
2	BP-250	L	2	Cushion seat	B
2	BP-300	L	2	Back vinyl cover	B
2	BP-350	L	2	Seat vinyl cover	B
2	BP-400	500	2	Buttons	B
3	BP-600	L	2	Chipboard sheet	B

▶ **MP:** manufactured part. These pieces have been manufactured from the parent material so that the piece can be used in the final product assembly.

▶ **CP:** contracted part. These pieces have been manufactured by another company according to the stool manufacturer's specifications.

▶ **BP:** bought in or purchased part.

Within a requirements planning system, the **planning horizon** refers to the span of time that the master production schedule covers, while the **time bucket** refers to the units of time into which the planning horizon is divided. In this example a planning horizon of thirteen weeks (a quarter of a year) and a time bucket of one week are used. In real systems we may well find that small time buckets, perhaps weeks or even days, are used in the early part of the planning horizon, while larger time buckets, perhaps months, tend to be used towards the end of the planning cycle.

In implemented requirements planning systems, the time horizons should extend beyond the longest cumulative lead time for a product. The data structures used to represent time can be bucketed or non-bucketed. In the bucketed approach, a predetermined number of data cells are reserved to accumulate quantity information by period. In the non-bucketed approach, each part-quantity information pair has associated with it a time label. Clearly the bucketless approach is more flexible and efficient, although somewhat more complex, from a data processing point of view. For the purposes of simplicity we will use the bucketed approach in our extended example.

Table 13.8 Simplified master production schedule

Week number	1	2	3	4	5	6	7	8	9	10	11	12	13
FP-100					55				75 *				50
FP-150							30					25	

* All entries in the tables associated with the order for 75 drawing office stools are emphasized by placing them in a frame. This will help to focus attention on the requirements planning explosion as it progresses down through the BOM.

Table 13.9 Inventory data

Part number	Current inventory
AP-300	10
AP-400	0
AP-700	10
BP-100	0
BP-200	50
BP-250	50
BP-300	50
BP-350	40
BP-400	0
BP-600	2
CP-100	50
CP-120	0
CP-150	150
FP-100	15
FP-150	10
MP-500	40
MP-550	5

The current week is assumed to be the beginning of week 1 and a simplified master production schedule is shown in Table 13.8. Table 13.9 indicates the current stock levels for each item. The **current inventory** represents the amount of material physically in stock. Table 13.10 lists those orders which are *open*, i.e. due as scheduled receipts. Scheduled receipts refer to orders which have been placed with suppliers, and which the supplier has committed to supply during a future time bucket.

There is now sufficient data available with which to illustrate a simple requirements planning calculation. The analysis begins with the top level items in the bill of materials. We will start with the drawing office stool (see Table 13.11). We take as our **gross requirements** for the office stool the requirements identified in the master production schedule. According to the inventory data there are 15 units in stock. Fifty units are scheduled to be received into stock in week 2 and hence the **net requirements** are as indicated in Table 13.11. The **order release** date is calculated

Table 13.10 Open orders data

Part number	Scheduled receipts	Due date
AP-300	25	2
AP-400	20	2
BP-300	25	3
BP-350	20	3
BP-400	200	2
CP-100	150	3
CP-150	150	2
FP-100	50	2

Table 13.11 Analysis of office stool

Item: Office stool									Part number: FP-100				
Week number	1	2	3	4	5	6	7	8	9	10	11	12	13
Gross requirements					55				75				50
Scheduled receipts		50											
Projected inventory	15	65			10				−65				−115
Net requirements									65				50
Planned order								65				50	

Table 13.12 Analysis of bar stool

Item: Bar stool									Part number: FP-150				
Week number	1	2	3	4	5	6	7	8	9	10	11	12	13
Gross requirements							30					25	
Scheduled receipts													
Projected inventory	10						−20					−45	
Net requirements							20					25	
Planned order						20					25		

simply by offsetting the net requirement due date by the lead time. The analysis of the bar stool is similarly carried out, and is presented in Table 13.12.

The next level in the bill of materials contains the three assemblies (AP-300, AP-400 and AP-700). We will deal initially with the back assembly, which is of course only used for the office stool. The gross requirements are equivalent to the planned orders

Table 13.13 Analysis of back assembly

Item: Back assembly								Part number: AP-300					
Week number	1	2	3	4	5	6	7	8	9	10	11	12	13
Gross requirements								65				50	
Scheduled receipts		25											
Projected inventory	10	35						−30				−80	
Net requirements								30				50	
Planned order						30				50			

Table 13.14 Analysis of seat

Item: Seat assembly								Part number: AP-400					
Week number	1	2	3	4	5	6	7	8	9	10	11	12	13
Gross requirements						20		65			25	50	
Scheduled receipts		20											
Projected inventory	0	20				0		−65			−90	−140	
Net requirements								65			25	50	
Planned order						65			25	50			

Table 13.15 Analysis of steel frame

Item: Steel frame								Part number: AP-700					
Week number	1	2	3	4	5	6	7	8	9	10	11	12	13
Gross requirements						20		65			25	50	
Scheduled receipts													
Projected inventory	10					−10		−75			−100	−150	
Net requirements						10		65			25	50	
Planned order				10		65			25	50			

for the office stool, as one back assembly is used per finished stool. The ten units currently in stock and the twenty-five units scheduled to be received in week 2 are taken into account in our calculation of net requirements as illustrated in Table 13.13.

Next, we consider the seat assembly. This assembly is common to both the office stool and the bar stool. Hence its gross requirements are equivalent to the combined planned orders for the office stool and the bar stool, as indicated in Table 13.14. The planned orders are computed as before. The analysis of the steel frame assembly in Table 13.15 is similar to that for the seat assembly.

Table 13.16 Analysis of leg

Item: Leg						Part number: CP-100							
Week number	1	2	3	4	5	6	7	8	9	10	11	12	13
Gross requirements				40		260			100	200			
Scheduled receipts			150										
Projected inventory	50		200	160		−100			−200	−400			
Net requirements						100			100	200			
Planned order				100			100	200					

Table 13.17 Analysis of cross-rails

Item: Frame bars						Part number: CP-150							
Week number	1	2	3	4	5	6	7	8	9	10	11	12	13
Gross requirements				80		520			200	400			
Scheduled receipts		150											
Projected inventory	150	300		220		−300			−500	−900			
Net requirements						300			200	400			
Planned order				300			200	400					

Table 13.18 Analysis of plastic covers

Item: Plastic covers						Part number: BP-100							
Week number	1	2	3	4	5	6	7	8	9	10	11	12	13
Gross requirements				40		260			100	200			
Scheduled receipts													
Projected inventory	0			−40		−300			−400	−600			
Net requirements				40		260			100	200			
Planned order	500						500						

We now move on to the third level of the bill of materials. There are four legs, eight cross-rails, four plastic covers and two back bars per steel frame assembly, and hence their gross requirements are calculated accordingly, as shown in Tables 13.16, 13.17 and 13.18. The gross requirements for the back bars are determined by doubling the planned orders for the back assembly (Table 13.19).

In Table 13.18 the planned order of 500 plastic covers in week 1 covers the requirements of weeks 1 to 9. Another order for 500 covers must be placed in week 7 to cover the requirements of week 10.

Table 13.19 Analysis of back bars

Item: Back bars						Part number: CP-120							
Week number	1	2	3	4	5	6	7	8	9	10	11	12	13
Gross requirements						60				100			
Scheduled receipts													
Projected inventory	0					−60				−160			
Net requirements						60				100			
Planned order				60				100					

Table 13.20 Analysis of chipboard back

Item: Chipboard back						Part number: MP-500							
Week number	1	2	3	4	5	6	7	8	9	10	11	12	13
Gross requirements						30				50			
Scheduled receipts													
Projected inventory	40					10				−40			
Net requirements										40			
Planned order									40				

Table 13.21 Analysis of chipboard seat

Item: Chipboard seat						Part number: MP-550							
Week number	1	2	3	4	5	6	7	8	9	10	11	12	13
Gross requirements						65			25	50			
Scheduled receipts													
Projected inventory	5					−60			−85	−135			
Net requirements						60			25	50			
Planned order					60			25	50				

The gross requirements for the chipboard back shown in Table 13.20 are equivalent to the planned orders for the back. Similarly, the gross requirements for the chipboard seat in Table 13.21 are the same as the planned orders for the seat.

The calculations for the cushion material and the vinyl cover for both the back and the seat are practically identical to the chipboard back/seat calculations (Tables 13.22–13.25). The gross requirements for buttons are generated by doubling the combined planned orders for the seat and back assemblies. As can be seen in Table 13.26 a planned order for 500 units is placed as required. Now consider the chipboard sheet.

Table 13.22 Analysis of cushion back

Item: Cushion back							Part number: BP-200						
Week number	1	2	3	4	5	6	7	8	9	10	11	12	13
Gross requirements						30				50			
Scheduled receipts													
Projected inventory	50					20				−30			
Net requirements										30			
Planned order								30					

Table 13.23 Analysis of cushion seat

Item: Cushion seat							Part number: BP-250						
Week number	1	2	3	4	5	6	7	8	9	10	11	12	13
Gross requirements						65			25	50			
Scheduled receipts													
Projected inventory	50					15			−10	−60			
Net requirements									10	50			
Planned order							10	50					

Table 13.24 Analysis of back vinyl cover

Item: Back vinyl cover							Part number: BP-300						
Week number	1	2	3	4	5	6	7	8	9	10	11	12	13
Gross requirements						30				50			
Scheduled receipts			25										
Projected inventory	50		75			45				−5			
Net requirements										5			
Planned order								5					

Fifteen chipboard backs can be manufactured from a single chipboard sheet. Hence 3 sheets are required for week 9. Similarly, as 10 chipboard backs can be manufactured from a single sheet, 6, 3 and 5 sheets are required in weeks 5, 8 and 9 respectively. Thus the chipboard sheet gross requirements are as shown in Table 13.27.

Screws are not included in the bill of materials, as they are a relatively inexpensive item. Although buttons and the plastic covers fall into the same inexpensive category, they can only be obtained from specific suppliers and hence are included in the BOM. The screws can be obtained from a number of suppliers whenever they are required. Such items are sometimes referred to as **free issue** items, suggesting that their supply and demand are not managed very rigorously.

Table 13.25 Analysis of vinyl seat cover

Item: Vinyl seat cover						Part number: BP-350							
Week number	1	2	3	4	5	6	7	8	9	10	11	12	13
Gross requirements						65			25	50			
Scheduled receipts			20										
Projected inventory	40		60			−5			−30	−80			
Net requirements						5			25	50			
Planned order					5			25	50				

Table 13.26 Analysis of buttons

Item: Buttons						Part number: BP-400							
Week number	1	2	3	4	5	6	7	8	9	10	11	12	13
Gross requirements						190			50	200			
Scheduled receipts		200											
Projected inventory	0	200				−10			−60	−260			
Net requirements						10			50	200			
Planned order				500									

Table 13.27 Analysis of chipboard sheet

Item: Chipboard sheet						Part number: BP-600							
Week number	1	2	3	4	5	6	7	8	9	10	11	12	13
Gross requirements					6			3	8				
Scheduled receipts													
Projected inventory	2				−4			−7	−15				
Net requirements					4			3	8				
Planned order			4			3	8						

13.4.1 Pegged requirements

Pegging allows the sources of demand for a particular component's gross require-ments to be identified. These gross requirements typically originate either from par-ent assemblies or from independent demand in the MPS, or from the demand for spare parts (normally considered to be independent demand items). Using the data from the requirements planning example, the pegged requirements for buttons are illustrated in Table 13.28. The gross requirements for the buttons arise from both the back and seat assemblies.

Table 13.28 Pegged requirement for buttons (BP-400)

Requirement		Source	
Component quantity	Week number	Parent	Parent quantity
60	6	AP-300	30
130	6	AP-400	65
50	9	AP-400	25
100	10	AP-300	50
100	10	AP-400	50

The pegged requirements report enables the sources of the total gross requirements for a particular item to be determined. The procedure of identifying each gross requirement with its source at the next immediate higher level in the BOM is termed **single level** pegging. Through a series of single level pegging reports, a set of requirements can be traced back to their source in the master schedule.

In order to link item demand to that schedule by means of a single enquiry, **full pegging** is required. For the full pegging approach each individual requirement for a planned item is identified against a master production scheduled item and/or a customer order. Factors such as the lot-sizing policy (see Section 13.4.2), safety stock and scrap allowances make it practically impossible to associate individual batches or lots with particular customer orders. Hence, the single level pegging facility is standard practice and full pegging is rarely used.

13.4.2 Lot-sizing techniques in requirements planning

In the examples illustrated in this chapter we have taken the net requirements for particular items, offset by the appropriate lead times, to constitute the planned order schedule. However, there are many situations where constraints on the order lot size make this an unsuitable procedure. For purchased items, vendors may supply only in multiples of a given number and the net requirements may have to be batched so as to accommodate this. Indeed, there may be quantity discounts which the purchasing department may wish to take advantage of, and which may justify the batching of individual orders. Similarly, for manufactured parts and assemblies a process which involves very high set-up times and therefore costs may dictate the use of a minimum lot size policy.

Any requirements planning system must, therefore, include a procedure which facilitates the calculation of lot sizes on some basis other than simple acceptance of the values that fall out from the net requirements calculation. Also, it should be noted that lot-sizing decisions made high up the BOM structure will have ripple effects right down through the planning of all components in the bill of materials.

A number of procedures are available to help to determine an appropriate lot size. These range from relatively simple procedures to very complicated algorithms.

We will now look briefly at the following methods:

▶ Lot for lot.

▶ Economic order quantity.

▶ Periodic order quantity.

▶ Least total cost.

It is essential to offer some definitions of certain terms before the various lot-sizing techniques can be understood:

▶ *Gross requirements* (GR_i) arise from the master production schedule, i.e. forecasts and customer orders that have already been received. These orders require that a specific quantity of the item will be available for the time period i.

▶ *Scheduled receipts* (SR_i) refer to orders that have already been placed with the supplier, but are not yet received. These orders are scheduled to be received into stock during period i.

▶ *Projected inventory* (PI_i) is the expected quantity of stock that will be held during period i, or the quantity of stock needed to meet requirements. The projected inventory for period i is equal to the projected inventory for period $i-1$ plus the scheduled receipts for period i, less the gross requirements for period i:

$$PI_i = PI_{i-1} - GR_i + SR_i \qquad\qquad \textbf{(13.35)}$$

e.g.

$$PI_2 = PI_1 - GR_2 + SR_2 \quad \text{(see Table 13.29 on page 472)}$$
$$= 5 - 60 + 70 = 15 \qquad\qquad \textbf{(13.36)}$$

▶ *Net requirements* (NR_i) are the quantity of extra stock needed to meet the requirements of period i:

$$NR_i = GR_i - PI_i - SR_i \qquad\qquad \textbf{(13.37)}$$

When $PI_i < 0$, PI_i is set equal to 0. For example:

$$NR_6 = GR_6 - PI_6 - SR_6 \quad \text{(see Table 13.29)}$$
$$= 40 - 0 - 0 = 40 \qquad\qquad \textbf{(13.38)}$$

▶ *Planned orders* are orders that will be placed with the supplier at specific time periods in the future. The net requirements are offset by the order lead time to determine when the order should be placed.

▶ The *planned order receipt* identifies the time period during which a planned order is assumed to be delivered into stock.

Lot for lot

Lot for lot is the simplest of the lot-sizing techniques. In essence the planned order quantity is equal to the quantity of the net requirements generated by the requirements planning procedure. In the example shown in Table 13.29, the net requirements are

Table 13.29 Lot for lot

Item: Office stool						Part number: FP-100							
Week number	1	2	3	4	5	6	7	8	9	10	11	12	13
Gross requirements		60	25	15		40	65		20	70	20	45	30
Scheduled receipts		70											
Projected inventory	5	15	−10	−25	−25	−65	−130	−130	−150	−220	−240	−285	−315
Net requirements			10	15		40	65		20	70	20	45	30
Planned order	10	15		40	65		20	70	20	45	30		

offset by a lead time of two weeks, to determine when the orders should be placed. Lot for lot is frequently used for expensive items and highly discontinuous demand items, as inventory carrying costs are minimized. Like other discrete lot-sizing techniques, the size of the latter lots may have to be recalculated as extra orders are received.

Economic order quantity

Large batch sizes result in high inventory levels, which are expensive in terms of the cost of capital tied up in inventory. Small batches imply a proportionately lower inventory cost. However, there is a set-up cost incurred with the placing of an order or the start-up of a new batch on a machine. The impact of the lot size on cost is represented by the economic order quantity (EOQ) model in Figure 13.12.

The economic order quantity attempts to minimize the sum of set-up and inventory costs. The EOQ model is based on an assumption of continuous steady state demand, and it will perform well in situations where the actual demand approximates this assumption. The more discontinuous and non-uniform the demand, the less effective the EOQ method will prove to be. The order quantity is specified by the economic order formula:

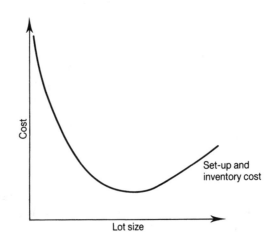

FIGURE 13.12
Economic order quantity model.

Table 13.30 Economic order quantity

Item: Office stool						Part number: FP-100							
Week number	1	2	3	4	5	6	7	8	9	10	11	12	13
Gross requirements		60	25	15		40	65		20	70	20	45	30
Scheduled receipts		70											
Projected inventory	5	15	−10	−25	−25	−65	−130	−130	−150	−220	−240	−285	−315
Net requirements			10	15		40	65		20	70	20	45	30
Planned order receipt			75				75			75	75		75
Planned order	75				75			75	75		75		

$$Q = \sqrt{\frac{2SD}{C}} \qquad \textbf{(13.39)}$$

where: Q = economic order quantity, S = set-up cost per batch, D = average demand for item per unit time, C = carrying cost per item per unit time.

In the given example, the demand for the stool is 390 over the given quarter, which represents a weekly demand of 30. Let us assume that the set-up cost is equal to £94. Furthermore, assume that the carrying cost = £1 per unit per week. This gives:

$$Q = \sqrt{\frac{2(94)(30)}{1}} = 75 \text{ units} \qquad \textbf{(13.40)}$$

As shown in Table 13.30, an order for 75 units is placed as required. If the net requirements are less than or equal to the lot size, then the amount specified in the lot size is ordered. Otherwise the order size is equal to the net requirements and is of course greater than the EOQ value. A weakness of the EOQ technique is that large quantities of units which are not immediately required are carried in stock. In the example, 50 units are carried unnecessarily in inventory in weeks 4 through 6.

Periodic order quantity

The periodic order quantity (POQ) technique is based on the same thinking as the EOQ method. For the EOQ technique the order quantity is constant while the ordering interval varies. However, for the POQ model the ordering interval is constant while the order quantity varies. Thus:

$$T = \frac{Q}{D} \qquad \textbf{(13.41)}$$

where: T = ordering interval, Q = economic order quantity, D = average demand per unit time.

For the example, the EOQ is equal to 75 units, while the average demand is 30 units per week, giving

$$T = \frac{75}{30} = 2.5 \text{ weeks} \qquad \textbf{(13.42)}$$

Table 13.31 Periodic order quantity

Item: Office stool							Part number: FP-100						
Week number	1	2	3	4	5	6	7	8	9	10	11	12	13
Gross requirements		60	25	15		40	65		20	70	20	45	30
Scheduled receipts		70											
Projected inventory	5	15	−10	−25	−25	−65	−130	−130	−150	−220	−240	−285	−315
Net requirements			10	15		40	65		20	70	20	45	30
Planned order receipt			25			105				90		95	
Planned order		25			105			90		95			

In this example, the ordering interval alternates between 2 and 3 weeks, except when zero requirements in a given period extend the ordering interval. Table 13.31 shows that the first order is required at week 3. The next order is expected two weeks later, i.e. week 5. However, the order is not taken until week 6, as there are no requirements for any units in week 5.

Least total cost

The least total cost (LTC) technique applies the assumption that stock is used at the beginning of each period. This means that a portion of the order, equal to the quantity of net requirements in the first period covered by the order, is used immediately upon arrival in stock and thus incurs no inventory carrying charge.

The LTC technique is based on the concept that the total cost is minimized when the set-up and inventory carrying costs are as near equal as possible. This is achieved through the economic part-period (EPP) factor. EPP is defined as that quantity of the inventory item which, if carried in inventory for one period, would result in an inventory carrying cost equal to the cost of set-up:

$$EPP = \frac{S}{C} \tag{13.43}$$

where: S = set-up cost, C = carrying cost per unit per period.

Again using the example, with S = £94 and C = £1 per stool per week, we obtain

$$EPP = \frac{94}{1} = 94 \tag{13.44}$$

The LTC technique selects that order quantity at which the part-period cost most closely matches the EPP value. Table 13.32 shows the least total cost calculation for the ongoing example:

$$PP_i = PP_{i-1} + (NR_i \times C_i) \tag{13.45}$$

where: PP_i = cumulative part-periods for period i, NR_i = net requirements for period i, C_i = duration for which inventory is carried.

Table 13.32 Calculation of least total cost

Period (week)	Net requirements	Carried in inventory (weeks)	Prospective lot size	Part-periods (cumulative)
3	10	0	10	0
4	15	1	25	15
5	0	2		15
6	40	3	65	135*
7	65	0	65	0
8	0	1		0
9	20	2	85	40*
10	70	3	155	250
10	70	0	70	0
11	20	1	90	20
12	45	2	135	110*
13	30	0	30	0*

* = closest match to EPP

Table 13.33 Least total cost

Item: Office stool							Part number: FP-100						
Week number	1	2	3	4	5	6	7	8	9	10	11	12	13
Gross requirements		60	25	15		40	65		20	70	20	45	30
Scheduled receipts		70											
Projected inventory	5	15	-10	-25	-25	-65	-130	-130	-150	-220	-240	-285	-315
Net requirements			10	15		40	65		20	70	20	45	30
Planned order receipt			65					85		135			30
Planned order	65			85					135		30		

For example:

$$PP_{10} = PP_9 + (NR_{10} \times C_{10})$$
$$= 40 + (70 \times 3) = 250 \qquad \textbf{(13.46)}$$

The quantity chosen for the first lot is 65, because 135 part-periods are the closest match to the EPP value of 94 (compared with 15 part-periods for a lot size of 25). This order covers the requirements of weeks 3 through 6, and the second order of 85 covers the requirements of weeks 7 through 9 etc., as shown in Table 13.33. In general the LTC technique is slightly biased towards larger order quantities.

13.5 Requirements planning in practice
....

Materials requirements planning (MRP) originated in the early 1960s in the United States as a computerized approach to the planning of materials acquisition and production. Early computerized applications of MRP were built around a bill of materials processor (BOMP) which converted a discrete plan of production for a parent item into a discrete plan of production or purchasing for component items and assemblies. This was done by exploding the requirements for the top-level product, through the bill of materials (BOM), to generate component demand, and then comparing the projected gross demand with available inventory and open orders, over the planning time horizon and at each level in the BOM. These systems were implemented on large mainframe computers and run in the centralized data processing departments of large companies.

One of the significant reasons that MRP was adopted so readily was that it made use of the computer's ability to store centrally and provide access to the large body of information that seemed necessary to run a company. It helped to coordinate the activities of various functions in the manufacturing firm, such as engineering, production and materials. Thus the attraction of MRP lay not only in its role in supporting decision-making, but perhaps equally importantly in its integrative role within the manufacturing organization.

Net change and regenerative MRP systems

In fact there are two basic styles of MRP system, termed the **regenerative** approach and the **net change** approach, respectively. These involve alternative approaches to the system-driven recalculation of an existing material plan based on changes in the input to that plan.

Regenerative MRP starts with the master production schedule and totally re-explodes it down through all the bills of materials to generate valid priorities. Net requirements and planned orders are completely *regenerated* at that time. The regenerative approach thus involves a complete re-analysis of each and every item identified in the master schedule, the explosion of all relevant BOMs, and the calculation of gross and net requirements for planned items. The entire process is carried out in a batch processing mode on the computer, and for all but the simplest of master schedules involves extensive data processing. Because of this, regenerative systems are typically operated in a weekly and occasionally monthly replanning cycle.

In the net change MRP approach, the materials requirements plan is continuously stored in the computer. Whenever there is an unplanned event, such as a new order in the master schedule, an order being completed late or early, scrap or loss of inventory or indeed an engineering change to one of the BOMs, a partial explosion is initiated only for those parts affected by the change. If an event is planned, for instance when an order is completed on time, then the original material plan should still be valid. The system is updated to reflect the new status, but replanning is not initiated. Net change MRP can operate in two ways. One mode is to have an on-line net change system, by which the system reacts instantaneously to unplanned changes as they occur. In most cases, however, change transactions are batched (typically by day) and replanning happens over night.

Data requirements for MRP systems

As is apparent from our discussion of requirements planning, the prerequisites to operate an MRP system include the following:

▶ A master production schedule exists. This master production schedule is a clear statement of the requirements in terms of quantities and due dates for top-level items.

▶ For every parent or top-level item (in fact MPS item), there must be a corresponding bill of materials (BOM) which gives an accurate and complete statement of the structure of that item.

▶ For every planned part, there must be available a set of inventory status information. Inventory status is a statement of physical stock on hand, material allocated to released orders, but not yet drawn from physical stock, and scheduled receipts for the item in question.

▶ For each planned part, either purchased or manufactured, a planning lead time must be available.

It is clear from our discussion thus far that an MRP system relies on a great deal of data. We now look in more detail at this data. Our intention is not to give an exhaustive list, but merely to discuss in general terms the more important sources of data used and maintained by MRP systems. We do not intend to discuss the implementation of the database. MRP systems are gradually migrating from file-oriented data storage to database management systems. Suffice it to say that data should be stored in a manner to avoid redundant storage, with links between related fields being system-maintained, and which facilitates the ease of access in any desired manner, either for inquiry or reporting purposes, or by applications external to the MRP system.

A typical MRP database contains several related major sources of information, including:

▶ The master parts information;

▶ Full inventory information;

▶ Bill of materials information;

▶ The manufacturing process or routing information for all manufactured and assembled items;

▶ Work centre information;

▶ Tooling information.

Master parts information contains detailed data on each planned item in the system. Each part is typically described in terms of static data and dynamic data. **Static data** refers to data whose values do not change very frequently. Furthermore, changes are typically initiated by the user, as distinct from being derived from calculations within the requirements planning procedure. Typical static data includes the part number, part description, unit of measurement, make or buy code, stores location, standard cost, material cost, shrinkage factor if appropriate, lead time, safety stock if appropriate, lot size policy etc. The **dynamic data** is so called because the values stored within the data fields change very frequently and many are generated as a consequence of MRP calculations. This data describes the full inventory status for the part, including requirements, allocations, open orders and planned orders. Typical dynamic data in the master parts file includes the current actual inventory, current open orders per time period or bucket, gross requirements per time period or bucket, net requirements per time period or bucket, planned order releases per time period or bucket etc.

The bill of materials file defines the structure of a product. Data is stored in a manner which facilitates the BOM inquiry options normally available in a bill of materials system. Such options include the ability to generate single-level assembly BOMs, indented bills of materials, summary bills of materials and 'where used' tables for individual assemblies and components.

Routing information defines the manufacturing and/or assembly operations which must be performed on a manufactured component. The data is primarily of an engineering nature. Typical data maintained on a manufactured parts routing includes the part number and, for each operation on that part, data on the operation number, the work centre at which it is to be performed, an alternative work centre if appropriate, tools required if appropriate, the set-up time, the processing time, the operation lead time etc.

Work centre information is used primarily for capacity planning purposes. It contains data on each work centre in the production facility. In this context, a **work centre** is a set of resources. Thus it may refer to a group of machines and/or operators with identical functionality and ability to discharge that functionality, or it may refer to a single resource.

Tooling information provides detailed data on tools which are available and are associated with particular operations and work centres. For a company engaged in substantial metal cutting or metal forming operations, one would certainly expect to find great emphasis on such information. Less emphasis would be placed on the same information by a firm engaged primarily in, say, electronics assembly.

The need for accurate data

The MRP procedure, although tedious, is deceptively simple. After all, what is involved but the calculation of net requirements from gross requirements taking the overall stock position into account, and then using some lot-sizing technique to generate firm orders? Perhaps the greatest requirement of all for successful MRP installation and operation is discipline. This includes the discipline to maintain accurate stock records, the discipline to report accurately and in good time the completion of jobs and orders, and the discipline to report to the system every event which it should be aware of. If stocks are withdrawn from stores then this fact should be notified to the system and the inventory status in the production database updated accordingly.

13.6 MRP and MRP II
·······················

Manufacturing resource planning (MRP II) represents an extension of the features of the MRP system to support many other manufacturing functions beyond material planning, inventory control and BOM control. In fact, manufacturing resource planning (MRP II) evolved from MRP by a gradual series of extensions to MRP system functionality. These extensions included the addition of transaction processing software to support the purchasing, inventory and financial functions of the firm. In supporting the extension of decision support, similar and quite reasonable assumptions are made and similar procedures are applied as those of MRP. In this way, MRP was extended to support master schedule planning, rough-cut capacity planning (RCCP), capacity requirements planning (CRP) and shop floor control.

RCCP is a relatively fast check on the feasibility of the master schedule from a capacity point of view. Essentially it involves identifying a number of critical, perhaps potential bottleneck, resources and checking that there is sufficient capacity available on them to meet the proposed master schedule. If the rough-cut capacity planning exercise reveals that the proposed master schedule is not feasible, then the master schedule must be revised or alternatively further resources must be acquired.

Capacity requirements planning (CRP) generates a more detailed capacity profile than that generated by RCCP. CRP is typically performed after each requirements planning run and is essentially a verification procedure to verify the feasibility of the planned orders generated by the MRP analysis.

Shop floor control refers to the operational element of the production planning and control system, and will be discussed in more detail in Chapter 14.

13.7 Distribution planning
·····························

Up to now we have concentrated in this chapter on the planning of the material flow through the manufacturing system. We have seen how MRP-style systems allow planners to manage and control the flow of purchased items into the manufacturing plant and the flow of manufactured parts and assembled products through the plant. But what about the flow of finished goods out of the plant and on to the customers? The distribution of finished product from manufacturing through warehousing and on to the customer is the subject of this section. Just as we have MRP-style systems to plan manufacturing, we have DRP (Distribution Requirements Planning) systems to plan distribution activities.

In illustrating the rationale and logic of DRP we will take the example of a manufacturer of canned pet food who has a single manufacturing facility in Dublin and a set of five regional warehouses located in, say, Glasgow, Middlesbrough, Manchester, Birmingham and London. We will look at the use of DRP to plan the distribution of one of this manufacturers products, namely 'DoggieMeat'. Let us further assume that 'DoggieMeat' is shipped from the manufacturing plant in cartons of 100 cans and that each distribution centre must order in multiples of 40 full cartons, that is a minimum of 40 cartons.

Table 13.34 London warehouse

Week no.		1	2	3	4	5	6	7
Order forecast		40	30	50	20	20	50	40
In transit	–							
Projected on hand	200	160	130	80	60	40	–10	–50

Table 13.35 London warehouse

Week no.		1	2	3	4	5	6	7
Order forecast		40	30	50	20	20	50	40
In transit	–							
Projected on hand	200	160	130	80	60	40	30	30
Planned receipt							40	40
Planned orders					40	40		

Table 13.36 London warehouse (safety stock = 100, order quantity = 120)

Week no.		1	2	3	4	5	6	7
Order forecast		40	30	50	20	20	50	40
In transit	–							
Projected on hand	200	160	130	200	180	160	110	190
Planned receipt				120				120
Planned orders		120				120		

Let us look at the situation in the London warehouse initially. Table 13.34 illustrates the inventory situation. Initially we will assume that the 'on-hand' balance of stock is 200 cartons, that there is no safety stock provision and that the lead time from dispatch of order to receipt of goods is two weeks. As Table 13.34 indicates, the London warehouse will experience stockouts and delayed orders unless some action is taken.

If there is no safety stock specified, and no ordering policy other than to meet short-term orders, then in order to avoid stockouts and delayed order deliveries, orders must be placed on the Dublin manufacturing plant in weeks 4 and 5 to deliver (planned receipts) in weeks 6 and 7 respectively. See Table 13.35.

Let us now consider the situation where the London warehouse had set a safety stock of 100 cartons and an order quantity of 120 cartons. Table 13.36 shows the effect. Now we need to order 120 cartons in week 1 for receipt in week 3 in order to ensure that the inventory level does not fall below 100 in any week. Similarly we need to order 120 cartons in week 5 for delivery in week 7.

Table 13.37 Glasgow warehouse (safety stock = 80, minimum order quantity 80)

Week no.		1	2	3	4	5	6	7
Order forecast		30	10	20	10	30	20	30
In transit	–							
Projected on hand	160	130	120	100	90	140	120	90
Planned receipt						80		
Planned orders				80				

Table 13.38 Middlesbrough warehouse (safety stock = 80, minimum order quantity = 80)

Week no.		1	2	3	4	5	6	7
Order forecast		20	30	20	20	40	20	20
In transit	–							
Projected on hand	160	140	110	90	150	110	90	150
Planned receipt					80			80
Planned orders			80			80		

Table 13.39 Manchester warehouse (safety stock = 70, minimum order quantity = 80)

Week no.		1	2	3	4	5	6	7
Order forecast		30	30	40	40	40	40	50
In transit	–							
Projected on hand	160	130	100	140	100	140	100	130
Planned receipt				80		80		80
Planned orders		80		80		80		

It is important to be clear on the meaning of the terms 'Planned receipt' and 'Planned orders' in Tables 13.34–13.36. 'Planned receipts' refer to the receipt of products in the warehouse from the manufacturing plant, that is the receipt of shipments. 'Planned orders' refers to the time bucket during which the orders are shipped from the manufacturing plant. In fact we could usefully relabel 'Planned receipts' as 'Shipments receipt' and 'Planned orders' as 'Order shipments'.

As we indicated earlier the manufacturer has five regional distribution centres. We now need to consider each of these distribution centres and show how their requirements are consolidated to generate the requirements for the manufacturing plant. The individual planned orders for the various distribution centres are outlined in Tables 13.37–13.40.

The consolidated requirements for the manufacturing plant are presented in Table 13.41.

Table 13.40 Birmingham warehouse (safety stock = 90, minimum order quantity = 80)

Week no.		1	2	3	4	5	6	7
Order forecast			30	40	40	40	50	50	40
In transit		–							
Projected on hand	170	140	100	140	100	130	160	120
Planned receipt				80		80	80	
Planned orders			80		80	80		

Table 13.41 Planned shipments from the manufacturing plant

Week no.	1	2	3	4	5	6	7
London	120				120		
Glasgow			80				
Middlesbrough		80			80		
Manchester	80		80		80		
Birmingham	80		80	80			
Total requirements	280	80	240	80	280	–	–

This table indicates to the manufacturing plant the individual requirements of the various warehouses so that it can plan its shipments. Also it indicates the orders coming from the various warehouses (which in this case are the only source of orders). In many DRP applications, the total requirements line of Table 13.41 feeds into the 'Customer order' line of the master production schedule (MPS) table (see Table 13.6). In the MPS table the DRP data could therefore be used to help determine total demand and ultimately the MRP quantity per time bucket.

'In transit'

In each of the DRP planning tableaux of Tables 13.34–13.40 the 'In transit' line appears. We now show how this line is used, by looking at the changes to the DRP tableau as time moves forward. We will use the London warehouse (Table 13.36) as an example.

Let us assume that the order forecast of 40 in week 1 turned out to have underestimated the demand, which in reality was for 60 cartons, and further that the forecast for week 2 has to be reduced from 30 to 25.

Table 13.42 represents the revised position for the London warehouse. Note that:

1. Table 13.42 covers weeks 2 to 8 inclusive (i.e. a rolling 7 week planning horizon).

2. Table 13.36 showed a 'Planned receipt' of 120 cartons in week 3, and a 'Planned order' for 120 cartons in week 1. In reality, as pointed out earlier, these 'Planned orders' are 'Planned shipments' from the manufacturing plant. By week 2 these

Table 13.42 Revised position for the London warehouse (safety stock = 100, minimum order quantity = 120)

Week no.		2	3	4	5	6	7	8
Order forecast		25	50	20	20	50	40	30
In transit			120					
Projected on hand	140	115	185	165	145	215	175	145
Planned receipt						120		
Planned orders				120				

'Planned shipments' should have become actual shipments and now appear in the 'In transit' line of the tableau, scheduled to arrive in the warehouse in week 3.

3. The overall effect of the changes documented in Table 13.42, compared with the original plan developed in Table 13.36, is to bring forward the order for 120 cartons by one week.

MRP and DRP

It is interesting to make explicit the similarities between the MRP and DRP approaches. In order to use MRP we need access to the following data:

▶ Product BOMs.

▶ Master parts data, which includes inventory data on all BOM items.

▶ Data on open purchase orders and open shop orders.

▶ A master production schedule.

A DRP system requires similar data:

▶ Bills of distribution.

▶ Inventory data on each product.

▶ Data on open orders and orders in transit.

▶ A forecast of customer requirements including existing orders.

A bill of distribution plays a somewhat analogous role to an engineering bill of materials. For example, the bill of distribution for the pet food manufacturer is illustrated in Figure 13.13.

The MRP system produces two outputs:

▶ A set of planned orders for manufactured and assembled parts.

▶ A set of planned orders for purchased parts.

Similarly the DRP system produced two outputs:

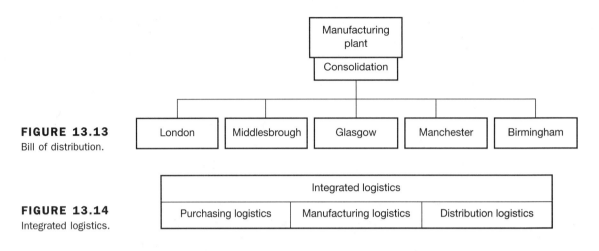

FIGURE 13.13
Bill of distribution.

FIGURE 13.14
Integrated logistics.

▶ A set of orders to be fed into the master production schedule of an MRP-style system.

▶ The detailed requirements of individual warehouses which are then used to plan the transport of product between the manufacturing plant(s) and the distribution warehouse(s).

Finally it is worth pointing out that MRP and DRP systems do not exist in isolation in the real world. Given the need to shorten the lead time from customer order to product delivery (i.e. the customer order fulfilment time), there is great interest today in developing integrated logistics systems. These integrated systems seek to provide seamless integration between the purchasing, manufacturing and distribution systems (see Figure 13.14).

MRP-style systems generate planned orders for purchasing (purchasing logistics) and manufacturing/assembly (manufacturing logistics). As we have seen, a DRP system used to manage distribution logistics will generate the required orders which are in turn fed back into the master schedule system of an MRP-style system.

Example 13.1 *MRP and the supply chain*

Thermo King produces transport refrigeration for truck bodies, trailers, seagoing containers, buses, and rail cars. These systems protect not only food, but also medicines, cosmetics, electronic gear, and other temperature-sensitive goods and products. Thermo King also manufactures air-conditioning systems for buses and rail cars, and provides management software for motor freight companies. Through the years, investments in technology, manufacturing and service have yielded strong performance in Thermo King, with excellent growth in revenue and profits. Thermo King's performance and strong customer service orientation make it the preferred supplier in the industry. Its European headquarters are located in Galway, Ireland. This plant primarily manufactures the SMX and the SuperBOSS refrigeration units and also supplies its sister plants in Europe and China with parts.

Importance of supply chain to Thermo King

Figure 13.15 outlines Thermo King's supply chain. Upstream in the channel of the supply chain orders are placed for parts to a number of trading partners. These include local, national and international vendors, Thermo King's head plant in Minneapolis, and its sister plants in Ireland and Europe. Some of these partners, in turn, share requirements information with a number of subcontractors who produce parts. The subcontractors must receive accurate information about the timing and quantity of parts required, since these items will be delivered to Thermo King's production facility for almost immediate use in manufacturing. Those companies that have to deliver the parts also need very accurate information in order to plan their production. Downstream in the channel the truck manufacturers that purchase the refrigeration units must provide demand information to Thermo King. Clearly, demand information is critical to achieve the supply chain goal, that is to meet customers' needs. In addition, other parties, such as consolidation warehouses and subassemblers, are also part of Thermo King's supply chain and they need to share the information required to meet customers' needs while carrying minimal inventory.

However, supply chain management is concerned with more than inventory. There are also information tools to be considered. The most widely used tool in this category is electronic data interchange (EDI) which allows the direct computer-to-computer transfer of data in standardized format so that firms with EDI installations can automatically process transactions. Use of EDI enables interchange of information from a final assembler to its suppliers, including information on forecasts, orders, pricing, invoices, payments, availability details, etc. As a result, these suppliers can meet orders on a JIT basis in the short term, plan materials in the medium term, and conduct strategic planning and customer terms negotiation in the long term.

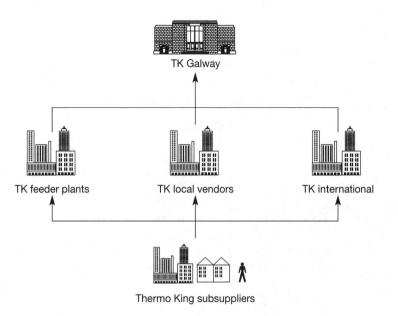

TK Galway

TK feeder plants   TK local vendors   TK international

Thermo King subsuppliers

FIGURE 13.15
Overall view of Thermo King Galway's role within the supply chain.

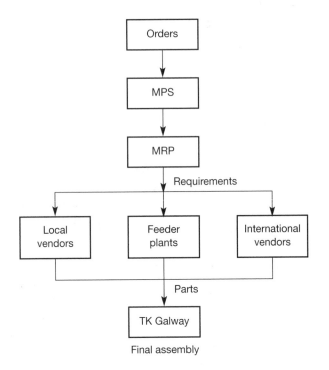

FIGURE 13.16

Local vendors within
Thermo King's
supply chain.

For the purpose of this example we will look at the role that Thermo King's local vendors play in the supply chain. Figure 13.16 shows that these local vendors are treated as part of Thermo King's overall supply chain.

An inventory management project was inaugurated in Thermo King to integrate its existing inventory management systems under one umbrella. By integrating its operations with its suppliers, customers, distributors and third-party logistics providers, Thermo King envisaged an overall improvement in channel efficiency.

The coordinated efforts of Thermo King and its suppliers allow Thermo King's supply chain partners to be responsive of its needs. The whole chain is managed almost as if it were one single entity to achieve improved customer service at reduced overall costs, and various decisions on production and distribution are viewed across the entire chain.

The computer system in Thermo King Galway

At present, most of Thermo King's critical systems are run on its mainframe, an IBM ES-9000. Much of the software running on this system is proprietary, written in the CICS language. In parallel with this, the plant is migrating towards a PC/LAN system. The software architecture of Thermo King Galway's system is shown in Figure 13.17. Barcoding has been implemented through the plant for some time now to support the tracking of material movement.

The mainframe systems handle two distinct types of system: manufacturing engineering systems and supply chain systems. Manufacturing engineering systems include the BTMS (the Barcode Tracking and Monitoring System), the FMS (Flexible

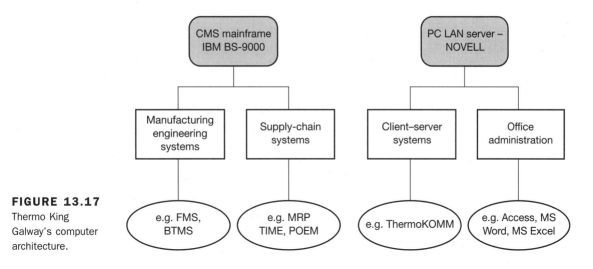

FIGURE 13.17
Thermo King Galway's computer architecture.

Manufacturing System), and other systems concerned with control at the shop floor level. Supply chain systems include the MRP system, TIME (Thermo King Inventory Management for Europe) and the POEM (Planning Order Entry Management) system.

The PCs host either client–server software, or office administration software, such as word processors, databases and spreadsheets. In general, the operating systems and software are mainly Microsoft, with the notable exception of Notes which is a Lotus product and uses OS/2 as its server. Most of the CAD tools are run on dedicated workstations.

Currently, most of the terminals to the mainframe have been replaced by sessions from Windows-based PCs. This closeness to the PC environment has led to a gradual porting of much of the presentation layer software over to the PCs. For example, the TIME system which is used for inventory management runs on the mainframe. It receives and analyses requests for parts through barcode wanding and performs calculations to find the optimal inventory at various points in the supply chain. Much of the front end for this application runs on PCs. All reports and much of the management and data entry functions run on an MS Access application which downloads/uploads data to and from the mainframe.

Thermo King is currently implementing EDI throughout its supply chain as an enabler of supply chain communications. Eirtrade is the EDI VAN which is providing the software, expertise and network for this data exchange. There are two pieces of software written by Eirtrade for the EDI system: the 'Thermo King Order Processing Module', and 'Intercept Plus'. The former module handles the translation of all data concerning orders, calloffs and receipts. This is illustrated in Figure 13.18. Intercept Plus is a generic system for management of the EDI account at Eirtrade, connection to the services, checking of mailboxes and posting of messages.

In general, interplant orders are managed through the shared CMS mainframe database, while communications with suppliers are largely fax based and migrating towards EDI. The main supply chain software at the moment is the mainframe MRP system and the related POEM system, the TIME inventory management system and

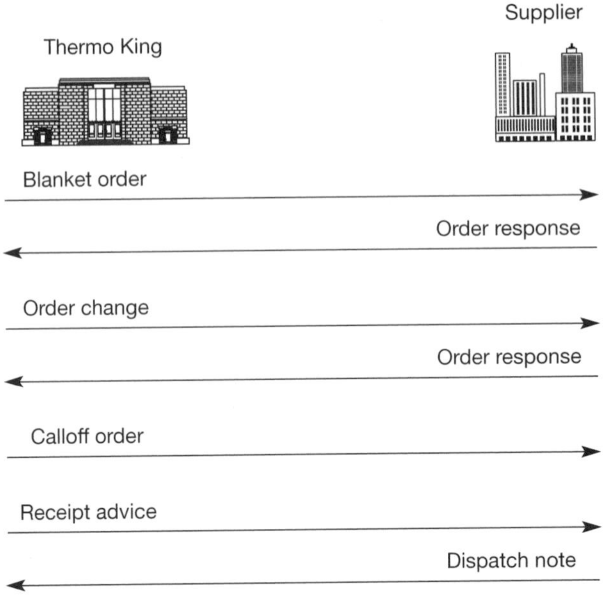

Thermo King

Supplier

Blanket order

Order response

Order change

Order response

FIGURE 13.18
Functional elements
of the Eirtrade
Thermo King Order
Processing EDI
module.

Calloff order

Receipt advice

Dispatch note

the EDI extension to TIME. The EDI extension to TIME allows the automated generation of electronic orders/calloffs as shown in Figure 13.18.

At present, the MRP module is used in all of the European plants. TIME is implemented fully in the Galway and Dublin plants, and partially in the Czech plant. The EDI extension to TIME is implemented fully only in the Galway plant at present, though plans are underway to bring the Dublin and Czech plants on line.

Profile of local vendor

Thermo King is supplied with parts for its refrigeration units by over 60 local vendors. For the purpose of this case study we will profile one of these vendors – ROM Plastics. ROM Plastics is a wholly owned Irish company that produces a wide range of rotational moulded products. The company has received ISO 9000 certification and operates a production environment to that standard as part of its commitment to world-class quality and manufacturing. ROM supplies Thermo King with plastic bulkheads for its refrigeration units. These bulkheads are hollow parts of complex and varied shapes.

Profile of the supply process

The pre-EDI situation is shown in Figure 13.19:

1. The MRP system dictated the local vendor parts requirements necessary to replenish Thermo King's existing supplies. The purchasing personnel then created a purchase order and sent it to the local vendor.

2. The local vendor processed the request and delivered the parts to Thermo King with the dispatch notice. On arrival at Thermo King the goods were unloaded and placed in the receiving and inspection area.

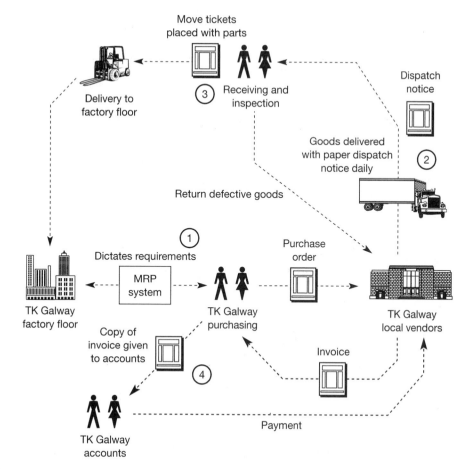

FIGURE 13.19
The pre-EDI module.

3. The parts received were checked against the dispatch notice to see that everything was in order. In addition, any defective goods were returned. Those that were not defective were delivered directly to the factory floor. The forklift operators knew what locations the parts were to be delivered to because 'move' tickets were generated by the receiving and inspection personnel.

4. Copies of the dispatch notices were sent to the purchasing department which in turn sent authorized receipts to the local vendors. These identified all the parts that had been received over a period of one month. This information was sent to the local vendor who used it to invoice Thermo King. It promptly sent a monthly invoice to Thermo King's purchasing department. The purchasing personnel created a copy of this invoice and sent it to the accounts department, who made the necessary adjustments to pay the local vendors.

The new situation is outlined in Figure 13.20:

1. On the factory floor progress chasers constantly check the quantities in the Kanban bins. If a particular bin is almost empty the barcode attached to the bin

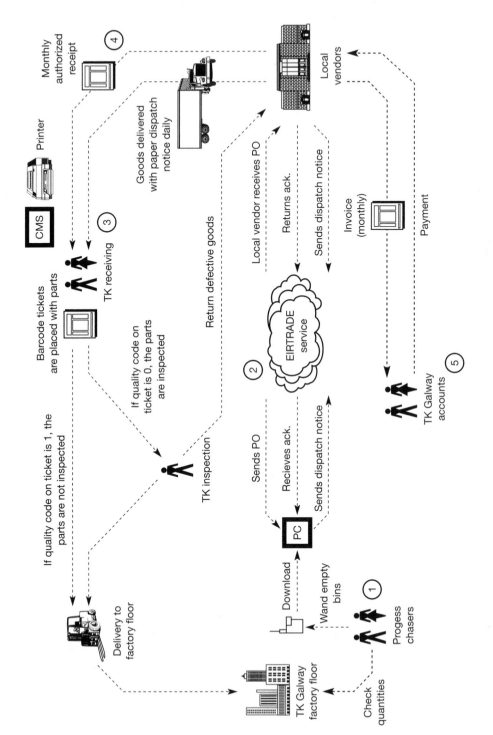

FIGURE 13.20

The new situation.

is wanded with a barcode reader. At the end of each day the barcode readers are downloaded onto Thermo King's CMS mainframe, and the system automatically routes the requests to an on-line file, which in turn routes them to a PC containing the Intercept Plus EDI software package.

2   This software package communicates with Telecom Eireann's EDI EIRTRADE service. The requests are formatted in such a way that a purchase order is generated and is sent electronically to the EIRTRADE 'cloud'. It resides there until the local vendor responsible for manufacturing the required parts logs onto its machine and sees that there is a message waiting. When the local vendor receives the purchase order it returns an acknowledgement via EIRTRADE to Thermo King and subsequently processes the order. When the request has been processed the vendor sends a dispatch notice, outlining the parts that will be delivered to Thermo King. Thermo King receives this notice and prints out barcode tickets corresponding to the parts that are due. The goods are then packed by the vendor and shipped with a copy of the dispatch notice.

3.   On arrival at Thermo King the parts are unloaded in the receiving and inspection department and their awaiting barcode tickets are placed with them. Those parts whose barcode tickets have a '1' quality code are delivered directly to the factory floor. However, those with a quality code of '0' are inspected. After inspection if the particular part is deemed defective, it is returned to the supplier. In some cases where the defect is minimal (e.g. the edges may need to be rounded), the part is reworked by Thermo King and is then delivered to the factory floor.

4.   Thermo King Galway then issues a monthly authorized receipt to its local vendors, containing all of the parts that were received during that particular month. This is used by the local vendors to invoice Thermo King.

5.   This invoice is sent by post and the accounts department within Thermo King deals with the necessary payment.

It is the vision of Thermo King eventually to utilize EDI to its maximum capability. This means that every document involved in the above process will be handled using EDI – for example, processing invoices and payment to the local vendor's bank account.

Benefits of the current system

The benefits of Thermo King's recent installation of EDI fall into two main areas: strategic benefits and operational benefits. Strategic benefits are of crucial long-term significance to the functioning of Thermo King. Operational benefits are probably the most clear and easily identifiable, and involve the day-to-day running of Thermo King. The strategic benefits include:

▶   faster trading cycle;

▶   quick response logistics;

▶   terms of trade dictated by bargaining power;

▶   ability to respond to a highly competitive market.

The operational benefits include:

▶ a reduction in stationery and postage bills;

▶ a reduction in money tied up in stock;

▶ improved cash flow;

▶ error reduction.

Conclusions

This case study has examined the difference new enabling technology has made to Thermo King's supply chain. Compared with the existing situation, the new one has the following technical and strategic advantages:

▶ It provides an integrated solution to all interfirm communications.

▶ The same system can be used to connect the sister plants in Europe and the United States.

▶ It is an expandable solution which embraces technologies which, as far as can be ascertained, will be in wide use for a considerable time.

▶ A system such as this compresses the time spent sourcing suppliers, placing orders, feeding out requirements and monitoring their performance. It should also decrease product development time for co-designed parts.

▶ Sending the requirements to the suppliers brings the benefit of better capacity forecasting to the rest of the supply chain, resulting in lower shortage statistics.

A solution such as this can be built on top of Thermo King's existing hardware infrastructure, without having to invest in expensive new systems.

Example 13.2 *MRP implementation*

Probe Inc. is a multinational supplier of sophisticated electronic sensors to the automotive, aerospace and general engineering industry. The company has three manufacturing plants: one plant is responsible for the production of the microchips on which the various sensors are based, the second plant assembles and tests the sensors, and a third plant assembles the completed sensors into probes. The company sells completed sensors from plant number 2 and probes from plant number 3 to its customers. The manufacture of the microchips in plant number 1 is done on a make to stock (MTS) basis, while the manufacture of sensors in plant number 2 is make to order (MTO) and the assembly of probes in plant number 3 is assemble to order (ATO). Given that the output of plant number 1, namely microchips, is not shipped to customers, but is sent for further processing into sensors to plant number 2, we can consider plant number 1 to be a feeder plant (see Figure 13.21).

The majority of customer orders (about 80%) are for completed probes supplied by plant number 3, with the remainder being sensors supplied by plant number 2.

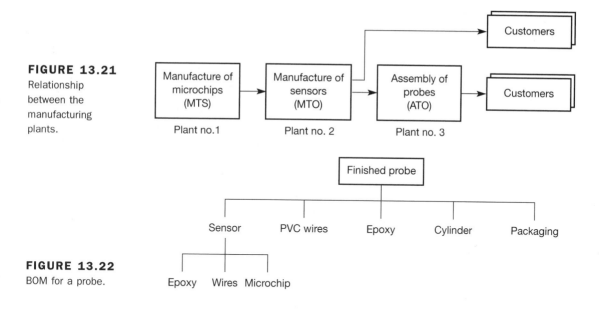

FIGURE 13.21
Relationship between the manufacturing plants.

FIGURE 13.22
BOM for a probe.

A typical phantom bill of materials (BOM) for a probe is presented in Figure 13.22.

Clearly the BOM is very flat. From the point of view of the probe assembly plant (plant number 3) the sensor is a 'purchased' plant. Similarly from the perspective of the sensor plant (plant number 2), the microchip is a 'purchased' plant. However, it is worth noting that individual customers buy customized probes and therefore the individual sensors are made to order at plant number 2 and the probes for individual customers require specific cylinders, PVC wires, packaging, etc.

Implementation of MRP at Probe Inc.

Prior to the introduction of MRP at the company, customers were quoted delivery dates based on standard lead times. Thus, for example, an order for sensors was assumed to have a lead time of 6 weeks, and a probe 10 weeks. These delivery lead times were based on 'pessimistic' production lead times and typically orders were delivered to customers earlier than their due date. This situation of a long quoted lead time and a somewhat shorter actual lead time was considered unsatisfactory by all concerned.

The system implemented in Probe Inc. is outlined in Figure 13.23. Three aspects of this system are worthy of note:

1. The MRP system is closely tied in with the company's accounts system. Note for example that the creation of purchase orders leads to the updating of the creditors' ledger. Also the creation of invoices by the shipping module updates the debtors' ledger.

2. The forecasting module is used to develop orders for the microchip manufacturing plant (plant number 1) while the sales order processing module creates

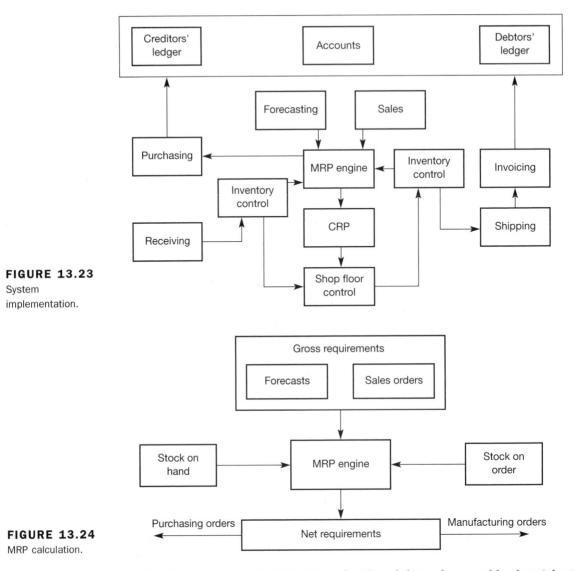

FIGURE 13.23
System
implementation.

FIGURE 13.24
MRP calculation.

orders for the sensors plant (plant number 2) and the probe assembly plant (plant number 3).

3. The MRP output of planned orders for the three plants is evaluated by a CRP module prior to its release to the shop floor control modules in the individual plants.

The details of the MRP calculation are illustrated in Figure 13.24.

The implementation of the system at Probe Inc. took approximately four months from selection of the software to finished installation and use of the system. The implementation of the system followed the outline implementation plan illustrated in Figure 13.25.

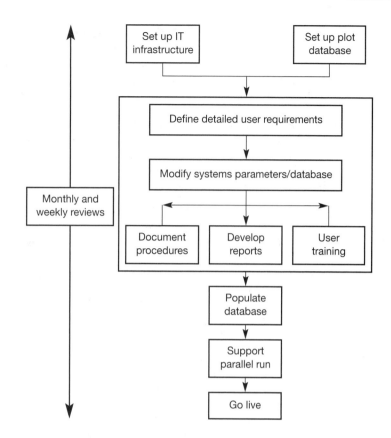

FIGURE 13.25
MRP system
implementation.

Note that the implementation of the system included a detailed review of the user requirements at the individual plants, which in turn allowed the modification of the system parameters, the sizing of the database and the development of reporting and documentation procedures tailored to the needs of each plant. Also it is important to emphasize the resources and time necessary for training at the end users in the individual plants. Well-trained and motivated users are critical to the success of any MRP installation.

··

13.8 Conclusion
··················

In this chapter we reviewed the basic principles of business planning in so far as they impact production planning and control and also looked at the background to master scheduling. Most of the chapter was taken up with a simple requirements planning example. We showed how the calculations are made and how the master schedule is exploded using the bill of materials. Also, in this chapter we looked at some of the more popular lot-sizing techniques in use today. In the following chapter we will look at some shop floor control techniques that are used to implement a company's strategic and tactical goals at operations level.

References and further reading

APICS Master Planning Committee (1988). *Master Planning Reprints*. The American Production and Inventory Control Society Inc., Virginia.

Burbidge J. L. (1987). *IFIP Glossary of Terms Used in Production Control*. Amsterdam: Elsevier Science Publishers.

Chambers J., Mullick S. and Smith D. (1971). How to choose the right forecasting technique. *Harvard Business Review*. July–August, 45–74.

Companys R., Falster P. and Burbidge J. L. (Editors) (1990). *Databases for Production Management*. Amsterdam: Elsevier Science Publishers.

Doumeingts G., Browne J. and Tomljanovich M. (Editors) (1991). *Computer Applications in Production and Engineering CAPE '91*. Amsterdam: Elsevier Science Publishers.

Falster P. and Mazumder R. B. (Editors) (1985). *Modelling Production Management Systems*. Amsterdam: Elsevier Science Publishers.

Friessnig R. (1979). Building a simple and effective forecasting system. *APICS Conference Proceedings*, pp. 156–8.

Gessner R. A. (1986). *Master Production Schedule Planning*. New York: John Wiley & Sons.

Hayes R. and Wheelwright S. C. (1984). *Restoring Our Competitive Edge, Competing Through Manufacturing*. New York: John Wiley.

Higgins P. and Browne J. (1992). Master production scheduling: a concurrent planning approach. *International Journal of Production Planning and Control*. **3**(1), 2–18.

Knox C. S. (1987). *Organizing Data for CIM Applications*. New York: Marcel Dekker Inc.

Krajewski L. J. and Ritzman L. P. (1987). *Operations Management*. Reading, MA: Addison Wesley Longman.

Makridakis S. and Wheelwright S. C. (1985). *Forecasting Methods for Management*. New York: John Wiley.

Orlicky J. (1975). *Material Requirements Planning*. New York: McGraw-Hill.

Skinner W. (1974). The focused factory. *Harvard Business Review*. May–June, 113–21.

Vollmann T., Berry T. and Whybark D. (1988). *Master Production Scheduling: Principles and Practice*. Falls Church VA: American Production and Inventory Control Society.

Wight O. W. (1981). *MRP II. Unlocking America's Productivity Potential*. Vermont: The Book Press.

Womack J. P., Jones D. T. and Roos D. (1991). *The Machine That Changed the World*. Rawson and Associates.

Exercises

13.1 Identify the six decision categories involved in the development of a manufacturing strategy.

13.2 What is the long-range production plan? How does it relate to the master production schedule?

13.3 In terms of the MPS record, distinguish clearly between the 'manual forecast' and the 'system forecast'.

13.4 How is total demand calculated in the MPS record?

13.5 How is the MPS line calculated in the MPS record?

13.6 Distinguish clearly between the projected available balance (PAB) and the available to promise (ATP) lines in the MPS record. Which should be used to support customer order promising? Why?

13.7 Complete the following MPS record. Assume a safety stock of 20 items and a lead time of one month. Further, assume PAB(O), or the starting inventory, is 30.

Item: Product B			Part No. FP-20			
Month number	1	2	3	4	5	6
Manual forecast	40	50	50	60	40	50
System forecast	50	50	50	50	60	60
Customer orders	45	40	20	10	–	–
Total demand						
MPS						
PAB						
ATP						
Cumulative ATP						

13.8 Alpha Manufacturing Company's master production scheduler is seeking to develop a forecasting model for a major product line. He has collected unit sales data for the past six months (i.e. January through to June inclusive). The data is presented in the table below.

Month:	January	February	March	April	May	June
Unit sales:	2100	2400	2300	2700	2600	2900

Develop a simple exponential smoothing model for this product, using a starting average (i.e. December) of 2200, and an exponential smoothing constant value of $\alpha = 0.2$. Forecast the unit sales figure for July, based on the data given.

13.9 Beta Retail Ltd has collected the following sales data on its best-selling product line for the past twelve months:

Month:	1	2	3	4	5	6	7	8	9	10	11	12
Sales (000s):	40	42	39	43	44	42	46	45	48	49	47	52

(a) Calculate the four-month moving average for month 10, as made at the end of month 9.
(b) Calculate the three-month moving average for month 12, as made at the end of month 10.
(c) Using a three-month moving average, calculate the forecast demand for months 4 through to 12 inclusive. Further, calculate the mean absolute deviation and the mean squared error for the forecasts.

13.10 Boston Manufacturing Ltd manufactures two products, Product X and Product Y. The bills of material for the two products are as illustrated in Figure 13.26.

A01 refers to an assembly composed of two components, C02 and C03. Note that there are common components between the two products (e.g. C01) and also assembly A01 is common to the two products. The number in brackets under a component indicates the number of that component required to build the assembly or product. Thus two of item C02 are required to assemble item A01.

Given the short master schedule outlined below, calculate the net requirements for components C01 and C02. Assume no inventory and no outstanding orders.

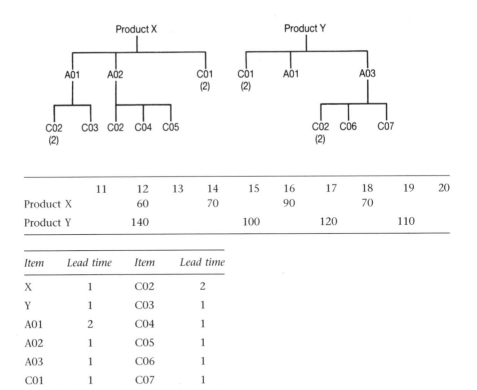

FIGURE 13.26
Bills of material.

	11	12	13	14	15	16	17	18	19	20
Product X		60		70		90		70		
Product Y		140			100		120		110	

Item	Lead time	Item	Lead time
X	1	C02	2
Y	1	C03	1
A01	2	C04	1
A02	1	C05	1
A03	1	C06	1
C01	1	C07	1

13.11 Based on the net requirements for component C02 (see Exercise 13.10), generate the planned orders releases for component C02, using the EOQ algorithm.

   Assume the order set-up cost is £120 and the inventory cost is £1 per unit per time period.

13.12 Using the cost data of Exercise 13.11 and the net requirements for C02 generated in Exercise 13.10, generate the planned order releases for C02 using the least total cost technique.

13.13 Distinguish clearly between net change and regeneration MRP systems.

13.14 Why is 'pegging' necessary in MRP systems? How does 'single level pegging' differ from 'full pegging'?

13.15 Using the cost data of Exercise 13.11, and the net requirements for C01 generated in Exercise 13.10, generate the planned order releases for C01, using the periodic order quantity approach.

13.16 Comment briefly on the data requirements of MRP systems.

13.17 Distinguish clearly between MRP and MRP II.

14 Shop floor control systems

··

Chapter objectives

When you have completed studying the material in this chapter you should be able to:

▶ **understand the role and structure of a shop floor control system;**
▶ **describe the architecture of a production activity control (PAC) system;**
▶ **define clearly the functionality of the different modules of a PAC system;**
▶ **identify the various performance measures used to evaluate scheduling systems;**
▶ **classify scheduling problems;**
▶ **apply simple scheduling algorithms and heuristics;**
▶ **understand the OPT (optimized production technology) approach to scheduling, and the implications of bottlenecks;**
▶ **describe the architecture of a factory coordination system;**
▶ **define clearly the functionality of the different modules of the factory coordination system.**

Chapter contents

14.1 Introduction
·····················

In this chapter we present an outline of the activities which occur at the operational level of the production management system hierarchy (see Chapter 12), namely the day-to-day tasks involved in planning and controlling production on a shop floor. Production activity control (PAC) and factory coordination (FC) provide a framework which integrates the requirements planning functions of RP type systems and the planning and control activities on a shop floor, and in doing so close the loop between the tactical and operational layers of the production planning and control hierarchy (see Bauer *et al.* (1991) for a more complete treatment of shop floor control). The overall structure of this chapter is as follows:

► Firstly, we discuss an architecture for a PAC system and describe each of the individual functions, or building blocks, which are part of PAC. Through this discussion, we illustrate the interrelationships of the building blocks, the control hierarchies and the data requirements.

► Secondly, we review various approaches to scheduling which can be used at the production activity control and the factory coordination level.

► Thirdly, we describe an architecture for factory coordination, with particular reference to the combination of the control features and the production environment design tasks.

► Finally, we explain the production environment design task and the control task by detailing each of the individual functions associated with each of these tasks.

In the previous chapter we took a **top-down** approach to the production planning and control hierarchy, covering business planning and master scheduling prior to requirements planning. In this chapter we will take a **bottom-up** approach and discuss PAC prior to factory coordination. The reasons for this will become clear when we show that the structure of a major part of the factory coordination system is very similar to that of a PAC system.

14.2 Production activity control

We will now consider the typical activities used to plan and control the flow of products on any particular shop floor. Consider the following situation. Each supervisor has waiting on his or her desk a list of requirements which have to be fulfilled for the forthcoming week. The main task facing the supervisor at this point is to plan production over the following working week to ensure that the orders are fulfilled. Factors which influence the content of this plan include the likely availability of resources (operators, machines) and the capacity of the manufacturing system. This plan then acts as a reference point for production, and will almost certainly have to be changed because of any number of arising unpredictable events (e.g. raw material shortage, operator problems or machine breakdown). Therefore, the three main elements for shop floor control are (Bauer *et al.*, 1991):

1. To develop a short-term plan based on timely knowledge and data and which ensures that all of the production requirements are fulfilled. This is termed **scheduling**.

2. To implement that plan taking into account the current status of the production system. This is termed **dispatching**.

3. To **monitor** the status of vital components in the system during the dispatching activity, either with the naked eye or by using technology-based methods.

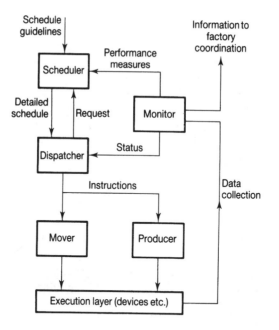

FIGURE 14.1
Production activity
control.

It is clear that activities of scheduling, dispatching and monitoring are in fact carried out, perhaps informally, by every competent shop floor manager or supervisor. We will now outline formally each of these separate tasks and show how they interact to control the work flow through a manufacturing system. The basis of our approach is to map the various shop floor activities onto an architecture which recognizes each individual component. The advantage of having an architecture is that it formalizes and simplifies the understanding of what occurs during production by establishing clear and separate functions which combine to form a complete shop floor control system.

Production activity control describes the principles and techniques used by management to plan in the short term and to control and evaluate the production activities of the manufacturing organization. The PAC architecture is illustrated in Figure 14.1, and the five basic building blocks of the PAC system are the **scheduler**, **dispatcher**, **monitor**, **mover** and **producer**. The **scheduler** develops a plan over a specified time period, based on the manufacturing data and the schedule guidelines from factory coordination. This plan is then implemented by the remaining four modules. The **dispatcher** takes the schedule and issues appropriate commands to the movers and producers, which carry out the required operation steps necessary to produce the different products. Given our inability to predict the future accurately, the need to modify the plan due to unforeseen circumstances (e.g. machine breakdown) may arise, and in this case the **monitor** notifies the dispatcher of any disturbances. The schedule may then be revamped to take account of any changes in the manufacturing environment. Based on the instructions from the dispatcher, the **producer** controls the execution of the various operations at each workstation. Further, the **mover** organizes the handling of materials between workstations within a cell by following the dispatcher's commands.

14.2.1 The scheduler

The task of the scheduler is to accept the production requirements from a higher planning system (i.e. a factory coordination system), and to develop a detailed plan which determines the precise use of the different manufacturing facilities within a specified time frame. Good scheduling practice is dependent on a number of factors including the structure of the manufacturing system (see Chapter 12 on manufacturing system typology), the design of the shop floor, the degree of complexity of the operations and the overall predictability of the manufacturing process. A well-designed, simply organized and stable manufacturing process is easier to schedule than a more complex and volatile system.

Much work has been reported on production scheduling, highlighting the fact that scheduling is a complex task, the technical difficulty being that of combinatorial explosiveness. For instance, sequencing twelve orders through six operations generates $(12!)^6$ or more than 10^{52} possible schedules in a simple job shop (although clearly the actual number of possible schedules is greatly reduced by precedence relationships among the various operations). This magnitude of possibilities makes the goal of schedule optimality an unattainable ideal, and there are relatively few situations in which general optimal solutions are known. Within manufacturing there are many diverse scheduling problems. No two scheduling problems are the same, and the production environment plays an important role in defining the requirements for an appropriate scheduling strategy. However, there are fundamental similarities between different scheduling problems which will be examined later in this chapter. The scheduling task within PAC is simplified due to the nature of the production management system hierarchy presented. Essentially, factory coordination and PAC perform the scheduling tasks based on a hierarchical decentralized production control model. The identification of self-contained tasks aids in reducing complexity and uncertainty in the execution of the overall task and also eases the coordination of decision making.

PAC is a *self-contained task* which controls a specific cell within the factory, and the scheduling function of PAC takes as its primary stimulus the schedule guidelines from the factory coordination system. These guidelines specify the time constraints within which a series of job orders are to be completed, and the role of the PAC scheduler is to take these guidelines and develop a plan which can then be released to the shop floor via the PAC dispatcher. The actual development of the schedule may be based on any one of a number of techniques, algorithms or computer simulation packages. (Simulation modelling is widely used as a tool to develop and test schedules. For a full discussion on the simulation approach see Carrie (1988). For a simple example of the use of simulation to support production management see Browne and Davies (1984). For an example of the use of simulation modelling in shop floor control see Biron *et al.* (1991).)

The scheduling function typically includes three activities which are carried out in order to develop a realistic schedule for the shop floor:

▶ Firstly, a check on the system capacity is required, the objective of which is to calculate whether or not the schedule constraints specified by the factory coordination or PAC system are realistic. The method of doing the capacity analysis depends on the type of manufacturing environment, and the results of the capacity analysis will have two possible outcomes: either the constraints are feasible or they are not. If the constraints are feasible, then they are included in the procedure for developing a schedule. If they are not, then clearly the higher level system (in this case the factory coordination system) will have to be informed and appropriate adjustments made to its plans.

▶ Secondly, a schedule must be generated. If there is a major problem with the available capacity, the scheduler may need to inform the factory coordination or requirements planning system, and the overall guidelines for scheduling that particular cell may have to be modified; for example, overtime may be authorized, or subcontracting may be necessitated.

▶ Finally, the schedule is released to the dispatcher so that it can be implemented on the shop floor. In an automated environment, this release will be achieved by means of a distributed software system, which passes the schedule between the scheduling and dispatching functions.

Scheduling represents one aspect of PAC, that is, the planning aspect. The schedule is developed taking different constraints and variables into account. When it is released to the shop floor it becomes susceptible to the reality of shop floor activity, and in particular unexpected events. The ability to deal with unexpected events is a true test of any system's flexibility and adaptability, and it is the role of the dispatcher to deal with the inevitable unplanned occurrences which threaten to disrupt the proposed schedule.

14.2.2 The dispatcher

Events such as machine breakdown or unexpected quality problems can have a serious effects on the production plans developed by the scheduler. In life, people 'dispatch' in many different situations; for instance, if when driving we see a major traffic jam, we search for an alternative route through a side street. The same principle applies to the dispatcher in a PAC system. Its main purpose is to react to the current state of the production environment and select the best alternative course of action, if one is available.

In order to function correctly, the dispatcher requires the following important information:

1. the schedule, which details the timing of the different operations to be performed;
2. manufacturing process data describing how the tasks are to be performed;
3. data describing the current shop floor status.

Thus access to the latest shop floor information is essential, so that the dispatcher can perform intelligent and informed decision-making. In fact, one of the greatest obstacles to effective shop floor control is the lack of accurate and timely data. In reality the possibility of a good decision is directly related to the integrity and timeliness of the manufacturing data. The dispatcher may use different algorithms and procedures to ensure that the schedule is followed in the most effective way. When a decision has been made on the next step to be taken in the production process, the dispatcher will send instructions to the mover and the producer so that these steps are carried out.

The three main activities of the dispatcher involve *receiving information, analyzing alternatives* and *broadcasting decisions*. The information received is the scheduling information, as well as both static and dynamic manufacturing data. The static data may be obtained from the manufacturing database, while the dynamic data describing the current status of the shop floor is received from the monitor. When received, this data is collated and manipulated into a format suitable for analysis. This analysis may be carried out using a range of software tools or performed manually by a supervisor, based on his or her experience and intuition. The analysis will most likely take place keeping the overall dispatching goals in mind, and the end result of it is to broadcast an instruction to the relevant building block, perhaps using a distributed software system.

The implementation of a dispatcher varies depending on the technological and manufacturing constraints of a production system. The dispatching task may be carried out manually, semi-automatically or automatically. Manual dispatching involves a human decision on what the next task should be in the system. Examples of this might be an operator deciding to select a job according to some preference. This preference might be generated using a **dispatching rule** or **heuristic** which prioritizes jobs in work queues according to a particular parameter (e.g. earliest due date, or shortest processing time). A semi-automatic dispatcher may be a computerized application which selects jobs, but this selection can be modified by an operator. An automatic dispatcher is a piece of computer software used in an automated environment, and it assumes responsibility for controlling the flow of jobs through the system. Typically we might find an automated dispatcher in a flexible manufacturing system.

To summarize, the dispatcher is the *controlling* element of the PAC architecture, and it ensures that the schedule is adhered to in so far as possible. It works in quasi-real-time by receiving data from the monitor on the current state of the system, and it issues instructions to the moving and producing devices so that the required tasks are performed.

14.2.3 The monitor

Within the different levels of manufacturing, from strategic planning down to PAC, informed and accurate decision-making relies on consistent, precise and timely information. Within PAC, the monitor function supplies the necessary data to the scheduler and dispatcher, so that they can carry out their respective tasks of planning and control. Thus the role of the monitor is to make sense of the multitude of data emanating from the shop floor, and to 'massage' that data into concise, relevant and understandable information for the scheduler and dispatcher. Put simply, the monitor can be seen as a translator of *data* into *information*, for the purpose of providing sensible decision support for the scheduling and dispatching functions.

There are three main activities of the monitor: **data capture**, **data analysis** and **decision support**. The **data capture** system collects data from the shop floor. This is then translated into information by the **data analysis** system, and can then be used as **decision support** for appropriate PAC activities.

Data capture

A vital part of the monitor is the data capture system, which makes the manufacturing data available in an accurate and timely format. This data capture function should perform reliably, quickly and accurately without detracting from the normal day-to-day tasks which are carried out by humans and machines on the shop floor. Ideally, data capture should be in real-time with real-time updating, and the data should be collected at source. Data might be captured using a variety of means, ranging from manual data collection systems where supervisors or indeed operators might collect data on machine and batch status, through semi-automated means where data might be keyed into a database using terminals situated throughout the plant, or indeed totally automated systems using bar code technology. Automatic or semi-automatic collection of data is often necessary for reasons of accuracy and speed of collection.

Monitoring the shop floor and the process of data capture are very much inter-linked, as information cannot be developed by the monitor unless the data has been collected. Therefore, data capture may be viewed as a subset of the monitor, the major difference being that data capture is only concerned with data transactions and making data available for other functions. However, the monitor analyses the data collected and either makes a decision by providing real-time feedback to the other applications within the PAC architecture, or provides a support tool with which management can make decisions at a later date. Data captured which may eventually be used for informed decision-making at a higher level in the PAC architecture includes: process times, job and part status, inspection data, failure data, rework data and workstation data.

Data analysis

The data analysis function of the monitor seeks to 'understand' the data emanating from the data capture system. It is a very important component of the monitor because it takes time and effort to filter important information from a large quantity of shop floor data. Thus this data analysis function effectively divides the monitor into different 'sub-monitors', which then keep track of different aspects of the manufacturing system. In a typical manufacturing situation there are three main classes of monitor:

▶ the production monitor;

▶ the materials monitor;

▶ the quality monitor.

We shall now discuss each of these in turn.

▶ *The production monitor*
The production monitor is responsible for monitoring work in progress status and resource status on the shop floor. Table 14.1 illustrates the type of information produced as a result of the data analysis performed by the production

Table 14.1 Typical information from the data analysis of the production monitor

Work in progress status	Job number
	Part name
	Current location
	Current operation
	Due date
	Number of remaining operations
Workstation status	Workstation name
	Current status
	Current job number
	Utilization
	Percentage time in set-up
	Percentage time processing
	Percentage time down

Table 14.2 Information from the data analysis of the materials monitor

Raw materials status	Material name
	Workstation name
	Buffer name
	Current quantity
	Reorder point
	Rate of usage

monitor. At a glance, production personnel can see the progress of the schedule. This information can then be used as the basis for informed decision-making. An important feature of the production monitor is the ability to recognize the point at which the schedule becomes infeasible and to request a new, more realistic schedule from the scheduler.

▶ *The materials monitor*
The materials monitor tracks the consumption of materials at each workstation in the process. Table 14.2 shows the type of information generated by this particular monitor. The main purpose of such a monitor is to ensure that there are no shortages of materials at a particular location. This is achieved by comparing current levels of a particular material with the recommended reorder point and indicating when materials need to be reordered.

▶ *The quality monitor*

As the name suggests, the quality monitor is concerned with quality-related data, and aims to detect any potential problems in this area. Quality problems may arise from internal or external sources. Quality problems arising from external sources may, for example, originate in the supply of raw material purchased from vendors, which can cause problems in later stages in the production process. Problems originating in the production process which affect the quality of products are classified as internal problems. These types of problem can be indicated by a drop in the yield of the cell or of a process within the cell. If the yield falls below a defined level, an investigation into the cause may be warranted. Possible causes of a drop in yield may include poorly maintained process equipment, sloppy operating procedures, poorly trained operators or perhaps poor quality raw materials.

Thus, the data analysis module makes information available so that accurate and informed decision-making can take place. It also prepares a historical reporting file so that a complete record of important manufacturing events can be kept for future reference. This type of historical reporting is particularly important if a company is required to track individual items or lots. This requirement frequently arises in the health care and food industries among others.

Decision support

The main function of the monitor's decision support element is to provide *intelligent* advice and information to the scheduling and dispatching functions within PAC in quasi-real-time. In effect, it is a form of expert analysis of output from the data analysis module of the monitor, sifting through a large quantity of data to detect trends which have a significant bearing on the shop floor control process. Examples of types of decision support provided by the monitor in each of the categories defined within the data analysis module are:

▶ *Overall decision support*

An overall decision support function might take aggregated information from each individual monitor and present it for the purposes of analysis to higher planning systems, such as factory coordination. This may illustrate how a particular cell is performing, and may highlight:

- the total number of jobs or batches completed in a defined period within the cell;
- the overall figures on individual workstation utilization and work in progress levels;
- the relationship between what was planned and what was produced (i.e. planned production versus actual production);
- the overall figures on raw material usage, and the number of raw material shortages that occurred in the cell;
- information on the quality of the products and the quality of the manufacturing process itself.

▶ *Decision support for the production monitor*
This decision support function can be used to assess how the current schedule is performing and if it is likely that the schedule passed down from the factory coordination system can be met. This feature of the monitor is important, as it ascertains whether or not a rescheduling activity may have to take place. Bottleneck workstations can be identified as well as under-utilized ones, and this information can then be used by the dispatcher and the scheduler to control the flow of work more effectively.

▶ *Decision support for the raw materials monitor*
If the quantity of a certain raw material has fallen below a certain pre-defined level, the raw materials monitor is in a position to tell the dispatcher that more raw materials need to be ordered. This approach is sometimes termed a **two bin system**.

▶ *Decision support for the quality monitor*
The monitor can use an early warning facility, such as a flashing signal on a terminal, to alert the operator to quality problems. This warning can be based on statistical process control data, which may indicate that the specified tolerance limits on a particular operation have been exceeded.

It is important to have a good decision support system within the monitoring function. This facility should operate on a **need-to-know** basis (i.e. only the most important and relevant information should be presented), and the existence of this function forces production personnel to identify the information requirements of the PAC system. One of the problems with management information systems (of which monitoring may be seen as a sub-function) is the over-abundance of irrelevant information, which may lead to confusion and inefficiency amongst decision-makers at all levels of the production management system hierarchy; hence the importance of an intelligent monitoring function to provide an efficient, informed and intelligent support service to the planning and control activities within PAC.

14.2.4 The mover

The mover coordinates the material handling function and interfaces between the dispatcher and the physical transportation and storage mechanisms on the shop floor. It supervises the progress of batches through a sequence of individual transportation steps. The physical realization of a mover depends on the type of manufacturing environment. It can range from an automatically guided vehicle (AGV) to a simple hand-operated trolley. The selection of the items to be moved is predetermined by the dispatcher and this decision is transferred as a command to the mover, which then carries out the instruction. The mover translates the commands from the dispatcher to specifically selected moving devices, and also issues messages to the dispatcher signalling the start and the completion of an operation. An automated mover system might use collision avoidance algorithms to ensure that no individual device will cross the path of another when parts are being transported to their destinations.

14.2.5 The producer

The producer is the process control system within PAC which contains (or has access to) all of the data required to execute the various operations at that workstation. The producer may be an automated function or a human. The main stimulus for a producer comes in the form of specific instructions from the dispatcher building block, and these instructions specify which batch, job or operation to process. In an automated environment the producer accesses the relevant part programs (detailed instructions on the operations which have to be performed) and also the configuration data which specifies the necessary set-up steps that are needed before an operation can commence. The producer translates the data into specific device instructions and informs the monitor when certain stages of activity have been completed (e.g. set-up completed, job started, job finished, producer failed etc.).

14.2.6 Overview of PAC

To summarize, a PAC system provides the necessary functions to control the flow of products *within* a cell, through the interaction of these five distinct building blocks:

▶ a scheduler, which develops a schedule based on the guidelines contained and the constraints imposed in the factory level schedule;

▶ a dispatcher, which controls the flow of work within the cell on a real-time basis;

▶ a monitor, which observes the status of the cell and passes any relevant information back to the scheduler, dispatcher and the higher level factory coordination system;

▶ a mover, which manages the movement of materials and semi-finished products between workstations;

▶ a producer, which controls the sequence of operations at each workstation.

14.3 Scheduling techniques

We have just seen that scheduling is an important aspect of PAC. Before going on to look at the factory coordination system we shall now review in detail some approaches to the scheduling of work through a manufacturing system. We shall review scheduling by firstly looking at the performance measures used to evaluate the performance of a schedule. We shall then go on to consider some well-known scheduling techniques.

14.3.1 Performance measures

The scheduling problem is one of timetabling the processing of jobs or batches on to machines or workstations so that a given measure of performance achieves its optimal value. The performance measures or objectives, which vary from manufacturer to manufacturer and sometimes from day to day, are numerous, complex and often conflicting. For example, it might be desirable to ensure a uniform rate of activity throughout the scheduling period so that demands for labour and power are stable. Conversely, it might be necessary to concentrate activity into periods when labour is available. At given times, senior management may focus strongly on reducing cost through reduced overtime and work in progress. At other times the emphasis may be on meeting the due dates of particular rush orders.

The following is a list of key terms that are used to define performance measures in mathematical terms:

r_i is the **ready time** of job J_i, i.e. the time at which J_i becomes available for processing.

d_i is the **due date** for job J_i, i.e. the time at which processing of J_i is required to be completed.

a_i is the **period allowed for processing** of job J_i:

$$a_i = d_i - r_i \qquad\qquad (14.1)$$

P_{ij} is the **processing time** of job J_i on machine M_j.

W_{ik} is the **waiting time** of job J_i preceding its kth operation.

W_i is the **total waiting time** of job J_i.

C_i is the **completion time** of job J_i.

F_i is the **flow time** of job J_i. This is the time that the job J_i spends in the workshop:

$$F_i = C_i - r_i \qquad\qquad (14.2)$$

L_i is the **lateness** of the job J_i : $L_i = C_i - d_i$. Clearly when a job is completed before its due date, L_i is negative.

T_i is the **tardiness** of J_i. $T_i = \mathrm{MAX}\,(L_i, 0)$

E_i is the **earliness** of J_i. $E_i = \mathrm{MAX}\,(-L_i, 0)$

I_j is the **idle time** on machine M_j.

N_u is the number of **unfinished jobs**.

N_w is the number of **jobs waiting between machines**.

N_p is the number of **jobs actually being processed**.

Depending on the individual measure of performance in question the maximum or the minimum or the mean of one or more of these variables may have to be considered. So, for example, if X_i is a variable relating to J_i, then $\overline{X} = (1/n)\sum_{i=1}^{n}X_i$ is the average over all the jobs and $X_{\max} = \mathrm{MAX}\,(X_1, X_2, \ldots, X_n)$, the maximum over all the jobs.

Equivalence of performance measures

When two performance measures are termed **equivalent** this implies that if a schedule is optimal with respect to one, it is also optimal with respect to the other, and vice versa. The usefulness of equivalent performance measures is that while it may not be practical to study a schedule on a particular criterion, a solution to the problem may be found by using another performance measure which is equivalent to it. Some equivalent performances are (French, 1982):

1. $\overline{C}, \overline{F}, \overline{W}, \overline{L}$

2. $C_{max}, \overline{N}_p, \overline{I}$

3.   A schedule which is optimal with respect to L_{max} is also optimal with respect to T_{max}. The opposite does not hold, which means that these two measures are only partially equivalent.

4.   For single machine problems the following performance measures are equivalent: $\overline{C}, \overline{F}, \overline{W}, \overline{L}, \overline{N}_u, \overline{N}_w$.

14.3.2 A classification of scheduling problems

A simple notation is used to represent the various types of scheduling problem. Problems can be classified according to four parameters: $n/m/A/B$, where:

n is the number of jobs.

m is the number of machines.

A describes the flow pattern or discipline within the manufacturing system.

A may take one of the following forms:

F for the flow-shop case, i.e. all of the jobs follow the same route through the manufacturing system;

P for the permutation flow-shop case. Here the search for a schedule is restricted to the case where the job order is the same for each machine;

G for the general job-shop case.

B describes the performance measure by which the schedule is to be evaluated.

For example: $3/2/F/\overline{F}$ describes a 3 job, 2 machine, flow-shop problem where the objective is to minimize the mean flow time, i.e. mean flow time is the measure of performance.

Now that we have defined the essential terminology, we will go on to discuss some of the more widely known and used scheduling techniques. Specifically, we will review the following approaches:

▶   operations research approaches to scheduling;

▶   scheduling algorithms;

▶   heuristic approaches to scheduling;

▶ the Gantt chart.

▶ the OPT (optimized production technology) approach.

Other approaches, for example PERT/CPM, which are frequently used to schedule projects, will not be considered.

14.3.3 Operations research approaches to scheduling

There are two reasonably well-known methods of scheduling which fall into the category of operations research approaches, namely:

▶ dynamic programming;

▶ branch and bound.

We shall now examine the branch and bound method of scheduling in some detail. We consider that the dynamic programming approach is beyond the scope of this book.

Branch and bound

Branch and bound is a form of implicit enumeration. It involves the formation of an elimination tree, which lists possible permutations. Branches in this tree are eliminated if it is evident that their solution will not approach the optimal. In theory, as with the dynamic programming approach, an optimal solution is found, but this can be costly in terms of computation time (Cunningham and Browne, 1986).

The branch and bound method uses a 'search tree' to check for feasible solutions to a problem and then compares these solutions to find the optimum. The process involves implicit enumeration of all the possible solutions, which means that it checks down along the various paths for the optimum solution. To illustrate the application of the branch and bound approach, consider the following example. The tree for the possible sequences of four jobs X, Y, Z and W is shown in Figure 14.2 (for the purposes of simplicity in the example we will assume for technological reasons that job X must be completed first). The numbers represent the cost of scheduling the jobs in that order. For example, the number 2 on the YZ branch indicates

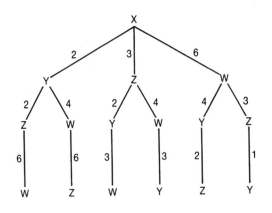

FIGURE 14.2
Possible sequence of four jobs X, Y, Z and W.

that it costs 2 units to set up job Z having completed job Y. The objective is to select the schedule for the four jobs which minimizes the total set-up time.

The partial schedules are examined as follows. The values in the brackets indicate the length of the branch.

1. First we branch on XY(2) producing XYZ(4) and XYW(6).

2. These are more costly than XZ(3).

3. So we branch on XZ producing XZY(5) and XZW(7).

4. The 'cheapest' is now XYZ(4) so we continue and get XYZW(10).

5. XYWZ(12) is eliminated as it is more expensive than XYZW(10).

6. XZYW(8) displaces XYZW(10).

7. Finally, XZWY(10), XWY(10) and XWZ(9) are eliminated as too expensive.

8. Therefore XZYW(8) is the optimal schedule, in this case the schedule with minimum set-up time.

The branch and bound approach, in general, has the following advantages over other methods:

▶ Many different objective functions may be employed, although the most frequently encountered is minimum flow time. This criterion is generally adopted if no other criterion or performance measure is set.

▶ The first pass solutions of branch and bound algorithms are frequently better than the solution obtained by heuristic methods.

▶ The 'quality' of the current solution is known, since it is possible to compare the value of the current solution with the lowest free bound in the branch and bound tree.

▶ Pre-loading and due dates are readily incorporated into the solution.

The major disadvantage with the branch and bound scheduling method is that the number of operations and hence the time required to solve a particular problem is unpredictable whatever search strategy is used. It might happen that the procedure has to explore fully virtually every node, in which case it would take almost as long as complete enumeration. In fact, it might take longer because branch and bound involves more computation per node than complete enumeration. Nevertheless, in general, branch and bound does perform a great deal better than complete enumeration.

14.3.4 Scheduling algorithms

An algorithm consists of a set of conditions and rules. If all the conditions for a particular algorithm are met and if the rules are applied properly an optimal schedule will be generated. The problem with using these algorithms is that they apply only to specific cases under very well defined and restrictive conditions.

For example, there are several algorithms which deal with so-called one machine problems. They generally involve the manipulation of due dates or processing times.

Table 14.3 Some algorithms and the performance measures or criteria they satisfy

Criteria	Algorithm	Problem
$\overline{C}, \overline{F}, \overline{W}, \overline{L}, \overline{N}_u, \overline{N}_w,$	Shortest processing time	1 machine
L_{max}, T_{max}	Earliest due date	1 machine
N_T (number of tardy jobs)	Moore's algorithm	1 machine
$\overline{F}$ subject to $T_{max} = 0$	SPT subject to $T_{max} = 0$ (Smith, 1956)	1 machine
$\overline{F}$ subject to $T_{max} \leqslant r$	SPT subject to $T_{max} \leqslant r$ $(r = 0, 1, 2, \ldots, r)$	1 machine
F_{max}	Johnson's algorithm	2 machines
F_{max}	Johnson's algorithm	3 machines

Rules such as shortest processing time (SPT) and earliest due date (EDD) can be used as algorithms in the one machine environment. However they are usually associated with multiple machine environments, where they are used as heuristics. The shortest processing time (SPT) and earliest due date (EDD) rules will be discussed in more detail in the section dealing with heuristics.

A number of optimizing algorithms are available for one machine problems, a smaller number for two machine problems and one for a specific three machine problem. Table 14.3 lists some of those algorithms (Cunningham and Browne, 1986), which we will now present in some detail.

While there may be very few systems in which there is only one machine to schedule, the methods available for one machine scheduling are often useful when certain conditions arise in the multi-machine environment. An example might be where a bottleneck occurs in the system, i.e. an individual machine holding up production and keeping machines further down the production line idle. In this case an appropriate algorithm is used to develop an optimal sequence for the bottleneck machine. This sequence is then used as the basis on which the remainder of the schedule is constructed, i.e. a schedule is generated forward and backward of the bottleneck machine. An approach similar to this is used in OPT scheduling, which will be discussed later.

We shall now review some of the algorithms presented in Table 14.3. The shortest processing time (SPT) and the earliest due date (EDD) methods will be looked at later when we come to consider heuristic approaches.

Moore's algorithm

In some cases it makes sense to penalize all late or tardy jobs equally, no matter how late they are. Essentially we are suggesting here that it may cost as much to miss a due date by a day as to miss it by a month. Moore's approach to the scheduling task is to minimize the number of tardy jobs (N_T), i.e. an $n/1/N_T$ problem. The algorithm proceeds as follows:

Step 1: Sequence the jobs in the order of the earliest due date (EDD) to find the current sequence $(J_{i(1)}, J_{i(2)}, \ldots, J_{i(n)})$ such that $d_{i(k)} \leqslant d_{i(k+1)}$ for $k = 1, 2, \ldots, n - 1$.

Step 2: Find the first tardy job, say $J_{i(l)}$, in the current sequence. If no such job is found, go to Step 4.

Step 3: Find the job in the sequence $(J_{i(1)}, \ldots, J_{i(l)})$ with the largest processing time and reject this from the current sequence. Return to Step 2 with a current sequence one shorter than before.

Step 4: Form an optimal schedule by taking the current sequence and appending to it the rejected jobs, which may be sequenced in any order.

The rejected jobs which are placed at the end of the schedule will be tardy jobs.

Example 14.1 *The 8/1/N$_T$ problem (shown in Table 14.4)*

First, the EDD sequence is formed (Step 1). The first cycle of the algorithm consists of computing the completion times until a tardy job is found (Steps 1 and 2). The first 'Completion time' row in Table 14.5 represents this first cycle. Job 4 is the first tardy job in the sequence. In this sequence (2,3,1,4), job 1 has the largest processing time and hence is rejected (Step 3). Job 1 is ignored in further cycles of the algorithm, by blanking its completion time with an asterisk.

The second cycle of the algorithm is represented by the second 'Completion time' row in Table 14.5. Job 8 is the first tardy job in the next sequence. In the new sequence (2,3,4,5,8) it has the largest processing time. Thus job 8 is rejected for the moment. For the third cycle of the algorithm, jobs 1 and 8 are ignored. No tardy jobs are found. Moving on to Step 4, jobs 1 and 8 are now brought back into consideration and the optimal sequence (2,3,4,5,7,6,1,8) is formed.

Table 14.4 8/1/N$_T$ problem

Job number	1	2	3	4	5	6	7	8
Due date	14	5	9	16	18	25	20	19
Processing time	6	3	5	3	4	5	4	5

Table 14.5 Completion time calculations

EDD sequence	2	3	1	4	5	8	7	6
Due date	5	9	14	16	18	19	20	25
Processing time	3	5	6	3	4	5	4	5
Completion time (1)	3	8	14	17				
Completion time (2)	3	8	*	11	15	20		
Completion time (3)	3	8	*	11	15	*	19	24

Johnson's algorithm for the n/2/F/F$_{max}$ problem

Johnson's algorithm constructs a schedule which minimizes the maximum flow time for a two machine flow-shop. The algorithm tries to push products with the shortest processing times on to the first machine (machine one) as near to the beginning of a sequence as possible, so that the first job will be available as soon as possible for machine two to start work. Likewise, it tries to push jobs with the shortest processing times on to machine two as near to the end of the schedule as possible. This is to reduce the time that machine one is left idle having completed its schedule, compared to the time that machine two takes to complete its schedule. The algorithm solves both the $n/2/P/F_{max}$ problem and the $n/2/F/F_{max}$ problem.

Thus the algorithm generates the processing sequence by working from both ends of the schedule towards the middle. The following example of a 6/2/F/F$_{max}$ problem shows how the algorithm works. Table 14.6 shows the processing times on each of two machines for six jobs (French, 1982).

Applying the algorithm the schedule builds up as follows:

Job 3 scheduled:	3	–	–	–	–	–
Job 1 scheduled:	3	–	–	–	–	1
Job 4 scheduled:	3	4	–	–	–	1
Job 5 scheduled:	3	4	–	–	5	1
Job 2 scheduled:	3	4	2	–	5	1
Job 6 scheduled:	3	4	2	6	5	1

Thus the jobs should be sequenced in the order (3,4,2,6,5,1).

This algorithm can only be used in situations where there are two machines involved. Sometimes machines can be grouped together because of their operation or because of the product routings. In this way a 'factory' or cell can be considered as a two machine situation and Johnson's algorithm used to create a schedule. Therefore this algorithm potentially has wider application then one might initially suspect.

Table 14.6 Processing times for six jobs on two machines

	Processing time (min)	
Job number	Machine 1	Machine 2
1	8	2
2	3	11
3	1	9
4	2	8
5	5	4
6	7	5

Johnson's algorithm for the n/3/F/F_{max} problem

Johnson's algorithm for the $n/2/F/F_{max}$ problem may be extended to a special case of the $n/3/F/F_{max}$ problem. This case arises when all of the processing times for all the jobs on machine two are either:

1. all less than the minimum processing time of all times on machine one; or

2. all less than the minimum processing times of machine three.

In other words the maximum processing time on the second machine cannot be greater than the minimum processing time on either the first or the third machine.

In effect, a special two machine problem is constructed from the data. The processing times on machines one and two are added for each job to give the times for the first machine of our constructed problem. Likewise, the times on the second and third machines are added to give the times for the second machine. Then the problem is treated as an $n/2/F/F_{max}$ problem, and a sequence of jobs is generated which is common to all three machines.

14.3.5 Heuristic approaches to scheduling

A heuristic is, as previously mentioned, a 'rule of thumb'. In other words, these methods are justified purely because, based on experience, they seem to work reasonably well. It is extremely unlikely that optimal solutions to realistic and large scheduling problems will ever be possible, except by partial enumerative methods such as branch and bound (Spachis and King, 1979). If an optimal schedule cannot be found within a reasonable time, knowledge and experience of the system can be used to find a schedule which, if not optimal, may at least be expected to perform better than average. Here we consider heuristics which do just that. The major drawback of the heuristic methods is that they may take a lot of computer time for large problems.

The shortest processing time heuristic

As was indicated earlier in Table 14.3 for the single machine environment, the shortest processing time rule (SPT) is optimal with respect to certain measures of performance. The jobs are queued in order of ascending processing times, i.e. the job with the shortest processing time is queued first. The schedule developed using this rule minimizes the mean flow time through the system, for a one machine problem. The SPT heuristic also develops optimal schedules for one machine systems with respect to the following criteria:

- ▶ $n/1//\overline{C}$ (minimizes the mean completion time);

- ▶ $n/1//\overline{W}$ (minimizes the mean job waiting time);

- ▶ $n/1//\overline{L}$ (minimizes the mean job lateness);

- ▶ $n/1//N_u$ (minimizes the mean number of unfinished jobs);

- ▶ $n/1//N_w$ (minimizes the mean number of jobs waiting between machines).

Conway and Maxwell (1962) explored the performance of the SPT rule in an *m*-machine environment. They found that in a multi-machine system the SPT rule retained the advantages of throughput maximization it had shown in the single machine situation, and that even imperfect data on the processing times had little effect on the operation of the SPT rule.

When using the SPT rule to schedule production in a multi-machine environment, the process time for a job is generally taken as the sum of the process times for that job through all the machines. Under this system, each machine has the same schedule. However, jobs can also be scheduled at a machine according to the process time for each job at that particular machine.

Example 14.2 *The SPT heuristic*

Assume four jobs A, B, C, D are ready for processing at machine J (M_j) in an *m*-machine environment. Take the data in Table 14.7; the SPT schedule using the total process time is (B,C,D,A), i.e. perform job B first, then job C and so on. Each machine has the same schedule. The SPT schedule for M_j using the process time for M_j is (C,B,D,A). However, the SPT schedule for M_j using the total process time is (B,C,D,A).

Table 14.7 SPT example

Job	A	B	C	D
Process time for M_j	8	4	3	6
Total process time	33	25	27	31

A problem with the SPT rule is that a job J_x which has a longer processing time than the other jobs being processed will remain at the bottom of the schedule list. The jobs ahead of J_x on the schedule list are replaced on the list by other jobs as they become available for processing. To overcome this, the SPT rule can be modified by placing jobs which have been at the bottom of the schedule list for a defined period of time to the top of the schedule list, in effect overriding the processing time priority. This procedure is known as a modified SPT rule.

The earliest due date heuristic

With this rule jobs are processed so that the job processed first has the earliest due date, the job processed second the next earliest due date, and so on. For a single machine problem the maximum job lateness is minimized by sequencing such that

$$d_{i(1)} \leq d_{i(2)} \leq d_{i(3)} \leq \ldots \leq d_{i(n)} \tag{14.3}$$

where $d_{i(k)}$ is the due date of the job that is processed *k*th in the sequence. Using this rule also minimizes T_{max}, i.e. maximum tardiness. The EDD rule can be applied to the data in Table 14.8 to obtain the schedule (C,B,A,D).

Table 14.8 Earliest due date example

Job	A	B	C	D
Due date	18	15	12	25

Another due date based rule is the critical ratio rule, which can take one of several forms. In its most general form the critical ratio is computed as follows:

$$\text{critical ration} = \frac{\text{due date} - \text{date now}}{\text{lead time remaining}} \qquad (14.4)$$

Thus, using the critical ratio rule requires an estimate of the lead time or queue time remaining for a job. The jobs are scheduled in descending order of their critical ratios. The principal advantage of due date based rules over processing time based rules (such as simple SPT) is a smaller variance of job lateness, and often a smaller number of tardy jobs.

Heuristic rules involving neither processing times nor due dates

The most commonly used rule in this category is first in first out (FIFO). A number of researchers have found that the FIFO rule performs substantially the same as a random selection with respect to mean flow time or mean lateness (Blackstone *et al.*, 1982). In fact, in general, FIFO performs practically the same as random selection with respect to many measurement criteria. However, FIFO is an attractive alternative because of its simplicity of definition and usage. In general, FIFO has been found to perform worse than SPT and EDD with respect to both the mean and variance of most measurement criteria.

The are a large number of other rules that have been developed, such as number in next queue (NINQ), which selects the job going next to the queue having the smallest number of jobs, or work in next queue (WINQ), which selects the job going next to the queue containing the least total work. However, they have greater mean flow time than SPT, and generally perform worse than the other rules.

14.3.6 The Gantt chart

A Gantt chart is a manual means of scheduling. It works by placing a time scale on one axis of a graph (usually the horizontal axis) and machines or work centres on the other (normally the vertical) axis. A simple chart is shown in Figure 14.3 with three machines and a time period of 4 hours (Duggan *et al.*, 1987). Three different jobs have been scheduled.

Each job has a process route through some or all of the machines. The user simply places a block on the correct machine axis for the particular job being scheduled at the time he wishes it to be processed. The length of the block corresponds to the process time of the operation. The process route for each job is worked through in this fashion, using a different coloured block for each job, until the chart is full – the number of blocks corresponds to the total number of operations carried out on the various jobs. Once this first attempt has been made at scheduling the different jobs,

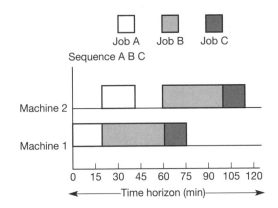

FIGURE 14.3
Simple Gantt chart.

there will be gaps between the blocks on the various machine axes. These correspond to time intervals when the machines are not being utilized. It usually becomes apparent at this stage that some of these gaps can be filled by rearranging the blocks. This is done and the chart is re-examined to determine if any further improvements can be made. The process is continued until it is felt that an acceptable result has been achieved. At this point the schedule can be released, with the option of further modification at any time in the future. This may become necessary because of unforeseen events, such as machine breakdown, absent operators etc.

While a Gantt chart has its limitations, since the placing of the blocks (i.e. the scheduling of the different jobs) lies with the user, it can be very useful in certain situations. If the number of jobs to be processed is small, then a realistic schedule can be worked out intuitively. Because the whole area of scheduling is so complex, often an intuitive approach is the only feasible method of achieving a realistic schedule. The value of a Gantt chart lies in its ability to present the scheduling problem in a graphical form which allows the user to see exactly where and how it is possible to achieve the best schedule.

The Gantt chart is usually used in batch type operations, where the number of products is small. In this case each block of processing time on the chart is taken as the processing time for the batch as a whole. This may or may not include the set-up time for the machine. However, it may also be used in certain types of job shop if the number of products is not too high, since the more jobs involved the more unlikely it is that they can be scheduled intuitively. In this case, each block of processing time corresponds to an individual job. Once again this may or may not include set-up time.

14.3.7 The optimized production technology (OPT) approach to scheduling

In response to the continued success of Japanese manufacturing, a new approach to the management of manufacturing has been proposed. The OPT (optimized production technology) approach contains many of the insights which underlie the Japanese JIT systems (see Chapter 15). From the OPT perspective there is one, and only one, goal for a manufacturing company – **to make money**. All activities in the business are but a means to achieve this goal. This goal can be represented by three **bottom-line** financial measurements as follows:

▶ net profit;

▶ return on investment;

▶ cash flow.

The OPT approach incorporates ten rules which, when followed, are claimed to help move the organization towards the goal of making profit. Eight of these rules relate to the development of correct schedules, while the other two are necessary for preventing traditional performance procedures from interfering with the execution of these schedules. The ten rules (see Browne *et al.*, 1989) are listed in Table 14.9.

▶ **Rule 1:** OPT argues that non-bottleneck resources should *not* be utilized to 100% of their capacity. Rather, they should be scheduled and operated based on the constraints in the system. If this were done, the non-bottleneck resources would not produce more than the bottlenecks can absorb, thereby preventing an increase in inventory and operating expenses.

▶ **Rule 2:** Traditionally, utilization and activation were considered to be the same. However, in OPT thinking, there is an important distinction to be made between doing the required work (what we *should* do – activation) and performing work not needed at a particular time (what we *can* do – utilization). Utilization is concerned with **efficiency**. Activation is concerned with **effectiveness**.

▶ **Rule 3:** To maximize the system-wide output, 100% utilization of all bottleneck resources should be a major goal of manufacturing.

Table 14.9 The ten OPT rules

Rule 1	The level of utilization of a non-bottleneck is determined not by its own potential but by some other constraint in the system.
Rule 2	Utilization and activation of a resource are not synonymous (i.e. efficiency vs. effectiveness).
Rule 3	An hour lost at a bottleneck is an hour lost for the total system.
Rule 4	An hour saved at a non-bottleneck is just a mirage.
Rule 5	Bottlenecks govern both throughput and inventory in the system.
Rule 6	The transfer batch may not, and many times should not, be equal to the process batch.
Rule 7	The process batch should be variable, not fixed.
Rule 8	Capacity and priority should be considered simultaneously, not sequentially.
Rule 9	Balance flow not capacity.
Rule 10	The sum of local optima is not equal to the optimum of the whole.

▶ **Rule 4:** Saving time at a non-bottleneck resource does not affect the capacity of the system, since system capacity is defined by the bottleneck resources.

▶ **Rule 5:** Traditionally, bottlenecks were believed to limit throughput temporarily and to have little impact on inventories. OPT argues that inventories (particularly work in progress) are a function of the amount of work required to keep the bottlenecks busy.

▶ **Rule 6:** This rule encourages the splitting of lots and the overlapping of batches. This leads to reduction of throughput time, but may also lead to non-bottleneck resources not being fully utilized (see Rule 2).

▶ **Rule 7:** This implies that the process batch at different work centres should not be the same. Traditional manufacturing practice would suggest that, except in exceptional cases, the batch size should be fixed over time and from operation to operation. In the OPT approach, however, process batches are a function of the schedule and potentially vary by operation and over time.

▶ **Rule 8:** Lead times are not known *a priori*, but depend on the sequencing at the limited capacity or bottleneck resources. Exact lead times, and hence priorities, cannot be determined in a capacity-bound situation unless capacity is considered.

▶ **Rule 9:** Traditionally, the approach was to balance capacity and then attempt a continuous flow. Line balancing (see Chapter 15) is a good example of this approach. The OPT approach suggests that production is controlled by considering product flow and capacity considerations simultaneously and not sequentially.

▶ **Rule 10:** The OPT approach seeks to measure the performance of the plant as a whole on the basis of raw material input and final product output, rather than by measuring only the efficiency of individual operators or machines or other elements of the subsystem.

It is clear that the OPT approach offers many useful insights into scheduling practice and in recent years many of the ideas discussed here have been implemented in practice.

Example 14.3 *ABC Company*

AB Ltd is an electronics manufacturing company. ABC is a subsidiary of AB Ltd, and is a small enterprise employing 50 design engineers and production technicians. Its main products are single-board computers for the telecommunications industry. It sells to a small niche market with small volumes but high returns on its products. The workforce at ABC is highly skilled from the designers through to the technicians on the shop floor. Because ABC is a subsidiary of a larger company it has a more formalized management structure than most SMEs.

Order fulfilment at ABC

The order fulfilment process begins at ABC when a customer places an order. Components are then selected, or purchased when necessary, and are kitted for assembly.

Assembly of the printed circuit boards is subcontracted. The assembled boards are then returned to ABC two weeks later where the processor is added and the board undergoes a series of tests. It is these tests that form the major part of the production process at ABC.

At each test there is a percentage of boards that fail. These boards are rerouted to either a previous stage or a repair station. Quality is the major concern of ABC. While delivery accuracy is important the company feels that reduction of its order fulfilment time is not crucial and it has installed an MRP system which plans availability of components and delivery dates. However, ABC did have a problem controlling and monitoring the shop floor where the boards are tested. The failure rates of boards at certain tests were high and the company did not know why. Often boards would 'get lost' in the test area without anyone knowing where they were. When a customer order delivery date was approaching and the board was found at one of the early production test stages this caused severe pressure.

ABC has a commission-based sales force which is measured yearly. Thus when the year end is approaching, sales people make an extra effort to sell more products. This results in a yearly glut in production during July, the end of the financial year. Unable to change the underlying problem the shop floor staff are left with a major problem at this time of year trying to get boards through the tests smoothly.

ABC's major problem was the quality of the boards and its principal concern was to get more information about why boards were failing and at which test they were failing.

Implementing production planning and control at ABC

ABC already has an MRP system which plans materials and sets delivery dates for its products (single-board computers). The problem is at the shop floor level where the emphasis is on quality. The PAC (Production Activity Control) system is a computer-based system developed using a relational database and a fourth-generation language to address the problems at the shop floor level (Figure 14.4).

The MRP system creates a sequence of orders to be produced. ABC feels that there is no need for a formal scheduler. What is needed is the ability to dispatch orders into production and a means of monitoring the start and stop times associated with these orders at each production or test station and record failure information for each test.

Each order represents a single board, so that the order quantity is always one. The PAC system takes these orders and displays them on a screen at the first station on the shop floor. On the left-hand side of the screen are the orders queuing for that

FIGURE 14.4
The PAC implementation at ABC.

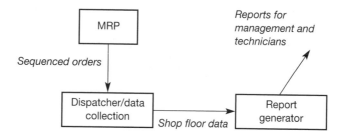

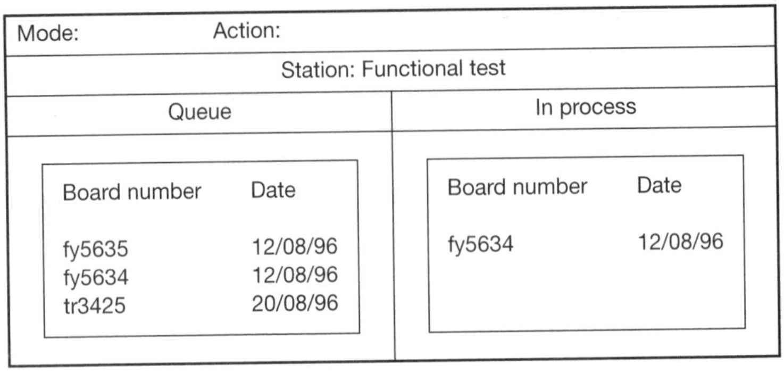

Mode:	Action:		
	Station: Functional test		
Queue		In process	

Board number	Date	Board number	Date
fy5635	12/08/96	fy5634	12/08/96
fy5634	12/08/96		
tr3425	20/08/96		

FIGURE 14.5
The dispatcher/data collection at ABC.

station and on the right-hand side of the screen are the orders currently being processed. When an order is completed the technician at the station selects that order and tags it as complete. The complete order then appears in the queue for the next station in the routing for that product and the technician selects a new order from the queue at his or her station.

The dispatcher screen is shown in Figure 14.5. It is this screen that technicians use to launch orders, record the movement of orders from station to station and to record failures.

The user interface for the system is considered to be quite difficult and a two-day course was needed to educate the technicians in its use. Underlying the interface is a comprehensive database which stores information on all the boards moving through production. Information on processing times, failures and delivery date adherence is subsequently used in many reports designed and written by ABC personnel. In many cases the technicians themselves indicate the need for a particular report which the production engineer then writes using data from the PAC database.

The ABC implementation of PAC can be considered a success. Three years after its implementation the software is still running. Probably the main component of the success can be attributed to the fact that the system collected the primary data, that is start and stop time and failure rates, and then allowed the shop floor personnel to access that data and design their own reports to present the data as information in a useful way.

Example 14.4 *XYZ Clothing Ltd*

XYZ Clothing produce men's and youth's trousers for the European markets. It employs 65 people and produces up to 7000 trousers each week to customer order. The customers of XYZ Clothing are major retail chain stores. In August 1991 new management took over at XYZ Clothing. The new manager is part owner and typical of the entrepreneurial SME owner/manager. He knew that radical changes were required to the business and he was determined to make the business a success. Although his background was in accounting he had a good insight into the importance of production and he took an active interest in the development of appropriate production planning and control systems.

Table 14.10 Business objectives for XYZ Clothing

Short-term objectives (0–12 months)	*Medium-term objectives (12–24 months)*
1 To remotivate the core production operators through enhanced training to produce an attitude change from 'volume produced' to 'quality produced'.	1 To broaden the product range by segmenting the market and by introducing designs focusing on trends in trousers to fit niches in the market.
2 To work with the main customers so as to rebuild confidence in the company.	2 To lower the dependence on existing customers by winning a broader customer base.
3 To restructure the manufacturing facilities and process to increase flexibility and improve production flows.	

The business plan, aimed at revitalizing XYZ Clothing and developed when the new manager took over the business in 1991, was set out in the form of a set of objectives. The objectives for the short and medium term are listed in Table 14.10.

Order fulfilment at XYZ Clothing

A global contract is received on a monthly basis and gives details on the style and approximate quantity of trousers the customer requires for the next month. These global contracts enable the production manager to plan the procurement of parts, for example belts, buttons, etc. An individual contract is then received which indicates the quantity required for a particular style of trouser. A 'scaling' is received from the customer against an individual contract which gives the breakdown of the quantity of each waist size and leg length that is required for a particular style of trouser. When the scaling is received for each individual contract a list of production orders with required delivery dates is generated and this is used as an aid to balance the workload on the shop floor and also to make sure that the required parts to complete the production order have been delivered by the relevant suppliers.

The process at XYZ Clothing involves mainly manual labour, working at sewing machines. There is a slight variation from one style to another, but most trousers go through a core 60 operations from cutting the material through sewing and finishing and on to final inspection. It is a classical flow shop with a history of the piecework system where each individual operator is rewarded on a basis of his or her individual performance. This tradition is somewhat unfortunate since it results in a build-up of work in process and a tendency to place more importance on quantity than quality.

Implementing production planning and control at XYZ Clothing

A functional architecture based on the PAC approach was used as the basis for implementing production planning and control in XYZ Clothing. The implementation was achieved in four steps.

Step I: Develop evaluation plan

The first step in implementing the PAC system at XYZ Clothing was to develop an evaluation plan:

1. Identify performance indicators. Production line performance indicators were identified and included internal/external failure costs, operator efficiency variance, excess material stock, obsolete finished stock, units in WIP (Work in Progress), units shipped per week, number of operators, number of garments per operator per day.

2. Measure current performance of the system in terms of these performance indicators.

These figures formed the basis for evaluation of the implementation and gave the operators and management a set of measures which they could use to monitor progress and improvement.

Step II: Generate a desire for change

Before implementing a new production activity control system it is first necessary to generate a desire for change. This involved:

1. Assigning responsibility for the implementation of the system.

2. Analysing current production control procedures.

3. Highlighting problems with these procedures.

A new production manager was hired and given responsibility for the implementation of the PAC system. The existing control procedures were analysed. Regular meetings between the production manager and supervisors helped to identify problems with these existing procedures and to create a desire to improve them.

Step III: Derive and implement improved procedures

Having identified the current tasks and their deficiencies in step II, improved procedures for production control based on the PAC architecture were derived. These procedures are described briefly below.

▶ Requirements planning was realized using a commercial MRP software package (the Xetal software from Kewill Systems).

▶ The planning of work in line with required shipments and a continuous 'analyse, review and replan' strategy was achieved through a form of input/output control. The result was a loading and finishing programme forming a schedule of production for one week at a time.

▶ Dispatch of cutting sheets into the line. Formal weekly and daily plans, or dispatch lists, are issued to supervisors and reviewed weekly and daily.

▶ The flow of trousers past key points in the line is monitored and compared with the planned flow.

Management introduced a process which continually reviews the performance of the shop floor against the planned performance by comparing the loading and finishing programmes with the actual overall performance.

Step IV: Evaluate and review implementation

The results of the evaluation of the PAC implementation (see Figure 14.6) are given in Table 14.11.

The quality figures improved dramatically. Part of the changeover process concentrated on convincing operators of the importance of quality. But because the work in process is lower and the line is better organized than before, it is easier for operators to do quality work and for examiners to identify flawed products.

This improved organization of the line was also reflected in operator efficiency figures. Operators are now rarely sitting around without work. This is due to the planning and scheduling of work into the line which identifies, in advance, slack

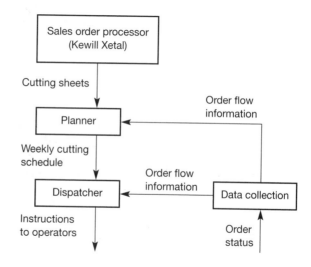

FIGURE 14.6

Implementation of PAC at XYZ Clothing.

Table 14.11 Improvement in performance indicators for XYZ Clothing

Performance indicator	Prior to change	After 12 months	After 24 months
Internal failure	£139 500	£55 800	£18 400
External failure	£27 900	£16 700	£8 350
Operator efficiency variance	25 %	17.5%	12.5%
Excess material stock	£50 000	£25 000	£10 000
Obsolete finished stock	£35 000	£10 000	£5 000
Average units in WIP	13 500	10 500	8 000
Average units/week shipped	3 950	4 900	6 350
No. of garments per operator per day	40.7	51.8	54

periods for a particular part of the line thus allowing the supervisor to move the flexible workers to different work centres and maintain overall flow.

The improved planning procedures make it possible to reduce work in process and throughput times. This also leads to a reduction in obsolete finished goods and an increase in the number of garments shipped per week.

Example 14.5 *Eurotechnology*

Eurotechnology produces gas detection equipment for the underground mining and offshore oil industries. In many ways Eurotechnology is quite similar to ABC (see Example 14.3). It too is a subsidiary of a larger manufacturer and although it only employs 37 full-time staff it has a formal management structure. The product is aimed at a small niche market where high-quality, highly reliable gas detectors are required. Production volumes are quite small, in the region of 200 units per week. There are three basic product models each with a set of revisions and each revision has certain variations for particular customers.

Order fulfilment at Eurotechnology

Customers call or fax Eurotechnology with an order which is then entered into the MRP system. In the past, customers were typically quoted a standard lead time of 6 weeks for one product line and 8 weeks for another. The MRP system is run weekly and creates work orders, which are released to the shop floor based on a rough-cut capacity planning (RCCP) calculation. The order release mechanism is a mixture of this capacity calculation and an informal backward scheduling approach which starts a work order approximately 2 weeks before its due date.

The process on the shop floor involves component preparation, component stuffing on to a printed circuit board, flow soldering, a sequence of testing operations and final assembly of the printed circuit board and the spray-painted mechanical housing. One interesting aspect of the production system is that the company has a tradition of multi-skilled operators. All operators work on one work order at one stage (station) at the same time. When that stage is complete they all move to the next stage and complete that operation on the order. The layout is similar to a flow shop with some excess capacity.

Implementing PPC at Eurotechnology

Management realized that a new system was required when a prolonged busy period was experienced and suddenly there was no excess capacity. A flow-shop-type production system was set up by hiring temporary staff and placing them at the production stages requiring low-skill operators. When the new system was introduced management found that it was difficult to plan production and delivery dates were starting to slip. It was decided that Eurotechnology should move towards customer-order-driven manufacturing. This meant that the work orders on the floor would be identical to the customer orders and the batch size would be reduced from an average size of 30 to 5. The main effect of the new proposed system was to implement

dynamic scheduling so that as an order is received it is entered directly on the shop floor schedule and the customer receives an exact due date rather than a standard lead time from the previous MRP-based system.

The implementation followed three steps.

Step I: Analysis of Eurotechnology production approach

The first step in implementing a new approach to production planning and control at Eurotechnology was to understand completely the manufacturing processes and document the roles of the people involved in the order fulfilment process.

Step II: Move to customer-driven production

The personnel in Eurotechnology were encouraged to change from work-order-driven manufacturing to customer-order-driven manufacturing. The sales personnel were encouraged to consider materials availability and capacity availability when quoting delivery dates. When orders are received customers are asked to wait until the next day to receive a delivery date. The order is entered to the MRP system. Each night the MRP system then regenerates the production plan. The delivery date given to the customer is therefore more accurate and shorter than the previously quoted standard lead time. Sales personnel noted that at first customers were unhappy with the change, but as they began to realize that it resulted in considerably shorter lead times, they became more satisfied.

Step III: Develop and implement shop floor control software

The shop floor control software was designed to implement what Eurotechnology called 'dynamic scheduling'. The intention was that customer orders would be scheduled on receipt and inventories of materials would be planned accordingly.

The scheduler was developed using a forward scheduling algorithm which utilized a capacity matrix. A printout of this system is designed to be released to the shop floor as a dispatch list each morning. A shop floor monitoring system was also developed which tracked work orders through the system using daily updating. Working together, these two modules allow the production manager to reschedule the shop floor each time a customer order is received. If a customer order is scheduled to finish after its original planned finish date then the scheduler software highlights this order, so that the customer can be informed.

14.4 Factory coordination
....

So far in this chapter, we have discussed some of the main issues involved in shop floor control and the use of production activity control (PAC) to control the flow of products *within* a cell. As indicated earlier, we visualize a typical manufacturing environment as consisting of a number of group technology cells, each controlled by a PAC system. The layout should be as close as possible to a product-based layout (see Chapters 9 and 15). This vision of a typical manufacturing environment is completed with the inclusion of a factory coordination system, which organizes the flow of products throughout a factory and ensures production in each cell is synchronized with the overall production goals of the factory.

FIGURE 14.7

The link between
production
environment
design and
control.

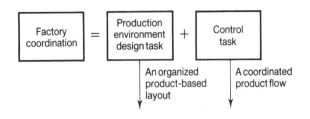

Traditionally the design of the production environment was considered separately from the control of product flow, but there is a close relationship between the two. The physical layout significantly influences the efficiency of the production system. Within the factory coordination architecture, we recognize a link between the tasks of production environment design and control, as illustrated in Figure 14.7.

Planning divides a problem and provides the means by which people can cope with the proliferation of variety within their area of responsibility. Within factory coordination, we take this approach by linking the tasks of production environment design and control. The production environment design module helps to reduce the variety of possible production-related problems by organizing the manufacturing system in so far as possible into a product-based layout and allocating new products to existing product families. The control module provides guidelines and goals with which each work group can manage its activities and deal with any problems that occur within its area of responsibility.

14.4.1 The production environment design task

A key role of the *production environment design* (PED) task is to *reorganize* the manufacturing system to simplify it and to accommodate new products coming into production. The production environment design task within factory coordination uses a range of static data and the future production requirements generated by an MRP-type system. Using the experience of manufacturing personnel together with some group technology analysis, the production process is reorganized to accommodate new products, and indeed new product mixes, subject to the various production constraints and the manufacturing goals of the organization.

The static data includes a bill of materials (BOM) and a bill of process (BOP) for each new product. As discussed earlier a **bill of materials** defines the structure of a product by listing the names and quantities of each component of each assembly and subassembly in a product's structure (Orlicky, 1975). A **bill of process** describes the process steps involved in the production of a product in terms of the required resources, operation procedures, process times and set-up procedures. In short, a BOM gives a description of a product's components and subassemblies, while a BOP gives a description of a product's process requirements.

As indicated earlier, the main aim of the production environment design task is to reorganize the initial layout of the manufacturing system, rather than create the layout initially. The initial layout of the manufacturing system should be, where possible, **product based**. The initial creation of a product-based layout is a one-off activity, which can be accomplished using a methodology such as group technology.

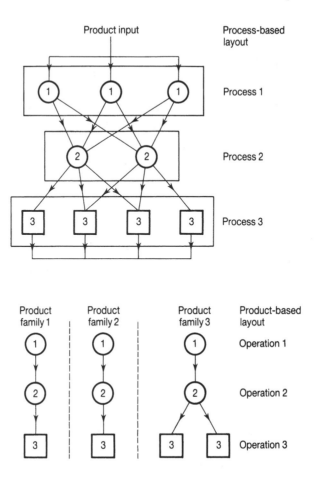

FIGURE 14.8
Process-based
layout vs. product-
based layout.

Burbidge (1989) defines **process-based** layout as involving organization units which specialize in particular processes, whereas **product-based** layout involves units which specialize in the completion of groups of products or subassemblies (see Figure 14.8). Each cell in a product-based layout is associated with the manufacture of a particular product family (see also Chapter 15).

It is clear that for the majority of manufacturing plants it will not be possible to define independent product-based cells. In fact, the product-based cells sketched in Figure 14.8 might be considered ideal, in that each product family is completed within its associated cell. Different components may be manufactured in individual cells and perhaps assembled in another cell. Also it may be necessary to share expensive equipment between cells. For example, the expensive equipment used in a heat treatment process is usually separated into one cell on a shop floor which all products share, rather than having individual heat treatment ovens and associated equipment in each cell. It is this failure to develop completely independent cells which makes the control task within factory coordination difficult. In fact, the degree of interdependence between the cells determines to a great extent the complexity of the factory coordination task.

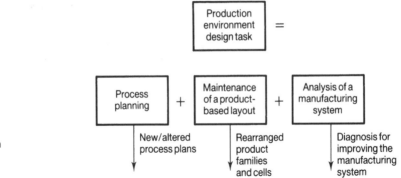

Using an initial product-based layout, the production environment design module integrates new products into the production environment with minimal disruption and reorganization to the existing product-based structure. The various procedures involved in production environment design may include the following (see Figure 14.9):

▶ the detailing of process plans for new products;

▶ the maintenance of a product-based layout;

▶ the analysis of a production system.

Process planning

The main function of the process planning procedure (see Chapter 9) is to generate a bill of process for each new product. By including a part of the process planning function* within the production environment design task, we are attempting to prevent any process plan proliferation. Often changes to process plans are made routinely, remain largely undocumented, and are accomplished by a variety of individuals using formal and informal systems. One consequence of process plan proliferation is the generation of a variety of product flow paths, which can reduce the benefits of a well-organized product-based layout. The inclusion of an element of the process planning activity within the factory coordination function helps to standardize and reduce the complexity in the planning task.

When new process plans are being developed, there may be two steps to the development process:

▶ *Determine production requirements.* Manufacturing personnel decide on suitable process requirements for each product given the product and process constraints.

▶ *Develop the process plan.* Based on the chosen process requirements, manufacturing personnel assign specific resources to carry out the operations. Other details, such as the tooling specification and set-up requirements, may also be added to complete the process plan at this stage.

* Clearly the bulk of the process planning work will be done within engineering (see Chapter 9); what we are talking about here is the final selection from alternative process plans if available.

It is clear that there may be more than one possible process plan for an individual component and that perhaps different workstations might be used to process a particular part, depending on availability of resources at any particular point in time. At the factory coordination stage, the production planning and control people should have the facility to select from alternative process plans, where feasible, in order to make best use of available resources. The process planning task also allows existing process plans to be altered, if such a need arises.

Maintenance of the product-based layout

The product-based layout must be maintained whenever a group of new products is introduced into production. Using a set of procedures based on group technology principles (see for example production flow analysis, outlined in Chapter 15), the new products are integrated into the existing range of product families and any necessary reorganization is carried out on the product-based layout. The reorganization of the product-based layout occurs with minimal disruption to the daily production activities. Group technology is a manufacturing philosophy that attempts to rationalize batch production by making use of design and/or manufacturing similarities among products. Families of products are established, based on the identified design or manufacturing similarities. With the formation of product families and cells, the factory layout changes from being process-based to being product-based, as previously illustrated in Figure 14.8.

Analysis of a manufacturing system

The main function of the analysis of a manufacturing system is to present information on various characteristics of the production environment, such as set-up times, throughput times and quality levels. The main purpose of this analysis is to pinpoint particular areas of the production process where there is room for potential improvement. Depending on the production environment, different categories of information are filtered and examined. For example, in a health-care products production environment, historical product and process data is considered important, and the monitor must track and maintain a record on the progress of each batch through the system. In the analysis procedure three steps may be taken:

1. *Collate information.* All the necessary information is firstly gathered by each of the PAC monitors and is then collated by the factory coordination monitor.

2. *Analyse alternatives.* Using various theories relating to manufacturing systems design, manufacturing personnel identify potential causes for any production problems; for example, the data might point to high set-up times on individual jobs or machines, or perhaps large queues at particular workstations might be highlighted.

3. *Develop diagnosis.* Based on the analysis of alternatives, a proposed solution to solve a particular problem is developed. For example, some of the techniques of set-up reduction, to be discussed in Chapter 15, might be used to reduce set-up times on a particular batch or machine.

The manufacturing systems analysis activity within factory coordination is based on the notion of *continuous improvement* to a production process, to simplify the control task. Schonberger (1982) places great emphasis on simple factory configurations and argues that by simplifying the process, products flow more efficiently through the system. The control task is relatively easier when operating in a well-organized factory configuration, because there is less variability and more stability in such a structured production environment. In fact the greater the effort expended in the production environment design task and the degree to which the resulting cells are independent, the simpler the control task within factory coordination becomes.

As indicated above, the thinking behind the manufacturing systems analysis is one of continuous pursuit of excellence. Initially the analysis should be regarded as a filter and medium for presenting information on the performance of a manufacturing system, from which the manufacturing personnel can decide which particular areas merit further attention. The analysis could be developed using the expertise and experience of the manufacturing personnel, perhaps encoded in a decision support system. This type of support system not only presents information, but recommends possible courses of action to solve problems. Manufacturing personnel can then choose to follow the recommended course of action or to use other approaches based on their own experience.

Overview of the production environment design (PED) task

The approach within the PED task can be summarized as follows. After the initial establishment of the product-based layout, new products are integrated within the existing families, a standardized process planning procedure is used to develop a selection of process plans for each new product, and the performance of the manufacturing system is continuously analysed so as to ensure that the benefits of product-based manufacturing are maintained. The integration of new products continues until there is a complete change in the product range or the families grow so large that the benefits diminish. If either of these situations occurs, new families and cells have to be established.

14.4.2 The control task within factory coordination

The production environment design task ensures that an efficient product-based manufacturing system is maintained within a manufacturing system. Product-based manufacturing facilitates the distribution of responsibility for the production of a family of products to each work group. With this distribution of responsibility the manufacturing system is better equipped to deal with any production problems or fluctuations in demand. Therefore the main purpose of the control task is to co-ordinate the activities of each PAC system through the provision of schedule and real-time control guidelines, while recognizing that each PAC system is responsible for the activities within its own cell.

The time horizon for coordination of the flow of products by the control task varies, depending on the manufacturing environment. However, it is influenced by the time horizon of the master production schedule (MPS), since the goal of the control task is to satisfy the production requirements and the constraints imposed by

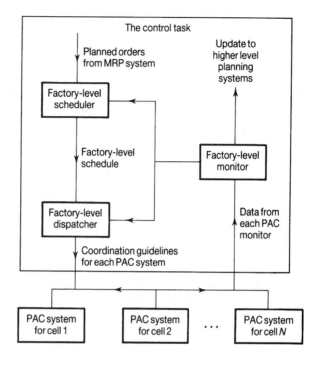

FIGURE 14.10

Data exchange between the control task of factory coordination and a number of PAC systems.

the MPS. The control task involves the development of schedule guidelines using a factory-level scheduler, implementing these guidelines and providing real-time guidelines for each of the PAC systems using a factory-level dispatcher, and monitoring the progress of the schedule using a factory-level monitor. The factory coordination control task, therefore, is in many ways a higher level recursion of a PAC system (see Figure 14.10).

As with a PAC system there are three individual building blocks associated with the factory coordination control task:

▶ **A factory-level scheduler** which develops a schedule which each PAC system uses as a guide when developing its schedule;

▶ **A factory-level dispatcher** which controls the movement of material between cells on a real-time basis and communicates with each PAC dispatcher;

▶ **A factory-level monitor** which observes the status of the entire factory based on information coming from each PAC monitor.

In addition to these three basic building blocks, each cell on the shop floor may be regarded as a virtual producer, because each cell receives guidelines on its production activities from the factory-level dispatcher. In relation to the movement of materials between cells, there may be two different types of factory-level mover.

▶ **The first type of mover.** The PAC mover which is used to organize materials handling within the cell can also coordinate the materials movement between cells, provided that the material handling between cells is a simple task. Information on the next cell on a product's process routing can be given to the mover by the particular PAC dispatcher of the cell which the batch is leaving.

▶ **The second type of mover.** This is a factory-level mover, which operates on the same principles as the PAC mover except that it is concerned with organizing the materials flow between the cells on the shop floor. The factory-level mover receives all of its instructions from the factory-level dispatcher. In a shop floor, where there is complex materials movement between cells, there may well be a requirement for a factory-level mover.

In relation to the movement of materials between cells, we shall think in terms of the first type of mover for the remainder of this chapter. Thus we shall now describe the basic building blocks of the control task in factory coordination, namely the scheduler, the dispatcher and the monitor.

Factory coordination – scheduler

The factory coordination scheduler is concerned with predictive scheduling, which involves the planning of work for an upcoming period to best optimize the system as a whole. Ideally, the scheduler develops a plan to coordinate the flow of products from cell to cell within the pre-defined production due dates. However, the plan may not be able to handle unpredictable events which may occur, such as resource breakdowns or component shortages, which are the responsibility of the factory-level dispatcher. The scheduler may have different schedule development strategies depending on the particular production environment. A production environment might be classified in terms of a job shop, batch manufacturing or a mass production environment. For example, in a production environment which is distinguished by a large production volume and a standardized product range, the process is predictable with little potential for variability. In such an environment a factory-level schedule can be very detailed in terms of guidelines to each of the PAC systems. This is in contrast to a production environment where there is a large variety of products being manufactured with fluctuating production volumes and where the potential for variability and unpredictability is greater. Here the corresponding factory-level schedule provides guidelines for each of the PAC systems, and allows for the increased variability by including less detail, and placing greater emphasis on the autonomy of each cell.

There are two approaches to developing a factory-level schedule: **infinite scheduling** or **finite scheduling**. Vollmann *et al.* (1988) draw a distinction between infinite and finite scheduling techniques:

▶ Infinite scheduling produces a schedule without any consideration for each resource's capacity or the other batches to be scheduled. The assumption is that each resource has infinite capacity.

▶ Finite scheduling produces detailed schedules for each product with defined start and finish times. With finite scheduling, each resource has finite capacity. Therefore full consideration is given to the resource's capacity and to the other batches being scheduled on that resource.

It is clear that requirements planning systems use infinite scheduling techniques, while finite scheduling techniques are more appropriate for PAC systems. In so far as is feasible, finite scheduling techniques should be used with the factory coordination scheduler also.

The scheduling procedure within factory coordination involves the following steps:

1. select appropriate criteria as measures of schedule performance;

2. allocate the requirements;

3. develop a schedule;

4. analyse the schedule.

Step 1 involves the selection of measures of performance for the scheduler. Measures of performance, such as the number of daily/weekly finished batches, average throughput times, average work in progress levels and average resource utilization, are identified to be used in Step 4.

Step 2 involves the transformation of the requirements, stated in the master production schedule and detailed through the requirements planning procedure, into well-defined batch orders with due dates spread throughout the time horizon. For example, using the production smoothing approach to planning in just in time systems (see Chapter 15), the batch orders are averaged evenly throughout the time horizon. In other types of production system, the spread of orders may not be so even, with particular product requirements being met before production of other products commences.

Step 3 involves developing a schedule proposal to suit the flow of products in a particular environment, which is analysed for its feasibility in Step 4. The main data inputs to Step 3 include data on all resources and products within the factory. The schedule proposal takes account of the production due dates of the required batches in determining coordination guidelines to enable the product flow to meet these due dates. Typically, one of the approaches discussed earlier, i.e. algorithms or heuristics, might be used to develop a schedule.

Step 4 examines each proposed schedule in relation to its suitability and efficiency with respect to a series of production criteria. The use of a range of criteria helps to ensure that the schedule proposals are analysed from the perspective of the overall production system.

Once a schedule proposal is accepted, it is regarded as a plan which can be used to coordinate each cell with respect to overall production goals. However, deviations from the plan may occur because of the occurrence of unexpected events and of trade-offs to decide between conflicting requirements and goals when the proposal was being developed. As in the case of the PAC system, it is the function of the dispatcher to implement the schedule and to manage unexpected events through real-time control at a factory level.

Factory coordination – dispatcher

The factory-level dispatcher implements the factory-level schedule by passing the relevant guidelines relating to each cell to the appropriate PAC system. In relation to the provision of real-time guidelines, the factory-level dispatcher only provides such guidelines when it can make an effective contribution to a problem arising in a manufacturing environment. Such guidelines include changes in product priorities and/or process data because of fluctuating production requirements and the regulation of the flow of raw material and work in progress stocks between cells.

In order to have a detailed picture of the production environment, the dispatcher has access to dynamic and static data. Bills of process for each product, and the factory-level schedule are examples of static data used by the dispatcher. Examples of dynamic data include the location of each work in progress batch, the status of the inter-cell transportation system and the status of the input buffer of each cell. The dispatching task can be carried out:

▶ by a production manager using his or her own expertise;

▶ by a production manager, using distributed software systems containing rules and other forms of intelligence in a decision support system;

▶ by a distributed software system, which automatically controls the group of cells.

Factory coordination – monitor

Similar to the PAC monitor discussed earlier, the factory coordination monitor has two tasks: the provision of accurate reports to management and the delivery of timely and accurate data to the scheduling and dispatching functions and higher level planning systems. With access to accurate data from the monitor, the scheduling and dispatching activities function more efficiently. One of the data exchanges with the scheduler may involve a request for a new schedule to be developed because of some problem on the shop floor. From the data provided by the monitor, the dispatcher is aware of the current status of the shop floor (e.g. work in progress buffer levels, raw material stock levels etc.). The reports to management summarize the production situation throughout the factory by filtering relevant information from each PAC monitor and compiling an overall picture of the performance of the manufacturing system. More detailed information on the performance inside each cell can be found in the reports provided by the particular PAC monitor.

The efficiency of a factory-level monitor can be assessed by the convenience and simplicity of its operations for manufacturing personnel and the promptness and accuracy of the information that the factory-level monitor generates. As with the PAC monitor, the factory-level monitor procedure might involve the following four steps:

1. capture the PAC data;

2. analyse the PAC data;

3. provide decision support;

4. provide historical reports.

Step 1 involves filtering and condensing data from each of the PAC monitors and gathering it into an organized form. According to previously identified monitoring reference goals, the data is then analysed in Step 2 and any necessary reports are prepared for management. The monitoring reference guidelines help identify different types of data, which should be analysed and presented by the monitor. For example, in a production environment producing high-quality products, the monitor could be instructed to provide all data on the quality levels of each batch.

In Step 3, higher level planning systems and the factory-level scheduler and dispatcher are kept fully informed of all activities throughout the factory through data generated by the monitor. This data feedback helps the dispatcher to carry out its real-time scheduling task.

The factory-level monitor also provides relevant data for higher level planning systems. For example, the factory-level monitor can provide regular updates on lead times to the requirements planning system. The regular update on lead times enables this system to produce more accurate plans for materials requirements. Step 4 involves providing reports to management, describing the performance of the factory in relation to different criteria, such as fulfilment of product orders, product quality etc.

The filtering and condensation of data by the factory-level monitor is important in order to avoid an overabundance of irrelevant information. Ackoff (1977) maintained that an explanatory model of the decision process within a production environment can assist in determining which information to provide to each department or function. This decision process model articulates the different data requirements for each department within an organization and how they influence the activities in other departments. For example, when the sales department gives a commitment to a customer for an order to be completed on a certain date, it is influencing the production planning task within manufacturing, who have to use the due date set by the sales department, when scheduling the production of that particular order. Problems such as capacity overload can occur when planning the production of a customer's order using the particular due date set by the sales department. Information drawn from the factory-level monitor can assist the sales department in determining a reasonable due date to a customer.

In summary, the factory-level monitor should be regarded as a filter for all data coming from each PAC system. Once the data is filtered and analysed, it can be used by:

▶ the scheduler and the dispatcher in their decision-making process;

▶ higher level planning systems such as RP systems, through for example more accurate estimates of manufacturing lead times;

▶ management in assessing the overall manufacturing performance of a factory.

14.4.3 Overview of factory coordination

We shall conclude this section on factory coordination by summarizing the architecture (see Figure 14.11):

▶ Factory coordination involves a production environment design task and a control task. By combining these two tasks in a single architecture, we are arguing that by improving the efficiency of the manufacturing environment through the production environment design task the control task is greatly simplified and

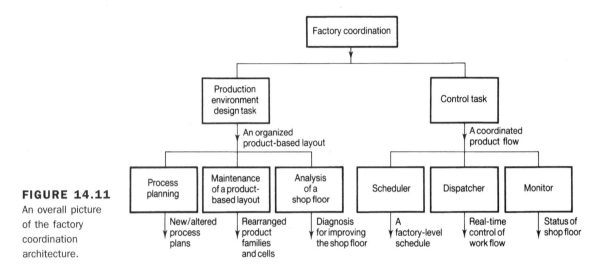

FIGURE 14.11
An overall picture of the factory coordination architecture.

the control system can coordinate the flow of products through the plant more effectively.

▶ The production environment design task is concerned with reorganizing a product-based layout to maintain its efficiency. It uses a selection of techniques involving process planning, maintenance of a product-based layout and manufacturing systems analysis.

▶ The control task coordinates the flow of products between cells to ensure that their production due dates are fulfilled with the highest quality standards and lowest costs. This is achieved by passing appropriate guidelines to the individual PAC systems.

14.5 Conclusion

The shop floor control task is an important and complex task in modern manufacturing. In this chapter we have described an approach to managing this control task efficiently which involves factory coordination and PAC systems coordinating the flow of work through a factory.

Factory coordination consists of two tasks: a production environment design task and a control task. The production environment design task is concerned with the reorganization of a manufacturing environment to support product-based manufacturing and to ensure the continuous improvement of the manufacturing environment. The control task involves using a scheduler, dispatcher and monitor. The scheduler develops a suitable factory-level schedule. The dispatcher implements the schedule and is charged with real-time control of the work flow within a factory. The monitor provides data on the status of the factory and the progress of the schedule. With these three factory-level systems all cells are coordinated to balance the flow of products through a factory. By establishing a relationship between the control and the production environment design tasks, we are trying to organize an efficient manufacturing environment so as to reduce the complexity of controlling the flow of products within the environment.

With the layout of the shop floor being as close as possible to a product-based layout, each PAC system has a definite area of responsibility. Using the guidelines from the factory coordination control task, each PAC system controls the work flow within each cell. To complete this control task, a PAC system uses a scheduler to develop a schedule based on the guideliness in the factory-level schedule, a dispatcher to control the work flow on a real-time basis and a monitor which gives progress reports on the schedule. Thus the factory coordination control task and the PAC task are similar, although operating at different levels.

References and further reading

Ackoff R. L. (1977). Optimization + objectivity = opt out. *European Journal of Operational Research*. **1**, 1–7.

Bauer A., Bowden R., Browne J., Duggan J. and Lyons G. (1991). *Shop Floor Control Systems – From Design to Implementation*. London: Chapman & Hall.

Biron B., Bel G., Cavaille J., Baraust O. and Bourrieres J. (1991). Integrating simulation for workshop control. In *Computer Applications in Production and Engineering CAPE '91* (ed. G. Doumeingts, J. Browne and M. Tomljanovich). Amsterdam: North-Holland.

Blackstone J. H., Phillips D. T. and Hogg D. L. (1982). A state of the art survey of dispatching rules for manufacturing job shop operations. *International Journal of Production Research*. **20**(1), 27–45.

Bowden R., Browne J. and Duggan J. (1989). The design and implementation of a factory coordination system. *Xth International Conference on Production Research*, Nottingham.

Browne J. (1988) Production activity control – a key aspect of production control. *International Journal of Production Research*. **26**(3), 415–27.

Browne J. and Davies B. J. (1984). A simulation study of a machine shop. *International Journal of Production Research*. **22**, 335–57.

Browne J., Boon J. E. and Davies B. J. (1981) Job shop control. *International Journal of Production Research*. **19**(6), 643–63.

Browne J., Harhen J. and Shivnan J. (1989). *Production Management Systems – A CIM Perspective*. Harlow: Addison Wesley Longman.

Burbidge J. (1989). *Production Flow Analysis for Planning Group Technology*. Oxford: Oxford Science Publications.

Carrie A. (1988). *Simulation of Manufacturing Systems*. New York: John Wiley.

Conway R. W. and Maxwell W. L. (1962). Network dispatching by shortest operation discipline. *Operations Research*. **10**, 51.

Conway R. W., Maxwell W. L. and Miller L. W. (1967) *Theory of Scheduling*. Reading, MA: Addison-Wesley.

Copas C. and Browne J. (1990). A rules-based scheduling system for flow type assembly. *International Journal of Production Research*. **28**(5), 981–1005.

Cunningham P. and Browne J. (1986). A LISP-based heuristic scheduler for automatic insertion in electronics assembly. *International Journal of Production Research*. **24**(6), 1395–1408.

Duggan J. and Browne J. (1988). ESPNET: Expert system based simulator of Petri nets. *IEE Proceedings – D Control Theory and Applications*. **135**(4), 239–47, July.

Duggan J., Fallon D., Higgins P., Jackson S. M. and Copas C. (1987). Building blocks within the application generator. *ESPRIT Project 447 Report*, UCG, January.

French S. (1982). *Sequencing and Scheduling*. Chichester: Ellis Horwood.

Goldratt E. and Cox J. (1986). *The Goal*. USA: North River Press, Inc.

Graves S. C. (1981). A review of production scheduling. *Operations Research*. **29**(4), 801–19, July–August.

Higgins P. D. and Browne J. (1989). The monitor in production activity control systems. *Production Planning and Control*. **1**(1), January–March.

Jackson S. and Browne J. (1989). An interactive scheduler for production activity control. *International Journal of Computer Integrated Manufacturing*. **2**(1), 2–15.

Kerr R. (1991). *Knowledge-Based Manufacturing Management (Applications of Artificial Intelligence to the Effective Management of Manufacturing Companies)*. Reading MA: Addison Wesley Longman.

Lundrigan R. (1986). What is this thing called OPT? *Production and Inventory Management*. **27**(2), 2–12.

O'Grady P. and Lee K. H. (1988). An intelligent cell control system for automated manufacturing. *International Journal of Production Research*. **26**(5), 845–61.

Orlicky J. (1975). *Material Requirements Planning: The New Way of Life in Production and Inventory Management*. New York: McGraw-Hill.

Rinnoy Kan, A. H. G. (1976). *Machine Scheduling Problems: Classification, Complexity and Computations*. The Hague: Martinus Nijhoff.

Schonberger R. (1982). *Japanese Manufacturing Techniques: Nine Hidden Lessons*. New York: Free Press.

Smith S. and Fox M. (1986). ISSIS: A knowledge based system for factory scheduling. *Expert Systems*. **1**, 25–49.

Smith W. E. (1956). Various optimizers for single-state production. *Naval Re. Logist. Quart.*, **3**, 59–66.

Spachis A. S. and King J. R. (1979). Job shop scheduling heuristics with local neighbourhood search. *International Journal of Production Research*. **17**, 507–26.

Vollmann T., Berry W. and Whybark D. (1988). *Manufacturing Planning and Control Systems*. New York: Dow Jones-Irwin.

Exercises

14.1 Differentiate clearly the respective roles of the scheduler and the dispatcher in a PAC system.

14.2 How does the monitor support the scheduler and dispatcher in a PAC system?

14.3 Identify and clearly define six performance measures used to evaluate the performance of a scheduling technique.

14.4 What do we mean when we say that two performance measures are equivalent?

14.5 Explain the $n/m/A/B$ notation used to classify scheduling problems.

14.6 Use Moore's algorithm to solve the following $6/1/N_T$ problem:

Job number	1	2	3	4	5	6
Due date	12	4	7	13	18	26
Production time	4	2	4	3	3	5

14.7 Use Johnson's algorithm to solve the following $4/2/F/F_{max}$ problem:

Job number	Processing time	
	Machine 1	Machine 2
1	4	6
2	7	13
3	3	8
4	5	10

14.8 Under what conditions can Johnson's algorithm be used to solve the $n/3/F/F_{max}$ problem?

14.9 What is a heuristic?

14.10 For which measures of performance is the SPT heuristic optimal for single machine environments?

14.11 What is the 'critical ratio'?

14.12 What is the modified SPT heuristic? When is it used?

14.13 What is a Gantt chart?

14.14 What is the role of the production environment design task in factory coordination?

14.15 Differentiate between a product- and process-based layout.

14.16 Differentiate clearly the role of the factory coordination system and the production activity control system.

14.17 In terms of the PAC monitor, distinguish clearly the three roles of data capture, data analysis and decision support.

14.18 Rule 5 of OPT says that 'Bottlenecks govern both throughput and inventory in a system'. Explain.

14.19 Why does OPT argue that 'the transfer batch may not, and many times should not, be equal to the process batch'.

14.20 'By including a part of the process planning function within the production environment design task of factory coordination, we are attempting to prevent any process plan proliferation'. Explain.

15 Just in time

··

When you have completed studying the material in this chapter you should be able to:

- ▶ describe the goals of the just in time (JIT) approach to manufacturing systems design and operation;
- ▶ understand the thinking behind flow-based production;
- ▶ understand the approach to suppliers in a JIT environment;
- ▶ understand and implement production smoothing systems;
- ▶ differentiate between mixed model and multi-model production systems;
- ▶ appreciate the breakdown of lead time in a typical manufacturing system and the approaches used to reduce lead time;
- ▶ understand what is meant by a repetitive manufacturing environment and the use of kanban cards to manage work flow through such an environment;
- ▶ apply simple line balancing techniques;
- ▶ appreciate the basic thinking behind WCM (world-class manufacturing) and its similarity to JIT thinking.

Chapter contents

15.1 Introduction

Just in time production has certainly attracted the attention of many industrial managers in recent times. Western industrial managers, aware of the success of their Japanese counterparts, now believe that a commitment to achieving just in time in manufacturing is essential in order to compete in world-wide markets. In this chapter, just in time (JIT) ideas and their influence on manufacturing systems will be discussed. (A more complete treatment than is possible here may be found in Browne *et al.* (1988).)

JIT will be discussed under the following headings: the just in time approach, which involves an examination of the goals and the key ideas which go to make up the approach; and the manufacturing systems design and planning for JIT, which looks at concepts such as design for ease of manufacture and quality control. Finally, there will be a brief discussion on the Kanban card system.

15.2 The just in time approach

The JIT approach involves a continuous commitment to the pursuit of excellence in all phases of manufacturing systems design and operation. JIT seeks to design a manufacturing system for efficient production of 100% good units. It seeks to produce only the required items, at the required time, and in the required quantities. This is probably the simplest statement of the JIT approach to manufacturing.

To be more specific, JIT seeks to achieve the following goals:

▶ Zero defects;

▶ Zero set-up time;

▶ Zero inventories;

▶ Zero handling;

▶ Zero breakdowns;

▶ Zero lead time;

▶ Lot size of one.

There are two aspects of the set of goals listed above which are worth pointing out. Firstly, in the minds of many manufacturing or industrial engineers trained in the Western approach to manufacturing systems design and operation, these goals seem very ambitious, if not unattainable. Secondly the attempt to consider all of these goals simultaneously is unusual in the context of the traditional approach to manufacturing systems. The traditional approach to manufacturing has been reductionist, which involves consideration of well-defined aspects of the overall manufacturing problem (in fact separate sub-problems), which are tackled and *solved* as separate problems. This approach has led to the proliferation of specialists in the various manufacturing functions, with a resulting absence of generalists whose role is to consider the totality of the manufacturing system. The JIT approach can clearly be characterized as holistic at least in terms of the range of goals it sets for itself.

Zero defects

In traditional manufacturing management there is a belief that a certain level of unacceptable product is unavoidable and that the emphasis should be on reaching an attainable or acceptable level of conformity to specification and to customer expectation. This contrasts with the JIT approach, which aims to eliminate, once and for all, the causes of defects, and so engenders an attitude of seeking to achieve excellence at all stages in the manufacturing process.

Zero inventories

In traditional manufacturing thinking, inventories, including work in progress (WIP) and the contents of finished goods stores, are seen as assets, in the sense that they represent added value which has been accumulated in the system. Inventories are often considered a buffer against uncertain suppliers. Outside suppliers are *distrusted* and the thinking is almost to assume that they may not deliver on time; hence the buffers – as *insurance* against uncertain availability of work by shop floor supervisors and as a buffer against an unexpected customer order.

The JIT view suggests that inventory is evidence of poor design, poor coordination and poor operation of the manufacturing system.

Zero set-up time

The concepts of zero set-up time and a lot size of one are interrelated. If the set-up times are approaching zero, then this implies that there is no advantage to producing in batches. The thinking behind the economic order quantity (EOQ)/economic batch quantity approach (see Chapter 13) is to minimize the total cost of inventory by effecting a trade-off between the costs of carrying stock and the costs of set-ups. Very large batches imply high inventory costs. Very small batches result in correspondingly lower inventory costs but involve a larger number of set-ups and consequently larger set-up costs. However, if set-up times and costs are zero then the ultimate small batch, namely the batch of one, is economic. The consequences of a lot size of one are of enormous benefit from an inventory and overall manufacturing performance perspective.

Zero lead time

Long planning lead times force the manufacturing system to rely on forecasts and to commit to manufacturing product prior to and in anticipation of customer orders. Small lots, combined with short lead times, mean that the manufacturing system is not committed to a particular production programme over a long period and can more readily adapt to short-term fluctuations in market demand. To approach zero lead time, the products, the manufacturing system and the production processes must be so designed as to facilitate rapid throughput of orders. Traditional approaches tended to treat product and process design separately. The JIT philosophy takes a holistic approach and recognizes the interdependence of these activities.

The importance of the zero lead time goal cannot be overstated when considering the demands the market places on manufacturers to respond quickly to orders for a diversity of products. While zero lead time is impossible, a manufacturing system that pursues such an ideal objective, and constantly strives to reduce the lead times for products to the absolute minimum, will clearly operate with far greater flexibility than its competitors.

Zero parts handling

Manufacturing and assembly operations frequently include a large number of non-value adding activities. Taking assembly operations as an example, one can view many assembly tasks as a combination of the following operations:

- ▶ component feeding;

- ▶ component handling;

- ▶ parts mating;

- ▶ parts inspection;

- ▶ special operations.

Operations such as component feeding and component handling are essentially non-value adding operations. If components and assemblies could be designed to minimize feeding and if manufacturing systems could be designed to minimize handling, significant reductions in assembly problems and assembly times could be achieved (see Chapter 9).

As was shown earlier (Chapter 14), the product-based manufacturing layout is preferred to the traditional process-based layout. One reason for this is that product-based layout results in much simpler patterns of material flow through the plant and consequently considerably reduces the planning and materials handling effort.

15.3 Key elements in the JIT approach

Arising from the goals discussed above one can recognize three essential elements of the JIT philosophy for product and manufacturing system design. These important elements are:

- ▶ An intelligent match of the product design with market demand, in an era of greatly reduced product life cycles, with the early consideration of manufacturing problems at the product design stage.

- ▶ The definition of product families, based upon a number of important manufacturing goals, and the design of manufacturing systems to facilitate flow-based production of these families, where possible.

- ▶ The establishment of relationships with suppliers to achieve just in time deliveries of raw materials and purchased components.

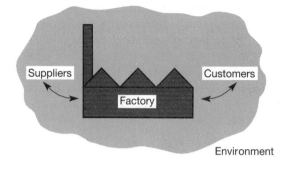

FIGURE 15.1
Plant environment from the JIT perspective.

These three elements can be seen as part of an overall approach to manufacturing which sees the factory sitting within an environment (see Figure 15.1), the front end of which involves the factory and its relations with its customers in the market place and the back end of which is the relationship of the factory with its suppliers. The fact that the JIT approach considers the total manufacturing picture is not surprising in view of the wide range of goals which JIT seeks to address and which have been outlined above.

The importance of this approach to manufacturing, i.e. not restricting attention to the *internals* of the factory, cannot be overstressed. The JIT approach to manufacturing incorporates a business perspective as distinct from a narrow, or strictly manufacturing (i.e. inside the four walls of the plant) perspective. We will now discuss each of the key elements in turn.

15.3.1 A match of product design to market demand

In Chapter 12, the changing environment of manufacturing was discussed, focusing on greatly increased product diversity and greatly reduced product life cycles as important factors in this new environment. The heightened expectations of today's consumers, who demand considerable choice in the configuration of options, was also discussed – the automotive market is an important example of this trend.

Of course, even with today's sophisticated and versatile manufacturing technology, companies cannot provide customized products at an economic price to the mass market. What is required is that industry interpret the wishes of the market place and in a sense direct the market in a manner which allows it (the industry) to respond to the market effectively. This involves designing a range of products which anticipates the market requirement and includes sufficient variety to meet consumers' expectations and can be manufactured and delivered to the market at a price which the market is willing and able to pay.

To achieve this objective, it is necessary to design products in a modular fashion. A large product range and a wide variety of product styles can result in high manufacturing and assembly costs, due to the high cost of flexibility in manufacturing systems. In general terms, it is true that the greater the flexibility required, the more expensive will be the manufacturing system, and therefore the products of that manufacturing system. Thus, too broad a product range and variety of product styles will result in products which are too expensive for the market.

Modular product designs are achieved by rationalizing the product range where possible and by examining the commonality of components and subassemblies across the product range with a view to increasing it to the maximum level possible. Rationalization of the product range results in reduced production costs through fewer manufacturing set-ups, fewer items in stock, fewer component drawings etc. These issues will be considered in more detail later in this chapter, when the product design issue will be reviewed in more detail.

15.3.2 Product families and flow-based manufacturing

A common approach to the identification of product families and the subsequent development of flow-based manufacturing systems is group technology (GT) (see Chapter 9). The use of GT in JIT systems to define product families is important for a number of reasons. Firstly, group technology is used to aid the design process and to reduce unnecessary variety and duplication in product design. Secondly, group technology is used to define families of products and components which can be manufactured in well-defined manufacturing cells. The effect of these manufacturing cells is to reorient production systems away from the process-based layout and towards the product- or flow-based layout. Group technology leads to cell-based manufacturing which seeks to achieve shorter lead times, reduced work in progress and finished goods inventories, simplified production planning and control, and increased job satisfaction. Group technology was not originally conceived by the Japanese, but its philosophy was adopted by them and drawn into the JIT approach to manufacturing (see Gallagher and Knight, 1987).

It is useful to consider in some detail the differences between a traditional functional or process-based plant layout and a group technology or product-based layout. In the functional or process layout, machines are organized into groups by function. Thus in a metal cutting machine shop, the lathes would be grouped together in a single department, as would the milling machines, the grinders, the drilling machines etc. A departmental supervisor/manager would be responsible for a particular function or group of functions. Individual components would *visit* some or maybe all departments, and thus would pass through a number of different supervisors'/managers' areas of responsibility. Individual operators and their supervisors/managers would be responsible for different operations on each component, but not for the resulting component or assembly itself. Given the variety of components associated with batch type production systems, the actual route individual batches take through the various departments or functions in the plant varies, and therefore the material flow system is complex. Furthermore, given this complex and virtually random material flow system, it is not easy at any point in time to say what progress has been made on individual batches.

The product- or cell-based layout, as shown in Figure 15.2, is clearly considerably simpler than the process-based layout. In fact, this simplicity is a hallmark of just in time systems, and for many writers and researchers on manufacturing systems, is a key characteristic of the system (see for example Schonberger (1984)). As we shall see later, this simplicity facilitates the use of a manual production activity control system, namely Kanban, on the shop floor itself.

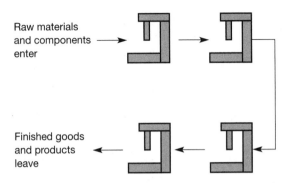

Raw materials
and components
enter

Finished goods
and products
leave

FIGURE 15.2
Cell layout.

A technique used to plan the change from a process- to a product-based plant organization is production flow analysis (see Burbidge, 1963). Production flow analysis (PFA) is based on the analysis of component route cards which specify the manufacturing processes for each component and indeed the manufacturing work centres which individual components must visit. PFA, according to Burbidge, is a progressive technique, based on five sub-techniques, namely:

▶ company flow analysis (CFA);

▶ factory flow analysis (FFA);

▶ group analysis (GA);

▶ line analysis (LA);

▶ tooling analysis (TA).

CFA is used in multi-plant companies to plan the simplest and most efficient inter-plant material flow system. FFA is used to identify the sub-products within a factory around which product-based departments can be organized. GA is used to divide the individual departments into groups of machines which deal with unique product families. LA seeks to organize the individual machines within a line to reflect the flow of products between those machines. TA looks at the individual machines in a cell or line and seeks to plan tooling so that groups of parts can be made with similar tooling set-up.

Group technology in a sense creates the conditions necessary for JIT because, as Lewis (1986) points out, it results in:

▶ control of the variety seen by the manufacturing system;

▶ standardization of processing methods;

▶ integration of processes.

In summary, the important issue from our point of view is that flow-based manufacturing is an important goal for manufacturing systems designers to aim towards, and it is certainly central to the whole JIT approach.

15.3.3 The relationship with suppliers in a JIT environment

As indicated earlier, the ideas of JIT are not restricted to the narrow confines of the manufacturing plant, but also reach out to customers and back to the vendor companies who supply the factory with raw materials and purchased items. The approach is to build strong and enduring relationships with a limited number of suppliers, to provide those suppliers with the detailed knowledge they need to be cost-effective, to help them to overcome problems which they might encounter, and to encourage them to apply their detailed knowledge of their own manufacturing processes to constantly improve the quality of the components they supply.

This involves taking a *long-term* view of the buyer/supplier relationship, and also involves commitment to building an enduring cooperative relationship with individual suppliers where information is readily shared and both organizations work to meet shared goals. JIT execution or implementation (i.e. the Kanban system) applied to purchasing gives rise to frequent orders and frequent deliveries. The ideal of single unit continuous delivery (delivery lot size of one) is impractical, but it can be approached by having as small a lot size as possible, delivered by the supplier, as frequently as possible. The physical distance of suppliers from the buyer's manufacturing plant plays an important role in determining the delivery lot size.

The closer the supplier is to the buyer's plant, the easier it is to make more frequent deliveries of smaller lots. This ideally may allow the supplier to initiate JIT production in its own plant and so link up with the buyer's JIT production system. In the case of suppliers at a distance from the buyer's plant, various techniques may be used to reduce what might otherwise be a high cost per unit load.

Example 15.1 *Reducing delivery costs*

Consider for example the following situation; four suppliers A, B, C and D each supply components to buyer E. The four suppliers are located in close proximity to each other, but all are at a distance from the buyer E. If they must all deliver four times each day then the possibility exists for them to cooperate in such a way that deliveries are made to the buyer four times each day but each supplier is responsible for only one delivery run per day. Supplier A might make the first delivery picking up products from B, C and D *en route*. Supplier B could make the second delivery, picking up the products of A, C and D, etc.

On the one hand, the buyer places great demands on the supplier in terms of frequent or just in time deliveries of components. On the other hand, by providing the supplier with commitments for orders over a long period and by ensuring that the supplier is aware of modifications to the company's master schedule as soon as is practicable, the buyer helps the supplier to meet the exacting demands of JIT. The ideal situation is where the supplier itself is able to focus a part of its plant to service each customer and the supplier starts to achieve a JIT environment in house.

The benefits from JIT purchasing include reduced purchased inventories, low rework, reduced inspection and shortened production lead time. These all combine to increase adaptability to demand and hence achieve just in time production. It is clear that the JIT approach to purchasing contrasts sharply with the traditional approach, which seeks to identify a number of competent suppliers and to have them compete for the business.

15.4 Product design for ease of manufacture and assembly

Earlier we identified some key elements in the JIT approach, one of which is an intelligent match of the product design with the perceived market demand. We indicated that this is important in an era of constantly changing market demand when a manufacturer must offer a diversity of products, within a given product range, to the market.

As suggested earlier, what is required of the product design team, among other things, is that it interpret the wishes of the market place and if possible lead the market by introducing a product range which allows the production system to respond effectively to the market. This involves designing products which both anticipate the market requirement and include sufficient variety to meet consumers' expectations, while being manufactured at a price which the market is willing to pay. This can be achieved in many ways – one approach is to increase the variety of products offered without simultaneously increasing the required process variety, associated complexity and increased cost. Consider Figure 15.3.

At present, designers of manufacturing systems are required to move along a diagonal which is bounded by both economic and technological constraints, as shown in Figure 15.3. The continuum of manufacturing mentioned in Chapter 12, which

FIGURE 15.3

Trade-off between product and process variety.

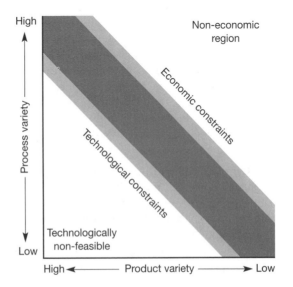

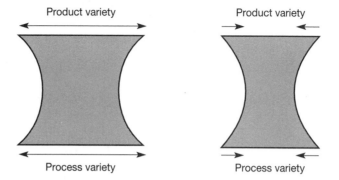

FIGURE 15.4
Product/process
variety relationship
(classical).

extends from mass production to jobbing shops, can be seen along this diagonal, with mass production in the bottom-right corner and jobbing shop production in the upper-left corner. However, given today's manufacturing environment, we might surmise that designers are attempting to move in the direction of low process variety and high product variety (i.e. the bottom-left corner of Figure 15.3). This effort is bounded by technological constraints, and the approach which seems to be prevalent in the West is often technologically driven, through the introduction of computer controlled, and consequently more flexible, production facilities.

The just in time approach represents a more comprehensive attempt to move towards low process variety and high product variety. Not only concerned with technological improvements, JIT also utilizes such techniques as product design for manufacture and assembly, flexible equipment, a flexible workforce and superior production engineering practice in areas such as the design of jigs and fixtures to achieve simple and therefore fast and inexpensive set-ups and change-overs between products. The concepts behind the use of flexible equipment and a flexible workforce will be brought out later in this chapter, as will the JIT approach to set-up reduction. For the moment we simply illustrate the effect of short set-up times using the following example. A machine which manufactures two distinct products A and B can be considered, from the process viewpoint, to be producing one product if the set-up or change-over time between the two products is very small, in effect approaching zero. To achieve this very desirable situation involves close collaboration between the product design, process engineering and manufacturing people in the plant.

Traditional thinking about the interaction between product or process variety can be represented by Figure 15.4. From this perspective, a widening of the product range results in an increase in the process variety required to cope with the increased product options. If a manufacturing plant increases the options within its product range this is normally expected to lead to increased process complexity because of increased process variety. Similarly, if the range of options in a product is reduced this might be expected to lead to a reduction in the complexity of the production system. In fact, the classical distinction between mass production, batch production and jobbing shop production is based at least partially on this notion – mass production uses specialized equipment to manufacture a narrow range of products in high volumes efficiently. However, where the product range is large and each product is required in relatively small volumes, more general purpose equipment is required and the

Product variety

Process variety

FIGURE 15.5
Product/process
variety relationship
under JIT.

resulting process variety is high. In effect, economies of scale cannot be realized in batch-based production systems. The impact of the introduction of computer-based automation into plants has been to allow the manufacturer to deal with greater variety, but the basic underlying relationship has not changed. Increased product variety involves more process complexity and therefore increased cost.

However, the JIT approach tries, through intelligent product design and through consideration of process issues at the product design stage, to increase the variety of products within a manufacturing plant while maintaining if not actually reducing process variety (see Figure 15.5). (It should be pointed out that design for manufacture and design for assembly are not unique to JIT. What is unique about the JIT approach is the emphasis it places on these issues and the fact that process and product design seem to have equal *status* and to work together effectively.)

This can be achieved by using techniques such as modular design, design for simplification and design for ease of manufacture and assembly (see Chapter 9).

Modular design

One of the consequences of good design is frequently a reduction in the number of components necessary to produce a given product, and hence a reduction in the production lead time. Similarly, products may be designed in a modular fashion so that components and assemblies are common across a given product range, and thus product variety is managed to good effect. With regard to the design process, it is possible to expand a basic model so as to increase the variety of products offered to the market. As illustrated in Figure 15.6, a common subassembly or module X is used across a number of products A, B and C. The effect of this is to increase the requirement for a single module X rather than having three different modules, each with a relatively low total requirement. Thus the use of standardized components and subassemblies results in increased production volumes of fewer different components and consequently reduced inventory levels.

This design philosophy is also reflected in the bill of materials (see Chapter 13) through attempts to keep the differences between products as high as possible in the product structure and thus minimize the consequences of variability for manufacturing.

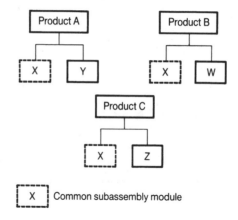

FIGURE 15.6

Common modules across bills of material.

Design for simplification

Design for simplification seeks to design products which are relatively simple to manufacture and assemble. New product designs should as far as possible include off the shelf items, standard items, or components that are possible to make with a minimum of experimental tooling. Product features such as part tolerances, surface finish requirements etc. should be determined while considering the consequences that unnecessary embellishment can have for the production process and therefore production costs. This approach can result in a major simplification of the manufacturing and assembly process.

Design for ease of automation

Design for ease of automation is concerned with the general concepts and design ideas which will, for example in the case of assembled components, help to simplify the automatic parts feeding, orienting and assembling processes. In the case of assembled components, it is important to design products to be assembled from the top down and to avoid forcing machines to assemble from the side or particularly from the bottom. The ideal assembly procedure can be performed on one face of the part with straight vertical motions, keeping the number of faces to be worked on to a minimum.

In fact, it is in the area of automated, and in particular robot-based, assembly that the importance of the design for assembly approach can be most clearly seen. Until recently the application of robots in industry has been confined to relatively primitive tasks – machine loading and unloading, spot and arc welding and spray painting. Relatively few applications in assembly have been realized. Researchers and manufacturing systems designers have adopted two main approaches: the development of sophisticated assembly robots and the redesign of products, components etc. for robot-based assembly. The first approach involves the development of universal grippers and intelligent sensor-based robots with sufficient accuracy, speed and repeatability and which are capable of being programmed in task-oriented languages. This approach seeks to mimic the flexibility and power of the human arm and hand. The second approach seems to be the more successful in practice. Laszcz (1985) points out '. . . a product designed in this manner reduces assembly to a series of pick-and-place operations, thereby requiring a less sophisticated robot. This results in manufacturing cost savings and increases the likelihood of financially justifying robotic assembly'.

15.5 Manufacturing planning techniques

Clearly an important purpose of JIT is to reduce costs. This is achieved in many ways, the most notable being the elimination of all wastes, especially unnecessary inventories. For example, in sales, cost reduction is realized by supplying the market with first class products in the quantities required at an affordable price, exactly when they are required. Stocks of finished goods are therefore minimized. To sell at a realistic price and in the quantities required, the production processes must be adaptable to demand changes and be capable of getting the required products quickly through manufacturing and to the market place. Similarly, the warehouses must only stock materials in the quantities required. To help production to respond effectively to short-term variations in market demand, just in time attempts to match the expected demand pattern to the capabilities of the manufacturing process and to organize the manufacturing system so that short-term, relatively small variations can be accommodated without a major overhaul of the system. The technique used to help achieve this is known as production smoothing.

Through production smoothing, single lines can produce many product varieties each day in response to market demand. Production smoothing utilizes the short production lead times to *mould* the market demand to match the capabilities of the production process. It involves two distinct phases, as illustrated in Figure 15.7.

The first phase adapts to monthly market demand changes during the year, the second to daily demand changes within each month. The possibility of sudden large changes in market demand and in seasonal changes is greatly reduced by detailed analysis of annual or even longer term projections and well thought out decisions on sales volumes, in so far as this is possible.

15.5.1 Monthly adaptation

Monthly adaptation is achieved though a monthly production planning process, i.e. the preparation of a master production schedule (MPS) (see Chapter 13). This MPS

FIGURE 15.7
Components of production smoothing.

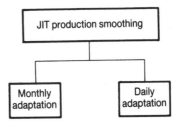

gives the averaged daily production level of each process, and is typically based on an aggregate three month and a monthly demand forecast. The precise planning horizon depends very much on the industry in question – in the automotive industry, where JIT originated, three months is typical. Thus the product mix and related product quantities are *suggested* two months in advance and a detailed plan is *fixed* one month in advance of the present month. This information is also transmitted to suppliers so as to make their task of providing raw materials as required somewhat easier. Daily schedules are then determined from the master production schedule.

In fact, the concept of production smoothing extends along two dimensions: firstly by spreading the production of products evenly over each day within a month, and secondly by spreading the quantities of individual products evenly over each day within a month. Both of these are typically incorporated into the dally schedule as in the following example.

Example 15.2 *Production smoothing*
....

Consider a production line which produces six different products, A, B, C, D, E and F. We assume that these products have different characteristics. Let us also assume that the master production schedule calls for 6000 units to be produced in a month which contains 20 working days. Then, by averaging the production of all products over each day, 300 units must be produced per day. If the 6000 products break down into the product quantities as in Table 15.1(a), then in the extreme case of traditional batch production the floor schedule would produce 1400 of Product A, followed by 600 of Product B, 1800 of Product C, 600 of Product D, 800 of Product E and finally 800 of Product F. However, by averaging the output of each product over all days within the month, and assuming that there are 20 working days in the month, the daily production schedule illustrated in Table 15.1(b) is calculated.

Therefore the required 300 units must be produced within a shift (i.e. 8 hours or 480 minutes). Simple mathematics tells us that a product must be produced every 1.6 minutes. This may be done in a batch of 70 of Product A followed by a batch of

Table 15.1 Monthly and daily product quantities

	(a)	(b)
Varieties	Monthly demand	Daily average output
Product A	1400	70
Product B	600	30
Product C	1800	90
product D	600	30
Product E	800	40
Product F	800	40
Demand	6000 per month	300 per day

Table 15.2 Production schedule

Varieties	Number of units
Product A	7
Product B	3
Product C	9
Product D	3
Product E	4
Product F	4
	30 every 48 minutes

30 of Product B and so on. However, by carrying the second concept further and spreading the production of all products evenly within each day we can develop a schedule for a small duration, e.g. 48 minutes, as in Table 15.2. This schedule is continuously repeated until the daily schedule is met.

15.5.2 Mixed model production

This process of manufacturing and assembling a range of products *simultaneously* is known as **mixed model** production and it is widely used within what are termed repetitive manufacturing systems (which will be discussed later on). Mixed model production should be differentiated from **multi-model** production where a variety of models are produced but not simultaneously. Clearly mixed model production is not feasible unless the set-up times for individual models are extremely small, so that there is no effective change-over in going from say Product A to Product B. This in turn can only be achieved if the designs of the products in question are such that they minimize process variety.

The benefits of mixed model assembly are potentially very great, particularly in an environment where customers expect rapid turn around on orders and where the ability to respond at short notice is considered important. Mixed model production offers a very high level of flexibility when compared to traditional production methods.

Example 15.3 *Mixed model production*

Consider the following situation. Let us assume that Table 15.1 reflects the expectation of requirements for the six products, A, B etc. at the start of the month. Based on this a basic production cycle as shown on Table 15.2 was developed. Now further assume that in the middle of the month a major customer changes its order – for example an important customer decides to change the order from 500 of Product C to 500 of Product B. How can this be accommodated? The expected requirement for the second half of the month has now been changed from that defined by Table 15.3 to that of Table 15.4.

Table 15.3 Half-monthly and daily product quantities

Varieties	Half-monthly demand	Daily average output
Product A	700	70
Product B	300	30
Product C	900	90
Product D	300	30
Product E	400	40
Product F	400	40
Demand	3000 per rest of month	300 per day

Table 15.4 Revised half-monthly and daily product quantities

Varieties	Half-monthly demand	Daily average output
Product A	700	70
Product B	800	80
Product C	400	40
Product D	300	30
Product E	400	40
Product F	400	40
Demand	3000 per rest of month	300 per day

Table 15.5 Revised production schedule

Varieties	Number of units
Product A	7
Product B	8
Product C	4
Product D	3
Product E	4
Product F	4
	30 every 48 minutes

Thus to meet this new situation all that is required is that the planner modify the production cycle in line with the new mix within the daily output. In effect all that is required is that the cycle represented by Table 15.2 be modified to that contained in Table 15.5.

••

This is clearly a simple example, but the point that it seeks to illustrate is nevertheless valid. Mixed model production results in a flexible production system and one which is responsive to sudden market changes. What would the situation have been if the system described above had been operated in the traditional manner where, in an admittedly extreme case, all of Product A had been manufactured first, followed by all of Product B etc.?

15.5.3 Daily adaptation

After the development of a monthly production plan, the next step in the smoothing of production is the breakdown of this schedule into the sequence of production for each day. This sequence specifies the assembly order of the units to be produced. The sequence is arranged so that when the cycle time expires, one group of units has been produced. At every work centre no new units are introduced until one is completed. This sequence schedule is *only* transmitted to the starting point of final assembly. Kanban cards (see Section 15.9) are used in order to transfer production instructions in a clear and simple manner to all other assembly and manufacturing processes.

Referring back to Table 15.2 we see that a mix of 30 units of the six products must be produced within 48 minute intervals. The sequence of production for these 30 units might be as follows:

AAAAAAA BBB CCCCCCCCC DDD EEEE FFFF

Or the sequence could be more varied such as:

ACAFECFBCDACDAEBFACBCACDCFEACE

Attaining the *optimal* sequence is difficult. Heuristic procedures (see Monden, 1983a) have been developed which produce a sequence that aims to achieve two plant-wide goals:

▶ an even load at each stage of the manufacturing process;

▶ a constant depletion rate for each component.

In greatly simplified terms, the objective of the heuristic is to minimize the variations in consumed quantities of each component at final assembly and at all of the work centres. By this smoothing of production, large fluctuations in demand and the amplification of these fluctuations back through the production system are prevented. Each day's schedule should resemble the previous day's schedule as closely as possible. Hence, uncertainties are eliminated and the need for dynamic scheduling and safety stocks is minimized.

The daily adaptation to the actual demand for varieties of a product during a month is the ideal of JIT production, which in turn requires the daily smoothed withdrawals of each part from the subassembly lines right back to the suppliers. Minor variations in demand are generally overcome by the Kanban system through increasing or decreasing the number of cards.

One might argue that the ideal of production smoothing is in fact very difficult to achieve in practice for many industries and individual companies. Nevertheless, it is clear that for all of manufacturing industry there are lessons to be learned from this approach. One lesson is the fundamental importance of a firm master schedule from the point of view of control of the production system and the advantages, in terms of flexibility, to be gained from moving towards mixed model production and assembly.

15.6 Techniques to simplify the manufacturing process and reduce lead times

The lead time or throughput time for a batch through the shop floor is typically much greater than the actual processing time for the batch in question. It is not unusual in conventional batch manufacturing systems for the actual processing (including set-up time) to represent less than 5% of the total throughput time. Furthermore, of that 5%, only 30% may be spent in value-adding operations. The throughput time or lead time for a product is composed of four major components, the actual process time (including inspection time), the set-up time, the transport time and the queueing time, as illustrated in Figure 15.8. In real life this latter component is frequently the largest, often representing in excess of 80% of total throughput time.

The single largest element of throughput time in traditional batch manufacturing systems is the queueing and transport time between operations. JIT encourages product-based plant layouts which greatly reduce throughput times for individual batches by reducing queueing time. At a plant level the product-based layout reduces throughput time by facilitating easy flow of batches between operations and work centres. At a line or work centre level, JIT reduces throughput time by using what are termed **U-shaped** layouts. In our view the effort to reduce throughput time must be seen in the context of the product-based layout at the macro level and the U-shaped layout at the micro level.

15.6.1 The layout of the production process

The major objectives in designing the production layout at the work centre level can be listed as follows:

▶ provide flexibility in the number of operators assigned to individual work centres so as to be able to adapt to small changes in market demand and consequently in the schedule;

▶ utilize the skills of **multifunction** operators;

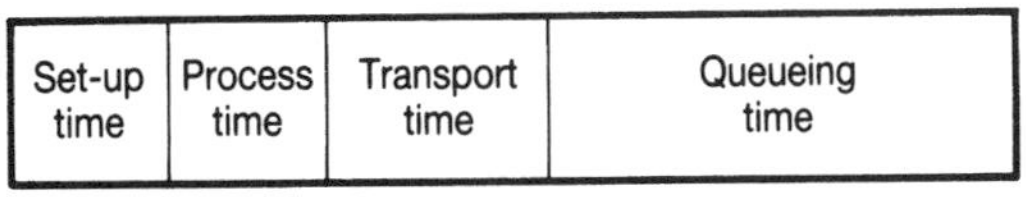

FIGURE 15.8
Breakdown of the lead time.

Set-up time	Process time	Transport time	Queueing time

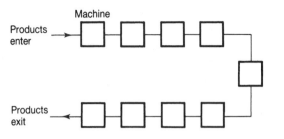

FIGURE 15.9
U-shaped work cell
layout.

▶ facilitate movement towards **single unit production and transport** between work centres;

▶ allow for the re-evaluation and revision of the standard operations.

To meet these objectives the U-shaped product-based layout was developed, as illustrated in Figure 15.9 (adapted from Monden (1983a)). This layout allows assignment of a multi-skilled operator to more than one machine owing to the close proximity of the machines.

Using this layout the range of jobs each operator does may be increased or decreased, allowing flexibility to increase or decrease the number of operators. It allows unit production and transport, given that machines are close together and may be connected with chutes or conveyers. Synchronization is achieved because one unit entering the layout means one unit leaving the layout and going on to the next work centre.

Clearly the use of the U-shaped layout, with its requirement for multi-skilled operators, implies an increased need for operator training as well as for very well defined and documented manufacturing instructions for operators. It is implicit in the JIT approach to manufacturing that no effort is spared in training and, where necessary, retraining operators in well-tested and refined work practices.

15.6.2 Reduction of the queueing time

Within the context of product-based and U-shaped layouts various techniques are used to reduce queueing time. Figure 15.10 identifies some of these techniques, which we will now go on to look at briefly.

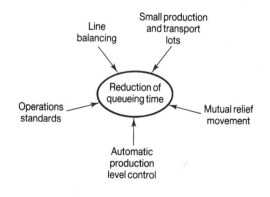

FIGURE 15.10
Methods of reducing
queueing time.

Small production and transport lots

In just in time manufacturing one unit is produced within every cycle, and at the end of each cycle a unit from each process in the line is simultaneously sent to the next process. This is already prevalent in the assembly line systems of virtually all companies engaged in mass production. However, processes supplying parts to the assembly lines are usually based on lot production. Just in time, however, seeks to extend the concept of unit production and transport to processes such as machining, welding, pressing etc. which feed the final assembly lines. Therefore, as in an assembly line, operations must start and end at each process at exactly the same time. This is often called **synchronization**, i.e. continuous flow production.

Example 15.4 *Synchronization*

Consider three operations with a cycle time of one minute each. One unit would take three minutes to go through all operations. If batch production is employed and the process lot is 200 then total throughput time is (200 + 200 + 200) minutes or 10 hours. In this case the transfer lot is equal to the process lot, as in Figure 15.11. In simple terms a single lot size is used and lots are not normally split to facilitate early dispatch of partial lots to subsequent operations.

However, if the transfer lot (conveyance or transport lot) is less than the process lot, say in the ultimate lot size one, then the total throughput time is greatly reduced, as is illustrated in Figure 15.12. In fact, the total throughput time is 3 hours and 22

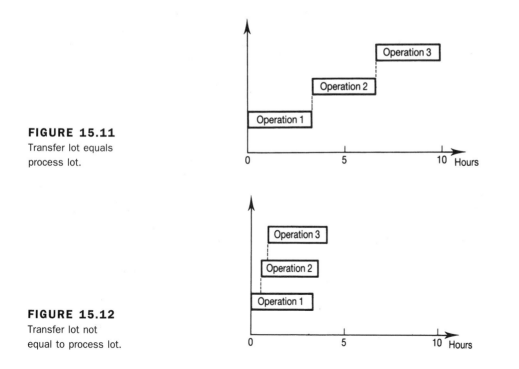

FIGURE 15.11
Transfer lot equals
process lot.

FIGURE 15.12
Transfer lot not
equal to process lot.

minutes. The total processing time is, of course, unaffected. In effect, the queueing time has been greatly reduced.

••

JIT, in separating production lots from transport lots in situations where production lots are large, is seeking to move away from batch-based production systems and towards flow-based systems.

Line balancing

Line balancing seeks to reduce the waiting time caused by unbalanced production times between individual work centres and ensures production is the same at all processes both in quantities and timing. Variances in operators' skills and capabilities are minimized through generating in advance well thought out and documented standard operations and by ensuring that all operators are trained in these *optimum* operation methods. What variances remain are smoothed through **mutual support** (discussed later). Line balancing is also promoted by the automatic control of production levels and unit production and transport. Synchronization also helps to balance the production timing between processes and facilitates line balancing.

It is interesting to compare briefly the notion of line balancing as seen from within a JIT perspective and the so called **line balancing problem** well known to generations of students of industrial engineering. Line balancing (see Appendix D for a short overview of line balancing techniques) is presented as a problem to be solved using algorithmic or heuristic procedures which seek to minimize what is termed the **balance loss**, or some similiar measure. The procedure is to take assumed elemental operations and operation precedence constraints and allocate the operations to assembly stations so as to divide the total work content of the job as evenly as possible between the assembly stations. The interesting point is that the emphasis is placed on allocating pre-defined operations to stations. The JIT approach places *as much emphasis on the design of the operations and on ensuring that individual operators are skilled in carrying them out*. Only then is the **analytical** approach to allocating the operations between stations brought to bear on the problem.

Automatic production level controls

In a particular work centre, a situation may exist where we have two machines operating on the same product. If the machine performing the first operation has a greater capacity than the second machine, it would traditionally build up a safety stock before the second machine. However the JIT approach would couple both machines, and the first machine will only produce when the number of parts between the two machines is below a pre-defined minimum. It will continue producing until the queue between the machines has reached a pre-defined maximum. This reduces the safety stock between machines and also reduces the queueing times of components.

Operations standards

Standardizing the operations to be completed at work centres attempts to attain three goals:

▶ minimum work in progress;

▶ line balancing through synchronization within the cycle time;

▶ high productivity.

Creating operations standards is a three-stage procedure, namely the determination of cycle time, the specification of operations for each operator, and, finally, the definition of a minimum quantity of WIP to allow smooth production.

The cycle time is determined by dividing the total available daily production time by the required daily output, with no allowance made for defective units, down time or idle time in the available daily production time.

For each component/subassembly at every work centre, the completion time per unit is determined, including manual and machine elements. By taking into account the number of components required for each finished product, the cycle time for the product and the completion times for each component and a list of operations for each operator are generated. This list of operations specifies the number and order of operations an operator must perform within the cycle time. This ensures the production of the correct number of components/subassemblies to allow the production of one finished product within each cycle time. Finally, the minimum quantity of WIP necessary to ensure production without material shortages is specified. This incorporates the minimum material between and on machines which are required for continuous production.

Once the three phases are completed, the cycle time, the order of operations and the standard WIP levels are combined to give a standard operations sheet which is then displayed where each operator can see it. With each new master planning schedule, gross estimates are presented to all processes of the demands likely to be made on them. At this point, re-evaluation of operations standards, through reassignment of tasks to operators for example, may result in a reassignment of the workforce to meet the projected requirement.

In our discussion of the U-shaped layout, we emphasized the need for good manufacturing documentation and for constant training and retraining of operators in good work practices. This approach to generating operations standards clearly facilitates this documentation and training. In turn, well-trained operators ensure that operations standards are adhered to.

Mutual support movement

As will be seen later, operators in a JIT environment tend to be very versatile and are trained to operate many different machines and carry out many operations within their particular work centre. As the plant and equipment layout are product-oriented, this means that advantage can be taken of the multi-skilled operator. The multi-function or multi-skilled operator also helps to reduce, if not eliminate, inventories between processes since when he or she unloads a part from one machine it may be loaded directly onto the next machine.

Operators regularly help each other on the shop floor. The ANDON board (see below) allows an operator to call for help if he or she is in difficulty. Since the work

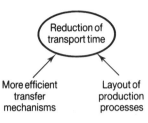

centres are close together and the operators are multi-functional, mutual support is feasible. Because an operator can go to the aid of a colleague who is temporarily overloaded, the queues in front of work centres can be reduced and the effect of what would otherwise constitute a bottleneck in the system is alleviated, again reducing the overall queueing time.

15.6.3 Reduction of the transport time

Figure 15.13 depicts two techniques that help to reduce the transport time in the just in time approach, namely the layout of the production processes and faster methods of transport between production processes. We have already discussed the product-oriented system of plant layout and the U-shaped layout of equipment, which tend to minimize transport needs between individual operations on a component or assembly.

It should, of course, be remembered that moving towards unit production and transport will most likely increase the transport frequency, i.e. the number of transports of partially completed units between operations. To overcome this difficulty, quick transport methods must be adopted along with improved plant and machine layout. Belt conveyers, chutes and fork lifts may be used. Generally, the close proximity of the subsequent process, as determined by plant layout, results in very low transport times between operations.

15.6.4 Reduction of set-up time

A major barrier to the reduction of the processing time and the ability to smooth production is the problem of large set-up times. The EOQ model is graphically represented in Figure 15.14.

The EOQ (economic order quantity) model (see Chapter 13) seeks to determine a lot size which marks an optimum trade-off between set-up and carrying costs in the case of manufactured items. EOQ calculations result in large lot sizes when set-up times and costs are high. However, large lot sizes and the resulting buffer stocks are incompatible with the JIT approach, and hence the concentration of effort on reduction of set-up times. This makes a smaller lot size feasible and is a step on the road to unit production and transport.

This JIT approach contrasts strongly with EOQ thinking and cultivates the idea that machine set-up time is a major source of waste that can and should be reduced. The influence of set-up time reduction is illustrated by the fact that if set-up time is reduced the process lot can also be reduced, without incurring extra costs. Therefore

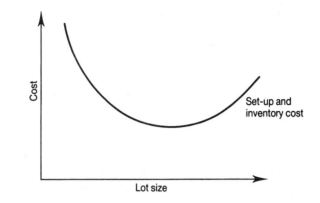

FIGURE 15.14
Economic order
quantity model.

the processing time is reduced, work in progress inventory is reduced and the ability to produce many different varieties is enhanced. This makes for better response to demand. Likewise, the ratio of machine utilization to its full capacity is increased without producing unnecessary inventory. In this way, productivity is enhanced. The techniques and concepts involved in reducing set-up are now briefly examined.

In order to shorten the set-up time, JIT offers four major approaches (see Monden, 1983a):

▶ Separate the internal set-up from the external set-up. Internal set-up refers to that element of the set-up process which requires that the machine be inoperative in order to undertake it.

▶ Convert as much as possible of the internal set-up to the external set-up. This is probably the most important practical approach for the reduction of set-up in practice and helps to achieve the goal of **single set-up**. Single set-up signifies that the set-up time can be expressed in terms of a single digit number of minutes (i.e. less than 10 minutes).

▶ Eliminate the adjustment process within set-up. Typically, adjustment accounts for a large percentage of the internal set-up time. The reduction of adjustment time is therefore very important in terms of reducing the total set-up time.

▶ Abolish the set-up where feasible.

In the JIT approach to reducing set-up the first step is to carry out a detailed study of existing practices. Invariably internal and external set-up overlap and need to be rigorously separated. A written specification outlining the procedures involved in the set-up and giving any necessary information is drawn up. By converting as much as possible of the set-up time to external set-up, which can be carried out off-line, a significant improvement in internal or **at the machine** set-up time can be achieved. The reader interested in a more detailed discussion on this topic of reducing set-up time is referred to Shingo (1985). He discusses the SMED System. SMED is an acronym for **single minute exchange of dies**, which connotes a group of techniques used to facilitate set-up operations of 10 minutes and under.

15.6.5 Reduction of processing time

The JIT approach to processing time is relatively straightforward. It sees processing time as the only time during a product's passage through the production system that real value is actually being added to it. Transport time, queueing time and set-up time are seen as non-value adding and therefore to be reduced to the absolute minimum where they cannot be simply eliminated. Given that the processing time represents value added, JIT takes care to ensure that this time is used to the best advantage and to produce high-quality products efficiently. Thus as we saw earlier in our discussion on the U-shaped layout and operations standards, great care is taken to ensure that the best manufacturing methods are refined to the highest degree, documented and communicated to the operators concerned through training sessions and practice sessions.

In fact, it is in the commitment to the best possible manufacturing methods practised by a skilled and trained workforce that the pursuit of excellence in the JIT approach to manufacturing can be most clearly seen. So often in the conventional approach to manufacturing operations manufacturing analysts and engineers forget the importance of good practice at the sharp end of manufacturing, namely the shop floor, and come to accept unnecessary deviation in operator performance as natural.

15.7 The use of manufacturing resources

The JIT approach to the resources available in a manufacturing plant is interesting. The approach could be summarized in a single dictum – *do not confuse being busy with being productive*. This philosophy is particularly applied to the use of labour resources and is also fundamental in the OPT (optimized production technique) approach to manufacturing (see Chapter 14). The way in which JIT seeks to use the major resources of labour and equipment efficiently and effectively will now be briefly reviewed.

15.7.1 Flexible labour

In JIT, those minor changes in demand which cannot be accommodated though the use of increased kanbans (see Section 15.9) are addressed through redeployment of the workforce. Ultimately, adaptation to increased market demand can be met through the use of overtime.

However, JIT has a more subtle and effective approach to meeting relatively small short-term demand changes. As mentioned previously, the basic tenet of the just in time philosophy is the production of only those products that are required and at the precise time they are required. Using the principle of multi-function operators and multi-process handling, one operator tends to a number of different machines simultaneously to meet this demand. Such a situation invariably results in the possibility of increasing output through introducing more operators into the system. Therefore, if market demand increases beyond a level where increased kanban utilization is able to cope, temporary operators may be hired. Each operator may then be required to tend fewer machines, thus taking up the equipment capacity slack. This approach presumes an economic and cultural environment where temporary operators of the required skill level are available and are willing to work in such a manner.

Adapting to decreases in demand is understandably more difficult, especially when one considers that many large Japanese companies offer life-time employment. However, the major approaches are to decrease overtime, release temporary operators and increase the number of machines handled by one operator. This will cause an increase in the cycle time, thus reducing the number of units produced. Operators are encouraged to remain *idle* rather than produce unnecessary stock. They may be redeployed to practice set-ups, maintain and/or modify machines or to attend quality circle meetings.

Therefore the workforce is flexible in two ways. It can be increased or decreased through temporary operators. It can also be relocated to different work centres. This latter flexibility demands a versatile, well-trained multi-function operator as well as good work centre layout.

The most important objective is to have a manufacturing system which is able to meet demand and to accommodate small, short-term fluctuations in demand with the minimum level of labour. This does not imply the minimum number of machines. Companies operating JIT often have some extra capacity in equipment, allowing for temporary operators when increased production is required.

15.7.2 Flexible equipment

Just in time requires production of different product variants on the same assembly line each day. This can involve a conflict between the market variety demanded by the customer and the production process available to service this market requirement, since in traditional manufacturing systems it is normally desirable to reduce the variety of product going through the system. As we have seen, the JIT approach seeks to overcome these difficulties. Through consideration of process requirements at the product design stage, multi-function equipment is developed to help resolve this conflict by providing the production process with the ability to meet the variety demanded by the market. The specialized machines developed for mass production are not suitable for repetitive manufacturing. By modifying these machines and adding minimum apparatus and tools they are transformed into multi-function machines capable of producing a product range which meets the marketplace demand. Such machines support just in time manufacturing and also facilitate production smoothing.

15.8 **Quality control aspects of JIT**

In more conventional production systems, work in progress inventories are often used to smooth out problems of defective products and/or machines. Batch production and the concept of acceptable quality levels (AQL) could be seen to promote this attitude. This approach is criticized by the promoters of JIT thinking on the basis that it is treating the symptoms while not attempting to understand and resolve the underlying fundamental problems. In JIT manufacturing, the emphasis is on the notion of total quality control (TQC) where the objective of eliminating all possible sources of defects from the manufacturing process and thereby from the products of that process is seen to be both reasonable and achievable.

We have already pointed out that JIT seeks zero defects. The zero defects approach involves a continuous commitment to totally eliminate all waste, including in this context yield losses and re-work due to product or process defects. The methods used to achieve zero defects are those of continuous steady improvement of the production process. Schneidermann (1986) offers an interesting analysis of the process of continuous improvement towards zero defects and suggests that it should be contrasted with an alternative improvement process – the innovation process. On the one hand the continuous improvement route involves groups seeking small steps forward on a broad range of issues, using the available know-how within the group. The innovation process on the other hand seeks to achieve great leaps forward in narrowly defined areas through the use of science and technology by well-qualified individuals.

Inspection is carried out to *prevent* defects rather than simply *detect* them. Machines, in so far as possible, are designed with an in-built capability to check all of the parts they produce as they are produced. The term **autonomation** was coined to describe this condition. This can be considered as one step on the road to total systems automation (i.e. a machine finds a problem, finds a solution, implements it itself and carries on).

Autonomation suggests automatic control of defects. It implies the incorporation of two new pieces of functionality into a machine:

▶ a mechanism to detect abnormalities or defects;

▶ a mechanism to stop the machine or line when defects or abnormalities occur.

When a defect occurs, the machine stops, forcing immediate attention to the problem. An investigation into the cause(s) of the problem is initiated and corrective action is taken to prevent the problem from recurring. Since, through autonomation, machines stop when they have produced enough parts and also only produce *good* parts, excess inventory is eliminated, thus making JIT production possible.

The concept of autonomation is not limited to machine processes. Autonomous checks for abnormal or faulty product can be extended to manual processes, such as an assembly line using the following approach. Each assembly line is equipped with a call light and an ANDON board. The call light has different colours signifying the different types of assistance and support which might be required. It is located where anybody who might be called upon to support the process (e.g. supervisor, maintenance, manufacturing engineering, nearby operators etc.) can easily see it.

The ANDON is a board which shows which operator on the line, if any, is having difficulties. Each operator has a switch which enables him or her to stop the line in case of breakdown or delay or problems with defective product. In many cases there are different colours to indicate the condition of the station on the assembly line which is having problems. The following are some colour signals which might be used and their respective meanings:

▶ Red – machine breakdown;

▶ White – end of a production run;

▶ Green – no work due to shortage of materials;

▶ Blue – defective unit;

▶ Yellow – set-up required.

When an ANDON lights up, nearby operators quickly move to assist and solve the problem and the supervisor takes the necessary steps to prevent it recurring. The ANDON also helps to ensure that completed products exiting the assembly line do not need re-work, i.e. that they are right first time. Individual operators have **line stop** authority to ensure compliance with standards. Hence the overall quality level is increased since each individual operator is encouraged to accept responsibility for the quality of the parts which he or she is involved with.

There are numerous other factors which assist in attaining extremely high quality levels. Small lot sizes, for example, will highlight quality problems very quickly as individual items are rapidly passed to the next process and any defects are quickly detected. Similarly, a good approach to **housekeeping** is encouraged and is considered important, as a clean, well-maintained working area leads to better working practices, better productivity and better personnel safety. Preventative maintenance is an important concept of the JIT approach. Using the **checklist technique**, machines are checked on a regular basis and repairs/replacements are scheduled to take place outside working time. This in turn helps to increase machine availability.

As a result of autonomation, only 100% good units are produced. Hence the need for re-work and buffer or insurance stocks is eliminated. This lends itself to adaptability to demand and JIT production.

15.9 Kanban

Now we focus our attention on the shop floor implementation of just in time. The techniques used at this level have been well documented in the last few years (APICS, 1981; Schonberger, 1982; Monden, 1983a) as interest in Japanese manufacturing techniques has increased. The system which executed JIT delivery on the shop floor level is known as Kanban. The cards which are used in this system are called kanban cards. Therefore to distinguish between the system and the cards we will use *Kanban* for the system and *kanban* for the cards. Our discussion will concentrate on JIT execution on the shop floor and will not cover JIT execution from outside suppliers in any detail.

Kanban was developed at the Toyota Car plants in Japan as a programme to smooth the flow of products throughout the production process. Its aim is to improve system productivity and secure **operator involvement** and participation in achieving this high productivity by providing a **highly visible** means to observe the flow of products through the production system and the build-up of inventory levels within the system. Later it was further developed as a means of **production activity control** to achieve the goals of JIT and to manage the operation of just in time production. Kanban also serves as an information system to monitor and help to control the production quantities at every stage of the manufacturing and assembly process. Kanban is normally applied in a repetitive manufacturing environment.

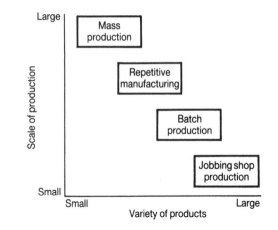

FIGURE 15.15
Classification of
discrete production.

Repetitive manufacturing

Repetitive manufacturing is 'the fabrication, machining, assembly and testing of discrete, standard units produced in volume, or of products assembled in volume from standard options . . . [it] is characterized by long runs of flows of parts. The ideal is a direct transfer of parts from one work centre to another' (Hall, 1983). Referring back to our discussion on the various categories of discrete parts manufacturing system in Chapter 12, we can position repetitive manufacturing in a modified version of our original Figure 12.5 as in Figure 15.15 above.

One could argue that the end result of rigorously applying the JIT approach and of using JIT manufacturing techniques as described earlier in this chapter is to move a manufacturing system away from jobbing shop or batch production and towards repetitive manufacturing. The greater the degree to which the manufacturing system approaches repetitive manufacturing the more relevant the Kanban technique is.

Production activity control with Kanban

The Kanban system has been described as a *pull* system. We will now explore how this system works by taking the example of a very simple assembly system and illustrating the flow of kanban cards through it. Under Kanban, the final assembly line knows the requirements for end products, and with this knowledge it controls what is produced in the total manufacturing system, using the following procedure.

The final assembly line, having received the schedule, proceeds to withdraw the components necessary, at the times they are required, and in the quantities they are required, from the feeding work centres or subassembly lines. These work centres or subassembly lines produce in lots just sufficient to replace the lots which have been removed. However, to do this, they also have to withdraw parts from their respective feeder stations, in the quantities necessary. Thus a chain reaction is initiated *upstream*, with work centres only withdrawing those components which are required, at the correct time and in the quantities required.

In this way, the flow of all material is synchronized to the rate at which material is used on the final assembly line. Amounts of inventory will be very small if a regular pattern exists in the schedule and if the deliveries are made in small quantities. Thus, just in time can be achieved without the use of controlling work orders for parts at each work centre.

The kanban card types

Kanban is the Japanese word for card. Kanbans are usually rectangular paper cards placed in transparent covers. There are two types of card mainly in use:

▶ *Withdrawal kanbans*
Withdrawal kanbans define the quantity which the subsequent process should withdraw from the preceding work centre. Each card circulates between two work centres only, the user work centre for the part in question and the work centre which produces it.

▶ *Production kanbans*
Production kanbans define the quantity of the specific part which the producing work centre should manufacture to replace those which have been removed.

Each standard container is assigned one of each card type. Examples of each type of card are shown in Figure 15.16 (based on Monden (1983a)).

The withdrawal kanban, for example, details both the name of the consuming work centre and the work centre which supplies the part described by the item name and number on the card. The precise location in the inventory buffer is detailed, as well as the type of standard container used and its capacity. The issue number in the case shown in Figure 15.16 reveals that it is the third kanban issued out of four.

The production kanban details the producing work centre name, the part to be produced, and where precisely in the buffer store it should be located.

There are other types of kanban differentiated by colour, shape or format such as subcontract, emergency, special and signal cards. However, the two cards just described are the basic types used in the Kanban system.

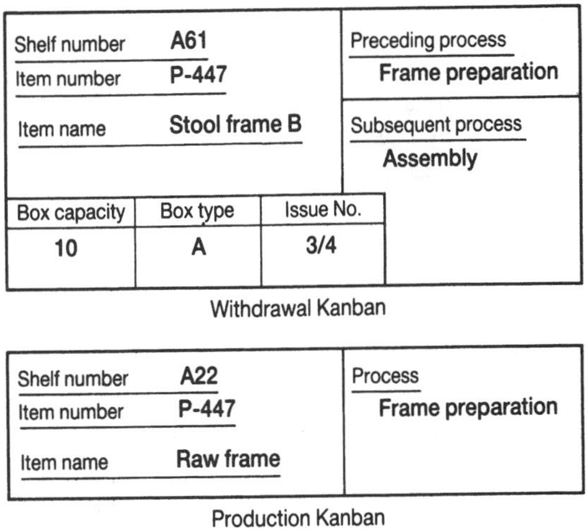

Shelf number	A61		Preceding process
Item number	P-447		**Frame preparation**
Item name	Stool frame B		Subsequent process
			Assembly

| Box capacity | Box type | Issue No. | |
| 10 | A | 3/4 | |

Withdrawal Kanban

Shelf number	A22		Process
Item number	P-447		**Frame preparation**
Item name	Raw frame		

Production Kanban

FIGURE 15.16
Kanban card types.

15.10 A note on WCM

In many ways the ideas of the WCM (world-class manufacturing) school (see e.g. Schonberger, 1987) developed from the experience of JIT implementations in factories in the United States. Issues of continuous improvement, training and cross-training of personnel and integration of product design and process design to facilitate efficient manufacturing were also emphasized. Hayes *et al.* (1988) for example identified the key characteristics of a WCM plant as follows:

1. Becoming the best competitor. Being better than almost every other company in the industrial sector in at least one aspect of manufacturing.

2. Growing more rapidly and being more profitable than competitors. World-class companies are able to measure their superior performance by observing how their products are accepted in the marketplace.

3. Hiring and retaining the best people. Having operators and managers who are so skilled and effective that other companies are continually seeking to attract them away from the organization.

4. Developing engineering staff. Being so expert in the design and manufacture of production equipment that equipment suppliers are continually seeking advice about possible modifications to their equipment, suggestions for new equipment and agreement to be a test site for one of their pilot models.

5. Being able to respond quickly and decisively to changing market conditions. Being more nimble and flexible than competitors in responding to market shifts or pricing changes, and in getting new products out into the market faster than they can.

6. Adopting a product and process engineering approach which maximizes the performance of both. Intertwining the design of a new product so closely with the design of the required manufacturing process that when competitors reverse engineer the product they find that they cannot produce a comparable one in their own factories without major retooling and redesign expenses.

7. Continually improving. Continually improving facilities, support systems and skills that were considered to be near optimal or state of the art when first introduced, so that they increasingly surpass their initial capabilities.

Hayes *et al.* (1988) went on to say that the emphasis on continuous improvement is the ultimate test of a world-class organization.

15.11 Conclusion

In this chapter the goals of JIT have been laid out. Also indicated are what are considered to be the key-elements in the JIT approach to manufacturing. These we have listed as:

▶ An intelligent match of product design with market demand in an era of greatly reduced product life cycles, with early consideration of manufacturing problems at the product design stage.

▶ The definition of product families, based upon a number of important manufacturing goals, and the design of manufacturing systems to facilitate flow-based production of these families, where possible.

▶ The establishment of relationships with vendors and suppliers to achieve just in time deliveries of raw materials and purchased components.

Clearly, within the JIT approach to manufacturing enormous planning and engineering effort is expended to ensure that the manufacturing environment is such that excellence can be achieved. The JIT approach to manufacturing systems design and operation has been considered in terms of a number of specific issues:

▶ product design for ease of manufacture and assembly;

▶ manufacturing planning techniques;

▶ techniques to facilitate the use of simple manufacturing control systems;

▶ an approach to the use of manufacturing resources;

▶ quality control and quality assurance procedures.

The JIT approach recognizes the importance of process and manufacturing system design. Perhaps in the past we have neglected this work and the organization of our manufacturing facilities reflect this neglect.

References and further reading

APICS (1981). JIT and MRPII: partners in manufacturing strategy. In *Report on 27th Annual APICS Conference Modern Materials Handling*, December, pp. 58–60.

Browne J., Harhen J. and Shivnan J. (1988). *Production Management Systems, A CIM Perspective*. Harlow: Addison Wesley Longman.

Burbidge J. L. (1963). Production flow analysis. *The Production Engineer*. **42**, 22–3.

Burbidge J. L. (1989). *Production Flow Analysis for Planning Group Technology*. Oxford: Oxford Science Publications.

Conway R. W. and Maxwell W. L. (1962). Network dispatching by shortest operation discipline. *Operations Research*. **10**, 51.

Corbett J., Donner M., Meleka J. and Pym C. (1991). *Design for Manufacturer – Strategies, Principles and Techniques*. Reading MA: Addison Wesley Longman.

Edwards G. A. B. (1971). *Readings in Group Technology*. London and Tonbridge: The Whitefriars Press.

Gallagher C. C. and Knight W. A. (1987). *Group Technology*. London: Butterworth.

Groover M. P. (1980). *Automation, Production Systems and Computer-Aided Manufacturing*. Englewood Cliffs NJ: Prentice-Hall.

Hall R. W. (1983). *Zero Inventories*. New York: Dow Jones-Irwin.

Hall R. W. (1987). *Attaining Manufacturing Excellence*. Illinois: Dow Jones-Irwin.

Hayes R. H., Wheelwright S. C. and Clark K. B. (1988). *Dynamic Manufacturing – Creating the Learning Organisation.* New York: The Free Press.

Hernandez A. (1989). *Just-In-Time Manufacturing – A Practical Approach.* Englewood Cliffs NJ: Prentice-Hall.

Imai M. (1986). *Kaizen: the Key to Japan's Competitive Success.* New York: Random House.

Knight W. A. (1974). The economic benefits of group technology. *Production Engineer.* May, 145–51.

Kusiak A. and Chow, W. (1987). Efficient solving of the group technology problem. *Journal of Manufacturing Systems.* **6**(2).

Laszcz J. Z. (1985). Production design for robotic and automatic assembly. In *Robotic Assembly: International Trends in Manufacturing Technology* (ed. K. Rathmill), pp. 157–72. Kempston: IFS Publications.

Lawrence A. (1986). Are CAPM systems just too complex? *Industrial Computing.* September, 5.

Lewis F. A. (1986) Statistics aid planning for JIT production. *Chartered Mechanical Engineer.* **33**, 27–30.

Lubben R. T. (1988). *Just in Time Manufacturing: An Aggressive Manufacturing Strategy.* New York: McGraw-Hill.

Monden Y. (1983a). Adaptable Kanban system helps Toyota maintain just in time production. *Industrial Engineering.* **15**, 29–46.

Monden Y. (1983b). *Toyota Production System: Practical Approach to Production Management.* Norcross, Georgia, USA. American Institute of Industrial Engineers.

Schneidermann A. M. (1986). Optimum quality costs and zero defects: are they contradictory concepts? *Quality Progress.* **19**, 28–31.

Schonberger R. (1982). *Japanese Manufacturing Techniques: Nine Hidden Lessons.* New York: The Free Press.

Schonberger R. J. (1984). Just in time production systems: replacing complexity with simplicity in manufacturing management. *Industrial Engineering.* **16**(10), 52–63.

Schonberger R. J. (1986). *World Class Manufacturing: The Lessons of Simplicity Applied.* New York: The Free Press.

Schonberger R. J. (1987). *World Class Manufacturing Casebook: Implementing JIT and TQC.* New York: The Free Press.

Shingo S. (1985). *A Revolution in Manufacturing: The SMED System.* New York: The Productivity Press.

Vollmann T., Berry W. and Whybark D. (1988) *Master Production Scheduling: Principles and Practice.* Falls Church VA: American Production and Inventory Control Society.

Exercises

15.1 Outline the goals of the JIT approach to manufacturing systems design and operation.

15.2 What is 'flow-based manufacturing'?

15.3 Outline the steps involved in using the production flow analysis technique.

15.4 Explain JIT purchasing.

15.5 How does the JIT approach to manufacturing deal with the relationship between product and process variety?

15.6 What is production smoothing?

15.7 Differentiate clearly between mixed model and multi-model production.

15.8 How does mixed model production facilitate unexpected changes in the planned schedule?

15.9 What approaches are available to reduce queueing time?

15.10 Differentiate clearly between the transfer lot and the process lot and show how the use of transfer lots reduces lead times.

15.11 Distinguish clearly between internal and external set-up.

15.12 What is an ANDON board?

15.13 What is the JIT approach to quality?

15.14 Define repetitive manufacturing.

15.15 What is meant by the term 'modular design'? How does it contribute to JIT manufacturing?

15.16 How does the U-shaped layout facilitate the use of multi-function operators?

15.17 Explain the often quoted dictum 'Do not confuse being busy with being productive'.

15.18 Show how Kanban is used to control work flow in repetitive manufacturing environments.

15.19 'The JIT approach recognizes the importance of process and manufacturing systems design. Perhaps in the past we have neglected this work and the organization of our manufacturing facilities reflects this neglect'. Discuss.

| Reuse ① |
| Remanufacture ② |
| Recycle ③ |
| Discard ④ |

PART FOUR

Future directions for CADCAM

· ·

Engineers have for many years been subjected to a relentless pressure for product quality improvement accompanied by reduced product introduction times and costs. In recent years two new challenges have been added in the increasing globalization of manufacturing, and in the growing awareness of the effect of human activities on the natural environment. Evidence of the first of these challenges may be seen in the increasing number of products – including aircraft, books, computers, foodstuffs, motor vehicles, software and indeed almost any manufactured product – that are produced by multinational teams. As engineering activities have become more global, we have also become more sensitive to the environmental consequences of products throughout their life cycle, from manufacture to eventual disposal.

As the new challenges have emerged, new technologies and techniques have been developed to meet them. Distributed product design teams use computer databases and high-speed communications networks to help them work together. New techniques assist in the assessment of the environmental impact of products throughout their life cycle, and provide advice on how designs should be modified to reduce this impact. In this section we will examine some of these developments and will speculate on the way that they will be applied in engineering, concentrating in particular on new developments in product modelling, on computer support for cooperative working, and on design for the environment.

Emerging challenges in CADCAM

....

Chapter objectives

When you have completed studying the material in this chapter you should be able to:

▶ understand the need for product data management and product modelling;

▶ describe the basic functionality of product data management systems;

▶ outline the techniques of assembly modelling, and describe the issues involved in tolerance modelling in CAD;

▶ describe the basis of the operation of the World-Wide Web, and outline the elements of HTML;

▶ appreciate the techniques and possibilities of computer-supported cooperative work;

▶ appreciate the challenge presented by environmentally benign production;

▶ understand the likely impact of design for the environment on the design of products;

▶ describe the generic business processes and the business infrastructure necessary to support end of life product recovery and recycling.

Chapter contents

16.1 Introduction

For many of us the revolution in our lives that has been brought about by the computer is as dramatic as the Industrial Revolution brought about by steam power and mechanized machines. The computer revolution continues at this moment, and indeed it can be argued that we are only just really beginning to understand how to use computers to the greatest effect. For the engineer, the opportunities of information technology come at a time of great pressure from international competition and globalization of supply chains, and also at a time of increasing concern about the effect of industry and its products on the natural environment. In this chapter we will consider current developments in CADCAM and in design and manufacture that we believe will be increasingly important in the future. We will first explore the present progress in product data representation and storage that allows all manner of product data to be collected and managed in globally distributed databases, and we will then discuss in some detail the developments in product representation to allow assembly and tolerance details to be stored. In Section 16.5 we will examine the World-Wide Web – the computing phenomenon of the 1990s that will have an enormous impact on the way that we all share and use information – and in Section 16.6 we will develop the theme of sharing information still further in a discussion of computer-supported cooperative work. In the remainder of the chapter we will draw away from computer applications to consider how the desire to reduce the environmental impact of products and industry is affecting the way that products are designed and manufacturing activities are organized.

16.2 Product data management

In a modern manufacturing company, there are a whole range of computer systems and indeed data systems. Every department and function concerned with production, including design engineering, manufacturing engineering, purchasing, quality, marketing, management information systems and accounting, use data which describes the products from their point of view. Ideally a product data management or PDM system should be in place to manage all of this product-related data **across the various functions** and **through the lifetime of the product**, irrespective of where in the company the data is located.

Thus, for example, an engineering change order (ECO) in the design department might have originated from a request from the quality department which in turn might have been motivated by a complaint from a customer received by the sales and marketing people. This ECO in turn may have consequences for the manufacturing engineers in terms of the changes to the manufacturing process parameters or indeed for the purchasing department in terms of the specification of a bought-in component. The PDM system seeks to manage the product data to ensure that all of the business process involvement in, for example, the implementation of an ECO is performed correctly and that the data remains consistent, accurate and up to date across the various computer applications. Thus PDM systems provide access and security controls, maintain relationships within the various strands of product data, enforce the rules that describe data flows and processes, and perform notification and messaging functions to appropriate personnel and functions within the organization. They are an extension of the engineering data management systems (EDMSs) introduced in Chapter 5, and are concerned with all of the documentation and data relating to a company's products.

PDM encompasses other approaches to information management that deal with specific subsets of the product information, including EDMSs, document management systems, technical information systems and so on. PDM is itself a subset of electronic data management (EDM) which is a general term for the computerized management of data of all sorts. Normally PDM systems work within a heterogeneous computing (and indeed partially paper-based) environment with individual applications (e.g. CAD, computer-aided process planning, computer-aided quality, computer-aided production management, etc.) running on different computers, workstations, PCs, etc.

According to CIMdata Inc. (1996), a PDM system should have two major groups of functions, namely **user functions** and **utility functions**. User functions include:

1. **Data vault and document management.** Management of the storage, security, access, version control, etc., of all product-related data.

2. **Process and workflow management.** Management and control of the business processes and associated workflows associated with the definition, revision, sign-off and scheduling of documents.

3. **Product structure management.** Provision of complete bills of materials, and bills of process data including planning bills.

4. **Data classification and retrieval.** Provision of software utilities to search for and retrieve data.

5. **Project management.** Provision of facilities for definition of work breakdown, scheduling, etc.

Utility functions include:

1. **Data communication and notification** functions to handle all data communication between the various applications subsystems and also to external systems.

2. **Data transport** facilities to move data between the various applications, users and systems. This is particularly important because in most cases PDM systems are implemented in distributed heterogeneous hardware and indeed software environments. Data transport and data communication between them cover electronic mail and file transfer.

3. **Data translation** facilities which allow the translation of data among applications. For example, CADCAM data might be translated into an appropriate format for a CNC programming application using IGES.

4. **Image services**, which provide a viewing capability to review graphical images – for example, to allow relatively low-cost PCs to view CAD images.

5. **System administration** utilities to support the system administration to set up and run the PDM system, including access control, authorizations, backup and archiving. The backup features are particularly important, and in situations that are most sensitive to system faults the data may be copied in real time to alternative disk systems.

Most PDM systems are built to a client–server architecture, and many are layered onto a large database supporting SQL (see Chapter 5). Clearly it is in the interests of PDM systems vendors to use standards and in this context STEP (STandard for the Exchange of Product data) is particularly important (see Chapter 7). Let us now consider some of the key features of PDM in more detail.

The information vault

The core of a PDM system is the information vault that is used for the storage and retrieval of the product definition information. The principal function of the information vault is to index the information using descriptive attributes, and where the information is computer based to store the computer records or files comprising the information. The vault also provides a capability to control the access and release of the information that it indexes. When engineering models are produced they often have to go through a checking and approval procedure. By enforcing data access only through the PDM, the vault can ensure that only those who need to have access to information at a certain stage in this release procedure may do so. The security mechanisms can also control the check-in and check-out of work so that there is no risk of conflicting access to information, and they can ensure that data is not inadvertently deleted or overwritten.

Engineering organizations are often spread across many sites in different locations and even in different countries. Databases are today capable of being distributed across many computers, but accessible from any of them. Large PDM systems may in this way integrate information from many parts of an organization in an apparently seamless way, accessible from a variety of computer types within the organization. PDM systems can often integrate data from many different CADCAM systems, and they can also reference data that is not computer based. For example, paper documents and files may be indexed into a PDM system, thus giving some of the search and find capabilities of the system, but without the information retrieval and security aspects.

Process and workflow management

The second key to PDM system operation is the incorporation of process and workflow management functions. The engineering of a product is undertaken by a number of different groups within an organization and within its suppliers. Process management aims to capture the process sequences undertaken by these groups, together with the flow of work between them, and then to use this information to manage and direct the diverse tasks and the movement of data between the tasks. This process management is also integrated with the information control activities of check-out and check-in, and release and approval control, to ensure that these information control activities are correctly carried out at each stage of the flow of work through the process.

Product structure

The hierarchical bill of materials is the main **product structure** used in PDM systems, and it is on the bill of materials that the product **configuration management** activity is based. The configuration of a product describes the parts used in the product and their relationships to each other in the product structure. Configuration management is the process of controlling the information relating to a product structure and its documentation over the life of the product from design through to use and eventual disposal (CIMdata, 1996). To the bill of materials are added version control, which allows identification of different versions of a product and different issues of engineering data (and the changes associated with these issues), and variant control, which allows variants of the same product to be modelled. In general the term **version** applies to variations in the product over time. A manufacturer will, for example, replace an old model with a new version. A variant, on the other hand, is one of a number of variations of a product offered concurrently. The latter is very important in automotive engineering, where a particular automobile may have many different customer options that may be added to different models of a particular vehicle. This introduces great complexity into the management of the product information, and indeed into the manufacture of the product. For example, for some prestige cars the number of customer options is so large that there are over a million possible variants – the manufacturer need never make the same vehicle twice! The PDM system will provide a number of facilities to assist in the management of versions and variants. For example, a function may allow the differences between different versions, or between different variants, to be highlighted within a structure diagram so that areas of change may be clearly seen. Alternatively, there may be a capability to show the products and subassemblies in which a particular part has been used to allow scope for part rationalization to be explored.

Information search and retrieval

While the core of the PDM system is the information vault, one of the keys to the success of a system is the facilities it provides for search and retrieval of information. These include search tools for locating and finding information based on the values of attributes, or perhaps the occurrence of key words in the text within a document or within the data attributes; documents will often be stored in full-text databases that index every word in a document. Of equal importance, however, are facilities to browse through graphical displays of the hierarchical structure of products such as the bill of materials that shows the decomposition of the product into assemblies and subassemblies in the form of a hierarchical tree. The nodes of this tree may be linked to the models describing individual parts, or assemblies.

Digital mock-up

When all of the geometric models describing a product are three-dimensional solid models then there is scope for **digital mock-up** (DMU) of the product. Engineers have traditionally built physical mock-ups of new products to ensure that the various parts may be correctly assembled, and also to explore the fitness for purpose and maintainability of the product. The availability of a complete computer-based record of the geometry of a product enables these evaluations to take place using a virtual three-dimensional assembly model of the product, thus allowing evaluation of these factors without the expense in time and money of constructing the physical mock-up. The digital mock-up allows engineers to 'walk through' the design, and to examine for clash between parts, or incorrect fit, without ever constructing a single physical part (this is sometimes known as **digital pre-assembly** (DPA) or **digital product definition** (DPD)). As an example, the Boeing Aeroplane Company traditionally constructed full-size (non-flying) physical mock-ups of its products before series construction. In the case of the 777, designed in the early 1990s, this was not done. The mock-ups used for this aircraft were digital, and by using this approach, Boeing achieved its fastest development time to date for a jet aircraft, and has achieved a dramatic reduction in the number of changes made to its drawings compared with the previous manual drawing practice.

Example 16.1 *An application of product data management*

A good example of the use of product databases is provided by the company BMW Rolls-Royce GmbH, a company formed by BMW and Rolls-Royce Aerospace in 1990 to design, manufacture and market a family of aero engines for large corporate aircraft and regional jets. The company has headquarters in Oberursel, near Frankfurt in Germany, but calls on the engineering resources of its parent companies in Germany and the United Kingdom, and in addition has a network of supply companies with which it wishes to share engineering data and information. Effective management of distributed information is essential to the company's activities. The company achieves this through engineering data management information vaults at Oberusel, and at its development and assembly centre in Dahlewitz, also in Germany. The Dahlewitz vault is the main R&D vault storing CAD and CAE documents. The Oberusel vault stores manufacturing information including NC and planning data. Work in progress designs are stored in local vaults, but can be accessed by authorized engineers from around the company. Once approved and released, designs are copied to all vaults to minimize network traffic. Hundreds of engineers have access to the company datastores, and yet security is maintained by sophisticated sign-on procedures.

In addition to the engineers from BMW Rolls-Royce itself, suppliers can access the databases. They connect to the databases through dial-up ISDN lines with access controlled by sophisticated security. The concept is that any approved or selected supplier anywhere in the world can concurrently engineer with BMW Rolls-Royce. Time is important to them.

Product data management is also used to maintain digital prototypes of the designs. Digital prototypes have the advantage over physical prototypes that they can be continually updated, and can be shared between as many sites as require to have access. The product data management approach may also track and maintain data from multiple CAD and non-CAD sources, through the use of the graphical presentation of product relationships, such as those shown in Figure 16.1 which also shows a three-dimensional model of part of the product.

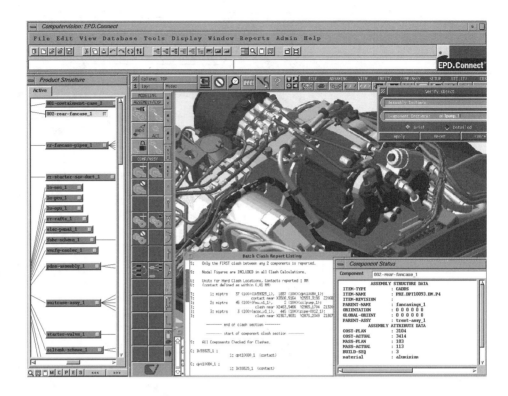

FIGURE 16.1
The screen
appearance of a
PDM system.
(Reproduced by
permission of
Rolls Royce and
Computervision.)

16.3 Product modelling

PDM has grown from the integration of geometric modelling, process planning and control, engineering analysis and engineering data management systems, which allowed the integration of diverse data structures into a common framework. The eventual aim of much CADCAM development is the integration of the data generated throughout the product life cycle from specification through to manufacture into a common logical framework. This may be termed **product modelling**, which has the aim of developing an integrated model to support all of the product life cycle aims. Figure 16.2 (Krause *et al.*, 1993) shows the range of product life cycle concerns to be dealt with by a product modelling system.

The process of developing the product is also important in product modelling. Krause *et al.* suggest that 'product modelling should be able to support product development process chains throughout the product life cycle and store all necessary information as product model data'. They suggest that process or workflow information is used not only to guide the product development processes, but also to record the history of the product development, and to provide a means to reconstruct the rationale behind design decisions. Long-term storage of the data model is necessary for product liability reasons, to allow manufacture of spare parts, and to allow data to be reused in the development of new products.

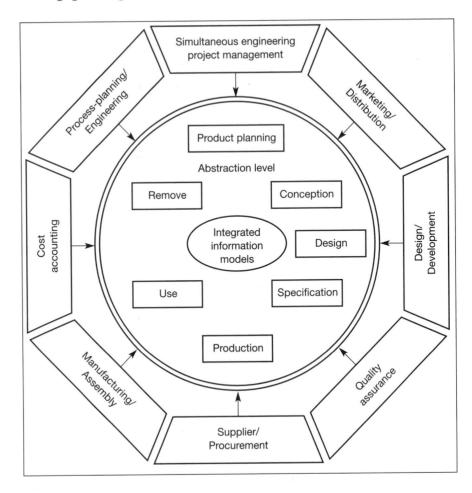

FIGURE 16.2
Product life cycle
concerns in product
modelling.
(Reproduced from
Krause *et al.* (1993)
by permission of
CIRP/Hallwag.)

There are a number of limitations in the traditional CADCAM approach to product modelling. Firstly, it is difficult to integrate specialist manufacturing process or analysis models with geometric models. Secondly, the various representations used in design, in process planning, in production control and so on have been developed independently and lack a common framework. Thirdly, a number of life cycle issues are supported by little in the way of formal representations. In order to tackle these limitations there have been a number of developments that we have seen in earlier parts of this book. A formal approach to modelling, based on the EXPRESS information modelling language, has been developed and is the basis of the STEP standard for the representation and exchange of product model data. Design representations have been enhanced by the use of **features**, which are modelling entities that allow a design model to be constructed using elements that have some specific manufacturing significance. Finally, significant emphasis is currently being placed on the way that different engineers have distinct viewpoints on the same underlying model data (Kugathasan and McMahon, 1997).

16.4 Assembly and tolerance modelling

The main product structure description used in EDMSs and in PDM systems is the bill of materials (BOM). A BOM describes the structure in terms of a hierarchical assembly/subassembly/part breakdown. It describes the product in terms of the parts that form an assembly, and the absolute or relative spatial position of the parts, but not **how** the parts go together and physically relate to each other. With a conventional system, if we combine the BOM structure with geometric models of the individual parts, then we can explore the visual appearance and mass properties of assemblies, and the interference between parts, but if we wish to explore how the assembly should be put together, how parts mate and move with respect to each other kinematically and dynamically, and how changes in one part affect others, then we need to store a richer model of the relationships between parts in the assembly. These relationships are provided in an **assembly modelling** system.

16.4.1 Assembly modelling

The essential basis of an assembly modelling system is the association of representations of the relationships between elements of an assembly with the description of the assembly. The elements can be at any level in the hierarchy – relationships can be between subassemblies, parts, or even elements of parts such as features or faces. The relationships describe constraints between parts, mating relationships and other factors relating to how parts interact, and are variously called **assembly constraints**, **assembly relationships** or **mating relationships**. As an example, an '**against**' relationship would store details of two parts that are in face-to-face contact with each other. It may be applied at the level of the parts, of the part features that are in contact, or at the level of part faces. Early experimental assembly models just allowed 'against' relationships between planar faces and 'fits' relationships between cylindrical part faces and cylindrical holes sharing a common axis (Ambler and Popplestone, 1975), but more recent developments have allowed a number of relationships and constraints including degrees of fit (tight and loose), contacts (e.g. cylindrical face against a plane face), mechanical transmission (e.g. mating gears or rack-and-pinion) and fastener constraints (e.g. screw threads). These allow kinematic simulation of the assembly as a machine or mechanism, as well as studying its characteristics as an assembly.

Shah and Rogers (1993) have classified the relationships that may be modelled between subassemblies and between parts into five groups:

▶ **Part-of** relations, which record that a part or subassembly belongs to a bigger assembly.

▶ **Structuring relations** (SRs), which nominally locate two elements with respect to each other.

▶ **Degrees of freedom** (DOFs), which are translational or rotational motion directions allowed after assembly, with or without limits.

▶ **Motion limits** (Lts), which are unilateral or bilateral limits on the DOF owing to obstructions or interferences.

▶ **Fits** – size constraints applied to dimensions, in order to maintain a given class of fit.

Part-of relationships are conventionally modelled in the assembly/subassembly/part hierarchy of the BOM, which would also hold information about the relative spatial positions of the parts or subassemblies. The remaining relationships may be modelled by attaching them to nodes in the assembly/part hierarchy as links between related elements. In Shah and Rogers' approach, parts are further subdivided into form features, feature volumes and faces and axes of the feature volumes. Relationships may be expressed between elements at any level, as shown in Figure 16.3. In this approach, one of the subassemblies is regarded as fixed in world coordinates, and is designated the *chassis*. Other subassemblies are located with respect to it. At part level, one part in each subassembly is *grounded*, or fixed with respect to the subassembly coordinate system, and one feature is the *base feature* in each part. Constraint reasoning may therefore be carried out using these frames of reference as a basis.

Several other assembly modelling systems use a graph-based approach. For example, the FROOM (Feature and Relation-based Object-Oriented Modelling) redesign support system from the University of Twente uses conceptual graphs to store both bottom-up relationships such as 'against' and 'fit' relations, and top-down relationships such as predefined assembly concepts that can be expanded to lower levels of abstraction (Salomons, 1995). Salomons notes that, once defined, the model can be used for a number of applications. Assembly constraints can be used to propagate dimensional changes between components, and can be the basis for assembly planning and kinematic or dynamic analysis. With the additional incorporation of

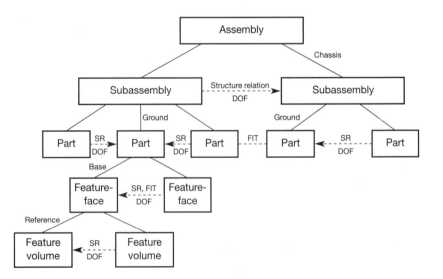

FIGURE 16.3

Relationships in an assembly modelling hierarchy. (Adapted from Shah and Rogers (1993) by permission of Springer Verlag, London Ltd.)

information about tolerances, it can be used as a basis for functional tolerancing and the exploration of tolerance stack-up (the effect of accumulation of tolerances within an assembly).

The satisfaction of assembly geometric constraints, for example to propagate dimensional changes between components, is mainly carried out either by solving the simultaneous algebraic equations that are derived from the constraints, as in variational geometry solvers (see Section 8.3), or by using the geometric constraints directly and applying domain knowledge. This is one of the methods adopted in FROOM, using an adaptation of a technique proposed by Kramer (1992). Kramer's approach first reasons with the DOF of parts, and relationships between parts, using rules to identify an assembly plan. This is then used to guide the solution of geometric constraints first by means of actions which are inferred based on geometric reasoning. Actions are effectively transformations such as rotations, translations and sometimes scaling. If proper actions cannot be found that may solve the constraint satisfaction problem, then Kramer's method may infer the equations belonging to that geometric constraint problem and solve them using conventional numeric iterative methods.

16.4.2 Tolerance modelling

Closely related to the modelling of assemblies is the modelling of tolerances on parts. Tolerances specify the allowed variations in dimension, position or form of parts, and are functions of the manufacturing processes used to make the parts (which determine how large the tolerances need to be), and the functional requirement of the parts (which determines how small they should be). Tolerances fall into two classes: **dimensional tolerances**, which specify allowable deviations from an actual dimension, and **geometric tolerances** of position, attitude or form, which are divided into a number of tolerance types, and specify how far from a nominal position, attitude or shape a part may deviate. Dimensional tolerances are traditionally the dominant way of specifying tolerance, but ambiguities in their application and interpretation are making the use of geometric tolerances more widespread in industrial practice. Tolerances are traditionally represented on engineering drawings using methods of presentation defined in a number of standards from organizations such as the BSI, ANSI or ISO.

Tolerances have been difficult to apply in CAD because they represent relationships *between* entities. A tolerance on a linear dimension represents the possible variation in dimension between two faces; a concentricity tolerance may represent the relationship between a cylindrical face and an axis. In the CAD model the face may in fact be represented by more than one separate face, and the axis may not exist as a geometric entity. Nevertheless, techniques are emerging that seem to offer a feasible and technically sound mechanism for tolerance representation in the context of B-rep and feature-based CAD models.

Salomons *et al.* (1995) suggest that there are four important aspects to computer-aided tolerancing:

▶ **Tolerance representation**, which concerns the theoretical basis for tolerancing, and consideration of how a tolerance can be linked to the CAD model.

▶ **Tolerance specification**, which concerns the definition of tolerances using types as described in a standard such as ISO 1101 (1983).

▶ **Tolerance analysis**, which involves computation of relationships and results derived from the set of tolerances of a part or assembly, for example to explore statistical variation in tolerance stack-up based on probabilistic analysis of tolerance chains.

▶ **Tolerance synthesis**, which is concerned with tolerance optimization, or with completing partial tolerance schemes.

A number of tolerance representations have been proposed, including offsetting nominal surfaces of a solid model (Requicha, 1984), defining limits on a vector relating a toleranced feature to a reference feature (Wirtz, 1993), Turner's feasibility approach, which defines tolerances as constraints on geometric variations (Turner, 1993), and others. Juster (1992) reviews a number of approaches to the representation of dimensions and tolerances, and the CIRP has sponsored a number of conferences on computer-aided tolerancing. Shape variation tolerances are also the subject of Part 47 of the current effort on the STEP standard (see Chapter 7). As an example of a tolerance representation, we will consider that incorporated in FROOM and described in Salomons *et al.* (1995). This is drawn from the approach of Clément *et al.* (1991) which is based on **technologically and topologically related surfaces** (TTRSs). A TTRS is defined as an assembly formed by two surfaces (or between a surface and a TTRS, or between two TTRSs) belonging to the same solid (defining the topological aspect) and located in the same kinematic loop in a mechanism – that is, functionally related in the assembly (the technological aspect). Clément *et al.* define seven elementary surface types and 28 tolerance cases between these face types, and also describe a **minimum geometric data element** (MGDE) which is the

Table 16.1 Elementary surfaces in TTRS, and their associated MGDEs

Elementary surface	MGDE
Sphere	Point
Plane	Plane
Cylinder	Line
Helical	Point and line or line and plane
Rotational	Point and line
Prismatic	Line and plane
Any	Point and line and plane

minimum set of points, lines or planes necessary and sufficient to define a reference frame so that tolerances can be transformed from one datum system to another. Clément *et al.*'s seven face types and their associated MGDEs are given in Table 16.1.

Clément *et al.* also use a **torsor** to represent tolerance zones. A torsor defines six DOFs – three cartesian directions and three rotations – in which small displacements are possible. In the context of a tolerance zone it defines constraints on the allowable movement of points in the tolerance zone. For example, for a cylinder, translations and rotations about the *x*-axis (due to small displacements) keep the cylinder surface invariant with respect to itself and can therefore be neglected when considering the tolerances since these influence the variations of the surface's orientation or position. For this case the torsor is $[0\ v\ w\ 0\ \beta\ \gamma]^{\mathrm{T}}$. The way that these approaches are used in a real system is shown in Figure 16.4, which shows the way tolerances are stored in FROOM. Once tolerances on a model have been defined, they can be used in conjunction with assembly constraints, such as 'against' relationships that establish kinematic loops within the assembly, as a basis for tolerance analysis and synthesis.

16.5 The World-Wide Web

PDM is the emerging technology for the sharing of data specifically relating to engineering products. The revolution in information sharing has extended much further, to encompass all manner of information ranging from academic papers to catalogues, timetables and reservation forms. At the end of the 1980s, a number of key information technologies were in place. The Internet was established as a means of exchanging data between networked computers. Hypertext applications were developing rapidly. Point and click user interfaces were in use on workstations and Apple Macintosh computers, and were beginning to be popular on PCs. The client–server computing model was in regular use in the X Window System and other applications. SGML had been introduced as a means of separating document content from structure, and other standards development was beginning to free users from proprietary formats. The technologies were, however, not all very easy to use. The Internet required Unix commands to move data from one system to another. Hypertext systems are a natural means of collecting large amounts of information, but required considerable effort to collect the data together into the systems in use at that time. But in 1989 Tim Berners-Lee, who was working for CERN, the European High-Energy Physics Laboratory near Geneva, came up with the visionary idea of linking networking and hypertext technologies to provide a distributed document handling and information sharing system. By 1990, CERN was the largest Internet site in Europe. Prototypes of the proposed system were available in this year, and the name World-Wide Web (routinely shortened to 'the Web', WWW or W3) was chosen by Berners-Lee, working with his colleague Robert Cailleau. In 1991, the first Web server in the United States was established at Stanford in California, and software distribution took place over the Internet. From these beginnings, the Web has developed phenomenally quickly.

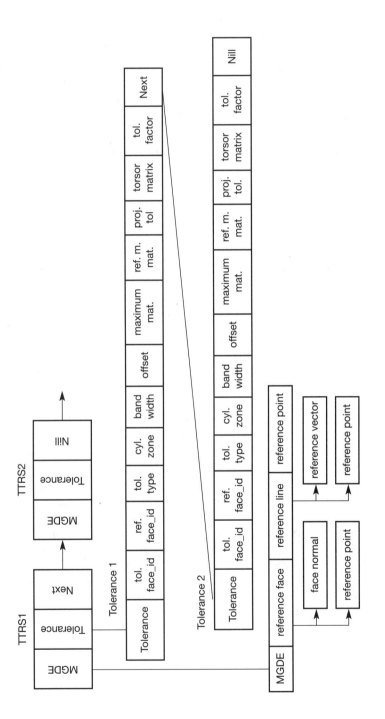

FIGURE 16.4
Tolerance
representation in
FROOM.
(Reproduced from
Salomons *et al.*
(1995) by
permission © ITP.)

Software for the X Window System was created in 1992, and the Mosaic software written by the National Center for Supercomputing Applications (NCSA) in the United States followed in 1993. This software allowed colour images to be incorporated into the hypertext, and was easy to install and robust. It led to an explosion of interest in the United States. In 1992 there were 50 computers providing a Web service (servers). In 1993 this grew to 250, in 1994 to 2500, and by 1995 there were 73 500 (Cailleau, 1995). There are no signs of this growth abating.

The WWW is a body of software, and a set of protocols and conventions, using networked hypertext and multimedia ideas. Key elements include:

▶ The client–server model is used as the mechanism for information exchange. Documents are displayed on the user's screen by **client** processes that obtain the documents from repositories managed by Web **servers**, which are processes whose objective is to deliver documents to other processes when requested to do so. The client processes are Web **browsers** (e.g. Mosaic, Netscape and other software systems). Browsers respond to user interaction by sending requests for documents to servers, and then configuring the returned documents to the local computing environment and displaying them on the screen.

▶ Hypertext documents are transferred between server and client using a protocol called the **hypertext transfer protocol** (HTTP). Clients can also exchange data using other protocols including FTP, gopher (a menu-based information system predating the WWW) and others.

▶ Documents and other information are located using **Uniform Resource Locators** (URLs). These are addresses for data that are like a combination of a computer filename and a telephone number. For example,

http://www.bris.ac.uk/about.htm

says that the document called 'about.htm' can be retrieved from the computer called 'www.bris.ac.uk' using http. The .uk element of the address indicates that the computer is in the United Kingdom, the .ac that it is connected to the academic network, and the .bris that it is at Bristol University. Additional elements in the URL can indicate the computing directory where the file is held, and even offsets within files, queries on databases and other information.

▶ Documents are described using the **hypertext markup language** (HTML). HTML documents are ASCII files with embedded codes (called **tags**) to represent the document format (text and paragraph styles, document titles and other embedded information) and the hyperlinks. HTML is a relatively simple implementation of SGML, and shares some of its features – it is more concerned with the logical structure of a document than with its appearance, and can therefore format a document for presentation for many different computer software and hardware environments. A brief description of HTML is given in the bracketed section below.

The hypertext markup language (HTML)

HTML is a specification for marking up documents for the WWW. It uses codes embedded in ASCII files comprising the document content. It is case insensitive, and ignores blank space ('white space') within the document. Codes in HTML are delimited by the < symbol which marks the start of the code and > which indicates the end. Commands are divided into two broad classes:

▶ **Container** commands, which surround text that has some role (e.g. <title> and </title> designate the beginning and end of the title to be displayed on the top bar of the browser window). A '/' character indicates the end of a container command.

▶ **Separator** commands which separate document elements. For example, <p> separates paragraphs, and <hr> provides a horizontal rule line.

There are a number of general rules for HTML documents. They should start by declaring themselves as such by using the <html> and </html> separators. The head of the document (<head> . . . </head>) contains items that are about the document, and the body (<body> . . . </body>) contains the content that is displayed.

Hyperlinks in HTML are made using a tag of the form <A HREF='URL'>link text</A>, which means 'link to Uniform Resource Locator "URL", with "link text" displayed as highlighted text'. Other widely used HTML commands are shown in Table 16.2.

An example of a very simple HTML file is therefore:

```
<HTML>
    <Head>
    <Title> An Example HTML File </Title>
    </Head>
    <Body>
    <H1> This is a visible header in the document </H1>
    . . . . This is a visible part of the document here. . . . <P>
    . . . . This is a second paragraph, followed by a horizontal ruled
line. . . . <P>
    <HR>
    </Body>
</HTML>
```

Table 16.2 Example HTML commands

Command	Meaning	Command	Meaning
<HTML> </HTML>	Start and end of HTML document.	<HEAD> </HEAD>	Start and end of document header.
<BODY> </BODY>	Start and end of document body.	<TITLE> </TITLE>	Start and end of browser window title.
<HX> </HX>	Heading start and end, level X (e.g. <H1>, <H2>, etc.).	<STRONG> </STRONG>	Start and end strongly emphasized text.
<EM> </EM>	Start and end emphasized text.	<I> </I>	Start and end italics (discouraged).
<B> </B>	Start and end bold face (discouraged).	<UL> </UL>	Start and end unnumbered list.
<OL> </OL>	Start and end numbered list.	<LI>	List element.
<P>	Paragraph separator.	<HR>	Horizontal rule.
 	Line break.		
<A HREF= 'URL'>link text</A>	Link to Uniform Resource Locator 'URL', with 'link text' displayed as highlighted text.	<A HREF= '#*name*'>link text</A>	Internal link in document to section labelled *name*, with 'link text' displayed as highlighted text.
<A NAME= '*name*'>label text</A>	Section label, with 'label text' displayed as section title.	<IMG SRC= '/image.gif'>	Insert image file 'image.gif'. Image file name can be full or relative (as shown here) URL.
ALIGN='TOP' (or 'MIDDLE' or 'BOTTOM')	Modification to IMG (*q.v.*) to indicate position of image relative to text.	ALT='alternative text'	Displays 'alternative text' in place of image if image is not displayed.

16.5.1 Developments in the WWW

The WWW is very dynamic, and new developments are being announced all the time (the reader is referred to the many sources of on-line information, such as the World-Wide Web Consortium (W3C (1997)) for the latest information). Three very significant developments from a CAD point of view are the development of browser plug-ins, the Java™ programming language and the virtual reality modelling language or VRML. Each of these assists in bringing the diversity of design information and data to the Web.

Plug-ins

Early Web browsers were only able to display text and static graphics. If sound or video files were accessed, then software had to be downloaded to play the files outside the browser. A plug-in is a piece of software that allows video, sound or some other file format to be dealt with inside the browser. It is a software module that can directly control the browser, although it will not execute as stand-alone software.

Java™

Java is an object-oriented programming language that can execute in a Web browser. It was created by Sun Microsystems, and allows programs to be written which can be downloaded to any compatible browser and executed to provide interactivity in a web page. Java applications, called **applets**, are different from ordinary computing applications in that they reside on the network in centralized servers and are delivered on request to the user's computer system. Applications created in Java can be used on any computing device capable of running the Java language, so software developers now do not have to worry about modifying their software to run on different devices. Perhaps more important is that, because the applications are downloaded on demand, there is no need for disks or CDs to distribute software (Sun, 1997). The language also offers the possibility of using simple systems without local hard disks and with minimal peripheral devices.

Virtual reality modelling language

The **virtual reality modelling language** (VRML) is, in the words of the specification for version 1.0, 'a language for describing multi-participant interactive simulations – virtual worlds networked via the global Internet and hyper-linked with the World-Wide Web' (VRML Version 1 Specification, 1995). What this means in practice is that VRML allows the creation of three-dimensional models that may be accessed via the Internet, and displayed using three-dimensional viewing in a Web browser. It achieves this by providing a specification for the representation of simple primitives (cubes, cylinders, cones, etc.) and polygonal face models in a right-handed cartesian coordinate space, and specifying viewing and lighting directions, together with surface properties of the geometric objects. Ultimately, VRML will allow for interaction between the user and the models, and for animations, motions and real-time interaction. At the time of writing, it is becoming possible to generate VRML models from many computer-aided engineering software systems, so that viewable three-dimensional models can be generated and distributed across the Internet. The implications of this are really very profound. In the past, expensive software was often required to view CAD models, and that has tended to limit the extent to which three-dimensional models have been used for communication to suppliers, customers or even end users. With VRML we have the prospect that anyone with a WWW browser will be able to download and view from arbitrary viewpoints CAD, finite element and other computer-based models of products. The challenge to the engineering community will be to identify the most appropriate ways to exploit these new technologies.

16.6 Computer-supported cooperative work

The WWW and the Internet are prime examples of technologies that help groups of people work together, and share information and data. A generic term for the combination of computing networking and the associated hardware, software, services and techniques with understanding of the way people work in groups is computer-supported cooperative work (CSCW) (Wilson, 1991). Wilson suggested in 1991 that there were four categories of CSCW enabling technologies, and noted examples of research topics in each of these:

▶ **Communications systems**, including advanced electronic mail systems, graphics and facsimile support, voice and video conferencing, X500 electronic mail directories.

▶ **Shared workspace systems**, including remote screen sharing (i.e. part of an individual's screen display reproduced on other screens) and electronically aided, intelligent whiteboards.

▶ **Shared information systems**, including multimedia, multi-user hypertext systems, large datastores making large numbers of documents available to a workgroup, and multi-user databases of various types.

▶ **Group activity support systems**, including workflow systems that enable electronic documents to be sent on predefined routes of people and roles, co-authoring tools for the joint writing of documents, decision support tools to help group decision making, and idea generating and prioritizing tools to help group creativity.

Some of these research topics have already led to significant practical applications. Mail systems, mail directories and workflow systems are routinely used, and of course the WWW provides a very effective shared information system. Many companies today are establishing company-internal versions of the Internet known as **intranets**. Video conferencing is now routine in many companies, and low-cost hardware capable of transmitting highly compressed video images along telephone connections between PC computers is available. Experimental work with high-speed digital communications in an **integrated broadband communications** (IBC) network has demonstrated a scenario whereby two designers on different sites may work simultaneously on the same CAD model, and at the same time have video and audio communication using the same workstation (with the video image being displayed in a window on the screen showing the CAD model) and the use of a shared whiteboard for the drawing of sketches and the posting of images. The University of Bristol participated in an experiment in 1995 in which such communications were established with Warwick in the UK and Darmstadt in Germany (SMAC, 1995), and more recently a research programme in the United States has seen a design activity distributed between universities throughout the country, entirely supported by CSCW technologies of the sort described (Coyne *et al.*, 1994). Maher and Rutherford (1997) propose an approach to collaborative design using the techniques of CSCW in CAD and database management. The topic is likely to be of increasing importance as design is distributed to supplier companies that are located throughout the world.

16.7 Environmentally benign production

In recent years society in general has been taking increasing interest in environmental issues and the impact of modern products and industrial processes on the environment. The concepts of environmentally benign production and sustainable industrial production have assumed a new importance for manufacturing companies.

According to Alting *et al.* (1993) sustainability implies that 'products are designed for their whole life cycle, i.e. production, distribution, usage and disposal with minimized (acceptable) influence on the environment, occupational health and use of resources'. The consequence of sustainability for the manufacturer is clear – the responsibility of the product manufacturer extends over the entire life cycle of the product, including 'end of life' disposal.

Increasingly governments are bringing forward legislation which requires manufacturers to deal with the waste products of their production processes. One concrete example of this is the requirement on product manufacturers in Germany to deal with the disposal of the packaging material in which their products are wrapped.

In fact, this issue of 'product take-back' to support resource sustainment and product or component recovery is a very live one for many manufacturers. Manufacturers of electronic products are setting up specialist recycling plants to reprocess returned products. Hewlett Packard processes approximately 1200 tons of returned computer equipment in Grenoble, France, each year. British Telecom in the UK employs 500 people to dismantle used telephone equipment each year. Multis, a small emerging Irish company, processes used Digital Equipment Corporation (DEC) equipment in Galway, Ireland. DEC also has a specialist computer recycling plant based in Nijmegen, Holland. A similar trend is emerging in the automotive sector where companies such as Mercedes Benz have developed recycling plants to refurbish returned car engines.

One multinational supplier of telecommunications equipment and services to the European market has developed a 'product life cycle management' programme which currently includes five major activities, namely:

1. Design and technology.

2. Purchasing of supplies and materials.

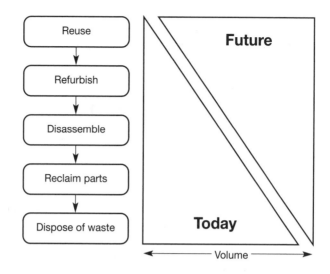

FIGURE 16.5
Resource recovery –
today's reality and
tomorrow's
potential.

3. Manufacturing processes.

4. Waste reduction and energy management.

5. Packaging and post-consumer materials management.

This company now includes environmental considerations as part of its supplier qualification process. The 'post-consumer materials management' activity represents a long-term challenge but is based on the following ideas: in the near future, manufacturers will refurbish and reuse products and recycle as much of their contents as possible; finally companies will source new markets for the recycled material and safely dispose of residual materials when necessary.

Figure 16.5 illustrates the current balance between reuse/refurbishing and waste disposal, and also a more desirable balance for the future (see Browne, 1995). Today the focus is on the control of harmful by-products from manufacturing processes and indeed products. Examples include avoidance of the use of fluorocarbon-based refrigerants in products and the gradual replacement of toxic solvents from fluxes and cleaners used in the assembly of printed circuit boards. In the future, as Figure 16.5 indicates, the emphasis will be on a total product life cycle approach to manufacturing and resource sustainment. The manufacturer will have to take increased responsibility for the products it has produced. The scope of its activities will be greatly enlarged as suggested by Figure 16.6.

Reay (1995) has developed a model of the resource sustainment cycle which is reproduced in amended form in Figure 16.7. This model fits within the vision of resource recovery suggested in Figure 16.5 and the product life cycle perspective suggested in Figure 16.6.

To indicate the importance of the resource sustainment issue it is worth briefly looking at the computer industry. In 1965 the PC did not exist. Today there are estimated to be 140 million PCs in use in the world (1 for every 35 to 40 people). By the year 2010, PCs may well outnumber people. Within 5 to 7 years virtually all

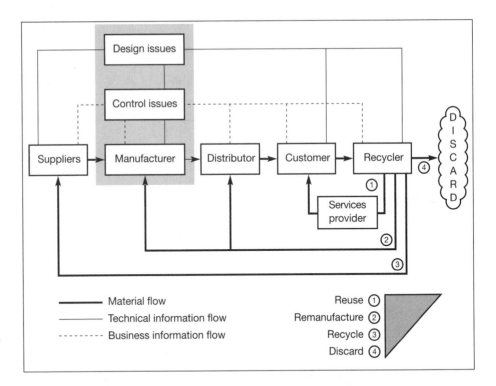

FIGURE 16.6
Total product cycle
perspective in
manufacturing.

current PCs will be discarded. It is estimated that plastics make up approximately 40% of the weight of a PC.

The development and widespread availability of portable PCs increases the volume of hazardous material used in PCs, for example rechargeable batteries. Computer manufacturers are recognizing the trends and are launching ecological programmes. They are beginning to offer 'green PCs'. The PC manufacturers are beginning to realize that a combination of product take-back, modular design and remanufacturing may offer an environmentally and economically productive path to new product development (RSA (1994), page 29). The take-back or resources recovery market is of course in its early stages, and today the volume of consumer products and materials is emerging slowly. However, its importance for the future must not be underestimated.

The reality today is that a small number of 'end of life' or retired computer products are being recycled. The majority are disposed of with inadequate attention to waste and potential environmental damage. There is an active and indeed a growing market for second-use computer products (particularly mid-range computers), and also for the options and components reclaimed from retired products. Many manufacturers are striving to be environmentally responsible and have introduced a number of 'point solutions' and services. Examples include product design to facilitate disassembly, material selection to maximize reuse at end of life, and environmental controls on manufacturing processes and their by-products. However, the perspective of the majority of manufacturers is that the environmental issue represents a 'cost' rather than an opportunity. Nevertheless there appears to be a growing

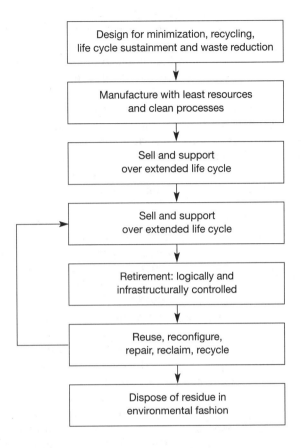

FIGURE 16.7
Model of the
Resource
Sustainment Cycle.
(Adapted from Reay
(1995).)

market for second-use product. Companies involved in this market suggest that the resale of retired product following remanufacture and reconfiguration offers a viable business opportunity. Through such resale, the reclamation of 'options', the reclamation of service parts and even the reclamation of base metals, between 30 and 50% of the value of the original computer system can be realized.

Manufacturers are also aware of emerging standards and legislation. In Europe, individual governments and the Commission of the European Union are increasingly aware of the 'electronic scrap' issue. Standards such as EMAS (Euro ECO Audit and Management Scheme) and BS7750 (British Standard on Environmental Management) are emerging. Large purchasers of electronic and computer products are beginning to raise questions about the suppliers' environmental and take-back policies. Many PC manufacturers have 'green PCs', which normally focus on energy efficiency. Although it is true that, as a statistical whole, consumers are wasteful and irresponsible, change is in the air. The ready availability of green products is beginning to offer a competitive edge in certain segments of the market, and manufacturers are aware of this.

The emergence of environmentally benign products and manufacturing processes has important consequences for manufacturing systems designers. The long-term objective must be maximum resource recovery. This will be achieved through maximizing our ability to recover products, subassemblies, components and materials and minimizing the need for disposal through reuse, recycling, reclamation, resale, reconditioning and remanufacturing. The extent to which this is possible depends on the technologies available (product technologies, manufacturing process technologies and information technologies), and emerging business processes will differ across individual industrial sectors. Today the focus seems to be on the automotive sector and the electronics and computing sectors. Research is focusing almost exclusively on the products (design for disassembly, design using compatible and recyclable materials) and the manufacturing processes (e.g. the safe disposal of effluents, the development of low-energy processes, the replacement of ozone-depleting chlorofluorocarbon (CFC) solvents from soldering systems).

Industrial practice is, however, rapidly moving towards achieving clean production. The automotive sector is a case in point. It is estimated that up to 24 million automobiles are scrapped world-wide each year. Clearly the potential for recycling in this industry is great. For example, most car bumpers are made from a relatively limited number of polymer types. Typically polypropylene and polycarbonate blends are used. Ford claims that it can recycle the radiator grill on the Mondeo model (see *Technology Ireland*, 1995). However, the trend towards using body-coloured painted bumpers is not a good one from a recycling perspective. The paint is of course a contaminant (from a recycling perspective!) and may seriously impair the mechanical properties of the recyclate. Tyre manufacturers are also actively involved in recycling. For example, Semperit (Ireland) Ltd, producing 12 000 tyres per day, used to generate approximately $1.5 million of waste material each year and dump it in landfill sites. Today this company recovers and recycles over 85% of its waste (by weight). Clegg and Williams (1994) report that Canon is remanufacturing printer and photocopier toner cartridges which were previously disposable. According to their research, the Canon plant in China receives retired cartridges shipped from Europe, Japan and the United States. Altogether about 2.5 million units are reprocessed each year, representing 15% of total production. Similarly, Xerox toner cartridges are returned to the United States at a cost of $4 per cartridge. The disassembly cost is between $10 and $15 per unit, and with design changes and increasing volume, the recycling activity is cost effective. According to Clegg and Williams, it costs $60 to manufacture a new product and $35 to remanufacture a cartridge.

Researchers have only begun to look at the possibility of using a recovery process to recycle products at their so-called end of life. Hentschel *et al.* (1995) identify very clearly the difficulties of the recovery process:

> Recovery is confronted with a huge variety of products from various producers and production years, as it usually cannot restrict itself to a spectrum of products from only one manufacturer. Uncertainty is caused by the varying product's life expectancies, creating a temporal dispersion of product abandonment. Arrival levels of each type of product and the product mix show non-deterministic properties. This is aggravated by the fact that products are usually distributed in many different places. In addition, used products, even when identical, often show heavy deviations caused by usage influences. Usage

influences result not only from the dedicated function of the product. Two other factors, time and media, can serve as examples of the influences that cause deviations from the original condition of the product. While deviations like wear, material fatigue, and maintenance activities can be predicted, the abuse of the product i.e. using a product for a purpose other than the dedicated one, creates deviations that cannot be foreseen. This creates an additional level of uncertainty in recovery, which is unknown in planning manufacturing systems.

Research teams are also beginning to consider the issues associated with the logistics of recycling and resource sustainment. A new European-Union-funded project started in late 1995, involving a mix of industrial and academic partners and labelled PAWS (Product Acquisition from Waste Streams), is looking at the information systems required to support resource recovery at product end of life. Issues such as the following will be addressed: When is resource recovery economically realistic? What type of business processes must be put in place to support resource recovery? What type of business relationships are appropriate between original product manufacturers and product recyclers? What type of markets exist for recycled products, components, subassemblies and materials? What type of information systems need to be put in place to support product take-back, disassembly and reuse? How do such information systems deal with issues such as common and unique subassemblies and components, reuse potential of components, disassembly difficulty, disassembly BOMs, etc.? (See PAWS, 1995.)

What is very clear, even from the limited experience and research reported to date, is that the environmental issue, the resource recovery issue or indeed the end of life disposal of product issue cannot be tackled by individual manufacturing firms operating independently. Suppliers, distributors, customers and specialist recyclers must be involved. Practices and procedures must be put in place across the whole value chain which facilitate an environmentally benign process. The issue cannot be addressed adequately by individual manufacturing firms seeking partial solutions. An extended enterprise approach must be adopted.

16.8 Lessons for designers arising from environmentally benign production

Today's designers are aware of the need to design for X, where X refers to assembly, safety, reliability, cost, test, etc. In the near future, designers will also need to consider design for sustainability or disassembly. Of course, design for disassembly (DFD) and design for sustainability (DFS) are not necessarily the same. DFD suggests a short-term approach where the designer is interested in ensuring that the product can be easily disassembled at the 'end of its life' so that, for example, subassemblies or components can be reused, possibly by the use of maintenance or service organizations. DFD also seeks to minimize the difficulties of disassembling products from the point of view of their safe and cost-effective disposal.

Design rules to support disassembly arise at a number of levels. At the level of product families, DFD seeks to control the proliferation of product variants and options. Too great a range makes control of disassembly difficult, as the disassembler needs to know which particular variant it is dealing with and the particular options the variant contains. Perhaps we need to evolve new forms of planning BOMs to support designers in this task. At the product and component level, a number of possible rules are already apparent. These rules seek to ensure that the disassembly or separation process for end of life products is carried out in a cost-effective and efficient manner, facilitating the recovery of subassemblies, components and indeed materials where possible. This process will require the development of a new type of BOM.

Typical rules for DFD include:

▶ where possible, use compatible materials (from a recycling point of view) in assemblies;

▶ where non-compatible materials must be used, ensure that the assembly process is so designed that the non-compatible parts can be easily separated;

▶ try to avoid using mechanical fasteners;

▶ where feasible, identify and date code the materials used in components;

▶ avoid labels and non-recyclable coatings and paints.

Table 16.3 gives more details on the DFD rules.

Table 16.3 Typical DFD rules

1	Use compatible materials.
2	Where non-compatible materials are used, design for ease of separation.
3	Use standardized parts.
4	Use tabs, snap-in and other non-mechanical fasteners.
5	Identify and date code materials on components.
6	Avoid the use of labels and non-recyclable paints and coatings.
7	Avoid the use of adhesives, welding or heatstaking to join incompatible plastics.
8	Minimize the number of material types.
9	Where feasible group high- and low-value components in separate areas (e.g. electronic printed circuit board assembly).
10	Locate high-value parts in easily accessible places in the product.
11	Design products for simple dismantling.
12	Clearly identify hazardous parts.

DFA, DFM and DFD

It is worth noting that the rules for DFM (Design for Manufacture), DFA (Design for Assembly) and DFD (Design for Disassembly) are by no means compatible. Thus for example a classic DFM rule is to keep mechanical or plastic components as simple as possible to avoid complex, time-consuming and expensive set-up on machines and expensive features on moulds. However, a well-known DFA rule is to seek to avoid assembly costs by manufacturing complex components which do not require to be assembled. The 'classic' example of this DFA rule in action comes from the electronics industry where conventional integrated circuits incorporate the functionality previously provided by a large number of individual discrete components which had to be assembled together on a printed circuit board. Of course the manufacture of these integrated circuits is an extremely complex and expensive task.

A similar incongruity occurs when we look at DFA and DFD. In terms of joining operations, DFA rules would advise designers to avoid, where possible, the use of screwed fasteners in high-volume products because assembly using screws is difficult to automate economically. However, DFD rules would presumably advise the use of such fasteners, precisely because they can be unfastened and thereby facilitate end of life product disassembly.

Design sustainability

Design for sustainability reflects a more profound perspective, which will have great consequences for designers in the longer term. Tomiyama (1991) takes a radical view. He quotes Professor Yoshikawa of Tokyo University who pointed out that:

> the measure of man's technical progress is given by the fact that the pyramids of Egypt have lasted for 5000 years, the castles of the middle ages for 500 years, the machines of the industrial revolution for 50 years, while a modern car lasts only five. It is astonishing to realise that while economic growth has been made possible largely by technological advances, these achievements are themselves only possible because of a quantitative sufficiency of artefacts with ever shorter lifetimes. That is, technological progress and advanced manufacturing techniques have only helped to shorten the lives of artefacts.

Tomiyama writes about a post mass production paradigm which extends the lifetime of an artefact infinitely and extends the value of that product indefinitely. As he points out:

> Of course, it is impossible to make something with an infinite lifetime and even if it were possible, an infinite lifetime would be wasteful. Instead, we are talking about an artefact that can be progressively developed into a system, a concept in which the manufacturing industry grows based on demands for renewals and maintenance.

Tomiyama suggests that in future we may distinguish two types of artefacts: a high-class product which will last indefinitely, and a completely recyclable item of social capital which 'provides functions and service in what is almost indistinguishable from a disposable product'.

Life cycle assessment

A second approach used by product designers, seeking to develop environmentally benign products, is life cycle assessment (LCA).

LCA is a tool which seeks to articulate and make visible the environment and resources consequences of product design choices. LCA seeks to measure the total environmental impact of a product throughout its life cycle, from product concept, through design, manufacture, use and on to and including end of life dispositioning. LCA analyses result in an environmental profile of a product in terms of its consumption of energy, production of ozone-depleting by-products, its impact on the human environment, etc.

16.9 BOMs for disassembly

As we have seen earlier, BOMs are used to define product structures and are an essential part of a production planning and control system. However, BOMs have been developed to support product manufacture and assembly and are less useful in planning disassembly operations. Simon *et al.* (1992) have developed an interesting disassembly BOM which is worth reviewing in detail because it indicates some of the difficulties associated with managing disassembly activities. This disassembly BOM is best understood by referring to the example presented by Simon and his co-workers.

This example uses the disassembly BOM to evaluate the optimal disassembly possibility for a domestic smoke alarm. A data structure is required which includes information about the relative location of parts and their connections. This can be obtained from the engineering drawing of the alarm. The first stage in the model involves constructing a simplified tree diagram of the product. This is similar to a BOM structure showing the parent/child relationships between parts/subassemblies within the product. At the top of the tree diagram is the completed smoke alarm. The subsequent level illustrates the next immediate subassemblies which are combined to form the smoke alarm. Lines in the diagrams represent 'ownership', the fact that parts belong to subassemblies which in turn belong to the complete unit. The completed tree diagram shows all the subassemblies represented by cubic shapes, and single components, represented by cylindrical shapes, and how they are related.

In Figure 16.8 the tree diagram for the smoke alarm is shown with sample disassembly costs and values filled in. The net value of the product is calculated, in this case just negative. This situation changes, however, if part 2.2, the circuit board subassembly, can be disposed of for 22 pence. In this case further disassembly is uneconomic and the net product value rises to 5 pence. The balance is tipped just in favour of substantial disassembly (Simon *et al.*, 1992).

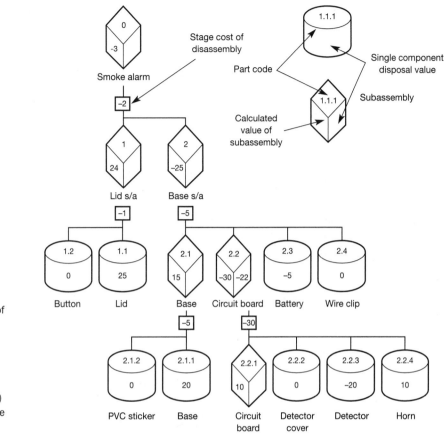

FIGURE 16.8
Structure diagram of the smoke alarm showing upward calculated part and assembly values. (Reproduced from Simon *et al.* (1992) by permission of the author.)

16.10 Conclusion

At the beginning of this chapter we said that we are still in the process of a computer revolution that is dramatically altering the way that we work in engineering, commerce and industry. Although this revolution has been going on for many decades, the pace of change can still be very fast. Consider, for example, that when the first edition of this book was being written, the World-Wide Web was concentrated on a handful of experimental sites. Today there are millions who have access to the Web and who use it on an everyday basis. So it is clear that attempting to predict the future is a risky business! The only certainty is that the pace of change will be maintained by technological developments, by the inexorable pressure of global competition, and by regulation and our increasing understanding of our effects on the natural environment.

References and further reading

Alting L., Hauschild M. and Wenzel H. (1993). Elements in a new sustainable industrial culture – environmental assessment in product development. In *Managing Enterprises –*

Stakeholders, Engineering, Logistics and Achievement (ed. D. T. Wright). Bury St Edmunds: Mechanical Engineering Publications.

Ambler A. P. and Popplestone R. J. (1975). Inferring the positions of bodies from specified spatial relationships. *Artificial Intelligence*. **6**, 157–74.

Andreasen M. M. and Hein L. (1987). *Integrated Product Development*. London: IFS Publications/Springer.

Arnold K. and Gosling J. (1997). *The Java Programming Language*. Reading, MA: Addison Wesley Longman.

Boston University, INSEAD, Waseda University (1991). Factories of the future. Executive Summary of the 1990 International Manufacturing Futures.

Bradley P., Browne J., Jackson S. and Jagdev H. (1995). Business process reengineering – a study of the software tools currently available. *Computers in Industry*. **25**, 309–30.

Browne J. (1995). The extended enterprise – manufacturing and the value chain. In *Balanced Automation Systems – Architecture and design methods* (ed. Luis M. Camarina-Matos and Hamideh Afsarmanesh). London: Chapman & Hall, 5–17.

Browne J., Sackett P. J. and Wortmann J. C. (1994). Industry requirements and associated research issues in the extended enterprise. *Proc. IMSE'94 Workshop on Integrated Manufacturing Systems Engineering*, Grenoble, France, 12–14 December.

Browne J., Sackett P. J. and Wortmann J. C. (1995). Future manufacturing systems – towards the extended enterprise. *Computers in Industry*. **25**, 235–54.

Bruno G., Agarwal R., Reyneri C., Chiavola B. and Varani M. (1994). Making CIMOSA operational. *Proc. European Workshop on Integrated Manufacturing Systems Engineering*, Grenoble, France.

Cailleau R. (1995). A short history of the web. Text of speech delivered to European W3 Consortium, Paris. *http://www.inria.fr/Actualites/Cailleau-fra.html*.

CIMdata, Inc. (1996). *Product Data Management: The Definition*. CIMdata, Ann Arbor, MI (*http://www.CIMdata.com*).

Clegg A. J. and Williams D. J. W. (1994). The strategic and competitive implications of recycling and design for disassembly in the electronics industry. Technical Report 9413, Department of Manufacturing Engineering, Loughborough University of Technology.

Clément A., Desrochers A. and Rivière A. (1991). Theory and practice of 3D tolerancing for assembly. *Proc. 2nd CIRP Seminar on Computer-aided Tolerancing*, Penn State University, 97–113.

Coyne R. *et al.* (1994). Creating an advanced collaborative open resource network. *Proc. 6th Int. Conf. on Design Theory and Methodology*, Minneapolis: American Society of Mechanical Engineers, 375–80.

Doll W. J. and Vonderembse M. A. (1992). The evolution of manufacturing systems: towards the post-industrial enterprise. In *Manufacturing Strategy – Process & Content* (ed. C. A. Voss). London: Chapman & Hall, 353–70.

Hentschel C. *et al.* (1995). Grouping of used products for cellular recycling system. *Annals of the CIRP*, **44**(1), 11–14.

Jovane F., Alting L., Armillotta A., Eversheim W., Feldmann K., Seliger G. and Roth N. (1993). A key issue in product life cycle: disassembly. *Annals of the CIRP*.

Juster N. P. (1992). Modelling and representation of dimensions and tolerances: a survey. *Computer-aided Design*. **24**(1), 3–17.

Kramer G. A. (1992). *Solving Geometric Constraint Systems: A Case-study in Kinematics*. Cambridge, MA: The MIT Press.

Krause F. -L., Kimura F., Kjellberg T. and Lu S. C. -Y. (1993). Product modelling. *Annals of the CIRP.* **42**(2), 695–706.

Kugathasan P. and McMahon C. A. (1997). Multiple viewpoint models for automotive body-in-white design. *Proc. 4th Int. Conf. on Concurrent Engineering, CE'97*, Oakland, MI, 75–82.

Maher M. L. and Rutherford J. H. (1997). A model for synchronous collaborative design using CAD and database management. *Research in Engineering Design.* **9**, 85–98.

Manufacturing Engineering (1993). Environmentally conscious manufacturing. **III**(4), 44–55.

Northern Telecom (1992). Environmental review.

Okino, N. (1994). Bionic manufacturing system. Manufacturing Systems.

PAWS (March 1995). Production acquisition from waste streams. Project submission to BRITE-EURAM, Technical University of Eindhoven, Dept of Industrial Engineering and Information Systems.

Reay, E. (1995). Private communication, Galway, Ireland.

Rehman, A. and Diehl M. B. (1993). Rapid modelling helps focus setup reduction at Ingersoll. *Industrial Engineering.* November.

Requicha A. A. G. (1984). Representation of tolerances in solid modelling: issues and alternative approaches. In *Solid Modelling by Computers: from Theory to Applications* (ed. M. S. Picket and J. W. Boyse). Plenum Press.

RSA Design (1994). Ecodesign in the telecommunications industry. *RSA Design Workshop.* London, UK: RSA.

Salomons O. W. (1995). Computer support in the design of mechanical products. Constraint specification and satisfaction in mechanical feature-based design and manufacturing. PhD Dissertation, University of Twente.

Salomons O. W., Jonge Poerink H. J., Slooten F. van, Houten F. J. A. M. van and Kals H. J. J. (1995). A computer-aided tolerancing tool based on kinematic analogies. *Proc. 4th CIRP Seminar on Computer-aided Tolerancing*, Tokyo, 53–72.

Shah J. J. and Rogers M. T. (1993). Assembly modelling as an extension of feature-based design. *Research in Engineering Design.* **5**, 218–37.

Simon M., Fogg B., Chambellant F. (1992). A design for cost-effective disassembly. Presented at the June, 1992 International Forum for DFA, Newport, RI, USA.

SMAC (1995). *Suppliers and Manufacturers in Automotive Collaboration.* European Community RACE Research Project R2112.

Society of Manufacturing Engineers (1988). Countdown to the future: the manufacturing engineer in the 21st century. Profile 21, Executive Summary.

Stendel H. J. and Desruelle P. (1992). *Manufacturing in the Nineties.* New York: Van Nostrand Reinhold.

Sun (1997). *http://java.sun.com/.* Java™ Web Server. Sun Microsystems.

Technology Ireland (1995). Environmental corner. July/August, 10.

Tomiyama T. (1991) The technical concept of intelligent manufacturing systems (IMS). Research paper, The University of Tokyo.

Turner J. U. (1993). A feasibility space approach for automated tolerancing. *ASME Journal of Engineering for Industry.* **115**, 341–5.

VRML Version 1 Specification (1995). *http://www.vrml.org/VRML1.0/vrml10c.html.*

Wilson P. (1991). *Computer Supported Cooperative Work: An Introduction.* Oxford: Intellect (UK)/Dordrecht: Kluwer.

Wirtz A. (1993). Vectorial tolerancing – a basic element for quality control. *Proc. 3rd. CIRP Seminar on Computer-aided Tolerancing*, Cachan, France, 115–28.

W3C (1997). World-Wide Web Consortium web server. *http://www.w3.org.*

Exercises

16.1 What do you understand by the terms product structure, configuration management, process management and digital mock-up in the context of product data modelling?

16.2 Suggest how database applications in product modelling may be extended in the future.

16.3 What information about an assembly needs to be stored in assembly modelling in addition to the part-of relationships of the bill of materials (BOM)? How can this information be associated with the assembly/subassembly/part hierarchy of the BOM?

16.4 Distinguish between dimensional and geometric tolerancing, and then outline the issues in computer-aided tolerancing.

16.5 Explain the meaning of technologically and topologically related surfaces, minimum geometric data element and torsor in the context of tolerance modelling.

16.6 Give an overview of the history and the technologies of the World-Wide Web, including explanations of what you understand by the terms or acronyms URL, HTML, client, server, tag, browser and search engine.

16.7 Write the HTML for a personal web page for yourself. It should include a page title, a header, sections describing your work or study and your interests, with internal links from a bulleted list to these, and a bitmap showing your photograph. You should also include external references to, for example, your place of work or study, and to your favourite web pages.

16.8 What do you understand by the terms environmentally benign manufacturing, total product perspective, remanufacturing and resource sustainment.

Appendices

Appendix A
Computer graphics techniques

··

A.1 The Cohen–Sutherland line clipping algorithm

··

The Cohen–Sutherland algorithm (Newman and Sproull, 1979) is for the clipping of lines to the boundaries of a graphics window. It is designed to accept entirely visible lines or to reject entirely invisible lines rapidly, and to compute the end points of visible parts of partly displayed lines. The first two cases are known as trivial acceptance or rejection respectively. The algorithm makes use of the fact that, for convex window boundaries, there is never more than one visible segment for any line. It has two parts:

1. Test the line for trivial acceptance/rejection.

2. If the line is not accepted/rejected it is divided into two parts at a window boundary and test 1 applied to each part.

The method employed is to:

1. Divide the picture area into nine areas by extending the window boundaries (Figure A.1), and then allocating a 4-bit (or four logical value) code to each picture region, such that bit 1 = 1 for regions to the left of the left edge and so on. The region codes are then allocated to line ends in the regions.

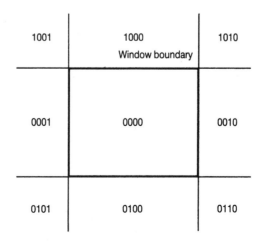

FIGURE A.1
Division of the picture area by extending the window boundaries.

2. Test the codes for the two line end points. If both codes are 0000 then the line is entirely within the window. If the logical intersection (i.e. logical AND) of the two codes is not 0000, then the line must lie entirely off the screen. For example, if the two end codes are 1001 and 1010, then the line is entirely above the top edge of the screen, because bit 4 is set to 1 in each end code.

3. If the line is not eliminated by the above tests it is subdivided at a window boundary and the tests repeated for each part.

Example A.1 ***The Cohen–Sutherland algorithm***

As an example of the application of the Cohen–Sutherland clipping algorithm, consider the line shown in Figure A.2. In this case, end point 1 has the code 1001 and end point 2,0000. The logical intersection of these is 1001 AND 0000 = 0000, which is neither trivially accepted nor rejected. The line is therefore subdivided at point A, giving:

$$x_A = x_1 + (x_2 - x_1) \times (w_{yt} - y_1)/(y_2 - y_1) \tag{A.1}$$

$$y_A = w_{yt} \tag{A.2}$$

The two parts of the line may now be tested again. That part from $(x_1\ y_1)$ to $(x_A,\ y_A)$ is off the screen, and may be rejected. The logical intersection of the end codes for that part from $(x_A\ y_A)$ to $(x_2\ y_2)$ is 0000, and we therefore need to subdivide at B and test again. This test shows the line segment from $(x_A\ y_A)$ to $(x_B\ y_B)$ to be off the screen, and that from $(x_B\ y_B)$ to $(x_2\ y_2)$ to be entirely visible. This latter line is therefore displayed.

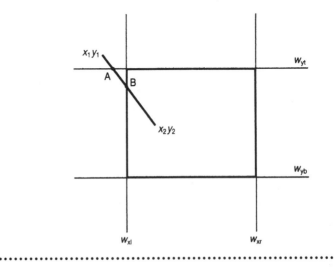

FIGURE A.2

Clipping of a line.

A.2 The scan-conversion hidden-surface algorithm

Scan conversion involves determining which pixels in a graphics image lie within the boundaries of a polygon. The simple approach to scan conversion is to test every pixel in the image against the polygon boundaries. This is rather inefficient and ignores the fact that, in general, sequences of adjacent pixels will be in the polygon. The **scan-line algorithm** exploits the limited changes in the sequences of visible pixels between adjacent scan lines (i.e. the **scan-line coherence**). It also exploits the fact that, for a given polygon, the same edges are likely to be intersected by adjacent scan lines (this is, incidentally, known as **edge coherence**).

A.2.1 The Y–X scan-line algorithm

The Y–X, or '**Y then X**' algorithm (Foley and Van Dam, 1982) is so called because it involves sorting the polygon information in the scene into order first by y coordinate and then by x coordinate. Let us consider the scene shown in Figure A.3, with three partly overlapping polygons. The algorithm involves first creating an **edge table** for all the non-horizontal edges of all the polygons in the scene, sorted in two ways:

▶ By y coordinate value into a **y-bucket** list – a table of y coordinate 'buckets' (0–15 in the case of Figure A.3). Assuming that sorting is by maximum y coordinate value, i.e. at each y coordinate at which there are the upper vertices of edges, a list of these edges is entered in the appropriate bucket.

▶ Within a bucket the edge list is sorted based on x value and change in x per scan line (dx/line).

Figure A.4 shows the edge table for the polygons shown in Figure A.3. For each edge, the x coordinate of the upper (maximum y) end is stored, together with the y coordinate of the other end (or the change in y), the change in x per scan line, and the polygon identification for the edge.

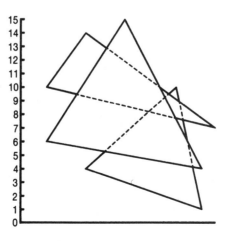

FIGURE A.3

Three overlapping polygons.

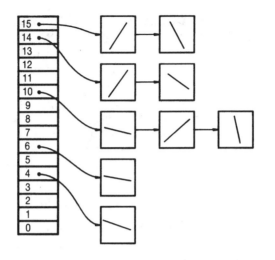

In addition, for each polygon there will be stored in a polygon table information about the orientation, colour and shade of the polygon, together with a **flag** used to record whether the scan line being processed is currently within the polygon boundary ('in'), or outside it ('out').

The actual generation of the scan-line data is achieved by taking each scan line in turn from the top to the bottom of the image, and by maintaining an **active-edge table** (AET) to record which edges are crossed by the scan line being currently processed. The active-edge table is similar to the edge list for a given entry in the y-bucket list. The edges are sorted by x value and slope. For a given scan line the process is (for non-intersecting polygons) to:

▶ Update the AET to reflect changes from the previous scan line, and add to the AET those edges which start at the current line (taken from the y-bucket list).

▶ Progress along the line to the first edge in the AET. At this edge, invert the in/out flag of the polygon containing the edge, and set the shade for the scan pixels to the shade for the polygon.

▶ Progress to the next edge in the AET. If the edge belongs to a polygon that has its in/out flag set to 'in', then:

– toggle the flag to 'out';
– if the scan line is not in any polygon, set pixel values to the background colour, otherwise do a depth comparison to find the nearest polygon whose in/out flag is set 'in' and use the shade of that polygon.

If the polygon has its in/out flag set 'out', compare the polygon depth with that polygon currently being displayed, and set the pixel shade to that for the nearer polygon.

▶ Repeat the previous step until all of the scan line has been processed.

If polygons may intersect each other, then a 'false edge' may be introduced at the intersection line.

References and further reading

Foley J. D. and Van Dam A. (1982). *Fundamentals of Interactive Computer Graphics*. Reading, MA: Addison Wesley Longman.

Newman W. M. and Sproull R. F. (1979). *Principles of Interactive Computer Graphics*. New York: McGraw-Hill.

Appendix B
Example parametric program

This appendix gives an example parametric program, written in a pseudo-code based on the Eagle programming language that is incorporated in the Auto-trol Series 7000™ CAD system. The program will draw metric nuts from a limited range of sizes.

B.1 Sequence of operation

The interactive sequence that the program user will see when the program is used is as follows:

1. A *menu* will be displayed asking:

    WHAT SIZE DO YOU REQUIRE?
    1   M4
    2   M5
    3   M6
    4   M8
    5   M12
    6   M16

    The user responds by selecting a number.

2. A *menu* will be displayed asking:

    WHAT GEOMETRY DO YOU REQUIRE?
    1   ACROSS CORNERS ELEVATION
    2   ACROSS FLATS ELEVATION
    3   PLAN

    The user responds by selecting a number.

3. A *menu* will be displayed asking:

    LOCATION OF CONSTRUCTION?
    1   SCREEN POSITION
    2   EXISTING POINT
    3   ENTER COORDINATES

Depending on the user's response, the user will be asked to indicate a position for the construction:

SELECT LOCATION POSITION

or the user will be asked to indicate a point (an existing entity) at which the construction is to be located:

SELECT LOCATION POINT

or the user will be asked to enter *x*, *y* and *z* coordinate values for the location of the construction:

ENTER COORDINATES
1   XT
2   YT
3   ZT

At this stage, the geometry will be constructed. (Note that it would be normal also to ask for the user to specify the construction angle. This has been omitted here in order to simplify the program.)

B.2 Program

```
%       The program commences with declarations of variables:
%       CONSTRUCTION_TYPE and SIZE are variables used to record
%       the user preference. IV and IV2 are 'information
%       variables' returned by procedure calls.
%
        INTEGER CONSTRUCTION_TYPE, SIZE, IV, IV2, NO_ENTS;
%
%       The real variables are the dimensions of the nut – the
%       nominal diameter and the across-corners and across-flats
%       dimensions. XYZ is an array for the construction
%       location.
%
        REAL    THREAD_DIA, A_F, A_C, THICKNESS, XYZ(3);
%
%       ENTITY declarations are used to define entities used in
%       construction or selection. SELECTED_PT is an entity used
%       to locate the construction.
%
        ENTITY  SELECTED_PT;
```

```
%
%       At this stage the program would normally record the
%       current values of system parameters such as line-style
%       and colour, and set the parameters to the values to be
%       used in the program.
%
%       The user is now asked what size is to be constructed.
%       SIZE__MENU is a label used for program jumps etc.
%
SIZE__MENU:
%
%       The next statement displays a menu with the title
%       'WHAT SIZE DO YOU REQUIRE?', and the options M4, M5, etc.
%       The user return is returned in IV
%
        IV := $MENU ('WHAT SIZE DO YOU REQUIRE?',
                         'M4', 'M5', 'M6', 'M8', 'M12', 'M16');
        IF IV < 0 THEN EXIT;
%
%       i.e. the user has selected 'go back a step'. Otherwise
%       set the SIZE variable according to the user return.
%
        SIZE := IV;
%
%       The user is now asked what two-dimensional construction
%       is required.
%
GEOM__MENU:
        IV :=    $MENU ('WHAT GEOMETRY DO YOU REQUIRE?',
                         'ACROSS CORNERS ELEVATION',
                         'ACROSS FLATS ELEVATION',
                         'PLAN');
%
%       If 'go back a step' is selected, then return to the
%       previous menu
%
        IF IV < 0 THEN GOTO SIZE__MENU;
%
%       otherwise set construction type
%
        CONSTRUCTION__TYPE := IV;
%
%       Now the user selects how he/she wishes to enter the
%       construction location point
%
```

```
LOCATION:
        IV := $MENU ('LOCATION OF CONSTRUCTION?',
                        'SCREEN POSITION',
                        'EXISTING POINT',
                        'ENTER COORDINATES');
        IF IV < 0 THEN GOTO GEOM__MENU;
%
%       The actual location is determined by a CASE statement:
%
        CASE IV OF
%
%       First screen position entry – the user is asked to
%       select a cursor position on the screen for construction
%
                1 :: BEGIN
                        IV2 := $POSITION ('SELECT POSITION', XYZ(1),
                                        XYZ(2), XYZ(3));
%
%       Again, go back to the previous menu if 'go back a step'
%       is selected.
%
                        IF IV2 < 0 THEN GOTO LOCATION;
                END;
%
%       Or select an existing point for construction
%
                2 :: BEGIN
%
%       '1' means select one entity, although NO__ENTS records the
%       number actually selected. The entity selected is
%       SELECTED__PT
%
                        IV2 := $SELECT ('INDICATE POINT', 1, NO__ENTS,
                                        SELECTED__PT);
                        IF IV2 < 1 THEN GOTO LOCATION;
%
%       The positional data is extracted from the entity using
%       this call
%
                        IV2 := $INFO (SELECTED__PT, 1, 3, XYZ);
                END;
%
%       The next section allows the user to enter the
%       construction position as x, y and z points.
%
```

```
            3 :: BEGIN
                    IV2 := $DATA ('ENTER COORDINATES',
                                    'X', XYZ(1),
                                    'Y', XYZ(2),
                                    'Z', XYZ(3));
                    IF IV2 < 1 THEN GOTO LOCATION;
            END;
%
%    The nut dimensions are now set according to the size
%    selected. These might be looked up from an array, or set
%    within a CASE statement, or in some other way.
%
        CASE SIZE OF

            1 :: BEGIN
                    THREAD__DIA :=      4.0;
%
%    the detail is omitted here
%
            .
            .
            .

    etc.
            .
            .
            .
%
%    The required geometry is now constructed – by calling
%    a subroutine (procedure) to carry out the construction.
%    Dimensional parameters are passed to the routines.
%
        CASE CONSTRUCTION__TYPE OF

            1 :: BEGIN
%
%    Across corners elevation
%
                        CALL DRAW__AC__ELEVATION (THREAD__DIA,
                                    A__F, A__C,
                                    THICKNESS,
                                    XYZ, IV);
            END;
            2 :: BEGIN
%
%    Across flats elevation
%
```

```
                    CALL DRAW__AF__ELEVATION (THREAD__DIA,
                                A__F, A__C,
                                THICKNESS,
                                XYZ, IV);
        END;
%
%       Plan view
%
            3 :: BEGIN

                    CALL DRAW__PLAN (THREAD__DIA, A__F, A__C,
                                THICKNESS, XYZ, IV);
        END;
%
%       At this stage the program would normally contain a
%       menu offering the user the opportunity to delete the
%       construction, or to group it, or perhaps to construct
%       an alternative view. In this simplified case, simply
%       return to the beginning
%
        GOTO SIZE__MENU;
        END;
%
```

An example of a construction routine is as follows (the Eagle syntax uses the word SUBR to identify a subroutine):

```
SUBR DRAW__AF__ELEVATION (THREAD__DIA, A__F, A__C,
THICKNESS, XYZ, IV);
%       This subroutine draws an across-flats elevation of a
%       metric nut of nominal diameter THREAD__DIA at location
%       XYZ.
%       Again, start with declarations. IV is simply an
%       information variable returned by the procedure calls.
%
        INTEGER    IV;
%
%       The REAL data is for construction dimensions and
%       location (see Figure B.1 for the dimensions and the
%       entities used)
%
        REAL       THREAD__DIA, A__F, A__C, THICKNESS, XYZ(3),
                                D, D1, H, H1;
%
%       The ENTITY definitions are for main construction
%       entities, and also for temporary entities used only
%       for construction purposes
```

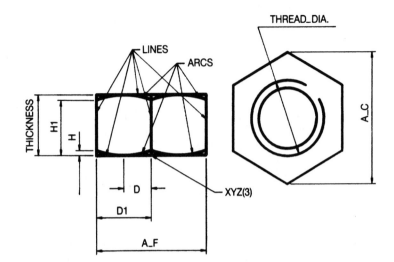

FIGURE B.1

Entities used in metric nut construction.

```
%
        ENTITY      LINES(5), ARCS(4), TEMPENTS(3);
%
%     This first section simply calculates dimensions used
%     in construction.
%

        H   := ((A_C – A_F)/2)*TAN(30);
        H1 := THICKNESS – H;
        D   := A_F/4;
        D1 := A_F/2;

%
%     The lines used in the nut construction are now drawn.
%

        LINES (1) := $LINE (XYZ(1) – D1, XYZ(2), 0.,
                                  XYZ(1) + D1, XYZ(2), 0.);
        LINES (2) := $LINE (XYZ(1) – D1, XYZ(2) + THICKNESS, 0.,
                                  XYZ(1) + D1, XYZ(2) + THICKNESS, 0.);
        LINES (3) := $LINE (XYZ(1) + D1, XYZ(2), 0.,
                                  XYZ(1) + D1, XYZ(2) + THICKNESS, 0.);
        LINES (4) := $LINE (XYZ(1) – D1, XYZ(2), 0.,
                                  XYZ(1) – D1, XYZ(2) + THICKNESS, 0.);
        LINES (5) := $LINE (XYZ(1), XYZ(2), 0.,
                                  XYZ(1), XYZ(2) + THICKNESS, 0.);

%
%     Now draw the  arcs – using three-point arcs through
%     temporary construction points TEMPENTS.
%

        TEMPENTS (1) := $POINT (XYZ(1) – D1, XYZ(2) + H, 0.);
        TEMPENTS (2) := $POINT (XYZ(1) – D, XYZ(2), 0.);
```

```
             TEMPENTS (3) := $POINT (XYZ(1), XYZ(2) + H, 0.);
             ARCS(1)        := $ARC__POINTS (TEMPENTS(1),
                                             TEMPENTS(2),
                                             TEMPENTS(3));
%
%      Now delete and redefine the temporary entities
%
             IV             := $DELETE (2, TEMPENTS);
             TEMPENTS (1) := $POINT (XYZ(1) + D, XYZ(2), 0.);
             TEMPENTS (2) := $POINT (XYZ(1) + D1, XYZ(2) + H, 0.);
%
%      and construct the next arc
%
             ARCS(1)        := $ARC__POINTS (TEMPENTS(3),
                                             TEMPENTS(1),
                                             TEMPENTS(2));
             IV             := $DELETE (3, TEMPENTS);
%
%      Repeat for the next arcs
%
             TEMPENTS (1) := $POINT (XYZ(1) + D1, XYZ(2) + H1, 0.);
             TEMPENTS (2) := $POINT (XYZ(1) + D, XYZ(2) + THICKNESS, 0.);
             TEMPENTS (3) := $POINT (XYZ(1), XYZ(2) + H1, 0.);
             ARCS(1)        := $ARC__POINTS (TEMPENTS(1),
                                             TEMPENTS(2),
                                             TEMPENTS(3));
             IV             := $DELETE (2, TEMPENTS); •
             TEMPENTS (1) := $POINT (XYZ(1) – D, XYZ(2) + THICKNESS, 0.);
             TEMPENTS (2) := $POINT (XYZ(1) – D1, XYZ(2) + H1, 0.);
             ARCS(1)        :=$ARC__POINTS (TEMPENTS(3),
                                            TEMPENTS(1),
                                            TEMPENTS(2));
             IV             := $DELETE (3, TEMPENTS);
      END;
```

Appendix C
The APT language

This appendix presents a summary of the automatically programmed tools (APT) language for the computer-assisted programming of numerically controlled machine tools. APT may be used to control a variety of machine types, with up to five motion axes. In this appendix we will consider only three-axis motion of milling and drilling machines.

An APT program comprises language statements that fall into the following four classes:

- **geometry statements,** which comprise definitions of these aspects of the part geometry relevant to the machining operations;

- **motion statements,** which define the motion of the cutting tool with respect to the part geometry;

- **post-processor statements,** which contain machine instructions that are passed unchanged into the CLDATA file to be dealt with by the post-processor;

- **auxiliary statements,** which provide additional information to the APT processor giving part name, tolerances to be applied and so on.

Details and examples of each of these are given below.

C.1 Geometry definition

The general form of an APT geometry statement is:

symbol = geometry__word/descriptive data

where symbol is a name for the geometric entity (using up to six characters commencing with a letter), and geometry__word is the **major** word name of a geometry type. The latter include POINT, LINE, PLANE, CIRCLE, PATERN (pattern) and CYLNDR (cylinder). The descriptive data for these elements comprises the numeric data to describe the entity and references to the names of other entities used in construction, separated by comma delimiters. Examples of complete geometry statements for common geometry types are as follows:

Description by coordinate data entry

P0 = POINT/1.25, 2.5, 0
{Point defined by x, y and z coordinate values}
L0 = LINE/25.0, 50.0, 0, 100.0, 50.0, 0
{Line defined by x, y and z of start and end points}

Description directly from other geometry

L1 = LINE/P0, P1   {Line between two points}
PL1 = PLANE/P0, P1, P2   {Plane through three points}

Description from geometry with 'modifiers' to specify geometry option to select

P1 = POINT/INTOF, L2, L3   {Intersection of two lines}
P2 = POINT/XSMALL, INTOF, L3, C1
{Intersection of line and circle with the point with the smaller x value chosen of the two possible solutions}
P3 = POINT/CENTER, C1   {Point at centre of circle}
L4 = LINE/P3, LEFT, TANTO, C2
{Line from a point tangent to a circle; the line to the left of the circle looking from the point is taken}
L5 = LINE/INTOF, PL1, PL2
{Line at intersection of two planes}
L6 = LINE/P3, PERPTO, L5
{Line through a point perpendicular to a line}
PL4 = PLANE/P4, PARLEL, PL2
{Plane through a point parallel to a plane}

In these definitions TANTO, INTOF, PERPTO and PARLEL are **minor** words. XSMALL is a modifier used to distinguish between possible positions. Other modifiers are YSMALL, XLARGE and YLARGE.

Description by a combination of geometric and numerical data

L2 = LINE/P0, 3.0, 4.0, 0
{Line defined by a point and the coordinates of a point}
L3 = LINE/P0, ATANGL, 50
{Line through a point and at an angle (to x axis)}

L4 = LINE/P1, ATANGL, 45, L3
{Line through a point and at an angle to another line}
C1 = CIRCLE/CENTER, P0, RADIUS, 5.0
{Circle defined by centre point and radius value}
PL5 = PLANE/PARLEL, PL4, YSMALL, 5.0
{Plane parallel to PL4, offset 5.0 units in the negative y direction}

In these definitions CENTER, RADIUS and ATANGL are **minor** words.

In APT, geometric entities are **unbounded**: lines and planes are infinite, and circles are always through a full 360°. They are also analytic entities, as opposed to the (generally) bounded parametric geometry used in CAD.

C.2 Motion statements

Once the part geometry has been defined the APT programmer may specify how the cutter is to move. This may be in absolute or incremental terms, using the commands GOTO/(absolute position) or GODLTA/(incremental move) respectively (e.g. to move into position to start a cut, or for point-to-point machining). It may also be with respect to the part, which is achieved by defining cutter moves with respect to geometric entities along paths bound by the **drive surface, part surface** and **check surface**, as discussed in Section 11.3.3 and shown in Figure 11.15. Let us consider that the tool is a cylindrical milling cutter, as shown in Figure 11.15. This cutter moves with its end against the part surface (which may not be an actual surface of the part), and its side against the drive surface, along which it travels until it meets the check surface. The way in which the check surface constrains the path is defined by the modifier words TO, ON, PAST and TANTO, the meaning of which is also shown in Figure 11.15.

The general form of a command for motion with respect to geometry is (where { } enclose alternative words):

motion__word/drive surface, {TO, ON, PAST, TANTO}, check surface

where motion__word defines the motion with respect to the move along the previous drive surface, and is one of GOLFT (go left), GORGT, GOFWD, GOBACK, GOUP or GODOWN – the meanings of which are shown in Figure C.1. The convention is that the workpiece is stationary and that the tool moves. The check surface of a move normally becomes the drive surface of the next move. The drive and part surfaces may be actual surfaces or planes, or may be curves (in which case the plane is assumed to be through the curve and parallel to the tool axis). If curves are used, the part surface might be defined by a plane or surface, or by the plane containing the drive and part curves.

At the beginning of the motion commands, the initial cutter position is specified by the statement FROM/(initial position), and the first move to the drive and part surfaces is defined using:

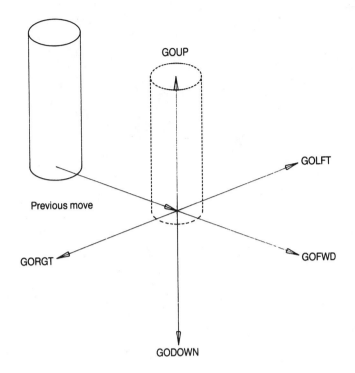

FIGURE C.1

APT motion words.

GO/{TO, ON, PAST}, drive surface, {TO, ON, PAST}, part surface, {TO, ON, PAST}, check surface

So, for example, if we consider points, a triangle and a plane described by the statements:

```
PT0 = POINT/–50, –50, 20
PT1 = POINT/0, 0, 0
PT2 = POINT/100, 0, 0
PT3 = POINT/50, 100, 0
LN1 = LINE/PT1, PT2
LN2 = LINE/PT2, PT3
LN3 = LINE/PT3, PT1
PL1 = PLANE/PT1, PT2, PT
```

then the motion shown in Figure C.2 would be defined by the statements:

```
FROM/PT0
GO/TO, LN1, TO, PL1, TO, LN3
GORGT/LN1, PAST, LN2
GOLFT/LN2, PAST, LN3
GOLFT/LN3, PAST, LN1
GOTO/PT0
```

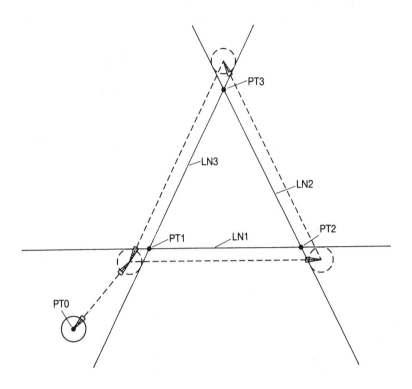

FIGURE C.2
APT geometry and
tool motion.

C.3 Post-processor and auxiliary statements

Post-processor statements control the operation of the spindle, the feed, and other features of the machine tool. Some common post-processor statements are (where the '/' indicates that some descriptive data is needed):

COOLNT/	for coolant control – for example, ON or OFF, MIST or FLOOD;
RAPID	to select rapid cutter motion;
END	to indicate the end of a section of program; FROM is used to restart;
SPINDL/	to select spindle on/off, speed and direction of rotation;
FEDRAT/	to select feedrate;
TURRET/	to select cutter number – from a turret or perhaps an automatic tool changer;
MACHIN/	to specify the machine type, number and post-processor.

Auxiliary statements are used to provide information required by the APT processor in processing the source. This includes for example the name of the part being processed and the details necessary for offset calculation including the cutter size and the accuracy to which approximations should be made when representing curved paths by straight lines. Examples are (again, '/' indicates that some descriptive data is needed):

CLPRNT used to obtain a computer printout of the cutter location sequence on the NC tape;

INTOL/ defines the inside tolerance – the allowable deviation from the inside of a curve or surface of any straight-line segments used to approximate the curve;

OUTTOL/ outside tolerance. As INTOL/ but the tolerance outside the curve;

CUTTER/ defines the cutter diameter to be used;

PARTNO/ used at the start of the program to identify the part program;

FINI the last statement in the APT program.

C.4 A complete program

We are now in a position to examine a complete program. Consider the simple example (text in braces { } is commentary):

```
{Initial auxiliary and post-processor statements}
PARTNO      APPENDIX C
            MACHIN/MILL,1
            INTOL/.01
            OUTTOL/.01
            CUTTER/20.0
{Geometry statements}
STRT      = POINT/–100.0, –100.0, 50.0
P0        = POINT/0.0, 0.0, 0.0
P1        = POINT/100.0, 0.0, 0.0
P2        = POINT/100.0, 50.0, 0.0
P3        = POINT/70.0, 70.0, 0.0
P4        = POINT/50.0, 100.0, 0.0
P5        = POINT/0.0, 100.0, 0.0
L1        = LINE/P0, P1
L2        = LINE/P1, P2
L3        = LINE/P2, PARLEL, L1
L4        = LINE/P4, PERPTO, L1
L5        = LINE/P4, PARLEL, L1
L6        = LINE/P5, P1
C1        = CIRCLE/CENTER, P3, RADIUS, 20.0
PL1       = PLANE/P0, P1, P5
{Start spindle and coolant, set up feedrate}
            SPINDL/600
            COOLNT/ON
            FEDRAT/30.0
```

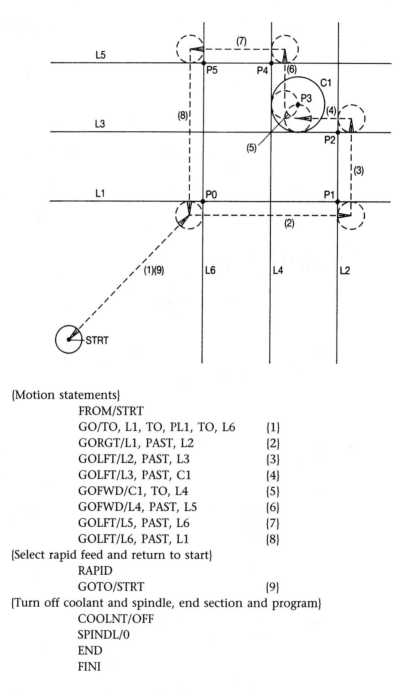

FIGURE C.3

Geometry and motion for example program.

```
{Motion statements}
        FROM/STRT
        GO/TO, L1, TO, PL1, TO, L6        {1}
        GORGT/L1, PAST, L2               {2}
        GOLFT/L2, PAST, L3               {3}
        GOLFT/L3, PAST, C1               {4}
        GOFWD/C1, TO, L4                 {5}
        GOFWD/L4, PAST, L5               {6}
        GOLFT/L5, PAST, L6               {7}
        GOLFT/L6, PAST, L1               {8}
{Select rapid feed and return to start}
        RAPID
        GOTO/STRT                        {9}
{Turn off coolant and spindle, end section and program}
        COOLNT/OFF
        SPINDL/0
        END
        FINI
```

The geometry and motion for this program are shown in Figure C.3. Note that the numbers marked against the tool moves correspond to those shown in braces { } in the program.

References and further reading

Bedworth D. D., Henderson M. R. and Wolfe P. M. (1991). *Computer-Integrated Design and Manufacturing*. New York: McGraw-Hill.

Groover M. P. and Zimmers, E. W. (1984). *CAD/CAM: Computer-Aided Design and Manufacturing*. Englewood Cliffs, NJ: Prentice Hall.

Kral I. H. (1987), *Numerical Control Programming in APT*. Englewood Cliffs, NJ: Prentice Hall.

Appendix D
Line balancing techniques

Line balancing involves arranging the individual processing and assembly tasks at the workstations so that the total time required at each workstation is approximately the same. If the work elements can be grouped so that all the station times are exactly equal, we have perfect balance on the line and production can be expected to flow smoothly. It is usually very difficult to achieve perfect balance. When the workstation times are unequal, the slowest station determines the overall production rate of the line (Groover, 1980).

D.1 A sample line balancing problem

A manual assembly line is to be designed to make a particular product. The total job of manufacturing the product has been divided into minimal rational work elements. The processing time for each element as well as the immediate predecessors are given in Table D.1. Production demand will be 120 000 units yr^{-1} at 40 h $week^{-1}$, equivalent to a production output of 60 units h^{-1} or 1 unit min^{-1}.

Before tackling the line balancing problem it is essential to have an appreciation of the line balancing terminology, which will now be defined.

Table D.1 Table of work elements

Element	Time (min)	Preceded by
1	0.25	–
2	0.45	1
3	0.35	1
4	0.40	1
5	0.32	2
6	0.20	2,3
7	0.27	4
8	0.70	4
9	0.60	5
10	0.38	6,7
11	0.50	8
12	0.43	9,10,11

D.2 Terminology

The **minimal rational work elements** are the smallest elements into which a job can be usefully divided. The time taken to carry out element j is specified as T_{ej}. For example, the element time, T_e, for element 5 in Table D.1 is 0.32 min.

The time T_{ej} of a work element is assumed constant. It is also assumed that the T_e values are additive, that is the time to perform two work elements is the sum of the times of the individual elements.

The **total work content** is the sum of all the work to be done on the line. Let T_{wc} be the time required for the total work content. Hence:

$$T_{wc} = \Sigma T_{ej} \tag{D.1}$$

From Table D.1, $T_{wc} = 4.85$ min.

A workstation is a location on the work line where work is done. The work consists of one or more of the individual work elements. The **workstation process time** (T_{si}) is the sum of the work elements done at station i.

The **cycle time** (T_c) is the time interval between parts coming off the line. The design value of T_c is specified according to the required production rate to be achieved by the flow line. In this example a cycle time of 1 unit min^{-1} is required.

The largest T_s value cannot exceed the required T_c value if the required production rate is to be achieved. If $T_c = \max T_{si}$, there will be idle time at all workstations whose T_s values are less than T_c. Also, the cycle time must be greater than any of the element times.

In nearly every processing or assembly job there are **precedence requirements** that restrict the sequence in which the job can be accomplished. The **precedence diagram** is a graphical representation of the sequence of work elements as defined by the precedence constraints. Figure D.1 shows the precedence diagram for this example. The nodes are used to represent the work elements, while the arrows connecting the nodes indicate the order in which the elements must be performed.

The **balance delay** is a measure of the line inefficiency which results from idle time due to unequal distribution of work among workstations. It is represented by the symbol d and can be computed for the flow line as follows:

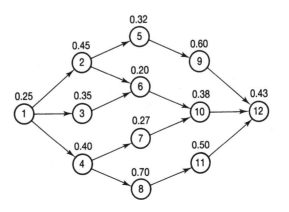

FIGURE D.1

Precedence diagram.

$$d = \frac{nT_c - T_{wc}}{nT_c} \tag{D.2}$$

The balance delay is often expressed as a percentage rather than as a decimal fraction.

D.3 Manual methods of line balancing

In this section we will consider two line balancing algorithms:

1. Largest-candidate rule.

2. Ranked positional weights method.

For the purpose of illustration we will apply these algorithms to the example above. None of the methods guarantee an optimal solution, but they are likely to result in good solutions which approach the true optimum.

D.3.1 Largest-candidate rule

The technique involves four simple steps, listed below.

1. List all elements in descending order of T_e values, as indicated in Table D.2.

2. Starting at the top of the list and working down, select the first feasible element for placement at the first workstation. A feasible element is one that satisfies the precedence requirements and does not cause the sum of the T_e values at the station to exceed the cycle time T_c.

3. Continue the process of assigning work elements to the station as in step 2 until no further elements can be added without exceeding T_c. Each time an element is allocated to a workstation, we go back to the top of the list.

Table D.2 Work elements arranged according to T_e value for the largest-candidate rule

Work element	T_e (min)	Immediate predecessors
8	0.70	4
9	0.60	5
11	0.50	7
2	0.45	1
12	0.43	9,10,11
4	0.40	1
10	0.38	6,7
3	0.35	1
5	0.32	2
7	0.27	4
1	0.25	–
6	0.20	2,3

Table D.3 Work elements assigned to stations according to the largest-candidate rule

Station	Work element	T_e (min)	ΣT_e at station
1	1	0.25	
	2	0.45	0.80
2	4	0.40	
	3	0.35	
	6	0.20	0.95
3	8	0.70	
	7	0.27	0.97
4	11	0.50	
	10	0.38	0.88
5	5	0.32	
	9	0.60	0.92
6	12	0.43	0.43

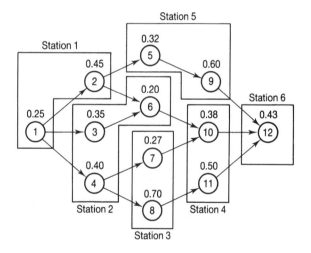

FIGURE D.2
Solution of sample problem using largest-candidate rule.

4. Repeat steps 2 and 3 for the other stations in the line until all the elements have been assigned. The assignment of work elements to stations is shown in Table D.3.

There are six stations. Hence, the balance delay is:

$$d = \frac{6(1.0) - 4.85}{6(1.0)} = 19\%$$

(D.3)

The solution is illustrated in Figure D.2. The largest-candidate rule is used only for simple line balancing problems. More sophisticated techniques are required for more complex problems.

D.3.2 Ranked positional weights method

A ranked positional weight value is computed for each element. The RPW takes account of both the T_e value of the element and its position in the precedence diagram. The elements are assigned to the workstations, according to the following procedure.

1. Calculate the RPW for each element by summing the element's T_e value with the T_e values for all the elements that follow it in the precedence diagram.

2. List the elements in descending order of RPW, largest RPW at the top of the list, as indicated in Table D.4. The T_e value and the immediate predecessor for each element are also included.

3. Assign elements to stations according to RPW, avoiding precedence constraints and time-cycle violations. As in the largest-candidate rule, we go back to the top of the list after the allocation of an element to a workstation. The assignment of work elements to stations is shown in Table D.5.

   A graphical representation of the solution is shown in Figure D.3. For this solution only five stations are required. This is a more efficient solution than that offered by the largest-candidate algorithm. The balance delay for the RPW solution is:

$$d = \frac{5(1.0) - 4.85}{5(1.0)} = 3\% \tag{D.4}$$

The balance delay value of 3% indicates that almost perfect balance has been achieved.

Table D.4 Work element arranged according to RPW

Work element	RPW	T_e (min)	Immediate predecessors
1	4.85	0.25	–
4	2.68	0.40	1
2	2.38	0.45	1
8	1.63	0.70	4
3	1.36	0.35	1
5	1.35	0.32	2
7	1.08	0.27	4
9	1.03	0.60	5
6	1.01	0.20	2,3
11	0.92	0.50	8
10	0.81	0.38	6,7
12	0.43	0.43	9,10,11

Table D.5 Work elements assigned to stations according to the RPW rule

Station	Work element	T_e (min)	ΣT_e at station
1	1	0.25	
	4	0.40	
	3	0.35	1.00
2	2	0.45	
	5	0.32	
	6	0.20	0.97
3	8	0.70	
	7	0.27	0.97
4	9	0.60	
	10	0.38	0.98
5	11	0.50	
	12	0.43	0.93

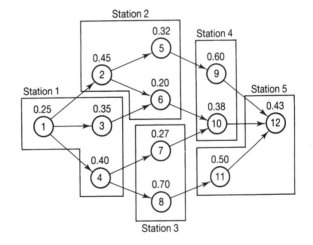

FIGURE D.3
Solution of sample problem using RPW method.

D.4 Notes

1. Occasionally a defined minimal rational work element can be divided into smaller task units. For example, welding the various pieces of a stool frame together can be divided into stages. It may be found useful to subdivide a work element j in cases where the T_{ej} value for that element exceeds the cycle time T_c.

2. It may be possible to alter the process time for a work element by changing the speed of a workhead, such as a drill.

3. Suppose a production rate of 1 unit min^{-1} is required. However, station n has a process time of 2 min. If two stations were arranged in parallel at the nth station position, their combined output would be 1 unit min^{-1}.

References and further reading

Groover M. P. (1980). *Automation, Production Systems and Computer-Aided Manufacturing.* Englewood Cliffs, NJ: Prentice Hall.

Index

·················

2-manifold, 46

active layer, 167
active matrix displays, 91
adjacency, 319
'against' relationship, 589, 590
aims of CAD, 14
aircraft manufacture, use of surface
    modelling, 41
algorithms
  Cohen-Sutherland, 100, 615–16
  definition, 513
  depth-buffer, 110–11
  earliest due date rule, 514
  Johnson's algorithm, 516–17
  Moore's algorithm, 514–15
  object-space, 115
  scan-conversion hidden surface, 111,
    617–19
  scheduling, 513–17
  shortest processing time rule, 514
  uses, 322
analysis
  finite element *see* finite element analysis
  geometric, 183–7
analysis of variance (ANOVA), 350
ANDON board, 570–1
annotation for drawings, 167–70
applets, 598
application programming interfaces (APIs),
    200, 202–4
  applications, 203–4
    examples, 204
  procedures library, 203
APT language *see* automatically programmed
    tools
arc construction
  drawing as series of vectors, 99–100
  geometric entities, 30

arc welding, use of robots, 396
ARPANET, 244
artificial intelligence, 254–70
  basic concepts, 255
  case-based reasoning, 266
  consistency maintenance, 267
  constraint-based reasoning, 264, 265
  decomposition, 263–4
  grammatical design, 266–7
  group technology, 304, 405
  inference schemes, 261–3
    chaining mechanisms, 262–3
  knowledge representation techniques,
    256–61
    frame systems, 256–7
    fuzzy sets and systems, 256, 260–1
    graphs and networks, 257–8
    hybrid representations, 258–9
    neural networks, 256, 259–60
    production systems, 256
  knowledge-based systems, 255, 267–9
    application example, 268–9
    elements, 255
  plan selection and refinement, 264
artificial neural networks, 259–60
  back propagation approach, 260
  hidden layers, 259
  net input, 259
  nodes/neurons, 259
  structure, 259
assemble to order (ATO), 417, 418
assembly constraints, 589, 590
assembly modelling, 588–90
  degrees of freedom, 590
  fits, 590
  graph-basd approach, 590
  motion limits, 590
  part-of relations, 590
  structuring relations, 590

643